The State of Old Testament Studies

"Do you want to know what Old Testament scholars are talking about to one another nowadays? It's a very different conversation from the one twenty-five years ago, and the conversation in another twenty-five-years' time will be different again. But this is a brilliant book to enable you to listen in on the conversation now, and perhaps join in."

—**John Goldingay**, Fuller Theological Seminary (emeritus)

"Informed, contemporary, accessible—this wonderful collection of essays orients readers to current trends in Old Testament study and provides guidance on how to take this research further. This volume is an essential addition to reading lists everywhere."

—**David G. Firth**, Trinity College Bristol

"*The State of Old Testament Studies* is now required reading not only for those entering this contemporary field of research but also for those wanting to ensure that they are up to speed on the latest developments. Its coverage is thorough, providing an overview of the state of the guild, with attention to the historical, literary, and hermeneutical dimensions of biblical interpretation. Be prepared for new insights into how the riches of the Old Testament can be assessed and accessed. An essential resource."

—**Mark J. Boda**, McMaster Divinity College

"What a wonderful thing for scholars and students alike to pick up a resource and know exactly where to begin because an incredible team of trusted scholars has recounted the current state of play! I highly commend the content of this volume for its utility and the posture of its authors in modeling hospitable academic discourse. A must-read for all those in or interested in the field of Old Testament studies."

—**Brittany N. Melton**, Regent College, Vancouver

"With so many varied approaches, the study of the Old Testament has become enormously complex in recent decades, and it is a challenge to see one's way through the thicket. This collection is a clear and reliable guide for navigating an intricate and fascinating landscape. Hardy and Carroll do a service to all who seek to understand the state of Old Testament studies in these days."

—**Jacqueline E. Lapsley**, Union Presbyterian Seminary

"*The State of Old Testament Studies* features cutting-edge essays by leading scholars delving into intriguing issues in the field. This thorough volume unites diverse contemporary perspectives, making it an indispensable resource for anyone interested in the evolving landscape of biblical studies. Whether you're a student, scholar, or simply curious about the latest insights, this book promises to deepen your understanding of academic discourse on Old Testament studies and related fields."

—**Dominick S. Hernández**, Talbot School of Theology, Biola University

"Our discipline needs these periodic updates to survey and evaluate developments of the last few decades. Hardy and Carroll are to be congratulated on recruiting and inspiring an impressive list of contributors. This volume is a worthy successor to its predecessors, not only updating earlier iterations of the genre but also engaging new topics and research agendas."

—**Bill T. Arnold**, Asbury Theological Seminary

The State of Old Testament Studies

A Survey of Recent Research

Edited by
H. H. Hardy II
and M. Daniel Carroll R.

Baker Academic
a division of Baker Publishing Group
Grand Rapids, Michigan

Published by Baker Academic
a division of Baker Publishing Group
Grand Rapids, Michigan
BakerAcademic.com

Printed in the United States of America

Library of Congress Cataloging-in-Publication Data

Names: Hardy, H. H., II, 1979– editor. | Carroll R., M. Daniel, editor.
Title: The state of Old Testament studies : a survey of recent research / edited by H.H. Hardy II and M. Daniel Carroll R.
Description: Grand Rapids, Michigan : Baker Academic, a division of Baker Publishing Group, [2024] | Includes bibliographical references and index.
Identifiers: LCCN 2024010429 | ISBN 9781540963659 (paperback) | ISBN 9781540968265 (casebound) | ISBN 9781493447411 (ebook) | ISBN 9781493447428 (pdf)
Subjects: LCSH: Bible. Old Testament—Criticism, interpretation, etc.—History—21st century.
Classification: LCC BS1160 .S85 2024 | DDC 221.07—dc23/eng/20240611
LC record available at https://lccn.loc.gov/2024010429

Baker Publishing Group publications use paper produced from sustainable forestry practices and postconsumer waste whenever possible.

25 26 27 28 29 30 31 8 7 6 5 4 3 2

Contents

Part 2: Old Testament Scripture

Part 3: Interpretive Approaches

Figures

Abbreviations

General and Bibliographic

*	indicates a hypothetical Hebrew form
[ ]	encloses alternate versification when different from English Bible verse numbering (e.g., Joel 2:28–32 [3:1–5 MT, LXX])
ANE	ancient Near East(ern)
BH	Biblical Hebrew
ca.	*circa*, about
cent.	century
chap(s).	chapter(s)
DSS	Dead Sea Scrolls
ed(s).	editor(s), edited by, edition
e.g.	*exempli gratia*, for example
esp.	especially
fig(s).	figure(s)
HB	Hebrew Bible
IAA	Israel Antiquities Authority
i.e.	*id est*, that is
LXX	Septuagint, Greek translation of the Hebrew Bible
mill.	millennium
MS(S)	manuscript(s)
MT	Masoretic Text
no(s).	number(s)
NT	New Testament
OG	Old Greek
OT	Old Testament
sec.	section
SP	Samaritan Pentateuch
suppl.	supplement
TAM	tense–aspect–mood
trans.	translation; translated by
v(v).	verse(s)
vs.	versus
VTE	Vassal Treaty of Esarhaddon

Era Designations

BCE	before the Common Era
BP	before the present
CE	Common Era
EH	Early Hellenistic period
ER	Early Roman period
Iron I	Iron Age I
Iron II	Iron Age II
LBA	Late Bronze Age
LH	Late Hellenistic period
MBA	Middle Bronze Age

Old Testament / Hebrew Bible

Gen.	Genesis
Exod.	Exodus
Lev.	Leviticus
Num.	Numbers

Deut.	Deuteronomy	Jer.	Jeremiah
Josh.	Joshua	Lam.	Lamentations
Judg.	Judges	Ezek.	Ezekiel
Ruth	Ruth	Dan.	Daniel
1–2 Sam.	1–2 Samuel	Hosea	Hosea
1–2 Kings	1–2 Kings	Joel	Joel
1–2 Chron.	1–2 Chronicles	Amos	Amos
Ezra	Ezra	Obad.	Obadiah
Neh.	Nehemiah	Jon.	Jonah
Esther	Esther	Mic.	Micah
Job	Job	Nah.	Nahum
Ps(s).	Psalm(s)	Hab.	Habakkuk
Prov.	Proverbs	Zeph.	Zephaniah
Eccles.	Ecclesiastes	Hag.	Haggai
Song	Song of Songs	Zech.	Zechariah
Isa.	Isaiah	Mal.	Malachi

New Testament

Matt.	Matthew	1–2 Thess.	1–2 Thessalonians
Mark	Mark	1–2 Tim.	1–2 Timothy
Luke	Luke	Titus	Titus
John	John	Philem.	Philemon
Acts	Acts of the Apostles	Heb.	Hebrews
Rom.	Romans	James	James
1–2 Cor.	1–2 Corinthians	1–2 Pet.	1–2 Peter
Gal.	Galatians	1–3 John	1–3 John
Eph.	Ephesians	Jude	Jude
Phil.	Philippians	Rev.	Revelation
Col.	Colossians		

Old Testament Apocrypha / Deuterocanonical Works

Bar.	Baruch	Sir.	Sirach
Bel	Bel and the Dragon	Sus.	Susanna
1–2 Esd.	1–2 Esdras	Tob.	Tobit
Jdt.	Judith	Wis.	Wisdom
1–4 Macc.	1–4 Maccabees		

Old Testament Pseudepigrapha

1 En.	1 Enoch	4 Ezra	4 Ezra

Qumran / Dead Sea Scrolls

1QIsa[a]	Isaiah[a]	1QS	Community Rule
1QM	War Scroll	11QT[a]	Temple Scroll[a]
1QpHab	Pesher Habbakuk		

Other Jewish and Patristic Sources

Abbreviations appearing before tractate names indicate the following sources: Mishnah (m.), Tosefta (t.), Babylonian Talmud (b.), and Jerusalem/Palestinian Talmud (y.).

Eusebius

Hist. Eccl. *Ecclesiastical History*
Vit. Const. *Life of Constantine*

Josephus

Ag. Ap. *Against Apion*
Ant. *Jewish Antiquities*
J.W. *Jewish War*

Modern Secondary Sources

ÄAT Ägypten und Altes Testament
AB Anchor Bible
ABD *Anchor Bible Dictionary*. Edited by David Noel Freedman. 6 vols. New York: Doubleday, 1992
ABS Archaeology and Biblical Studies
AcBib Academia Biblica
AcT *Acta Theologica*
AIL Ancient Israel and Its Literature
AION *Annali dell'Istituto Orientale di Napoli*
AKM Abhandlungen für die Kunde des Morgenlandes
AnBib Analecta Biblica Studia
ANEM Ancient Near East Monographs
ANEP *The Ancient Near East in Pictures Relating to the Old Testament*. Edited by James B. Pritchard. 2nd ed. Princeton: Princeton University Press, 1969
AOAT Alter Orient und Altes Testament
ARM Archives royales de Mari
ASTI *Annual of the Swedish Theological Institute*
AThANT Abhandlungen zur Theologie des Alten und Neuen Testaments
ATJ *Ashland Theological Journal*
AUS American University Studies
AUSS *Andrews University Seminary Studies*
AYB Anchor Yale Bible
AYBRL Anchor Yale Bible Reference Library
BA *Biblical Archaeologist*
BAR *Biblical Archaeologist Review*
BASOR *Bulletin of the American Schools of Oriental Research*
BBB Bonner biblische Beiträge
BBR *Bulletin for Biblical Research*
BBRSup Bulletin for Biblical Research, Supplements
BEATAJ Beiträge zur Erforschung des Alten Testaments und des antiken Judentum
BETL Bibliotheca Ephemeridum Theologicarum Lovaniensium
BHK *Biblia Hebraica*. Edited by Rudolf Kittel. Leipzig: Hinrichs, 1906; 2nd ed., 1913; 3rd ed., 1937
BHLXX The Baylor Handbook on the Septuagint
BHQ *Biblia Hebraica Quinta*. Edited by Adrian Schenker et al. Stuttgart: Deutsche Bibelgesellschaft, 2004–
BHS *Biblia Hebraica Stuttgartensia*. Edited by Karl Elliger and Wilhelm Rudolph. Stuttgart: Deutsche Bibelgesellschaft, 1983

Bib	*Biblica*
BibEnc	Biblical Encyclopedia
BibInt	*Biblical Interpretation*
BibInt	Biblical Interpretation Series
BJS	Brown Judaic Studies
BJS/UCSD	Biblical and Judaic Studies from the University of California, San Diego
BLS	Bible and Literature Series
BlTh	*Black Theology*
BN	*Biblische Notizen*
BRev	*Bible Review*
BSNA	Biblical Scholarship in North America
BT	*The Bible Translator*
BTB	*Biblical Theology Bulletin*
BZ	*Biblische Zeitschrift*
BZAW	Beihefte zur Zeitschrift für die alttestamentliche Wissenschaft
CBET	Contributions to Biblical Exegesis and Theology
CBQ	*Catholic Biblical Quarterly*
CHANE	Culture and History of the Ancient Near East
ChrCent	*Christian Century*
COMStB	*Comparative Oriental Manuscript Studies Bulletin*
COS	*The Context of Scripture*. Edited by William W. Hallo and K. Lawson Younger Jr. 4 vols. Leiden: Brill, 1997–2016
CSLC	Cambridge Semitic Languages and Cultures
CTR	*Criswell Theological Review*
CurBR	*Currents in Biblical Research*
CurBS	*Currents in Research: Biblical Studies*
CUSAS	Cornell University Studies in Assyriology and Sumerology
DCH	*Dictionary of Classical Hebrew*. Edited by David J. A. Clines. 9 vols. Sheffield: Sheffield Phoenix, 1993–2014
DJD	Discoveries in the Judaean Desert
DSD	*Dead Sea Discoveries*
ErIsr	*Eretz-Israel*
ESHM	European Seminar in Historical Methodology
EstBíb	*Estudios bíblicos*
ExAud	*Ex Auditu*
FAT	Forschungen zum Alten Testament
FCB	Feminist Companion to the Bible
FRLANT	Forschungen zur Religion und Literatur des und Neuen Testament
FSBP	Fontes et Subsidia ad Bibliam Pertinentes
GAT	Grundrisse zum Alten Testament
GBS	Guides to Biblical Scholarship
GDBS	Gorgias Dissertations: Biblical Studies
GPBS	Global Perspectives on Biblical Scholarship
HALOT	*The Hebrew and Aramaic Lexicon of the Old Testament*. By Ludwig Koehler, Walter Baumgartner, and Johann J. Stamm. Translated and edited under the supervision of Mervyn E. J. Richardson. 4 vols. Leiden: Brill, 1994–99
HBCE	The Hebrew Bible: A Critical Edition
HBM	Hebrew Bible Monographs
HBS	Herders biblische Studien
HBT	*Horizons in Biblical Theology*
HCOT	Historical Commentary on the Old Testament
HeBAI	*Hebrew Bible and Ancient Israel*
HS	*Hebrew Studies*
HSM	Harvard Semitic Monographs
HSS	Harvard Semitic Studies
HThKAT	Herders Theologischer Kommentar zum Alten Testament
HTR	*Harvard Theological Review*
IAA	Israel Antiquities Authority
IEJ	*Israel Exploration Journal*

Int *Interpretation*
IOSCS The International Organization for Septuagint and Cognate Studies
IVBS International Voices in Biblical Studies
JAAR *Journal of the American Academy of Religion*
JAJ *Journal of Ancient Judaism*
JAJSup Journal of Ancient Judaism Supplements
JAOS *Journal of the American Oriental Society*
JBL *Journal of Biblical Literature*
JBR *Journal of Bible and Religion*
JBTh *Jahrbuch für biblische Theologie*
JCS *Journal of Cuneiform Studies*
JEOL *Jaarbericht van het Vooraziatisch-Egyptisch Gezelschap (Genootschap) Ex oriente lux*
JETS *Journal of the Evangelical Theological Society*
JHebS *Journal of Hebrew Scriptures*
JJS *Journal of Jewish Studies*
JNES *Journal of Near Eastern Studies*
JNSL *Journal of Northwest Semitic Languages*
JPS Jewish Publication Society
JQR *Jewish Quarterly Review*
JSem *Journal of Semitics*
JSJ *Journal for the Study of Judaism in the Persian, Hellenistic, and Roman Period*
JSJSup Journal for the Study of Judaism in the Persian, Hellenistic, and Roman Period, Supplements
JSOT *Journal for the Study of Old Testament*
JSOTSup Journal for the Study of Old Testament Supplement Series
JSP *Journal for the Study of Pseudepigrapha*
JSPSup Journal for the Study of Pseudepigrapha Supplement Series
JSS *Journal of Semitic Studies*
JSSSup Journal of Semitic Studies Supplement
JTI *Journal for Theological Interpretation*
JTISup Journal for Theological Interpretation, Supplements
JTS *Journal of Theological Studies*
JTSA *Journal of Theology for Southern Africa*
KTU *Die keilalphabetischen Texte aus Ugarit, Ras Ibn Hani und anderen Orten*. 3rd enlarged ed. By Manfried Dietrich, Oswald Loretz, and Joaqíun Sanmartín. Alter Orient und Altes Testament 360/1. Münster: Ugarit-Verlag, 2013
KUSATU *Kleine Untersuchungen zur Sprache des Alten Testaments und seiner Umwelt*
LAI Library of Ancient Israel
LHBOTS Library of Hebrew Bible/Old Testament Studies
LSAWS Linguistic Studies in Ancient West Semitic
LSTS Library of Second Temple Studies
MARI *Mari: Annales de recherches interdisciplinaires*
MDAI *Mitteilungen des Deutschen archäologischen Instituts*
NEA *Near Eastern Archaeology*
NICOT New International Commentary on the Old Testament
NIGTC New International Greek Testament Commentary
NIVAC NIV Application Commentary Series
NSBT New Studies in Biblical Theology
OBO Orbis Biblicus et Orientalis
OBO.SA Orbis Biblicus et Orientalis, Series Archaeologica

OBT	Overtures to Biblical Theology
OEAE	*The Oxford Encyclopedia of Ancient Egypt*. Edited by Donald Redford. 3 vols. Oxford: Oxford University Press, 2001
OIS	Oriental Institute Seminars
OLA	Orientalia Lovaniensia Analecta
ORA	Orientalische Religionen in der Antike
OTE	*Old Testament Essays*
OTL	Old Testament Library
OTS	Old Testament Studies
OtSt	Oudtestamentische Studiën
OTT	Old Testament Theology
PEQ	*Palestine Exploration Quarterly*
PLoS ONE	*Public Library of Science One*
ProEccl	*Pro Ecclesia*
Proof	*Prooftexts: A Journal of Jewish Literary History*
RA	*Revue d'assyriologie et d'archéologie orientale*
RB	*Revue biblique*
RBL	*Review of Biblical Literature*
RBS	Resources for Biblical Study
RevQ	*Revue de Qumrân*
RHR	*Revue de l'histoire des religions*
RIH	Ras Ibn Hani
RRBS	Recent Research in Biblical Studies
SAA	State Archives of Assyria
SAAS	State Archives of Assyria Studies
SAHS	Scripture and Hermeneutics Seminar
SAOC	Studies in Ancient Oriental Civilizations
SBL	Society of Biblical Literature
SBLCS	Society of Biblical Literature Commentary on the Septuagint
SBLDS	Society of Biblical Literature Dissertation Series
SBLIVBS	Society of Biblical Literature International Voices in Biblical Studies
SBLMS	Society of Biblical Literature Monograph Series
SBLSS	Society of Biblical Literature Symposium Series
SCS	Septuagint and Cognate Studies
SEÅ	*Svensk exegetisk årsbok*
SemeiaSt	Semeia Studies
SemeiaSup	Semeia Supplements
SHANE	Studies in the History of the Ancient Near East
SHS	Scripture and Hermeneutics Series
SJ	Studia Judaica
SJOT	*Scandinavian Journal of the Old Testament*
SOTSMS	Society of Old Testament Studies Monograph Series
SPiL Plus	*Stellenbosch Papers in Linguistics Plus*
SSLL	Studies in Semitic Languages and Linguistics
SSN	Studia Semitica Neerlandica
StBibLit	Studies in Biblical Literature (Lang)
STDJ	Studies on the Texts of the Desert of Judah
STI	Studies in Theological Interpretation
SubBi	Subsidia Biblica
SWBA	Social World of Biblical Antiquity
TA	*Tel Aviv*
TAD	*Textbook of Aramaic Documents from Ancient Egypt*. By Bezalel Porten and Ada Yardeni. 4 vols. Jerusalem: Hebrew University Press, 1986–99
Textus	*Textus: A Journal on Textual Criticism of the Hebrew Bible*
THOTC	Two Horizons Old Testament Commentary
ThTo	*Theology Today*
TQ	*Theologische Quartalschrift*
TSAJ	Texte und Studien zum antiken Judentum

TUGAL Texte und Untersuchungen zur Geschichte der altchristlichen Literatur
TynBul *Tyndale Bulletin*
UF *Ugarit-Forschungen*
VT *Vetus Testamentum*
VTSup Vetus Testamentum Supplement
WAW Writings from the Ancient World
WAWSup Writings from the Ancient World Supplement Series
WBC Word Biblical Commentary
WO *Die Welt des Orients*
WTJ *Westminster Theological Journal*
WUNT Wissenschaftliche Untersuchungen zum Neuen Testament
ZAW *Zeitschrift für die alttestamentliche Wissenschaft*
ZTK *Zeitschrift für Theologie und Kirche*

Editors' Preface

Twenty-five years ago, *The Face of Old Testament Studies* was published and offered a one-volume survey of the discipline. Its essays focused on sixteen "contemporary approaches" and their developments from 1970 to the cusp of the new millennium.[1] While much of that volume remains a valuable resource—primarily as a historical sounding of the field at that time—the discipline of OT studies today looks significantly different from how it looked at the end of the last century. The modes of inquiry have proliferated, diversified, and intermingled with related disciplines, yielding productive outcomes. New questions are being asked, novel approaches have emerged, and old paradigms are resurfacing in fresh ways. Scholars are finding innovative techniques to query the ancient contexts of the Scriptures, read the texts, and interrogate their own cultural situations and interpretive traditions.

The State of Old Testament Studies provides an overview of current academic study of the HB/OT. It is more than an update of *The Face of Old Testament Studies* since the essays engage new topics and research agendas. Several subdisciplines considered here did not exist only a few decades ago, while others were widely unexplored or nascent areas of inquiry. The wealth of scholarly research annually continues to increase prodigiously. Even those who attempt to keep up with research in the various disciplines find themselves unaware of some interesting, innovative approaches, while others remain entrenched in outmoded views of the scholarly landscape. As the field fragments and, at times, clusters in new arrangements, it is even more of a desideratum to reconsider in one place its shared assumptions, comparable goals, and multifaceted questions. We hope that in small measure these essays advance a greater interest in the study of the OT and motivate broader awareness of the field.

1. David W. Baker and Bill T. Arnold, *The Face of Old Testament Studies: A Survey of Contemporary Approaches* (Grand Rapids: Baker, 1999), 9–11.

Organization

The present volume is organized around three broad categories of OT studies. These three parts subdivide the field into distinct realms of inquiry, and each comprises almost the same number of essays. The collection could be ordered otherwise to different ends and with a variety of results. But although the editors' proclivities and assumptions have inevitably molded the presentation, we have attempted to represent the breadth of current research in the field. Achieving this breadth of coverage, however, has necessarily prevented pursuing some topics in greater depth.

Part 1 covers advances in the study of the cultural contexts of Scripture. The essays consider the languages and text of the Hebrew Bible (Hardy and Fresch), ancient versions and textual criticism (Tully), and the earliest textual evidence from the Judean Desert (Longacre). The archaeology and history of Syria and Palestine is subdivided into four eras: Late Bronze Age to Iron Age I (Hawkins), Iron Age II (Shafer-Elliott and Fulton), Neo-Babylonian and Persian periods (Silverman), and the Hellenistic period (Ryan). Treatments of Israelite religion (Hess), iconography (Strawn), and the ANE context for Israelite prophecy (Hilber) complete the initial section.

Part 2 surveys research on distinct books or genres of the canonical text. The field of OT studies customarily groups certain texts together. While these groupings are not innate to the texts, for convenience we have divided the chapters according to these textual groupings. The first essay summarizes matters involved in defining the OT canon (Dempster). Subsequent chapters follow the canonical order of most English Bibles: the Pentateuch (Boyd), Joshua, Judges, and Ruth (Lamb), Samuel-Kings (Gilmour), Chronicles (Ristau), Ezra-Nehemiah and Esther (Buster), Psalms (Grant), Wisdom literature (Kynes), Isaiah, Jeremiah, and Ezekiel (Kelle), and the book of the Twelve (Timmer). A final chapter is dedicated to apocalyptic literature (Cook).

Part 3 examines interpretive approaches from a variety of traditions and situations. The essays look at ideological readings (Brett), Old Testament ethics (Carroll R.), and environmental (Richter), literary (Longman), contextual (Lim), and sociological (Coomber) interpretive approaches. Other studies focus on recent work on gender and sexuality (Davis), inner-biblical exegesis (Dell), migration (Strine), theological interpretation (Thomas), and OT theology (Chapman).

Essay Content

All thirty-two essays reflect on the past and present of OT research. Each chapter surveys the subfield, presents different points of view, and gives proportional coverage to a diverse range of issues, including contemporary trends in research and ongoing controversies. Key bibliography is provided along with hospitable analysis of critical questions, major disputes, and methodologies. Although the essays concentrate mostly on developments over the past three decades, some offer additional historical analysis that could impact understandings today. Each chapter ends with a short reflection on the state of the discipline and suggested directions for future research.

The contributors are experts in their respective fields and often express their own opinions and preferences but at the same time seek to represent current research fairly and to evaluate the work of other scholars, even those with opposing opinions, with generosity.

Goals, Limitations, and Audience

Cross-disciplinary study is broadly valued within academia. The enlargement of any field is not, however, without adverse consequences. As research continues to expand, most find the resulting diversity beyond their ability to manage or appropriately cultivate. Researchers discover an unwieldy, sprawling, and oftentimes esoteric set of disciplines that can resist the admission of fresh voices. Without curated points of entry, there is the danger of overlooking important work, duplicating others' efforts, or neglecting voices that could expand one's expertise and experience. This volume seeks to mitigate these potential negatives by presenting the contemporary study of the OT with a wide range of contributors and topics.

A volume of this size and scope necessarily makes concessions. Each subdiscipline included deserves a volume to itself, and additional subdisciplines could have been included, but doing so would have expanded the volume beyond what was practical. Even so, overlap in some of the areas discussed was unavoidable.

The contributors come from a broad diversity of Christian faith and practice. Although located within the Western (mostly Protestant) scholastic tradition, they also reflect a range of backgrounds and experience. Some articles required more engagement with specific sectarian commitments than others. In those cases, the contributors make their commitments explicit, properly qualifying these preferences and avoiding exclusionary rhetoric.

We have attempted to offer a lucid presentation for a broad readership. The intended readership includes those interested in the academic study of the OT, so scholars, teachers, and students will find this survey of scholarship beneficial. To make the discussions accessible to nonspecialists, transliteration accompanies Hebrew and Greek words wherever feasible; however, the specialized vocabulary of each field, including its respective nomenclature and abbreviations, may occasionally pose a challenge to some readers. In such instances, consulting other resources, such as standard Bible dictionaries and encyclopedias, may be necessary.

We desire that this volume will help those invested in OT research to listen to, engage with, and learn from one another. The participants, both the contributors and potential readers, represent a vibrant future in this shared endeavor. We hope that *The State of Old Testament Studies* will promote collaboration so that the next quarter century will achieve further expansion and deepening of our knowledge.

On the Use and Limitations of the Term "Old Testament" in This Volume

On the one hand, the choice of title is intended to complement the companion volume, *The State of New Testament Studies*.[2] On the other hand, "Old Testament" is unavoidably positioned alongside "New Testament" as the Christian name for the Hebrew Scriptures. While the fields of study discussed in this volume are generally associated in the academy with "Old Testament studies," this convention also reflects a mostly Christian approach to this literature. Alternative descriptors such as Hebrew Bible, Tanak (תנ״ך), Hebrew Scriptures, Jewish Bible, and the bulky Hebrew Bible/Old Testament have their merits, but none is completely free of its own assumptions. Hence, for convenience contributors employ "Old Testament" (OT), "Hebrew Bible" (HB), or both, and where necessary, they qualify and explain their usage. The tetragrammaton is rendered YHWH throughout the volume except when alternative representations appear in direct quotations from other works.

Acknowledgments

We thank the good people at Baker Academic, especially Bryan Dyer and Jim Kinney, for their support of this project. Ms. Billie Goodenough provided assistance by proofreading the essays, and Auburn Powell Josephs, Andrew Panaggio, and Faith Steele helped to create several of the indexes.

2. Scot McKnight and Nijay K. Gupta, eds., *The State of New Testament Studies: A Survey of Recent Research* (Grand Rapids: Baker Academic, 2019).

PART 1

Ancient Linguistic and Cultural Contexts

1

Language and Text of the Hebrew Bible

H. H. Hardy II and Christopher J. Fresch

This essay surveys recent advances in the ways scholars construct Biblical Hebrew (BH) as a language and the Hebrew Bible (HB) as a text. The former focuses on the language of the documents; the latter describes the materiality of the writings, including the constituent parts of textualization.

The study of language and text is intertwined and coalesces under the traditional label philology. Some specialists bifurcate between *linguistics* as the analysis of language function and structure and *philology* as the examination of physical artifacts as materially embodied works.[1] However, linguists and philologists employ overlapping tools and methods to examine and construct knowledge about BH and the HB.[2] Their explorations regularly lead to implications beyond the narrower scope of linguistics or philology.

Historical Overview

Appraising more than two thousand years of inquiry into BH is impractical, but heuristically, four historical movements highlight important trends in its study:

1. Jacobus A. Naudé and Cynthia L. Miller-Naudé, "Linguistics and Philology—Separate, Overlapping or Subordinate/Superordinate Disciplines?," *JSem* 29, no. 2 (2020): 1–28, https://doi.org/10.25159/2663-6573/8573.

2. H. H. Hardy II, "The Table of Grammar: *lqr't* as Test Case," *JSem* 29, no. 2 (2020): 11–14, https://doi.org/10.25159/2663-6573/8515.

integrative approach; textual, grammatical, and lexical specialization; maturation of comparative philology; and new science. While this overview narrates these movements successively, each overlaps with the next and builds through time.

Integrative Approach

Readers have studied the language of the HB from its formation. The material itself prompts such investigations. Language intelligibility (and unintelligibility) plays a role in various stories. For example, Babel serves as a foundational etiology onto which are mapped early concepts of language origins. Code-switching is a product of political expansion and nation building (2 Kings 18:26). The *shibboleth* password delimits linguistic diversity among related but geographically disparate groups (Judg. 12:6), and assumptions about naming (i.e., onomastics, Judg. 1:10–11, 23) and diachronic semantic change (1 Sam. 9:9) are important cultural signifiers. Parallel passages (e.g., Exod. 20 and Deut. 5) invite comparison of similarities and differences.

Early Jewish and Christian interpreters interacted with these and other matters. Their discussion of language was an extension of exegetical—rather than linguistic—inquiry, and they engaged textual concerns as part of an integrated interpretive procedure.[3] Similar approaches, with modern subtleties, continue today.

Textual, Grammatical, and Lexical Specialization

As specializations emerged, the object of study shifted in the first millennium CE. Specialists began to study language and text as goals in themselves, rather than merely as instruments for ascertaining divine revelation. Late medieval scholasticism, paralleling developments within Syriac Christianity and early Islam, formed a trivium of text, grammar, and lexicon that portended later humanistic inquiry.

In the seventh-to-tenth centuries CE, scholars began to codify the physical representation of the HB in view of their textual and pronunciation traditions. Parallel movements to textualize the vocalization of underdetermined consonantal texts had started earlier in the Syriac world and were later employed by Arabic scribes.[4] The so-called proto-MT archetype provided the predominant orthographic form of the Scriptures from at least the time of Bar Kokhba (2nd cent. CE).[5]

3. Julio Trebolle Barrera, *The Jewish Bible and the Christian Bible: An Introduction to the History of the Bible* (Leiden: Brill, 1998).

4. Nick Posegay, *Points of Contact: The Shared Intellectual History of Vocalisation in Syriac, Arabic, and Hebrew*, CSLC 10 (Cambridge: Open Book, 2021).

5. Ian Young, "The Contrast between the Qumran and Masada Biblical Scrolls in the Light of New Data," in *Keter Shem Tov: Collected Essays on the Dead Sea Scrolls in Memory of Alan Crown*, ed. Shani Tzoref and Ian Young, Perspectives on Hebrew Scriptures and Its Contexts 20 (Piscataway, NJ: Gorgias, 2013), 113–19.

Late first-millennium Jewish communities in Babylon, Palestine, and Galilee textualized their readings, using sub-, intra-, and supralinear sigla as supplements to this inherited text. Cairo Geniza manuscripts reveal the incipient codification of several of these reading traditions.[6] One of these traditions is epitomized by the tenth-century Aleppo Codex, which less than a century later was replicated in the Firkovich ("Leningradensis") B19A Codex.[7] The Aleppo Codex emerged as "the most renowned model codex," enshrining the Tiberian Hebrew tradition with its venerable status as *the* Masoretic Text (MT).[8] The conventions of the Ben Asher manuscripts have been copied for more than a millennium and form the basis of many modern translations. Even as most Jewish communities adopted the MT, the Tiberian pronunciation evanesced around the end of the eleventh century and was replaced by discontinuous local readings.[9] The vocalized codex did not ultimately signal the end of the unvocalized scroll; unvocalized manuscripts continue to be used in synagogue recitation.

In Renaissance Europe, the MT became synonymous with Daniel Bomberg's *Mikraot Gedolot*, the so-called Rabbinic Bible; however, various MT manuscripts formed the textual basis of this early printed edition. Bomberg's sixteenth-century text persisted through two editions of *Biblia Hebraica* (*BHK*, 1906, 1913) until Paul Kahle produced the third (1937) and fourth editions (*BHS*, 1968–76) as diplomatic representations of Leningradensis.[10] Westminster Leningrad Codex, a widely used digital resource, is similarly a normalized edition. *Biblia Hebraica Quinta* (*BHQ*, 2004–) updates only the textual apparatuses and adds commentary. Representing a more eclectic text, the Hebrew University Bible Project defaults to the Aleppo Codex in its extant sections.[11] *Hebrew Bible: A Critical Edition* (formerly *Oxford Hebrew Bible*) reproduces the "earliest inferable text," or archetype, by comparing all ancient versions.[12]

The Masoretes developed extensive aids for proper written and oral transmission. Condensed lists of similar words, oddities in the spelling, and *ketiv/qere* were appended to manuscript margins, later called "Masorah parva" and

6. Geoffrey Khan, *A Short Introduction to the Tiberian Masoretic Bible and Its Reading Tradition*, 2nd ed. (Piscataway, NJ: Gorgias, 2013).

7. Yosef Ofer, *The Masora on Scripture and Its Methods*, FSBP 7 (Berlin: De Gruyter, 2019).

8. Maimonides legitimizes only the sections and layout of the Aleppo Codex and not its general textual authority or orthography; see M. H. Goshen-Gottstein, "The Aleppo Codex and the Rise of the Massoretic Bible Text," *BA* 42, no. 3 (1979): 145–63.

9. Shelomo Morag, "Pronunciations of Hebrew," *Encyclopaedia Judaica*, 2nd ed. (Detroit: Thomas Gale/Keter, 2007), 16:547–62.

10. In contrast to an eclectic text, which is compiled by comparing all variant manuscripts of a text and choosing the best reading, a diplomatic text is an edition that reproduces an existing manuscript. A photo-facsimile is available as David Noel Freedman, ed., *The Leningrad Codex: A Facsimile Edition* (Grand Rapids: Eerdmans; Leiden: Brill, 1998).

11. Michael Segal, "The Hebrew University Bible Project," *HeBAI* 2, no. 1 (2013): 38–62.

12. Michael V. Fox, *Proverbs: An Eclectic Edition with Introduction and Textual Commentary*, HBCE 1 (Atlanta: SBL Press, 2015); Ronald Hendel, *Steps to a New Edition of the Hebrew Bible*, Text-Critical Studies 10 (Atlanta: SBL Press, 2016).

"Masorah magna." Their compilations inspired lexicographic and grammatical studies. Independent works included lexical lists (e.g., *ʾOklah we-ʾOklah*) and early grammatical treatises (e.g., *Diqduqe ha-Ṭeʿamim*, *Hidāyat al-Qāriʾ*, and *Diqduq*).[13] These treatments detail the correct articulation of letters, of vowel letters, and of syllables, analogy, and even "fieldwork" in their own language use, yet the explanations were never fully dissociated from their interpretive application.[14]

The following centuries evidence the development and dissemination of these traditions in and beyond the Middle East. Cross-pollinating influences came from Syriac and Arabic grammarians, such as Sībawayh (d. 793), prompting more comprehensive language descriptions. The theory of the derivational root (Arabic *ʾaṣl*) and its triliteral nature, particularly in the work of ibn Janāḥ and Ḥayyūj, is one example. Medieval Hebrew grammar culminated in Spain,[15] Byzantium, and the Egyptian Sultanate.[16]

Renaissance Christianity engaged with the HB alongside other classical works but mostly dismissed its autochthonous interpretive traditions. With some notable exceptions—Origen, Jerome, and other Christians in the Middle East—interest in Hebrew waned in much of Christendom as OT translations (Septuagint, Peshitta, Vulgate, etc.) gained religious prominence. By the thirteenth century, the newly formed European universities taught Hebrew, with early Christian Hebraists predominantly assimilating the grammatical traditions of Joseph Qimḥi (ca. 1105–1170), Abraham ibn Ezra (ca. 1089–1164), and Yehuda Ḥayyūj (ca. 940–1000). Sixteenth-century Christian Hebraism flourished in collaboration with Jews like Elias Levita (1469–1549), reflected in the work of Johann Reuchlin (1455–1522) and Sebastian Münster (1488–1552), and moved toward innovation with Johannes Buxtorf (1564–1629).[17] With few exceptions, Christian Hebraists diverged from the exegetical concerns of their Jewish contemporaries, focusing instead on vernacular translation and apologetic (even polemical) tomes. This fragmentation accelerated as Christian scholastics formed their own grammatical acuity and, fueled by growing anti-Semitism, separated from Jewish traditions that were increasingly focused on the Talmud.

The Masoretic word lists led to more comprehensive lexicographic works. Disagreement between the Hebrew-only approach of Menaḥem ben Saruq (ca. 910–960) and the comparative Semitic approach of Dunaš ben Labraṭ (ca. 920–985)

13. Geoffrey Khan, *The Tiberian Pronunciation Tradition of Biblical Hebrew*, 2 vols., CSLC 1 (Cambridge: Open Book, 2020).

14. Geoffrey Khan, "Biblical Exegesis and Grammatical Theory in the Karaite Tradition," in *Exegesis and Grammar in Medieval Karaite Texts*, JSSSup 13 (Oxford: Oxford University Press, 2001), 127–49.

15. Ángel Sáenz-Badillos and Judit Targarona Borrás, *Gramáticos hebreos de al-Andalus (siglos X–XII): Filología y biblia* (Córdoba: El Almendro, 1988).

16. Ze'ev Ben-Ḥayyim, *The Literary and Oral Tradition of Hebrew and Aramaic amongst the Samaritans* (Hebrew), 5 vols. (Jerusalem: Bialik Institute, 1957–79).

17. Stephen Burnett, *From Christian Hebraism to Jewish Studies: Johannes Buxtorf (1564–1629) and Hebrew Learning in the Seventeenth Century* (Leiden: Brill, 1996).

presages debates in lexicography today. Medieval lexical studies culminated in the widely influential *Sefer ha-Šorašim* of David Qimḥi, employing root-based morphology and Semitic cognates.

Maturation of Comparative Philology

Early grammarians drew on their native languages of Arabic and Aramaic to explain similarities and differences in relation to BH. Comparative studies can be traced from at least the work of Saʿadiah Gaʾon (882–942) through the Spanish grammatical tradition into Christian Hebraism.[18] The full maturation of comparative philology coincided with advances in diachronic linguistics, particularly nineteenth-century lexicography.

Many Hebrew grammars still used today follow the comparative-diachronic approach. As an epigone of the grammatical tradition from Reuchlin to Buxtorf,[19] Wilhelm Gesenius provides the wellspring for nearly all later grammars.[20] Emil Kautzsch continued this descriptive tradition,[21] and others constructed similar treatments.[22] These grammars are arranged using categories based on Latin or other Indo-European languages. They list common and rare forms almost exhaustively, and their prescriptionist evaluations of corrupt and correct forms reflect their time.

Under the influence of eighteenth-century Indo-European studies, Hebraists enhanced the descriptive approach with comparative data from Semitic languages and developed diachronic methodologies. Early examples include Eduard König[23] and Gotthelf Bergsträsser's revision of *Hebräische Grammatik*.[24] Following the Neogrammarians and Semiticist Carl Brockelmann,[25] some reconstructed the

18. Aharon Maman, *Comparative Semitic Philology in the Middle Ages: From Saadiah Gaon to Ibn Barun (10th–12th cent.)*, SSLL 40 (Leiden: Brill, 2004).

19. Stephen G. Burnett, *From Christian Hebraism to Jewish Studies: Johannes Buxtorf (1564–1629) and Hebrew Learning in the Seventeenth Century* (Leiden: Brill, 1996), 114–15, 242.

20. Wilhelm Gesenius, *Hebräische Grammatik* (Halle: Rengerschen Buchhandlung, 1813).

21. *Wilhelm Gesenius' Hebräische Grammatik*, 28th ed., rev. Emil Kautzsch (Leipzig: Vogel, 1909); English translation, *Gesenius' Hebrew Grammar*, 2nd ed., trans. A. E. Cowley (Oxford: Clarendon, 1910).

22. Heinrich Ewald, *Ausführliches Lehrbuch der hebräischen Sprache*, 8th ed. (Göttingen: Dieterich, 1870); Andrew Bruce Davidson, *Introductory Hebrew Grammar: Hebrew Syntax*, 3rd ed. (Edinburgh: T&T Clark, 1902); Mayer Lambert, *Traité de Grammaire Hébraïque* (Paris: Leroux, 1931).

23. Eduard König, *Historisch-kritisches Lehrgebäude der hebräischen Sprache*, 3 vols. (Leipzig: Hinrichs, 1881, 1895, 1897).

24. Gotthelf Bergsträsser, *Wilhelm Gesenius' Hebräische Grammatik*, 29th ed. (Leipzig: Vogel, 1918); Bergsträsser, *Introduction to the Semitic Languages*, trans. Peter T. Daniels (Winona Lake, IN: Eisenbrauns, 1983); see also Rudolf Meyer, *Hebräische Grammatik*, 3rd ed. (Berlin: De Gruyter, 1992).

25. Carl Brockelmann, *Grundriss der vergleichenden Grammatik der semitischen Sprachen*, 2 vols. (Berlin: Reuther & Reichard, 1908, 1913).

historical grammar(s) of BH.[26] These comparative-historical approaches continue to be held in high regard.[27]

The lexicographic work of Gesenius, posthumously completed by Rödiger, embodies nineteenth-century philology.[28] Gesenius employs "the *historico-logical* method of lexicography," which "first investigates the primary and native signification of a word, and then deduces from it in logical order the subordinate meanings," according to Edward Robinson, "which, in short, presents a logical and historical view of each word."[29] Translating Gesenius's work into English, the Brown-Driver-Briggs lexicon arranges words by root, expands its etymological considerations, and separates the Hebrew and Aramaic words.[30] Later revisions of Gesenius's *Handwörterbuch* share similar innovations. Between the twelfth and sixteenth editions, Frants Buhl completely revised the work (popularly called the *Gesenius-Buhl Lexicon*), and the eighteenth edition, begun by Rudolf Meyer, was completed in 2013.[31] This latest *Handwörterbuch* expands usage collocations and provides updated cognate, onomastic, and textual information but excludes earlier literary-critical assessments.

Following the Second World War, Ludwig Koehler compiled a dictionary based on comparative methods and organized alphabetically that used "logical" semantic development. Along with Walter Baumgartner, who produced the Aramaic volume and completed the work, Koehler updated the cognate information and referenced the Dead Sea Scrolls, Sirach, Secunda (the second column of Origen's Hexapla), and Jerome.[32] The English translation appeared in the 1990s.[33] Franz

26. Hans Bauer and Pontus Leander, *Historische Grammatik der hebräischen Sprache des alten Testamentes* (Halle: Niemeyer, 1922); Paul Joüon, *Grammaire de l'hébreu biblique*, 2nd ed. (Rome: Biblical Pontifical Institute, 1947); Paul Joüon and T. Muraoka, *A Grammar of Biblical Hebrew*, 2nd ed., SubBi 27 (Rome: Pontifical Biblical Institute, 2006); Alexander Sperber, *A Historical Grammar of Biblical Hebrew* (Leiden: Brill, 1966).

27. Joshua Blau, *Phonology and Morphology of Biblical Hebrew*, LSAWS 2 (Winona Lake, IN: Eisenbrauns, 2010); Benjamin D. Suchard, *The Development of Biblical Hebrew Vowels*, SSLL 99 (Leiden: Brill, 2019).

28. Wilhelm Gesenius, *Hebräisch-deutsches Handwörterbuch*, 2 vols. (Leipzig: Vogel, 1810–12).

29. Wilhelm Gesenius, *A Hebrew and English Lexicon of the Old Testament, including Biblical Chaldee*, trans. Edward Robinson (Boston: Crocker & Brewster, 1836), iv.

30. Francis Brown, S. R. Driver, and Charles A. Briggs, eds., *A Hebrew and English Lexicon of the Old Testament with an Appendix Containing the Biblical Aramaic* (Oxford: Clarendon, 1898); Stefan Schorch and Ernst-Joachim Waschke, eds., *Biblische Exegese und hebräische Lexikographie*, BZAW 427 (Berlin: De Gruyter, 2013).

31. Wilhelm Gesenius, *Hebräisches und Aramäisches Handwörterbuch über das Alte Testament*, 16th ed., ed. Frants Buhl (Leipzig: Vogel, 1915); 18th ed., ed. Herbert Donner (Berlin: Springer, 2013).

32. Ludwig Koehler and Walter Baumgartner, *Lexicon in Veteris Testamenti Libros* (Leiden: Brill, 1953); Ludwig Koehler, Walter Baumgartner, and J. J. Stamm, *Hebräisches und aramäisches Lexikon zum alten Testament*, 6 vols. (Leiden: Brill, 1967–96).

33. Ludwig Koehler, Walter Baumgartner, and Johann J. Stamm, *The Hebrew and Aramaic Lexicon of the Old Testament*, trans. and ed. under the supervision of M. E. J. Richardson, 4 vols. (Leiden: Brill, 1994–99).

Zorell produced a comparatively oriented Hebrew lexicon in the mid-twentieth century.[34] An English edition of Ernst Vogt's Aramaic portion was published separately.[35] These lexicons realize Gesenius's vision, amassing current data within a comparative framework.

New Science

In the mid-nineteenth century, the Neogrammarians initiated the scientific approach to language study, adhering to the strict application of the comparative-historical method and the principle of exceptionless sound change.[36] With the turn toward the synchronic investigation of language (i.e, *langue*), Ferdinand de Saussure is credited with initiating the new science of linguistics.[37] Ensuing approaches would mature with the work of Leonard Bloomfield until supplanted in the 1960s both by the generative theories of Noam Chomsky and by several nongenerative approaches. Functional linguistics, including the Prague school of linguistics, emerged independently and focused on the usage-based purpose of language as an adaptive organic system. Further fragmentation continued in the twentieth century with language universals,[38] functional discourse grammar,[39] functional grammar,[40] emergent grammar,[41] cognitive grammar,[42] construction grammar,[43] and more.

BH grammarians were slow to adopt theoretical linguistic research and favored more traditional approaches. They often focused on accumulating data rather than contributing to general linguistics.[44] Toward the end of the twentieth century, however, several grammars integrated linguistic analysis using

34. Franz Zorell, *Lexicon Hebraicum et Aramaicum Veteris Testamenti* (Rome: Pontifical Biblical Institute, 1954).

35. Ernst Vogt, *Lexicon of Biblical Aramaic*, trans. and rev. Joseph Fitzmyer, SubBi 42 (Rome: Gregorian and Biblical Press, 2011).

36. Kurt Jankowsky, *The Neogrammarians: A Re-evaluation of Their Place in the Development of Linguistic Science* (Hague: Mouton, 1972).

37. Ferdinand de Saussure, *Cours de linguistique générale*, ed. C. Bally and A. Sechehaye (Lausanne and Paris: Payot, 1916).

38. Joseph Greenberg, *Language Universals* (Hague: Mouton, 1966); William A. Croft, *Typology and Universals*, 2nd ed. (Cambridge: Cambridge University Press, 2002).

39. Talmy Givón, *Functionalism and Grammar* (Amsterdam: John Benjamins, 1995).

40. Simon C. Dik, *The Theory of Functional Grammar*, ed. Kees Hengeveld, 2 vols. (Berlin: De Gruyter, 1997).

41. Paul Hopper, "Emergent Grammar," *Berkeley Linguistics Society* 13 (1987): 139–57.

42. Ronald W. Langacker, *Cognitive Grammar: A Basic Introduction* (Oxford: Oxford University Press, 2008).

43. George Lakoff, *Women, Fire, and Dangerous Things: What Categories Reveal about the Mind* (Chicago: CSLI, 1987); William A. Croft, *Radical Construction Grammar* (Oxford: Oxford University Press, 2001).

44. Though see the contribution to corpus-based linguistics by Cynthia Miller-Naudé and Jacobus Naudé, "New Directions in the Computational Analysis of Biblical Hebrew Grammar," *JSem* 27, no. 1 (2018): 1–17.

transformational-generative grammar,[45] "modern linguistic study,"[46] or what may be called linguistic eclecticism.[47] Twenty-first-century studies proliferated in number and in the methodologies employed. Geoffrey Khan's *Encyclopedia of Hebrew Language and Linguistics* is a paradigmatic example that includes many historically and linguistically related topics from ancient to modern Hebrew.[48] These topics extend to and overlap with the realities of manuscript materiality and codicology.[49]

Linguistic approaches were even slower to infiltrate lexicography. While not restricted to BH, Eliezer Ben-Yehuda's *A Complete Dictionary of Ancient and Modern Hebrew* signaled an inflection point.[50] By the mid-twentieth century, lexicographers were no longer willing to demarcate a boundary between biblical and later Hebrew.[51] The *Dictionary of Classical Hebrew* (*DCH*) includes all evidence through the second century CE.[52] Additionally, it employs "a theoretical base in modern linguistics," semantic and syntagmatic-paradigmatic analysis instead of the traditional comparative, diachronic, and developmental arrangements.[53] Focusing on contextual domains, the *Semantic Dictionary of Biblical Hebrew* takes a cognitive-semantic approach.[54] Elsewhere, advances in understanding function words[55] and loanwords[56] result from current linguistic insights.[57] These recent dictionaries and lexical studies signal the value of

45. Wolfgang Richter, *Grundlagen einer althebräischen Grammatik*, 3 vols. (Ottilien: EOS, 1978–80).

46. Bruce Waltke and Michael P. O'Connor, *An Introduction to Biblical Hebrew Syntax* (Winona Lake, IN: Eisenbrauns, 1989), x.

47. Christo H. J. van der Merwe, Jacobus A. Naudé, and Jan H. Kroeze, *A Biblical Hebrew Reference Grammar*, 2nd ed. (London: Bloomsbury, 2017), xxix.

48. Geoffrey Khan, ed., *Encyclopedia of Hebrew Language and Linguistics*, 4 vols. (Berlin: Brill, 2013).

49. Liv Ingeborg Lied and Hugo Lundhaug, *Snapshots of Evolving Traditions: Jewish and Christian Manuscript Culture, Textual Fluidity, and New Philology*, TUGAL 175 (Berlin: De Gruyter, 2017).

50. Eliezer Ben-Yehuda, *A Complete Dictionary of Ancient and Modern Hebrew*, 17 vols. (Berlin: Schöneberg, 1908–59).

51. See Ma'agarim: The Historical Dictionary Project (https://isaw.nyu.edu/publications/awol-index/html/maagarim.hebrew-academy.org.il/Pages-PMain-aspx.html). For a fuller description of the project, see https://en.hebrew-academy.org.il/historical-dictionary-project/.

52. David J. A. Clines, ed., *Dictionary of Classical Hebrew*, 9 vols. (Sheffield: Sheffield Academic/Sheffield Phoenix, 1993–2016).

53. *DCH* 1:14.

54. Reinier de Blois and Enio R. Mueller, eds., *Semantic Dictionary of Biblical Hebrew* (United Bible Societies, 2000–2021), https://semanticdictionary.org/semdic.php. For additional information about this resource, see https://translation.bible/tools-resources/semantic-dictionary-of-biblical-hebrew/.

55. H. H. Hardy II, *The Development of Biblical Hebrew Prepositions*, ANEM 28 (Atlanta: SBL Press, 2022).

56. Benjamin Noonan, *Non-Semitic Loanwords in the Hebrew Bible: A Lexicon of Language Contact*, LSAWS 14 (Winona Lake, IN: Eisenbrauns, 2019).

57. Christo H. J. van der Merwe, "Biblical Hebrew and Cognitive Linguistics: A General Orientation," in *New Perspectives in Biblical and Rabbinic Hebrew*, ed. Aaron D. Hornkohl and

usage-based and cognitive-linguistic research in furthering our understanding of BH.

Recent Trends in Biblical Hebrew Grammar

Our review of advances in BH grammar is organized by phonology, morphology, syntax, pragmatics, and verbal semantics.

Phonology

Much of the current work in Hebrew phonology details language diversity within both the corpus of the HB and later reading traditions. The Hebrew contained within the HB is not a single uniform language. It is widely held that "Biblical Hebrew" reflects a combination of linguistic strata, registers, and dialects.[58] The traditional tripartite periodization of Ancient, Standard, and Late Biblical Hebrew has been challenged by scholars who proscribe clear boundaries.[59] Even those who ascribe more static divisions debate the extent of the dialectal and diachronic overlap.[60]

Ongoing research explores how the HB was pronounced in various Jewish communities that preserved their reading of the Scriptures. Even the earliest manuscripts, as evidenced in the DSS, demonstrate phonetic variation.[61] Comparing the Hebrew phonologies recorded in Origen's Secunda, Jerome's Latin transcriptions, and the reading traditions of Samaritan, Tiberian, Babylonian, and Palestinian Hebrew highlight disparities and developments from the Second Temple through the end of the first millennium CE.[62] These changes are further studied as the outcome of bilingualism and language contact, particularly with various dialects of Aramaic.[63]

Geoffrey Khan, CSLC 7 (Cambridge: Open Book, 2021), 641–96; Ellen van Wolde, *Reframing Biblical Studies* (Winona Lake, IN: Eisenbrauns, 2009).

58. Gary Rendsburg, "Israelian Hebrew, Inscriptions from the North of Israel, and Samaritan Hebrew: A Complex of Northern Dialects," *JSem* 30, no. 2 (2021): 1–19; Edward Greenstein, "The Language of Job and Its Poetic Function," *JBL* 122, no. 4 (2003): 651–66; Aaron Hornkohl, *Ancient Hebrew Periodization and the Language of the Book of Jeremiah: The Case for a Sixth-Century Date of Composition*, SSLL 74 (Leiden: Brill, 2014).

59. Ian Young, Robert Rezetko, and Martin Ehrensvärd, *Linguistic Dating of Biblical Texts*, 2 vols. (London: Equinox, 2008).

60. Cynthia Miller-Naudé and Ziony Zevit, eds., *Diachrony in Biblical Hebrew*, LSAWS 8 (Winona Lake, IN: Eisenbrauns, 2012).

61. Eric Reymond, *Qumran Hebrew: An Overview of Orthography, Phonology, and Morphology*, RBS 76 (Atlanta: SBL Press, 2014).

62. Benjamin Kantor, *The Linguistic Classification of the Reading Traditions of Biblical Hebrew: A Phyla-and-Waves Model*, CSLC (Cambridge: Open Book, 2023).

63. Aaron Koller, "Hebrew and Aramaic in Contact," in *A Companion to Ancient Near Eastern Languages*, ed. Rebecca Hasselbach-Andee (Hoboken, NJ: Wiley-Blackwell, 2020), 439–55; Samuel Boyd, *Language Contact, Colonial Administration, and the Construction of Identity in Ancient Israel*, HSM 66 (Boston: Brill, 2021).

While the textualization of the HB began to coalesce in the Middle Ages, different communities pronounced the text in diverse ways according to long-standing reading traditions.[64] Even after the Tiberian Masoretic text achieved near authoritative status, Tiberian Hebrew pronunciation was lost early in the second millennium, and subsequent phonetic realizations varied significantly. Readers reimagined the Tiberian Hebrew signs using their own community's phonology, as with the traditional quantitative description based on David Qimḥi's *Compedium Michlol*. Khan connects three main evidential strains to reconstruct a more sophisticated phonetic description of Tiberian Hebrew: the pointings of various traditions, descriptions of vowels in grammatical treatises, and the Karaite transcriptions.[65] He concludes that vowel length was not phonemic but conditioned, and syllables were structured as nonphonological (one to three moras) or phonological encoding (strictly two moras).[66] The results have transformed our understanding of the Tiberian Hebrew reading tradition, its impermanence, and the diversity of BH phonologies. Ernest John Revell investigates the prosaic changes in pausal forms and their connection with the Tiberian diacritics.[67] Other studies present competing cantillation and intonation models.[68] Finally, insights from formalist phonology have made slow inroads,[69] but constraint-based models like Optimality Theory have produced generative results for a number of persistent quandaries.[70]

Morphology

Comparative-historical research, incorporating methods from historical linguistics, dialectology, and language typology, has advanced our understanding of morphology through reconstructions of both Hebrew and the broader Semitic language family. Significant progress continues to hone the place of the Canaanite languages, including Hebrew, within the Semitic language

64. W. Randall Garr and Steven E. Fassberg, eds., *A Handbook of Biblical Hebrew*, 2 vols. (Winona Lake, IN: Eisenbrauns, 2016).

65. Khan, *Tiberian Pronunciation Tradition.*

66. Geoffrey Khan, "Vowel Length and Syllable Structure in the Tiberian Tradition of Biblical Hebrew," *JSS* 32, no. 1 (1987): 23–82.

67. E. J. Revell, *The Pausal System: Divisions in the Hebrew Biblical Text as Marked by Voweling and Stress Position* (Sheffield: Sheffield Phoenix, 2015).

68. Sung Jin Park, *Fundamentals of Hebrew Accents* (Cambridge: Cambridge University Press 2020); Sophia Pitcher, "Towards a Prosodic Model for Tiberian Hebrew: An Intonation-Based Analysis," *SPiL Plus* 63 (2021): 1–27.

69. Edward Greenstein, "An Introduction to the Generative Phonology of Biblical Hebrew," in *Linguistics and Biblical Hebrew*, ed. Walter R. Bodine (Winona Lake, IN: Eisenbrauns, 1992), 29–40.

70. Silje Alvestad and Lutz Edzard, La-ḥšōḇ, *but* la-ḥăzōr? *Sonority, Optimality, and the Hebrew* פ"ח *Forms*, AKM 66 (Wiesbaden: Harrassowitz, 2009); Hadas Yeverechyahu and Outi Bat-El, "Biblical Hebrew Segholates: Universal and Language-Specific Effects," *Brill's Journal of Afroasiatic Languages and Linguistics* 12, no. 1 (2020): 31–73.

family.[71] These studies demonstrate clear morphological isoglosses within the Central and Northwest Semitic subgroupings and areal diffusion in more closely related Iron Age languages,[72] although some have questioned Hebrew's place among its Canaanite neighbors.[73]

Cross-linguistic comparisons provide insights into BH morphology. Joshua Fox presents the derivational noun patterns in Semitic using comparative lexicography and semantics.[74] Dennis Pardee outlines the development and loss of vocalic case endings through external reconstruction and comparing vestigial internal features.[75] A broad consensus considers the Hebrew narrative preterite (*wayyiqtol*) as deriving from a short **yiqtul* form.[76] Others use historical linguistics to trace the linguistic incorporation and development of various grammatical items.[77] Within the framework of distributed morphology, both root- and word-based approaches have been used to describe word-formation.[78]

Syntax

Peter Bekins demonstrates that BH utilizes a differential object marking (DOM) system.[79] These systems interact with the semantic roles and pragmatics of clause constituents. BH exhibits both asymmetric (overt vs. null object marking) and symmetric patterns (accusative vs. oblique cases). Regarding asymmetric marking, the likelihood that the object is overtly marked with אֶת־/אֵת (*ʾet-*/*ʾēt*) increases with the referent's information status (more known), animacy, and persistence in the discourse. For symmetric marking, the accusative or an oblique case for the direct object correlates with "semantic motivations related to parameters

71. John Huehnergard and Na'ama Pat-el, eds., *The Semitic Languages*, 2nd ed. (London: Routledge, 2019); Leonid Kogan, *Genealogical Classification of Semitic: The Lexical Isoglosses* (Berlin: De Gruyter, 2015).

72. W. Randall Garr, *Dialect Geography of Syria-Palestine, 1000–586 BCE* (Winona Lake, IN: Eisenbrauns, 1985).

73. Anson Rainey, "Whence Came the Israelites and Their Language?," *IEJ* 57, no. 1 (2007): 41–64.

74. Joshua Fox, *Semitic Noun Patterns*, HSS 59 (Winona Lake, IN: Eisenbrauns, 2003).

75. Dennis Pardee, "Vestiges du système casuel entre le nom et le pronom suffixe en hébreu biblique," in *Grammatical Case in the Languages of the Middle East and Europe*, ed. Michèle Fruyt, Michel Mazoyer, and Dennis Pardee, SAOC 64 (Chicago: Oriental Institute, 2011), 113–21.

76. Dennis Pardee, "The Biblical Hebrew Verbal System in a Nutshell," in *Language and Nature: Papers presented to John Huehnergard on the Occasion of His 60th Birthday*, ed. Rebecca Hasselbach and Na'ama Pat-El, SAOC 67 (Chicago: Oriental Institute, 2012), 285–317.

77. Hardy, *Biblical Hebrew Prepositions*, 26–28.

78. Outi Bat-El, "The Fate of the Consonantal Root and the Binyan in Optimality Theory," *Recherches linguistiques de Vincennes* 32 (2003): 31–60; Maya Arad, *Roots and Patterns: Hebrew Morpho-Syntax*, Studies in Natural Language and Linguistic Theory 63 (Dordrecht: Springer, 2005).

79. Peter Bekins, *Transitivity and Object Marking in Biblical Hebrew: An Investigation of the Object Preposition ʾEt*, HSS 64 (Leiden: Brill, 2014).

such as affectedness and aspect."[80] The less affected the object or less bounded the event, the more likely it is that an oblique case is used for the object. For accusative objects, higher transitivity (i.e., exhibiting semantic features such as definiteness, boundedness, and patient semantics) results in a greater likelihood that the overt marker will be used.

Daniel Wilson discusses the syntax and semantics of היה (*hyh*, be), copular clauses, and verbless clauses.[81] Since BH evinces both verbless and copular clauses, he argues the option to use היה is dependent on interrelated controlling features, including tense, aspect, and mood marking, *Aktionsart* (inchoative and telic achievements), and disambiguation.[82] Wilson clarifies two related issues. In the left (initial) periphery of a clause, היה is used pragmatically to signal "not-at-issue" content, information that updates the common ground among participants and serves as a foundation for the following discourse. Second, the pronoun הוּא (*hûʾ*, he; and הֵם, *hēm*, they) can function as a present-tense copula in verbless clauses.[83] It correlates to individual-level predicates that characterize individuals in terms of their inherent or permanent properties.

Robert Holmstedt describes relative clauses through generative syntax and typological comparisons. The relative clause is a syntactically subordinate element—marked with אֲשֶׁר (*ʾăšer*), -שֶׁ (*še-*), מָה (*mâ*), a near demonstrative, or the definite article—that serves as an adnominal modifier of a relative head.[84] The relative head plays a role in both the embedded clause and the matrix clause. Sometimes the head is null. Semantically, a restrictive relative clause indicates necessary information about its referent, while a nonrestrictive clause, which offers optional information, is essentially unmarked.

Other studies examine edge constructions (*casus pendens*). Explorations of edge constructions, pronouns, and anaphora require multifaceted descriptions at the intersection of syntax and pragmatics. Fronting, extraposition, and dislocation identify clause constituents in unconventional locations, often motivated by topicalization.[85] Related is the use of pronouns in a variety of constructions related to anaphora (e.g., resumption, tripartite nominal clauses, covert constituency, and pro-drop).[86]

80. Bekins, *Transitivity and Object Marking in Biblical Hebrew*, 198.

81. Daniel Wilson, *Syntactic and Semantic Variation in Copular Sentences: Insights from Classical Hebrew*, Linguistics Today 261 (Amsterdam: John Benjamins, 2020); Wilson, "הָיָה in Biblical Hebrew," in Hornkohl and Khan, *New Perspectives*, 455–71.

82. Wilson, "הָיָה in Biblical Hebrew," 461–65; Wilson, *Copular Sentences*, 44–54, 65–88.

83. Wilson, *Copular Sentences*, 54–56.

84. Robert Holmstedt, *The Relative Clause in Biblical Hebrew*, LSAWS 10 (Winona Lake, IN: Eisenbrauns, 2016).

85. Robert Holmstedt, "Critical at the Margins: Edge Constituents in Biblical Hebrew," *KUSATU* 17 (2014): 109–56; Cynthia Miller-Naudé and Jacobus Naudé, "Differentiating Dislocations, Topicalisation, and Extraposition in Biblical Hebrew: Evidence from Negation," *SPiL Plus* 56 (2019): 179–99.

86. Cynthia Miller-Naudé and Jacobus Naudé, "Theoretical Approaches to Anaphora and Pronouns in Biblical Hebrew," *JSem* 28, no. 2 (2019): 1–22.

Pragmatics

Despite its absence in most BH grammars, pragmatics constitutes a significant portion of contemporary BH linguistic scholarship. The "pragmatic turn" of the 1970s led to research in the 1980s on emphatic structures,[87] extraposition and word order,[88] and discourse analysis.[89] Each decade since has seen its expansion.

One ongoing discussion concerns default word order in verbal clauses. Two positions dominate: (1) BH as a verb-subject (VS) language,[90] or (2) BH as a subject-verb (SV) language.[91] Both camps acknowledge that most clauses are verb-initial and that clauses in which a nominal or phrasal constituent precedes the verb exhibit fronting, a phenomenon drawing attention to the sentence topic or focus.[92] In actual analysis of BH information structure, the two positions often agree.

Recent scholarship on fronting expands beyond information structure, particularly where notions of topic and focus do not appear relevant. Adina Moshavi posits four alternate functions in narrative: anteriority, simultaneity, background information, and a new unit or scene within the narrative.[93] Aaron Hornkohl similarly suggests that discourse discontinuity is the overarching pragmatic principle for clauses with a fronted constituent.[94] Ian Atkinson, though in considerable agreement, argues that theticity better accounts for nontopic/focus-fronting constructions.[95] Unlike categorical sentences (i.e., predications about a known/presupposed topic), thetic sentences do not convey information about a referent. They convey the announcement or presentation of an entire state of affairs (i.e., the whole utterance).

87. T. Muraoka, *Emphatic Words and Structures in Biblical Hebrew* (Jerusalem: Magnes, 1985).

88. Geoffrey Khan, *Studies in Semitic Syntax*, London Oriental Series 38 (Oxford: Oxford University Press, 1988).

89. Robert Longacre, *Joseph: A Story of Divine Providence; A Text Theoretical and Textlinguistic Analysis of Genesis 37 and 39–48*, 2nd ed. (Winona Lake, IN: Eisenbrauns, 2003).

90. Adina Moshavi, *Word Order in the Biblical Hebrew Finite Clause*, LSAWS 4 (Winona Lake, IN: Eisenbrauns, 2010); Aaron Hornkohl, "Biblical Hebrew Tense–Aspect–Mood, Word Order and Pragmatics: Some Observations on Recent Approaches," in *Studies in Semitic Linguistics and Manuscripts: A Liber Discipulorum in Honour of Professor Geoffrey Khan*, ed. Nadia Vidro et al., Studia Semitica Upsaliensia 30 (Uppsala: Uppsala Universitet, 2018), 27–56.

91. Robert Holmstedt, "Word Order and Information Structure in Ruth and Jonah: A Generative-Typological Analysis," *JSS* 54, no. 1 (2009): 111–39; Elizabeth Cowper and Vincent DeCaen, "Biblical Hebrew: A Formal Perspective on the Left Periphery," *Toronto Working Papers in Linguistics 38* (2017): 1–33.

92. Since subject-verb proponents tend to utilize generative linguistics, their position concerns "deep structure." Accordingly, the surface structure appears most commonly as verb-subject with certain "triggers" (e.g., relatives, interrogatives, causal words, negators, modal words, covert modal operators) that cause verb raising and word-order inversion (Holmstedt, "Word Order and Information Structure," 120–26).

93. Moshavi, *Word Order*, 112–15.

94. Hornkohl, "Biblical Hebrew Tense–Aspect–Mood," 44–53.

95. Ian Atkinson, "In Pursuit of a More Comprehensive Framework for Fronting in Classical BH Prose" (PhD diss., University of Stellenbosch, 2021), 99–134.

Thetics are typically used for discourse-management purposes, providing background information or a jumping-off point for ensuing discourse. Khan and van der Merwe posit three types of fronting constructions: focus, topic, and thetic.[96] They consider fronting to be an exploitation of information structure for the purposes of discourse organization. Though disagreements remain, the consensus is that fronting often conveys thematic (topical) or salient (focal) information. Discussions on discontinuity, theticity, and discourse organization evince general agreement that non-verb-initial (X + V) clauses denote similar pragmatic phenomena.

Discourse grammar investigates grammatical phenomena with discourse implications,[97] such as quotative frames,[98] participant reference,[99] and discourse markers.[100] Discourse grammar is one aspect of the method known as discourse analysis. A comprehensive discourse analysis of the HB is a daunting task, but JoAnna Hoyt and Todd Scacewater provide pathways for future research.[101]

Finally, pragmatics involves other areas of study, such as sociolinguistics and discourse pragmatics. Sociolinguistics offers a social parameter to view linguistic variation rather than relying exclusively on traditional explanations, such as diachrony.[102] Advances include studies in forms of address[103] and kinship reference.[104]

Verbal Semantics

A number of studies seek to define and nuance the prevailing representation of the verbal semantics of the stems (*binyanim*) and the conjugations.

96. Geoffrey Khan and Christo H. J. van der Merwe, "Towards a Comprehensive Model for Interpreting Word Order in Classical Hebrew," *JSS* 65, no. 2 (2020): 347–90.

97. See a summary of BH discourse features in Steven Runge and Joshua Westbury, *The Lexham Discourse Hebrew Bible: Introduction* (Bellingham, WA: Lexham, 2012).

98. Cynthia Miller[-Naudé], *The Representation of Speech in Biblical Hebrew Narrative: A Linguistic Analysis*, HSS 55 (Leiden: Brill, 2003).

99. Steven Runge, "Pragmatic Effects of Semantically Redundant Anchoring Expressions in Biblical Hebrew Narrative," *JNSL* 32, no. 2 (2006): 87–104; Frank Polak, "Participant Tracking, Positioning, and the Pragmatics of Biblical Narrative," in *Advances in Biblical Hebrew Linguistics: Data, Methods, and Analyses*, ed. Adina Moshavi and Tania Notarius, LSAWS 12 (Winona Lake, IN: Eisenbrauns, 2017), 153–72.

100. Adina Moshavi, "הלא as a Discourse Marker of Justification in Biblical Hebrew," *HS* 48 (2007): 171–86; Cynthia Miller-Naudé, "הִנֵּה and Mirativity in Biblical Hebrew," *HS* 52 (2011): 53–81. See also van der Merwe, Naudé, and Kroeze, *A Biblical Hebrew Reference Grammar* (§40).

101. JoAnna Hoyt and Todd Scacewater, eds., *Discourse Analysis of Biblical Hebrew Narratives* (Dallas: Fontes, forthcoming).

102. Frank Polak, "Sociolinguistics: A Key to the Typology and the Social Background of Biblical Hebrew," *HS* 47 (2011): 115–62; Dong-Hyuk Kim, *Early Biblical Hebrew, Late Biblical Hebrew, and Linguistic Variability: A Sociolinguistic Evaluation of the Linguistic Dating of Biblical Texts*, VTSup 156 (Leiden: Brill, 2013).

103. Young Bok Kim, *Hebrew Forms of Address: A Sociolinguistic Analysis*, ANEM 31 (Atlanta: SBL Press, 2023).

104. Raffaele Esposito, "Kinship Terms as Forms of Address in Biblical Hebrew: Fictive and Literal Use," *AION* 69 (2009): 127–40.

Despite the semantic complexity and polysemy, the verbal stems coalesce around encoding grammatical voice, completion, plurality, and other semantic notions. Five grammatical categories provide a holistic picture of verbal stems:[105]

1. Grammatical voice (active, passive, reflexive, or middle voice),
2. Duration (fientive or stative),
3. Completion (transitive, intransitive, ditransitive, or ambitransitive) and Valency (avalent, univalent, bivalent, trivalent),
4. Causation (causative or anticausative; resultative or factitive), and
5. Plurality of action (iterative, habitual, distributive, intensive, or reciprocal).

These interconnected categories provide a robust framework to understand the prototypical semantics encoded with each stem and their interactions with clause syntax.[106]

Ongoing research has specifically enhanced our understandings of the N (Niphal) and D (Piel) stems.[107] Regarding the Niphal, Ellen van Wolde argues against the traditional designations of passive and reflexive, claiming instead that the stem marks middle voice. The Niphal portrays the verb's subject as both agent/experiencer/mover and patient, while "focusing on the action, the resultative state, the disposition or modal conditions of this action, but not on its cause, source, or external Agents."[108] Van Wolde admits the Niphal is used for passive voice with transitive verbs, but this rare use only occurs if an external agent is present.[109] Ethan Jones agrees that the Niphal expresses the middle voice but critiques van Wolde's position as too narrow.[110] Giving consideration to typological research and the role that context plays in communication and comprehension, Jones concludes that passive semantics are more common than van Wolde claims and suggests a more variegated situation.[111]

Building from N. J. C. Kouwenberg's research on the D-stem in Akkadian,[112] John Charles Beckman critiques the dominant view that the Piel is factitive/

105. H. H. Hardy II and Matthew McAffee, *Going Deeper with Biblical Hebrew* (Nashville: B&H Academic, 2024), §3.6, reworking of *An Introduction to Biblical Hebrew Syntax*, §20.2o.

106. For a helpful summary of how these categories interact and can be mapped onto the *binyanim*, see Hardy and McAffee, *Going Deeper*, chaps. 3–4.

107. Benjamin Noonan, *Advances in the Study of Biblical Hebrew and Aramaic: New Insights for Reading the Old Testament* (Grand Rapids: Zondervan Academic, 2020), 92–113.

108. Ellen van Wolde, "The Niphal as Middle Voice and Its Consequence for Meaning," *JSOT* 43, no. 3 (2019): 453–78.

109. Van Wolde, "Niphal," 467–73.

110. Ethan Jones, "Hearing the 'Voice' of the Niphal: A Response to Ellen van Wolde," *JSOT* 45, no. 3 (2021): 291–308.

111. Ethan Jones, "Middle and Passive Voice: Semantic Distinctions of the Niphal in Biblical Hebrew," *ZAW* 132, no. 3 (2020): 427–48.

112. N. J. C. Kouwenberg, *The Akkadian Verb and Its Semitic Background*, Languages of the Ancient Near East 2 (Winona Lake, IN: Eisenbrauns, 2010).

resultative. Beckman confirms several general properties for the Piel. Two are noteworthy: (1) only verbs with low transitivity in the G (Qal) stem add an additional agent in the D stem; (2) the D stem has higher verbal plurality or higher transitivity than the G stem.[113] This research demonstrates that BH does not exhibit a single unifying semantic meaning for the Piel. Rather, the Piel is polysemous, chosen for varying reasons with particular verbal roots.

The semantics of the verbal conjugations, particularly the finite conjugations, continues to be debated. This primarily concerns the encoding of tense, aspect, and mood (TAM) but also relates to issues of grounding status and discourse structure. In response to the plethora of publications,[114] we review a few recent claims that attempt to advance the conversation.

John Cook analyzes the verbal system through diachronic typology and grammaticalization. He posits typological pathways for each conjugation and situates distinct synchronic states.[115] The *wayyiqtol* and *qatal* represent different stages along a resultative path: the *wayyiqtol* is further along as a simple past, and the *qatal* is perfective. The *yiqtol* and *qotel* (participle) are placed on a progressive path: the former is imperfective and the latter progressive. Other uses (e.g., perfect *qatal* or irrealis *yiqtol*) are explained as expected, given the intergenerational nature of language change and of the text of the HB. Though recognizing the complexity of language and its multiple strategies for expressing TAM, Cook does regard aspect and mood (in some ways) to be expressed by BH verb forms. He argues aspectual grams (*qatal, yiqtol, qotel*) have default temporal interpretations that can be canceled. Concerning discourse, Cook resists positions that replace semantic explanations with discourse-pragmatic ones, maintaining that discourse functions of verb forms are motivated by their semantics.

Ulf Bergström presents a similar model using a stage-based model of aspect and communicative appeal.[116] He reconstructs the evolutionary developments from the primary aspectual senses (*qatal* and *wayyiqtol* as resultative, *qotel* and *yiqtol* as progressive) that were reanalyzed through situational ambiguity to become temporal (past, future). In addition, "communicative appeal" provides a semiotic characteristic describing the effect an utterance has on the receiver. The short and long *yiqtol* encode "reduced appeal," associated with more relaxed speech and less imminent reactions from the listener; *qotel* and *qatal* default to "full appeal," signaling the demand for an immediate reaction.

Hornkohl draws on typological research to demonstrate that in most verbal systems, one member of TAM tends to be the organizing semantic principle,

113. John Charles Beckman, "Toward the Meaning of the Biblical Hebrew Piel Stem" (PhD diss., Harvard University, 2015), 211–12.

114. See the summary in Noonan, *Advances*, 123–39.

115. John A. Cook, *Time and the Biblical Hebrew Verb: The Expression of Tense, Aspect, and Modality in Biblical Hebrew*, LSAWS 7 (Winona Lake, IN: Eisenbrauns, 2012).

116. Ulf Bergström, *Aspect, Communicative Appeal, and Temporal Meaning in Biblical Hebrew Verbal Forms*, LSAWS 16 (University Park, PA: Eisenbrauns, 2022).

while the others are present to lesser degrees.[117] He acknowledges the perfective (*qatal/wayyiqtol*) and imperfective (*yiqtol/weqatal/qotel*) aspects but notes that future verbs default to perfective or undefined semantics, thereby overriding the aspectual semantics of the *yiqtol/weqatal*. Regarding modality, *yiqtol* and *weqatal* are generally restricted to events in the future, which precludes mood-prominence, given that mood-prominent languages tend to mark modality "across the full range of tenses and/or aspects, not in one alone."[118] The result is a taxonomy organized by tense as the primary semantic characteristic, with aspect and mood less prominent.

Utilizing cognitive linguistics, historical linguistics, grammaticalization, and linguistic typology, Elizabeth Robar demonstrates the complexity of positing semantic cores for *wayyiqtol*, *weqatal*, and *weyiqtol*; she argues that these forms often convey schematic coordination.[119] Robar suggests the following:

1. The *wayyiqtol* is a narrative present with perfective aspect that nevertheless relies on the preceding schematically coordinate verb for its TAM.
2. The *weqatal* has two functions: a schematically coordinated past perfective (analogous to the *wayyiqtol*) or a contingent modal/consecutive future.
3. The *weyiqtol* schematically coordinates with a preceding volitive to express a consecutive volitional or schematically *incorporates* with a preceding indicative form to express purpose/result modality.

The alternation of these forms distinguishes schematic levels within a discourse. Discourse units are embedded as offline (background) within the mainline framework (foreground).

The Path Ahead

Significant developments have been made in our understanding of the language and text of the HB. We have mentioned only a fraction of them here. While some may question what else could be said about ancient texts and languages, novel approaches give life to many persistent questions and provide new avenues of exploration. The current state of the field attests to a rigorous dialectic, utilizing emerging methodologies and testing the limits of theoretical frameworks, all the while relying on and building upon previous scholarship. The path ahead is widening and lengthening, inviting us to continue the work.

117. Hornkohl, "Tense–Aspect–Mood," 27–33. For the typological research on verbal systems and the prominence of one member of TAM, see D. N. S. Bhat, *The Prominence of Tense, Aspect and Mood*, Studies in Language Companion Series 49 (Amsterdam: John Benjamins, 1999).

118. Hornkohl, "Tense–Aspect–Mood," 31–32.

119. Elizabeth Robar, *The Verb and the Paragraph in Biblical Hebrew: A Cognitive-Linguistic Approach*, SSLL 78 (Leiden: Brill, 2014), 61–147.

2

Ancient Versions and Textual Criticism of the Old Testament

Eric J. Tully

Textual criticism is a complex but fascinating subfield of OT studies. Traditionally, readers of any text[1]—whether Shakespeare's *Hamlet*, Austen's *Sense and Sensibility*, or Wells's *The Invisible Man*—have wanted to read the words that the author actually wrote. This is especially true in faith communities who are reading and preaching Scripture. If the Bible is inspired by God, authoritative, and teaches "what man is to believe concerning God, and what duty God requires of man,"[2] then it is critical that we know what the biblical authors actually *wrote* before we can ask what they meant. Variant readings exist. Therefore, we can choose a text to exegete based on careful study of the evidence, or we can choose a text by privileging a certain version, ignoring other evidence, and pretending that textual difficulties do not exist. The former option is preferable.

The discipline of textual criticism is constantly evolving. Ancient readers decided between readings in multiple languages (such as Hebrew and Greek), manuscripts with different wording, and texts that held different authority in

1. A "text" is the work of an author containing content. A "manuscript" is a physical document that contains this text and may have different "readings" or wordings as compared with other manuscripts of the same text. A "version" refers to the text in different editions or languages, sometimes in differing faith communities.

2. "Westminster Shorter Catechism," Westminster Shorter Catechism Project, https://bpc.org/shorter-catechism.

different communities. Today we have easy access to more biblical manuscripts and textual evidence than ever before, thanks to digitization and the ability to view texts online. Yet, like the ancients, we are still attempting to make sense of a tension: every word of the biblical text is significant, but that text exists in a variety of forms.

This chapter contains two parts. First, I survey significant recent research on the ancient versions of the OT. Second, I discuss the primary, controversial question for scholars: What text are we aiming to reconstruct with this evidence?

The Evidence in Old Testament Textual Criticism

If there were only one extant manuscript of the OT, there would be no need for textual criticism. Even if that text were filled with errors, we would not know it without other manuscripts with which to compare it. Textual criticism exists as a discipline because there *are* a number of different texts and readings that must be compared, weighed, and reconciled. The OT's eclectic variety of witnesses includes documents from the Judean Desert (which are fragmentary and incomplete), the Samaritan Pentateuch (SP), the Masoretic Text (MT), and major ancient translations such as the Greek Septuagint (LXX), Aramaic targums (T), the Syriac Peshitta (S), and the Latin Vulgate (V), as well as other minor versions, each of which has its own transmission history. These witnesses span hundreds of years and came long after the OT books were composed but also long before our time. This adds a great deal of complexity to the task and is quite different from the NT situation, where thousands of Greek manuscripts are known and date from a relatively short time after the composition of the NT.

Recent research on the various versions focuses on six main areas. First, scholars continue to produce new or revised editions of the versions, with apparatuses containing variant readings and texts that either follow one key manuscript or one that is judged to be the best combination of readings of that version. Second, new translations of the versions into modern languages are being created, giving nonspecialists access, and aiding in comparative studies. Third, scholars are investigating the translation technique of particular books in certain versions. One benefit of this type of study is that it enables us to distinguish actual textual variants from readings produced by translator interference. Fourth, scholars are focusing on the textual history of specific versions and how the versions relate to each other. Fifth, new textual commentaries on biblical books in various versions are being produced. Sixth, scholars are examining the ideology and theology of ancient translators and how these versions were received in faith communities. The third and fourth areas in this list tend to focus on the versions primarily as witnesses to the original Hebrew text. By contrast, the fifth and sixth areas tend to focus on the versions as biblical texts in their own right, without comparison to the Hebrew text.

In this section, I survey recent advancements in scholarship for each of the major versions. However, space limitations prevent me from reviewing the prodigious scholarship on historical and archaeological backgrounds, textual transmission and reception, and lexical and grammatical tools.

Hebrew/Aramaic Documents

The Hebrew and Aramaic textual evidence is especially significant because it has not undergone transformation through translation from another language. We have three primary groups of such witnesses: documents from the Judean Desert, the Samaritan Pentateuch, and the Masoretic Text.

The Judean Desert

In the late 1940s, eleven caves containing biblical and nonbiblical manuscripts were discovered in the region of Khirbet Qumran, a settlement on the western shore of the Dead Sea. Cave 4 was the jackpot, containing fragments of every book of the OT except Esther as well as fragments of a few books from the Apocrypha and Pseudepigrapha. Additional biblical texts were discovered elsewhere in the Judean Desert, primarily at Masada, Naḥal Ḥever, and Wadi Murabbaʿat.

The fragments were published in a series titled Discoveries in the Judaean Desert, and since 2005, two final volumes of biblical texts have appeared.[3] Eugene Ulrich, one of the series editors, has also produced a three-volume edition that contains only the biblical material, with a basic apparatus indicating differences from the other major versions.[4] Another edition is *Biblia Qumranica*, a synopsis of the biblical books among the scrolls. This work reflects a paradigm shift in textual criticism: rather than attempting to reconstruct the urtext, the textual witnesses are considered "literary works in their own right."[5]

Several commentaries analyze the readings of biblical books from the Judean Desert, including the historical books,[6] Lamentations,[7] Joshua,[8] and Leviticus.[9] These summarize the evidence and reflect on the implications for exegesis and our

3. Frank Moore Cross et al., *Qumran Cave 4, XII: 1–2 Samuel*, DJD 17 (Oxford: Clarendon, 2005); Eugene Ulrich, Peter W. Flint, and Martin G. Abegg, *Qumran Cave 1, II: The Isaiah Scrolls*, DJD 32 (Oxford: Clarendon, 2010).

4. Eugene Ulrich, ed., *The Biblical Qumran Scrolls: Transcriptions and Textual Variants*, 3 vols. (Leiden: Brill, 2013).

5. Beate Ego et al., eds., *Biblia Qumranica*, vol. 3B, *Minor Prophets* (Leiden: Brill, 2005), ix.

6. Hans Ausloos, Bénédicte Lemmelijn, and Julio C. Trebolle Barrera, *After Qumran: Old and Modern Editions of the Biblical Text—The Historical Books*, BETL 246 (Leuven: Peeters, 2012).

7. Gideon R. Kotzé, *The Qumran Manuscripts of Lamentations: A Text-Critical Study*, SSN 61 (Leiden: Brill, 2013).

8. Ariel Feldman, *The Rewritten Joshua Scrolls from Qumran: Texts, Translations and Commentary*, BZAW 438 (Berlin: De Gruyter, 2014).

9. Robert A. Kugler and Kyung S. Baek, *Leviticus at Qumran: Text and Interpretation*, VTSup 173 (Leiden: Brill, 2017).

knowledge of those who created the scrolls. Although the scrolls were discovered more than seventy years ago, in some ways their impact on textual criticism has reached a climax just in the past two decades (see "The Aim of Old Testament Textual Criticism" below).

The Samaritan Pentateuch

The Samaritans are a people group and religious sect that emerged in Palestine in the Second Temple period. They considered themselves to be the "pure" Israel.[10] While their exact origins are unknown, they may have come from those who lived in Palestine during the time of the Babylonian exile.[11] Apparently they selected a Hebrew text of the Pentateuch (the only part of the Bible they accepted as Scripture) and made changes to the text to reflect their own religious views. An example includes the conversion of verb forms related to YHWH's choice of a place of worship (Deut. 12:5) from future tense (יבחר, *ybḥr*, will choose) to past tense (בחר, *bḥr*, has chosen). This suggests that God had already chosen Mount Gerizim before the Israelites even entered the promised land.[12] Other readings, such as the reading "Gerizim" rather than "Ebal" in Deut. 27:4 and the so-called Samaritan Tenth Commandment prioritizing Mount Gerizim are evidenced in the Old Latin and Dead Sea Scrolls (4QpaleoExod^{m}) respectively and are no longer viewed as later ideological changes.[13]

August von Gall's critical edition of the Samaritan Pentateuch[14] is now regarded as "outdated," "reliant on deficient manuscripts," and "founded on erroneous assumptions that render it obsolete."[15] A new *editio maior* is underway, and two volumes have already appeared.[16] These volumes present a diplomatic text plus five apparatuses presenting variants internal to the SP transmission history, translations of the SP (e.g., into Aramaic and Arabic), other versions, vocalization, and punctuation. In addition to this new critical text, two recent volumes compare the SP to the MT, with differences marked by the layout of the text and by font or style.[17] Benyamim Tsedaka has produced an English translation that compares the SP to MT, with

10. Robert T. Anderson and Terry Giles, *The Samaritan Pentateuch: An Introduction to Its Origin, History, and Significance for Biblical Studies*, RBS 72 (Atlanta: Society of Biblical Literature, 2012), 8.

11. Magnar Kartveit, *The Origin of the Samaritans* (Boston: Brill, 2009), 370; Anderson and Giles, *Samaritan Pentateuch*, 14–16.

12. Anderson and Giles, *Samaritan Pentateuch*, 90–91.

13. Emanuel Tov, *Textual Criticism of the Hebrew Bible*, 4th ed. (Minneapolis: Fortress, 2022), 192.

14. August von Gall, *Der hebräische Pentateuch der Samaritaner* (Giessen: Töpelmann, 1918).

15. Stefan Schorch, ed., *The Samaritan Pentateuch*, vol. 3, *Leviticus* (Berlin: De Gruyter, 2015), xxxi.

16. Stefan Schorch, ed., *The Samaritan Pentateuch*, vol. 1, *Genesis* (Berlin: De Gruyter, 2021); vol. 3, *Leviticus* (Berlin: De Gruyter, 2015).

17. M. Shoulson, *The Torah: Jewish and Samaritan Versions Compared* (Mhaigh Eo: Evertype, 2006); Abraham Tal and Moshe Florentin, *The Pentateuch: The Samaritan Version and the Masoretic Version* (Tel Aviv: Haim Rubin Tel Aviv University Press, 2010).

differences indicated by style and layout of the text.[18] Finally, several important studies analyze the character of the SP and its relationship to other versions.[19]

The Masoretic Text

The MT—or rather, the text tradition that *became* the MT—has been transmitted within Judaism since the Second Temple period. It is the basis of almost all English versions and other modern translations today. However, for text-critical purposes, it should not be considered the "default" version when weighing multiple variant readings. It is not "innocent (of error) until proven guilty." The MT is our most significant OT text, but it is only one of many significant witnesses, all of which deserve attention. Text critics must weigh each variant on a case-by-case basis, allowing all the evidence to speak. We must remember that even though several significant ancient translations have a Hebrew source similar to the MT, the MT is not the source text of those versions. Those translations also contain variant readings that reflect a Hebrew text that differs from the MT.

For a full discussion of recent research, see chapter 1 by Hardy and Fresch in the present volume. Here we will simply note that the long-awaited *Biblia Hebraica Quinta* (*BHQ*) continues in development. Since 2005, seven volumes have appeared: Ezra and Nehemiah (2006), Deuteronomy (2007), Proverbs (2008), the Twelve Prophets (2010), Judges (2011), Genesis (2016), and Leviticus (2021). Volumes containing Exodus, Numbers, and Joshua are currently in preparation. The critical apparatus of *BHQ* is far superior to that of the current standard text, *Biblia Hebraica Stuttgartensia*, which contains incomplete information and far too many (and dubious) judgments by the editors.

Ancient Translations of the Old Testament

The Greek Septuagint

The most important of the ancient translations is commonly called the Septuagint. This name overlaps with "Old Greek" in describing the original translation but is also used of later translations and revisions in the Greek tradition. The Pentateuch was translated between 285 and 240 BCE, and the rest of the books were translated by 130 BCE.[20] The earliest extant codices are Vaticanus

18. Benyamim Tsedaka, *The Israelite Samaritan Version of the Torah: First English Translation Compared with the Masoretic Version* (Grand Rapids: Eerdmans, 2013).

19. Jörg Frey, Ursula Schattner-Rieser, and Konrad Schmid, eds., *Die Samaritaner und die Bibel: Historische und literarische Wechselwirkungen zwischen biblischen und samaritanischen Traditionen*, Studia Samaritana 7 (Berlin: De Gruyter, 2012); Magnar Kartveit and Gary N. Knoppers, eds., *The Bible, Qumran and the Samaritans*, SJ 104 (Berlin: De Gruyter, 2018); Michaël Langlois, *The Samaritan Pentateuch and the Dead Sea Scrolls*, CBET 94 (Leuven: Peeters, 2019).

20. Peter J. Gentry, "The Text of the Old Testament," *JETS* 52, no. 1 (2009): 24; Jennifer M. Dines, "The Minor Prophets," in *T&T Clark Companion to the Septuagint*, ed. James K. Aitken (London: Bloomsbury T&T Clark, 2015), 441.

(4th cent. CE), Alexandrinus (5th cent. CE), and Sinaiticus (4th cent. CE). Multiple authors were responsible for the translation, so each book or collection of books has its own translation character. Within the Greek tradition, later revisions such as Theodotion, Aquila, and Symmachus attempted to ensure that the Greek text corresponded to the proto-MT (the text tradition antecedent to the Masoretic Text).[21]

There has been continued progress on the standard critical edition of the Septuagint in the past two decades. The Göttingen Septuagint has been produced in three phases. The first phase, Göttingen Septuaginta-Unternehmen, ran for almost a century and officially closed in 2015.[22] The two final volumes were Ruth[23] and 2 Chronicles.[24] The second phase (2016–19), the Forschungskommission zur Edition und Erforschung der Septuaginta, saw the publication of Ecclesiastes.[25] The third phase, *Editio critica maior des griechischen Psalters*, began in 2020 and will run for 21 years. The aim is to prepare a new critical edition of the Septuagint Psalms and Odes.[26]

Important work is being done on Origen's Hexapla through the Hexapla Institute. The institute is producing a new series called "Origen's Hexapla: A Critical Edition of the Extant Fragments," a critical text of hexaplaric fragments from the "most up-to-date evidence and sources available."[27] Thus far, only the volume on Job 22–42 has appeared,[28] but most books have been assigned.

Three commentary series on the Septuagint are notable. First, the Septuagint Commentary Series provides a literary commentary of the Greek text as it appears in a single manuscript (e.g., Codex Vaticanus) without reference to the Hebrew text of that book. Recent volumes include Leviticus, Proverbs, and Isaiah.[29] Second, the Baylor Handbook on the Septuagint (BHLXX) is similar to the Baylor Handbook on the Hebrew Bible and Baylor Handbook on the Greek New Testament series. The volumes focus on syntax, translation, and other linguistic issues relevant to reading the Greek text accurately. A third series is the

21. Peter J. Gentry, "Pre-Hexaplaric Translations, Hexapla, Post-Hexaplaric Translations," in *Textual History of the Bible*, vol. 1A, *The Hebrew Bible: Overview Articles*, ed. Armin Lange and Emanuel Tov (Leiden: Brill, 2016), 225–28.

22. This phase included the publication of the Pentateuch, Prophetic books, Job, Ruth, Ezra-Nehemiah, Esther, 2 Chronicles, and Deuterocanonical books.

23. Udo Quast, ed., *Ruth*, Septuaginta: Vetus Testamentum Graecum, vol. 4.3 (Göttingen: Vandenhoeck & Ruprecht, 2006).

24. R. Hanhart, ed., *Paralipomenon Liber II*, Septuaginta: Vetus Testamentum Graecum, vol. 7.2 (Gottingen: Vandenhoeck & Ruprecht, 2014).

25. Peter J. Gentry, ed., *Ecclesiastes*, Septuaginta: Vetus Testamentum Graecum, vol. 11.2 (Göttingen: Vandenhoeck & Ruprecht, 2019).

26. F. Albrecht, "Report on the Göttingen Septuagint," *Textus* 29, no. 2 (2020): 201–20.

27. The Hexapla Institute, http://www.hexapla.org/about.

28. John D. Meade, *A Critical Edition of the Hexaplaric Fragments of Job 22–42*, Origen's Hexapla: A Critical Edition of the Extant Fragments (Leuven: Peeters, 2020).

29. Brill, Septuagint Commentary Series, https://brill.com/display/serial/SEPT.

Society of Biblical Literature Commentary on the Septuagint (SBLCS),[30] but no volumes have yet appeared.[31]

Recent years have seen a number of important translations of the Septuagint into modern languages, including two English translations[32] as well as Spanish,[33] French,[34] and German translations.[35] A number of handbooks on the Septuagint provide readers with an overview of the field.[36] One of the most important books on the use of the Septuagint in textual criticism is Emanuel Tov's *The Text-Critical Use of the Septuagint in Biblical Research*, now in a third edition.[37] For a more comprehensive discussion of recent research on the Septuagint, see the article by William Ross.[38]

Aramaic Targums

At the turn of the era, around the time of Jesus, Aramaic was the lingua franca in Palestine and had replaced Hebrew as the language of everyday discourse for most Jews. Targums were created for use in synagogue worship and for personal reading. When they faithfully follow the Hebrew text, they are quite literal and follow certain rules.[39] On the other hand, they can exhibit significant expansions and renderings that support rabbinic interpretations. The targums allowed for commentary on the Hebrew text without fully replacing it; the translation/commentary could be read as a kind of authoritative guide.

Flesher and Chilton released a new critical introduction to the targums in 2011.[40] Although there have not been more recent critical editions of the targums,

30. The series is sponsored by the International Organization for Septuagint and Cognate Studies. See https://ccat.sas.upenn.edu/ioscs/commentary.

31. Dirk Büchner, *The SBL Commentary on the Septuagint: An Introduction*, SCS 67 (Atlanta: SBL Press, 2017).

32. Albert Pietersma and Benjamin G. Wright, *A New English Translation of the Septuagint* (New York: Oxford University Press, 2007); Ken M. Penner, Rick Brannan and Israel Loken, eds., *The Lexham English Septuagint: A New Translation* (Bellingham, WA: Lexham, 2020).

33. Natalio Fernández Marcos, *La Biblia Griega Septuaginta* (Salamanca: Sígueme, 2013).

34. Marguerite Harl, ed., *La Bible d'Alexandrie LXX*, vol. 1, *Genesis* (Paris: Cerf, 1986). Since 2005, new volumes by different editors include Ruth, Esther, Song of Songs, Haggai, Zechariah, and Malachi.

35. Wolfgang Kraus and Martin Karrer, eds., *Septuaginta Deutsch: Das griechische Alte Testament in deutscher Übersetzung* (Stuttgart: Deutsche Bibelgesellschaft, 2009).

36. James K. Aitken, ed., *T&T Clark Companion to the Septuagint* (London: T&T Clark, 2015); William A. Ross and W. Edward Glenny, eds., *T&T Clark Handbook of Septuagint Research* (London: T&T Clark, 2021); Alison G. Salvesen and Timothy Michael Law, eds., *The Oxford Handbook of the Septuagint* (Oxford: Oxford University Press, 2021).

37. Emanuel Tov, *The Text-Critical Use of the Septuagint in Biblical Research*, 3rd ed. (Winona Lake, IN: Eisenbrauns, 2015).

38. William A. Ross, "The Past Decade in Septuagint Research (2012–2021)," *CurBR* 21, no. 1 (2022): 293–337.

39. Paul V. M. Flesher and Bruce Chilton, *The Targums: A Critical Introduction*, Studies in the Aramaic Interpretation of Scripture 12 (Boston: Brill, 2011), 23.

40. Flesher and Chilton, *Targums*.

Accordance Bible Software has developed the Targums Wordmap.[41] This is a database that aligns each word of the MT with Targum Onkelos, Neofiti, Pseudo-Jonathan, fragmentary targums, and manuscripts from Cairo Geniza. The software highlights corresponding words in the various texts, and the user can conduct sophisticated searches.

Syriac Peshitta

"Peshitta" means "simple," as it is a straightforward translation of the OT and NT into Syriac, a late dialect of Aramaic. The translation must have been completed by the third century CE at Edessa in northern Mesopotamia (now Urfa in southeastern Turkey).[42] The Peshitta OT was created from a Hebrew source text with influence from the Greek Septuagint. It shows influence from Jewish exegetical traditions. However, it manifests a Christian context because it also shows influence from the Greek Septuagint and was transmitted within the Christian Church. Michael Weitzman explains the dual Jewish/Christian character of the translation by arguing that it was made by Jewish converts to Christianity.[43] The Hebrew source text is similar to the proto-MT and does not contain many significant textual variants. Some agreement with the Greek and Aramaic versions against the MT is due to "polygenesis"—that is, when two translators solve the same translation problem in the same way by coincidence rather than direct influence.[44]

In the past two decades, two volumes in the standard critical edition appeared: one containing Ezra and Nehemiah,[45] and one containing Jeremiah and Lamentations.[46] In addition, Gorgias Press began the Syriac Peshitta Bible with English Translation series. Each volume contains a newly prepared Syriac text with a parallel English translation on the facing page. Recent volumes include the Book of Women (Ruth, Susanna, Esther, and Judith); Psalms; and Proverbs, Qoheleth, and Song of Songs. Several volumes in the Monographs of the Peshitta Institute series focus on translation technique and the textual traditions of the Peshitta of particular books.[47]

41. Accordance Bible Software, https://www.accordancebible.com/new-targums-wordmap.

42. Jonathan Loopstra, "The Syriac Bible and Its Interpretation," in *The Syriac World*, ed. Daniel King (London: Routledge, 2019), 293–308.

43. Michael Weitzman, *The Syriac Version of the Old Testament* (Cambridge: Cambridge University Press, 1999), 258–59.

44. Eric J. Tully, "Translation Universals and Polygenesis: Implications for Textual Criticism," *BT* 65, no. 3 (2014): 292–307.

45. M. Albert and A. Penna, *The Old Testament in Syriac according to the Peshiṭta Version*, part IV, fasc. 4, *Ezra and Nehemiah, 1 and 2 Maccabees* (Leiden: Brill, 2013).

46. B. Albrektson, *The Old Testament in Syriac according to the Peshiṭta Version*, part III, fasc. 2, *Jeremiah, Lamentations, Epistle of Jeremiah, Epistle of Baruch* (Leiden: Brill, 2019).

47. Janet W. Dyk, *Language System, Translation Technique, and Textual Tradition in the Peshitta of Kings*, Monographs of the Peshitta Institute 19 (Boston: Brill, 2013); Eric J. Tully, *The Translation and Translator of the Peshitta of Hosea*, Monographs of the Peshitta Institute

Latin Vulgate

In the second century CE, translations were made from the Greek Septuagint into Latin by Christians (Old Latin), but no complete manuscript survives. Later, in the late fourth century, Jerome made a fresh translation into the "common" Latin language (thus "vulgate") from the Hebrew text with some help from the Greek. Michael Graves writes, "In most cases, it can be assumed that Jerome's translation reflects a Hebrew text that is in front of him, and that he has selected his translation—even when following a Greek source—on the basis of its perceived agreement with his Hebrew text."[48] The Vulgate does not offer many textual variants that differ from the MT.

In the past twenty years, the only new critical edition of the Vulgate to appear is *Biblia Sacra: Iuxta vulgatam versionem*,[49] an *editio minor* of *Biblia Sacra* with a slightly revised text and an abridged apparatus. Important translations of the Vulgate into modern languages include two multivolume translations in English and German.[50] There have also been some new studies on the translation technique and exegesis of the Vulgate, including Matthew Kraus's study.[51]

The Aim of Old Testament Textual Criticism

What should we do with all this textual evidence? The most important way that the field of OT textual criticism has developed in the past several decades is in addressing the question of the goal of textual criticism. There has traditionally been a division between "higher criticism" (dealing with the composition of the text, literary issues, source criticism, redaction criticism, etc.) and "lower criticism" (dealing with establishing the text and transmission). Today, these two areas have merged.

What text are we trying to reconstruct? What is the "best" or "most original" text? The answer depends heavily on one's view of the literary composition and history of the biblical text. Although the practical methods of comparing textual witnesses might *seem* neutral, our presuppositions, including our theology and view of Scripture, form an important starting point.

---

21 (Leiden: Brill, 2015); Kristian Heal, *Genesis 37 and 39 in the Early Syriac Tradition*, Monographs of the Peshitta Institute 20 (Leiden: Brill, 2022).

48. Michael Graves, "6–9.1.7 Latter Prophets: Primary Translations: Vulgate," in *Textual History of the Bible*, vol. 1B, *The Hebrew Bible: Pentateuch, Former and Latter Prophets*, ed. Armin Lange and Emanuel Tov (Leiden: Brill, 2016), 646.

49. Robert Weber and Roger Gryson, eds., *Biblia Sacra: Iuxta Vulgatam Versionem*, ed. altera emendata (Stuttgart: Deutsche Bibelgesellschaft, 2007).

50. Edgar Swift, ed., *The Vulgate Bible*, 5 vols. (Cambridge, MA: Harvard University Press, 2010–12); Andreas Beriger, Widu-Wolfgang Ehlers, and Michael Fieger, eds., *Biblia Sacra Vulgata: Lateinisch-deutsch*, Sammlung Tusculum (Berlin: De Gruyter, 2018).

51. Matthew A. Kraus, *Jewish, Christian, and Classical Exegetical Traditions in Jerome's Translation of the Book of Exodus: Translation Technique and the Vulgate*, Supplements to Vigiliae Christianae (Leiden: Brill, 2017).

Possible Aims Suggested by Scholars

About thirty-five years ago, Bruce Waltke suggested six possible aims or goals of text critics.[52] From our perspective now, Waltke was almost prescient about the future of the field. His list is helpful, although I will mention only the four most relevant today.

First, some scholars have sought to *restore the original composition*. For example, R. K. Harrison writes, "If the doctrine of inspiration means anything at all for the written word of God, it surely refers to the original autographs, since subsequent copyists, however gifted or diligent, were not themselves inspired. The true objective of the textual critic, therefore, should be the restoration of the Hebrew to the point where it is as near as possible to what the original author is deemed to have written."[53] Harrison sharply separates authorship from transmission or copying. This view might work in the case of a book like Ruth. It is short and relatively simple, with no evidence of development over time. It seems probable that an author sat down and wrote its four chapters. At that time, the composition was finished, and it began to be copied. Over time, the text was changed as scribes made mistakes or minor additions, or a manuscript was damaged. The goal of the text critic would therefore be to reconstruct that original work.

Other OT books clearly were written over the course of a long time. If certain Psalm titles indicate authorship, then one psalm was written by Moses (Ps. 90), many were written by David, and some were written in the postexilic period (e.g., Ps. 137). While there may have been earlier collections of psalms, someone in the postexilic period gathered them all and arranged and completed the book. Similarly, Proverbs contains section headings informing us that some of the book comes from Solomon (Prov. 10:1), some from anonymous wise men (22:17), some from proverbs of Solomon that were collected at the time of Hezekiah (25:1), and some from other individuals (30:1; 31:1). At some point, an editor put the collections together into the book that we have now.

Biblical scholars working in source criticism and redaction criticism have gone further than these kinds of explicit statements and argued that much of the biblical text—including the Pentateuch, the Deuteronomistic History, and most of the Latter Prophets—has undergone development over time as the contents (narratives, legal material, oracles, etc.) were constructed from sources, adapted, and then redacted in multiple stages until they arrived at the books we have now. Therefore, a second possible aim is to *restore the final text*. "Final text" refers to the end of literary development when a book reached its final intended form. For example, Paul Wegner writes, "The goal, then, of OT text criticism is to determine the earliest, final, authoritative form which then was maintained by the scribes and

52. Bruce K. Waltke, "Aims of OT Textual Criticism," *WTJ* 51, no. 1 (1989): 93–108.
53. R. K. Harrison, *Introduction to the Old Testament* (Peabody, MA: Prince, 1999), 259.

was later recorded in the canon." This is possible, he says, in "the vast majority of cases."[54]

A third possible aim is to *restore final text(s)*. For some books of the OT, the differences between two text versions are more significant than variations arising from copying or translation. Jeremiah is the most well-known case. In the MT, the prophetic oracles against the nations are located at the end of the book (chaps. 46–51). In the Septuagint, the book is one-sixth shorter (but also includes pluses),[55] and the oracles against the nations occur in the middle of the book, after 25:13. Thus the two versions represent not just two texts but two different literary editions. Similarly, the Septuagint version of Joshua, when compared with the MT, has some shorter elements, some longer, and some differences in structural sequence.[56] Books containing more significant differences between versions include 1–2 Samuel, Ezekiel, and Proverbs.[57]

In these cases, Tov explains, a text came to a (temporary) final form, began to be copied in one tradition, and then was revised into a second final form. Because these significant differences are due to the merging of composition and transmission, the text critic is at an impasse and must remain agnostic about which is more original. (Of course, literary criticism may determine that one is more authoritative, original, canonical, etc., but textual criticism does not have the tools to make that judgment.) Therefore, the goal of textual criticism is not the composition written by the biblical author, which is "beyond the horizon" of available evidence; rather, "we must try to reconstruct the earliest texts themselves. . . . We are not aiming at the words of the Scripture authors, but at the final literary products."[58]

Finally, a fourth possible aim is to *reconstruct all literary editions*. Whereas the previous view recognizes different literary editions for *some* books, this view understands all books to have undergone multiple redactional adaptations that result in a plethora of literary editions and pluriformity among biblical texts. The most important proponent of this view is Eugene Ulrich, whose scholarship has been quite influential on the entire discipline.[59]

54. Paul D. Wegner, "Current Trends in Old Testament Textual Criticism," *BBR* 23, no. 4 (2013): 477.

55. "Plus" is a neutral term that text critics use to refer to content that is present in a version (but not others) without predetermining the question of whether the material is original but has disappeared from other textual witnesses or has been added to the original text at a later stage of transmission.

56. Tov, *Textual Criticism*, 244.

57. Tov, *Textual Criticism*, 232. Tov argues that Judges, Isaiah, Psalms, Job (possibly), Ruth, Ecclesiastes, and Lamentations all exhibit a "unified textual tradition," which is "not challenged by Qumran fragments" (373).

58. Tov, *Textual Criticism*, 398.

59. Ulrich first proposed this aim in 1991. Eugene Ulrich, "Pluriformity in the Biblical Text, Text Groups, and Questions of Canon," in *The Madrid Qumran Conference: Proceedings of the International Congress on the Dead Sea Scrolls, Madrid, 18–21 March 1991*, ed. Julio Trebolle Barrera and Luis V. Montaner, STDJ 11 (Leiden: Brill, 1992), 1:37–40.

Ulrich maintains that Tov's four classifications for texts from the Judean Desert (MT-like, pre-Samaritan, close to the Hebrew source of the Septuagint, and "non-aligned") are pedagogically helpful but anachronistic and oversimplified.[60] Rather, the pluriformity seen among the scrolls shows that the biblical texts were still in development at that time as scribes not only copied but also continued to *create* the text that would become Scripture. As scribes copied the text, they also adjusted it, added to it, changed it to make it relevant to their current circumstances, and so on. It was "the deliberate activity of a series of creative scribes who produced the new or multiple literary editions of the books of the Bible."[61] Ulrich uses Exod. 32:10–11 as an example (see table 2.1).

For these two verses, Ulrich posits four different literary editions. The edition represented by the Septuagint is earliest and was revised and rearranged in what is now the MT. The text from 4QpaleoExod^{m} and the SP represent a third edition, which has been further expanded. Finally, the SP as a whole, with its changes to support certain ideological commitments, should be considered a fourth edition.[62] In addition, "many creative new editions . . . preceded our surviving textual witnesses."[63]

In this view, it makes no sense to speak of an "original" form because every text was continually reshaped by a series of scribes over the centuries. Ulrich writes, "Each book is not the product of a single author, such as Plato or Shakespeare, but of multiple, anonymous bards, sages, religious leaders, compilers or tradents."[64] This constant evolution means that it is also meaningless to speak of a "final" text or texts "until the organic development of the texts was halted due to extraneous circumstances [i.e., in history]."[65]

It is instructive to compare Ulrich with Tov. When encountering differences between texts, Tov distinguishes those that arise in transmission from those that arise in composition, recognizing that the two are not always easily distinguished: "In most cases of assumed revisions . . . no textual evidence is available (e.g., Judges, Isaiah). In other cases, when the literary development was simple, that is, when the composition presumably was not rewritten, textual transmission started upon its literary crystallization."[66] By contrast, Ulrich makes no distinction between transmission and composition. Scribes are authors, editors, and copyists at every stage, at least up to the first century CE. Therefore, the textual

60. Eugene Ulrich, *The Dead Sea Scrolls and the Developmental Composition of the Bible*, VTSup 169 (Leiden: Brill, 2015), 26.

61. Eugene Ulrich, "Multiple Literary Editions: Reflections toward a Theory of the History of the Biblical Text," in *Current Research and Technological Developments on the Dead Sea Scrolls: Conference on the Texts from the Judaean Desert, Jerusalem 30 April 1995*, ed. Donald W. Parry and Stephen D. Ricks, STDJ 20 (Leiden: Brill, 1996), 88.

62. Ulrich, "Multiple Literary Editions," 82–84.

63. Ulrich, "Multiple Literary Editions," 84.

64. Ulrich, *Dead Sea Scrolls*, 2.

65. Ulrich, *Dead Sea Scrolls*, 313.

66. Tov, *Textual Criticism*, 326.

Table 2.1. Textual Witnesses to Exodus 32:10–11 Compared

1	LXX	καὶ ποιήσω σὲ εἰς ἔθνος μέγα. . . . ἐν ἰσχύι μεγάλῃ καὶ ἐν τῷ βραχίονί σου τῷ ὑψηλῷ	And I will make you into a great nation. . . . with great power and your uplifted arm.
2	MT *(expanded)*	וְאֶעֱשֶׂה אוֹתְךָ לְגוֹי גָּדוֹל: . . . בְּכֹחַ גָּדוֹל וּבְיָד חֲזָקָה	I will make you a great nation. . . . with great power and a strong hand.
3	4QpaleoExod^{m} *(expanded)*	[ואעשה] או[תך] לגוי גדול [ובאהרון התאנף יה]וה מאד להשמידו ו[י תפלל משה בעד א[הרון] . . . [ ]בזרוע חזק[ה]	[I will make] you a great nation, [but against Aaron the Lo]rd was very angry [enough] to destroy him, so Moses prayed on behalf of A[aron] . . . with a strong arm
	SP *(expanded)*	. . . אתך לגוי גדול ובאהרן התאנף יהוה מאד להשמידו ויתפלל משה בעד אהרן . . . בכוח גדול ובזרוע נטויה	[I will make] you a great nation, but against Aaron the Lord was very angry [enough] to destroy him, so Moses prayed on behalf of Aaron . . . with great power and an outstretched arm
4	SP—final text (ideological)	(various changes)	(e.g., ideological readings)

critic should not evaluate variants in search of some pristine, original text but rather should restore all literary editions of a text, since each one is the work of a different author and a different time.

Critique

Ulrich's view, although influential, has been criticized for discounting the central role of the proto-MT in Judaism during the Second Temple period. Whereas many scholars believe that pluriformity (as evidenced at Qumran) finally gave way to a standardized text, Peter Gentry argues that we should not overstate the nature or the significance of the pluriformity at Qumran. He writes, "The text of the OT in arrangement, content, and stability was fixed by the time of Ben Sira or more probably, at the end of the fifth century BC by Ezra and Nehemiah."[67] He gives several reasons for this view. First, the scrolls from the Judean Desert are dominated by the proto-MT tradition. Second, a pre-Samaritan updating toward the proto-MT by 200 BCE shows that the proto-MT was already significant. Third, many of the variants in the Judean Desert are either insignificant or may be due to adaptation by various groups.[68] We should also acknowledge that pluriformity does not preclude one authoritative text in Judaism. Scribes could repeat the text faithfully, while others could "resignify"

67. Peter John Gentry, "The Text of the Old Testament," *JETS* 52, no. 1 (2009): 19.
68. Gentry, "Text of the Old Testament, 35–39.

the text to make it relevant for their own times. According to Gentry, scribes in the temple took the former approach. What looks like standardization of a pluriform text after the fall of the temple reflects the end of resignification. The faithful copying of the proto-MT continued, while other scribes stopped their creative work.[69] Wegner makes a similar argument, stating that a standard authoritative tradition was always maintained by temple scribes throughout Israel's history, regardless of the pluriformity that existed elsewhere in Judaism.[70]

Assessment of these approaches partly depends on one's theology of inspiration and the distinction between divine authority and reception. Even if scribes and communities reworked Scripture over time, this does not mean that those additions are on equal authoritative ground or that they are all what God intended. While different communities even today recognize different versions as canonical, the question remains: What did the Holy Spirit inspire?

So, what is the aim of textual criticism? Taking seriously the manuscript evidence and the internal claims of the biblical books, we must exercise some flexibility according to the nature of each book.[71] We need to adjust the sense of the word "autograph" so that it does not imply that, in every case, an author simply sat down and wrote a book. Some books, such as Psalms and Proverbs, developed over time, but at some point the text was completed and recognized as a canonical, authoritative book. In my estimation, the second option, "restore the final text," is the best approach. This aim acknowledges that some biblical books have developed over time, and the goal is to seek the final, intended form. As Ellis Brotzman and I have written elsewhere, "Our goal, therefore, is the final form of the text. This is the 'published' copy that was intended to be promulgated. Whatever processes occurred prior to this in the development phase are the domain of literary or compositional studies. Textual criticism is concerned with working back through the transmission history of the text and establishing this final, authoritative version."[72]

However, in some cases, such as the book of Jeremiah, the third view, "restore the final *texts*," may be the necessary approach. We must acknowledge that in such situations, we are dealing not just with two different texts but with two different literary editions in two different canons. Therefore, "in these relatively rare situations, our goal . . . may be limited to the earliest form of each tradition: one reflected in the Greek Septuagint and one reflected in the Hebrew MT."[73]

69. Gentry, "Text of the Old Testament, 45.

70. Wegner, "Current Trends," 466.

71. Waltke, "Aims of OT Textual Criticism," 107–8. See also Ellis R. Brotzman and Eric J. Tully, *Old Testament Textual Criticism: A Practical Introduction*, 2nd ed. (Grand Rapids: Baker Academic, 2016), 130–33, 225–26.

72. Brotzman and Tully, *Old Testament Textual Criticism*, 132.

73. Brotzman and Tully, *Old Testament Textual Criticism*, 225.

Conclusion

Textual criticism of the OT is an exciting academic discipline that intersects with multiple other disciplines, including exegesis, the history of interpretation, linguistics, translation studies, diachronic studies of the text's composition, and the history of Israel and the church. Much has been written, but more is yet to be worked out. Although the scrolls in the Qumran caves were discovered over seventy years ago, we continue to assess their implications for the text of the OT. Another avenue of future study is further assessment of the character of individual books in major translations such as the Septuagint, targums, and the Peshitta. Only after this is done can the versions be used accurately for textual criticism.

3

Qumran and the Scrolls from the Judean Desert

Drew Longacre

The study of the Dead Sea Scrolls (DSS) has developed into a full-fledged, mature discipline with connections to countless related disciplines, and today hardly any critical research on the HB/OT can justifiably ignore it. There are several good general introductions to the study of the DSS,[1] as well as handbooks and encyclopedias offering focused introductions to specific topics and texts in the field.[2] In this brief article I will survey some of the main recent developments in theoretical approaches, methods, and resources that define the state of DSS research in the twenty-first century.

Theoretical Developments

Some of the most notable changes have come in the form of shifting theoretical frameworks that have added considerable nuance to several key areas of DSS research.

1. James C. VanderKam, *The Dead Sea Scrolls Today*, 2nd ed. (Grand Rapids: Eerdmans, 2010); Daniel Stökl Ben Ezra, *Qumran: Die Texte vom Toten Meer und das antike Judentum*, Jüdische Studien 3 (Tübingen: Mohr Siebeck, 2016); Timothy H. Lim, *The Dead Sea Scrolls: A Very Short Introduction*, 2nd ed. (Oxford: Oxford University Press, 2017).

2. Lawrence H. Schiffman and James C. VanderKam, eds., *Encyclopedia of the Dead Sea Scrolls*, 2 vols. (Oxford: Oxford University Press, 2000); Timothy H. Lim and John J. Collins, eds., *The Oxford Handbook of the Dead Sea Scrolls* (Oxford: Oxford University Press, 2010); George J. Brooke and Charlotte Hempel, eds., *T&T Clark Companion to the Dead Sea Scrolls* (London: Bloomsbury, 2018).

The Nature and Origins of the Qumran Community

Probably the most frequently asked question by non-specialists about the Qumran scrolls is whether or not the site of Khirbet Qumran and its associated community are to be identified with the Essenes of Josephus and other Greco-Roman writers. Ironically, among DSS scholars interest in this and related historical questions has waned in recent years, and attempts to identify specific individuals and historical circumstances in the origins of the community—so common and significant in early DSS studies—have all but ceased. Sidnie Crawford provides the most robust recent defense of the classic Essene sectarian identification for the Qumran community.[3] Support for this position remains strong in the field, even though most scholars today acknowledge that the Qumran community was likely only one group within a larger movement.[4] Other scholars remain skeptical about the association of Qumran with the Essenes, considering it an unwarranted conclusion. They prefer to treat Qumran in its own right without imposing ideas about the Essenes from external sources, while generally refraining from proposing alternative identifications between Qumran and other known Jewish groups.[5]

Whether or not one accepts some sort of association between the community of the scrolls and the Essenes, recent studies generally reinforce the nature of the site of Khirbet Qumran as an ascetic religious community closely connected to the scroll deposits around the site.[6] Some of the scroll caves can be considered part of the Qumran site proper, and even the more distant ones in the vicinity are still close to Qumran and share similar material culture.[7] Most DSS scholars today also read the archaeology of Qumran as indicative of a small, ascetic, predominantly (if not exclusively) male community oriented around the study of religious texts, who inhabited the site from the early or mid-first century BCE until its destruction by the Romans in 68 CE.[8] This seems required by the plainness of the site, the large numbers of ritual baths, the large collection of plain eating dishes, the relative lack of small everyday objects, and the substantial material evidence for

3. Sidnie White Crawford, *Scribes and Scrolls at Qumran* (Grand Rapids: Eerdmans, 2019).

4. John J. Collins, *Beyond the Qumran Community: The Sectarian Movement of the Dead Sea Scrolls* (Grand Rapids: Eerdmans, 2009).

5. Steve Mason, "The Historical Problem of the Essenes," in *Celebrating the Dead Sea Scrolls: A Canadian Collection*, ed. Peter W. Flint, Jean Duhaime, and Kyung S. Baek (Atlanta: Society of Biblical Literature, 2011), 201–51.

6. Crawford, *Scribes and Scrolls*.

7. In addition to Crawford, *Scribes and Scrolls*, see Mladen Popović, "Qumran as Scroll Storehouse in Times of Crisis? A Comparative Perspective on Judaean Desert Manuscript Collections," *JSJ* 43 (2012): 551–94, who contrasts the profiles of the Qumran caves with those of refugee caves from other sites.

8. See esp. Jodi Magness, *The Archaeology of Qumran and the Dead Sea Scrolls*, 2nd ed. (Grand Rapids: Eerdmans, 2021).

writing, which includes at least five inkwells,[9] materials for scroll manufacture and repair, and a large library of scrolls preserved in its environs. This picture is further supported by the unusually high proportion of older males buried in the graves around Qumran, though scholars continue to debate to what extent women may have been present at Qumran.[10] There remain, nevertheless, archaeologists who propose that the site may have been used for a time or throughout its occupation for other functions, such as a fortress, a villa, or a pottery production center, which highlights the ambiguities inherent in interpreting the archaeological evidence from the site.[11]

Despite the general consensus in favor of an ascetic religious community at Qumran, there has been lively debate about how to describe this community in sociological terms. Recent studies using models from the social sciences have questioned or nuanced the classic model of a Jewish religious "sect," such that one can no longer assume a common, well-established definition. Discussion has focused on whether the concept entails voluntary association, boundary markers, attitudes toward outsiders and social transformation, and/or separation from a "mainstream" or "normative" Judaism.[12] Many DSS scholars now speak in general terms of a Jewish "movement," emphasizing the larger group of which the Qumran community was only a part.[13] The Qumran community and its associated movement were not completely isolated but rather were situated within broader Jewish and Mediterranean contexts, which may help to explain phenomena such as the discovery of the Damascus Document in the Cairo Genizah.

Rethinking Canonical and Literary Classifications

One of the biggest scholarly challenges since the full publication of the scrolls is classifying and describing major categories or groups of texts. Many terms once casually applied to texts in the early stages of DSS research have since been shown to imply thought structures that later scholars deem problematic.[14] The first such difficulty regards traditional canonical categories such as "(non)biblical,"

9. Juhana Saukkonen, "A Few Inkwells, Many Hands: Were There Scribes at Qumran?," in *Houses Full of All Good Things: Essays in Memory of Timo Veijola*, ed. Juha Pakkala and Martti Nissinen (Helsinki: Finnish Exegetical Society, 2008), 538–53.

10. For a recent evaluation of the burial sites, see Yossi Nagar et al., "Conclusive Palaeodemographic Analysis, Based on New Anthropological Data from the Cemetery of Qumran," *RevQ* 34, no. 1 (2022): 3–70. Some of the graves in the area seem to have been dug later than the occupation of Qumran, which complicates the question.

11. For a brief survey and critique of these alternative views, see Dennis Mizzi, "Archaeology of Qumran," in Brooke and Hempel, *T&T Clark Companion to the Dead Sea Scrolls*, 17–36.

12. Jutta Jokiranta, "Sociological Approaches to Qumran Sectarianism," in Lim and Collins, *Oxford Handbook of the Dead Sea Scrolls*, 200–231.

13. Collins, *Beyond the Qumran Community*.

14. See esp. the programmatic article by Hindy Najman and Eibert J. C. Tigchelaar, "A Preparatory Study of Nomenclature and Text Designation in the Dead Sea Scrolls," *RevQ* 26, no. 3 (2014): 305–25.

"parabiblical," "apocryphal," "pseudepigrapha," etc. The world of the DSS exhibits little evidence for an explicit, well-defined, and authoritative "canon" of the Hebrew Scriptures. Granted, frequent references to the Law and Prophets in Second Temple literature reflect a clear scripture consciousness and at least a general idea about which books might function in this way, but many scholars question whether—at least on the margins—"canon" was an operative concept in the period or, if it was, which books were included. In many respects, books like Enoch, Sirach, and Jubilees were apparently more popular and influential than many "biblical" books, some of whose scriptural status remained debated well after the destruction of the Second Temple.[15] Furthermore, the idea of a "Bible" conjures modern connotations of a single composite volume containing all inspired Scripture, whereas in the time of the DSS, Hebrew books were generally copied separately onto different scrolls, and it was presumably rare to have scrolls of all the books that are now considered part of the HB collected and available in one location. Thus, the common—and still functional—designation "biblical" is often considered problematic and treated with scare quotes and/or caveats. Furthermore, classifications like "apocrypha" and "pseudepigrapha" that depend on canonical categories are likewise drawn into question as anachronistic.

Similarly, the term "sectarian" documents only makes sense within a framework that considers the Qumran community and its affiliates a "sect" (see above) and sees distinctive terminology and ideology clustering in a set of documents deemed characteristic of that community.[16] But the Qumran community used a great many texts that circulated more generally in contemporary Judaism and may have composed a good number of texts that lack what is often considered to be distinctive "sectarian" terminology. Thus, even scholars who apply the category "sectarian" to the texts continue to debate what features are truly indicative and which specific texts should be included in the category. Add to this the possibilities of diachronic development and/or different subgroups within the movement, and reliably identifying a discrete corpus of "sectarian" texts remains a challenge.

One of the most lively discussions in recent years relates to the phenomenon of textual rewriting.[17] The category of "rewritten Bible/Scripture" in particular has been challenged, and not only because it depends on the concept of an established body of scripture (see above). Rather than viewing it as a distinct genre of narrative texts reworked in new literary contexts, many scholars now treat rewriting as an

15. Crawford, *Scribes and Scrolls*, prefers to speak of Israel's "classical" texts, a corpus that overlaps considerably but not perfectly with the later canon of the HB.

16. See the classic study of Devorah Dimant, "The Qumran Manuscripts: Contents and Significance," in *Time to Prepare the Way in the Wilderness: Papers on the Qumran Scrolls by Fellows of the Institute for Advanced Studies of the Hebrew University, Jerusalem, 1989–1990*, ed. Devorah Dimant and Lawrence H. Schiffman, STDJ 16 (Leiden: Brill, 1995), 23–58.

17. See the literature and synthesis in Molly M. Zahn, *Genres of Rewriting in Second Temple Judaism: Scribal Composition and Transmission* (Cambridge: Cambridge University Press, 2020).

editorial process that was broadly applied to different text genres and in varying degrees. It then becomes essential, and yet extremely difficult, to delineate when divergences from a base text change from being merely indicative of a revised version of the same composition to being a distinct, derivative composition. A famous example of this conundrum is the 4QReworked Pentateuch manuscripts. At first, they were understood as new, interpretive retellings of the pentateuchal traditions, but they have increasingly come to be understood as heavily revised versions of the Pentateuch itself.[18] Similarly, it is now widely accepted that the DSS reveal alternative editions of several books of the HB, including at least Exodus, Numbers, Joshua, Psalms, and Jeremiah.[19] And yet, even with all this discussion of revisions and derivative works, it is important to observe the creative contributions of Hellenistic- and Roman-period Jewish authors who not only interpreted and revised prior works but also innovated and produced a wide array of related religious literature.[20]

Interdisciplinarity

Another major development in the field is an increase in interdisciplinary studies. The emphasis has shifted from simply making the data available to those in related fields to situating the DSS within broader historical and theoretical discussions within the humanities. The sophisticated interaction with modern sociological models mentioned above provides one good example. Another is the collaboration between DSS scholars and experts in the physical and computer sciences.

One particularly noteworthy trend is the use of comparative approaches such as setting ancient Jewish science in its ANE and Greco-Roman contexts.[21] Several scholars seek to understand Jewish book and writing culture in light of Greco-Roman parallels.[22] Examples could be multiplied, but it is important to recognize how thoroughly integrated DSS studies has become with diverse approaches and perspectives within the humanities. As scholars increasingly recognize that the

18. For the history of research, see Molly M. Zahn, *Rethinking Rewritten Scripture: Composition and Exegesis in the 4QReworked Pentateuch Manuscripts*, STDJ 95 (Leiden: Brill, 2011).

19. Eugene Ulrich, *The Dead Sea Scrolls and the Developmental Composition of the Bible*, VTSup 169 (Leiden: Brill, 2015); Emanuel Tov, *Textual Criticism of the Hebrew Bible*, 4th ed. (Minneapolis: Fortress, 2022).

20. Eva Mroczek, *The Literary Imagination in Jewish Antiquity* (Oxford: Oxford University Press, 2016).

21. Mladen Popović, *Reading the Human Body: Physiognomics and Astrology in the Dead Sea Scrolls and Hellenistic-Early Roman Period Judaism*, STDJ 67 (Leiden: Brill, 2007); Jonathan Ben-Dov and Seth Sanders, eds., *Ancient Jewish Sciences and the History of Knowledge in Second Temple Literature* (New York: New York University Press, 2014).

22. Pieter B. Hartog, *Pesher and Hypomnema: A Comparison of Two Commentary Traditions from the Hellenistic-Roman Period*, STDJ 121 (Leiden: Brill, 2017); Mladen Popović, "Reading, Writing, and Memorizing Together: Reading Culture in Ancient Judaism and the Dead Sea Scrolls in a Mediterranean Context," *DSD* 24, no. 3 (2017): 447–70; Drew Longacre, "Comparative Hellenistic and Roman Manuscript Studies (CHRoMS): Script Interactions and Hebrew/Aramaic Writing Culture," *COMStB* 7, no. 1 (2021): 7–50.

Qumran community/corpus was less an isolated special case and more a particular expression of a highly interconnected Jewish culture, we are better able to understand the nature of these connections with the world around them.

Manuscript Studies

Major theoretical developments in the interpretation and categorization of the DSS remain heavily dependent on the manuscripts themselves.

Material Analysis

Some of the most innovative aspects of manuscript studies relate to material analyses of the DSS as artifacts. Most prominently, radiocarbon dating has provided independent material evidence to check, correct, and/or refine traditional paleographic typologies. Two rounds of radiocarbon dating were conducted in the 1990s,[23] but some scholars raised concerns about contamination of the results, because scrolls were treated with castor oil by the early generation of DSS scholars.[24] The recent European Research Council project "Hands That Wrote the Bible" at the University of Groningen aims to provide new, reliable radiocarbon dating of ancient Hebrew and Aramaic scripts, the results of which are forthcoming.[25] In all, over sixty DSS have now been radiocarbon dated, amounting to more than 5 percent of the entire corpus, an enviable state of affairs compared to most ancient corpora. Thus the field is in a much better position today than it was even a decade ago in dating the DSS, and the dates proposed in the early DJD volumes should always be used with due awareness of the limitations and ambiguities inherent in paleographic dating.[26]

Another interesting avenue of material study of the DSS relates to DNA analysis of the animal skins.[27] This can indicate what type of animal was used and

23. Georges Bonani et al., "Radiocarbon Dating of Fourteen Dead Sea Scrolls," *Radiocarbon* 34, no. 3 (1992): 843–49; A. J. Timothy Jull et al., "Radiocarbon Dating of Scrolls and Linen Fragments from the Judean Desert," *Radiocarbon* 37, no. 1 (1995): 11–19.

24. Kaare Lund Rasmussen et al., "The Effects of Possible Contamination on the Radiocarbon Dating of the Dead Sea Scrolls I: Castor Oil," *Radiocarbon* 43, no. 1 (2001): 127–32.

25. Mladen Popović, "Digital Palaeography for Identifying the Unknown Scribes and Dating the Undated Manuscripts from the Dead Sea Scrolls," presented at Digital Palaeography and Hebrew/Aramaic Scribal Culture: The 2021 International Online Groningen Symposium (6 April 2021), https://youtu.be/JZeyWBbWawM.

26. Drew Longacre, "Reconsidering the Date of the En-Gedi Leviticus Scroll (EGLev): Exploring the Limitations of the Comparative-Typological Paleographic Method," *Textus* 27, no. 1 (2018): 44–84; Eibert J. C. Tigchelaar, "Seventy Years of Palaeographic Dating of the Dead Sea Scrolls," in *Sacred Texts and Disparate Interpretations: Qumran Manuscripts Seventy Years Later*, ed. Henryk Drawnel, STDJ 133 (Leiden: Brill, 2020), 258–78.

27. Sarit Anava et al., "Illuminating Genetic Mysteries of the Dead Sea Scrolls," *Cell* 181, no. 6 (2020): 1218–1231.e27.

provide conclusive evidence of which separated fragments belong to the same sheet of a reconstructed scroll.

Recent advances in scientific imaging and image processing techniques also provide new avenues for material analysis. Scholars have made initial forays into semi-automated matching of papyrus fibers for purposes of manuscript reconstruction.[28] Raman spectroscopy and X-ray fluorescence (XRF) imaging have been used to study inks and writing materials to answer questions about authenticity, provenance, and how skins were prepared and changed over time.[29] The most noteworthy result of such studies—in conjunction with paleographic analysis—is confirmation that most (if not all) of the purported DSS fragments that have appeared on the market in the twenty-first century are modern forgeries or at least highly suspicious.[30]

Material Reconstructions

While scrolls with known texts can often be reconstructed based on the preserved texts and column boundaries, Hartmut Stegemann developed a method for reconstructing even unknown texts based on recurring patterns of damage in fragmentary remains.[31] When a scroll is damaged across multiple layers while still rolled up, the damage appears similar from layer to adjacent layer. By observing these patterns, scholars can reverse engineer and reconstruct the scroll. This method allows the relative placement of separated fragments and an approximation of scroll length based on material indications, though highly fragmentary remains often leave many uncertainties and ambiguities. The method was refined and applied numerous times by Stegemann's students and successors at the University of Göttingen and has gained significant

28. Roy Abitbol, Ilan Shimshoni, and Jonathan Ben-Dov, "Machine Learning Based Assembly of Fragments of Ancient Papyrus," *Journal on Computing and Cultural Heritage* 14, no. 3 (2021): 33.1–21.

29. Emanuel Tov, "The Sciences and the Reconstruction of the Ancient Scrolls: Possibilities and Impossibilities," in *The Dead Sea Scrolls in Context: Integrating the Dead Sea Scrolls in the Study of Ancient Texts, Languages, and Cultures*, vol. 1, ed. Armin Lange, Emanuel Tov, and Matthias Weigold, VTSup 140 (Leiden: Brill, 2011), 10–14; Ira Rabin, "Instrumental Analysis in Manuscript Studies," in *Comparative Oriental Manuscript Studies: An Introduction*, ed. Alessandro Bausi et al. (Hamburg: Tredition, 2015), 27–30.

30. Kipp Davis, "Caves of Dispute: Patterns of Correspondence and Suspicion in the Post-2002 'Dead Sea Scrolls' Fragments," *DSD* 24, no. 2 (2017): 229–70; Kipp Davis et al., "Nine Dubious 'Dead Sea Scrolls' Fragments from the Twenty-First Century," *DSD* 24, no. 2 (2017): 189–228; Colette Loll et al., *Museum of the Bible, Dead Sea Scroll Collection: Scientific Research and Analysis; Final Report*, November 2019, https://d2f7x7uhr2xem7.cloudfront.net/sixteen_by_nine/MOTB-DSS-Report-FINAL-web.pdf.

31. Hartmut Stegemann, "Methods for the Reconstruction of Scrolls from Scattered Fragments," in *Archaeology and History in the Dead Sea Scrolls: The New York University Conference in Memory of Yigael Yadin*, ed. Lawrence H. Schiffman, JSPSup 8 (Sheffield: Sheffield Academic, 1990), 189–220.

prominence.[32] The past two decades have seen a proliferation of such material reconstructions in DSS studies, and they are becoming standard in the field. The so-called Göttingen method relies on precise measurement and extrapolation, and scholars often offer very precise reconstructions.[33] Several studies using mathematical models for reconstructing scroll length, however, question the degree of precision possible with such methods and suggest large margins of error that must be factored in as part of the process.[34]

Scribal Practices

Recent decades have seen significant progress in the study of scribal practices in the DSS. Emanuel Tov produced a comprehensive monograph surveying these scribal practices, which is an essential reference work for anyone working with the scrolls as artifacts.[35] And Daniel Machiela published a thorough study of the scribal practices evident in the Aramaic scrolls.[36]

The study of ancient Hebrew/Aramaic paleography has progressed significantly in the last decade, primarily through the "Hands That Wrote the Bible" project. In addition to using new radiocarbon dates to provide material grounds for dating the DSS and using digital paleographic tools to produce automated date predictions for undated scrolls,[37] this project also uses computer-aided writer identification, where scholars attempt to identify multiple manuscripts written by the same writer, which provides additional evidence for scribal profiling.[38] Furthermore, I have suggested a new approach to the stylistic and functional

32. Annette Steudel, "Assembling and Reconstructing Manuscripts," in *The Dead Sea Scrolls after Fifty Years: A Comprehensive Assessment*, ed. Peter W. Flint and James C. VanderKam (Leiden: Brill, 1998), 516–34.

33. Eva Jain, *Psalmen oder Psalter? Materielle Rekonstruktion und inhaltliche Untersuchung der Psalmenhandschriften aus der Wüste Juda*, STDJ 109 (Leiden: Brill, 2014).

34. Eshbal Ratzon and Nachum Dershowitz, "The Length of a Scroll: Quantitative Evaluation of Material Reconstructions," *PLoS ONE* 15, no. 10 (2020), https://doi.org/10.1371/journal.pone.0239831; Drew Longacre, "Methods for the Reconstruction of Large Literary (Sc)rolls from Fragmentary Remains," in *The Hebrew Bible Manuscripts: A Millennium*, ed. Élodie Attia and Antony Perrot, Supplements to the Textual History of the Bible 6 (Leiden: Brill, 2022), 110–41.

35. Emanuel Tov, *Scribal Practices and Approaches Reflected in the Texts Found in the Judean Desert*, STDJ 54 (Leiden: Brill, 2004).

36. Daniel A. Machiela, *A Handbook of the Aramaic Scrolls from the Qumran Caves: Manuscripts, Language, and Scribal Practices*, STDJ 140 (Leiden: Brill, 2022).

37. See the preliminary work in Maruf A. Dhali et al., "Feature-Extraction Methods for Historical Manuscript Dating Based on Writing Style Development," *Pattern Recognition Letters* 131 (2020): 413–20.

38. Maruf A. Dhali et al., "A Digital Palaeographic Approach towards Writer Identification in the Dead Sea Scrolls," in *Proceedings of the 6th International Conference on Pattern Recognition Applications and Methods (ICPRAM 2017)*, ed. Maria De Marsico, Gabriella Sanniti di Baja, and Ana L. N. Fred (Porto, Portugal: SciTePress, 2017), 693–702; Mladen Popović, Maruf A. Dhali, and Lambert Schomaker, "Artificial Intelligence Based Writer Identification Generates New Evidence for the Unknown Scribes of the Dead Sea Scrolls Exemplified by the Great Isaiah

classification of the Hebrew/Aramaic scripts[39] by relating many of the most notable developments in this writing tradition to Greco-Roman influence.[40]

The language and orthography of the scrolls remain issues of dispute. Research on literacy generally reinforces the conclusion that Aramaic, Hebrew, and Greek were all spoken and not-infrequently written/read in Judea around the turn of the era in various degrees and in different social/reading circumstances.[41] Studies of the Hebrew and Aramaic of the scrolls provide a good starting point for understanding the vernaculars reflected in the Qumran manuscripts, especially some of the distinctive features characteristic of many of the Hebrew scrolls.[42] Some scholars have gone so far as to argue that the distinctive features amount to a language system intentionally fostered by the Qumran community and associates in order to enhance group cohesion in distinction from other Jewish groups,[43] though others contest that this sociolinguistic conclusion is unwarranted by the inconsistent and unsystematic nature of the evidence.[44] Tov's well-known theory of a distinct Qumran scribal practice—consisting of a set of morphological and orthographic features and scribal practices that correlate with the Qumran "sectarian" texts—continues to be a source of controversy with respect to both its internal consistency and its association with Qumran.[45] Some studies statistically support the idea of two distinct systems of scribal practice,[46] while others suggest that the unsystematic nature of the orthographic distributions is incompatible with such a binary differentiation.[47]

Scroll (1QIsa[a])," *PLoS ONE* 16, no. 4 (2021), https://doi.org/10.1371/journal.pone.0249769; Gemma Hayes, "Searching for Dead Sea Scribes" (PhD diss., University of Groningen, 2023).

39. Drew Longacre, "Disambiguating the Concept of Formality in Palaeographic Descriptions: Stylistic Classification and the Ancient Jewish Hebrew/Aramaic Scripts," *COMStB* 5, no. 2 (2019): 101–28; Drew Longacre, "Paleographic Style and the Forms and Functions of the Dead Sea Psalm Scrolls: A Hand Fitting for the Occasion?," *VT* 72, no. 1 (2022): 67–92.

40. Longacre, "Comparative Hellenistic and Roman Manuscript Studies."

41. See, e.g., Catherine Hezser, *Jewish Literacy in Roman Palestine*, Texts and Studies in Ancient Judaism 81 (Tübingen: Mohr Siebeck, 2001); Michael Owen Wise, *Language and Literacy in Roman Judaea: A Study of the Bar Kokhba Documents* (New Haven: Yale University Press, 2015).

42. E.g., Takamitsu Muraoka, *A Grammar of Qumran Aramaic*, Ancient Near Eastern Studies Supplement Series 38 (Leuven: Peeters, 2011); Eric D. Reymond, *Qumran Hebrew: An Overview of Orthography, Phonology, and Morphology* (Atlanta: SBL Press, 2014).

43. William M. Schniedewind, "Language and Group Identity in the Dead Sea Scrolls: The Case for an 'Essene Hebrew,'" in *Hebrew Texts and Language of the Second Temple Period: Proceedings of an Eighth Symposium on the Hebrew of the Dead Sea Scrolls and Ben Sira*, ed. Steven E. Fassberg, STDJ 134 (Leiden: Brill, 2021), 280–91.

44. Eibert J. C. Tigchelaar, "Sociolinguistics and the Misleading Use of the Concept of Anti-Language for Qumran Hebrew," in *The Dead Sea Scrolls and the Study of the Humanities*, ed. Pieter B. Hartog, Alison Schofield, and Samuel I. Thomas, STDJ 125 (Leiden: Brill, 2018), 195–206.

45. For details, see Tov, *Scribal Practices*.

46. E.g., Martin Abegg, "Qumran Scribal Practice: Won Moor Thyme," in *Scribal Practice, Text and Canon in the Dead Sea Scrolls*, ed. John J. Collins and Ananda Geyser-Fouché, STDJ 130 (Leiden: Brill, 2019), 175–204.

47. E.g., Eibert J. C. Tigchelaar, "Assessing Emanuel Tov's 'Qumran Scribal Practice,'" in *The Dead Sea Scrolls: Transmission of Traditions and Production of Texts*, ed. Sarianna Metso, Hindy Najman, and Eileen Schuller, STDJ 92 (Leiden: Brill, 2010), 173–207.

Digital Resources

In addition to the use of innovative technologies for material analysis and digital paleography, it is worth highlighting the ways digital resources have proliferated in the field and greatly facilitated research on the DSS.

Digital Imagery

Undoubtedly, one of the most important developments in the study of the DSS has been the Israel Antiquities Authority's (IAA) ongoing project to digitize all the DSS and make them available online (https://www.deadseascrolls.org.il). Although this project is still ongoing, scholars can now access color images of the full IAA plates where the fragments are physically stored, high-resolution color and infrared photographs of each fragment, and a selection of scans from the old Palestine Archaeological Museum photographs. Additional photographs (including different lighting arrangements and color/scale bars for measurement) are available upon request directly from the IAA. The IAA-provided images are of excellent quality and enhance the reading of difficult fragments, often making it easier and more productive to read the scrolls from the pictures than to consult the originals. Furthermore, images of five of the best-preserved DSS (1QS, 1QIsa[a], 1QM, 1QpHab, and 11QT[a]) can be viewed on the website of the Israel Museum (http://dss.collections.imj.org.il).

Easy and free access to the DSS has greatly facilitated and even democratized the study of the scrolls. However, while all are allowed to use the images for their own private research, inclusion of the images in formal publications or public presentations requires explicit permission from the IAA.[48] Under current copyright law, it remains unclear to what extent the credited reproduction of small extracts from images or modified images qualifies as "fair use."

One further particularly exciting development in digital imagery and processing relates to the virtual unrolling of a charred Leviticus scroll from En-Gedi.[49] Using three-dimensional microtomography scans, Brent Seales and his team at the University of Kentucky were able to unroll and read the scroll virtually, without physically opening the artifact. I argue that this scroll was written later than most of the other DSS.[50] The value of this technology for the study of earlier scrolls with carbon-based ink and less metallic content than the En-Gedi scroll (and thus less contrast between the background and the ink) remains to be seen, but recent advances with the Herculaneum papyri are encouraging.

48. See https://www.deadseascrolls.org.il/terms.

49. Michael Segal et al., "An Early Leviticus Scroll from En-Gedi: Preliminary Publication," *Textus* 26, no. 1 (2016): 1–30; William Brent Seales et al., "From Damage to Discovery via Virtual Unwrapping: Reading the Scroll from En-Gedi," *Science Advances* 2, no. 9 (2016): e1601247.

50. Longacre, "Reconsidering the Date of EGLev."

Digital Workspaces

The field of DSS studies has made great strides in the creation of digital workspaces, though to date none are fully functional and publicly available. Most prominently, the Scripta Qumranica Electronica project is currently in the testing phase and has enormous potential for facilitating research on the DSS (https://sqe.deadseascrolls.org.il).[51] It intends to provide an online workspace for accessing and processing images, a canvas for digital reconstructions, and an interface for creating and aligning transcriptions.

Transcriptions of the DSS are also readily available (in the original languages and translation) in commercial software platforms like Accordance and Logos. These can be purchased in modules containing the biblical scrolls and/or the nonbiblical ones. These modules are lexically and morphologically tagged to facilitate reading and electronic searches.

Commentaries on Specific Texts

In the early generations of DSS scholarship, scholars focused on piecing together manuscripts from scattered fragments. As the full corpus of scrolls has been published and many manuscripts have been reconstructed and studied, the field has matured to the point of offering full scholarly commentaries on Qumran texts, similar to what is common practice for biblical texts. Eerdmans has a DSS commentary series that has published comprehensive volumes on the liturgical and wisdom texts from Qumran.[52] An Oxford University Press commentary series has published volumes on Pesher Habakkuk and the Damascus Document.[53] Charlotte Hempel has recently published a scholarly commentary on the Community Rule texts from Qumran.[54] A complicating factor in many of these commentaries is that they study textual traditions preserved in multiple fragmentary manuscripts that only partially overlap and often exhibit significant differences. But commentaries such as these increasingly provide nonspecialists with easily accessible explanations of the DSS as well as concise, up-to-date summaries of the complex scholarly debates and steadily growing body of secondary literature that characterize the field of DSS studies in the twenty-first century.

51. Bronson Brown-deVost, "Scripta Qumranica Electronica (2016–2021)," *HeBAI* 5, no. 3 (2016): 307–15.

52. James R. Davila, *Liturgical Works*, Eerdmans Commentaries on the Dead Sea Scrolls (Grand Rapids: Eerdmans, 2000); John Kampen, *Wisdom Literature*, Eerdmans Commentaries on the Dead Sea Scrolls (Grand Rapids: Eerdmans, 2011).

53. Timothy H. Lim, *The Earliest Commentary on the Prophecy of Habakkuk*, Oxford Commentary on the Dead Sea Scrolls (Oxford: Oxford University Press, 2020); Steven D. Fraade, *The Damascus Document*, Oxford Commentary on the Dead Sea Scrolls (Oxford: Oxford University Press, 2021).

54. Charlotte Hempel, *The Community Rules from Qumran: A Commentary*, TSAJ 183 (Tübingen: Mohr Siebeck, 2020).

Conclusion

Modern study of Qumran and the Dead Sea Scrolls is a vast and complex discipline, with voluminous secondary literature that even specialists can no longer comprehensively master. This creates great challenges for nonspecialist scholars who seek responsibly and knowledgeably to incorporate the scrolls into their research. Yet the DSS are firmly established as critical resources for the study of ancient Judaism, early Christianity, and the text and interpretation of the Bible and simply cannot be ignored. This brief survey highlights conceptual and technological developments that scholars need to be aware of when interacting with the DSS and cites key literature that can serve as entry points for studying the various issues in greater depth. In this way, I hope to have made the task a little less daunting and thus encourage nonspecialists to incorporate the DSS thoroughly into their own research agendas, because the scrolls have much to contribute.

4

Archaeology and History

Late Bronze Age–Iron Age I

Ralph K. Hawkins

The Late Bronze Age (LBA, 1550–1200 BCE) through the Iron Age I (Iron I, 1200–1000 BCE) corresponds with significant events in the life of ancient Israel, notably the exodus, the emergence of Israel in Canaan, and the rise of the monarchy. Written texts and material evidence have survived only in fragments and require correlated interpretation, "historical archaeology." The archaeology of a society with written records can only be meaningfully interpreted in relation to its context(s). This survey considers the history recounted in the biblical and epigraphic texts and their relationship to current archaeology.

The Period of the Exodus

Since the 1960s, the fortunes of OT history have waxed and waned. The exodus traditions have not fared well, and some conclude that they cannot be correlated with anything in ancient Egypt. William Dever judges that "there [is] no archaeological evidence for an exodus" and that "the history of the Exodus [is] a dead issue."[1] Israel Finkelstein and Neil Silberman assume the exodus traditions are simply a "brilliant product of the human imagination."[2]

1. William G. Dever, "Is There Any Archaeological Evidence for the Exodus?," in *Exodus: The Egyptian Evidence*, ed. Ernest S. Frerichs and Leonard H. Lesko (Winona Lake, IN: Eisenbrauns, 1997), 67–86.

2. Israel Finkelstein and Neil Asher Silberman, *The Bible Unearthed: Archaeology's New Vision of Ancient Israel and the Origins of Its Sacred Texts* (New York: Free Press, 2001), 8.

The Absence of Direct Material Evidence for the Exodus

Current negative conclusions about the exodus are not based on new discoveries but, rather, on the *lack* of direct archaeological evidence. This interpretation corresponds to three areas. First, there is no indisputable reference to enslaved "Hebrews" or "Israelites" in any Egyptian record. Second, no inscription refers to any event in the book of Exodus. Third, there is no noninscriptional evidence from the Egyptian Delta that mentions "Hebrews," "Israelites," or the exodus events.

The lack of reference to "Hebrews" or "Israelites" is unsurprising because "the Egyptians referred to all of their West Semitic slaves simply as 'Asiatics,' with no distinction among groups."[3] Since monumental stelae were designed to laud the pharaoh's achievements and not embarrassing failures, it is predictable that no inscription would commemorate the exodus.[4] Furthermore, that no papyrus mentions anything related to the exodus events is unsurprising. Almost no papyri are known from dynastic times, and none exist from the eastern Nile Delta.[5]

The lack of data raises the methodological question of how to view the absence of evidence. David Fischer discredits the myth of "negative proof," which is "an attempt to sustain a factual proposition merely by negative evidence."[6] Historiographic evidence must be positive. He asserts: "Negative evidence is a contradiction in terms—it is no evidence at all."[7] Many claims of historical records—such as that of the battle of Megiddo in 1457 BCE—are universally accepted by historians without any archaeological evidence. Unfortunately, a double standard is often applied to the biblical texts, which are viewed as "guilty until proven innocent."[8] The absence of evidence is viewed as negative proof. A consistent methodology requires that we consider the biblical text "innocent until proven guilty," unless compelling evidence exists to do otherwise.[9]

Positive Evidence of a Viable Context for the Exodus

There is in fact positive evidence of a viable context for the exodus around 1280–1260 BCE. The most important comes from Tell el-Rataba and Qantir, which may be identified with the Pithom and Rameses of Exod. 1:11. Tell el-Rataba is one of several places named "Pithom" in the Wadi Tumilat but is the only one occupied in the Ramesside period. At this site, Ramesses II built a

3. Joshua Berman, *Ani Maamin: Biblical Criticism, Historical Truth, and the Thirteen Principles of Faith* (Jerusalem: Maggid, 2020), 44.

4. G. Wheeler, "Ancient Egypt's Silence about the Exodus," *AUSS* 40, no. 2 (2002): 257–64.

5. Bridget Leach and John Tait, "Papyrus," *OEAE* 3:22–24.

6. David Hacket Fischer, *Historians' Fallacies: Toward a Logic of Historical Thought* (New York: Harper & Row, 1970), 47.

7. Fischer, *Historians' Fallacies*, 62.

8. William G. Dever, *What Did the Biblical Writers Know and When Did They Know It? What Archaeology Can Tell Us about the Reality of Ancient Israel* (Grand Rapids: Eerdmans, 2002), 128.

9. Ralph K. Hawkins, *How Israel Became a People* (Nashville: Abingdon, 2013), 3–18.

defensive enclosure wall and gate, a temple of Atum, and storerooms in the region of Tjeku/Succoth.[10] Qantir was first identified with Pi-Ramesses around 1930, an equation that gained full acceptance over the next several decades. Excavations have revealed that Seti I (1294–1279 BCE) established a small palace there and that Ramesses II built it into a great city that in effect served as the capital until it was abandoned in about 1135 BCE. The new administrative site of Pi-Ramesses flourished only in the Nineteenth Dynasty (ca. 1270–1120 BCE). No evidence exists during the Eighteenth Dynasty that the region was known as Rameses or that a city known as Rameses existed.[11] And the portrayal of the pharaoh residing in Rameses occurs only in this era.[12] The account of the Israelites avoiding the "Way of the Philistines"[13] (see Exod. 13:17), a system of stations and forts built as part of the renewal of Egypt's presence in north Sinai, accords with the beginning of the Nineteenth Dynasty.

Several texts suggest a viable context for the exodus during Egypt's Nineteenth Dynasty. The Amarna tablets record more than three hundred communications between the Eighteenth-Dynasty Pharaoh Amenophis IV (1353–1337 BCE) and vassal city-states of Syria-Palestine. Canaanite rulers address Pharaoh as "my lord" and ask him to intervene in local power conflicts, illustrating that Egypt had authority over Canaan in the fourteenth century BCE.[14] Around 1250 BCE, however, the LBA system in the eastern Mediterranean began to crumble, and Egypt's domination waned. This political vacuum created the opportunity for new settlements. Several New Kingdom letters attest to movements of Bedouin throughout the southern Levant. Papyrus Anastasi V describes two Asiatic laborers fleeing from Egypt through the northern Sinai; Papyrus Anastasi VI refers to the arrival of Bedouin from the northern Sinai desert at an Egyptian border

10. James K. Hoffmeier and Gary A. Rendsburg, "Pithom and Rameses (Exodus 1:11): Historical, Archaeological, and Linguistic Issues (Part I)," *Journal of Ancient Egyptian Interconnections* 33 (2022): 1–19.

11. Hawkins, *How Israel Became a People*, 63–65; Hoffmeier and Rendsburg, "Pithom and Rameses (Exodus 1:11)," 2–4; see also Gary A. Rendsburg and James K. Hoffmeier, "Pithom and Rameses (Exodus 1:11): Historical, Archaeological, and Linguistic Issues (Part II)," *Journal of Ancient Egyptian Interconnections* 34 (2022): 36–52.

12. Manfred Bietak, "On the Historicity of the Exodus: What Egyptology Today Can Contribute to Assessing the Biblical Account of the Sojourn in Egypt," in *Israel's Exodus in Transdisciplinary Perspective: Text, Archaeology, Culture, and Geoscience*, ed. Thomas E. Levy, Thomas Schneider, and William C. H. Propp, Quantitative Methods in the Humanities and Social Sciences (New York: Springer, 2015), 17–37.

13. The "Way of the Philistines" is an anachronistic name for a route known as "The Ways of Horus" in Egyptian sources. James K. Hoffmeier and Stephen O. Moshier, "'The Ways of Horus': Reconstructing Egypt's East Frontier Defense Network and the Military Road to Canaan in New Kingdom Times," in *Tell el-Borg I: Excavations in North Sinai*, ed. James K. Hoffmeier (Winona Lake, IN: Eisenbrauns, 2014), 34–61.

14. Nadav Na'aman, "The Egyptian-Canaanite Correspondence," in *Amarna Diplomacy: The Beginnings of International Relations*, ed. Raymond Cohen and Raymond Westbrook (Baltimore: Johns Hopkins University Press, 2000), 125–38.

fortress built during the Ramesside period; Papyrus Anastasi I repeatedly mentions the presence of Bedouin populations in Canaan.[15]

Early Israelite Settlement in Canaan

Early Israelite settlement in Canaan took place at the LBA to Iron I transition. Discussion of Israel's appearance in Canaan focuses on the books of Joshua and Judges, the description of the land and territory, and the interpretation of the material evidence from this period.

Classical and Recent Models for the Appearance of Israel in Canaan

Several models purport to interpret this period of early Israelite settlement. William Albright coined the Conquest Model as the view that the Israelite tribes settled Canaan primarily through violent warfare. Initially, Albright looked for burn levels at Jericho, Ai, and Hazor that coincided with the time of the Eighteenth Egyptian Dynasty. Hazor appeared to have a destruction layer at about 1400 BCE, but no burn layers could be found at the same time from Jericho or Ai. Canaanite sites, such as Bethel, Debir, Eglon, Hazor, and Lachish, showed evidence of a thirteenth-century destruction. Albright associated their destruction with invading Israelites,[16] and decided that archaeology and philological study of the Bible made it "absolutely certain" that the main phase of the conquest should be dated to the second half of the thirteenth century.[17] His disciples promoted this model in America and Israel. Although it stood in some tension with a "face-value" reading of the biblical data, which appear to suggest a fifteenth-century exodus-conquest, G. Ernest Wright agreed with the later date, interpreting some biblical numbers symbolically.[18]

Other archaeological research challenged the Conquest Model. Several sites mentioned in the biblical account were either unoccupied in the thirteenth century BCE or did not neatly correlate with thirteenth-century destructions. Other destructions seemed too widely separated for a single or even a drawn-out campaign. In response, Albright and Wright recognized the need to temper the Conquest Model. Albright later admitted, "At present we cannot propose any safe reconstruction of the actual course of events during the period of the Israelite settlement in Palestine."[19] Wright likewise observed that a closer reading indi-

15. *COS* 3.4:16; 3.5:16–17; 3.2:9–14.

16. W. F. Albright, "The Israelite Conquest in the Light of Archaeology," *BASOR* 74 (1939): 11–23.

17. W. F. Albright, *The Biblical Period from Abraham to Ezra: An Historical Survey* (New York: Harper & Row, 1963), 27.

18. G. Ernest Wright, *Biblical Archaeology* (Philadelphia: Westminster, 1957), 84.

19. W. F. Albright, *Archaeology and the Religion of Israel: The Ayer Lectures of the Colgate-Rochester Divinity School, 1941* (Baltimore: Johns Hopkins University Press, 1965), 95.

cates that the author of the book of Joshua was "quite aware of much left to be done" in terms of taking the land.[20] John Bright, another of Albright's students, recognized that the Israelite conquest must have been "vastly more complex than a simplistic presentation . . . would suggest."[21] As new data emerged that did not seem to cohere, Bright continued to argue that "impressive" evidence indicated a violent conquest at the end of the thirteenth century and that none of these data "can be held flatly to refute the theory."[22] Likewise, Yigal Yadin reflected that "in its broad outline the archaeological record supports the narrative in Joshua and Judges as Albright said."[23]

The Conquest Model came under increasing fire. James Maxwell Miller criticized a wholesale destruction of Canaan that reached beyond what the biblical text required or the archaeological record supported.[24] He stated that "the cities which do present archaeological evidence of having been destroyed at the end of [the LBA] are, for the most part, not the ones which figure prominently in the biblical conquest traditions" and that the LBA destructions may be due to localized causes.[25] Dever also emphasizes the difficulties in harmonizing the biblical and archaeological data.[26]

Other accounts of Israel's emergence in Canaan were proposed in the early twentieth century. Albrecht Alt proposed what came to be known as the Peaceful Infiltration Model.[27] He hypothesized that the Israelites entered from outside the land through peaceful migration over hundreds of years. This theory views the account in Judges as more reliable than Joshua's.

George Mendenhall's Peasant Revolt hypothesis represented a radical departure from the Conquest and Peaceful Infiltration Models. Mendenhall postulated that many Israelites were disenfranchised Canaanites who fled from oppressive feudalistic situations in the urban centers of the lowlands and settled in the highlands. They were joined by a band of Hebrews who had escaped from Egypt and brought faith in YHWH. These two groups made a covenant with one another and became Israel.[28] Departing from Mendenhall's feudalistic understanding,

20. Wright, *Biblical Archaeology*, 69–70.

21. John Bright, *A History of Israel*, 3rd ed. (Philadelphia: Westminster, 1981), 129–30.

22. Bright, *History of Israel*, 132.

23. Yigal Yadin, "Is the Biblical Account of the Israelite Conquest of Canaan Historically Reliable?," *BAR* 8, no. 2 (1982): 16–23.

24. J. Maxwell Miller, "The Israelite Occupation of Canaan," in *Israelite and Judaean History*, ed. John H. Hayes and J. Maxwell Miller, OTL (London: SCM, 1977), 256.

25. Miller, "Israelite Occupation of Canaan," 236–37.

26. William G. Dever, *Who Were the Early Israelites and Where Did They Come From?* (Grand Rapids: Eerdmans, 2003), 23–74.

27. Albrecht Alt, *Essays on Old Testament History and Religion*, trans. R. A. Wilson, The Biblical Seminar (Sheffield: JSOT Press, 1989), 175–221.

28. George E. Mendenhall, "The Hebrew Conquest of Palestine," *BA* 25, no. 3 (1962): 66–87; Mendenhall, *The Tenth Generation: The Origins of the Biblical Tradition* (Baltimore: Johns Hopkins University Press, 1973).

Norman Gottwald adopted Marx's concept of an "Asiatic mode of production" and applied it to Canaanite society. Israel's emergence stemmed from peasant uprisings against ruling groups, who took advantage of the peasantry.[29] Later, Gottwald preferred the name Social Revolution Model.[30]

In the 1950s, archaeologists began conducting surface surveys in Israel and, by the 1980s, new data allowed scholars to reevaluate these models. A network of hundreds of small, unwalled villages, most of which were in the hill country extending from Lower Galilee to the northern Negev, were occupied in the late thirteenth to eleventh centuries BCE.[31] A clear demographic change had occurred in the central hill country from LBA to Iron I that represented a major influx of new population elements.

The interpretation of the origins and ethnic identity of these newcomers was initially influenced by the Peaceful Infiltration and Social Revolution Models. Robert Coote and Keith Whitelam argued that, at the end of the LBA, a decline in interregional trade in the eastern Mediterranean led to the collapse of local economies. Bandits, nomads, and peasant groups joined together in the highlands, where they established agricultural settlements and developed an identity as "Israel."[32]

Finkelstein proposed that those who settled the highlands were seminomadic "peaceful infiltrators."[33] Although this Pastoral Canaanite Model is sometimes regarded as a variation of the Peaceful Infiltration Model, Finkelstein identifies these settlers as indigenous and their settlement as one phase in an ordinary cyclic demographic process. The highland settlement was part of a process that began with the destruction of LBA urban culture and the displacement of population groups in different areas, some of whom settled in the highlands of Canaan.[34] Dever suggests a model of indigenous agrarian reform, having continuities with the preceding LBA Canaanite society.[35]

Another recent reconstruction is Ann Killebrew's Mixed Multitude Model. She proposes that the population increase consisted of elements of LBA Canaanite society, especially the rural population, displaced peasants and pastoralists, and

29. Norman K. Gottwald, *The Tribes of Yahweh: A Sociology of the Religion of Liberated Israel, 1250–1050 BCE* (Maryknoll, NY: Orbis Books, 1979).

30. Norman K. Gottwald, "Israel's Emergence in Canaan: *BR* Interviews Norman Gottwald," *BRev* 5, no. 5 (1989): 26–34.

31. Israel Finkelstein, *The Archaeology of the Israelite Settlement* (Jerusalem: Israel Exploration Society, 1988).

32. R. B. Coote and K. W. Whitelam, *The Emergence of Early Israel in Historical Perspective*, SWBA 5 (Sheffield: Almond, 1987), 117–38.

33. Finkelstein, *Archaeology of the Israelite Settlement*, 302–6.

34. Israel Finkelstein and Nadav Na'aman, "Introduction: From Nomadism to Monarchy—the State of Research in 1992," in *From Nomadism to Monarchy: Archaeological and Historical Aspects of Early Israel*, ed. I. Finkelstein and N. Na'aman (Jerusalem: Israel Exploration Society, 1994), 9–17.

35. Dever, *Who Were the Early Israelites?*

lawless Habiru and Shasu. These included "outside elements," such as "Semitic slaves from Twentieth-Dynasty New Kingdom Egypt," as well as other nonindigenous groups mentioned in the Bible, such as the Midianites, Kenites, and Amalekites. This "mixed multitude" (Exod. 12:38 ESV) underwent a process of ethnogenesis, identifying "as 'Israelite' in its broader sense . . . based on the reference 'Israel' in the Merneptah stela."[36]

Today, empire is frowned upon, colonialism is rejected, and indigenous models of early Israelite origins are in vogue.[37] Many contend that debate about early Israelite origins is "almost at an end," with a consensus that early Israel originated from the indigenous population in Canaan.[38] Others argue that at least some elements of early Israel were nonindigenous. Lawrence Stager maintains, "There is something to be said for a migration, if not an actual invasion, of Israelites into Canaan toward the end of the Bronze Age." He believes the dramatic population increase cannot be accounted for by natural growth, although it is "doubtful that archaeologists can distinguish one highland group from another."[39] In his Ruralization Model, the decline of LBA city-state systems led to peasant farmers settling beyond areas of state control, especially in the less accessible highlands.

Volkmar Fritz argues, based on dissimilarities in the material culture of the early Israelites and Canaanites, that the new settlers were unrelated to former inhabitants of the Canaanite cities. Recognizing some similarities, he postulates close contact with Canaanites over a long period. In this Symbiosis Model, cultural similarities developed when nomadic Israelites entered the land and gradually formed close economic relationships with Canaanites. The Israelites eventually became self-sufficient in the highlands but retained aspects of the shared Canaanite material culture.[40]

Baruch Halpern rejects the Social Revolution Model because he sees no evidence for a retreat from the cities to the hill country.[41] The collared-rim jar and the four-room house do not characterize LBA Canaanite centers but are typical

36. Ann E. Killebrew, "The Emergence of Ancient Israel: The Social Boundaries of a 'Mixed Multitude' in Canaan," in *"I Will Speak the Riddles of Ancient Times": Archaeological and Historical Studies in Honor of Amihai Mazar on the Occasion of His Sixtieth Birthday*, ed. A. M. Maeir and P. de Miroschedjui (Winona Lake, IN: Eisenbrauns, 2006), 2:571; Avraham Faust, *Israel's Ethnogenesis: Settlement, Interaction, Expansion and Resistance* (London: Equinox, 2006).

37. William G. Dever, "Earliest Israel: God's Warriors, Revolting Peasants, or Nomadic Hordes?," *ErIsr* 30 (Jerusalem: Israel Exploration Society, 2011), 4.

38. Neils P. Lemche, "Early Israel Revisited," *CurBS* 4 (1996): 9–34.

39. Lawrence E. Stager, "Forging an Identity: The Emergence of Ancient Israel," in *The Oxford History of the Biblical World*, ed. Michael D. Coogan (New York: Oxford University Press, 1998), 134–37.

40. Volkmar Fritz, *The Emergence of Israel in the Twelfth and Eleventh Centuries BCE*, trans. James W. Barker, BibEnc 2 (Atlanta: Society of Biblical Literature, 2011), 135–38.

41. Baruch Halpern, *The Emergence of Israel in Canaan*, SBLMS 29 (Chico, CA: Scholars Press, 1983), 81–94.

of Iron I Israelite settlements at Cisjordanian and Transjordanian sites.[42] In his view, the textual and archaeological data suggest an origin for the early Israelites from outside Canaan, particularly from Haran and east of the Jordan. Some migrants "may have been propelled into Transjordan by the stick of Assyrian expansion at the end of the thirteenth century" and developed into the nations of Ammon, Moab, and Edom.[43] Other pastoralists migrated out of Egypt to the "land of the Shasu of YHWH" to avoid corvée. These Yahwists met others who were homesteading down the King's Highway in Transjordan and together coalesced into "Israel."[44]

Recent studies build on points of contact between Transjordan and the Shasu. Randall Younker observes that during the LBA–Iron I transition, a rise in rural kin-based groups evolved into more complex tribal organizations that opposed Egypt. Local groups implemented an avoidance strategy by retreating to marginal frontier zones in the deserts or highlands, in some cases reverting to nomadism. One group, the Shasu, migrated to Transjordan, outside the direct sphere of Egyptian influence. When Egyptian domination waned in the latter part of the thirteenth century, the Shasu settled in the highlands of both Cisjordan and Transjordan. Because of the social fluidity provided by tribal genealogies, the Shasu, along with other sedentarizing peoples, coalesced into "Israel."[45] This reconstruction, the so-called Shasu Model, is closely associated with Anson Rainey.[46] He argues that the Shasu, who had settled east of the Jordan River during the LBA–Iron I transition, were "at least one major group of those settlers who migrated from Transjordan [into Canaan] and bore the ethnicon 'sons of Israel.'"[47]

Most models of the early Israelite settlement, except for the Shasu Model, are based primarily on the archaeological remains discovered during the twentieth century from the Upper Galilee, the Lower Galilee, the hill country of Manasseh and Ephraim, the hill country of Judah, and the Negev. Iron I sites in the eastern part of the land, especially the Jordan Valley, are often ignored, and this almost universal tendency results in dismissing the Transjordan as a possible source for early Israel in the Canaanite highlands.[48]

Beginning in 1978 until his death in 2015, Adam Zertal conducted the Manasseh Hill Country Survey, which is continued today by Shay Bar. The survey

42. Baruch Halpern, "Settlement of Canaan," *ABD* 5:1132–35.

43. Halpern, "Settlement of Canaan," 1139.

44. Baruch Halpern, "The Exodus from Egypt: Myth or Reality?," in *The Rise of Ancient Israel*, ed. Hershel Shanks (Washington, DC: Biblical Archaeology Society, 1992), 104–7.

45. Randall W. Younker, "The Emergence of Ammon: A View of the Rise of Iron Age Polities from the Other Side of the Jordan," in *The Near East in the Southwest: Essays in Honor of William G. Dever*, ed. B. A. Nakhai, Annual of ASOR 58 (Boston: American Schools of Oriental Research, 2004), 153–76.

46. Anson F. Rainey, "Whence Came the Israelites and Their Language?," *IEJ* 57, no. 1 (2007): 41–64; Rainey, "Shasu or Habiru: Who Were the Early Israelites?," *BAR* 34, no. 6 (2008): 51–55.

47. Rainey, "Whence Came the Israelites and Their Language?," 57.

48. Dever, "Earliest Israel," 4–12.

has produced a wealth of data about this largely unknown territory, and much of the information is pertinent to the discussion of early Israelite origins.

First, the survey reveals an almost complete absence of inhabitants in the region during the LBA and a demographic shift toward settlement in Iron I. Potsherds indicative of the later period were found at sixty-nine sites and account for 30.8 percent of the total collected there. Since most of these sites were founded on virgin soil, with no preceding settlement, Zertal and Bar conclude that the settlers originated from outside the region.[49]

Second, Iron I pottery in East Manasseh is related to that of highland settlers. The unique ceramic decorations do not appear in the LBA or Iron II and connect the Manasseh Hill Country with northern Mount Ephraim, concentrated in the Shechem Syncline. Zertal proposes that "the indented decoration can be utilized, with certain reservation, as an additional guide for the relative chronology of Iron Age I."[50]

Third, the distribution of cooking pots suggests the gradual foundation of sites from east to west. Zertal qualifies this, however, by noting that "these preliminary conclusions are based on a surface survey; their significance should not be overestimated and must be proven or refuted in stratigraphic excavations."[51]

Fourth, most newly discovered Iron I sites are simple enclosures with few associated finds. Previously, scholars assumed that initial Israelite highland settlements consisted of a circle of houses serving as the village's outer wall, like ʿIzbet Ṣarṭah.[52] Zertal and Bar propose that the Israelites first traversed the Jordan Valley as nomads or seminomads, and while living in tents, they built enclosures for corralling their cattle and only later constructed enclosed settlements like the one at ʿIzbet Ṣarṭah.[53]

Fifth, among the sites in the Jordan Valley and eastern Samaria, the survey associates several walled enclosures with a similar "sandal"-shaped curvature.[54] These early Iron I enclosures share similar masonry and an absence of nearby dwellings. No other parallels are known in the southern Levant. Zertal and Dror Ben-Yosef propose that they may have been cultic assembly areas for the (semi-) nomadic tribes living in the Jordan Valley and eastern Samaria.[55]

49. Adam Zertal and Shay Bar, *The Manasseh Hill Country Survey*, vol. 4, *From Nahal Bezeq to the Sartaba*, CHANE 21 (Leiden: Brill, 2017), 58.

50. Adam Zertal, *The Manasseh Hill Country Survey*, vol. 2, *The Eastern Valleys and the Fringes of the Desert*, CHANE 21 (Leiden: Brill, 2007), 54.

51. Zertal, *Eastern Valleys and the Fringes of the Desert*, 55.

52. Ze'ev Herzog, "Enclosed Settlements in the Negeb and the Wilderness of Beer-Sheba," *BASOR* 250 (1983): 41–49; Finkelstein, *Archaeology of the Israelite Settlement*, 235–50.

53. Zertal and Bar, *From Nahal Bezeq to the Sartaba*, 61–63.

54. Dror Ben-Yosef, "Excavations at Bedhat esh-Shaʿab, an Early Iron Age Enclosure in the Jordan Valley: 2002–2003 Excavation Seasons," in Zertal and Bar, *The Manasseh Hill Country Survey*, 4:667–702; Shay Bar, "Shaʿab Romani: A Newly Discovered Iron Age Foot-Shaped Enclosure near Wadi al-Makuk," *Judea and Samaria Studies* 29, no. 1 (2020): *29–*51.

55. Adam Zertal and Dror Ben-Yosef, "Bedhat esh-Shaʿab: An Iron Age I Enclosure in the Jordan Valley, in *Exploring the Longue Durée: Essays in Honor of Lawrence E. Stager*, ed. J. David Schloen (Winona Lake, IN: Eisenbrauns, 2009), 517–29.

Sixth, the westernmost "sandal" enclosure is the LBA–Iron I cultic site on the northern slopes of Mount Ebal. The site is strategically situated on the highest mountain in northern Samaria, elevated above nearby Shechem, as the premier regional and cultic center in the region. It featured a monumental altar functioning as a central sanctuary.[56] This early Israelite central sanctuary served to establish YHWH as the sovereign over the land.[57]

Some criticize the Manasseh Hill Country Survey and its conclusions.[58] Excavations are ongoing in the Jordan Valley and in the central highlands to confirm the surveys.[59] Following Zertal's death, the Jordan Valley Excavation Project was founded to excavate further the Manasseh Hill Country Survey sites.[60] Additionally, scholars increasingly recognize the Ebal site as cultic in nature.[61] Strong interest continues with the renewal of work on the final report for the 1982–87 excavations and the launch of a field project to wet-sift the original excavation dump, which has led to further discoveries and renewed debate.[62]

Contrary to those claiming that debate about early Israelite origins is settled and Israel's indigenous origins are certain, new data is emerging from the Jordan Valley and eastern Samaria that will stimulate ongoing research.

56. Adam Zertal, *The Manasseh Hill Country Survey*, vol. 1, *The Shechem Syncline*, CHANE 21 (Leiden: Brill, 2004), 532–37; Ralph K. Hawkins, *The Iron Age I Structure on Mt. Ebal: Excavation and Interpretation*, BBRSup 6 (Winona Lake, IN: Eisenbrauns, 2012).

57. Sandra L. Richter and Ralph K. Hawkins, "The Mt. Ebal Site in the Context of the History of Biblical Scholarship," in *His Inheritance: A Memorial Volume for Adam Zertal*, ed. Ralph K. Hawkins, Erasmus Gaß, and Dror Ben-Yosef, AOAT 454 (Münster: Ugarit-Verlag, 2021), 341–42.

58. William G. Dever, "Israelite Origins and the 'Nomadic Ideal': Can Archaeology Separate Fact from Fiction?," in *Mediterranean Peoples in Transition: Thirteenth to Early Tenth Centuries BCE*, ed. Seymour Gitin, Amihai Mazar, and Ephraim Stern (Jerusalem: Israel Exploration Society, 1998), 220–36.

59. Adam Zertal and Shay Bar, *The Manasseh Hill Country Survey*, vol. 5, *The Middle Jordan Valley: From Wadi Fasael to Wadi ʿAuja*, CHANE 21 (Leiden: Brill, 2019).

60. Ralph K. Hawkins, David Ben-Shlomo, and Michael Freikman, "The Jordan Valley Excavation Project: Retrospects and Prospects," in Hawkins, Gaß, and Yosef, *His Inheritance*, 281–317.

61. William G. Dever, *Beyond the Texts: An Archaeological Portrait of Ancient Israel and Judah* (Atlanta: SBL Press, 2017), 161; Mark S. Smith and Elizabeth Bloch-Smith, *Judges 1*, Hermeneia (Minneapolis: Fortress, 2021), 153.

62. Zvi Gal, "Mount Ebal Site in the Context of Archaeological Research," in Hawkins, Gaß, and Yosef, *His Inheritance*, 321–30; S. Stripling, G. Galil, I. Kumpova, J. Valach, P. G. van der Veen, and D. Vavrik, "'You Are Cursed by the God YHW': An Early Hebrew Inscription from Mt. Ebal," *Heritage Science* 11, no. 105 (2023): 1–24. The identification of a folded lead object as a defixio by Stripling et al. has recently been challenged in a series of articles, including the following: Aren M. Maeir and Christopher Rollston, "The So-Called Mount Ebal Curse Tablet: A Critical Response," *IEJ* 73, no. 2 (2023): 132–42; Amihai Mazar, "The Lead Object from Mount Ebal as a Fishing Net Sinker," *IEJ* 73, no. 2 (2023): 143–52; Naama Yahalom-Mack, "The Source of the Lead of the Mount Ebal 'Tablet,'" *IEJ* 73, no. 2 (2023): 153–59.

The Book of Joshua and Archaeology

Another area of ongoing reconsideration is the relationship between the book of Joshua and early Iron I archaeology. While the evidence contradicts the idea of a sweeping "conquest," some argue that an Israelite blitzkrieg is a modern scholarly construct imposed on the biblical narrative and that a close reading reveals a more complex and protracted settlement process.[63] The account reports initial victories, but the Israelites did not follow through with widespread settlement. Following the two campaigns—one in the south and the other in the north—much of the land was not possessed (Josh. 13:1–7), the Israelites remained in Gilgal (14:6), and some had failed to drive out the indigenous inhabitants of the land (15:63). Even the prologue to Judges (1:1–2:5) affirms that, following Joshua's death, the Israelites failed to complete the conquest.

Many contradictions result from misconceptions about the biblical account. For example, if the book of Joshua does not claim that the Israelites conquered and destroyed every city in Canaan, then the tension between the archaeological data and the expectation to find evidence of a wholesale destruction disappears.[64] Richard Hess engages the conquest accounts from this perspective, giving careful attention to the biblical account and its ANE background, and I undertake a close reading of the accounts of Jericho, Ai, Hazor, and Dan.[65] For the tensions that remain, more dialogue is required between the biblical text and the archaeological data to understand the relationship between the two.[66]

The Rise of the Monarchy

The reigns of David and Solomon are central to scholarly discussion of the rise of the Israelite monarchy. The Bible portrays this "united kingdom" as a golden age and devotes more space to it than to any other in ancient Israel's history (1 Sam. 8–1 Kings 11; 1 Chron. 32–2 Chron. 9). Synchronisms between biblical and extrabiblical evidence date David and Solomon to the tenth century BCE.[67] According to the early historical

63. Hawkins, *How Israel Became a People*, chaps. 2, 6–10.

64. P. David Merling, "The Book of Joshua, Part II: Expectations of Archaeology," *AUSS* 39, no. 2 (2001): 209–21.

65. Richard S. Hess, "The Jericho and Ai of the Book of Joshua," in *Critical Issues in Early Israelite History*, ed. Richard S. Hess, Gerald A. Klingbeil, and Paul J. Ray Jr., BBRSup 3 (Winona Lake, IN: Eisenbrauns, 2008), 33–46; Hawkins, *How Israel Became a People*, 91–120.

66. Baruch Halpern, "Text and Artifact: Two Monologues?," in *The Archaeology of Israel: Constructing the Past, Interpreting the Present*, ed. N. A. Silberman and D. Small, JSOTSup 237 (Sheffield: Sheffield Academic, 1997), 311–38; R. L. Zettler, "Written Documents as Excavated Artifacts and the Holistic Interpretation of the Mesopotamian Archaeological Record," in *The Study of the Ancient Near East in the 21st Century: The William Foxwell Albright Centennial Conference*, ed. Jerrold S. Cooper and Glenn M. Schwartz (Winona Lake, IN: Eisenbrauns, 1996), 81–101.

67. M. Cogan, "Chronology," *ABD* 1:1002–11.

books, however, the kingdom of Israel formed under the leadership of Saul, who is usually dated toward the end of the eleventh century (ca. 1030–1009 BCE).[68]

In this final stage of early settlement, Israelite tribes developed into a state-level society and dominated the region. Reconstructing the process of transitioning from a network of tribes to a state-level society is controversial. Since at least the 1960s, the rise of the state has been seen as an inevitable stage in an evolutionary process, commonly referred to as "politicization."[69] At this stage social power is concentrated in a ruling class, while ordinary households are subordinated.[70] Four subprocesses typically accompany this stage: taxation, specialization, militarization, and urbanization. Politicization concentrates social power with political elites, a coercive process with inherent inequity. This negative conception of politicization predominates today.[71]

In *Economy and Society*, Max Weber proposes an alternative patrimonial model for social structure, where forces of tradition and personal association, natural in the ancient Israelite household, shape the concept of authority.[72] Patrimonial societies express authority primarily in terms of kinship. Weber applies this logic to larger, more centralized societies, deducing the idea of a "patrimonial state." Lawrence Stager reconstructs this patrimonial state as a recursive series of "nested households," at the base of which is the "house of the father."[73] The king functions as the state's head of the household. Subjects depend on loyal personal relationships and, in return, receive security and support. Just like the father of a household, the king presides over a house that includes all the households under his rule.

While older approaches regarded the Israelite monarchy as an "alien" urban institution grafted onto a reluctant, egalitarian, kin-based, and tribal society, the patrimonial model reflects a higher level of kinship. In this approach, the king was perceived not as an oppressor taking advantage of his people, but as a caring kinsman. Tribes retained decision-making structures, which could be mobilized for or against the king. This arrangement does not conform to the centralized

68. Thiele places Saul's reign in the 10th cent. (930–909 BCE). Hayes and Hooker date it 927–906 BCE. Edwin R. Thiele, *The Mysterious Numbers of the Hebrew Kings*, rev. ed. (Grand Rapids: Zondervan Academic, 1983), 10; John H. Hayes and Paul K. Hooker, *A New Chronology for the Kings of Israel and Its Implications for Biblical History and Literature* (Atlanta: John Knox, 1988), 24.

69. William G. Dever, "Archaeology, Urbanism, and the Rise of the Israelite State," in *Urbanism in Antiquity: From Mesopotamia to Crete*, ed. Walter E. Aufrecht, Neil A. Mirau, and Steven W. Gauley, JSOTSupp 244 (Sheffield: Sheffield Academic, 1997), 172.

70. J. H. Bodley, "Socioeconomic Growth, Culture Scale, and Household Well-Being: A Test of the Power-Elite Hypothesis," *Current Anthropology* 40, no. 5 (1999): 595–620.

71. Victor H. Matthews and Don C. Benjamin, *Social World of Ancient Israel: 1250–587 BCE* (Peabody, MA: Hendrickson, 1993), 159–61.

72. Max Weber, *Economy and Society*, ed. G. Roth and W. Wittick (Berkeley: University of California Press, 1978), 2:1007.

73. Lawrence E. Stager, "The Patrimonial Kingdom of Solomon," in *Symbiosis, Symbolism, and the Power of the Past: Canaan, Ancient Israel, and Their Neighbors from the Late Bronze Age through Roman Palaestina*, ed. William G. Dever and Seymour Gitin (Winona Lake, IN: Eisenbrauns, 2003), 63–74.

concept of the European state, in which a king is the only legitimate source of authority, and is better articulated as a "tribal kingdom."[74] In this paradigm, "it is not so difficult to imagine a farmer such as Saul . . . becoming king."[75]

The Impetus for Kingship

The impetus for kingship in ancient Israel is debated. Certainly peer-polity interaction contributed to the development of monarchy (1 Sam. 8:5).[76] The Philistine threat was an important contributing factor (1 Sam. 9:16), along with technological advances, economic prosperity, population growth, demographic pressures, and competition for scarce resources.[77] By the eleventh century BCE, the Philistine enclave was concentrated, rich in resources, and organized as a palace economy around five city-states in Canaan. Ekron is estimated to have been populated by as many as five thousand people, Ashkelon five thousand, and Ashdod ten thousand. The total population of the pentapolis approached twenty-five thousand, equaling the entire population of Judah.[78] The Philistines posed a substantial challenge as they expanded into the Shephelah, approaching the natural border of Judah. The formation of the early Israelite state would be a fitting response. It is "indisputable" that Saul's Benjaminite tribal kingdom was founded "on the periphery of Ekron."[79] Some scholars attribute the evidence of destruction at Ashdod XI, Ekron IVB, and Tell Qasile X in the late eleventh century to the campaigns of Saul.

Material Correlates for the Kingship of Saul

Material engagement theory emphasizes that as social structures and religious concepts develop, they find expression in material correlates.[80] Likewise,

74. Daniel M. Master, "State Formation Theory and the Kingdom of Ancient Israel," *JNES* 60, no. 2 (2001): 117–31.

75. Philip J. King and Lawrence E. Stager, "Of Fathers, Kings, and the Deity: The Nested Households of Ancient Israel," *BAR* 28, no. 2 (2002): 62.

76. Colin Renfrew and John F. Cherry, eds., *Peer Polity Interaction and Socio-Political Change*, New Directions in Archaeology (Cambridge: Cambridge University Press, 1986).

77. Walter Dietrich, "Israelite State Formation and Early Monarchy in History and Biblical Historiography," in *The Oxford Handbook of the Historical Books of the Hebrew Bible*, ed. Brad E. Kelle and Brent A. Strawn (New York: Oxford University Press, 2020), 94–108; Baruch Halpern, "The United Monarchy: David between Saul and Solomon," in *The Old Testament in Archaeology and History*, ed. Jennie Ebeling et al. (Waco: Baylor University Press, 2017), 337–62.

78. Lawrence E. Stager, "The Impact of the Sea Peoples in Canaan (1185–1050 BCE)," in *The Archaeology of Society in the Holy Land*, ed. Thomas E. Levy (London: Leicester University Press, 1995), 332–48.

79. Ernst Axel Knauf and Philippe Guillaume, *A History of Biblical Israel: The Fate of the Tribes and Kingdoms from Merenptah to Bar Kochba*, Worlds of the Ancient Near East and Mediterranean (Sheffield: Equinox, 2016), 67.

80. Elizabeth DeMarrais, Chris Gosdon, and Colin Renfrew, eds., *Rethinking Materiality: The Engagement of Mind with the Material World*, McDonald Institute Monographs (Cambridge: McDonald Institute, 2005).

the power strategies of new sociopolitical systems find expression in material correlates.[81] Dever suggests that a political-scale society produces at least five material correlates: (1) a topographical unit with a fortification wall; (2) dense occupation; (3) reflection of social differentiation and centralized administration; (4) evidence of economic accumulation (surplus) and distribution; (5) constitution of a "central place."[82] In historical archaeology, buildings and other material correlates are viewed as gauges of political control. The only building activities attributed to Saul are the erection of a monument on Carmel (1 Sam. 15:12) and an altar in an unknown location (14:35). One might thus conclude that Saul was not the head of a "state" but only a permanent judge, a self-appointed protector, or maybe a chieftain.[83] However, Saul's residence qualifies as a monumental building (10:26; 15:34; 18:10; 19:9).[84] The terminology used of it, בַּ֫יִת (*bayit*, house) rather than הֵיכָל (*hêkāl*, palace), does not negate its political status.

Settlement patterns in the late eleventh century BCE support the biblical portrayal of the emergence of the early Israelite kingdom in the densely inhabited regions of the central highlands. At that time, many small, isolated highland villages were destroyed or abandoned.[85] These destructions and abandonments were probably due to the Philistines, and the inhabitants relocated to safer locations.[86] Three sites in particular attest to the centrality and importance of Benjamin for state formation in the late eleventh century: Khirbet ed-Dawwara, where massive fortifications make it the first fortified settlement in the central highlands; Tell el-Ful, where a fort of some kind may be connected with Saul; and Gibeon (Tell el-Jib), where major public structures date to this period. Avraham Faust concludes that society in this region was more complex than in other regions of the highlands, suggesting that this area was the "core" of the state formation process and where resistance to the Philistines would have been expected.[87]

The archaeological data coheres with the biblical story, which describes the emergence of the monarchy in the central highlands. The seat of Saul's kingdom was in Benjamin and extended northward toward the border of Manasseh, near the southern tip of the Jezreel Valley. To the south, he held some sway over parts

81. Elizabeth DeMarrais, Luis Jaime Castillo, and Timothy Earle, "Ideology, Materialization, and Power Strategies," *Current Anthropology* 37 (1996): 15–31.

82. Dever, "Archaeology, Urbanism, and the Rise of the Israelite State," 187.

83. D. V. Edelman, "Saul," *ABD* 5:989–99.

84. K. H. Keimer, "Evaluating the 'United Monarchy' of Israel: Unity and Identity in Text and Archaeology," in *Jerusalem Journal of Archaeology* 1 (2021): 68–101.

85. Avraham Faust, "Abandonment, Urbanization, Resettlement and the Formation of the Israelite State," *NEA* 66 (2003): 147–61.

86. Avraham Faust, "Settlement Patterns and State Formation in Southern Samaria and the Archaeology of (a) Saul," in *Saul in Story and Tradition*, ed. C. S. Ehrlich (Tübingen: Mohr Siebeck, 2006), 14–38.

87. Faust, "Settlement Patterns and State Formation," 26–29.

of northern Judah, but Jerusalem remained under Canaanite control until Iron II. To the east, his kingdom reached Gilead in Transjordan and encompassed Jabesh-Gilead and Mahanaim.

Saul's capital at Tell el-Ful was in a strategic political and economic location along a north-south road.[88] While some argue against early attempts to extend military power outside of this immediate vicinity (contra 1 Sam. 14:47–48),[89] Saul would surely have "striven to control local trade routes and find markets for the few natural resources he would have controlled: olive oil, wine, wool, iron ore, possibly red dye, and foodstuffs and spices from oasis areas in the Jordan Valley."[90] Axel Knauf and Phillippe Guillaume imagine that Saul built an economic base on the trade between the Jordan Valley and Philistia.[91] If Saul was able to use trade routes to expand his economic reach, he could also use them to extend his military reach.

Ultimately, Saul primarily brought regions or towns into his realm through societal means. When the Ammonites attacked Jabesh-Gilead, the elders went throughout the territories of Israel, looking for aid; when they came to Saul of Gibeah, he took up their cause (1 Sam. 11). In return, they remained loyal to him even after his death (1 Sam. 31:11–13; 2 Sam. 2:4b–7). Keimer notes that Saul's power "is not expressed uniformly across the landscape, nor is there anything expressly tangible in the way his power is manifested." Yet, "through his actions a unifying identity, i.e., 'Israel,' is established."[92]

Conclusions

We have reviewed the relationship between the history and archaeology of the LBA through Iron I periods with some key biblical events that correspond to these periods, including the exodus, the emergence of Israel in Canaan, and the rise of the Israelite monarchy.

Regarding the LBA and the exodus, recent Egyptological data present opportunities for fresh historical, archaeological, and linguistic interpretations. In relation to the LBA–Iron I transition, new data from archaeological surveys, site excavations, and synthetic studies provide new directions for research and theoretical models for the emergence of early Israel. In connection with the late Iron I

88. David Dorsey, *The Roads and Highways of Ancient Israel* (Eugene, OR: Wipf & Stock, 2018), 117.

89. A. Lemaire, "The Early Monarchy: Saul, David, and Solomon," in *Ancient Israel: From Abraham to the Roman Destruction of the Temple*, 4th ed., ed. John Merrill and Hershel Shanks (Washington, DC: Biblical Archaeology Society, 2021), 103.

90. D. V. Edelman, "Saul ben Kish in History and Tradition," in *The Hebrew Bible and History: Critical Readings*, ed. Lester L. Grabbe, Critical Readings in Biblical Studies (London: T&T Clark, 2019), 222–35.

91. Knauf and Guillaume, *History of Biblical Israel*, 67.

92. Keimer, "Evaluating the 'United Monarchy,'" 80.

period and the rise of the monarchy, new sociological theories and data show the need for renewed inquiry. Study in each of these areas has not been exhausted, and questions are far from answered. We are witnessing constant pressure to reevaluate old ideas and generate new solutions.

5

Archaeology and History

Iron Age II

Cynthia Shafer-Elliott
and Deirdre N. Fulton

The Face of Old Testament Studies, the predecessor of the present work, contained only one chapter on OT archaeology. This lone chapter endeavored to cover a range of issues, most of which were related to controversial topics of the day.[1] The present volume has multiple chapters on archaeology, which reflects the rising importance of archaeological excavations and their various methodologies and interpretations for our understanding of ancient Israel and Judah. This chapter will survey the present state of archaeological studies relating to ancient Israel and Judah during the Iron Age II (Iron II) period (ca. 1000–586 BCE).[2] Rather than focus on controversial topics, this chapter surveys the Iron II period in a way the authors think will be most helpful to the unacquainted reader—that is, by highlighting current trends and methodologies used in archaeology and explaining how they contribute to the ongoing conversation about the histories of Iron II Israel and Judah. We must be selective, but the more impactful areas of interest include state formation, cult and economy, collaboration with various scientific fields, and those digging into daily life.

1. Mark W. Chavalas and Murray R. Adamthwaite, "Archaeological Light on the Old Testament," in *The Face of Old Testament Studies: A Survey of Contemporary Approaches*, ed. David W. Baker and Bill T. Arnold (Grand Rapids: Baker, 1999), 59–96.

2. Since the split of the kingdom of Israel occurred within the Iron II period, it is helpful to refer to both "Israel and Judah."

State Formation

Summarizing Iron II archaeology is a difficult task. Margreet Steiner appropriately observes, "The Iron II period may easily be the most extensively excavated and intensively researched era of the Levant, especially in the southern part of the region, but it is not the best understood period under investigation."[3] This era is characterized by the rise of small kingdoms throughout the southern Levant. By the end of Iron II, most of these small kingdoms had been subsumed by the larger empires of Assyria and Babylon.

In an earlier stage of this discipline, state formation was an important topic with regard to Israel and Judah, particularly in light of chronological issues such as the rise of the kingdom of Israel. Aspects of state formation continue to be part of the conversation, but archaeological studies have increasingly expanded to include both the southern Cisjordan (that is, Israel, Judah, and Philistia) and the Transjordan, with its various political entities of Ammon, Moab, and Edom. The shift to understanding ancient Israel and Judah within the broader Levantine context is most evident in the *Oxford Handbook of the Archaeology of the Levant: c. 8000–332 BCE*, with individual chapters devoted to Judah and Israel, as well as Ammon, Moab, and Edom.[4] These studies describe the process of state formation in several regions across the southern Levant—specifically Ammon, Moab, Edom, Israel, and Judah—that were relatively contemporaneous with each other. They also highlight the connection between the rise of the state and the rise of a national deity, revealing certain universal features of state formation in the southern Levant in the Iron II period.

Cult and Economy in Israel and Judah

Another avenue of research focuses on Jerusalem and its political, economic, and religious role throughout the Iron II period. Ongoing excavations in the City of David, specifically its upper and lower portions and the Givati Parking Lot excavations on the northwestern slope, have expanded the archaeological record regarding the size and wealth of the city during the Iron II period. Work on the Upper City—namely, the area south of the Akra—has uncovered the foundations of a large, monumental structure, though the exact date and nature of the structure is debated. While the excavators assign the monumental structure to the Davidic era, others argue for a later date.[5] Excavations on the

3. Margreet L. Steiner, "Introduction to the Levant During the Iron Age II Period," in *The Oxford Handbook of the Archaeology of the Levant: c. 8000–332 BCE*, ed. Margreet L. Steiner and Ann E. Killebrew, Oxford Handbooks in Archaeology (Oxford: Oxford University Press, 2013), 677.

4. Steiner and Killebrew, *Oxford Handbook of the Archaeology of the Levant*.

5. Eilat Mazar directed the excavations of the upper city and argues for a 10th-cent. Davidic date for the earliest structure (*The Palace of King David* [New York: Shoham Academic

western slope have also uncovered signs of monumental architecture (specifically Structure 100) that may have functioned as a public or elite structure.[6] Seals, ivory fragments, and other luxury remains uncovered in and around Structure 100 support this conclusion. Finally, archaeologists have uncovered evidence of a massive conflagration dating to the Babylonian conquest and destruction of Jerusalem in 586 BCE.[7]

Excavations continue to reveal Judah and Israel's economic and religious complexity during the Iron II period. Current excavations at the site of Tel Moẓa, located in the modern outskirts of Jerusalem, provide evidence for religious practices in Judah external to the Jerusalem temple cult in the Iron II period. The excavations uncovered a temple, designed in a tripartite structure corresponding to the description of the Jerusalem temple in 1 Kings, with clear cultic vessels dating to the ninth century onward. Storage silos, cultic statues, and animal bone remains also support the excavator's conclusion that this was an important religious center during the early to mid-Iron II period.[8]

According to 1 Sam. 7:1, the ark of the covenant was kept at Kiriath Jearim (Abu Ghosh) before it was moved to Jerusalem.[9] Excavations at the site reveal that it served as a cultic center into the Iron II period, with a large platform that may have supported some kind of cultic structure. Tel Moẓa and Kiriath Jearim offer archaeological remains from cultic practices outside of Jerusalem in the Iron II period, revealing a lack of cultic centralization and more local, regional control for much of the Iron II period. Cultic sites from the kingdom of Israel, specifically Tel Dan and other sites such as Bethel and Shiloh, also reveal the prevalence of regional cultic centers during the Iron II period.[10]

Remains of regional economic centers near Jerusalem reflect a more complicated tax collection system than previously understood. The Ramat Raḥel site, located between Jerusalem and Bethlehem, contains the remains of an

---

Research and Publications, 2009]). For a different perspective, see Israel Finkelstein, "A Great United Monarchy? Archaeological and Historical Perspectives," in *One God, One Cult, One Nation: Archaeological and Biblical Perspectives*, ed. Reinhard G. Kratz et al. (Berlin: De Gruyter, 2010), 3–27.

6. Yoav Vaknin et al., "The Earth's Magnetic Field in Jerusalem during the Babylonian Destruction: A Unique Reference for Field Behavior and an Anchor for Archaeomagnetic Dating," *PLoS ONE* 15 (2020): https://doi.org/10.1371/journal.pone.0237029.

7. Vaknin et al., "Earth's Magnetic Field."

8. Shua Kislev and Oded Lipschits, "Another Temple in Judah! The Tale of Tel Moẓa," *BAR* 46, no. 1 (2020): 40–49.

9. Israel Finkelstein and Thomas Römer, "Kiriath-jearim, Kiriath-baal/Baalah, Gibeah: A Geographical History Challenge," in *Writing, Rewriting, and Overwriting in the Books of Deuteronomy and the Former Prophets*, ed. Ido Koch, Thomas Römer, and Omer Sergei (Leuven: Peeters, 2019), 211–22.

10. Jonathan S. Greer, *Dinner at Dan: Biblical and Archaeological Evidence for Sacred Feasts at Iron II Age Tel Dan and Their Significance*, CHANE 66 (Leiden: Brill, 2013); Israel Finkelstein et al., *Shiloh: The Archaeology of a Biblical Site* (Tel Aviv: Institute of Archaeology of Tel Aviv University, 1993).

eighth-century Judahite palace that was later rebuilt to contain a large garden and was in use throughout the Iron II period.[11] Stamped handles on storage jars mark its importance as a tax collection center, particularly when Judah was under Assyrian and Babylonian control. Estates under the control of the monarchy have been discovered in other areas of Judah and Israel. These estates were used to collect taxes in kind and reveal important information regarding the ancient economy as well as agricultural and foodways practices.[12]

Archaeological Methods

Scientific methods performed in tandem with archaeological excavations constitute another major area of research. With the rise of processual archaeology in the 1960s, excavations began using specialists to broaden the scope of knowledge that can be obtained. Processual archaeology, also referred to as "New Archaeology," is an anthropological movement that employs the scientific method to help prove or disprove an idea or theory.[13] Aspects of biology, earth science, chemistry, and physics are all part of the contemporary archaeological conversation. These methods have helped to inform our interpretations of archaeological data.[14]

Studies of botanical and bone remains reveal a more complete picture of practices related to diet and economy. Questions related to paleodietary practices may be understood from the food remains, both plant and animal. Animal remains tell us what people were eating, but bones, teeth, and even hair also help us understand other aspects of dietary practices. Through the study of stable isotopes in bones and teeth—specifically, carbon, oxygen, strontium, and nitrogen—we can trace where animals were born, where they grazed, and where they died.[15] Bones can also be used to help date archaeological sites through radiocarbon dating. Analysis of paleoenvironments is a growing field in archaeology, particularly in the Iron II period. In what follows, we discuss specific examples of how new approaches elucidate the picture of life in Iron II Israel.

11. Oded Lipschits et al., "Palace and Village, Paradise and Oblivion: Unraveling the Riddles of Ramat Raḥel," *NEA* 74, no. 1 (2011): 2–49.

12. Yuval Gadot, "In the Valley of the King: Jerusalem's Rural Hinterland in the 8th–4th Centuries BCE," *TA* 42, no. 1 (2015): 3–26.

13. Sally R. Binford and Lewis Binford, *New Perspectives in Archaeology* (Chicago: Aldin, 1968); Bruce Trigger, *A History of Archaeological Thought* (Cambridge: Cambridge University Press, 1989).

14. Steve Weiner, *Microarchaeology: Beyond the Visible Archaeological Record* (Cambridge: Cambridge University Press, 2010).

15. Elizabeth Arnold et al., "'Come, O Pilgrim'—but Buy Local: An Isotopic Investigation of Animal Provisioning at Iron Age II Tel Dan," *Archaeological and Anthropological Sciences* 13 (2021): https://doi.org/10.1007/s12520-021-01291-7.

Everyday Life

While the field has moved past debates about processual archaeology, the impact is still being felt in the discussion of how the archaeology of ancient Israel and Judah can assist in HB studies. One benefit of this dialogue is the shift of focus within the last couple of decades from the study of the monumental to that of the mundane. Historically, the archaeology of ancient Israel/Judah has prioritized the places, people, and performances of prestige, such as palaces and temples, priests and kings, battles, and official religious rituals.[16] While important, the monumental seldom provides information on the lived experience of the average Israelite/Judahite man, woman, or child. Methods that have shed light on the daily life of other ancient peoples are being applied to the study of Israel/Judah and are proving immensely helpful and informative. Some of these methods include household archaeology, gender archaeology, and the archaeology of food. Below, we briefly summarize each approach and highlight its impact on the archaeology of Israel and Judah during Iron Age II.

Household Archaeology

Household archaeology is "a branch of archaeology concerned with the study of the material culture and activities associated with ancient households."[17] In their landmark paper introducing household archaeology, Richard Wilk and William Rathje state that even though the household is the smallest social unit, it is the most common and abundant group. Furthermore, they argue that all households have three common features that provide building blocks for studying households, regardless of geography and time period: the household's material, social, and behavioral aspects. The material aspect is the actual physicality of the household (e.g., buildings, features, artifacts, etc.), while the social aspect concerns the members of the household and their relationships to each other. The activities the household engaged in, both daily and on special occasions, form the behavioral aspect.[18] Although only the material aspect can be excavated, the social and behavioral aspects can be inferred from the material aspect and from secondary sources, such as comparative archaeological data, texts, ethnography, ethnoarchaeology, and iconography.

One may conduct household archaeology in the field by using spatial analysis, which allows an archaeologist to recognize and understand patterns and regularities that would otherwise be missed. James Hardin writes that by mapping in detail the vertical and horizontal relationships of the dwelling and the remains

16. Carol Meyers, "Having Their Space and Eating There Too: Bread Production and Female Power in Ancient Israelite Households," *Nashim: A Journal of Jewish Women's Studies & Gender Issues* 5 (2002): 14–44.

17. "Glossary," s.v. "Household Archaeology," Archaeological Institute of America, https://www.archaeological.org/programs/educators/introduction-to-archaeology/glossary/.

18. Richard Wilk and William L. Rathje, "Household Archaeology," *American Behavioral Scientist* 25, no. 6 (1982): 617–39.

found within it, spatial relationships of and patterns in the material culture are recognized and can then be linked to specific activities, where these activities occurred, and who possibly carried them out.[19]

Two sites known for their use of spatial analysis in uncovering Iron II households are Tell en-Naṣbeh and Tell Halif. The former was a fortified village located twelve kilometers northwest of Jerusalem. Excavations uncovered several Iron II houses, including one cluster of five attached houses. Based on his spatial analysis of this housing cluster, Aaron Brody classified it as a compound made up of related households (בֵּית אָב, *bêt ʾāb*) that perhaps constituted an extended family or clan (מִשְׁפָּחָה, *mišpāḥâ*).[20] In this instance, one can see how household archaeology helps us understand the social aspect of households.

The second example, Tell Halif, is a Iron II fortified town located in a liminal zone between the Shephelah and the Negev in southern Israel. Documenting not only the type of artifact but also its detailed location in relation to the house, its features, and other artifacts allowed the excavators to determine that these households were engaged in expected activities related to food production and preparation, storage, and weaving. However, some houses had artifacts that distinguished them from other households. For instance, in the F7 house, artifacts used in religious ritual (a polished triangular-shaped stone, two standing stones squared with beveled edges, the broken pillar figurine, and the fenestrated stand) were uncovered in the back room along with artifacts related to food preparation and consumption (cooking pots, a krater, and bowls), suggesting that religious domestic feasting occurred in this space.[21] In the D7 house, the floor of one room was covered with artifacts including 110 loom weights, some of which were arranged in lines suggesting that they were attached to a loom. The large quantity of loom weights and the spatial analysis indicated that three looms once occupied this room. The chief function of this space was textile production, but one that far exceeded the needs of a typical household, hinting that the household was engaged in both the production and trade of textiles.[22] This raises questions

19. James W. Hardin, *Lahav II: Households and the Use of Domestic Space at Iron II Tell Halif: An Archaeology of Destruction* (Winona Lake, IN: Eisenbrauns, 2010), 10, 26–27.

20. Aaron J. Brody, "The Archaeology of the Extended Family: A Household Compound from Iron II Tell en-Naṣbeh," in *Household Archaeology in Ancient Israel and Beyond*, ed. Assaf Yasur-Landau, Jennie R. Ebeling, and Laura B. Mazow, CHANE 50 (Leiden: Brill, 2011), 237–54.

21. Hardin, *Households and the Use of Domestic Space,* 133–43; Cynthia Shafer-Elliott, "The Role of the Household in the Religious Feasting of Ancient Israel and Judah," in *Feasting in the Archaeology and Texts of the Hebrew Bible and Ancient Near East*, ed. Peter Altmann and Janling Fu (Winona Lake, IN: Eisenbrauns, 2014), 199–221.

22. Oded Borowski et al., *Life in the Iron Age II at Tell Halif* (University Park, PA: Eisenbrauns, forthcoming), 61–62; Oded Borowski, *Lahav Research Project, Phase IV: 2016 Field Season, Field V Report* (Atlanta: Emory University Press, 2017), 166–67; Cynthia Shafer-Elliott, "Putting One's House in Order: Household Archaeology at Tell Halif, Israel," in *The Hunt for Ancient Israel: Essays in Honour of Diana Edelman*, ed. Cynthia Shafer-Elliott, Kristin Joachimsen, Ehud Ben Zvi, and Pauline A. Viviano (Sheffield: Equinox, 2022), 233–57.

regarding the economic security of the household and of Tell Halif before its destruction by the Neo-Assyrian campaign in 701 BCE.[23]

As evident from the examples above, household archaeology provides a glimpse of the physical reality of the daily lives of ancient societies. By concentrating on the lived environment and daily activities of the home and household, a more accurate representation of daily life in Iron II Israel and Judah can be achieved.

Gender Archaeology

If we take into consideration the increasing interest in contemporary sex and gender identities, preferences, and roles, it should come as no surprise that gender-informed archaeology, also referred to as gender archaeology, has been widely used in the fields of anthropology and archaeology and has made its way to the study of Iron Age Israel/Judah.[24] Here it would be helpful to clarify how Western sociologists have *historically* differentiated the terms "sex" and "gender." Sex has been defined as a biological concept that "refers to the anatomical and other biological differences between females and males," while gender has been seen as a social concept that "refers to the social and cultural differences a society assigns to people based on their biological sex."[25] Additionally, the concept of gender roles has historically been seen as referring to "a society's expectations of people's behaviors and attitudes based on their biological sex."[26] However, many today would argue against such a normative male-female dichotomy, opting for approaches that treat sexual and gender identities as more fluid.[27] Keeping these definitions in mind along with the current conversations about sex and gender identities, preferences, and roles, gender archaeology can be loosely defined as "approaches to interpretation that examine the social construction of gender and its representation in the archaeological record."[28] Jennie Ebeling expands this definition by stating, "Gender roles, behaviors, and ideology vary between cultures and must be learned. . . . Gender studies examine how different cultures

23. Borowski et al., *Life in the Iron Age II at Tell Halif*, 87 (unpublished manuscript page).

24. Margaret W. Conkey and Janet D. Spector, "Archaeology and the Study of Gender," *Advances in Archaeological Method and Theory* 7 (1984): 1–38.

25. Erica Hill, "Gender-Informed Archaeology: The Priority of Definition, the Use of Analogy, and the Multivariate Approach," *Journal of Archaeological Method and Theory* 5, no. 1 (1998): 102.

26. "Understanding Sex and Gender," in *Sociology: Understanding and Changing the Social World* (Minneapolis: University of Minnesota Libraries, 2010), https://open.lib.umn.edu/sociology/chapter/11-1-understanding-sex-and-gender/.

27. Hill, "Gender-Informed Archaeology," 102. Karen Dempsey writes, "Gender archaeology challenges the notion that gender is timeless, biologically determined, and universal." Karen Dempsey, "Gender and Archaeology," *Oxford Bibliographies in Anthropology*, https://doi.org/10.1093/OBO/9780199766567-0274.

28. Timothy Darvill, "Gender Archaeology," in *The Concise Oxford Dictionary of Archaeology* (Oxford: Oxford University Press), https://doi.org/ 10.1093/acref/9780199534043.001.0001.

determine appropriate behaviors for biological females and males and the social construction of femininity and masculinity."[29] Investigation into gendered roles and identities can be carried out by addressing questions to the various types of material evidence, including but not limited to landscapes, space, architecture, food, bodies, and artifacts.[30]

As mentioned earlier, in order to focus on the daily lives of the average ancient Israelite/Judahite man, woman, and child, we must shift our attention to the stage where daily life occurred: the home. Similarly, gender archaeology attempts to make visible the often overlooked average person, especially women, who too often have been pushed to the margins of history. Consequently, a gender-focused approach to archaeology uses several of the same methodologies as those that focus on households, including household archaeology, spatial analysis, ethnography, ethnoarchaeology, iconography, and various texts. In this way, archaeologists can shed light on the ordinary people, places, and activities of daily life. But gender archaeology goes beyond questions about the daily activities of the average woman by focusing on societal questions related to gendered roles and identities. Gender *roles* are composed of societal expectations, including how people are expected to walk, talk, dress, and act. Gendered *identities*, on the other hand, consist of personal conceptions of self, which can be less straightforward than gender roles. We must also keep in mind that the performance of genders can be embodied differently throughout the various stages of the life cycle. In other words, gender performance is not static; rather, people and the societies in which they live are continually negotiating and renegotiating gender roles and identities.[31]

A concrete example of how gender archaeology informs our understanding of women in ancient Israel/Judah relates to food preparation. Conducting a spatial analysis of a house and its rooms is imperative in reconstructing a room's function(s), which is the "necessary prelude" to interpret what gendered activities were performed in that space.[32] In one of our earlier examples from household archaeology, we considered the spatial analysis of a couple of houses at Tell Halif. In this same neighborhood a house was excavated (the A8 house) that uncovered a semicircular, permanent grinding installation built against a main wall of a three-room house. Inside the installation was a large stone grinding quern with some oven (תַּנּוּר, *tannûr*) fragments, faunal remains, and worked stone immediately

29. Jennie Ebeling, "Gender in Ancient Israel," in *The Ancient Israelite World*, ed. Kyle H. Keimer and George A. Pierce (London: Routledge, 2022), 278. See also Stephanie L. Budin, "Finding a World of Women: An Introduction to Women's Studies and Gender Theory in Biblical Archaeology," in *The Social Archaeology of the Levant: From Prehistory to the Present*, ed. Assaf Yasur-Landau, Eric H. Cline, and Yorke M. Rowan (Cambridge: Cambridge University Press, 2019), 254.

30. Dempsey, "Gender and Archaeology."

31. Dempsey, "Gender and Archaeology."

32. Carol Meyers, "Engendering Syro-Palestinian Archaeology: Reasons and Resources," *NEA* 66, no. 4 (2003): 185–97.

outside it. On the beaten earth floor around the installation was a large quantity of restorable pottery, including many whole-mouth storage jars, numerous pockets of carbonized micro-remains, pounders, fragmented loom weights, and a cosmetic bowl.[33] The poorly preserved remains of another oven are located not far from the grinding installation. Grinding installations and ovens are permanent features, typically located within a dwelling in a common space where it was convenient to conduct numerous household tasks.[34] The presence and location of the grinding installation along with the numerous artifacts related to food preparation and storage indicate that food preparation, including the storage and grinding of grain for flour, baking, and cooking, were performed in this space.

Various strands of evidence (archaeological, ethnographic, and textual) indicate that household women were responsible for the preparation of food. Christine Hastorf notes that in cross-cultural studies of 185 societies, women completed most food preparation and cooking tasks, performing more than 80 percent of these tasks in each group. Furthermore, the men in these same societies tended to dominate only certain food-related tasks such as hunting, butchering, generating fire, and farming (plowing).[35] Ethnographic studies of traditional villages in the Middle East also highlight that women were in charge of the household food and the spaces where its preparation occurred.[36] Women would share ovens and fuel while they prepared bread together, creating a social space out of a work space.[37] Ovens found in ancient Israelite/Judahite houses are often found in the larger central spaces both inside and outside the dwelling, suggesting that the baking of bread was also a communal activity. Furthermore, the HB usually links the domestic preparation of bread with women (Exod. 11:5; Lev. 26:26; Judg. 9:53–54; 1 Sam. 8:13; 28:24; 2 Sam. 11:21; 13:6–8; Job 31:10; Eccles. 12:3; Isa. 47:2; Jer. 7:18).[38] The spatial analysis of the A8 house at Halif illustrates how common household spaces were used for the preparation of food. Coupled with the textual and ethnographic sources, it is easy to imagine that the women of the Halif house were overseeing and conducting the tasks related to the household's food preparation.

33. Tyler Mowery and Cynthia Shafer-Elliott, "Area L8 Season 2016 Report," in Borowski, *Lahav Research Project*, 117–46.

34. Nicholas Cahill, *Household and City Organization at Olynthus* (New Haven: Yale University Press, 2002), 165–66.

35. Christine Hastorf, *The Social Archaeology of Food: Thinking about Eating from Prehistory to the Present* (Cambridge: Cambridge University Press, 2017), 183.

36. Yizhar Hirschfeld, *The Palestinian Dwelling in the Roman-Byzantine Period* (Jerusalem: Franciscan Printing Press and Israel Exploration Society, 1995), 148–49, 152, 182; Meyers, "Having Their Space," 14–44.

37. Bradley J. Parker, "Bread Ovens, Social Networks and Gendered Space: An Ethnoarchaeological Study of Tandir Ovens in Southeastern Anatolia," *American Antiquity* 76, no. 4 (2011), 603–27.

38. Meyers, "Having Their Space," 25–26.

Archaeology of Food

Food did not become a serious topic of intellectual inquiry until well into the twentieth century. "Food studies" started mainly in the social sciences; later, anthropologists took the lead.[39] The focus on the daily life of ancient Israel/Judah has only somewhat recently (within the last 20 years or so) included food studies in its repertoire and has done so with enthusiasm.[40] Since food is an essential part of life and survival, it should come as no surprise that the study of food in ancient Israel/Judah has taken off. The question should be, rather, why did it take so long? A primary obstacle has been that the study of food requires contributions from multiple disciplines within archaeology and the social sciences.[41] Scholars of the HB were not typically trained in these disciplines and, therefore, did not include food-related research in their own analyses. As a result, little consideration was given to the study of food in ancient Israel/Judah and the HB, an unfortunate oversight that is happily being rectified.[42]

One example of how the archaeology of food directly influences our understanding of what products the ancient Israelites cultivated can be found in that well-known biblical phrase "a land flowing with milk and honey." This idiom is used to describe the abundance of the land of Canaan (Exod. 3:8, 17; 33:3; Lev. 20:24; Num. 13:27; 14:8; Deut. 6:3; etc.), but until recently it was commonly thought that the "honey" (*dəbaš*) referred not to honey from bees but to a syrup made from pressed dates or figs. The rationale for this stems from a couple of factors. First, there was no evidence for apiculture (beekeeping) in either the HB or the archaeological record. Second, the few references in the HB to eating honey from bees indicate that it was acquired by chance encounters with wild sources, not from cultivated beehives (Deut. 32:13; Judg. 14:8–9; 1 Sam. 14:27; Ps. 81:16).[43] The archaeological excavations at the site of Tel Reḥov, however, altered what was commonly thought regarding bees and honey in ancient Israel.

Tel Reḥov is a ten-hectare mound located in the Beit Shean Valley in northern Israel, with excavations focusing on the site's Iron IIA (10th to 9th centuries BCE)

39. Carol Meyers, Cynthia Shafer-Elliott, and Janling Fu, "Introduction: Food, the Hebrew Bible, and the Ancient Israelites," in *T&T Clark Handbook of Food in Ancient Israel and the Hebrew Bible*, ed. Janling Fu, Cynthia Shafer-Elliott, and Carol Meyers (London: T&T Clark, 2022), 1–14.

40. Oded Borowski, *Every Living Thing: Daily Use of Animals in Ancient Israel* (Walnut Creek, CA: Alta Mira, 1997); Borowski, *Agriculture in Iron Age Israel* (Boston: American Schools of Oriental Research, 2002); Carol L. Meyers, *Discovering Eve: Ancient Israelite Women in Context* (New York: Oxford University Press, 1988); Nathan MacDonald, *What Did the Ancient Israelites Eat? Diet in Biblical Times* (Grand Rapids: Eerdmans, 2008); Nathan MacDonald, *Not Bread Alone: The Uses of Food in the Old Testament* (Oxford: Oxford University Press, 2008).

41. Meyers, Shafer-Elliott, and Fu, "Introduction," 2–3.

42. Meyers, Shafer-Elliott, and Fu, "Introduction," 3–4.

43. Joshua Walton and Lauren M. Santini, "Spices, Herbs, and Sweeteners," in Fu, Shafer-Elliott, and Meyers, *Handbook of Food*, 157–70.

occupation.[44] In 2005 a large-scale apiary was uncovered, which had an estimated 180 hives.[45] The hives were cylinder shaped and constructed from unbaked clay, straw, and animal dung, with four-centimeter-thick walls. The hives were identical in size, eighty centimeters in length, with an external diameter of about forty centimeters. Each hive is estimated to have a capacity of fifty-six liters. The best-preserved hives were closed with packed clay at one end and had a round hole at the center that allowed the bees to enter and exit the hive. On the other end of the hive was a removable lid with a handle made from the same material as the hive, which allowed for easy access. The hives were arranged in three parallel rows, each containing at least three tiers.[46]

It's been estimated that each hive could produce between three to five kilograms of honey and between 0.5 and 0.7 kilograms of beeswax annually. Assuming there were at least one hundred active hives in the Tel Reḥov apiary, the estimated annual yield of honey would have been three to five hundred kilograms and fifty to seventy kilograms of beeswax, indicating that the inhabitants of this region were engaged in industrial-scale beekeeping.[47]

The type of bees cultivated at Rehov is noteworthy. Morphometric analyses indicate that the hives were occupied by Anatolian honeybees (*Apis mellifera anatoliaca*) and not the local Syrian subspecies (*Apis mellifera syriaca*). Considering the scale of the apiary, this different subspecies of bee may have been imported for its milder temper and improved honey yield. The cultivation of a foreign subspecies would have required sophisticated beekeeping skills as well as reliable supply lines.[48] Consequently, it is now safe to say that Israel was indeed a land of honey.

Summary

Much has happened within the archaeology of Iron II Israel and Judah within the last twenty-plus years, so much so that this brief survey barely scratches the surface. This chapter has highlighted the tremendous work that has been achieved and that continues to be realized. We hope that this summary encourages readers to seek out more detailed information on the current trends and methodologies discussed here, such as state formation, cult and economy, collaboration with other scientific fields, and a focus on the daily life of Israel and Judah in the Iron II period.

44. Amihai Mazar and Nava Panitz-Cohen, "It Is the Land of Honey: Beekeeping at Tel Reḥov," *NEA* 70, no. 4 (2007): 202–19.

45. Mazar and Panitz-Cohen, "Land of Honey," 207.

46. Mazar and Panitz-Cohen, "Land of Honey," 205.

47. Mazar and Panitz-Cohen, "Land of Honey," 209.

48. Guy Bloch et al., "Industrial Apiculture in the Jordan Valley during Biblical Times with Anatolian Honeybees," *Proceedings of the National Academy of Sciences* 107, no. 25 (2010): 11240–44.

6

Archaeology and History

Neo-Babylonian and Persian Periods

Jason M. Silverman

The Neo-Babylonian Empire asserted hegemony over the Levant in 605 BCE in the wake of Nebuchadnezzar's defeat of Assyria and Egypt at Carchemish. Control shifted to the Persian Empire in 539 BCE when Cyrus took Babylon. The southern Levant remained in Persian hands until 331 BCE, when Alexander moved down the coast toward Egypt after his victory at Issus. In the past, this era was traditionally split into the exilic and postexilic periods, after the dominant narrative arc in the HB. However, historians are increasingly referring to these periods as the Neo-Babylonian and Persian periods, though the earlier stages (ca. 620–484 BCE) are also called "the long sixth century," due to the wealth of Babylonian archives in this period and the continuity visible therein.[1] In Assyriology, texts from this period are often merely labeled Neo-Babylonian; in Egyptology, this is the Late Period or Twenty-Sixth to Thirty-First Dynasties. The era also overlaps with the late archaic and classical periods in Greece.

This essay was written as part of the Academy of Finland Center of Excellence in Ancient Near Eastern Empires, University of Helsinki.

1. E.g., Michael Jursa, *Aspects of the Economic History of Babylonia in the First Millennium BC* (Münster: Ugarit-Verlag, 2010), 4; cf. Pamela Barmash and Mark W. Hamilton, eds., *In the Shadow of Empire: Israel and Judah in the Long Sixth Century BCE*, ABS 30 (Atlanta: SBL Press, 2021). For a closer look, see Tero Alstola et al., *Handbook of the Babylonian Exile*, ANEM (Atlanta: SBL Press, forthcoming).

From Marginal to Crucial

Once considered a hiatus in the development of the southern Levantine traditions behind the HB, the brief hegemony of the Neo-Babylonian Empire and then the longer rule of the Persian (Achaemenid) Empire over the region has taken a central role in many scholars' historical reconstructions. Already noted by H. G. M. Williamson in the previous iteration of this volume,[2] in the subsequent twenty years this trend has only accelerated.

Several series are essential and comprise too many books to list here. Especially important are the Achaemenid History series from the Nederlands Institute voor het Nabije Oosten (Leiden), the Classica et Orientalia series from Harrassowitz (Wiesbaden), the Persika series from de Boccard (Paris), and the Achaemenid Research on Texts and Archaeology journal (ARTA) from Achemenet (http://www.achemenet.com). The most important history of the period remains Pierre Briant's,[3] though a number of shorter histories are now available.[4] Increasing numbers of synthetic volumes continue to appear, including a Blackwell Companion,[5] Routledge Worlds volumes,[6] Oxford Handbooks,[7] and studies placing the Persian Empire in a wider discursive frame.[8]

2. H. G. M. Williamson, "Exile and After: Historical Study," in *The Face of Old Testament Studies: A Survey of Contemporary Approaches*, ed. David W. Baker and Bill T. Arnold (Grand Rapids: Baker Academic, 1999), 236–65.

3. Pierre Briant, *From Cyrus to Alexander: A History of the Persian Empire*, trans. Peter T. Daniels (Winona Lake, IN: Eisenbrauns, 2002).

4. Matt Waters, *Ancient Persia: A Concise History of the Achaemenid Empire (550–330 BCE)* (Cambridge: Cambridge University Press, 2014); Maria Brosius, *A History of Ancient Persia: The Achaemenid Empire*, Blackwell History of the Ancient World (Hoboken, NJ: Wiley-Blackwell, 2021).

5. Bruno Jacobs and Robert Rollinger, eds., *A Companion to the Achaemenid Persian Empire*, 2 vols. (Hoboken, NJ: Wiley & Sons, 2021).

6. Gwendolyn Leick, ed., *The Babylonian World*, Routledge Worlds (London: Routledge, 2009); Javier Álvarez-Mon, Gian Pietro Basello, and Yasmina Wicks, eds., *The Elamite World*, Routledge Worlds (London: Routledge, 2018); Roger Matthews and Hasan Fazeli Nashli, eds., *The Archaeology of Iran from the Palaeolithic to the Achaemenid Empire*, Routledge World Archaeology (London: Routledge, 2022).

7. Karen Radner and Eleanor Robson, eds., *The Oxford Handbook of Cuneiform Cultures* (Oxford: Oxford University Press, 2011); Daniel T. Potts, ed., *The Oxford Handbook of Ancient Iran* (Oxford: Oxford University Press, 2013); Touraj Daryaee, ed., *The Oxford Handbook of Iranian History* (Oxford: Oxford University Press, 2012); Margreet L. Steiner and Ann E. Killebrew, eds., *The Oxford Handbook of the Archaeology of the Levant: c. 8000–332 BCE*, Oxford Handbooks in Archaeology (Oxford: Oxford University Press, 2014); Brad E. Kelle and Brent A. Strawn, eds., *The Oxford Handbook of the Historical Books of the Hebrew Bible* (Oxford: Oxford University Press, 2020).

8. Lori Khatchadourian, *Imperial Matter: Ancient Persia and the Archaeology of Empires* (Oakland: University of California Press, 2016); Matthew P. Canepa, *The Iranian Expanse: Transforming Royal Identity through Architecture, Landscape, and the Built Environment, 550 BCE–642 CE* (Berkeley: University of California Press, 2020); Touraj Daryaee, Ali Mousavi, and Khodadad Rezakhani, eds., *Excavating an Empire: Achaemenid Persia in Longue Durée* (Costa Mesa, CA: Mazda, 2014).

New Sources: Material and Texts

Historians now benefit from many new primary source publications in the past two decades, including texts, artifacts, and architectural remains. Amélie Kuhrt offers a convenient sourcebook for the Persian Empire.[9] No comparable sourcebook exists for the Neo-Babylonian Empire, though there are a few useful overviews.[10] For convenience an overview of these new sources is organized below by broad region.

Babylon

The Neo-Babylonian period is one of the most densely documented periods in Babylonia, though many tablets remain unpublished. Publication proceeds apace, however, improving our understanding.[11] These include new editions of the Neo-Babylonian royal inscriptions.[12] One exciting new data set has been the unprovenanced evidence of new settlements of Judeans in Babylonia, including one known as (Al-)Yahudu.[13]

Cisjordan

New Cisjordan excavations and surveys have brought increased attention to the period and have greatly increased the number of sources, especially material sources. Unfortunately, many of the inscribed objects (such as seals and coins)

9. Amélie Kuhrt, *The Persian Empire: A Corpus of Sources from the Achaemenid Period* (London: Routledge, 2007).

10. Michael Jursa, *Neo-Babylonian Legal and Administrative Documents* (Münster: Ugarit-Verlag, 2005); Jursa, "The Neo-Babylonian Empire," in *Imperien und Reiche in der Weltgeschichte*, ed. Michael Gehler and Robert Rollinger (Wiesbaden: Harrassowitz, 2014), 121–48.

11. Hanspeter Schaudig, *Die Inschriften Nabonids von Babylon und Kyros' des Grossen samt den in ihrem umfeld Entstandenen Tendenzschriften* (Münster: Ugarit-Verlag, 2001); Jean-Jacques Glassner, *Mesopotamian Chronicles*, WAW 19 (Atlanta: Society of Biblical Literature, 2004); Kathleen Abraham, *Business and Politics under the Persian Empire* (Bethesda, MD: CDL, 2004); Caroline Waerzeggers and Maarje Seire, eds., *Xerxes and Babylonia: The Cuneiform Evidence*, OLA 277 (Leuven: Peeters, 2018).

12. Schaudig, *Die Inschriften Nabonids*; Rocío Da Riva, *The Twin Inscriptions of Nebuchadnezzar at Brisa* (Vienna: Institut für Orientalistik der Universität Wien, 2012); Frauke Weiershäuser and Jamie Novotny, *The Royal Inscriptions of Amēl-Marduk (561–560 BC), Neriglissar (559–556 BC), and Nabonidus (555–539 BC), Kings of Babylon* (University Park, PA: Eisenbrauns, 2020).

13. Laurie E. Pearce and Cornelia Wunsch, *Documents of Judean Exiles and West Semites in Babylonia in the Collection of David Sofer* (Bethesda, MD: CDL, 2014); Cornelia Wunsch, *Judeans by the Waters of Babylon: New Historical Evidence in Cuneiform Sources from Rural Babylonia Primarily from the Schøyen Collection* (Dresden: ISLET, 2022); Yigal Bloch, "Judeans in Sippar and Susa during the First Century of the Babylonian Exile," *Journal of Ancient Near Eastern History* 1, no. 2 (2014): 119–72; Tero Alstola, *Judeans in Babylonia: A Study of Deportees in the Sixth and Fifth Centuries BCE*, CHANE 109 (Leiden: Brill, 2020).

are unprovenanced. Ephraim Stern's overviews remain useful.[14] Knowledge of the former kingdom of Judah has improved with the discovery of stamp seals, the excavation of Ramat Raḥel, and the reanalysis of Mizpah.[15] Jerusalem continues to be heavily debated, though it is clear that the settlement was small throughout the period.[16] Data on the former territory of the kingdom of Israel has likewise increased, with extensive survey data and coinage now available.[17] The most famous discoveries have been the archives at Wadi ed-Daliyeh, dating to the end of the Persian era,[18] and the temple complex at Gerizim.[19] New finds have spurred discussion of a wide array of Levantine remains.[20]

Five volumes of unprovenanced ostraca from Idumea have been published, most probably deriving from Persian and early Hellenistic administration of the region.[21] New archaeology is improving understanding of the coast and the Phoenician polities in the period.[22]

14. Ephraim Stern, *Material Culture of the Land of the Bible in the Persian Period, 538–332 B.C.*, trans. Essa Cindorf (Warminster: Aris & Philips, 1982); Stern, *Archaeology of the Land of the Bible* (New York: Doubleday, 2001).

15. Oded Lipschits and David Vanderhooft, *The Yehud Stamp Impressions: A Corpus of Inscribed Impressions from the Persian and Hellenistic Periods in Judah* (Winona Lake, IN: Eisenbrauns, 2011); Oded Lipschits, Manfed Oeming, and Yuval Gadot, *Ramat Raḥel IV* (University Park, PA: Eisenbrauns, 2020); Oded Lipschits et al., *Ramat Raḥel VI: The Babylonian-Persian Pit* (University Park, PA: Eisenbrauns, 2021); Jeffrey R. Zorn and Aaron J. Brody, eds., *"As for Me, I Will Dwell at Mizpah . . .": The Tell en-Naṣbeh Excavations after 85 Years* (Piscataway, NJ: Gorgias, 2014).

16. Kenneth A. Ristau, *Reconstructing Jerusalem: Persian Period Prophetic Perspectives* (Winona Lake, IN: Eisenbrauns, 2016), chap. 2.

17. Shay Bar and Adam Zertal, *The Manasseh Hill Country Survey*, 6 vols. (Leiden: Brill, 2004–21); Patrick Wyssmann, *Vielfältig geprägt* (Leuven: Peeters, 2020).

18. Douglas M. Gropp et al., *Wadi Daliyeh II and Qumran Miscellanea, Part 2: Samaria Papyri from Wadi Daliyeh*, DJD 28 (Oxford: Clarendon, 2001); Jan Dušek, *Les manuscrits araméens du Wadi Daliyeh et la Samarie vers 450–332 av. J.-C.* (Leiden: Brill, 2007).

19. Yitzhak Magen, Haggai Misgav, and Levana Tsfania, *Mount Gerizim Excavations*, 2 vols. (Jerusalem: Israel Antiquities Authority, 2004–8); Jan Dušek, *Aramaic and Hebrew Inscriptions from Mt. Gerizim and Samaria between Antiochus III and Antiochus IV Epiphanes*, CHANE 54 (Leiden: Brill, 2012).

20. Assaf Yasur-Landau, Jennie R. Ebeling, and Laura B. Mazow, eds., *Household Archaeology in Ancient Israel and Beyond*, CHANE 50 (Leiden: Brill, 2011); Eric H. Cline, Yorke M. Rowan, and Assaf Yassur-Landau, eds., *The Social Archaeology of the Levant: From Prehistory to the Present* (Cambridge: Cambridge University Press, 2019); Izaak J. de Hulster, *Figurines in Achaemenid Period Yehud: Jerusalem's History of Religion and Coroplastics in the Monotheism Debate*, ORA 26 (Tübingen: Mohr Siebeck, 2017).

21. Bezalel Porten and Ada Yardeni, *Textbook of Aramaic Ostraca from Idumea*, 5 vols. (Winona Lake, IN: Eisenbrauns, 2014–23).

22. Oren Tal, "Some Remarks on the Coastal Plain of Palestine under Achaemenid Rule—an Archaeological Synopsis," in *L'archéologie de l'empire Achéménide: Nouvelles recherches*, ed. Pierre Briant and Rémy Boucharlat (Paris: De Boccard, 2005), 71–96; Vadim S. Jigoulov, *The Social History of Achaemenid Phoenicia: Being a Phoenician, Negotiating Empires*, BibleWorld 42 (London: Routledge, 2019).

Egypt

Additional papyri and ostraca not published in *TAD* have appeared, as well as a new English translation of some of the previous material (numbered differently from *TAD*).[23] Excavation continues at Elephantine, improving the contextualization of that site.[24] Late Period Egypt beyond Elephantine has also attracted attention.[25]

Iran

The trilingual royal inscriptions (Old Persian, Achaemenid Elamite, and Babylonian Akkadian) have long been key resources for the Persian Empire, including Darius I's Bisitun inscription, though most editions include only the Old Persian text. More recent scholarship has increasingly pointed to differences between the Akkadian and Elamite versions.[26]

A massive project underway since 2004 aims to publish fully the most important central imperial sources, the so-called Fortification and Treasury Tablets. These are roughly seven thousand administrative tablets written mostly in Elamite that were found on the Persepolis terrace in the fortifications and treasury, respectively.[27] They offer detailed information on the minutiae of imperial praxis in the Persian heartland, including the officially supported cult.

The majority of Achaemenid archaeology has focused on the famous royal complexes at Susa, Pasargadae, and Persepolis. More recent work describes the

23. Hélène Lozachmeur, *La collection Clermont-Ganneau: Ostraca, épigraphes sur jarre, étiquettes de bois*, 2 vols. (Paris: De Boccard, 2006); Bezalel Porten, *The Elephantine Papyri in English: Three Millennia of Cross-Cultural Continuity and Change*, 2nd ed., Documenta et Monumenta Orientis Antiqui 22 (Atlanta: Society of Biblical Literature, 2011); James D. Moore, *New Aramaic Papyri from Elephantine in Berlin*, Studies on Elephantine 1 (Leiden: Brill, 2022).

24. Cornelius von Pilgrim, "Tempel des Jahu und 'Strasse des Konigs'—Ein Konflikt in der Späten Perserzeit auf Elephantine," in *Egypt—Temple of the Whole World: Studies in Honour of Jan Assmann*, ed. Sibylle Meyer, Studies in the History of Religions 97 (Leiden: Brill, 2003), 303–17; Martin Ziermann, "Elephantine wiederentstanden–zeichnerische dreidimensionale Rekonstruktion," *MDAI, Abteilung Kairo* 70 (2014): 505–22.

25. Melanie Wasmuth, *Ägypto-persische Herrscher- und Herrschaftspräsentation in der Achämenidenzeit* (Stuttgart: Steiner, 2017); Henry P. Colburn, *Archaeology of Empire in Achaemenid Egypt*, Edinburgh Studies in Ancient Persia (Edinburgh: Edinburgh University Press, 2020).

26. Pierre Lecoq, *Les inscriptions de la Perse achéménide* (Paris: Éditions Gallimard, 1997); Rüdiger Schmitt, *Die altpersischen Inschriften der Achaimeniden* (Wiesbaden: Reichert, 2009); Saber Amiri Parian, "A New Edition of the Elamite Version of the Behistun Inscription (II)," *Cuneiform Digital Library Bulletin* 1 (2020): 1–15.

27. Abdol Majid Arfaee, *Persepolis Fortification Tablets, Fort. and Teh. Texts*, Ancient Iranian Studies 5 (Tehran: Center for the Great Islamic Encyclopedia, 2008); Annalisa Azzoni et al., "The Persepolis Fortification Archive Project" (Chicago: University of Chicago, 2006), https://oi.uchicago.edu/research/projects/persepolis-fortification-archive; Mark B. Garrison, *The Ritual Landscape at Persepolis* (Chicago: Oriental Institute of the University of Chicago, 2017); Pierre Briant, Wouter Henkelman, and Matthew W. Stolper, eds., *L'archive des fortifications de Persépolis* (Paris: De Boccard, 2008).

space around and between these sites, with increasing evidence for the actual settlements and rural sites.[28]

Transjordan

The Neo-Babylonian and Persian periods in the Transjordan have long been lumped into the Iron Age III period and somewhat ignored,[29] but the fate of the old Iron Age polities (Ammon, Moab, and Edom) in the imperial age has gained increased attention.[30] Related to this discussion is the nature of Nabonidus's stay in Teman, an oasis and trading hub, with recent archaeology in Saudi Arabia revealing more information about this era.[31] The Persian era remains understudied, though the region was clearly administered.

Wider Persian Empire

An assessment of the above main sources requires knowledge of the wider empire as well. A number of caches of administrative letters and documents survive in Imperial Aramaic. The most important include an unprovenanced satchel of letters from a satrap of Egypt named Aršama and unprovenanced leather and

28. Erich F. Schmidt, *Persepolis I–III*, 3 vols. (Chicago: University of Chicago Press, 1953–70); Wouter F. M. Henkelman, "The Achaemenid Heartland," in *A Companion to the Archaeology of the Ancient Near East*, ed. Daniel T. Potts, 2 vols. (Malden, MA: Wiley & Sons, 2012), 2:931–62; Silvia Balatti, Hilmar Klinkott, and Josef Wiesehöfer, eds., *Paleopersepolis: Environment, Landscape and Society in Ancient Fars*, Oriens et Occidens 33 (Stuttgart: Franz Steiner, 2021); Gian Pietro Basello and Adriano V. Rossi, *Dariosh Studies II*, Università degli Studi di Napoli l'Orientale 78 (Naples: Ismeo, 2012).

29. Aurelie Jouvenel, "The Iron Age and the Persian Period (1200–332 BC)," in *Atlas of Jordan*, ed. Myriam Ababsa (Beyrouth: Presses de l'Ifpo, 2013), 126–30.

30. Paul J. Ray Jr., "Connectivity: Transjordan during the Persian Period," in *Connectivity in Antiquity: Globalization as a Long-Term Historical Process*, ed. Øystein Sakala LaBianca and Sandra Arnold Scham (London: Equinox, 2006); Walter E. Aufrecht, *A Corpus of Ammonite Inscriptions*, 2nd ed. (University Park, PA: Eisenbrauns, 2019); Bradley L. Crowell, *Edom at the Edge of Empire: A Social and Political History*, ABS 29 (Atlanta: SBL Press, 2021); Benedikt Hensel, Ehud Ben Zvi, and Diana V. Edelman, eds., *About Edom and Idumea in the Persian Period: Recent Research and Approaches from Archaeology, Hebrew Bible Studies and Ancient Near Eastern Studies*, Worlds of the Ancient Near East and Mediterranean (Bristol, CT: Equinox, 2022); Benedikt Hensel, ed., *Transjordan and the Southern Levant: New Approaches regarding the Iron Age and the Persian Period from Hebrew Bible Studies and Archaeology*, Archaeology and Bible 8 (Tübingen: Mohr Siebeck, 2024).

31. Ricardo Eichmann, Hanspeter Schaudig, and Arnulf Hausleiter, "Archaeology and Epigraphy at Tayma (Saudi Arabia)," *Arabian Archaeology and Epigraphy* 17, no. 2 (2006): 163–76; Bradley L. Crowell, "Nabonidus, as-Silaʿ, and the Beginning of the End of Edom," *BASOR* 348 (2007): 75–88; Bruno Jacobs and M. C. A. MacDonald, "Felszeichnung eines Reiters aus der Umgebung von Taymāʾ," *Zeitschrift für Orient-Archäologie* 2 (2009): 364–76; Arnulf Hausleiter and Hanspeter Schaudig, "Rock Relief and Cuneiform Inscription of King Nabonidus at al-Ḥāʾiṭ (Province of Ḥāʾil, Saudi Arabia), Ancient Padakku," *Zeitschrift für Orient-Archäologie* 9 (2016): 224–40.

wood dockets from Bactria.[32] Wider sets of Aramaic inscriptions from the general period also survive.[33] In addition there is important archaeology from Anatolia, the Caucasus, and central Asia.[34]

Significant Moments and Historical Developments in the Long Sixth Century

Nabonidus

The status of Yehud under the Babylonians remains debated. Was it a client kingdom, province, or buffer zone?[35] The reign of the last Neo-Babylonian king, Nabonidus, is significant for understanding both the transition to Persian rule and the imperial involvement in the southern Levant. His ten-year campaign in the region and his religious policies remain issues of debate.[36] Recent scholarship has argued that the cuneiform sources for his reign are in fact later, Hellenistic reflections,[37] providing new impetus to query the reasons for his being remembered and forgotten in Judaism.[38]

32. Christopher Tuplin and John Ma, eds., *Aršāma and His World: The Bodleian Letters in Context*, 3 vols. (Oxford: Oxford University Press, 2020); Joseph Naveh and Shaul Shaked, *Aramaic Documents from Ancient Bactria*, Studies in the Khalili Collections (London: Khalili Family Trust, 2012).

33. Dirk Schwiderski, *Die alt- und reichsaramäischen Inschriften 2* (Berlin: De Gruyter, 2004); Dirk Schwiderski, Walter Bührer, and Benedikt Hensel, *Die alt- und reichsaramäischen Inschriften 1* (Berlin: De Gruyter, 2008); Michael C. A. MacDonald, *Taymāʾ II: Catalogue of the Inscriptions Discovered in the Saudi-German Excavations at Taymāʾ 2004–2015* (Oxford: Archaeopress, 2021).

34. Briant and Boucharlat, *L'archéologie de l'empire Achéménide*; Lori Khatchadourian, "The Achaemenid Provinces in Achaeological Perspective," in Potts, *Companion to the Archaeology of the Ancient Near East*, 2:963–83; Bruno Genito, "Eastern Iran in the Achaemenid Period," in Potts, *Oxford Handbook of Ancient Iran*, 622–37.

35. Oded Lipschits and Joseph Blenkinsopp, eds., *Judah and the Judeans in the Neo-Babylonian Period* (Winona Lake, IN: Eisenbrauns, 2003).

36. Paul-Alain Beaulieu, "Nabonidus the Mad King," in *Representations of Political Power*, ed. Marlies Heinz and Marian H. Feldman (Winona Lake, IN: Eisenbrauns, 2007), 137–66; Kabalan Moukarzel, "The Religious Reform of Nabonidus," in *Melammu: The Ancient World in an Age of Globalization*, ed. Markham J. Geller (Berlin: Edition Open Access, 2014), 157–90; Piotr Michalowski, "Biography of a Sentence," in *Extraction and Control: Studies in Honor of Matthew W. Stolper*, ed. Michael Kozuh et al., SAOC 68 (Chicago: Oriental Institute of the University of Chicago, 2014), 203–10.

37. Stefan Zawadzki, "The Portrait of Nabonidus and Cyrus in Their(?) Chronicle," in *Who Was King? Who Was Not King? The Rulers and the Ruled in the Ancient Near East*, ed. Petr Charvát and Petra Maříková Vlčková (Prague: Institute of Archaeology of the Academy of Sciences of the Czech Republic, 2010), 142–54; Caroline Waerzeggers, "Facts, Propaganda, or History?," in *Political Memory in and after the Persian Empire*, ed. Jason M. Silverman and Caroline Waerzeggers, ANEM 13 (Atlanta: SBL Press, 2015), 95–124.

38. Carol Newsom, "Now You See Him, Now You Don't," in *Remembering Biblical Figures in the Late Persian and Early Hellenistic Periods: Social Memory and Imagination*, ed. Diana V.

Transition from Neo-Babylonian to Persian Rule

The regime changed when Cyrus captured Nabonidus, yet scholars debate the relative levels of continuity and discontinuity in administration and society in Babylonia and in the Levant.[39] The material culture of the Levant between the Neo-Babylonian and early Persian periods is hard to distinguish.[40] The same is true for Yehud and its practices.[41]

Crisis around Darius I's Accession

Cambyses II's death and Darius I's accession to the throne (522–521 BCE) brought a moment of upheaval and renegotiation,[42] which is the raison d'être for the famous Bisitun inscription. It marked the end of the Teispid dynasty and the beginning of the Achaemenid dynasty, spurred multiple revolts, and ended in a reorganization of the empire. Scholars have posited various impacts on Yehud in political positioning and literary presentations, often in relation to Zerubbabel, a governor of Yehud.[43]

Edelman and Ehud Ben Zvi (Oxford: Oxford University Press, 2013), 270–82; Caroline Waerzeggers, "The Prayer of Nabonidus in Light of Hellenistic Babylonian Literature," in *Jewish Cultural Encounters in the Ancient Mediterranean and Near Eastern World*, ed. Mladen Popović, Myles Schoonover, and Marijn Vandenberghe, JSJSup 178 (Leiden: Brill, 2017), 64–75.

39. Michael Jursa, "The Transition of Babylonia from the Neo-Babylonian Empire to the Achaemenid Rule," in *Regime Change in the Ancient Near East and Egypt*, ed. Harriet Crawford, Proceedings of the British Academy 136 (Oxford: Oxford University Press, 2007), 73–94; Caroline Waerzeggers, *Marduk-Remanni: Local Networks and Imperial Politics in Achaemenid Babylonia*, OLA 233 (Leuven: Peeters, 2015); Heather D. Baker and Michael Jursa, eds., *Documentary Sources in Ancient Near Eastern and Greco-Roman Economic History* (Oxford: Oxbow, 2014).

40. Ephraim Stern, "Persian Period," in *The Ancient Pottery of Israel and Its Neighbors from the Iron Age through the Hellenistic Period*, ed. Seymour Gitin (Jerusalem: Israel Exploration Society, 2015), 2:565–617; Lipschits et al., *Ramat Raḥel VI*.

41. Rainer Albertz and Bob Becking, eds., *Yahwism after the Exile: Perspectives on Israelite Religion in the Persian Era*, Studies in Theology and Religion 5 (Assen: Royal Van Gorcum, 2003); Jill Middlemas, *The Troubles of Templeless Judah*, Oxford Theological Monographs (Oxford: Oxford University Press, 2005); Melody D. Knowles, *Centrality Practiced: Jerusalem in the Religious Practice of Yehud and the Diaspora during the Persian Period*, ABS 16 (Atlanta: Society of Biblical Literature, 2006); José Balcells Gallarreta, *Household and Family Religion in Persian-Period Judah*, ANEM 18 (Atlanta: SBL Press, 2017).

42. Stefan Zawadzki, "Bardiya, Darius and Babylonian Usurpers in the Light of the Bisitun Inscription and Babylonian Sources," *Archäologische Mitteilungen aus Iran* 27 (1994): 127–45; Christopher Tuplin, "Darius' Accession in (the) Media," in *Writing and Ancient Near Eastern Society*, ed. Piotr Bienkowski, Christopher Mee, and Elizabeth Slater (London: T&T Clark, 2005), 217–44; Robert Rollinger, "The Relief at Bisitun and Its Ancient Near Eastern Setting," in *Diwan: Studies in the History and Culture of the Ancient Near East and the Eastern Mediterranean*, ed. Carsten Binder, Henning Börm, and Andreas Luther (Duisburg: Wellem Verlag, 2016), 5–51; Uzume Z. Wijnsma, "The Worst Revolt of the Bisitun Crisis," *JNES* 77, no. 2 (2018): 157–73.

43. Rüdiger Lux, *Prophetie und zweiter Tempel: Studien zu Haggai und Sacharja* (Tübingen: Mohr Siebeck, 2009), 241–65; Antonios Finitsis, *Visions and Eschatology: A Socio-Historical*

484 BCE

Numerous northern Babylonian archives end in 484 BCE, marking the conclusion of the long sixth century.[44] It coincides with the suppression of revolts against Xerxes in his second year. The crisis has prompted scholars to reevaluate classical historians' depictions of Xerxes and consider possible social changes in northern Babylonia relevant to the Judeans visible in the later Murashu archive.

Temple Rebuilding: Jerusalem, Gerizim, Elephantine

The (re)building of Yahwistic temples in the Persian period exercises much scholarship. Herod's massive building project probably destroyed all archaeological evidence for the earlier temple in Jerusalem, so the discussion centers on the three building accounts in Ezra-Nehemiah and the nature of the Persian Empire's involvement therein.[45] A Yahwistic temple was built on Mount Gerizim, but the date is debated.[46] The date of the building of the temple to Yaho in Elephantine is uncertain, though it was destroyed and rebuilt during the Persian domination (destroyed in 410 BCE, rebuilt before 404 BCE).[47] The other two known temples in the Levant were aware of this temple and its troubles (*TAD* A4.7 and 8; *TAD*

Analysis of Zechariah 1–6, LSTS 79 (New York: T&T Clark, 2011); Jason Silverman, *Persian Royal–Judaean Elite Engagements in the Early Teispid and Achaemenid Empire*, LHBOTS 690 (London: T&T Clark, 2019).

44. Caroline Waerzeggers, "The Babylonian Revolts against Xerxes and the 'End of Archives,'" *Archiv für Orientforschung* 50 (2003): 150–73; Andrew George, "Xerxes and the Tower of Babel," in *The World of Achaemenid Persia*, ed. John Curtis and John Simpson (London: I. B. Tauris, 2010), 471–80; Amélie Kuhrt, "Xerxes and the Babylonian Temples," in Curtis and Simpson, *World of Achaemenid Persia*, 491–94; Waerzeggers and Seire, *Xerxes and Babylonia*.

45. James M. Trotter, "Was the Second Jerusalem Temple a Primarily Persian Project?," *SJOT* 15, no. 2 (2001): 276–94; Lisbeth S. Fried, "Temple Building in Ezra 1–6," in *From the Foundations to the Crenellations: Essays on Temple Building in the Ancient Near East and Hebrew Bible*, ed. Mark J. Boda and Jamie Novotny, AOAT 366 (Münster: Ugarit-Verlag, 2010), 319–38; Diana Edelman, *The Origins of the "Second" Temple: Persian Imperial Policy and the Rebuilding of Jerusalem* (London: Equinox, 2005); James D. Moore, "Who Gave You a Decree?," *JBL* 140, no. 1 (2021): 69–89.

46. Eran Arie, "Revisiting Mount Gerizim: The Foundation of the Sacred Precinct and the Proto-Ionic Capitals," in *New Studies in the Archaeology of Jerusalem and Its Region: Collected Papers*, vol. 14, ed. Yehiel Zelinger et al. (Jerusalem: Israel Antiquities Authority, 2021), 39*–63*; Dalit Regev, "The Persian Pottery from Salvage Excavations at Har Gerizim (2019–2021) Preliminary Findings," in *Social Groups behind Biblical Traditions*, ed. Benedikt Hensel, Bartosz Adamczewski, and Dany R. Nocquet, FAT 167 (Tübingen: Mohr Siebeck, 2023), 65–88.

47. Bob Becking, "'That Evil Act: A Thick Description of the Crisis around the Demolition of the Temple of "Yahô" at Elephantine,'" in *Elephantine in Context: Studies on the History, Religion and Literature of the Judeans in Persian Period Egypt*, ed. Reinhard G. Kratz and Bernd U. Schipper, FAT 155 (Tübingen: Mohr Siebeck, 2022), 183–207.

A4.9). The relationships between these temples (and any other temples) and wider structures are debated.[48]

"Restoration"

Based on the narrative in Kings/Chronicles and Ezra-Nehemiah, it has traditionally been accepted that, after a group of Judeans were taken to Babylonia, a number of their descendants returned to the Levant to "restore" Yehud. Archaeological surveys of the region of the kingdom of Judah, however, show two qualifications. First, the pattern of Babylonian destruction was uneven, with the area around Jerusalem destroyed but the Benjamin region left largely untouched.[49] Second, no large influx of settlers is visible with new farmsteads on virgin sites.[50] The largest collection of new farmsteads appears only in Idumea in the fifth to fourth centuries. This raises a problem for understanding what "restoration" or "end of exile" means for Persian Yehud.[51]

Idumea

The southern regions of the kingdom of Judah saw extensive changes in the Persian period. No longer a part of Yehud, new administrative structures, farms, and populations appear, including an influx of people from Edom.[52] The

48. Reinhard Kratz, *Das Judentum in Zeitalter des Zweiten Tempels*, FAT 42 (Tübingen: Mohr Siebeck, 2004), 60–78; Tova Ganzel and Shalom E. Holtz, eds., *Contextualizing Jewish Temples*, Brill Reference Library of Judaism 64 (Leiden: Brill, 2020); Reinhard Achenbach, ed., *Persische Reichspolitik und lokale Heiligtümer* (Wiesbaden: Harrassowitz, 2019).

49. Avraham Faust, "Social, Cultural and Demographic Changes in Judah during the Transition from the Iron Age to the Persian Period and the Nature of the Society during the Persian Period," in *From Judah to Judaea: Socio-Economic Structures and Processes in the Persian Period*, ed. Johannes Unsok Ro (Sheffield: Sheffield Phoenix, 2012), 106–32.

50. Oded Lipschits and Manfred Oeming, eds., *Judah and the Judeans in the Persian Period* (Winona Lake, IN: Eisenbrauns, 2006); Diana V. Edelman, "Settlement Patterns in Persian-Era Yehud," in *A Time of Change: Judah and Its Neighbours in the Persian and Early Hellenistic Periods*, ed. Yigal Levin, LSTS 65 (New York: T&T Clark, 2008), 52–56; Edelman, "Different Sources, Different Views," *EstBíb* 76 (2018): 411–51.

51. Gary N. Knoppers, Lester L. Grabbe, and Deirdre Fulton, eds., *Exile and Restoration Revisited: Essays on the Babylonian and Persian Periods in Memory of Peter R. Ackroyd*, LSTS 73 (London: T&T Clark, 2009).

52. Alexander Fantalkin and Oren Tal, "Identifying Achaemenid Imperial Policy at the Southern Frontier of the Fifth Satrapy," in Lipshits and Oeming, *Judah and the Judeans in the Persian Period*, 167–88; Fantalkin and Tal, "Judah and Its Neighbors in the Fourth Century BCE," in Unsok Ro, *From Judah to Judaea*, 133–96; Hensel, Ben Zvi, and Edelman, *About Edom and Idumea in the Persian Period*; Levin, *Time of Change*; Yigal Levin, "Judea, Samaria, and Idumea," in Unsok Ro, *From Judah to Judaea*, 4–53; Diana V. Edelman, "The Economy and Administration of Rural Idumea at the End of the Persian Period," in *The Economy of Ancient Judah in Its Historical Context*, ed. Marvin Lloyd Miller, Ehud Ben Zvi, and Gary N. Knoppers (Winona Lake, IN: Eisenbrauns, 2015), 175–206.

publication of a corpus of unprovenanced ostraca is providing a basis for evaluating the nature of these changes and the imperial reasons behind them.

Late Persian Period

Sources for the late Persian Empire (essentially the late 5th to 4th cent.) are less abundant but by no means nonexistent.[53] A number of the relevant sources listed above derive from the later periods, including the Idumean ostraca and Wadi ed-Daliyeh papyri. Key moments for the southern Levant include the so-called Inaros revolt (460 BCE), loss of Persian control of Egypt (404–343 BCE), Artaxerxes III's successful reconquest of Egypt (343 BCE), and finally, the campaign of Alexander, including the sieges of Tyre, Gaza (332 BCE), and Samaria (331 BCE).

Trends in the Study of the Neo-Babylonian and Persian Periods

Increased Importance of Communities in Samaria and outside the Levant

Scholarship has traditionally focused on Yehud, the province formed after the fall of the kingdom of Judah to Nebuchadnezzar. The past few decades have seen an increased interest in communities of Yahweh worshipers and Judeans outside Yehud.[54] The unprovenanced tablets from several Babylonian villages noted above and those from some other urban Judeans[55] have greatly increased the available documentation for the Judeans in Babylonia.[56] These new data help scholars to reassess the implications for understanding the Judeans' lives in Babylonia, particularly in light of migration studies.[57]

53. Oded Lipschits, Gary N. Knoppers, and Rainer Albertz, eds., *Judah and the Judeans in the Fourth Century BCE* (Winona Lake, IN: Eisenbrauns, 2007); Lester L. Grabbe and Oded Lipschits, eds., *Judah between East and West: The Transition from Persian to Greek Rule (ca. 400–200 BCE)*, LSTS 75 (London: T&T Clark, 2011).

54. Gard Granerød, *Dimensions of Yahwism in the Persian Period: Studies in the Religion and Society of the Judaean Community at Elephantine*, BZAW 488 (Berlin: De Gruyter, 2016); Benedikt Hensel, Dany R. Nocquet, and Bartosz Adamczewski, eds., *Yahwistic Diversity and the Hebrew Bible: Tracing Perspectives of Group Identity from Judah, Samaria, and the Diaspora in Biblical Traditions*, FAT 2/120 (Tübingen: Mohr Siebeck, 2020).

55. Yigal Bloch, "Judeans in Sippar and Susa during the First Century of the Babylonian Exile," *Journal of Ancient Near Eastern History* 1, no. 2 (2014): 119–72; Tero Alstola, "Judean Merchants in Babylonia and Their Participation in Long-Distance Trade," *WO* 47, no. 1 (2017): 25–51.

56. Previously the most important had been the so-called Weidner Tablets and the Murašu Archive.

57. See the essay by C. A. Strine, "Migration Studies," which is chap. 28 of the present volume; Uri Gabbay and Shai Secunda, eds., *Encounters by the Rivers of Babylon: Scholarly Conversations between Jews, Iranians, and Babylonians in Antiquity*, TSAJ 160 (Tübingen:

The importance of Yahwists in the former kingdom of Israel (Samerina after the Assyrian conquest), long overshadowed by the narratives of strife in Ezra-Nehemiah and Josephus, has increasingly come to the fore. The discovery of the temple complex at Gerizim, papyri, and the Dead Sea Scrolls have prompted a reanalysis of the relationships between the two provinces.[58]

Scholars have also given increased attention to the Judean community on the island of Elephantine in the southern Egyptian Nile cataract as evidence for contemporary social and religious practice. This is perhaps the most thoroughly documented Judean community of the era, with archives that can be connected to excavated houses. Scholarly reappraisal has been facilitated by the increasing publication of ostraca and material culture and by recognition of the contrast between the cult as practiced here and the biblical portraits of Judean religion.[59]

Increased Awareness of the Lateness of "Judaism"

Over the three decades following the historiographical battlefield often called the minimalist-maximalist debate,[60] it has become increasingly accepted that the history of Judean religion in the Neo-Babylonian and Persian periods is distinct from both the biblical account and later Second Temple practice.[61] This has had the effect of seriously qualifying the historiographic usefulness of the biblical narrative.

Mohr Siebeck, 2014); Jonathan Stökl and Caroline Waerzeggers, eds., *Exile and Return: The Babylonian Context*, BZAW 478 (Berlin: De Gruyter, 2015); Jakob Wöhrle, ed., "Mass Deportations to and from the Levant during the Age of Empires in the Ancient Near East," *HeBAI* 11, no. 5 (2022).

58. Gary N. Knoppers, *Jews and Samaritans: The Origins and History of Their Early Relations* (Oxford: Oxford University Press, 2013); Benedikt Hensel, *Juda und Samaria: Zum Verhältnis zweier nach-exilischer Jahwismen*, FAT 110 (Tübingen: Mohr Siebeck, 2016); Magnar Kartveit and Gary N. Knoppers, eds., *The Bible, Qumran, and the Samaritans* (Berlin: De Gruyter, 2018); Dany R. Nocquet, *La Samarie, la Diaspora et l'achèvement de la Torah: Territorialités et internationalités dans l'Hexateuque*, OBO 284 (Fribourg: Academic Press, 2017); Gary N. Knoppers, *Judah and Samaria in Postmonarchic Times: Essays on Their Histories and Literatures*, FAT 129 (Tübingen: Mohr Siebeck, 2019).

59. Annalisa Azzoni, *The Private Lives of Women in Persian Egypt* (Winona Lake, IN: Eisenbrauns, 2013); Angela Rohrmoser, *Götter, Tempel und Kult der Judäo-Aramäer von Elephantine: Archäologische und schriftliche Zeugnisse aud dem perserzeitlichen Ägypten*, AOAT 396 (Münster: Ugarit-Verlag, 2014); Bob Becking, *Identity in Persian Egypt: The Fate of the Yehudite Community of Elephantine* (University Park, PA: Eisenbrauns, 2020); Margaretha Folmer, ed., *Elephantine Revisited: New Insights into the Judean Community and Its Neighbors* (University Park, PA: Eisenbrauns, 2022); Kratz and Schipper, *Elephantine in Context*.

60. Emanuel Pfoh, "On Biblical Minimalism in Hebrew Bible/Old Testament Studies," *Annali di storia dell'esegesi* 38, no. 2 (2021): 283–300.

61. Summing up three decades of "minimalist" argumentation are Yonatan Adler, *The Origins of Judaism: An Archaeological-Historical Reappraisal*, AYBRL (New Haven: Yale University Press, 2022); and Gard Granerød, "Canon and Archive: Yahwism in Elephantine and Al-Yāhudu as a Challenge to the Canonical History of Judean Religion in the Persian Period," *JBL* 138, no. 2 (2019): 345–64.

Another trend focuses on other sources of information to create a more complex picture, including the political and material evidence for temples in the era,[62] in particular the practices attested at Elephantine[63] and attested figurines and coins.[64]

It is widely accepted that Judean religious practice was originally polytheistic, and many scholars still place the beginnings of more monotheistic practices or beliefs in the context of the Persian Empire.[65]

Selected Themes in the Study of Biblical Literature within the Babylonian and Persian Periods

Much of the literature that survives in the HB is now accepted to have been written, edited, and/or collated in the Babylonian and Persian periods and later, though there is no consensus concerning the process or the dating of precise passages.[66] Nonetheless, the past decades have seen some significant scholarly interest in several lines of investigation of texts believed to date to these periods.

The most significant and clear trend is an increasing awareness of the importance of the Babylonian and especially Persian imperial contexts. This includes the nature of the ancient empires and their impacts on local polities.[67] In many

62. Achenbach, *Persische Reichspolitik*.

63. Karel van der Toorn, "Eshem-Bethel and Herem-Bethel," *ZAW* 128, no. 4 (2016): 668–80; Ryan Thomas, "Reconstructing the Pantheon of Judaean Elephantine," *UF* 51 (2020): 225–97; Gad Barnea, "*Interpretatio Ivdaica* in the Achaemenid Period," *JAJ* 14 (2023): 1–37.

64. Ya'akov Meshorer, *A Treasury of Jewish Coins* (Jerusalem: Yad Ben-Zvi Press, 2001); Christian Frevel, Katharina Pyschny, and Izak Cornelius, eds., *A "Religious Revolution" in Yehud? The Material Culture of the Persian Period as a Test Case*, OBO 267 (Fribourg: Vandenhoeck & Ruprecht, 2014); Hulster, *Figurines in Achaemenid Period Yehud*; Collin Cornell, "The Forgotten Female Figurines of Elephantine," *Journal of Ancient Near Eastern Religions* 18 (2018): 111–32.

65. John Barton and Francesca Stavrakopoulou, eds., *Religious Diversity in Ancient Israel and Judah* (London: T&T Clark, 2010); Philip R. Davies, "Monotheism, Empire, and the Cult(s) of Yehud in the Persian Period," in *Religion in the Achaemenid Persian Empire: Emerging Judaisms and Trends*, ed. Diana V. Edelman, Anne Fitzpatrick-McKinley, and Philippe Guillaume, ORA 17 (Tübingen: Mohr Siebeck, 2016), 24–35; Shawn W. Flynn, *A Story of YHWH: Cultural Transition and Subversive Reception in Israelite History*, SHANE (London: Routledge, 2020); Michael B. Hundley, *Yahweh among the Gods: The Divine in Genesis, Exodus, and the Ancient Near East* (Cambridge: Cambridge University Press, 2022).

66. Richard J. Bautch and Mark Lackowski, eds., *On Dating Biblical Texts to the Persian Period: Discerning Criteria and Establishing Epochs*, FAT 2/101 (Tübingen: Mohr Siebeck, 2019).

67. James W. Watts, *Persia and Torah: The Theory of Imperial Authorization of the Pentateuch*, SBLSS 17 (Atlanta: Society of Biblical Literature, 2001); Alejandro F. Botta, ed., *In the Shadow of Bezalel: Aramaic, Biblical, and Ancient Near Eastern Studies in Honor of Bezalel Porten*, CHANE 60 (Leiden: Brill, 2012); Stökl and Waerzeggers, *Exile and Return*; Myles Lavan, Richard E. Payne, and John Weisweile, eds., *Cosmopolitanism and Empire: Universal Rulers, Local Elites, and Cultural Integration in the Ancient Near East and Mediterranean*, Oxford Studies in Early Empires (Oxford: Oxford University Press, 2016); Clifford Ando and

cases scholars are keen to detect "resistance" to imperial rule.[68] An increase in comparative views of exile/migration can be seen, especially those positing various forms of social trauma.[69]

Another major trend assesses the biblical narrative in terms of social memory.[70] This school of thought tries to tease out why the community would have valued memories and ways of remembering. One major subset of this is remembrance of or expectations for the defunct Davidic dynasty.[71] Many have explored the connection between writing and identity construction.[72] Of particular interest is how the biblical texts relate to social roles, especially those of scribes[73] and priests.[74]

Much work remains in synthesizing this new material and in applying the many new methods gaining ground in the wider field.

Seth Richardson, eds., *Ancient States and Infrastructural Power: Europe, Asia, and America*, Empire and After (Philadelphia: University of Pennsylvania Press, 2017).

68. Jon L. Berquist, "Resistance and Accommodation in the Persian Empire," in *In the Shadow of Empire: Reclaiming the Bible as a History of Faithful Resistance*, ed. Richard A. Horsley (Louisville: Westminster John Knox, 2008), 41–58; John J. Collins and J. G. Manning, eds., *Revolt and Resistance in the Ancient Classical World and the Near East: In the Crucible of Empire*, CHANE 85 (Leiden: Brill, 2016); Marc Van De Mieroop, *Before and after Babel: Writing as Resistance in Ancient Near Eastern Empires* (New York: Oxford University Press, 2022).

69. Daniel Smith-Christopher, *A Biblical Theology of Exile*, OBT (Minneapolis: Fortress, 2002); Brad E. Kelle, Frank Ritchel Ames, and Jacob L. Wright, eds., *Interpreting Exile: Displacement and Deportation in Biblical and Modern Contexts*, AIL 10 (Atlanta: Society of Biblical Literature, 2011); Jeremiah W. Cataldo, "Memory, Trauma, and Identity in Ezra-Nehemiah," in *Methods, Theories, Imagination: Social Scientific Approaches in Biblical Studies*, ed. David J. Chalcraft, Frauke Uhlenbruch, and Rebecca S. Watson (Sheffield: Sheffield Phoenix, 2014), 147–58.

70. Ehud Ben Zvi and Christoph Levin, eds., *Remembering and Forgetting in Early Second Temple Judah*, FAT 85 (Tübingen: Mohr Siebeck, 2012); Ian Douglas Wilson and Diana V. Edelman, *History, Memory, Hebrew Scriptures: A Festschrift for Ehud Ben Zvi* (Winona Lake, IN: Eisenbrauns, 2015); Ian Douglas Wilson, *Kingship and Memory in Ancient Judah* (Oxford: Oxford University Press, 2017); Ehud Ben Zvi, *Social Memory among the Literati of Yehud*, BZAW 509 (Berlin: De Gruyter, 2019).

71. Silverman and Waerzeggers, *Political Memory*; David Janzen, *Chronicles and the Politics of Davidic Restoration: A Quiet Revolution*, LHBOTS 655 (London: T&T Clark, 2017); Diana V. Edelman and Ehud Ben Zvi, eds., *Leadership, Social Memory, and Judean Discourse in the Fifth–Second Centuries BCE*, Worlds of the Ancient Near East and Mediterranean (Sheffield: Equinox, 2016).

72. Oded Lipschits, Gary N. Knoppers, and Manfred Oeming, eds., *Judah and the Judeans in the Achaemenid Period* (Winona Lake, IN: Eisenbrauns, 2011); Rainer Albertz and Jakob Wöhrle, eds., *Between Cooperation and Hostility: Multiple Identities in Ancient Judaism and the Interaction with Foreign Powers*, JAJSup 11 (Göttingen: Vandenhoeck & Ruprecht, 2013); Joanna Töyräänvuori, ed., "The Construction of Identity in the Ancient World," *WO* 50, no. 2 (2020): 201–376; Hensel, Nocquet, and Adamczewski, *Yahwistic Diversity and the Hebrew Bible*; Hensel, Adamczewski, and Nocquet, *Social Groups behind Biblical Traditions*.

73. Philip R. Davies and Thomas Römer, eds., *Writing the Bible: Scribes, Scribalism and Script* (Durham, NC: Acumen, 2013); Mark Leuchter, ed., *Scribes and Scribalism*, Hebrew Bible in Social Perspective (London: T&T Clark, 2020).

74. Jeremiah W. Cataldo, *A Theocratic Yehud? Issues of Governance in a Persian Province*, LHBOTS 498 (London: T&T Clark, 2009); Alice Hunt, *Missing Priests: The Zadokites in Tradition and History*, LHBOTS 452 (New York: T&T Clark, 2006).

7

Archaeology and History

Hellenistic Period

Jordan J. Ryan

The Hellenistic period in the southern Levant began *circa* 332 BCE, when Alexander the Great brought the region under his control. The Early Hellenistic period (EH) thus saw the rise of Alexander's empire in the southern Levant, as well as the subsequent emergence of the Hellenistic successor states to that empire, particularly the Egypt-based Ptolemaic kingdom and the Syria-based Seleucid kingdom, following Alexander's death. The author of 1 Maccabees colorfully describes the emergence of these successor states, remarking that after Alexander died, "his officers began to rule, each in his own place. They all put on crowns after his death, and so did their descendants after them for many years; and they caused many evils on the earth" (1:8–9 NRSV). The Late Hellenistic period (LH) in the region is defined by the rise of the Hasmonean state (ca. 164–64 BCE), which bloomed into a largely autonomous Jewish kingdom that stretched from Galilee in the north to Judea in the south and included regions east of the Sea of Galilee and the Jordan River, such as the Golan and Perea. The Roman conquest of the region in 63 BCE marks the end of the Hellenistic period.

Thanks is due to Bethany Grainger, my teaching assistant, for proofreading this piece. Gratitude is also due to Andrea Berlin for correspondence and several conversations about Galilee in the Late Hellenistic and Early Roman periods that helped to shape its direction.

These two major shifts in the region—the rise of the Hellenistic kingdoms in the EH period and the rise of the Hasmonean state in the LH period—correspond to two movements in the archaeological record: the introduction and enduring influence of Hellenistic material culture in the EH period and the emergence of a distinctive Jewish material culture throughout what became the Hasmonean state in the LH period.

"Hellenistic" and "Jewish" should not be viewed as two categories in opposition to one another; instead, we should seek to understand the complex ways in which the two interface. Martin Hengel's landmark studies in the latter half of the twentieth century made a strong case that, to varying degrees, *all* Judaism was Hellenized in the Hellenistic period, both in Judea and in the diaspora.[1] Although Hengel's work is beginning to show its age and has not been without detractors over the years,[2] this core insight remains influential.[3] Subsequent scholarship develops Hengel's hypothesis and further erodes a dichotomous understanding of Judaism and Hellenism.[4]

The impact of Hellenistic civilization and culture on Jewish culture in the southern Levant can be seen in the EH and LH archaeological record. A certain tradition is also identifiable in the archaeological record that we can and should associate with an emergent Jewish material culture. This is particularly clear in Galilee, where new settlements exhibit an emerging coherent material culture and profile during the rise of the Hasmonean kingdom. Interpreting the complex relationship between Hellenism and Judaism in the archaeological record, recognizing the substantial overlap between them, and rejecting essentializing notions are all major topics in current scholarship that are crucial for our understanding of the Hellenistic period in the southern Levant.

1. Martin Hengel, *Jews, Greeks, and Barbarians: Aspects of the Hellenization of Judaism in the Pre-Christian Period*, trans. John Bowden (Philadelphia: Fortress, 1980); Hengel, *Judaism and Hellenism: Studies in Their Encounter in Palestine during the Early Hellenistic Period*, trans. John Bowden (Eugene, OR: Wipf & Stock, 2003).

2. Louis H. Feldman, "Hengel's *Judaism and Hellenism* in Retrospect," *JBL* 96, no. 3 (1977): 371–82; Feldman, *Jew and Gentile in the Ancient World: Attitudes and Interactions from Alexander to Justinian* (Princeton: Princeton University Press, 1993), 42–44, 416–22; Eric M. Meyers and Carol Meyers, "The Material Culture of Late Hellenistic–Early Roman Palestinian Judaism: What It Can Tell Us about Earliest Christianity and the New Testament," in *Neues Testament und hellenistisch-jüdische Alltagskultur*, ed. Roland Deines, Jens Herzer, and Karl-Wilhelm Niebuhr, WUNT 274 (Tübingen: Mohr Siebeck, 2011), 3–23.

3. E.g., Erich S. Gruen identifies Hengel's *Judaism and Hellenism* as still "the classic study of Greek influences in Palestine." See Gruen, *Constructs of Identity in Hellenistic Judaism: Essays on Early Jewish Literature and History*, Deuterocanonical and Cognate Literature Studies 29 (Berlin: De Gruyter, 2016), 113n4.

4. Notable developments of Hengel's hypothesis include Gruen, *Constructs of Identity*; Lee I. Levine, *Judaism and Hellenism in Antiquity: Conflict or Confluence?* (Seattle: University of Washington Press, 1998); Tessa Rajak, *The Jewish Dialogue with Greece and Rome: Studies in Cultural and Social Interaction* (Boston: Brill, 2002), 1–11.

The Impact of Hellenization

Evidence for the impact of Hellenistic culture on the southern Levant is widespread and varied in the archaeological record.[5] Perhaps the most overt examples are the non-Jewish Hellenistic cities of the region. These include not only cities founded as Hellenistic settlements, such as the Decapolis cities like Hippos and Scythopolis (Beit Shean), but also cities like Marisa (Maresha), an Idumean city with a strong Phoenician community, and Dor, a city on the Phoenician coast, both of which exhibit thoroughly Hellenistic culture blended with local traditions and cultures.[6] Greek inscriptions, such as the Hefzibah inscription and the Yavneh-Yam inscription, which represent decrees of Seleucid authorities, bear witness to the rise of the Greek language in the region.

Elements of Hellenistic influence are attested in Jewish contexts as well. Hellenistic architectural traditions—particularly the classical Doric, Ionic, and Corinthian orders in combination with the post and lintel system—come to prominence in Jewish contexts in the Hellenistic period. One dramatic early example can be seen at Qaṣr al-ʿAbd, a palatial estate located at ʿIraq el-Amir in the Jordan Valley.[7] Qaṣr al-ʿAbd is solidly linked to a prominent Jewish family, the Tobiads, on the basis of inscriptions (the name Tobiah [Neh. 2:10] is inscribed over the facades of two different rock-carved halls on the site) and textual evidence (Josephus, *Ant.* 12.230–33). The architecture is Hellenistic, featuring Corinthian columns and a post-and-lintel construction, though with local influence, as the palace's corner towers and terrace roof resemble temple architecture of Syria-Palestine.[8] Most striking are the carved lions or leopards that appear in relief on a frieze and the two stone carved leopards with spouts in their mouths, meant to be used as fountains; their artistic style is decidedly Hellenistic.[9] While uncommon, finding

5. Jordan J. Ryan, "Archaeology of the Hellenistic Period," in *Behind the Scenes of the Old Testament: Cultural, Social, and Historical Contexts*, ed. Jonathan S. Greer, John W. Hilber, and John H. Walton (Grand Rapids: Baker Academic, 2018), 79–82.

6. For summaries in connection to Hellenism, see, e.g., Robert Harrison, "Hellenization in Syria-Palestine: The Case of Judea in the Third Century BCE," *BA* 52, no. 2 (1994): 98–108; Andrea M. Berlin, "Manifest Identity: From *Ioudaios* to Jew, Household Judaism as Anti-Hellenization in the Late Hasmonean Era," in *Between Cooperation and Hostility: Multiple Identities in Ancient Judaism and the Interaction with Foreign Powers*, ed. Rainer Albertz and Jakob Wöhrle, JAJSup 11 (Göttingen: Vandenhoeck & Ruprecht, 2013), 151–75; Berlin, "Between Large Forces: Palestine in the Hellenistic Period," *BA* 60, no. 1 (1997): 3–51.

7. Nancy L. Lapp, *The Excavations at Araq el-Emir*, 2 vols. (Ann Arbor, MI: American Schools of Oriental Research, 1983, 2019), 1:133–47; cf. Paul W. Lapp and Nancy L. Lapp, "ʿIraq el-Emir," in *New Encyclopedia of Archaeological Excavations in the Holy Land*, ed. Ephraim Stern, Ayelet Lewison-Gilboa, and Joseph Aviram (Jerusalem: Israel Exploration Society; Jerusalem: Carta, 1993), 2:646–49. For a more recent summary, see Jodi Magness, *The Archaeology of the Holy Land: From the Destruction of Solomon's Temple to the Muslim Conquest* (Cambridge: Cambridge University Press, 2012), 73–75.

8. P. Lapp and N. Lapp, "ʿIraq el-Emir," 648; cf. Magness, *Archaeology*, 74.

9. Dorothy Kent Hill, "The Animal Fountain of ʿArâq el-Emîr," *BASOR* 171 (1963): 55.

such figurative images in a Jewish context is noteworthy and demonstrates that such a thing is possible.

More examples of Hellenistic influence can be seen in Jewish burials,[10] particularly the monumental rock-cut tombs of LH and Early Roman period (ER) Jerusalem.[11] Unlike traditional tombs of Iron Age Judah, Hellenistic tombs typically featured external decoration. The Tomb of Benei Ḥezir in the Kidron Valley prominently features the Doric classical order, with entablature, architrave, frieze, and Doric columns.[12] An inscription identifies this tomb as belonging to a priestly family. The so-called Tomb of Zechariah, located adjacent to the Tomb of Benei Ḥezir, is a monolith carved entirely out of the rock. Its facade boasts two decorative, nonfunctional columns of the classical Ionic order carved in relief in the stone, as well as two Ionic pilasters.[13]

The Hasmoneans embraced certain Hellenistic influences. The palaces at Jericho exemplify the complexities of the Hasmoneans and the intertwining of Hellenistic and Jewish material culture. They contain Hellenistic features such as swimming pools (typical of Hellenistic palaces), Greek baths, and Hellenistic-style decor, including Doric columns and frescos.[14] At the same palaces, numerous ritual baths have been discovered, and the pottery is overwhelmingly of common local varieties,[15] which is surprising given the palace context.

Magdala-Tarichaea, located on the western shore of the Sea of Galilee, is a small city founded in the LH period around the time of a boom in settlements in Galilee typically connected to the Hasmonean annexation of the region.[16] It was the capital of a toparchy (Josephus, *J.W.* 2.252; *Ant.* 20.159) and had strong ties to

10. Rachel Hachlili, *Jewish Funerary Customs, Practices and Rites in the Second Temple Period*, JSJSup 94 (Boston: Brill 2005), 515–16.

11. Andrea M. Berlin, "Power and Its Afterlife: Tombs in Hellenistic Palestine," *NEA* 65, no. 2 (2002): 138–48; Ryan, "Archaeology of the Hellenistic Period," 80–81.

12. Dan Barag, "The 2000–2001 Exploration of the Tombs of Benei Ḥezir and Zechariah," *IEJ* 53, no. 1 (2003): 79.

13. Barag, "Tombs of Benei Ḥezir and Zechariah," 95–99. Barag holds that the Tomb of Zechariah dates to the latter half of the 1st cent. BCE, during the LH–ER transition, but its architecture is instructive of the broader trends of the late Second Temple period.

14. Ehud Netzer, *Hasmonean and Herodian Palaces at Jericho: Final Reports of the 1973–1987 Excavations*, vol. 1, *Stratigraphy and Architecture* (Jerusalem: Israel Exploration Society, 2001); Orit Peleg-Barkat, "The Architectural Decoration from the Hasmonean and Herodian Palaces at Jericho and Cypros," in Netzer, *Hasmonean and Herodian Palaces at Jericho*, vol. 5, *The Finds from Jericho and Cypros*, ed. Rachel Bar-Nathan and Judit Gärtner (Jerusalem: Israel Exploration Society, 2013), 235–69. See summary in Eyal Regev, "The Hellenization of the Hasmoneans Revisited: The Archaeological Evidence," *Advances in Anthropology* 17, no. 4 (2017): 177–82.

15. Regev, "Hellenization of the Hasmoneans Revisited," 181–82.

16. Stefano De Luca and Anna Lena, "Magdala/Taricheae," in *Galilee in the Late Second Temple and Mishnaic Periods: The Archaeological Record from Cities, Towns, and Villages*, ed. David A. Fiensy and James Riley Strange (Minneapolis: Fortress, 2015), 2:303; Danny Syon, "Coins," in Marcela Zapata-Meza et al., "The Magdala Archaeological Project (2010–2012): A Preliminary Report of the Excavations at Migdal," *ʿAtiqot* 90 (2018): 117–19.

the Hasmoneans.[17] Magdala-Tarichaea was built in Hellenistic fashion according to the "Hippodamian grid," an orthogonal street plan characteristic of Greek and Roman cities.[18] It featured public architecture, most significantly the Greek-style bathhouse. In fact, the city's urban character leads Richard Bauckham to argue that Magdala could be classified as a Greco-Roman polis.[19] By the ER period, the same city boasted two synagogue buildings, the famed "Magdala stone" (a carved stone block found in one of the synagogues that prominently features a menorah), and groundwater-fed ritual baths along with chalkstone vessels and Kefar Ḥananyah ware (a pottery type common only at Jewish sites in Galilee and the Golan). The city's Hellenistic features make it no more or less Jewish, and its Jewish features make it no more or less Hellenistic. The site is instructive, reflecting the broader Hasmonean state's dual identity as an ethnically Jewish state that was also a Hellenistic kingdom.

The evidence discussed thus far demonstrates the diffusion of Hellenistic culture through Jewish locales and material culture during the entire Hellenistic period. Hellenistic influence does not disappear but is actually ubiquitous in the LH period. It is reasonable to think that elites such as the Hasmonean royal family, the Jerusalem priesthood, and the Tobiads adopted Hellenistic influences because aligning themselves with the architectural iconography and cultural markers associated with the dominant powers of the day was a statement of their own refinement, taste, power, and class.

Hellenistic Jerusalem before the Hasmoneans

Our archaeological knowledge of Hellenistic Jerusalem prior to the rise of the Hasmonean dynasty is relatively scant. However, recent excavations in East Jerusalem in the Tyropoeon Valley (known as the Givati Parking Lot) have shed light on Jerusalem under the Ptolemies and Seleucids. Also, a public building on the western slope of the City of David is dated to the EH period.[20] This identification

17. R. Steven Notley, "Genesis Rabbah 98:17—'And Why Is It Called Gennosar?' Recent Discoveries at Magdala and Jewish Life on the Plain of Gennosar in the Early Roman Period," in *Talmuda de-Eretz Israel: Archaeology and the Rabbis in Late Antique Palestine*, ed. Steven Fine and Aaron Koller (Berlin: De Gruyter, 2014), 141–57; Jordan J. Ryan, "The Ideology of Restoration and the Archaeology of Galilee: The Hasmonean Transformation of Galilee as Context for Jesus and the Gospels," *CTR* 16, no. 1 (2018): 61–65.

18. De Luca and Lena, "Magdala/Tarichaea," 303–5; Richard Bauckham, "Magdala as We Now Know It," in *Magdala of Galilee: A Jewish City in the Hellenistic and Roman Period*, ed. Richard Bauckham (Waco: Baylor University Press, 2018), 23.

19. Bauckham, "Magdala as We Now Know It," 23–26.

20. Yiftah Shalev et al., "New Evidence on the Location and Nature of Iron Age, Persian and Early Hellenistic Period Jerusalem," *TA* 47, no. 2 (2020): 162–65; Yiftah Shalev et al., "Jerusalem in the Early Hellenistic Period: New Evidence for Its Nature and Location," in *The Middle Maccabees: Archaeology, History, and the Rise of the Hasmonean Kingdom*, ed. Andrea M. Berlin and Paul J. Kosmin, ABS 28 (Atlanta: SBL Press, 2021), 23–31.

is further supported by small finds, including a gold bead and earring, and twenty clay bullae found in the fills associated with this structure.[21] The iconography of these finds speaks to the cultural character of the inhabitants of the building. The earring is in the form of an animal (either an antelope or a gazelle), and ten bullae depict Greek mythological motifs.[22] The gold jewelry indicates the connection of the space to people of high status with decidedly Hellenistic tastes, and the bullae are certainly at home in administrative contexts.[23] Although earlier scholarship tended to suggest that EH Jerusalem was relatively small, excavators have rightly observed that this discovery of a public building in an area where occupation in this period was uncertain suggests that the city was significantly larger than previously thought.[24]

Another recent discovery further brings our picture of Jerusalem under the Seleucids into sharper relief. Major military architecture dating to the second century BCE has been uncovered on the northwestern side of the Givati Parking Lot excavation.[25] According to the preliminary excavation report, the complex includes a fortification wall, a glacis, and a rectangular tower.[26] The excavators have suggested that this military complex should be identified with the Seleucid Akra (citadel),[27] a structure featuring prominently in the narrative of the Maccabean revolt (1 Macc. 1:31–36; 3:45; 4:2, 41; 6:18–27; 9:52–53; 10:6–9; 11:20–21; 13:49–52; cf. 2 Macc. 4:12, 28; 5:5; 15:31, 35; Josephus, *Ant.* 12.252). The identification of this military complex as the Akra will likely be an ongoing topic of debate. These recent discoveries shed some light on Jerusalem as a city under the rule of the Ptolemies and Seleucids and provide a window into how the Hellenistic successor states contributed to the shaping of Jerusalem through public and defense architecture.

21. Shalev et al., "Early Hellenistic Period Jerusalem," 165.
22. Shalev et al., "Jerusalem in the Early Hellenistic Period," 30.
23. On comparative examples of bullae, see Sharon C. Herbert and Andrea M. Berlin, "A New Administrative Center for Persian and Hellenistic Galilee: Preliminary Report of the University of Michigan/University of Minnesota Excavations at Tel Kedesh," *BASOR* 329 (2003): 13–59.
24. Shalev et al., "Early Hellenistic Period Jerusalem," 166–68.
25. Doron Ben-Ami, Yana Tchekhanovets, and Salome Dan-Goor, "Jerusalem, Giv'ati Parking Lot," *Hadashot Arkheologiyot* 133 (2021); Ayala Zilberstein, "Hellenistic Military Architecture from the Givʿati Parking Lot Excavations, Jerusalem," in Berlin and Kosmin, *Middle Maccabees*, 37–52. On the fortifications, see Ayala Zilberstein, "'On Your Walls, City of David': The Line of the Western Fortification of the City of David Hill during the Hellenistic Period, in Light of New Finds" [Hebrew], in *New Studies in the Archaeology of Jerusalem and Its Region XIII*, ed. Orit Peleg-Barkat et al. (Jerusalem: Tel Aviv University; Jerusalem: Israel Antiquities Authority, 2019), 31–50.
26. Ben-Ami, Tchekhanovets, and Dan-Goor, "Jerusalem, Giv'ati Parking Lot."
27. Doron Ben-Ami and Yana Tchekhanovets, "'Then They Built Up the City of David with a High, Strong Wall and Strong Towers, and It Became Their Citadel' (1 Maccabees 1:33)," *City of David Studies of Ancient Jerusalem* 11 (2016): 19–29.

Rise of the Hasmonean State and Emergence of Jewish Material Culture

The LH period saw the advent of a new material culture that was distinctive to Jewish locales and thus to Jews. Finds such as stepped pools, Hasmonean coins, new locally made pottery types, and folded wheel-made lamps emerge. While scholars widely agree that these things are associated with Jews, ongoing discussions include how to interpret the finds, how they relate to Jewish ethnic and religious identity (if at all), whether they constitute identity markers, how they relate or do not relate to Hellenization, and what they can or cannot tell us about early Judaism.

The appearance of this assemblage at Galilean sites is particularly significant because it appears across newly settled sites throughout the LH and ER periods. Contemporary scholarship typically relates this to the emergence of Jewish Galilee and a major ethnic change and settlement process, which is almost certainly tied to the growth of the Hasmonean state. The questions of *when* Galilee became predominantly Jewish and *what* the ethnic identity of Galileans was during the Hasmonean and Herodian periods dominated previous scholarship.[28] The current prevailing opinion is that Galilee was populated primarily by non-Jews in the EH period and was relatively sparsely settled. However, beginning in LH and ER, the Jewish population of Galilee was made up primarily of Judean Jews who migrated to the north in the late second and early first centuries BCE and founded new settlements.[29] The settlement pattern and emergence of a new material culture in Galilee speaks not only to Jewish identity but also to the northern expansion of the Hasmonean kingdom.

Hasmonean Coinage

Hasmonean coins are, by their nature, connected in a direct way to the Jerusalem-based Jewish kingdom and are datable to the reigns of the rulers that minted them. For these reasons, the presence of large quantities of Hasmonean coinage at a site indicates the site's connection to the Hasmonean kingdom and is thus a reasonable basis for inferring the Jewish ethnic identity of its occupants.[30] According to Danny Syon, "the coinage of the Hasmoneans, apart from supplying currency, was definitely a political statement of a new ethnic power."[31] The act of minting coins

28. E.g., Mark A. Chancey, *The Myth of a Gentile Galilee*, Society for New Testament Studies Monograph Series 118 (Cambridge: Cambridge University Press, 2002), esp. 11–17; Uzi Leibner, *Settlement and History in Hellenistic, Roman, and Byzantine Galilee: An Archaeological Survey of the Eastern Galilee*, Texts and Studies in Ancient Judaism 127 (Tübingen: Mohr Siebeck, 2009), 319–27.

29. Leibner, *Settlement and History*, 307–45.

30. Danny Syon, *Small Change in Hellenistic-Roman Galilee: The Evidence from Numismatic Site Finds as a Tool for Historical Reconstruction* (Jerusalem: Israel Numismatic Society, 2015), 59, 155–59, 161–65. On coins as an ethnic marker, see Danny Syon, "The Hasmonean Settlement in Galilee: A Numismatic Perspective," in Berlin and Kosmin, *Middle Maccabees*, 182.

31. Syon, *Small Change*, 59.

was a proclamation of Hasmonean authority, and the circulation and preferred use of the coins indicated an orientation toward Judea and the Hasmonean state.

Hasmonean coins are characteristically nonfigurative, meaning that they do not depict rulers, deities, or any other living beings. This coheres with a broader tendency in the LH and ER periods toward nonfigurative artwork and is often connected to the Torah's injunction against graven images. Since nonfigurative coinage was, as Syon puts it, "a radical departure from the customs of the period, which normally included the head of the king or some deity on the obverse,"[32] this was likely a conscious choice and reflects broader patterns of behavior against figurative imagery among people aligned with the Hasmonean state. The coins can be reasonably interpreted as contributing toward the construction of Jewish identity by virtue of simultaneously proclaiming Hasmonean political power and differentiating themselves and the state from the figurative coins minted and circulated by other authorities.[33] At the same time, it would be a mistake to see the coins as a wholesale rejection of Hellenism. The very act of minting coins situated the Hasmoneans among the Hellenistic rulers of their time. Moreover, while John Hyrcanus typically minted coins with Paleo-Hebrew script, they also included some Greek characters and monograms, and some of the issues of Alexander Jannaeus and Mattathias Antigonus included both Greek and Semitic inscriptions.[34] Thus the coins should be seen as representing *both* movements: the construction of a distinct Jewish material culture *and* the ongoing influence of Hellenistic culture.

Syon's recent work on coinage in Galilee shows a dividing line between Galilean sites where Hasmonean issues are dominant, indicating ties to Jerusalem, and sites where coins were minted at the coastal cities of Tyre, Sidon, and Ptolemais (Akko), indicating ties to the (Seleucid) Phoenician coast.[35] The clear divide allows Syon to locate the potential boundaries between the Hasmonean state, in which Hasmonean coins predominate, to the south and east in Galilee and settlements oriented toward the Phoenician coast to the north and west.[36] Coins also contribute important evidence of when the Jewish settlement of Galilee began. As Syon argues, the wide distribution of coins north of Judea dating to the reign of John Hyrcanus suggests "a substantial Jewish presence already in the time of Hyrcanus I."[37] This is further supported by the surprisingly widespread presence of coins of the Seleucid ruler Antiochus VII, which were minted in Jerusalem between 132 and 130 BCE, suggesting a connection

32. Syon, *Small Change*, 59.

33. Eric M. Meyers and Mark A. Chancey, *Archaeology of the Land of the Bible*, vol. 3, *Alexander to Constantine* (New Haven: Yale University Press, 2012), 46.

34. Meyers and Chancey, *Alexander to Constantine*, 46; Jodi Magness, *Archaeology*, 105.

35. Syon, *Small Change*; see also Syon, "Hasmonean Settlement."

36. Syon, *Small Change*, 157–59. See also Uzi Leibner, "Galilee in the Second Century BCE: Material Culture and Ethnic Identity," in Berlin and Kosmin, *Middle Maccabees*, 127.

37. Syon, "Hasmonean Settlement," 181–83.

between these Galilean sites and Jerusalem.[38] The numismatic data serves to illuminate the ethnic transition and Hasmonean annexation of Galilee, a key historical event with major implications for the history of early Judaism and for Christian origins.

Pottery

Although finds from the EH period are sparse, the pottery indicates that, under the Ptolemies and Seleucids, Jerusalem residents regularly owned and used imported goods, including tableware, luxury items, and amphorae with stamped handles used to transport wine or olive oil.[39] However, Andrea Berlin observes that, in the years following the rise of the Hasmoneans in the second century BCE, "people lived simply with only the most basic of household goods, all manufactured in the immediate environs of the city."[40] The situation in smaller Judean locales is similar.[41] Imported wares did not entirely disappear: small numbers of imported amphorae are found in Hasmonean contexts at Jerusalem and Jericho.[42] Nevertheless, the small quantities of amphorae relative to the EH period and to nearby non-Jewish sites is surely significant.

The situation in Galilee and the Golan differs but speaks to a similar process. Red-slipped vessels made on the Phoenician coast (Eastern Sigillata A) were common throughout Galilee through the late second century BCE. However, over the course of the first century BCE, there was a shift among residents of Jewish sites toward a preference for new, locally made wares resembling the pottery of Judea.[43] By the early first century CE, Eastern Sigillata A continues at non-Jewish sites but essentially disappears from Jewish sites, while locally made Kefar Ḥananyah wares and Shikhin wares become prevalent.[44] This change was gradual. Berlin estimates that each household at Gamla in the first century BCE would have had a relatively small number of Eastern Sigillata A bowls and dishes (specifically 7 to 9), perhaps used as common serving vessels, while small, locally made vessels, which were in greater quantity, were used for individual

38. Syon, "Hasmonean Settlement," 179–80.

39. Andrea M. Berlin, "Manifest Identity," 157–60. On amphorae, see Donald T. Ariel, *Excavations at the City of David 1978–1985 Directed by Yigal Shiloh*, vol. 2, *Imported Stamped Amphora Handles, Coins, Worked Bone and Ivory, and Glass*, Qedem 30 (Jerusalem: Hebrew University, 1990), 13–24.

40. Berlin, "Manifest Identity," 154. See also Jodi Magness, *Stone and Dung, Oil and Spit: Jewish Daily Life in the Time of Jesus* (Grand Rapids: Eerdmans, 2011), 54–56.

41. Berlin, "Manifest Identity," 156.

42. See the discussion in Magness, *Stone and Dung*, 55.

43. Andrea M. Berlin, "Identity Politics in Early Roman Galilee," in *The Jewish Revolt against Rome: Interdisciplinary Perspectives*, ed. Mladen Popović, JSJSup 154 (Leiden: Brill, 2011), 85–86. At Gamla specifically, see Berlin, *Gamla: Final Reports*, vol. 1, *The Pottery of the Second Temple Period*, IAA Reports 29 (Jerusalem: Israel Antiquities Authority, 2006), 137–43. See also Syon, *Small Change*, 88–91.

44. Berlin, "Identity Politics," 96–106; Berlin, *Gamla*, 151.

servings.[45] Although this scenario does not present a complete rejection of non-Jewish wares, Berlin observes that it does present dining behavior that differs from typical Hellenistic norms. By the first century CE, Eastern Sigillata A pottery all but disappears from Gamla. This scenario is instructive: the shift is not immediate, but it is eventually decisive.

Galilean Course Ware is another ceramic group that was produced and used by non-Jewish residents of Galilee. Prior to the late second century BCE, Galilean Course Ware was common throughout Galilee and could be found alongside Eastern Sigillata A.[46] However, in the time that follows, many sites with a concentration of Galilean Course Ware were abandoned; in some of them, a new layer of occupation lacking Galilean Course Ware and containing Hasmonean coins is established, which suggests a shift in ethnic groups in the region.[47]

The confluence of data in Judea and Galilee is sufficient. Pottery itself is not "ethnic," and anyone could use it. Jews could and did use red-slipped pottery. Nevertheless, the data suggests particular behavior, choices, and preferences related to pottery usage and ownership among Jews in the LH period. Although objects themselves do not have ethnicity,[48] what objects we choose to own and use can express identity, behavior, self-understanding, and preferences. Widespread shifts suggest an emerging material culture, and when taken alongside the other developments, material culture may speak to particular ideologies, allegiances, and emerging identities.

Folded Oil Lamps

Closed lamps made in molds featuring elongated nozzles were common throughout the southern Levant throughout the Hellenistic period. However, sometime in the mid-second century BCE, a type of open lamp, the wheel-made folded oil lamp, became the most common form of lamp in Jerusalem and throughout Judea. This is yet another aspect in which the material culture of the Hasmonean state differentiated itself from that of its neighbors.

Omri Abadi and Eyal Regev suggest that these folded lamps functioned as a Jewish identity marker and contributed to the formation of Jewish ethnic identity.[49] Folded lamps appear concurrently and in the same region as standing-pit

45. Berlin, *Gamla*, 138.

46. Leibner, *Settlement and History*, 327–28.

47. Mordechai Aviam, "The Transformation from *Galil Ha-Goyim* to Jewish Galilee: The Archaeological Testimony of an Ethnic Change," in *Galilee in the Late Second Temple and Mishnaic Periods*, ed. David A. Fiensy and James Riley Strange, 2 vols. (Minneapolis: Fortress, 2015), 9–21; Aviam, "People, Land, Economy, and Belief in First-Century Galilee and Its Origins: A Comprehensive Archaeological Survey," in *The Galilean Economy in the Time of Jesus*, ed. David A. Fiensy and Ralph K. Hawkins, Early Christianity and Its Literature 11 (Atlanta: SBL Press, 2013–15), 2:5–7; Leibner, *Settlement and History*, 327–28.

48. Cf. Berlin, *Gamla*, 133.

49. Omri Y. Abadi and Eyal Regev, "Folded Wheel-Made Oil Lamps, Standing Pit Burial Caves and Judaean Ethnic Identity in the Hasmonean Period," *PEQ* 152, no. 3 (2020): 248–72.

burials, which are also unique to Judea in this period. Abadi and Regev rightly note the marked similarity between the Hasmonean folded lamps and the open lamps of Iron Age Judah in the First Temple period, and between the standing burial pits of the LH period and the burial caves of the First Temple period. They suggest that the appearance of both "was nothing less than a deliberate and tendentious imitation of the past culture," in keeping with the cultural memory of the Davidic monarchy.[50] Thus they suggest that the lamps and burials are examples of archaism, similar to the Paleo-Hebrew featured on Hasmonean coinage, helping Judean Jews to create "an 'authentic' ethnic identity rooted in past history."[51]

The strength of Abadi and Regev's argument lies in the confluence of data. The folded lamps sit alongside other examples of archaism in the same period and, moreover, alongside other examples of distinctive material culture that emerge at Hasmonean-aligned locales during the LH period. This strongly suggests that the lamps are part of a broader trend rather than an isolated accident of local style or form.

Stepped Pools (Ritual Baths)

By the ER period, stepped pools designed for full immersion were ubiquitous in Jewish locales. These pools first begin to appear in the LH period, where they are attested at sites in both the north (e.g., Gamla and Keren Naftali) and south (e.g., Jerusalem and Jericho).[52] The stepped pools in question are widely interpreted as ritual baths used for purification and were referred to as מִקְוָאוֹת (*miqwāʾôt*) in rabbinic literature.[53]

The Torah contains injunctions pertaining to washing for ritual purification (Lev. 14:8–9; 15:2–30; 16:23–28; 17:15–16; 22:4–7; Num. 19:9–10, 19; Deut. 23:10–11). However, as Yonatan Adler observes, "There is no reason to assume that in any of these cases the authors or early receivers of these regulations might have had in mind *immersion* in water as the specific method whereby such 'washing' was to be performed."[54] By contrast, Jewish texts from the Hellenistic and Roman periods specifically discuss or describe immersion for ritual purification, often using the Greek term βαπτίζω (*baptizō*; Jdt. 12:7–9; Sir. 34:30; Mark 7:3–4; Luke 11:38; Josephus, *Ant.* 3.263, using καθίημι [*kathiēmi*]). Thus the confluence of the archaeological evidence of the stepped pools and textual evidence of immersion suggests a particular development and widespread reception and practice of the ritual purification rites described in the Torah.

50. Abadi and Regev, "Oil Lamps," 263.

51. Abadi and Regev, "Oil Lamps," 263.

52. The literature on this is extensive. For a recent review, see Yonatan Adler, "The Hellenistic Origins of Jewish Ritual Immersion," *JJS* 69, no. 1 (2018): 7–10.

53. See m. Mikwa'ot.

54. Adler, "Hellenistic Origins," 2–3 (emphasis original).

That these stepped pools reflect behavior particular to Jewish culture and religion in the Second Temple period does not necessarily mean that there is nothing Hellenistic about them or the associated behavior. For example, Adler has argued that Hellenistic hip baths (partial immersion baths introduced to the southern Levant earlier in the Hellenistic period) may have shaped the understanding of washing as immersion in the region and thus may have been precursors to the stepped pools used for ritual immersion by Jews.[55] Magdala-Tarichaea—a Jewish city featuring typical Jewish material culture of the Hellenistic and Roman periods, including Hasmonean coins, stone vessels, Kefar Ḥananyah ware, ritual baths, and a synagogue[56]—also boasted a Hellenistic-style bathhouse. This exemplar suggests that we should not regard Jewish and Hellenistic forms of bathing as dichotomous or incompatible.[57]

Conclusion

Our overview of recent scholarship and current archaeological evidence demonstrates that Judaism and Hellenism should be viewed not as opposite poles but as overlapping, complex categories that are expressed diversely and cannot be essentialized. At the same time, the two should not be completely collapsed into one another. We can identify the diffusion of Greek culture among Jews in the southern Levant and in the diaspora, and we likewise can recognize distinctly Jewish cultural expressions. Nevertheless, Hellenistic qualities do not preclude Jewish ones: that something is Hellenistic does not necessarily mean that it is not also Jewish, and vice versa. This extends to material culture, although more work is required in this area to combat assumptions about what elements can be categorized as Jewish or Hellenistic.

Aspects of Jewish material culture could be and frequently were intertwined with aspects of Hellenistic culture. Jewish identity in antiquity, or any ethnic identity, need not be defined by what it rejects or by something that it defines itself against. It is worth remembering that our literary sources, particularly 1–2 Maccabees, do not situate the revolution solely as a response to Hellenization but as a response to oppression (1 Macc. 1:44–53, 57–61). Although the authors of those texts are admittedly critical of accommodation to forms of Hellenization that they consider to be incompatible with Jewish religious practice and belief, the spark that lit the flame of revolution in the narratives was the oppressive policies enacted by Antiochus IV and not, for example, Jason's reforms (see 2 Macc. 4:7–22). According to 1 Maccabees, Antiochus IV attempted to enforce conformity to Hellenistic norms in order to encourage a unified identity within his kingdom, issuing a decree that "all should be one people, and that all should give up their particular customs" (1 Macc.

55. Adler, "Hellenistic Origins," 15–17.

56. Zapata-Meza et al., "Magdala Archaeological Project," 83–125; Richard Bauckham, "Magdala as We Now Know It."

57. Joseph Scales, "Bathing Jewish, Bathing Greek: Developing an Approach to De-Categorising Hellenism and Judaism," *PEQ* 154, no. 3 (2022): 1–14, esp. 8, 10.

1:41–42). This was accomplished through forced abandonment of Jewish cultural and religious identity and practice (1 Macc. 1:44–53, 57–61). The use of the classical orders of architecture or orthogonal urban planning is not necessarily incompatible with Jewish practice, belief, and identity, but the decree that anyone who holds to the Torah or practices circumcision should be put to death certainly is.

The archaeological record shows that there was never a wholesale rejection of Hellenism, not even by the royal family that led the revolt against Antiochus IV. There was, however, an assertion of the political power and independence that the Hasmonean state represented, as reflected in Hasmonean coinage, the founding of new settlements in Galilee, and royal architecture such as the palaces at Jericho. The concurrent emergence of a distinctively Jewish material culture is not coincidental. These examples simultaneously bear both Jewish and Hellenistic influences and speak to the ongoing incorporation of Hellenistic culture into the emergent Jewish identity of the Hasmonean state.

The current academic discourse could be enriched through further exploration of how factors such as imperialism, coloniality, and class might contribute to our understanding of the relationship between Hellenistic and Jewish material culture. As the culture of the dominant imperial, colonizing power in the region, Hellenism was not politically neutral. The power dynamic at play needs to be considered. Similar work has been done with respect to the Roman period, and perhaps these perspectives could illuminate the Hellenistic period.[58]

One theme of the Jewish material culture that emerges during the LH period is the relationship between certain aspects of that culture and a certain interpretation of Torah. As discussed above, the aniconic Hasmonean coins may reflect a particular understanding of the injunction against graven images (Exod. 20:4; Deut. 5:8). Likewise, the practice of immersion in stepped pools for ritual purification reflects a particular understanding of washing for ritual purity, and the widespread attestation of these pools speaks to an understanding of the wide applicability of the practice for Jews beyond the immediate temple sphere. Thus material culture may serve as a potential avenue for illuminating the reception of Torah and its interpretation. The earliest extant synagogue building in Judea or Galilee, located at Khirbet Umm el-ʿUmdan, dates to the LH.[59] As the place where Torah was read and interpreted publicly,[60] the synagogue enabled the popular spread of Torah and particular interpretations of it. Torah may thus have served as a rallying point for Jewish religious and national identity in this period.[61]

58. Benjamin H. Isaac, *The Limits of Empire: The Roman Army in the East* (Oxford: Clarendon, 1993); David J. Mattingly, *Imperialism, Power, and Identity: Experiencing the Roman Empire* (Princeton: Princeton University Press, 2011).

59. Shlomit Weksler-Bdolah, "Khirbat Umm el-ʿUmdan," *Hadashot Arkheologiyot* 126 (2014), https://www.hadashot-esi.org.il/report_detail_eng.aspx?id=14718&mag_id=121.

60. See Jordan J. Ryan, *The Role of the Synagogue in the Aims of Jesus* (Minneapolis: Fortress, 2017), 39–45; Anders Runesson, *The Origins of the Synagogue: A Socio-Historical Study* (Stockholm: Almqvist & Wiksell, 2001), 193–232.

61. Ryan, "Ideology of Restoration," passim, esp. 48.

8

Archaeology and Israelite Religions

Richard S. Hess

This study focuses on the religion of ancient Israel from its origins until the exile, especially on areas most affected by extrabiblical textual and artifactual materials. A half century ago, in the wake of scholars such as W. F. Albright and Albrecht Alt, one might be forgiven for assuming that the broad contours of Israelite religion were fixed,[1] but the study of Israelite religions has continued to progress since that time. Discoveries and further research have brought about significant transformations in our understanding. This has brought with it the realization that the biblical text can no longer be viewed as providing a sufficiently thorough and nuanced picture of religious life in ancient Israel.

Of course, the biblical text was never intended to be used in this manner. Nevertheless, much of the history of its study has tended to organize extrabiblical texts and artifacts into a set of categories generated by the biblical text. Discoveries such as Kuntillet ʿAjrud defy conceptions of Israelite religion as consisting of only two options: either orthodox faith in one God YHWH as represented by the prophets or the opposing worship of Baal, Asherah, and other deities. Instead, multiple deities and permutations in a variety of Israelite religions captured hearts and minds in the southern Levant.[2]

1. William F. Albright, *Yahweh and the Gods of Canaan: A Historical Analysis of Two Contrasting Faiths* (Garden City, NY: Doubleday, 1968); Albrecht Alt, "The Gods of the Fathers," in *Essays on Old Testament History and Religion*, trans. R. A. Wilson, The Biblical Seminar (Sheffield: Sheffield Academic, 1989), 1–77.

2. John Day, *Yahweh and the Gods and Goddesses of Canaan*, JSOTSup 265 (Sheffield: Sheffield Academic, 2000); Mark S. Smith, *The Early History of God: Yahweh and the Other*

Before Israel

The Middle Bronze Age (MBA) ended ca. 1550 BCE, with a major change in culture occurring in the MBA IIB (early 18th cent.). Mary Buck argues that the Amorite culture at Ugarit and elsewhere appeared in MBA IIB.[3] She identifies several phenomena related to religion.[4] There are some forty theophoric elements found in the names from this region. Divine names frequently found in the Amorite personal names from Alalakh, Mari, and elsewhere include ʾIlu, Haddu, IM (a weather deity), ʿAmmu, ʾAbu, Dagan, Baʿlu, Šamšu/Šapšu/ᵈUTU, Ḥamu, Liʿm, ʾAḫu, Rāpiʾ, and Yaraḥ.[5] Although yielding no MBA texts, the thirteenth-century BCE city of Ugarit has provided us with thousands of LBA texts, and a similarly high distribution of the same names occurs (ʾIlu, Haddu, Baʿlu, Šapšu/ᵈUTU), with the addition of the Hurrian deity Teššub.[6] These divine names are also found in personal names in the fourteenth-century Amarna texts from across the western Levant, omitting the solar deity Šamšu/Šapšu/ᵈUTU.[7] Terms expressing kinship with a deity occur frequently in names from both MBA and Ugarit collections. However, at Ugarit they are limited to immediate relations: *ảb* (father), *ảḫ* (brother), and *ảḫt* (sister). Frequent at Mari but absent at Ugarit are the terms *liʾm* (kin-based extended family), *ḫamu* (father-in-law), and *ḫālu* (maternal uncle). *ʿAmmu* (paternal ancestor) appears in both.[8] Urban Ugarit thus attests to the importance of close family relations, but there is less evidence of connections with the extended family.

The ritual texts from the West Semitic city of Emar along the Euphrates parallel various Levitical rituals: the installation of the high priestess (cf. Exod. 29; Lev. 8–10), the *zukru* festival (cf. Passover and Unleavened Bread), and the half-year ritual calendar (cf. Lev. 23).[9] As an agrarian-based inland city, Emar mirrors the

Deities in Ancient Israel, 2nd ed. (Grand Rapids: Eerdmans, 2003); Ziony Zevit, *The Religions of Ancient Israel: A Synthesis of Parallactic Approaches* (London: Continuum, 2001).

3. Mary E. Buck, *The Amorite Dynasty of Ugarit: Historical Implications of Linguistic and Archaeological Parallels*, Studies in the Archaeology and History of the Levant 8 (Leiden: Brill, 2020).

4. Buck's use of the term "religion" and its identification from a particular analysis of exclusively personal names has been criticized by J. Caleb Howard, "Some of What's New in Amorite Language," in *"Now These Records Are Ancient": Studies in Ancient Near Eastern and Biblical History, Language and Culture in Honor of K. Lawson Younger, Jr.*, ed. James K. Hoffmeier, Richard E. Averbeck, J. Caleb Howard, and Wolfgang Zwickel, ÄAT 114 (Münster: Zaphon, 2022), 213–42.

5. Buck, *Amorite Dynasty*, 250.

6. Buck, *Amorite Dynasty*, 253, citing W. H. van Soldt, "Divinities in Personal Names at Ugarit," in *Ras Shamra-Ougarit 24*, ed. V. Matoïan and M. Al-Maqdissi (Paris: Peeters, 2016), 95–108, esp. 100–101.

7. Richard S. Hess, *Amarna Personal Names*, American Schools of Oriental Research Dissertation Series 9 (Winona Lake, IN: Eisenbrauns, 1993), 233–42.

8. Frauke Gröndahl, *Die Personennamen der Text aus Ugarit*, Studia Pohl 1 (Rome: Papal Biblical Institute, 1967), 109.

9. Respectively, Emar texts 369, 373, and 446. See Richard S. Hess, *Israelite Religions: An Archaeological and Biblical Survey* (Grand Rapids: Baker Academic, 2007), 112–22. For the

agrarian-based inland world of ancient Israel, and its ritual texts offer important comparative material to accompany the myth and ritual texts from the urban international trading city-state of Ugarit. These two cities are contemporary with the earliest traditions of Israel as a nation, sharing a common West Semitic background, so evidence of similar religious emphases is not surprising. Unique in Israel, however, are both the historical/narrative significance of the festivals (e.g., Passover's association with the exodus) and the connection of ethics with religion, something found elsewhere in the West Semitic world only in the laws at Hazor (*COS* 4:87D).

The continued publication and study of MBA texts from Mari and LBA texts from Ugarit illuminate many aspects of pre-Israelite West Semitic religion and provide windows into the earliest world of Abram and his family. For example, the eighteenth-century Mari letters indicate that Harran, the biblical home of Abram and Laban, was a sacred center for the Binu Yamina (cf. Benjamin) tribal coalition. One text records how the tribal leaders killed a donkey and swore an oath of alliance in the temple of the moon god Sin at Harran.[10] Among the mythological and ritual texts from Ugarit, the example of RIH 98/02 provides the first identification in West Semitic literature of the goddess ʿAṯtartu (Astarte/Ashtoreth) with leonine imagery. Specifically, her name appears in parallel with *lbʾi* (lion).[11] This lyric poem also represents one of many MBA and LBA attestations of music performance as part of the cult. The ritualists mimicked the actions of the deities as seen in the iconography of the nineteenth-century BCE Beni Hassan depiction of an Asiatic lyre player; the royal procession with the lyre player on the Megiddo LBA ivory plaque;[12] the discovery of cymbals, rattles, and clay drums in cultic contexts; and the mention of singers, cymbalists, lyre players, flute players, and drum players in Ugarit ritual contexts.[13]

An important MBA text from southern Canaan is the Tell er-Rumeide tablet. This fragment records the presence of a king and of sacrifices (sheep, lambs, and possibly goats) made in a cultic context, presumably at the site identified with ancient Hebron (*COS* 4:77). The presence of a possible Hurrian personal name,

---

calendar of Emar 446, see Bryan C. Babcock, *Sacred Ritual: A Study of the West Semitic Ritual Calendars in Leviticus 23 and the Akkadian Text Emar 446*, JSOTSup 9 (Winona Lake, IN: Eisenbrauns, 2014).

10. The oath was sworn along with an alliance of four towns in the Balikh River basin. Cf. ARM 26 24, lines 10–12; Daniel E. Fleming, "Genesis in History and Tradition: The Syrian Background of Israel's Ancestors, Reprise," in *The Future of Biblical Archaeology: Reassessing Methodologies and Assumptions*, ed. James K. Hoffmeier and Alan Millard (Grand Rapids: Eerdmans, 2004), 193–212, esp. 217.

11. Dennis Pardee, "A Preliminary Presentation of a New Ugaritic Song to *ʿAṯtartu* (RIH 98/02)," in *Ugarit at Seventy-Five*, ed. K. Lawson Younger Jr. (Winona Lake, IN: Eisenbrauns, 2007), 27–39, lines 1–2 of the text.

12. See Hess, *Israelite Religions*, 138, for a drawing of the plaque.

13. Matthew Susnow, *The Practice of Canaanite Cult: The Middle and Late Bronze Ages*, ÄAT 106 (Münster: Zaphon, 2021), 215.

Inti, suggests an international cultural connection. The religious picture is not unlike that of the Hebron near where Abram and his family lived, as described in Gen. 12–25.[14]

YHWH the Name

Both El and YHWH appear as the chief deity in Israel. Although ʾIlu (El) is clearly the name of the pantheon head at Ugarit, the distinction between this divine name and the title *ʾil* ("god," related to the more common biblical אֱלֹהִים [*ʾĕlōhîm*]) is unclear. Nevertheless, most scholars accept the origins of the name Israel with אֵל (*ʾēl*) as the final element on the name. Further, the name YHWH is seen as secondary. Early poetic texts such as Exod. 6:3, Deut. 32:8–9, and Ps. 82 may attest that YHWH was originally one of El's pantheon who somehow became the leader. Sometimes related to this is the theory that the name YHWH was originally an Amorite verbal form (*yahwî*) added to El as a verbal epithet to identify El as living, giving life, or creating.[15]

Austin Surls argues that the appearance of the divine name in Exod. 3 and 6 was a wordplay using a largely unobtainable etymology of the name YHWH.[16] After surveying the later evidence, he concludes that the pronunciation was also uncertain (though probably not Yahweh). Examining Exod. 3:13–15; 6:2–8; 33:12–23; and 34:5–7, Surls argues for a gradual revelation of the character of God as represented by the divine name. This climaxes in Exod. 34:6–7, where YHWH is prepared to forgive his rebellious covenant people who have repented. Surls tries to understand the revelation of the divine name to Israel within the final form of Exodus.

Daniel Fleming takes a different approach. While some assume that the divine name was brought by an outside (and southern) group that influenced Israel to accept it, he argues that it is best understood as a personal name rather than part of a verbal sentence attached to a divine ancestor.[17]

14. Richard S. Hess, "Second-Millennium BC Cuneiform from the Southern Levant and the Literature of the Pentateuch," in *Exploring the Composition of the Pentateuch*, ed. L. S. Baker Jr. et al., BBRSup 27 (University Park, PA: Eisenbrauns, 2020), 66–72. In addition to what is described in this section, Andrew George and Mandred Krebernik ("Two Remarkable Vocabularies: Amorite-Akkadian Bilinguals," *RA* 116, no. 1 [2022]: 113–66) have published ca. 18th cent. BCE texts that are housed in private collections in New York and London. Related to early West Semitic religion are the names of ten Amorite deities, Amorite blessings from a god, and phrases on giving sacrifices.

15. William F. Albright, "Contributions to Biblical Archaeology and Philology," *JBL* 43, no. 3/4 (1924): 363–93; Albright, *Yahweh and the Gods of Canaan*; Frank Moore Cross, *Canaanite Myth and Hebrew Epic* (Cambridge, MA: Harvard University Press, 1973).

16. Austin Surls, *Making Sense of the Divine Name in Exodus: From Etymology to Literary Onomastics*, BBRSup 17 (Winona Lake, IN: Eisenbrauns, 2017), esp. the summary on 182–84.

17. Daniel E. Fleming, *Yahweh before Israel: Glimpses of History in a Divine Name* (Cambridge: Cambridge University Press, 2021).

Theodore Lewis's massive study on the origin and character of God devotes a chapter to the origin of the name and presence of YHWH.[18] Following the position of Albright and Frank Moore Cross, Lewis argues that Israel originated with the worship of El as their chief deity. Much later, YHWH became prominent, and his name was inserted into earlier accounts. Lewis considers the fourteenth-century Egyptian mention of the "Shasu of *yh(w)* [= Yhwꜣ]" and the eighth-century appearance of personal names at the Syrian site of Hamath that bear a possible Yahwistic suffix as bona fide elements related to YHWH.[19] While it is unlikely that the name Azri-Yau from Hamath would appear as Idri-Yau in Aramaic,[20] the three attested occurrences of this name do not demonstrate the presence of YHWH as a major deity in Hamath.

Lewis also discusses the Midianite hypothesis. Among its various forms, the theory argues that YHWH originated in the southern desert of Paran, Edom, and Sinai and is connected with Reuel/Jethro/Hobab, the father-in-law of Moses and possible priest of YHWH, who introduced this deity to his son-in-law and then to all Israel. The threefold name of Moses's father-in-law suggests some disjunction in the biblical sources. Lewis overstates the biblical account when he claims that Num. 31 requires the annihilation of all Midianites, as opposed to those involved in Baal Peor and the subsequent battle.[21] However, the discussion of Moses's father-in-law and its problems are well presented. Moses's mother, Jochebed, possesses a uniquely Yahwistic name, the only one in Exodus other than Joshua (who is given a Yahwistic name by Moses in Num. 13:16). This argues against YHWH's revelation of himself to Moses first and only through Midianite traditions as conveyed by Jethro. Genesis 49:3 demonstrates the special role of Reuben, whose tribe is southernmost in Transjordan and through whom Yahwistic traditions may have come from the south. In particular, Midianite trading caravans may have moved through this region (cf. Gen. 37:28) and carried knowledge of YHWH. Of interest are the relevant texts of Judg. 5, Ps. 68, Deut. 33, Hab. 3, and Kuntillet ʿAjrud. All these recite the march of YHWH from the south as warrior and storm god. Lewis finds references to this past event by translating the imperfect verbs in Exod. 15:15–16 as past tense. This is more likely a prophecy of how the neighboring peoples will respond to YHWH's victory over Egypt in the exodus (cf. the language in Rahab's confession presented as occurring decades later, Josh. 2:9–11). Thus, the reality of YHWH's presence and salvation is rooted in the historical past, present, and future experiences of Israel, not merely in a mythical past.

18. Theodore J. Lewis, *The Origin and Character of God: Ancient Israelite Religion through the Lens of Divinity* (Oxford: Oxford University Press, 2020), 209–86.

19. Cf. Richard S. Hess, "The Divine Name Yahweh in Late Bronze Age Sources?," *UF* 23 (1991): 181–88.

20. Cf. K. Radner, ed., *The Prosopography of the Neo-Assyrian Empire, 1/I: A Neo-Assyrian Text Corpus Project* (Helsinki: University of Helsinki, 1998), 240, who cites four other non-Israelite, non-Judean bearers of this name (Azri) from Syria and Mesopotamia.

21. Lewis, *Origin and Character*, 272–73.

The strength of Lewis's arguments and their connection with past scholarship make this reconstruction more convincing. However, Fleming's model provides a welcome challenge to the long-standing idea of a foreign presence introducing YHWH and his worship into Israel in Canaan. Surls positions the divine name in the canonical context of Exod. 3, 6, and 34, while Fleming redirects our attention to its development from a personal name to a divine name within the Israelite community. Lewis returns to the connection made earlier by Albright and Cross in which YHWH replaced El in various biblical sources.

YHWH the Warrior

YHWH's early appearance also provides a connection with the warrior role of leading West Semitic gods. Some of the earliest biblical poetry is often dated to the early Iron Age and, with it, the presence of the picture of YHWH as a warrior in the ANE tradition of the warrior deity. Lewis points to the inscription of King Mesha of Moab (mid-9th cent. BCE).[22] Mesha recognized that his deity Chemosh was angry with the Moabites and thus allowed Israel to oppress them. Chemosh called Mesha to go to battle and saved him from enemy kings. The deity restored Moab's cities. Mesha uses the root חרם (*ḥrm*) to describe how he devoted the war booty from Israel and the cultic items of YHWH to Chemosh. In thirteenth-century Ugarit, this type of warfare is associated with ʿAnat (*KTU* 1.13.3–7). The South Arabian Sabaean text RES 3945 mentions how the city of Nashan is devoted as *ḥrm* by burning it for the moon god Almaqah. Another early Sabaean text, DAI Ṣirwāḥ 2005-50, mentions cities devoted in this manner. Lewis compares Joshua's assault on Jericho. YHWH gives similarly worded orders to Joshua, the army, and the priests (Josh. 5:13–6:26). While the Mesha stele commemorates the building of cult places, as does Josh. 8:30–31, the biblical text also emphasizes intercessory prayer, fasting, and sacrifice (Judg. 20:26; 1 Sam. 7:5–11; 13:9, 12).

Closer to Israel, texts from Aleppo and Ugarit betray similar themes of the Chaoskampf (cosmic war). The artists of Aleppo portray the lord of Aleppo, their storm god, riding on a chariot pulled by a bull. In the Ugaritic Baal myth, Baal fights Sea (Yammu) and Death (Motu). Baal defeats Sea, who also appears under the names of Litanu and Tunnanu, a dragon of many heads. He has victory with the assistance of the divine artisan Koṯar-wa-Ḫasis. ʿAṯtartu provides incantations that scatter or dry up Yammu. ʿAnat, the warrior goddess, also defeats Sea and later assists with Motu. In the Bible, YHWH appears as a warrior deity fighting on a cosmic scale, with enemies of similar names (Yam, Leviathan, Rahab, Tannin, and Mot), and on a national level (alongside Israelite troops).

22. Lewis, *Origin and Character*, 427–73.

Early Israel

The warrior role of YHWH at the beginning of Israel's history also coincides with the contemporary appearance of the earliest archaeological evidence of distinctive cult sites in and around Israel. The first two hundred years of the Iron Age (ca. 1200–1000 BCE) saw the disappearance of great Bronze Age civilizations, such as the Hittites and the city-state of Ugarit. While some states such as Egypt remained, the appearance of new "mobile pastoralist" groups such as Israel, Aram, and the Philistines created a new world, especially in southern Canaan. Many cult centers continued in population centers, with architecture and objects similar to the LBA. At Iron I Hazor, a stone pavement in Area B included a tall, curved basalt standing stone (מַצֵּבָה, *maṣṣēbâ*). From this position one could gaze down on the ruins of the great LBA cult site, which had been violently destroyed in fire. Similar standing stones appear in dozens of clusters in the Negev and, in many cases, are dated by carbon 14 to more than five thousand years ago. Also, in the Negev, in the Timna Valley, a shrine to the Egyptian god Hathor was built and maintained during the copper mining in the region. After the departure of Egypt in the mid-twelfth century, the shrine was adapted by locals (perhaps connected with the biblical traditions of Midianites). A copper snake (cf. Num. 21) was found there as well as pieces of red and yellow cloth. The latter indicate a tent shrine, perhaps not unlike the biblical tabernacle (Exod. 25–30; 35–40).[23]

Two early Iron I cult sites in the Israelite hill country differ from a mere continuation of LBA-type sites. The first is the Bull Site east of Dothan.[24] The site has an oval-shaped low wall, a standing stone, and a bronze statue of a bull. It is close to a few villages and might be their center of worship. This Iron I site does not give evidence of sacrifice. Thus this stone may not have been worshiped. Lewis identifies Israelite El as the best candidate for the bull, although YHWH or Baal are possible contenders.[25]

A second site is the altar installation on Mount Ebal's third highest peak, away from the ridge. Adam Zertal excavated this site in the 1980s, and Ralph Hawkins provides the most extensive study.[26] Zertal identified two levels, the first forming an ashpit and the second a structure of fieldstones over the ashpit, which was filled with dirt and animal bones. There were other stone installations, and the

23. Richard S. Hess and Denys Pringle, "Sacred Spaces and Holy Places," in *The Oxford Illustrated History of the Holy Land*, ed. Robert G. Hoyland and H. G. M. Williamson (Oxford: Oxford University Press, 2018), 317–51, esp. 320–21.

24. For a summary, see Robert Mullins, "Bull Site," in *Encyclopedia of the Bible and Its Reception* (Berlin: De Gruyter, 2012), 4:590–92.

25. Lewis, *Origin and Character*, 200–202. Daniel E. Fleming, "If El Is a Bull, Who Is a Calf? Reflections on Religion in Second-Millennium Syria-Palestine," *ErIsr* 26 (1999): 23*–27*; William G. Dever, *Beyond the Texts: An Archaeological Portrait of Ancient Israel and Judah* (Atlanta: SBL Press, 2017), 178.

26. Ralph K. Hawkins, *The Iron Age I Structure on Mt. Ebal: Excavation and Interpretation*, BBRSup 6 (Winona Lake, IN: Eisenbrauns, 2012).

whole area was surrounded by a temenos wall. Pottery and two scarabs dated the ashpit to ca. 1250–1200 BCE and the later stratum to ca. 1200–1150. The more than twenty-seven hundred animal bones were largely sheep, goats, cattle, and a small percentage of fallow deer, but no pig bones. The absence of customary farm implements and donkey bones, as well as the absence of nearby occupation, suggests that this was neither a farm nor a watchtower. Its role as a public outdoor cult center is enhanced by the sizable, adjacent area that could have accommodated thousands of people. Unlike other LBA cult sites, however, no traditional cultic objects (e.g., figurines) appear. If this Mount Ebal complex is a cult center, it evokes the aniconic worship of Israel's "orthodox" Yahwistic cult and relates to the nation's earliest recorded worship in the hill country (Josh. 8:30–35).

The Hathor temple site, the Bull Site, and Mount Ebal preserve examples of a tent sanctuary in the desert, a bronze bull image, and a single altar of fieldstones. These suggest, for example, people in and around the hill country at the time of Israel's appearance there, who used a tent/tabernacle (Exod. 25–30; 35–40), compared a bull to their deity (Ps. 106:19–20), and used fieldstone altars (Exod. 20:25–26).

Israel's Monarchy

The tabernacle and elements of Israelite worship come together at the time of the monarchy, especially in Solomon's Temple. The period from around 1000 BCE until Babylon's destruction of Jerusalem and its temple in 586 (archaeologically Iron II and III) leaves no direct evidence for the architecture of Solomon's Temple. However, the tenth-century temple at ʿAin Dara in northern Syria closely resembles its layout. The structure had three parts, corresponding to the outer court, holy place, and holy of holies. Surrounding the structure and attached to it were multistory rooms for storage (cf. 1 Kings 6:5, 10), something found only here and in Solomon's Temple. Significantly, giant footprints carved into the stone entrance suggest a divine figure some sixty-five feet in height entering the temple.[27] To the west, at Tell Tayinat along the Orontes River, a temple was excavated where a vassal treaty with the Assyrian overlord Esarhaddon (680–669 BCE) was found, the first physical evidence of such preservation of treaties in temples by the vassal (cf. Deut. 31:26).[28]

A tenth-century cult stand at Taanach features important religious iconography. The "front" side portrays images in four panels. The bottom panel shows

27. John Monson, "The New ʿAin Dara Temple: Closest Solomonic Parallel," *BAR* 26, no. 3 (2000): 20–35, 67. On the larger context of a divine "body," see Mark S. Smith, "The Three Bodies of God in the Hebrew Bible," *JBL* 134, no. 3 (2015): 471–88.

28. Jacob Lauinger, "Esarhaddon's Succession Treaty at Tell Tayinat: Text and Commentary," *JCS* 64 (2012): 87–123; Timothy P. Harrison and James F. Osborne, "Building XVI and the Neo-Assyrian Sacred Precinct at Tell Tayinat," *JCS* 64 (2012): 125–43.

a nude female between two lions. Ugaritic leonine imagery identifies Astarte with lions, which may also be true of Asherah. The second panel has a space left intentionally empty and flanked by two sphynx or cherubs, calling to mind the aniconic YHWH in the Jerusalem temple. The third panel exhibits a tree flanked by two ibex, who are then flanked by two lions. The lions appear identical to the first panel and may suggest that the tree is a symbol of the goddess. The top panel may have at its center a calf or a horse with a winged sun disk over top and columns flanking the image. Is this a symbol of the calves that Jeroboam I constructed for the worship of YHWH at Bethel and Dan? Or is it reminiscent of the horses dedicated to the sun and kept in the Jerusalem temple (2 Kings 23:11)? In either case, the association with the aniconic deity, YHWH, creates an alternating set of images on the four panels: goddess/YHWH/goddess/YHWH.[29] If so, who is the goddess?

The site of Kuntillet ʿAjrud was discovered in the northeastern Sinai desert.[30] It appears to be a caravansary, a way station overlooking trade and pilgrimage routes, used in the ninth century BCE. It includes an entry room with benches containing votive gifts of pottery with images and inscriptions. Writing and drawings appear on the plastered walls. While the various images are much discussed, with some key figures likely identified as the Egyptian god Bes, the various texts mention Baal, YHWH, and Asherah. YHWH is given two epithets: YHWH of Samaria and YHWH of Teman. Several blessings join YHWH and "Asherah" or "his Asherah." While the form of the word "Asherah" is debated, it is best interpreted as the goddess "Asherah/Asherata" rather than "his Asherah."[31] These ancient "authors" believed that YHWH had a consort, just as ʾIlu at Ugarit had Asherah and other Iron Age pantheons had consorts for their chief male deities. YHWH and Asherah are similarly connected in a Khirbet el-Qom inscription from southern Judah. Many preexilic Hebrew texts mention only YHWH, but some connect these two deities, including perhaps the Taanach cult-stand artist.

Throughout Iron II, the sanctuary at Dan was active. Although groups of standing stones at various places inside and outside the gate to Dan may witness to other religious activity, the main sanctuary at the city's highest point seems to have prominently displayed a huge altar (based on one of the altar horns found there) and a place at the northern end for display of an image, such as the gold calf erected by Jeroboam I (1 Kings 12:28–29). The location and prominence suggest a state-supported cult site.

A significant part of the fort of Arad, along the southern boundary of Judah, was set aside for a three-part sacred space. The outer court contained a single

29. This is not the only interpretation of the panels. See the discussion and photo in Hess, *Israelite Religions*, 321–24.

30. The full publication of the site, drawings, and inscriptions is Ze'ev Meshel, *Kuntillet ʿAjrud (Ḥorvat Teman): An Iron Age II Religious Site on the Judah-Sinai Border* (Jerusalem: Israel Exploration Society, 2012).

31. Richard S. Hess, "Asherah or Asherata?," *Orientalia* 65 (1996): 209–19.

altar of fieldstones (like the one at Ebal; cf. Exod. 20:25–26). The middle court was a smaller, broad room accessed only from the outer court and provided a small closet-sized holy of holies at the opposite end. With three steps and two incense altars, one wonders whether there were two standing stones or a single stone here. Or were these pieces lintels for the entrance to this sacred spot? Correspondence between the leader of this fort and his commander in Jerusalem, which was found at the gate, mentions a "house of YHWH." This refers either to the Jerusalem temple or to the structure at Arad.[32]

Four and a half miles west of Jerusalem, a large cultic site was uncovered at Tel Moẓa. With figurines, some five standing stones (מַצֵּבָה, *maṣṣēbâ*), and other paraphernalia associated with temples of various deities, the site's purpose is unclear. It may have been one of the more prominent "high places" condemned by the prophets, and yet it remained active until such high places were partially eliminated by Hezekiah (2 Kings 21:3) and completely eliminated by Josiah (cf. 23:5–19).

This last point raises the issue of when belief in one deity began in Judah and especially the question of the reforms of Josiah. Nathan MacDonald argues that layers of redaction lasted well into the exilic period, one of which introduced the concept of the "book" that Josiah found; these redactions significantly modified an earlier monotheistic perspective or perhaps introduced it entirely.[33] On the other hand, I argue that the reforms of 2 Kings 23 fit well into the late seventh century, and I do not see a difficulty with the discovery of a "book" that invigorated such a reform. For example, the destruction of the Asherah pole at Bethel in 23:15 clearly reflects the syncretism there of YHWH and his consort, Asherah. The biblical silence regarding this heterodox "YHWH" preserved the prophetic view that no other deities could be mentioned alongside YHWH. This is more likely under Josiah and less likely in the exilic/postexilic period, when memories of these syncretisms, especially at a northern Israelite site such as Bethel, dimmed.[34]

The cult of Judah (and Israel) had its priest and other officiants. Women also exercised a role in the cult. Biblical mentions of Hannah at Shiloh, the Queen of Heaven cult, Micah's mother and her divine image, the cultic practices of Solomon's wives, female prophets (e.g., Miriam, Deborah, Huldah, the unnamed woman of Isa. 8:3), and necromancers (1 Sam. 28) reveal that women participated in both Yahwistic and non-Yahwistic activities. While female priests are not known in Israel or Ugarit, there was a female priestess at thirteenth-century BCE Emar and a fifth-century BCE Phoenician priestess of Astarte. Lewis reviews

32. On Dan, Arad, and other contemporary sites, see Hess, *Israelite Religions*, 297–307.

33. Nathan MacDonald, "Did Josiah Enact a Monotheistic Reform?," in *Conversations on Canaanite and Biblical Themes: Creation, Chaos, and Monotheism*, ed. R. S. Watson and A. H. W. Curtis (Berlin: De Gruyter, 2022), 151–75.

34. Richard S. Hess, "Belief in One God in Preexilic Judah?," in Watson and Curtis, *Conversations on Canaanite and Biblical Themes*, 135–50. Additional discussion between the two authors appears in subsequent responses in the book.

the arguments against cultic prostitution in ancient Israel.[35] The much-discussed Hebrew קְדֵשָׁה (*qədēšâ*) may have been a noncultic prostitute or a temple officiant who was not a prostitute but polemically portrayed as such. Phyllis Bird suspects that these were not necessarily prostitutes but rather unmarried women dependent on the temple or cult center with which they were affiliated.[36]

Starting in the eighth century BCE, the inscriptions and the personal names that contain divine names mention YHWH almost exclusively.[37] The meanings of the names suggest that YHWH was worshiped through personal names, with qualities of grace, mercy, and salvation that have no parallel in the naming practices or inscriptional material found in neighboring states.[38] Something special was going on in Judah.

Naming practices introduce the important topic of family religion. Of the many aspects, notable are the pillar figurines and burials, especially in eighth- and seventh-century Judah until 586 BCE. In that period, many hundreds of pillar-based female figurines appear within (but rarely outside) Judah. Made of clay, naked from the waist up, and having either a face or simply a pinch of clay, these mass-produced images do not suggest the lavish attention given to a chief deity. Rather, they may be minor or middle-tier deities (so Erin Darby), votive objects, or symbols of prayers for giving birth and lactation.[39]

Burials were generally unvarying in Israel and Judah during the Iron Age. The bench tomb became popular in Jerusalem and throughout Judah, to the point

35. Lewis, *Origin and Character*, 668–70.

36. Phyllis A. Bird, *Harlot or Holy Woman? A Study of Hebrew* Qedešah (University Park, PA: Eisenbrauns, 2019). For the various biblical roles of female diviners, see Esther J. Hamori, *Women's Divination in Biblical Literature: Prophecy, Necromancy, and Other Arts of Knowledge* (New Haven: Yale University Press, 2015).

37. For inscriptions, see Shmuel Aḥituv, *Echoes from the Past: Hebrew and Cognate Inscriptions from the Biblical Period*, trans. Anson F. Rainey (Jerusalem: Carta, 2008); Peter Bekins, *Inscriptions from the World of the Bible: A Reader and Introduction to Old Northwest Semitic* (Peabody, MA: Hendrickson Academic, 2020). For personal names and analysis, see Rainer Albertz and Rüdiger Schmitt, *Family and Household Religion in Ancient Israel and the Levant* (Winona Lake, IN: Eisenbrauns, 2012). This resource does not evaluate the names diachronically. See Richard S. Hess, review of R. Albertz and R. Schmitt, *Family and Household Religion in Ancient Israel and the Levant*, *BBR* 23, no. 4 (2013): 565–68.

38. Jeaneane D. Fowler, *Theophoric Personal Names in Ancient Hebrew: A Comparative Study*, JSOTSup 49 (Sheffield: Sheffield Academic, 1988); Richard S. Hess, "Aspects of Israelite Personal Names and Pre-exilic Israelite Religion," in *New Seals and Inscriptions, Hebrew, Idumean and Cuneiform*, ed. M. Lubetski, HBM 8 (Sheffield: Sheffield Phoenix, 2007), 301–13; Hess, "Deities in the Ammonite Personal Names," in Hoffmeier et al., "*Now These Records Are Ancient*," 177–82. The Ammonite onomastica are closest to Judah as a contemporary neighbor with many similar names.

39. Hess, *Israelite Religions*, 308–11; Erin D. Darby, *Interpreting Judean Pillar Figurines: Gender and Empire in Judean Apotropaic Ritual*, FAT 2/69 (Tübingen: Mohr Siebeck, 2014); Darby, "Sex in the City? Judean Pillar Figurines and the Archaeology of Jerusalem," in *Iron Age Terracotta Figurines in the Southern Levant in Context*, ed. Erin D. Darby and Izaak J. de Hulster, CHANE 125 (Leiden: Brill, 2021), 178–214; Beth Alpert Nakhai, "Response to Darby and Deutsch," in Darby and de Hulster, *Terracotta Figurines*, 215–19.

of exclusive use after the eighth century BCE. After the body decomposed on the stone bench(es) in the tomb, the bones were collected and deposited with the remains of other deceased family members in the recesses of the same tomb. The discovery of eating and drinking plates and bowls in the tombs evokes the question of purpose, whether to feast in some way with one's deceased family or to feed them (cf. Deut. 26:14), but it is not possible to know with certainty.[40]

Ketef Hinnom, a group of tombs on the west side of the Hinnom Valley, was excavated by Gabriel Barkay. Written parts of the blessing of Aaron (Num. 6:24–26) and possibly Deut. 7:9 were discovered on two small silver scrolls. Dated ca. 600 BCE, with the actual writing of the scrolls predating this by some decades, these tombs preserve the earliest known textual material from the HB.[41] They witness to the continuity between this period and the exclusive worship of YHWH in the postexilic world of those returning after 539 BCE.

The vast array of inscriptional and archaeological evidence from Iron II and III point to the emergence of biblically approved shrines (especially Solomon's Temple and its similarities to temples at ʿAin Dara and Tell Tayinat) and heterodox centers (at Tel Dan, Tel Moẓa, Tel Arad, and possibly Kuntillet ʿAjrud). Naming practices, inscriptions (e.g., at Khirbet el-Qom and Ketef Hinnom), figurines, and burial practices provide examples of the worship of various deities alongside a gradual emergence of texts that, by the end of this period, witness to worship of YHWH with characteristics similar to those found in the HB.

The Exile

The important cuneiform records of Al-Yahudu, Našar, and other Babylonian Jewish communities record the lives of the deportees from Judah. More than one hundred cuneiform documents dating through the sixth and fifth centuries BCE have been published, testifying to a vibrant community whose names remained Yahwistic, continuing worship of the God of Israel there and among the fifth-century returnees who rebuilt the temple and resumed worship in Jerusalem.[42]

40. For the archaeology, see Elizabeth Bloch-Smith, *Judahite Burial Practices and Beliefs about the Dead*, JSOTSup 123 (Sheffield: Sheffield Academic, 1992). For a biblical perspective, see Philip S. Johnston, *Shades of Sheol: Death and Afterlife in the Old Testament* (Downers Grove, IL: InterVarsity, 2002). For expansion of the "cult" of caring for dead kin, see Kerry M. Sonia, *Caring for the Dead in Ancient Israel*, ABS 27 (Atlanta: SBL Press, 2020). Scholars continue to debate whether the biblical sacrifices of children were to Molech or YHWH. See Heath D. Dewrell, *Child Sacrifice in Ancient Israel*, Explorations in Ancient Near Eastern Civilizations 5 (Winona Lake, IN: Eisenbrauns, 2017). For an alternative view of the biblical texts, see Hess, *Israelite Religions*, 102, 132, 257–59, 293; for the undoubted existence of the West Semitic deity Malik in personal names, cf. G. C. Heider, *The Cult of Molek: A Reassessment*, JSOTSup 43 (Sheffield: JSOT, 1985).

41. Gabriel Barkay et al., "The Amulets from Ketef Hinnom: A New Edition and Evaluation," *BASOR* 334 (2004): 41–71.

42. Laurie E. Pearce and Cornelia Wunsch, *Documents of Judean Exiles and West Semites in Babylonia in the Collection of David Sofer*, CUSAS 28 (Bethesda, MD: CDL, 2014). Cf.,

That temple was understood by the writers of the postexilic texts of Haggai and Zechariah, as well as Ezra and Nehemiah of the fifth century, as a restoration and continuation of the preexilic worship, now devoid of polytheism or syncretism with other deities.

Conclusion

As we have seen, the Kuntillet ʿAjrud inscriptions changed the understanding of religions in Iron II and III of ancient Israel. Further study and the publication of texts from Mari, Emar, Ugarit, and southern Levant sites such as Tell er-Rumeide have revealed religious deities that the ancestors of Israel encountered and many types of religious practices already hinted at in Genesis that provide close comparisons with elements of Leviticus and Deuteronomy. The emergence of the name YHWH forms a unique part of early Israel's faith and worship, as do his role as a warrior on behalf of his people, the descriptions of tent structures for worship, altars of fieldstones, and the contrast with forbidden images such as bulls. Solomon's Temple fits well in the tenth century BCE, just as the later shrines, figurines, cult stands, and other imagery and texts witness to competing and syncretistic worship forms. Burial practices demonstrate special care for the dead, just as female and male cultic roles are suggestive of non-Israelite religious practices. The personal names with confessional elements about YHWH, as well as texts both religious (e.g., Ketef Hinnom's priestly blessing texts) and nonreligious (e.g., letters from Arad), bear witness to a unique emphasis on a single deity, YHWH, and his kindness and mercy. The emphasis continues and becomes solely devoted to YHWH during the exile. Research continues as new discoveries of texts, sites, and artifacts bring to light possibilities for expanding understanding of the diverse religious life of ancient Israel.

e.g., W. G. Lambert, "A Document from a Community of Exiles in Babylonia," in Lubetski, *New Seals and Inscriptions*, 201–5.

9

Biblical Iconography

Brent A. Strawn

> Biblical iconography . . . needs to be viewed as an additional and corrective tool to traditional text-oriented historical-critical biblical studies.
>
> Angelika Berlejung[1]

Iconography refers to the study of visual material or to the visual data that are the object of such study. After an account of the origins of iconography and its application to the study of ancient Israel and the HB, I discuss some of the main achievements in previous research with regard to theory, method, and practice. I conclude with a case study on the imprecatory psalms in light of iconography.

Situating Biblical Iconography among the Disciplines

Iconography is part of, if not coterminous with, the academic study of art. When applied to the study of ancient Israel and the biblical text, iconography becomes a meeting place of three discrete but related areas of inquiry: art history, archaeology, and exegesis.

I am grateful for the input I received from several students: Matt Arakaky, Victor Knight IV, Jon Mansen, Imhotep Newsome, Isabel Packevicz, and Caleb Punt.

1. Angelika Berlejung, "Methods," in *T&T Clark Handbook of the Old Testament: An Introduction to the Literature, Religion and History of the Old Testament*, ed. Jan Christian Gertz et al. (London: T&T Clark, 2012), 55.

Art history encompasses art from all human history. The "story of art" begins with prehistoric wall paintings, the earliest of which date to the Upper Paleolithic period (50,000–12,000 years BP), and with three-dimensional objects like the Lion-man of Hohlenstein-Stadel and the Venus of Willendorf that date to the same horizon (figs. 9.1–2).[2]

Art history, then, includes art from the "biblical world," a convenient term to describe the regions and periods pertinent to the Bible, its history, and its analysis. The biblical world may be defined as the ANE (including Egypt) from the advent of writing (late 4th or early 3rd mill. BCE) through the Hellenistic and Roman periods.[3] The biblical world represents only a small piece of the history of art but encompasses a large swath of time and territory and, as a result, offers a vast number of archaeological finds.

Archaeology is the study of human antiquity, involving careful excavation, documentation, and interpretation of evidence from ancient human habitation.[4] Archaeological investigation uncovers great amounts of data including, not infrequently, art. Analysis of ancient art with the tools of art history properly comes *after* archaeologists excavate materials from antiquity. Since artistic media come in a host of forms—sculpture, paintings, architecture, and the like—iconography is related to the study of "materiality," a term used for how people interact with various material objects.[5]

Figure 9.1. Lion-man from the Stadel Cave in Hohlenstein; mammoth ivory; 12.2 inches high (41,000–45,000 years BP)
Photograph by Dagmar Hollmann / CC BY-SA 4.0 / Wikimedia Commons

Archaeology and art history have been around for quite some time, as has the attempt to use archaeological discoveries to help understand the biblical world. The combination of these disciplines and their joint employment with reference to the Bible is a more recent development. "Biblical

2. E. H. Gombrich, *The Story of Art* (London: Phaidon, 2006), 36–60.

3. Silvia Schroer and Othmar Keel, *Die Ikonographie Palästinas/Israels und der Alte Orient: Eine Religionsgeschichte in Bildern*, Die Ikonographie Palästinas/Israels und der Alte Orient 1 (Fribourg: Academic Press, 2005); Annette Weissenrieder, Friederike Wendt, and Petra von Gemünden, eds., *Picturing the New Testament: Studies in Ancient Visual Images*, WUNT 2/193 (Tübingen: Mohr Siebeck, 2005).

4. Cynthia Shafer-Elliott, ed., *The 5 Minute Archaeologist in the Southern Levant* (Sheffield: Equinox, 2016); Suzanne Richard, ed., *Near Eastern Archaeology: A Reader* (Winona Lake, IN: Eisenbrauns, 2003).

5. Manfred Oeming, *Contemporary Biblical Hermeneutics: An Introduction*, trans. Joachim F. Vette (Burlington, VT: Ashgate, 2006), 49–54; Alice Mandell and Jeremy Smoak, "The Material Turn in the Study of Israelite Religions: Space, Things, and the Body," *JHebS* 19, no. 5 (2019): 1–43; Angelika Berlejung, ed., *Encyclopedia of Material Culture in the Biblical World* (Tübingen: Mohr Siebeck, 2022); Ishaq al-Hroub, *Atlas of Palestinian Rural Heritage*, trans. Khalid Amayreh, ed. Thomas Staubli (Bethlehem: Diyar, 2015).

iconography" synthesizes what has been unearthed archaeologically and analyzed artistically, applying it to ancient Israelite literature, with *exegesis*, the disciplined study of textual data, as a third component. Biblical iconography, sometimes called "iconographic exegesis,"[6] can be categorized within historical-critical approaches because it is especially, though not exclusively, concerned with the original author(s) and first audience(s) of a text within its ancient context(s). Attention to a text's earliest context(s) means iconography is also related to comparative approaches in at least two ways. First is the comparison of a visual image to/with a written text—a comparison that is intrinsic to iconographic exegesis but rarely, if ever, easy.[7] Second, iconography often requires cross-cultural comparison of one image with images from other cultures.[8]

One final matter of classification deserves mention: insofar as iconographic exegesis has frequently focused on metaphors and other instances of figurative language, it also benefits from literary and theological approaches.[9]

Figure 9.2. Venus of Willendorf; limestone with red ochre; 4.4 inches high (25,000 years BP)
Photograph by Thirunavukkarasye-Raveendran / CC0 / Wikimedia Commons

Origins of Biblical Iconography

The pioneer of the study of ANE iconography and the Bible is Othmar Keel. His work *Die Welt der altorientalischen Bildsymbolik und das Alte Testament*

6. Izaak J. de Hulster, Brent A. Strawn, and Ryan P. Bonfiglio define iconographic exegesis as "an interpretive approach that explains aspects of the Hebrew Bible with the help of ancient Near Eastern visual remains" ("Iconographic Exegesis: Method and Practice," in *Iconographic Exegesis of the Hebrew Bible/Old Testament: An Introduction to Its Method and Practice*, ed. Izaak J. de Hulster, Brent A. Strawn, and Ryan Bonfiglio [Göttingen: Vandenhoeck & Ruprecht, 2015], 20). Silas Klein Cardoso calls it "an umbrella term for interartistic comparative practices correlating biblical texts and ancient images" ("The Genesis of Iconographic Exegesis," *CurBR* 21 [2023]: 179).

7. Ryan P. Bonfiglio, *Reading Images, Seeing Texts: Towards a Visual Hermeneutics for Biblical Studies*, OBO 280 (Fribourg: Academic, 2016).

8. Brent A. Strawn, "Comparative Approaches: History, Theory, and the Image of God," in *Method Matters: Essays on the Interpretation of the Hebrew Bible in Honor of David L. Petersen*, ed. Joel M. LeMon and Kent Harold Richards, RBS 56 (Atlanta: Society of Biblical Literature, 2009), 117–42.

9. Klein Cardoso, "Genesis of Iconographic Exegesis," 182; Martin Klingbeil, *Yahweh Fighting from Heaven: God as Warrior and as God of Heaven in the Hebrew Psalter and Ancient Near Eastern Iconography*, OBO 169 (Fribourg: University Press, 1999); William P. Brown, *Seeing the Psalms: A Theology of Metaphor* (Louisville: Westminster John Knox, 2002); Brent A. Strawn, *What Is Stronger than a Lion? Leonine Image and Metaphor in the Hebrew Bible and the Ancient Near East*, OBO 212 (Fribourg: Academic, 2005).

inaugurated a new field of study and has achieved classic status.[10] Keel urged biblical scholars to "see through the eyes of the ancient Near East" with the help of ancient visual remains.[11] Before Keel's work, there had been countless art historical investigations, and an equally large number of archaeological explorations had been offered; Keel's genius was in bringing those two things together and employing them in tandem to better understand the book of Psalms. The psalms had been subjected to careful exegetical analysis numerous times prior to *Symbolism*, but by including hundreds of images with his analysis, Keel made a new dataset available. Instead of depending solely on one's own imagination or on analogous textual data when encountering a literary image in a psalm, one could and *should*, Keel argued, compare artistic depictions from the ANE. What we imagine in our own modern mind's eye is one thing, but if one is interested in the original context(s), the real question is What did *the ancients* imagine? The artistic record "compels us," Keel wrote, to see with ANE eyes, thus correcting our own often myopic and mistaken imaginations.[12] Iconography provides access to *ancient* eyes and *ancient* imaginations, to nothing less than ancient cognition.[13]

For example, the Psalms mention God's wings no less than six times (Pss. 17:8; 36:7; 57:1; 61:4; 63:7 [36:8; 57:2; 61:5; 63:8 MT]; 91:4). In ANE iconography, we find hundreds of images of wings, including images of winged deities (figs. 9.3–5).[14] Such images help us "see" what ancient people would have envisioned as the wings of God.

Keel went on to produce a series of monographs in which he refined his approach with reference to many different texts (and genres) in the HB, in the process inspiring a generation of students in Switzerland and beyond.[15] As many pioneers do, Keel tended to focus on the primary evidence (images and texts) and did

10. Translated into English as Othmar Keel, *The Symbolism of the Biblical World: Ancient Near Eastern Iconography and the Book of Psalms*, trans. Timothy J. Hallett (New York: Seabury, 1978).

11. Keel, *Symbolism*, 8.

12. Keel, *Symbolism*, 8.

13. Brent A. Strawn, "The Iconography of Fear: *Yir'at YHWH* (יראת יהוה) in Artistic Perspective," in *Image, Text, Exegesis: Iconographic Interpretation and the Hebrew Bible*, ed. Izaak J. de Hulster and Joel M. LeMon, LHBOTS 588 (London: Bloomsbury, 2014), 91–134; Brett E. Maiden, *Cognitive Science and Ancient Israelite Religion: New Perspectives on Texts, Artifacts, and Culture*, SOTSMS (Cambridge: Cambridge University Press, 2020), 133–76; Justin Walker, *The Power of Images: The Poetics of Violence in Lamentations 2 and Ancient Near Eastern Art*, OBO 297 (Leuven: Peeters, 2022).

14. Joel M. LeMon, *Yahweh's Winged Form in the Psalms: Exploring Congruent Iconography and Texts*, OBO 242 (Fribourg: Academic, 2010).

15. Brent A. Strawn, "Introduction: Othmar Keel, Iconography, and the Old Testament," in Othmar Keel, *Jerusalem and the One God: A Religious History*, ed. Brent A. Strawn (Minneapolis: Fortress, 2017), xxv–xlii; Izaak J. de Hulster, *Illuminating Images: An Iconographic Method of Old Testament Exegesis with Three Case Studies from Third Isaiah* (Utrecht: Universiteit Utrecht, 2007), 21–164; Klein Cardoso, "Genesis of Iconographic Exegesis," 178–217.

Figure 9.3. Glazed tile of Tukulti Ninurta II; 28 cm high (888–884 BCE)
LeMon, Yahweh's Winged Form, 97, fig. 1.4 (used by permission)

Figure 9.4. Relief from Tell Halaf (9th cent. BCE)
Strawn, *What Is Stronger?*, 471, fig. 4.213; cf. LeMon, *Yahweh's Winged Form*, 110, fig. 3.27

not always take time to explain his methodology.[16] It fell largely to his academic offspring to articulate a method for biblical iconography. Even then, advances in methodological technique were typically achieved, not in the abstract, but in the course of studies devoted to particular texts and images.

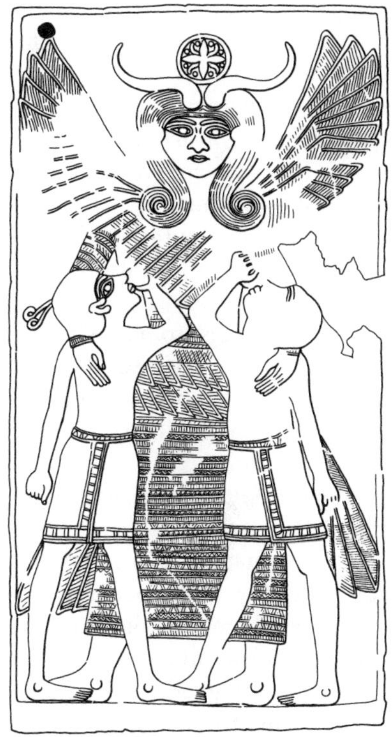

Figure 9.5. Ivory relief from Ugarit; LBA IIB; Middle Syrian
LeMon, *Yahweh's Winged Form*, 166, fig. 7.1 (used by permission)

The Theory, Method, and Practice of Biblical Iconography

The application of iconography ideally involves attention to *theory* (the rationale for what is done), *method* (how it is to be done), and *practice* (what is, in fact, done). Keel's own work, and much of what followed, has been dominated by practice, no doubt with an operative but unexpressed method and underlying theory. Until recently, methodological discussions and theoretical reflections have been rare in biblical iconography, though from the outset Keel expressed concerns over "a double fragmentation."[17] This problem, Keel acknowledges, is inherent to his approach in *Symbolism*, which sought "not only to offer illustrative material, but also to confront this material, picture by picture, with the texts of the biblical book."[18] Keel stages these confrontations around six major themes: conceptions of the cosmos, destructive forces, the temple, conceptions of God, the king, and the human being before God. Figure 9.6 illustrates Keel's method and the fragmentation problem. Keel "confronts" this image with two different psalms, which he included under the image as a kind of caption:

> Joseph's feet hurt in his shackles;
>   his neck was in an iron collar. (Ps. 105:18 CEB)

16. Klein Cardoso, "Genesis of Iconographic Exegesis," 180, 185; Othmar Keel, "*Minima methodica* und die Sonnengottheit von Jerusalem," in *Iconography and Biblical Studies: Proceedings of the Iconography Sessions at the Joint EABS/SBL Conference, 22–26 July 2007, Vienna, Austria*, ed. Izaak J. de Hulster and Rüdiger Schmitt, AOAT 361 (Münster: Ugarit-Verlag, 2009), 213–24.

17. Klein Cardoso, "Genesis of Iconographic Exegesis," 182.

18. Keel, *Symbolism*, 12.

> Some of the redeemed had been sitting in darkness and deep gloom;
> they were prisoners suffering in chains. (Ps. 107:10 CEB)[19]

In his accompanying discussion of this image, Keel claims that "prisoners were often bound by iron fetters on the hands, neck, or feet. . . . Under such conditions, escape from misery was inconceivable."[20]

The connections forged by juxtaposing these two verses with this image reasonably merit Keel's more discursive comment. The problem of double fragmentation is that this type of "confrontation" presents (1) only a portion of a psalm (usually just a verse or two) selected from a larger, integral whole and (2) selectively excerpted images from larger artistic tableaus. In Keel's own words, "A problem arises the moment one examines the psalms from a thematic point of view, for each psalm represents a whole which is fragmented by systematic-thematic treatment. The same often holds true of ancient Near Eastern pictures and their context."[21]

To his credit, Keel recognizes this problem and knows that debate over texts and images will be ongoing. At the same time, his approach has real merit, and "the advantages of this procedure are obvious: in a thematic arrangement, one picture or one psalm verse can illustrate another, and a positive overall impression can be obtained."[22] The "positive overall impression" results from setting image with text and text with image and does "not merely . . . present objective facts" but also "explore[s] fundamental orders and religious propositions."[23]

Iconographic exegesis is a matter not simply of illustration but of illumination, of applying an interpretive lens. The image-text engagement is generative, not merely illustrative. This is particularly true given the nature of ANE art, which was "not intended to be viewed, like paintings of nineteenth- or twentieth-century European art (*Sehbild*), but rather to be read (*Denkbild*)."[24] A *Sehbild* (visual image) is designed to be seen as an artistic object; a *Denkbild* (mental picture), by contrast, is meant to be thought. Ancient Egyptian depictions of the pharaoh, for instance, are not akin to

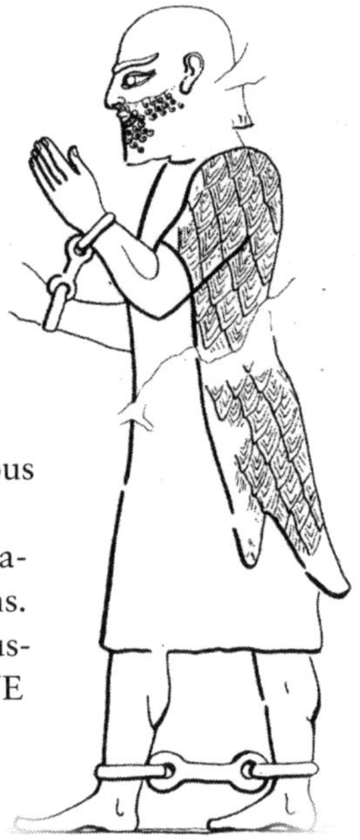

Figure 9.6. Portion of relief from Khorsabad, Hall VIII, 18; reign of Sargon II (721–705 BCE)
Keel, *Symbolism*, 70, fig. 77 (used by permission)

19. Keel, *Symbolism*, 70, fig. 77.
20. Keel, *Symbolism*, 69.
21. Keel, *Symbolism*, 12.
22. Keel, *Symbolism*, 12.
23. Keel, *Symbolism*, 12.
24. Keel, *Symbolism*, 7.

modern portraiture or contemporary photographs. While some representations may be taken concretely (e.g., commemorating a specific battle), most appear to portray a larger, more abstract idea (e.g., "the conquest of an enemy"), which may not have happened historically but which communicates a generalized or universalized principle nevertheless.[25] It appears that images, no less than animals, per a well-known line from Claude Lévi-Strauss, are "good to think" (*bonnes à penser*).[26]

Symbolism demonstrated the numerous advantages of an iconographic approach. In subsequent work, Keel refined his approach, eventually writing a full commentary on the Song of Songs to counter the issue of literary fragmentation.[27] He also addressed the problem of artistic fragmentation, arguing for the importance of the entire work of art, not just excerpts, because "the original message" and "purpose" of these works "was not the illustration of perceptual material culture, but of concepts like divine rule, world order, kingship and the gods,"[28] and so forth. Keel paid special attention to minor art: the thousands of stamp seals and other small objects bearing images from archaeological excavations in ancient Israel/Palestine.[29] Publishing a complete catalog of all these seals has been the focus of his most recent research.[30] The minor art is important for several reasons, including its mobility: seals functioned in antiquity as the equivalent of modern mass media.[31] Another advantage of minor art is that, unlike large, complex depictions, its imagery can be seen and grasped as a whole. Given their small size and often dense composition, seals allowed Keel and his fellow researchers to address iconographic constellations (how certain images appear with and relate to others)

25. Keel, *Symbolism*, 9.

26. Claude Lévi-Strauss, *Totemism* (Harmondsworth: Penguin, 1969), 162, cited in Maiden, *Cognitive Science*, 133.

27. Othmar Keel, *The Song of Songs*, trans. Frederick J. Gaiser, Continental Commentary (Minneapolis: Fortress, 1994); Keel, *Deine Blicke sind Tauben: Zur Metaphorik des Hohen Liedes*, Stuttgarter Bibelstudien 114/115 (Stuttgart: Katholisches Bibelwerk, 1984).

28. Othmar Keel, "Iconography and the Bible," *ABD* 3:369.

29. Klein Cardoso, "Genesis of Iconographic Exegesis," 182–85; Allison Karmel Thomason, "The Impact of the 'Portable': Integrating 'Minor Arts' into the Ancient Near Eastern Canon," in *Critical Approaches to Ancient Near Eastern Art*, ed. Brian A. Brown and Marian H. Feldman (Boston: De Gruyter, 2014), 133–58.

30. Othmar Keel, *Corpus der Stempelsiegel-Amulette aus Palästina/Israel: Von den Anfängen bis zur Perserzeit; Einleitung*, OBO.SA 10 (Fribourg: Academic, 1995); Keel, *Corpus der Stempelsiegel-Amulette aus Palästina/Israel: Von den Anfängen bis zur Perserzeit*, 5 vols. to date (Fribourg: Fribourg University Press / Academic, 1997–); Jürg Eggler and Othmar Keel, *Corpus der Siegel-Amulette aus Jordanien: Vom Neolithikum bis zur Perserzeit*, OBO.SA 25 (Fribourg: Academic, 2006); Keel, *700 Skarabäen und Verwandtes aus Palästina/Israel: Die Sammlung Keel*, OBO.SA 39 (Leuven: Peeters, 2020).

31. Othmar Keel and Christoph Uehlinger, *Altorientalische Miniaturkunst: Die ältesten visuellen Massenkommunikationsmittel; Ein Blick in die Sammlungen des Biblischen Instituts der Universität Freiburg Schweiz*, 2nd ed. (Freiburg: Universitätsverlag Freiburg, 1996); Klein Cardoso, "Genesis of Iconographic Exegesis," 183.

and visual grammar or syntax (how images, especially in their interrelation, communicate messages).[32]

More than thirty years after the publication of Keel's seminal work, LeMon returned to the problem of literary fragmentation, offering a study focused on Psalms. Building on Brown's notion of iconic structure, "the various ways particular images and metaphors interact in the text,"[33] LeMon showed how an entire psalm and the totality of its imagery could be analyzed and compared with ANE iconography.[34] Having a sense of the iconic structure of an entire psalm meant that there was both more and less to use in comparison with the artistic record. There was *less* to compare in the sense that the image-to-text comparison did not traffic in the disconnected (i.e., fragmented) pieces of a psalm and/or possibly related images. Yet there was *more* to compare because the various parts were now seen to operate in service to a whole psalm, thus permitting a more productive text-image assessment, what LeMon called the "congruence" between psalm and picture.[35] Such congruence is rarely, if ever, one to one, however. Typically, several iconographic tropes help to assess the iconic structure of any given psalm.[36]

LeMon delineates three types of iconographic pursuits:

- the *iconographic-artistic* approach, which is art historical in nature with attention to diachronic developments;
- the *iconographic-historical* approach, which considers the historical relevance or pertinence of the artistic data; and
- the *iconographic-biblical* approach, which looks at how iconography informs the reading of the biblical text.[37]

It is not always easy to separate these three approaches from each other, nor is it always desirable or advisable to do so. Iconographic study should pay attention to the artistic aspects of an object (iconographic-artistic), analyses of ancient art are irreducibly historical (iconographic-historical), and artistic and historical investigations have real import when they intersect with the biblical world and its texts (iconographic-biblical).

32. On the other hand, the small size of the seals not infrequently complicates their interpretation, not least because the tableaus they contain are often devoid of the more fulsome details present in larger works. See, e.g., Brent A. Strawn, "The Human Being before God: The Iconography of Worship (and Prayer) after Keel's *Symbolism* and Keel's *Corpus*, with a Focus on Jerusalem" (forthcoming).

33. Brown, *Seeing the Psalms*, 14.

34. LeMon, *Yahweh's Winged Form*, esp. 16–17, 21–22, 24, and 73–74.

35. LeMon, *Yahweh's Winged Form*, 24. Bonfiglio, *Reading Images*, 69–89, has expanded the discussion to include image-text *congruence*, *correlation*, and *contiguity*. See also de Hulster, Strawn, and Bonfiglio, "Iconographic Exegesis," 22–32.

36. LeMon, *Yahweh's Winged Form*, 192.

37. LeMon, *Yahweh's Winged Form*, 8–16; LeMon, "Iconographic Approaches: The Iconic Structure of Psalm 17," in LeMon and Richards, *Method Matters*, 143–68.

Another breakthrough book—*Gods, Goddesses, and Images of God in Ancient Israel*—is a case in point.[38] Keel and Christoph Uehlinger set out to write a history of Israelite religion based on the iconographic record, with minimal recourse to textual material. The iconographic-historical approach adopted here is thoroughgoing, but the authors cannot avoid using biblical and epigraphic texts along the way. This is neither a critique nor a demerit; rather, this is exactly as it should be. Iconography is not art history alone: it is art history coupled with archaeology and exegesis, at least when the iconography is of the biblical variety. The larger point is that the same author can produce analyses that fall into one or more of LeMon's approaches. Images and texts can and properly do go together in the interpretation of either. In this way, even if Keel and Uehlinger's book cannot fully escape some dependence on textual evidence, it nevertheless serves as a crucial corrective to text-only approaches. In their words,

> Anyone who systematically ignores the pictorial evidence that a culture has produced can hardly expect to recreate even a minimally adequate description of the culture itself. Such a person will certainly not be able to describe the nature of the religious symbols by which such a culture oriented itself. . . . In our opinion, the sadly neglected pictorial evidence from Canaan and Israel must be treated as being equally important as textual evidence, offering its own unique type of information.[39]

Gods, Goddesses, and Images of God is considerably removed from Keel's *Symbolism*. The earlier work of Keel and the Fribourg School is thoroughly iconographic-biblical and exegetically driven; the later work is iconographic-historical, archaeologically driven, and concerned with origins, dating, and probable lines of influence. Although Keel has remained equally dexterous, there are nevertheless two primary sides to his work. These two sides can be diachronically mapped. The "early Keel" of *Symbolism* is comfortable with wide-scale phenomenological comparisons concerned with "fundamental orders and religious propositions."[40] The "later Keel" (and his circle) presses for more precision about the artistic remains undergoing analysis, a process often pursued independently of any overt interest in biblical interpretation.

Even so, the "later Keel" did not forsake the study of the HB. Even his most decidedly nontextual, or *a*-textual, studies engage textual evidence, especially the Bible. This holds true for *Gods, Goddesses, and Images of God* and also for Keel's work on the seal corpus or on the history of Jerusalem.[41] The development has been toward ever more precision, with great attention to matters

38. Othmar Keel and Christoph Uehlinger, *Gods, Goddesses, and Images of God in Ancient Israel*, trans. Thomas H. Trapp (Minneapolis: Fortress, 1998).

39. Keel and Uehlinger, *Gods, Goddesses, and Images of God*, xi.

40. Keel, *Symbolism*, 12; Klein Cardoso, "Genesis of Iconographic Exegesis," 182–83; Walker, *The Power of Images*, 1–33.

41. For the former, see n. 30 above; for the latter, see Keel, *Jerusalem and the One God*; and, most extensively, Keel, *Die Geschichte Jerusalems und der Entstehung des*

of chronological proximity and geographical propinquity, matters important in comparative analysis more generally.[42]

Much has transpired in the fifty years since Keel inaugurated biblical iconography, and not all developments fall within the iconographic-historical approach. Several iconographic exegetes have paid attention to the metaphorical language used in the HB. Since metaphorical language is a subset of figurative language and often imagistic, it is ripe for analysis with *visual* images and figures. Other developments in biblical iconography include the following.

1. Several iconographic studies map onto other types of biblical exegesis. Eleanor Beach attempts to align iconography with form criticism,[43] and recent works relate iconographic exegesis to translation, textual criticism, literary analysis, emotion studies, social-historical analysis, and more.[44]

2. Some scholars have returned to aspects of the phenomenological approach found in the "early Keel" but do so informed by advances in iconographic-historical approaches.

3. Iconographic exegesis has benefited from increased attention to visual culture studies. Visual culture studies may be differentiated from art history by the fact that the former considers any manner of object as worthy of visual analysis. A society's visual culture includes things that many moderns would likely not regard as art, certainly not well-executed art. Further, visual culture studies assign as much importance to viewers' reception of objects, including religious objects, as to the intention of the one who produced it.[45] What an artist *meant* is one thing, but what (and how) their work *means* to viewers thereafter is another thing, and these do not necessarily align.

4. Since ancient visual remains are testimony to ancient ways of thinking, iconography has begun to engage with cognitive science in intriguing ways.[46] Art

---

Monotheismus, 2 vols., Orte und Landschaften der Bibel IV/1 (Göttingen: Vandenhoeck & Ruprecht, 2007).

42. Strawn, "Comparative Approaches," 118–29.

43. Eleanor Ferris Beach, "Image and Word: Iconology in the Interpretation of Hebrew Scriptures" (PhD diss., Claremont Graduate School, 1991).

44. See, e.g., de Hulster, Strawn, and Bonfiglio, *Iconographic Exegesis*; M. Justin Walker, "Samson's Lion Encounter (Judges 14:5–6) and Persian Period Leonine Iconography," *VT* 72 (2022): 769–820 (source/composition criticism); Michael J. Chan, *The Wealth of Nations: A Tradition-Historical Study*, FAT 2/93 (Tübingen: Mohr Siebeck, 2017) (tradition history).

45. Bonfiglio, *Reading Images*, 171–310; David Freedberg, *The Power of Images: Studies in the History and Theory of Response* (Chicago: University of Chicago Press, 1989); David Morgan, *The Sacred Gaze: Religious Visual Culture in Theory and Practice* (Berkeley: University of California Press, 2005).

46. Strawn, "Iconography of Fear"; Strawn, "'Mischmetaphors': (Re-)Presenting God in Unusual and Sophisticated Ways," in *Image as Theology: The Power of Art in Shaping Christian Thought, Devotion, and Imagination*, ed. C. A. Strine, Mark McInroy, and Alexis Torrance, Arts and the Sacred 6 (Turnhout: Brepols, 2021), 19–54; Maiden, *Cognitive Science*, 133–76; Walker, *Power of Images*, 12–20.

is a way of thinking that is composed of mental images, so (ancient) images, no less than (ancient) texts, are sites of (ancient) meaning-making.[47]

5. As a result of these developments, recent iconographic studies consider other ways of comparing images and texts beyond their surface content. Are there ways to compare how meaning is made in these distinct forms: the picture and the word? The answer would seem to be yes, and such an endeavor is nothing less than an exercise in comparative poetics.[48]

More could be added to this list.[49] The major observation is that the study of iconography is now "an almost self-sufficient intellectual domain."[50] Iconography thus warrants further attention and more studies that benefit from and contribute further to its already considerable results.

A Case Study: The Iconography of Imprecation

A case study may be helpful in bringing together several of the strands mentioned above. The imprecatory, or cursing, psalms are known for their vitriolic comments about enemies (e.g., Pss. 58, 79, 83, 94, 109, and 137). A full list is difficult to finalize, because enemy curses are found in psalms not normally considered imprecatory (e.g., Pss. 5:5–6, 9–10; 12:3–4; 41:10).[51] For instance, Ps. 139 celebrates the watchful care of God and ends in imprecation before making a final appeal to God.

47. Rudolf Arnheim, *Visual Thinking*, 35th anniversary ed. (Berkeley: University of California Press, 2004); Steven Pinker, ed., *Visual Cognition* (Boston: MIT Press, 1986); Stephen Kosslyn, William Thompson, and Giorgio Ganis, *The Case for Mental Imagery* (Oxford: Oxford University Press, 2006).

48. Walker, *Power of Images*; Walker, "Historical Narrativity in the Song of the Sea (Exodus 15:1–18) and the Throneroom Reliefs of Ashurnasirpal II," *HeBAI* 13 (2024): 105–33; Brent A. Strawn, "*Ut pictura poesis*: The Historical Psalms and the Reliefs from Ashurnasirpal II's Throneroom in the Northwest Palace at Nimrud," in *Architecture, Iconography, and Text: New Studies on the Northwest Palace Reliefs of Ashurnasirpal II*, ed. J. Caleb Howard, OBO 301 (Leuven: Peeters, 2023), 139–80.

49. Urs Winter, *Frau und Göttin: Exegetische und ikonographische Studien zum weiblichen Gottesbild im Alten Israel und in dessen Umwelt*, 2nd ed., OBO 53 (Fribourg: Universitätsverlag, 1987); Thomas Staubli and Silvia Schroer, *Body Symbolism in the Bible* (Collegeville, MN: Liturgical Press, 2001); Staubli and Schroer, *Menschenbilder der Bibel* (Stuttgart: Patmos, 2014); Silvia Schroer, ed., *Images and Gender: Contributions to the Hermeneutics of Reading Ancient Art*, OBO 220 (Fribourg: Academic, 2006); Brian C. DiPalma, "Intersections between Iconographic and Gendered Approaches to Biblical Interpretation," *BibInt* 25 (2017): 430–41; Shawna Dolansky, "Interpreting Iconography: A Polysemic and Multivalent Approach to Understanding Judean Pillar Figurines," in *Epigraphy, Iconography, and the Bible*, ed. Meir Lubetski and Edith Lubetski, HBM 98 (Sheffield: Sheffield Phoenix, 2021), 137–71; Brady Beard, "Seeing Visions with the Prophet: Toward an Iconographical Hermeneutic of Joel" (PhD diss., Emory University, 2023).

50. Klein Cardoso, "Genesis of Iconographic Exegesis," 195.

51. Trevor Laurence, *Cursing with God: The Imprecatory Psalms and the Ethics of Christian Prayer* (Waco: Baylor University Press, 2022).

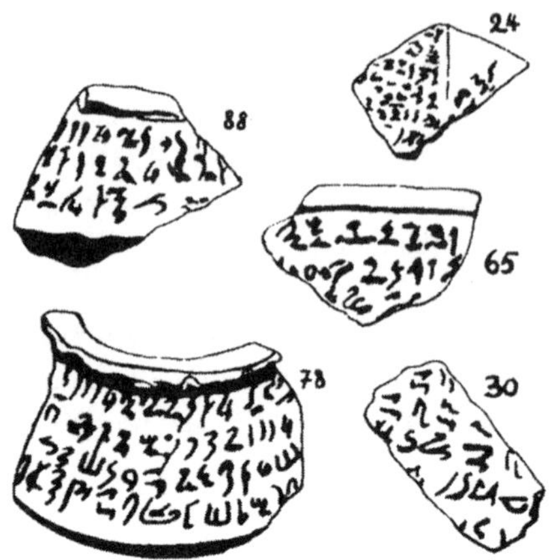

Figure 9.7. Potsherds from Thebes; Dynasties 11–13 (2052–1770 BCE)
Keel, *Symbolism*, 267, fig. 359 (used by permission)

Figure 9.8. Clay statuette; 33 cm high; Saqqara; Dynasties 12–13 (1991–1770 BCE)
Keel, *Symbolism*, 267, fig. 360 (used by permission); cf. *ANEP* 196, no. 593

If only, God, you would kill the wicked!
If only murderers would get away from me—
the people who talk about you, but only for wicked schemes;
the people who are your enemies,
who use your name as if it were of no significance.
Don't I hate everyone who hates you?
Don't I despise those who attack you?
Yes, I hate them—through and through!
They've become my enemies too. (Ps. 139:19–22 CEB)

How might this text be illuminated by iconography?

We might begin, broadly, with various ANE ritual activities related to cursing one's enemies. Actions include burning a witch's effigy or substitution rituals that enact or displace divine punishment on someone other than the one performing the rite.[52] This pattern is "especially visible" (!), according to Kenton Sparks, in the Egyptian execration texts, a genre attested from the Old Kingdom through the Roman era.[53] These texts curse adversaries by, first, writing the enemies' names on various types of media—red pots, for example, or clay figurines—and second, smashing them. Thousands of potsherds with names (fig. 9.7) and broken figurines of bound prisoners with inscribed names have been recovered (fig. 9.8). A New Kingdom relief shows Amenhopis III "shattering the red pots" (*sd dšrwt*) before

52. Kenton L. Sparks, *Ancient Texts for the Study of the Hebrew Bible* (Peabody, MA: Hendrickson, 2005), 180, 185.

53. Sparks, *Ancient Texts*, 185; Stephen J. Seidlmayer, "Execration Texts," *OEAE* 1:487–89.

Figure 9.9. Relief from Luxor Temple, Room XVII, interior of east wall, second register; Amenophis III (1413–1377 BCE)
Keel, *Symbolism*, 266, fig. 357a (used by permission)

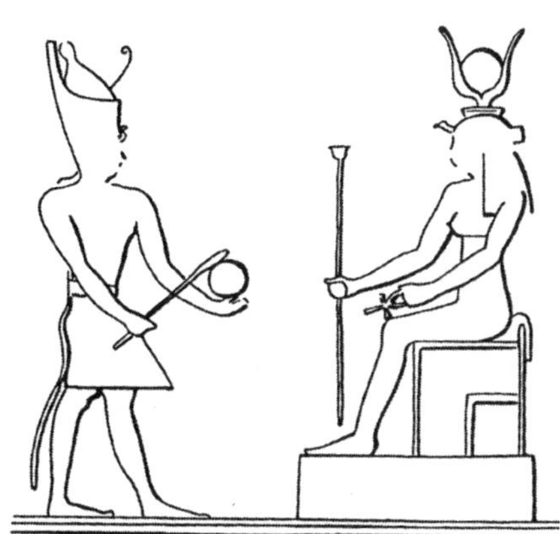

Figure 9.10. Relief from Edfu Temple, exterior east wall of the naos (237–57 BC)
Keel, *Symbolism*, 267, fig. 358 (used by permission)

a deity (fig. 9.9); another, later relief represents Apophis, the enemy of the sun, ritually smashing a clay globe in the presence of the goddess Hathor (fig. 9.10).[54]

The listing of enemy names in the execration texts was highly formalized, including mention of Nubians, Asiatics, Libyans, living and/or deceased Egyptians, and other hostile rulers or forces. These texts contain no explicit curses, just lists of enemy names, sometimes accompanied by the "rebellion formula" (a generic mention of all who might rebel with the named enemies); it is the ritual breaking itself that constitutes or enacts the curse.[55] Biblical scholars have found traces of execration rites in Jer. 19:1–13 and notably Ps. 2, where the Lord says to the anointed king,

> Just ask me, and I will make the nations your possession;
> the far corners of the earth will be your property.
> You will smash them with an iron rod;
> you will shatter them like a pottery jar. (Ps. 2:8–9 CEB)[56]

54. Keel, *Symbolism*, 266–67.

55. The act of smashing, figs. 9.9–10 notwithstanding, is not found in the execration texts proper but is nevertheless part of a visual-culture-studies approach to these broken pots and figurines, engaging viewers as further testimony to the complex interaction of art and viewer. W. J. T. Mitchell, *What Do Pictures Want? The Lives and Loves of Images* (Chicago: University of Chicago Press, 2005); David Morgan, *Images at Work: The Material Culture of Enchantment* (New York: Oxford University Press, 2018).

56. Keel, *Symbolism*, 268; cf. Choon-Leong Seow, *Ecclesiastes: A New Translation with Introduction and Commentary*, AB (New York: Doubleday, 1997), 381–82, on Eccles. 12:6.

Another route into the imprecatory psalms and the iconographic record considers the dynamics of prayer. The enemies in the imprecatory psalms are never merely the psalmist's own enemies; they are ultimately *God's* enemies.[57] This is captured with remarkable clarity in Ps. 139:21–22:

> Don't I hate everyone who hates *you*?
> Don't I despise those who attack *you*?
> Yes, I hate them—through and through!
> *They've become my enemies too.* (CEB, emphasis added)

This dynamic means that the cry for vengeance is most basically a cry for divine justice.[58] Imprecatory prayers function rhetorically to urge God's involvement, to align divine purpose with the plight of the imperiled psalmist because the problem is God's. Such cries also align the psalmist with God and God's purposes. In this prayer dynamic, a harmony is achieved between God and the psalmist, which is no doubt what allows the poet to conclude:

> Examine me, God! Look at my heart!
> Put me to the test! Know my anxious thoughts!
> Look to see if there is any idolatrous way in me,
> then lead me on the eternal path! (Ps. 139:23–24 CEB)

Divine scrutiny is possible, even welcomed, because in the dynamics of imprecatory alignment, the praying self and the divine self are united in concern over the wicked and their ways.

This same dynamic seems apparent, artistically, on a seventh-century silver bowl from Cyprus (fig. 9.11). LeMon has likened the center image of this bowl, which depicts a winged anthropomorphic deity fighting a lion, to the presentation of YHWH in Ps. 17. The iconic structure of that psalm depicts God as "a winged anthropomorphic deity, encountering enemies in the form of lions . . . [who] dispatches these lion-enemies with his sword in a brutal and efficient manner (v. 13)."[59] LeMon then shows that such a constellation is found "with relative frequency in seventh-century Cypro-Phoenician art."[60] That is, despite figure 9.11's origin in Cyprus, its style evidences Phoenician and Mesopotamian influence, along with Egyptianizing elements, indicating that it belongs to a larger ANE artistic tradition.[61]

57. Erich Zenger, *A God of Vengeance? Understanding the Psalms of Divine Wrath*, trans. Linda M. Maloney (Louisville: Westminster John Knox, 1996), 71–72; Brent A. Strawn, "Who's Afraid of the Old Testament? Tough Texts for Rough Times," in *The Oxford Handbook of the Bible in Orthodox Christianity*, ed. Eugen J. Pentiuc (Oxford: Oxford University Press, 2022), 539–55.

58. Zenger, *God of Vengeance?*, 66–67.

59. LeMon, *Yahweh's Winged Form*, 107.

60. LeMon, *Yahweh's Winged Form*, 107.

61. Glenn Markoe, *Phoenician Bronze and Silver Bowls from Cyprus and the Mediterranean*, University of California Publications in Classical Studies 26 (Berkeley: University of California Press, 1985), 40–41, 46–47.

Following LeMon's analysis, one might consider the constellation(s) of the entire bowl and map the bowl's iconic structure. Several image clusters on the three registers seem particularly important and interrelated. First, the central medallion depicts the divine figure in hand-to-hand combat with a lion, about to thrust it through with a sword. Behind and above an Assyrian four-winged genie are two Horus falcons in protective postures. The divine figure is clearly the victor over the lion, which represents a real threat by means of its rampant posture, extended paws, and open mouth. No matter: the divine sword is about to pierce this lion's heart. The danger posed by the lion is also in the second, next-inmost register. In two constellations, the lion encounters human, not divine, figures. In the first scene, directly above the central medallion, a lion strides right over a prone figure, with its paw on the head of its human victim. Moving counterclockwise, another scene shows a lion on top of a doubled-over human figure, only this time the animal is confronted from both directions by armed individuals (an

Figure 9.11. Silver bowl (Cy8); Kourion, Cyprus (7th cent. BCE)
Strawn, *What Is Stronger?*, 472, fig. 4.214; cf. LeMon, *Yahweh's Winged Form*, 107, fig. 3.21

archer and a spearman), who apparently attempt a rescue (cf. Amos 3:12). There is no indication of an arrow meeting its target (indeed, the bowstring appears still taut), but the spear appears to almost make contact with the lion's mouth.[62] Finally, on the outmost register are three additional scenes of domination. In the first, directly above the central medallion, "a hero in Assyrian garb" slays a rampant griffin in a posture quite like that of the Assyrian four-winged genie.[63] Moving clockwise, an Egyptian pharaoh is depicted smiting a cluster of enemy captives. Behind Pharaoh is an attendant with fan, spear, and a dead body; in front of Pharaoh is the god Re-Horakhty, who approves of the smiting. Finally, still moving clockwise, another hero, this one Egyptian, stands in combat with a griffin in a fallen pose. After this comes a winged Isis-type goddess and, after some heraldic pairs of sphinxes and goats, another combat scene in which a human figure wearing a lion skin wrestles a rampant lion.[64]

When these scenes are viewed together within the "iconic structure" of this bowl, one may perceive a dynamic not unlike that discerned in the imprecatory psalms. It is a matter of divine-human mirroring vis-à-vis real threats that are at times human, at times mammalian, and at times supernatural. The human figures on the outmost register, especially the Assyrian hero, strike poses similar to the divine hero in the central medallion. This similarity, and the combat more generally, suggests a transferability of the enemy that is encountered. These images are *Denkbilder*: mental images good to think with. The enemy can be a real lion, something quite unreal, or supra-real (supernatural), like a griffin; or the enemy can be a host of enemies. Whatever the case, both victor and vanquished are cipher-like, abstract, general if not universal, and thus capable of redefinition and re-presentation. Given its size and positioning, however, the conflict in the central medallion is the most important for the visual field.[65] And so what is happening there, in the divine realm, is transferred—hoped or prayed for—onto the other more or less "realistic" depictions of humans in the outer register.

Seen in this way, the bowl "prays" in a way not unlike the imprecatory psalms: the enemies encountered by the human figures in the outer register are not merely human: they are beastly, even preternatural. The bowl's iconic structure aligns these enemies, in all their instantiations, with *something more*, ultimately as reflexes of the central divine conflict. These enemies are, finally, of a piece: indexes of threat and conflict. The victory that comes can only be due to the divine

62. These details are clearer in the plates found in Markoe, *Phoenician Bronze and Silver Bowls*, 256–57.

63. Markoe, *Phoenician Bronze and Silver Bowls*, 178. The similarity is even more pronounced than fig. 9.11 reveals, since the line drawing lacks what is clear from the plates (178, 258)—namely, another Horus falcon hovering in the field to the left and above the hero.

64. Markoe, *Phoenician Bronze and Silver Bowls*, 178. This last detail is clearer in the plate (259).

65. Morgan, *Images at Work*, 70–112.

power(s) represented at the center of the bowl in the winged warrior and by the Horus falcons there, and then in the outermost register, by another Horus falcon, Re-Horakhty, and the protective winged goddess. If the various enemies depicted on the bowl are of a piece, deliverance from or victory over them is somewhat similarly accomplished only because of and with the help of divine power(s).[66] Alignment of the divine will and the human supplicant, and vice versa, is thus of utmost importance and is accomplished in the imprecatory psalms as well as the Cyprian bowl. Both media offer a petition that can be expressed in the words of a much later prayer, "Your will be done, / on earth as it is in heaven" (Matt. 6:10 NIV). In such acts of prayer, as in worship more generally, "the believer becomes one with God."[67]

66. Markoe, *Phoenician Bronze and Silver Bowls*, 46.
67. Keel, *Symbolism*, 352.

10

Israelite Prophecy in Its Ancient Near Eastern Context

John W. Hilber

The Face of Old Testament Studies devoted a chapter to developments in the study of "Israelite Prophets and Prophecy."[1] Such a broad chapter could afford only scant treatment of prophets and prophecy in their ANE context, but then, not much was expected. Aside from the well-known Mari prophecies (early 2nd mill. BCE) and a couple of other texts, the crucially important data from the Neo-Assyrian period (7th cent. BCE) was hardly known outside specialist circles.[2] However, significant advances in the study of ancient prophetism have occurred over the past twenty years. Just four years after *The Face of Old Testament Studies* was released, Martti Nissenen made available for the first time a nearly exhaustive compilation of extrabiblical texts relevant to prophecy, which numbered 142 texts in the first edition and expanded to 176 texts in the second.[3] The expansion of

1. David W. Baker, "Israelite Prophets and Prophecy," in *The Face of Old Testament Studies: A Survey of Contemporary Approaches*, ed. David W. Baker and Bill T. Arnold (Grand Rapids: Baker, 1999), 266–94.

2. Simo Parpola, *Assyrian Prophecies*, SAA 9 (Helsinki: University of Helsinki Press, 1997); Martti Nissinen, *References to Prophecy in Neo-Assyrian Sources*, SAAS 7 (Helsinki: University of Helsinki Press, 1998). The corpus of the State Archives of Assyria is now available online: http://oracc.museum.upenn.edu/saao/.

3. Martti Nissinen, C. L. Seow, and Robert K. Ritner, *Prophets and Prophecy in the Ancient Near East*, WAW 12 (Atlanta: Society of Biblical Literature, 2003); Martti Nissinen et al., *Prophets and Prophecy in the Ancient Near East*, 2nd ed., WAW 41 (Atlanta: SBL Press, 2019).

the bibliography from approximately 520 entries in the first edition to more than 760 in the second illustrates the ongoing fruitfulness of this material for scholarly reflection. The currently known geographical and chronological distribution is extensive, spanning from the late third millennium to the third century BCE and ranging across the fertile crescent: Ur, Babylon, Eshnunna, Mari, Assyria, Emar, Hatti, Ugarit, Byblos, Hamath, Amman, Deir ʿAlla, and Egypt. The texts include reports of prophetic speech in diplomatic correspondence; prophetic speech to kings transcribed directly and preserved in administrative archives; prophetic speech embedded in royal annals; descriptions of prophetic activity in letters, annals, and epic narrative; descriptions of cultic rituals; lexical lists; and records of rations to temple functionaries. While Greece is not generally considered in discussions of ANE prophecy, the evidence is nonetheless relevant and recently integrated with ANE discussion by Nissinen.[4]

Definition of Prophecy

Scholars in OT studies have traditionally maintained a clear distinction between "prophecy" and "divination" (cf. Deut. 18:9–22).[5] More recent discussion, particularly in the context of broader ANE religion, has nuanced the definitions differently. In contemporary discussion, "divination" simply refers to any means by which humans gain access to secret information known only from the divine realm.[6] According to this definition, "prophecy" is a subtype of "divination" in the sense that God discloses the secrets of his heavenly council to his prophets (e.g., Jer. 23:18, 22). "Divination" is a neutral description for processes by which humans receive divine revelation. Even in the OT, the orthodox tradents regarded the Urim and Thummim (Exod. 28:30; 1 Sam. 28:6) as a legitimate form of revelation even though it qualifies as "technical divination" under the contemporary definition.[7]

In spite of this redefinition, it remains useful to differentiate between "prophecy" on the one hand and "technical divination" on the other.[8] "Prophecy" is a divine message, intuitively received by a human agent with a commission to transmit it to a

4. Martti Nissinen, *Ancient Prophecy: Near Eastern, Biblical, and Greek Perspectives* (Oxford: Oxford University Press, 2017); cf. Armin Lange, "Greek Seers and Israelite-Jewish Prophets," *VT* 57, no. 4 (2007): 461–82.

5. The definitions in this section follow John W. Hilber, "Prophecy, Divination, and Magic in the Ancient Near East," in *Behind the Scenes of the Old Testament: Cultural, Social, and Historical Contexts*, ed. Jonathan S. Greer, John W. Hilber, and John H. Walton (Grand Rapids: Baker Academic, 2018), 368–69.

6. Lester L. Grabbe, *Priests, Prophets, Diviners, Sages: A Socio-Historical Study of Religious Specialists in Ancient Israel* (Valley Forge, PA: Trinity Press International, 1995), 136–41; Esther J. Hamori, *Women's Divination in Biblical Literature: Prophecy, Necromancy, and Other Arts of Knowledge* (New Haven: Yale University Press, 2015), 4.

7. See C. Van Dam, "Divination, Magic," in *Dictionary of the Old Testament: Prophets*, ed. Mark J. Boda and J. Gordon McConville (Downers Grove, IL: InterVarsity, 2012), 160–62.

8. Nissinen, *Ancient Prophecy*, 19.

third party.[9] This process involves direct, divine intervention into a person's cognitive processes, with the result that they perceive reception of a divine message. If this divine communication is intended only for the immediate recipient (e.g., in a dream), then it is revelation. It becomes "prophecy" only when it is a message intended for another party. David Petersen expresses reservations about Manfred Weippert's definition because it relies too heavily on interpreting the experience of the intermediary, to which we have no access. He prefers the more objective descriptions of a prophet's social behavior witnessed in texts.[10] But the ancients themselves thought in terms of cognitive state (see below under discussion of the *muḫḫûm* prophet).

"Technical divination" refers to practices in which one receives information from the gods by ritual manipulation and/or observation of objects exterior to the human agent. In the case of prophecy, the agent is a passive recipient of the message, and any individual might be qualified to receive such a message. With technical divination, the agent is more actively involved, employing a learned skill. The line between the two is sometimes blurred, such as when an individual induces a dream experience in a temple or when a diviner interpretively expands upon a liver inspection. But even in these cases, one can differentiate the stages between mechanical inducement of the revelatory experience and the intuitive reception of an associated message. Whether by intuitive prophecy or by the exercise of technical skill, these human agents had special access to divine knowledge, either by divine call or by training.[11]

The Titles, Social Identity, Location, and Function of Prophets

Various terms were used in ancient sources to refer to those who spoke on behalf of deities, and the distribution of the terms varied by geographical locale as well as time period.

Old Babylonian (ca. 1800 BCE)

Letters and other administrative documents from the royal archive at Mari (18th cent. BCE) refer to variously titled functionaries who received divine messages

9. Following Manfred Weippert, "Aspekte israelitischer Prophetie im Lichte verwandter Erscheinungen des Alten Orients," in *Ad bene et fideliter seminandum: Festgabe für Karlheinz Deller zum 21. Februar 1987*, ed. Gerlinde Mauer and Ursula Magen, AOAT 220 (Kevelaer: Butzon & Bercker, 1988), 289–90. Cf. Ann K. Guinan, "A Severed Head Laughed: Stories of Divinatory Interpretation," in *Magic and Divination in the Ancient World*, ed. Leda Ciraolo and Jonathan Seidel, Ancient Magic and Divination 2 (Leiden: Brill, 2002), 18; Martti Nissinen, "What Is Prophecy? An Ancient Near Eastern Perspective," in *Inspired Speech: Prophecy in the Ancient Near East; Essays in Honour of Herbert B. Huffmon*, ed. John Kaltner and Louis Stulman, JSOTSup 378 (London: T&T Clark, 2004), 20.

10. David L. Petersen, "Defining Prophecy and Prophetic Literature," in *Prophecy in Its Ancient Near Eastern Context: Mesopotamian, Biblical, and Arabian Perspectives*, ed. Martti Nissinen, SBLSS 13 (Atlanta: Society of Biblical Literature, 2000), 39–41.

11. Hamori, *Women's Divination*, 6.

intuitively, sometimes in a dream or a vision. The term *āpilum* has often been translated "answerer" or "respondent" and is related to the verb *apālum*, "to answer."[12] Abraham Malamat likens this term to biblical descriptions of divine response to human inquiry (cf. 1 Sam. 9:17; Jer. 23:37; Mic. 6:5).[13] However, the *āpilum*'s messages are not ordinarily set in a context of response to oracular inquiry.[14] These individuals carry diplomatic messages for the king *and* speak spontaneously as mouthpieces for deities. Consequently, the broader designation "spokesperson" or in some contexts "interpreter" is perhaps more accurate.[15] Karel van der Toorn argues that "Old Babylonian gods grant prophetic revelations only in the sanctuary," but the prophets could deliver their messages elsewhere.[16] However, the location of revelation is not always stated, so this argument is in some cases an assumption.[17] It is at least certain that prophetic *performance* could be outside the temple.[18] The *āpilum* rising in a temple might suggest recovery from a trancelike state before delivering a communicable message.[19] Unlike the case of the *muḫḫûm* below, the mental status or behavior of the *āpilum* is unclear.[20] The early suggestion that the *āpilum*(s) travelled in bands or functioned in groups, like the "sons of prophets" in the OT, is not supported in the texts.

12. Jean-Marie Durand, "Les prophéties des textes de Mari," in *Oracles et prophéties dans l'antiquité: Actes du colloque de Strasbourg 15–17 Juin 1995*, ed. Jean-Georges Heintz (Paris: Université des Sciences Humaines de Strasbourg, 1997), 117; Herbert B. Huffmon, "A Company of Prophets: Mari, Assyria, Israel," in Nissinen, *Prophecy in Its Ancient Near Eastern Context*, 49, 52; Hans M. Barstad, "Sic dicit dominus: Mari Prophetic Texts and the Hebrew Bible," in *Essays on Ancient Israel in Its Near Eastern Context: A Tribute to Nadav Na'aman*, ed. Yairah Amit et al. (Winona Lake, IN: Eisenbrauns, 2006), 30.

13. Abraham Malamat, "A Forerunner of Biblical Prophecy: The Mari Documents," in *Ancient Israelite Religion: Essays in Honor of Frank Moore Cross*, ed. Patrick D. Miller Jr., Paul D. Hanson, and S. Dean McBride (Philadelphia: Fortress, 1987), 39–41.

14. Paolo Merlo, "Āpilum at Mari: A Reappraisal," *UF* 36 (2004), 331; Jonathan Stökl, *Prophecy in the Ancient Near East: A Philological and Sociological Comparison*, CHANE 56 (Leiden: Brill, 2012), 44, 47–50. A possible exception is ARM 26 199. See Jean-Marie Durand, *Archives épistolaires de Mari I/1*, ARM 26/1 (Paris: Éditions Recherche sur les Civilisations, 1988), 388–89.

15. Merlo, "Āpilum at Mari," 326; Stökl, *Prophecy in the Ancient Near East*, 42–43; Nissinen, *Ancient Prophecy*, 35.

16. Karel van der Toorn, "Mesopotamian Prophecy between Immanence and Transcendence: A Comparison of Old Babylonian and Neo-Assyrian Prophecy," in Nissinen, *Prophecy in Its Ancient Near Eastern Context*, 80. Cf. Beate Pongratz-Leisten, *Herrschaftswissen in Mesopotamien: Formen der Kommunikation zwischen Gott und König im 2. und 1. Jahrtausend v. Chr.*, SAAS 10 (Helsinki: University of Helsinki Press, 1999), 57.

17. John W. Hilber, *Cultic Prophecy in the Psalms*, BZAW 352 (Berlin: De Gruyter, 2005), 58–59; cf. Daniel Fleming, "Prophets and Temple Personnel in the Mari Archives," in *The Priests in the Latter Prophets: The Portrayal of Priests, Prophets and Other Religious Specialists in the Latter Prophets*, ed. Lester L. Grabbe and Alice Odgen Bellis, JSOTSup 408 (London: T&T Clark, 2004), 53n32.

18. Nissinen, *Ancient Prophecy*, 35.

19. Huffmon, "Company of Prophets," 56.

20. Stökl, *Prophecy in the Ancient Near East*, 50.

The second and most common designation for prophetic functionaries in Old Babylonian sources is the *muḫḫûm*, commonly translated "ecstatic" prophet. Both etymology (the verb *maḫḫû* means "to become crazy") and usage indicate that the term designates an individual who is acting without a sound mind or behaving in an unusual way.[21] A Neo-Assyrian prayer to the god Nabu offers a helpful window into the ancient psychological perspective on the *muḫḫûm*: "I have become struck like a prophet [*muḫḫûm*]: what I do not know I bring forth."[22] In a copy of the Poem of the Righteous Sufferer found at Ugarit, the poet describes his brothers' mourning rights: "My brothers bathe in their blood like prophets [*maḫḫûm*]."[23] So some sort of altered state of consciousness and eccentric behavior is suggested by the term.

The terms *āpilum* and *muḫḫûm* are never used of the same person, so they are distinct titles.[24] Decades ago, Malamat suggested that these two functionaries were both "professional prophets," differentiated from ordinary people outside the cultic community whom he regarded as "lay prophets."[25] But more recently, Jonathan Stökl has argued that while the *āpilum* prophesied regularly as a primary official function in the role of a royal prophet, the *muḫḫûm* functioned ecstatically in other ways in cultic performance and only occasionally prophesied. Whether these individuals were socially located in the temple community or were ordinary laypeople, their occasional prophetic speech was not necessarily an expression of their ecstatic performance.[26] Although some ritual descriptions of the *muḫḫûm*'s activity are vague, Nissinen questions Stökl's distinction, arguing that their ecstasy could only serve the purpose of prophesying.[27] He furthermore questions the distinction between professional and lay prophets altogether.[28] However, ecstatic behavior and articulate speech were not incompatible.[29]

Another individual who functioned prophetically at times was the *assinnum*, who was also connected to the temple, perhaps as a dancer or singer.[30] On one occasion the *assinnum*'s oracle is revealed while in a trance (ARM 26 213, line 7).[31] On another occasion the oracular procedure is associated with giving drink of

21. Martti Nissinen, "Prophetic Madness: Prophecy and Ecstasy in the Ancient Near East and in Greece," in *Raising Up a Faithful Exegete: Essays in Honor of Richard D. Nelson*, ed. K. L. Noll and Brooks Schramm (Winona Lake, IN: Eisenbrauns, 2010), 7–17.

22. Nissinen et al., *Prophets and Prophecy* (2nd ed.), no. 118b, line 12′.

23. Nissinen et al., *Prophets and Prophecy* (2nd ed.), no. 122, line 11′.

24. Nissinen, *Ancient Prophecy*, 35.

25. Malamat, "Forerunner," 43–44. Cf. Huffmon, "Company of Prophets," 52.

26. Stökl, *Prophecy in the Ancient Near East*, 37, 44, 50, followed by Brad E. Kelle, "The Phenomenon of Israelite Prophecy in Contemporary Scholarship," *CurBR* 12, no. 3 (2014): 296.

27. Nissinen, *Ancient Prophecy*, 34.

28. Nissinen, *Ancient Prophecy*, 37.

29. Nissinen, "Prophetic Madness," 29.

30. Herbert Huffmon, "The *assinnum* as Prophet: Shamans at Mari?," in *Nomades et sédentaires dans le Proche-Orient ancien*, ed. Christophe Nicolle (Paris: Éditions Recherche sur les Civilisations, 2004), 241; Stökl, *Prophecy in the Ancient Near East*, 58.

31. The named individual is identified in ARM 26 197 (line 4) as an *assinnum*.

some sort (ARM 26 212, lines 1′–2′).[32] The *assinnum*'s gender identity is ambiguous and disputed.[33] Evidence in the Neo-Assyrian period suggests that the *assinnum* played cross-gendered roles, but this is less clear for Old Babylonian times. The *assinnum*'s service seems confined to the cult of the goddess Ištar-Annunītum, consistent with same-gender identity between goddess and prophet.[34]

Other prophetic functionaries at Mari include the *qammātum* and the *nābûm*. The meaning of the former term remains uncertain, although the derivation from the verb *qābûm* (to speak) is now considered incorrect.[35] The latter term has generated considerable interest due to its cognate relationship to the Hebrew word for prophet, נָבִיא (*nābîʾ*). A difficulty arises in that the phrase translated "deliver an oracle" (*epēšum têrtam*) is used of the *nābûm* in ARM 26 216, but it ordinarily refers to technical divination.[36] So are they prophets or are they specialists in extispicy? It is possible that this group merely interpreted the results of extispicy.[37] Alternatively, there may have been two separate revelatory events (extispicy, then prophetic word).[38] Even the meaning of the word itself (prophet? invocation specialist?) at both Mari and Emar remains an open question.[39]

Outside of the Mari archive, two Old Babylonian prophetic texts from Ishchali attest to oracles of well-being in the form of a divine letter.[40] A ration list from the same temple from which these oracles likely originated lists prophets (*muḫḫûm*)

32. For succinct discussion, see Nissinen, *Prophets and Prophecy* (2nd ed.), 41–43, n. b.

33. For evidence of gender crossover, see Gwendolyn Leick, *Sex and Eroticism in Mesopotamian Literature* (London: Routledge, 1994), 159–62, 224–25; Martti Nissinen, *Homoeroticism in the Biblical World: A Historical Perspective* (Minneapolis: Fortress, 1998), 28–36; Nissinen, *Ancient Prophecy*, 308–10; and Huffmon, "*Assinnum* as Prophet," 244–45. Ilona Zsolnay stresses the functions that symbolize the martial aspect of the goddess and questions some of the evidence for gender crossover. See Ilona Zsolnay, "The Misconstrued Role of the Assinnu in Ancient Near Eastern Prophecy," in *Prophets Male and Female: Gender and Prophecy in the Hebrew Bible, the Eastern Mediterranean, and the Ancient Near East*, ed. Jonathan Stökl and Corrine L. Carvalho, AIL 15 (Atlanta: SBL Press, 2013), 81–99. See also Jonathan Stökl, "Gender 'Ambiguity' in Ancient Near Eastern Prophecy? A Reassessment of the Data behind a Popular Theory," in Stökl and Carvalho, *Prophets Male and Female*, 69–77.

34. Nissinen, *Ancient Prophecy*, 309.

35. See Stökl, *Prophecy in the Ancient Near East*, 61; and Nissinen, *Ancient Prophecy*, 37n185. Contrast Malamat, "Forerunner," 38.

36. See Daniel Fleming, "*Nābû* and *munabbiātu*: Two New Syrian Religious Personnel," *JAOS* 113, no. 2 (1993): 179–80.

37. Fleming, "*Nābû* and *munabbiātu*," 180–81; cf. Maria de Jong Ellis, "Observations on Mesopotamian Oracles and Prophetic Texts: Literary and Historiographical Considerations," *JCS* 41, no. 2 (1989): 136n36.

38. Pongratz-Leisten, *Herrschaftswissen*, 69–70.

39. For discussion, see John Huehnergard, "On the Etymology and Meaning of Hebrew *nābîʾ*," *ErIsr* 26 (Jerusalem: Israel Exploration Society, 1999), 91*, 93*n40; Stökl, *Prophecy in the Ancient Near East*, 161–66; and Daniel Fleming, review of Jonathan Stökl, *Prophecy in the Ancient Near East: A Philological and Sociological Comparison*, *NEA* 78, no. 4 (2015): 312–13.

40. Maria de Jong Ellis, "The Goddess Kititum Speaks to King Ibalpiel: Oracle Texts From Ishchali," *MARI* 5 (1987): 235–66.

as recipients.[41] These suggest that Old Babylonian prophecy enjoyed wide geographical distribution and was not an exclusively Western Semitic phenomenon as was once surmised.[42] From roughly the same time, a seal impression discovered at a village in Egypt names a "seer" (Canaanite, *ḥzy*; cf. Hebrew חֹזֶה, *ḥōzeh*).[43] This reference constitutes the earliest attestation to prophecy in a West Semitic language. Diverse evidence fills the chronological gap between Old Babylonian prophecy and the Neo-Assyrian archive dating a millennium later.[44]

Neo-Assyrian (ca. 700 BCE)

The words *āpilu* and *assinnu* do not appear in conjunction with prophetic activity in Neo-Assyrian records. Rather, in addition to the continued use of *maḫḫû*, the term *raggimu* (feminine, *raggintu*) is predominant. The verb *ragāmu* (to call out) is used in descriptions of prophetic performance.[45] Simo Parpola and Nissinen suggest that *raggimu* was the more colloquial term for prophet in letters and in colophons of prophetic texts, whereas *maḫḫû* was retained in other genres.[46] This is contested by Stökl, who maintains a technical distinction between the *raggimu* and the *maḫḫû*.[47]

Van der Toorn suggests that Neo-Assyrian prophecy differs from Mari by the degree to which prophets received messages outside the temple and away from the divine image.[48] Not only did prophets serve in the royal court and probably accompany the king on military expeditions, but a prophetess of Ishtar of Arbela hails from an unknown mountain village where there was likely no cultic site.[49] On one occasion, a spontaneous prophetic word comes to two men, facilitating the repatriation of the Marduk statue.[50]

Gender representation changes from the Old Babylonian period to the Neo-Assyrian. Of those whose gender can be determined, the Mari sources indicate that about 60 percent were male. However, Neo-Assyrian prophets are about 60 percent female. Perhaps the predominance of the goddess Ishtar as the chief deity of prophecy in the later period accounts for this, since in both periods there is a

41. Nissinen, *Prophets and Prophecy* (2nd ed.), no. 67a, line 12′.

42. Stökl, *Prophecy in the Ancient Near East*, 88–90.

43. Nissinen, *Prophets and Prophecy* (2nd ed.), no. 141a. See Stökl, *Prophecy in the Ancient Near East*, 22–23.

44. Brigitte Lion, "Les mentions de 'prophètes' dans la seconde moitié du IIe millénaire av. J.-C.," *RA* 94, no. 1 (2000): 21–32.

45. Martti Nissinen, "The Socioreligious Role of the Neo-Assyrian Prophets," in Nissinen, *Prophecy in Its Ancient Near Eastern Context*, 92–93.

46. Parpola, *Assyrian Prophecies*, xlv–xlvi; Nissinen, "The Socioreligious Role," 91; Nissinen, *Ancient Prophecy*, 38–39.

47. Stökl, *Prophecy in the Ancient Near East*, 111–15.

48. Van der Toorn, "Mesopotamian Prophecy," 82–84.

49. SAA 10 109, lines o 9′–10′; SAA 7 9, lines r i 20–24 (see Nissinen, *References to Prophecy*, 65); SAA 9 1.3.

50. SAA 10 24.

correlation between the gender of the deities and their prophets.[51] In spite of the esteem given women in the palace at Mari, female prophets were subjected to verification of their prophecies significantly more than their male counterparts.[52] Regarding prophetic function itself, there appears to be no difference based on gender at Mari or Nineveh.[53]

Prophecy beyond Mesopotamia

The breadth of prophetic activity geographically was noted in the introduction. Some recent discussion has involved the possibility of prophecy in Hittite Anatolia and in Egypt.

The Hittite culture exhibits a plethora of divinatory practices.[54] This elaborate revelatory apparatus suggests that intuitive prophecy might be expected as well, and the Hittite "man of god" might have functioned in ways similar to other ANE prophets.[55] However, in Nissinen's second edition of prophetically related texts, he cautiously omits references to divine messages from a "man of god" in the Hittite plague prayers due to the lack of clear evidence of intuitive rather than technical means of revelation.[56] Another candidate for divine speech might be the "Old Woman" listed with the "man of god" in the plague prayers. However, Hannah Marcuson's work on the Hittite "Old Woman" shows that these women used traditional methods of magic and divination rather than intuitive prophecy.[57] This adds little confidence to our knowledge that the "man of god" discerned the divine will any differently. Revelation through dreams was common, but for words to count as prophecy, the report must be messenger speech from the deity to a third party.[58] A Luwian text from a Neo-Hittite state uses an equivalent Luwian

51. Nissinen, *Ancient Prophecy*, 298–99, 303.

52. Esther J. Hamori, "Gender and the Verification of Prophecy at Mari," *WO* 42, no. 1 (2012): 22.

53. Jonathan Stökl, "Female Prophets in the Ancient Near East," in *Prophecy and the Prophets in Ancient Israel*, ed. John Day, LHBOTS 531 (London: T&T Clark, 2010), 56; Martti Nissinen, "Gender and Prophetic Agency in the Ancient Near East and in Greece," in Stökl and Carvalho, *Prophets Male and Female*, 58; Nissinen, *Ancient Prophecy*, 325.

54. Richard H. Beal, "Hittite Oracles," in Ciraolo and Seidel, *Magic and Divination in the Ancient World*, 57–81.

55. Meindert Dijkstra, "Prophets, Men of God, Wise Women: Dreams and Prophecies in Hittite Stories," in *Prophecy and Prophets in Stories: Papers Read at the Fifth Meeting of the Edinburgh Prophecy Network, Utrecht, October 2013*, ed. Bob Becking and Hans M. Barstad, OtSt/OTS 65 (Leiden: Brill, 2015), 13–14.

56. Nissinen, *Prophets and Prophecy* (2nd ed.), 9. For texts, see Itamar Singer, *Hittite Prayers*, WAW 11 (Atlanta: Society of Biblical Literature, 2002), no. 4a, §§6, 11, and no. 11, §11.

57. Hannah Marcuson, "'Word of the Old Woman': Studies in Female Ritual Practice in Hittite Anatolia" (PhD diss., University of Chicago, 2016).

58. Alice Mouton, "Portent Dreams in Hittite Anatolia," in *Perchance to Dream: Dream Divination in the Bible and the Ancient Near East*, ed. Esther Hamori and Jonathan Stökl, ANEM 21 (Atlanta: SBL Press, 2018), 27–28.

term for "man of god," who speaks a command on behalf of the storm god.[59] In addition, Meindert Dijkstra quotes a salvation oracle from a priest that could be construed as prophecy.[60] Both of these examples offer evidence of prophecy from this region.

Ancient Egyptians expected revelation from the divine realm to be received through divination, oracular movement of the god's barque/barge, dreams, communication with the dead, and divine words from the "wise woman"; stories of divine speech are also embedded in their narrative literature.[61] In spite of these socioreligious prerequisites for prophecy, the scholarly consensus is that prophecy, in the sense of divine-messenger speech, did not exist in ancient Egypt.[62] The texts usually discussed are correctly classified as a subspecies of wisdom literature.[63] However, a class of Egyptian texts has been overlooked in previous discussions of Egyptian prophecy. Numerous royal inscriptions record first-person divine speech that is framed with introductory speech formulas attributing the words to a god and delivered by a priest to the king in public, cultic rituals.[64] These Egyptian royal oracles satisfy the same criteria applied to Mesopotamian texts, where, in Nissinen's words, "the prophet is not mentioned but the form and content suggest a prophetic origin."[65] The only difference between the Egyptian texts and prophecies from Mesopotamia or the Bible is that the divine message is delivered by a priest rather than a formally titled prophet, for which Egyptian does not have a distinct word. Schneider summarizes clear evidence of prophecy in Hellenistic Egypt but critiques my use

59. Nissinen, *Prophets and Prophecy* (2nd ed.), no. 143, §§22–23; Nissinen, *Ancient Prophecy*, 275–78. I thank Robert Marineau for helping me sort out the Luwian and Hittite terms under discussion.

60. Dijkstra, "Prophets, Men of God, Wise Women," 14. Cf. Nissinen, *Ancient Prophecy*, 73.

61. John W. Hilber, "Prophetic Speech in the Egyptian Royal Cult," in *On Stone and Scroll: Essays in Honour of Graham Ivor Davies*, ed. James K. Aitken, Katharine J. Dell, and Brian A. Mastin, BZAW 420 (Berlin: De Gruyter, 2011), 42–46.

62. Nissinen, *Ancient Prophecy*, 42; Stökl, *Prophecy in the Ancient Near East*, 16, although he remains open to the possibility; see Jonathan Stökl, review of Martti Nissinen et al., *Prophets and Prophecy in the Ancient Near East*, *RBL* 11 (2020), https://www.sblcentral.org/home/bookDetails/13314.

63. Nili Shupak, "Egyptian 'Prophecy' and Biblical Prophecy: Did the Phenomenon of Prophecy, in the Biblical Sense, Exist in Ancient Egypt?," *JEOL* 31 (1989): 5–40; Shupak, "The Egyptian 'Prophecy'—A Reconsideration," in *Von reichlich ägyptischem Verstande: Festschrift für Waltraud Guglielmi zum 65. Geburtstag*, ed. Karol Zibelius-Chen and Hans-Werner Fischer-Elfert, Philippika: Marburger altertumskundliche Abhandlungen 11 (Wiesbaden: Harrassowitz, 2006), 133–44.

64. John W. Hilber, "Royal Cultic Prophecy in Assyria, Judah, and Egypt," in *"Thus Speaks Ishtar of Arbela": Prophecy in Israel, Assyria, and Egypt in the Neo-Assyrian Period*, ed. Robert P. Gordon and Hans M. Barstad (Winona Lake, IN: Eisenbrauns, 2013), 162–63. See Hilber, "Prophetic Speech," 46–52; Hilber, "Prophetic Ritual in the Egyptian Royal Cult," in *Prophecy and Its Cultic Dimensions*, ed. Lena-Sofia Tiemeyer, JAJSup 31 (Göttingen: Vandenhoeck & Ruprecht, 2019), 51–62.

65. Nissinen, *Prophets and Prophecy* (2nd ed.), 8.

of the royal texts.[66] He maintains that these speeches did not originate from a cognitive experience of a human mediator and lack the "momentary" element of initial performance. But I contend that, whether composed in advance of cultic performance or more spontaneously delivered, these texts do constitute prophecy.[67]

Another issue is whether priests in procession rituals were thought to have been transformed into gods themselves, thereby eliminating human agency (and prophecy) altogether because the gods were effectively speaking in person.[68] But in ritual processions before human audiences, the divine image in the barque/barge already manifested the deity's presence and was usually veiled. It is unlikely that these procession rituals would feature the redundant appearance of the god walking among the people for them to gaze directly upon his sacred presence. Rather, the Egyptians seem not to have imagined the complete elimination of the humanness of the intermediary.[69] One iconographical portrait of ritual masking even shows an animal head on a priest (representing the deity) but with a human head inside.[70] The simpler explanation is that some form of prophetic "possession" of the human agent is in view.

Royal Concerns, Covenant, and Social Justice

Considerable royal attention was given to monitoring and, when possible, controlling the means by which the will of the gods could be ascertained.[71] Since most extant texts relevant to prophecy are from palace records, it is not surprising to see prophecy providing divine knowledge to the king in order to support and advance more effective rule.[72] A letter from the scholar Urad-Gula to Assurbanipal shows that a private individual could, at least on occasion, seek the word of a god from a prophet for help.[73] Letters from Mari frequently bring prophetic citations to bear on international relations. In the Neo-Assyrian texts, one finds secondary use of prophetic oracles in archival form and cited in royal annals to validate the king's

66. Thomas Schneider, "A Land without Prophets? Examining the Presumed Lack of Prophecy in Ancient Egypt," in *Enemies and Friends of the State: Ancient Prophecy in Context*, ed. Christopher A. Rollston (University Park, PA: Eisenbrauns, 2018), 68–73. See Hilber, "Prophetic Speech," 44–45.

67. Hilber, "Prophetic Ritual."

68. Schneider, "Land without Prophets?," 68–69.

69. For further discussion, see John W. Hilber, "Egyptian Prophecy—Some Clarifying Issues," in *Egypt and Hebrew Prophecy*, ed. Christopher B. Hays, John Huddlestun, and Thomas Schneider, ÄAT (Münster: Zaphon, forthcoming).

70. M. A. Murray, "Ritual Masking," in *Mélanges Maspero I* (Cairo: French Archaeological Institute of Cairo, 1934), 255.

71. Pongratz-Leisten, *Herrschaftswissen*, esp. 16, 286–88.

72. Martti Nissinen, "Biblical Prophecy from a Near Eastern Perspective: The Cases of Kingship and Divine Possession," in *Congress Volume: Ljubljana 2007*, ed. André Lemaire, VTSup 133 (Leiden: Brill, 2010), 445–47; Nissinen, *Ancient Prophecy*, 263–65.

73. SAA 10 294.

legitimacy against rival claimants and enemies of the state. A few relatively mild admonitions are directed toward the king regarding cultic responsibilities, but wholesale condemnation appears in only one report of prophecy that emerged among what might be regarded as the opposition party.[74] Technical divination was a more highly regarded source of divine knowledge, and so at Mari a sample of a prophet's "hair and hem" was sometimes submitted to be tested by divinatory inquiry. It is debated whether the inquiry tests the credibility of the prophet or of the message, but the fact that an official *āpilum* or the queen mother herself could be tested suggests that the reliability of the message is the concern.[75]

Closely related to political stability is the treaty system. In Esarhaddon's succession treaty, vassals swore to inform the king of any prophetic words that might encourage sedition.[76] One of the Neo-Assyrian archival tablets (SAA 9 3) preserves rubrics that suggest its use in Esarhaddon's coronation proceedings; it reports the goddess Ishtar brokering a covenant between the gods, the king, and vassals (cf. 2 Kings 11:4–12).[77] The king was responsible to help maintain world order, and there is evidence at Mari, at least, that prophets might demand social justice, though this is only a modestly attested theme.[78] Nissinen argues that because of the social function of temples in the welfare system of the ancient world and because prophets generally hail from temple contexts, they likely had a more visible role as advocates for social justice than the extant texts indicate.[79]

Ritual and Cult

Ancient Near Eastern sources portray prophets actively engaged in the temple and as advocates of temple welfare.[80] They admonished the king to follow appro-

74. Martti Nissinen, "Das kritische Potential in der altorientalischen Prophetie," in *Propheten in Mari, Assyrien und Israel*, ed. Matthias Köckert and Martti Nissinen, FRLANT 201 (Göttingen: Vandenhoeck & Ruprecht, 2003), 4–7, 29–30; Nissinen, "Biblical Prophecy," 453; Matthijs J. de Jong, *Isaiah among the Ancient Near Eastern Prophets: A Comparative Study of the Earliest Stages of the Isaiah Tradition and the Neo-Assyrian Prophecies*, VTSup 117 (Leiden: Brill, 2007), 308–13.

75. Stökl, *Prophecy*, 81–86.

76. SAA 2 6, lines 116–17.

77. Antti Laato, *History and Ideology in the Old Testament Prophetic Literature: A Semiotic Approach to the Reconstruction of the Proclamation of the Historical Prophets*, Coniectanea biblica, Old Testament 41 (Stockholm: Almquist & Wiksell, 1996), 274.

78. Robert P. Gordon, "From Mari to Moses: Prophecy at Mari and in Ancient Israel," in *Of Prophets' Visions and the Wisdom of Sages: Essays in Honour of R. Norman Whybray on His Seventieth Birthday*, ed. Heather A. McKay and David J. A. Clines, JSOTSup 162 (Sheffield: JSOT Press, 1993), 75–78; Nissinen, "Das kritische Potential"; Robert P. Gordon, "Prophecy in the Mari and Nineveh Archives," in Gordon and Barstad, *"Thus Speaks Ishtar,"* 47–49.

79. Nissinen, "Das kritische Potential," 9; Nissinen, *Ancient Prophecy*, 213.

80. John W. Hilber, "Liturgy and Cult," in Boda and McConville, *Dictionary of the Old Testament: Prophets*, 514–15; Nissinen, *Ancient Prophecy*, 204–23.

priate cultic customs and not to neglect the temple. There is good evidence that Neo-Assyrian prophets responded to inquiries and in an intercessory manner to laments.[81] But Lena-Sofia Tiemeyer reviews the evidence and observes a general contrast with biblical prophets. In Neo-Assyrian texts, deities intercede directly with one another in the divine council on behalf of the petitioner, whereas biblical material stresses the role of the human as an independent intercessor.[82] Little is known about the actual activity of prophets in the cult, but a couple of texts hint at the nature of their responsibility. An important Old Babylonian festival of Ishtar depended in part on whether or not the prophet became ecstatic in the context of a musical performance, and prophets played a role in the Neo-Assyrian "Marduk Ordeal."[83] A Neo-Assyrian healing ritual also involved the ecstatic performance of prophets.[84]

Prophets and Writing

Another important area is the textualization of prophecy. Are written texts a reliable guide to the oral performance of prophets? How do texts develop individually and in relation to one another? Discussion of these questions for ANE texts cannot be easily disentangled from the interests of scholars regarding biblical prophetic books. A paradigm shift occurred in the 1980s as scholars began to question whether biblical prophetic books could reveal anything about the historical prophets.[85] About the same time, the emerging knowledge of ANE prophecy was brought to bear, bringing a more positive outlook.[86] However, doubts about the usefulness of the parallels between the textualization of prophecy in Mesopotamia and in the OT have persisted, arising in large part because of the longer redactional and social history of the biblical texts.[87] Consequently, Nissinen cautions

81. Hilber, *Cultic Prophecy in the Psalms*, 62–74; de Jong, *Isaiah among the Ancient Near Eastern Prophets*, 298–300.

82. Lena-Sofia Tiemeyer, "Were the Neo-Assyrian Prophets Intercessors? A Comparative Study of Neo-Assyrian and Hebrew Texts," in Gordon and Barstad, *"Thus Speaks Ishtar,"* 253–72.

83. Nissinen, *Prophets and Prophecy* (2nd ed.), nos. 51, 52, and 103.

84. Nissinen, *Prophets and Prophecy* (2nd ed.), no. 118.

85. A. Graeme Auld, "Prophets through the Looking Glass: Between Writings and Moses," *JSOT* 8, no. 27 (1983): 3–23; Robert Carroll, "Poets Not Prophets: A Response to 'Prophets through the Looking-Glass,'" *JSOT* 8, no. 27 (1983): 25–31. Cf. Robert R. Wilson, "Current Issues in the Study of Old Testament Prophecy," in Kaltner and Stuhlman, *Inspired Speech*, 40–41; Martti Nissinen, "The Historical Dilemma of Biblical Prophetic Studies," in *Prophecy in the Book of Jeremiah*, ed. Hans M. Barstad and Reinhard G. Kratz, BZAW 388 (Berlin: De Gruyter, 2009), 106–8.

86. Alan R. Millard, "La prophétie et l'écriture: Israël, Aram, Assyrie," *RHR* 202, no. 2 (1985): 125–45; Gordon, "From Mari to Moses"; Gordon, "Where Have All the Prophets Gone? The 'Disappearing' Israelite Prophet against the Background of Ancient Near Eastern Prophecy," *BBR* 5, no. 1 (1995): 67–86.

87. Ernst Axel Knauf, "Prophets That Never Were," in *Gott und Mensch im Dialog: Festschrift für Otto Kaiser zum 80. Geburtstag*, ed. Markus Witte, BZAW 354 (Berlin: De Gruyter,

against "apologetic" tendencies to use parallels to support the reliability of OT prophetic books as a historical witness to preexilic prophets.[88] Representing one mainstream voice, he maintains a Persian-period scribal origin for the production of prophetic books that may witness to a social reality of preexilic prophecy but not in any reliable way reporting the actual words of preexilic prophets.[89] Others, using ANE models, accommodate varying degrees of scribal editing and reinterpretation in the production of prophetic books without necessarily relegating the majority of it to Persian-period production.[90]

In large measure, this discussion revolves around a broader assessment of the textualization and transmission process. Viewing prophetic books as "scribal artifacts" represents only half of the story.[91] Scribes and prophets worked in concert in the ANE. Tradents preserved the link between a text and its authorial source, and the culture of writing guarded prophetic speech as diplomatic language, not to be tampered with or fabricated as other genres of writing were. Correspondents and scribes transmitted oracles in letters and literary texts with relative accuracy. Furthermore, often overlooked in discussion are "divine letters," which textualized prophecy at the point of revelation. Some have suggested that "literary predictive texts" provide the best model for imagining the final literary cast of prophetic books.[92] But this genre of texts is a form of historiography connected to omen series and not related in any way to prophetic speech. The literary predictive texts from Egypt are also historiographic in nature and representative of the wisdom tradition, not prophecy.[93]

Conclusion

As Brad Kelle says, the main current of scholarship stresses the distinction between "ancient Hebrew prophecy" as a sociological phenomenon and "biblical prophecy" as a literary/scribal phenomenon.[94] With regard to sociological features,

2004), 451–53; Nissinen, "What Is Prophecy?," 28–29; Nissinen, "How Prophecy Became Literature," *SJOT* 19, no. 2 (2005): 153–72; Nissinen, *Ancient Prophecy*, 154–56.

88. Nissinen, "Biblical Prophecy," 443n4.

89. Nissinen, "How Prophecy Became Literature," esp. 157–59, 166–67; Nissinen, "Historical Dilemma," 115.

90. E.g., de Jong, *Isaiah among the Ancient Near Eastern Prophets*.

91. John W. Hilber, "The Culture of Prophecy and Writing in the Ancient Near East," in *Do Historical Matters Matter to Faith?*, ed. James K. Hoffmeier and Dennis Magary (Wheaton: Crossway, 2012), 219–41.

92. De Jong, *Isaiah among the Prophets*, 420–39; Stuart Weeks, "Predictive and Prophetic Literature: Can Neferti Help Us Read the Bible?," in Day, *Prophecy and the Prophets in Ancient Israel*, 25–46. For description of the genre, see Ellis, "Observations."

93. John W. Hilber, "Isaiah as Prophet and Isaiah as Book in Their Ancient Near Eastern Context," in *Bind Up the Testimony: Explorations in the Genesis of the Book of Isaiah*, ed. Daniel I. Block and Richard L. Schultz (Peabody, MA: Hendrickson, 2015), 165–69.

94. Kelle, "Phenomenon of Israelite Prophecy."

ANE parallels are widely seen as a helpful window into the Bible's portrait of Israelite prophetism. While differences in degree are evident, the assessment by Robert Gordon three decades ago remains true: "In the end the difference between Israelite prophecy and the rest may simply have to be expressed in terms of its conception of its God."[95] But ANE literature offers no parallels to the Bible's prophetic *books*. So opinions about the extent to which biblical texts preserve the words of the historical prophets depend largely on prejudgments about the composition and redaction processes that resulted in the prophetic books.

95. Gordon, "Where Have All the Prophets Gone?," 86.

PART 2

Old Testament Scripture

11

Old Testament Canons

Stephen G. Dempster

"Neither Judaism or Christianity is conceivable without the Bible. Without Scripture, either religion turns into simply what Christians or Jews happen to believe or do at the moment, and then there is no criterion against which to measure their beliefs."[1] This is because both Jews and Christians can be described as "people of the Book." Neither religion is conceivable without the Old Testament (for Christians) or the Hebrew Bible (for Jews). The Jews' origin as a people and their raison d'être are found in the Hebrew Bible (HB); for Christians the New Testament (NT) is incomprehensible without the Old Testament (OT).

A further question arises for Christians: Which OT is Scripture? The major denominations disagree on this matter, but despite differences, there is remarkable unity. For all Christians, there is a solid core of OT books—the very same books of the HB—with some blurred boundaries. The Protestant OT differs from the HB only in its enumeration,[2] arrangement,[3] and nomenclature;[4] Roman Catholics and the Orthodox communions add books to this common core.[5]

I thank John Meade and Peter Gentry for their helpful comments.

1. John Barton, *A History of the Bible: The Book and Its Faiths* (New York: Viking, 2019), 485.

2. The HB has 24 books, versus the OT's 39 (Protestant), 46 (Roman Catholic), and 49 (Orthodox).

3. The HB is divided into Law, Prophets, and Writings, whereas the OT arrangement is Law, Historical Books, Poetic Books, and Prophetic Books.

4. In the HB, e.g., the Minor Prophets are simply The Twelve, whereas the OT counts each book individually. Also, the HB identifies the books of Samuel and Kings as 1–4 Kings (or Kingdoms), whereas the OT identifies them as 1–2 Samuel and 1–2 Kings.

5. The Roman Catholic canon adds Tobit, Judith, 1 and 2 Maccabees, Wisdom of Solomon, Ecclesiasticus, Baruch, and additions to Daniel (3), Esther (6), and Baruch (the Epistle of Jeremiah). The Orthodox canon adds to these 1 Esdras, 3 Maccabees, the Epistle of Jeremiah as a separate book, Psalm 151, and the Prayer of Manasseh. The Orthodox Tehawedo canon, of

Despite these differences, the HB and OT (in all its forms) show remarkable cohesion. The first half of the HB (Genesis–2 Kings) is virtually mirrored in Christian Bibles. And though arranged differently, all the remaining books in the HB appear in the various OT canons without exception.[6] Until recently many Protestant Bibles printed the "extra books" of the other OT canons—sometimes called "the Apocrypha" or Deuterocanonical books—either at the end of the Bible or in between the Testaments.[7] So while Protestants distinguished them from the other books, they were still viewed as profitable.

The Old Testament Canon: Theories of Evolution

In the last two decades of the twentieth century, the consensus view of the HB/OT canon, put forth by Herbert Edward Ryle, was jettisoned. This had been based on the tripartite structure of the HB: the Law, the Prophets, and the Writings.[8] The structure was assumed to have evolved over a long period of time, with the Law canonized during the time of Ezra (450–400 BCE), the Prophets later (200 BCE), and the Writings at a council of rabbis at Yavneh (90 CE). The assumption was that, when a section closed, nothing more could be added. This explained why Daniel was not included in the Prophets but in the Writings since the Prophets corpus was closed by the time Daniel was written.[9] Since this process took place in Palestine, it also explained the difference between a Palestinian Hebrew canon and a Greek one in Alexandria among Greek-speaking Jews, for whom the Septuagint translation was provided. The larger Alexandrian canon was later adopted by the Christian church.

Two studies demolished these conclusions. First, the theory of a wider Alexandrian canon in Judaism was refuted by Albert Sundberg.[10] He noted that all the manuscripts containing the "Septuagintal plus" came from Christian sources in the fourth to fifth centuries CE. He accepted Ryle's model but assumed that the Jews closed their canon in 90 CE in response to Christians who accepted more

Ethiopian and Eritrean provenance, adds more books to the Orthodox canon, while subtracting a few, but fully accepts the books of the narrower Jewish canon.

6. Some in the early church questioned Esther's canonicity (cf. for Jewish sources, b. Megillah 7a). John Meade, "The Disputed Reception of Esther: A Case Study in the Formation of Canon," in *The Law, the Prophets, and the Writings: Studies in Evangelical Old Testament Hermeneutics in Honor of Duane A. Garrett*, ed. Andrew M. King, Joshua M. Philpott, and William R. Osborne (Nashville: B&H, 2021), 327–50.

7. The Westminster Confession (1646), chap. 1, sec. 3, greatly diminished the authority of these books in Reformed circles.

8. Herbert Edward Ryle, *The Canon of the Old Testament: An Essay on the Gradual Growth and Formation of the Hebrew Canon of Scripture* (London: Macmillan, 1914).

9. This assumed a late (ca. 165 BCE) date for the book of Daniel.

10. Albert Sundberg, *The Old Testament of the Early Church* (Cambridge, MA: Harvard University Press, 1964).

books. This explained the two canons—a narrower *Jewish* canon and a wider *Christian* one.

Second, one of the foundations of Sundberg's theory was eliminated when Jack Lewis questioned the tenuous evidence for the council at Yavneh.[11] Such a "council" was an anachronistic concept. The Jewish rabbis were discussing the rationale for the inclusion of certain books in their canon, not their canonical status.

With the dissolution of these views, the way was cleared for different proposals. Some now argue for an earlier canon pushed back to the Maccabean revolt or before, others for a later canon pushed as far forward as the fourth century CE.[12]

Terminology

Although the terms "canon" and "Old Testament" originate in Christian sources, they point to the priority of the Hebrew Scriptures. "Old Testament" is a way of describing the covenant God made with Israel at Sinai in contrast to the New Covenant prophesied by Jeremiah (Jer. 31:31–34). "Canon" is a loanword from Hebrew קָנֶה (*qāneh*, reed), which came into Greek as κανών (*kanōn*). The Hebrew term signified a "stalk" or "reed" (1 Kings 14:15) and by extension could be used of a measuring stick or standard (Ezek. 40:3, 5). The Greek term was often used to describe a model, a pattern, or a ruler used by masons or carpenters.[13] In the NT it describes a circumscribed sphere or norm (2 Cor. 10:13, 15–16; Gal. 6:16).

The use of "Old Testament" to describe a collection of sacred documents is first found in a letter of Bishop Melito of Sardis around 170 CE, in which he states that he went to Syria-Palestine "to learn the correct number and order of the books . . . [understood as] Moses and the Prophets." He later names this collection τὰ τῆς παλαιᾶς διαθήκης βιβλία, "the books of the Old Testament" (*ta tēs palaias diathēkēs biblia*).[14] This first reference to the OT describes a body of literature whose content, if not arrangement, is essentially identical to the HB.

"Canon" is first used in a Christian context in 367 CE in Bishop Athanasius's thirty-ninth Easter Letter.[15] The letter evinces a growing concern in Christian circles about literature being used as if under the stamp of divine authority but without this imprimatur. "Apocryphal" books were making their way into the divinely inspired collection, so Athanasius identified the canonical works. He

11. Jack P. Lewis, "What Do We Mean by Jabneh?," *JBR* 32, no. 2 (1964): 25–32.

12. Lee Martin McDonald and James A. Sanders, eds., *The Canon Debate* (Peabody, MA: Hendrickson, 2002).

13. Henry George Liddell and Robert Scott, *A Greek-English Lexicon with Revised Supplement* (Oxford: Clarendon, 1996), 875.

14. Eusebius, *Hist. eccl.* 4.26.12–14.

15. Athanasius, *De Decretis* 18.3.2. Edmon L. Gallagher and John D. Meade, *The Biblical Canon Lists from Early Christianity: Texts and Analysis* (Oxford: Oxford University Press), 118–29.

distinguishes (1) canonized books, (2) noncanonized books useful for edification, and (3) heretical, apocryphal books.

Although the terminology first appears in the fourth century CE, the concept of an authoritative body of writing can be traced back to Judaism and ancient Israel. The first canon dates back to the Ten Words spoken from Mount Sinai.[16] In time, more words of inspired representatives were added to this collection and placed in a nearby sacred zone,[17] including the Book of the Covenant (Exod. 21:1–24:7) and the Deuteronomic document renewing the covenant (Deut. 31:26), which was written under the supervision of a priestly class (17:18–20). These words were to transform the hearts and homes of the Israelites (6:4–9). Later Judaism called the collection of such documents "books which defile the hands," probably meaning that they were so holy that one had to purify oneself after contact since one had been in touch with the divine.[18] These same books were later called "canonical" by Athanasius. During the first century CE, rabbis discussed why some of these books were included among such a collection, but there was little doubt about their status.[19]

Some scholars have begun to use a distinction between "scripture" as an open collection of authoritative documents and "canon" as a closed collection of authoritative books.[20] The distinction is problematic, for it implies a qualitative difference between canonical books and those on the way to canonical status; thus the idea of an open canon becomes an oxymoron.[21] Moreover, this distinction implies the need for a formal council "imbued with the authority to make such judgments."[22] Such a state of affairs would seem absurd because all agree that a core collection held a functional, if not formal, authority by the first century CE. Thus, there was probably not a qualitative difference between Scripture and canon, merely a quantitative one.[23]

16. Exod. 20:1–18; 25:10–16; 40:20; Deut. 10:5; 1 Kings 8:9.

17. Josh. 24:26. Roger T. Beckwith, *The Old Testament Canon of the New Testament Church and Its Background in Early Judaism* (Grand Rapids: Eerdmans, 1985), 80–86.

18. Mishnah, Yadayim 4.6; b. Shabbat 14a. See F. F. Bruce, *The Canon of Scripture* (Downers Grove, IL: InterVarsity, 1988), 34.

19. Mishnah, Yadayim 3.5–6. See Lewis, "What Do We Mean by Jabneh?"

20. Eugene Ulrich, "The Notion and Definition of Canon," in McDonald and Sanders, *Canon Debate*, 21–30; John Barton, "The Old Testament Canons," in *The New Cambridge History of the Bible*, vol. 1, *From the Beginnings to 600*, ed. James Carleton Paget and Joachim Schaper (Cambridge: Cambridge University Press, 2013), 152.

21. Julius Steinberg and Timothy J. Stone, "The Historical Formation of the Writings in Antiquity," in *The Shape of the Writings*, ed. Julius Steinberg and Timothy J. Stone, Siphrut 16 (Winona Lake, IN: Eisenbrauns, 2016), 8–10.

22. Steinberg and Stone, "Historical Formation of the Writings," 6. Only the Council of Trent (1546) for the Roman Catholic Church and the Synod of Jerusalem (1672) for the Orthodox Church functioned to close the canon.

23. I use the terms "Canon 1" and "Canon 2" to indicate the organic unity between these labels. See Stephen Dempster, "Canons on the Right and Canons on the Left: Finding a Resolution in the Canon Debate," *JETS* 51, no. 1 (2009): 47–77.

Book versus Scrolls

The OT was not originally a book in the modern sense, where all the canonical "books" were found in one volume. The earliest pandects (Bibles in one volume) that included the OT are not attested until the fourth century CE and were relatively rare until the second millennium CE.[24] The codex, or book in our modern sense, seems to have been embraced first in Christian circles and then much later by Jews because of their veneration for the scroll.[25] For the most part, in earlier times the "books" of the HB/OT were written on individual scrolls.[26] The original texts consisted of twenty-four scrolls but could be numbered as twenty-two by combining short books with longer ones. This was probably done in order to view the canon as an alphabet for theological literacy since there are twenty-two letters in the Hebrew alphabet.[27] Translating the HB into Greek increased the number of scrolls because representing vowels made the Greek script less compact than the Hebrew script and required that some books be divided into two scrolls.[28] This accounts for the larger number of scrolls in Christian circles that adopted the Greek manuscripts as their Bible.

It is sometimes mentioned that sequence would have been unimportant during early times while individual scrolls were being used and that the codex forced scribes to consider the importance of sequence.[29] But it is easy to see how there could be conceptual unity even with the technological constraints of multiple scrolls. After all, the volumes of a modern multivolume work are numbered to be read in a particular sequence. In early Jewish and Christian circles, sequence and arrangement were important.[30] This is proved not only by explicit statements but also by the resultant subcollections within the HB/OT.

24. One exception may be provided from Eusebius, who mentions that Constantine wrote to him about producing fifty copies of the Scriptures for the churches. If this happened, only one may have survived, Codex Sinaiticus (Eusebius, *Vit. Const.* 4.36). T. C. Skeat, "The Codex Sinaiticus, the Codex Vaticanus and Constantine," *JTS* 50, no. 2 (1999): 583–625.

25. The first evidence for codices of complete Hebrew Bibles occurs in the 10th cent. CE (e.g., the Aleppo Codex). A codex of the Prophets (Cairensis) was previously dated to the 9th cent., but this has been revised. See Colin H. Roberts and T. C. Skeat, *The Birth of the Codex* (Oxford: Oxford University Press, 1999).

26. The Babylonian Talmud (Bava Batra 13b–14b; Megillah 1.11; 3.1) gives rules for including more than one book on a scroll. Qumran supplies manuscript evidence: Genesis-Exodus (4Q1, 4Q11), Exodus-Leviticus (4Q17), and Leviticus-Numbers (4Q23).

27. Jerome, *Prologus Galeatus*; Origen, *Selecta in Psalmos 1*. The number twenty-four may reflect the Greek alphabet for similar reasons. See Guy Darshan, "The Twenty-Four Books of the Hebrew Bible and Alexandrian Scribal Methods," in *Homer and the Bible in the Eyes of Ancient Interpreters*, ed. Maran I. Niehoff (Leiden: Brill, 2012), 221–44.

28. Samuel, Kings, Chronicles, and Ezra-Nehemiah.

29. Peter Brandt, *Endgestalten des Kanons: Das Arrangement der Schriften Israels in der jüdischen and christlichen Bible*, BBB 131 (Berlin: Philo, 2001), 371.

30. This is the assumption behind Melito's quest for the OT, which is also reflected in Jewish circles (b. Bava Batra 14b) and in the late medieval period (Joseph of Constantinople, *Adath Deborim*), with a polemic against a Babylonian order of the Writings. Later Judaism has several orders for the Writings, based on liturgy and other factors.

Important Considerations for Origins of a Closed Canon

Josephus (*Ag. Ap.* 1.8) explicitly addresses the matter of canon at the end of the first century CE. He argues for a defined list of twenty-two books, a specific epoch for this list (Moses until Artaxerxes), a consensus among Jews about this list, a standardization of the texts, and even a tripartite structure for the order.

Around the same time, 4 Ezra/2 Esdras (14:44–46) mentions a similar list of ninety-four books, twenty-four of which are to be read in public. While the author extends the canon, he reveals the standard default position. The Gospel of Thomas (52), a document contemporary with 4 Ezra, describes "twenty-four prophets who spoke in Israel," another probable reference to the canon. By the end of the second century, a baraita (an external source in the Talmud dating to the time of the Mishnah, 10–200 CE) indicates twenty-four books in the Jewish Scriptures (b. Bava Batra 14b). They are named and in a particular order: the Torah is assumed (Genesis, Exodus, Leviticus, Numbers, Deuteronomy), Prophets (Joshua, Judges, Samuel, Kings, Jeremiah, Ezekiel, Isaiah, The Twelve), and Writings (Ruth, Psalms, Job, Proverbs, Ecclesiastes, Songs, Lamentations, Daniel, Esther, Ezra-Nehemiah, Chronicles). Variation between twenty-two and twenty-four may seem a problem, but Christian sources beginning a century or so later mention two Jewish enumerations.[31] The lower number is reached by combining Ruth with Judges and Lamentations with Jeremiah.

Other facts need to be considered. The Mishnah was codified in 200 CE, but its oral traditions date to much earlier times. When the rabbis want to support their words with absolute authority, they appeal only to books named in the previously mentioned baraita, prefaced by the formula "as it is said."[32] Over one hundred years earlier, the vast majority of Scripture citations by the NT authors come from the writings listed in the baraita.[33] At Qumran, the use of authoritative citations virtually coheres with this picture.[34] One further piece of evidence is highly suggestive. The early church fathers, particularly from the East and some

31. Origen (180–250 CE) notes that the Jews have twenty-two books, according to the letters of the Hebrew alphabet (Eusebius, *Hist. eccl.* 6.25). Jerome (340–420 CE) notes the two Jewish enumerations (*Prologus Galeatus*).

32. Only Daniel is not cited, but elsewhere in the Mishnah (Yadayim 4.5; Yoma 1.6), it is regarded as authoritative.

33. The Enoch quote in Jude 14–15 is the exception, but some argue that the reference is not an authoritative citation. Cf. Peter J. Gentry and Andrew M. Fountain, "Reassessing Jude's Use of Enochic Traditions," *TynBul* 68, no. 2 (2017): 261–86. In my judgment, the exception proves the rule. There are allusions to other literature, and not all the "canonical" books are explicitly quoted in the NT (such as Judges, Ruth, Ecclesiastes, Song of Songs, Esther, Lamentations), but the evidence for a closed authoritative collection is massive.

34. The one exception, with 43 citations, may be Jubilees (4Q228 1 1.9; CD 16.2–3), but see Johann Lust, "Quotation Formulae and Canon in Qumran," in *Canonization and Decanonization: Papers Presented to the International Congress of the Leiden Institute for the Study of Religions*, ed. A. van der Kooij and K. van der Toorn, Studies in the History of Religions 82 (Leiden: Brill, 1998), 67–77.

from the West, make clear that they inherited a closed authoritative collection from the Jews that was restricted to either twenty-two or twenty-four books.[35] Even when the number is increased to twenty-seven, the books are the same and the number is regarded as another way to view the alphabet since the Hebrew alphabet contains five letters with final forms (see Epiphanius). This is impressive corroboration for the early existence of a Jewish canon.

Those arguing for a late CE canon interpret this evidence differently. Josephus is viewed as an "outlier," as exaggerating the situation or being "out of step with his contemporaries."[36] In some of the evidence, exceptions are emphasized. First Enoch seems to be cited as Scripture in the NT and Jubilees at Qumran. Moreover, Esther is omitted in some early church lists and is questioned in rabbinic discussions. Other evidence includes a passage in 2 Maccabees (2:13–16) regarding the possible structure and formation of the canon and references to canonical structure in the prologue to Sirach (2, 8, 25), Philo (*De vita contemplativa* 25), and the NT (Luke 24:44). Other issues cannot be considered here, and the literature is vast.[37] Nevertheless, the evidence strongly suggests that the Christian church "was born with a canon in its hands." There may have been divergent collections of Scriptures. The Samaritans accepted only the Torah, and Qumran may have had a wider canon, but the evidence converges to indicate a restricted canon among many Jews, which the first-century church inherited.[38]

In the subsequent years, many references to the number twenty-four and the tripartite structure of the canon appear in the Midrash and the Talmud.[39] Medieval Jewish scribes produced the first large Hebrew codices encompassing the second division of the Prophets (Codex Cairensis, ca. 11th cent. CE) and two complete Hebrew Bibles (the Aleppo Codex, 925 CE; Codex Leningradensis, 1008 CE). A tenth-century list attests to a sequence conforming to that of Bava Batra 14b.[40] Codex Cairensis exhibits a more chronological order of the Latter

35. Origen, Cyril of Jerusalem, Athanasius, Synod of Laodicea, Gregory of Nazianzus, Epiphanius, Hilary of Poitiers, Jerome.

36. Stephen Dempster, "The Old Testament Canon, Josephus, and Cognitive Environment," in *The Enduring Authority of the Christian Scriptures*, ed. D. A. Carson (Grand Rapids: Eerdmans, 2016), 321–61. For a CE canon, see Lee Martin McDonald, *The Biblical Canon: Its Origin, Transmission, and Authority*, 3rd ed. (Peabody, MA: Hendrickson, 2007); and Barton, "Old Testament Canons."

37. Different perspectives are represented in Beckwith, *Old Testament Canon*; McDonald, *Biblical Canon*; and Gallagher and Meade, *Biblical Canon Lists*, 3–25.

38. Philip S. Alexander, "The Formation of the Biblical Canon in Rabbinic Judaism," in *The Canon of Scripture in Jewish and Christian Tradition*, ed. Philip S. Alexander and Jean-Daniel Kaestli (Prahins: Éditions du Zèbre, 2007), 65; Gallagher and Meade, *Biblical Canon Lists*, 25.

39. See b. Taʿanit 8a; b. Ḥagigah 77b; b. Sanhedrin 90b; Leviticus Rabbah 16.4. Sid Z. Leiman, *The Canonization of Hebrew Scripture: The Talmudic and Midrashic Evidence* (Hamden: Archon, 1976), 53–58.

40. Hans Peter Rüger, "Ein Fragment der bisher ältesten datierten hebräischen Bibelhandschrift mit babylonischer Punktation," *VT* 16, no. 1 (1966): 65–73.

Prophets than Bava Batra. Others present a different order than Bava Batra's for the Writings, and this becomes the source for polemics by the early thirteenth century CE. A treatise comparing Masoretic schools, *Adath Deborim*, argues for the correctness of a western sequence of the Writings found in Aleppo and Leningradensis.[41]

After this time there seems to be an explosion of proposed orders. Virtually all are based on a tripartite scheme of twenty-four books. In some more liturgical orders, the Megillot (Song of Songs, Ruth, Lamentations, Ecclesiastes, Esther) are placed after the Torah. These books are publicly read in their entirety in the synagogue every year—the Torah in scheduled readings and the Megillot on relevant Festal Days. Peter Brandt categorizes the main orders of the Writings as eastern, western, and rabbinic (which represents a blending of the two).[42]

Canonical Order of the Writings

Eastern Sequences	Western Sequences	Rabbinic Bibles
Ruth	Chronicles	Psalms
Psalms	Psalms	Proverbs
Job	Job	Job
Proverbs	Proverbs	Song of Songs
Ecclesiastes	Ruth	Ruth
Song of Songs	Song of Songs	Lamentations
Lamentations	Ecclesiastes	Ecclesiastes
Daniel	Lamentations	Esther
Esther	Esther	Daniel
Ezra-Nehemiah	Daniel	Ezra-Nehemiah
Chronicles	Ezra-Nehemiah	Chronicles

The western and rabbinic orders are based on liturgy, since in each, the Megillot are grouped together. The western order arranges the Megillot chronologically, and the rabbinic order, calendrically. Despite the variety, the tripartite order is basic. The Torah represents the great acts of God for Israel; the Prophets call on the people to remember the Torah and to prepare for the future acts of God; and the Writings convey the response of the people as they pray and sing, reflect and ponder, in the midst of suffering and hope.[43] The variation in later arrangements results from the freedom of scribes to change sequences for liturgical and other purposes, where the books were less chronologically constrained.[44]

41. Beckwith, *Old Testament Canon*, 201.

42. Brandt, *Endgestalten des Kanons*, 132–71; Brandt, "Final Forms of the Writings," in Steinberg and Stone, *Shape of the Writings*, 71–75.

43. Dempster, "Canons on the Right," 68–77.

44. Beckwith, *Old Testament Canon*, 211.

Whither Old Testament Canons?

As the church was leaving its Jewish roots, expanding to the gentiles, and adopting the Septuagint as its default Bible, there was a growing confusion about the books of the OT. Melito made a journey to rectify this problem. This first explicit Christian list matches the Hebrew canon, but it has a different tripartite structure and excludes Esther. The Prophets, including Daniel, shift toward the end. This becomes a tendency in the early Christian lists.[45]

The Latin West continued placing the Prophets toward the end.[46] Jerome is an exception with his two enumerations of the Jewish order, placing the Prophets in the middle.[47] The greatest difference is "extra" books outside the Jewish canon placed among the canonical books.[48] At the same time, some lists exhibit an awareness that these "intermediate books" are different. The farther from the East one goes, the less connection there is to the root of the HB. But again Jerome is the exception, listing the noncanonical books as apocrypha after the OT books because of his knowledge of Hebrew.[49] Others, like Rufinus and Hilary, are also aware of some of the differences.[50]

By the fourth or fifth century, complete Greek pandects were produced on single codices. While surviving manuscripts are minimal, they include all the books of the Jewish canon. The "intermediate" books are included with no apparent distinction (although no two lists are the same). The structure of the books is based on genre, with historical books coming first, followed by poetic books, and then prophetic books (e.g., Vaticanus) or the reverse of the last two categories (e.g., Sinaiticus, Alexandrinus). The earliest examples of the Syriac and Latin pandects, which date to the seventh and eighth centuries, show similar generic categories, with the so-called apocryphal books shifting closer to the end (Syriac)[51] or simply occurring within the arrangement (Latin).[52] But one must be cautious about identifying pandects as Bibles in a contemporary sense. Because of the labor and cost of producing them, other books may have been included for edification, to make them more like "service manuals."[53]

45. Origen, Cyril of Jerusalem, Athanasius, Synod of Laodicea, Gregory of Nazianzus, Apostolic Canons 85, Amphilocus, and the three lists of Epiphanius.

46. Mommsen Catalogue, Hilary of Poitiers (*Instructio Psalmorum* 15), Augustine (*On Christian Doctrine*).

47. Jerome, "Prologus Galeatus."

48. Codex Claromontanus, Mommsen Catalogue, lists of Innocent I, and Augustine.

49. Jerome, "Prologus Galeatus." See also his preface to the Solomonic books.

50. Rufinus, *Commentary on the Apostles' Creed*; Hilary, *Instructio Psalmorum* 15.

51. See Codex Ambrosianus. The Wisdom of Solomon is among the Wisdom literature, the Epistle of Jeremiah and Baruch among the Prophets, and Susanna and Judith join Ruth and Esther to compose the "Book of Women."

52. Codex Amiatinus.

53. E. Earl Ellis, *The Old Testament in Early Christianity in the Light of Modern Research* (Eugene, OR: Wipf & Stock, 2003), 34–35. Codex Sinaiticus ends with the Epistle of Barnabas and the Shepherd of Hermas, which do not appear in any canonical list.

Clearly Jerome's influence had dissipated for separating the extra "intermediate" books from the core, canonical books. Nevertheless, there is some fluidity. The oldest complete copy of a Latin Bible, Codex Amiatinus, includes the extra books within its arrangement and has several lists of books in the prologue, one of which matches Jerome's.

At the turn of the millennium, the ambiguity regarding the extra books continued as the manuscripts multiplied. Samuel Berger's classic study collects over two hundred various orders for books of the OT, which he divides into seven basic categories.[54] Some individuals follow Jerome with his belief that the extra books are useful but not canonical (Hugh of St. Victor, 1096–1141; John of Salisbury, 1120–1180; Nicholas of Lyra, 1270–1349). Many, however, disagree.[55] Pandects become much more numerous in the 1200s. In Paris the scholarly pandects "harden" the arrangement so that the influential Prophets provide closure for the OT. This order becomes the norm for the Vulgate, when it becomes the official Bible of the Roman Catholic Church.[56] It is not a coincidence that the first Gutenberg Bible follows a similar order, with the Prophets being at the end followed by Maccabees.[57]

Influence of the Protestant Reformation

The Reformation forced the Roman Catholic Church to settle the issue of canon and resolve any ambiguity about the books outside the HB. Martin Luther's decision to rely on the "Hebrew truth" of Jerome in polemics, and his German translation of the Bible in 1534, which placed the Apocrypha between the Testaments, show Jerome's influence. These books were not considered equal to Scripture but were useful to read. The influence of Luther's Bible resulted in the Council of Trent's promulgation of a decree concerning the Sacred Scriptures (1546), in which these books were included after significant debate.[58] In 1566 any ambiguity was finally eliminated when Sixtus of Siena declared these books "deuterocanonical"—that is, not lesser in status but later in reception. The Bible for the Roman Catholic Church was the Vulgate. A definitive edition was promoted by Pope Sixtus V in 1590. Revised in 1592 under orders by Pope

54. Samuel Berger, *Histoire de la Vulgate pendant les premiers siècles du Moyen Âge* (Paris: Librairie Hachette, 1893), 331–39.

55. Armin Lange, "The Canonical Histories of the Jewish Bible and the Christian Old Testament with Special Attention to the Deuterocanonical Books—A Synthesis," in *Textual History of the Bible*, vol. 2A, *The Deuterocanonical Scriptures: Overview Articles*, ed. Frank Feder and Matthias Henze (Leiden: Brill, 2020), 181–82.

56. Brandt, *Endgestalten des Kanons,* 239–40.

57. First and Second Esdras follow Ezra and Nehemiah in the Gutenberg Bible but are lacking in the Clementine Vulgate.

58. Edmon L. Gallagher, "The Latin Canon of the Old Testament in the Sixteenth Century," in *Textual History of the Bible*, vol. 2, ed. Armin Lange and Emmanuel Tov (Leiden: Brill, 2020), 183–90.

Clement VIII and known as the Sixto-Clementine Vulgate, it was the official Latin text for the Roman Catholic Church until 1979.

Greek Orthodoxy

After the Great Schism of the Eastern Churches from the West in 1054, the situation of the OT canon for the East had the same ambiguity as in the West. Other books besides those in the HB could be read for edification. One early Eastern council (Laodicea) included only the books of the Jewish Bible,[59] while the later Apostolic Canons included other books. Later lists alternate between accepting the Jewish core and excluding others. John of Damascus (*Expositio Fidei* 4.17) accepted only the books of the HB while noting the didactic value of some others. In other lists, some of these additional books are included in the core. Consequently, the situation in Orthodoxy was much like the Roman Catholic Church before the Council of Trent. The Synod of Jerusalem in 1672 responded to a previous confession three decades earlier that adopted the canon of the Council of Laodicea. To the Laodicean list, the Synod added the Wisdom of Solomon, Judith, Tobit, the History of the Dragon, the History of Susannah, the Maccabees, and Sirach. In contemporary Orthodoxy, there is a looser understanding of canon, and a considerable number of scholars view these books to be on a lower level than the books of the HB.[60]

Recent Developments in Canonical Studies

Several important studies of the OT canon have led to new developments. First, Timothy Lim has reevaluated the evidence for the Jewish canon. On his reading, a number of scriptural collections existed among the sectarian groups of the Jews in the first century, but the collection of the majority, the Pharisees, eventually triumphed.[61] Evidence for the different collections comes from Qumran (where books such as Jubilees and Enoch had a high level of authority), from a postulated larger collection mentioned in Sirach's Prologue, and from the disputed status mentioned in the Mishnah of certain books such as Ecclesiastes and Song of Songs. After the destruction of Jerusalem, only the Pharisaic majority and their collection survived. This collection did not achieve canonical status until the second or third century CE. In short, it was the canon of the "winners."

Lim's book is an advance over the views of scholars such as Lee Martin McDonald, since Lim's dating for the CE canon is earlier, but he still regards

59. This explicitly included Baruch and the Letter of Jeremiah as part of Jeremiah.

60. T. Kallistos Ware, *The Orthodox Church* (New York: Penguin, 1993), 200–209. For further developments, see n. 5 above. See also Eugen J. Pentiuc, *The Old Testament in Eastern Orthodox Tradition* (New York: Oxford University Press, 2014), 128–31.

61. Timothy H. Lim, *The Formation of the Jewish Canon* (New Haven: Yale University Press, 2013).

Josephus's explicit statements about the canon as exaggeration, and some of his interpretations of the evidence are questionable. Particularly difficult for his view is the problem of accounting for not only the evidence from Josephus but also the evidence from 4 Ezra and the Gospel of Thomas and for the remarkable coordination of the lists of the early church fathers, all of which assume a similar tradition.

Julius Steinberg and Timothy Stone have edited a significant study on the Jewish canon, particularly the Writings. Their introductory essay is a lucid discussion of the conceptual issues related to canon.[62] They emphasize the sequence and arrangement of the scrolls and the importance of the temple as the site for the storing and organization of the holy books. The scrolls would not have been haphazardly arranged. Other essays also argue for the hermeneutical significance of these arrangements.

Two essays demonstrate the influence of German scholarship. Building on his earlier work on the OT canon, Brandt shows the relevance of the various sequences of the Writings for Jews and Christians.[63] With respect to the Writings, he wonders whether interpreters of the HB should be guided by the eastern, western, or rabbinic order. He argues that the historical evidence allows for "a certain plurality of arrangement" and urges us "to appreciate the potential of several of the historically important orders for exegesis."[64]

Developing an earlier study, Georg Steins argues that Chronicles was explicitly written as a conclusion to the canon.[65] He concludes that the book is a fitting ending since it recapitulates Israel's history from Adam to Cyrus, with a reading based on Torah observance.[66] While Steins's thesis has many strengths, his argument that the Maccabean crisis produced Chronicles and thus was the catalyst for the closing of the canon is highly questionable, since the scholarly consensus dates Chronicles between 400 and 300 BCE. The earliest possible date is determined by the termination of the generational sequence of David's line after the exile (1 Chron. 3:19–24) and the latest date by the absence of Hellenistic influence, particularly the struggles of the Maccabean period.[67]

While his dating of Chronicles is doubtful, Steins's study of signals of canonical closure points to evidence of canonical consciousness among the documents of the canon and forcefully puts the question as to whether an internal force of

62. Steinberg and Stone, "Historical Formation of the Writings," 1–58.

63. Brandt, *Endgestalten des Kanons*.

64. Brandt, "Final Forms of the Writings," 84.

65. Georg Steins, *Die Chronik als kanonisches Abschlussphänomen: Studien zur Entstehung und Theologie von 1/2 Chronik*, BBB 93 (Weinheim: Beltz Athenäum, 1995).

66. Georg Steins, "Torah Binding and Canonical Closure: On the Origin and Canonical Function of the Book of Chronicles," in Steinberg and Stone, *Shape of the Writings*, 274–76.

67. David Janzen, *Chronicles and the Politics of Davidic Restoration: A Quiet Revolution* (London: Bloomsbury T&T Clark, 2017), 10–14; Isaac Kalimi, "The Date of the Book of Chronicles: Biblical Text, Elephantine and Ibrahimiah's Aramaic Grave Inscription," in *An Ancient Israelite Historian: Studies in the Chronicler, His Time, Place and Writing*, SSN 46 (Leiden: Brill, 2005), 41–65.

canon is operative within the texts. Such signs have been observed at the seams of the bipartite[68] or tripartite canon[69] and suggest the possibility of closure at the end of the biblical period.

Edmon Gallagher and John Meade's study is an excellent resource for examining the canon in antiquity. While not taking a specific stance on the canon debate, two conclusions are especially significant. First, they emphasize a remarkable unity to the canon in spite of the absence of any hierarchical imposition.[70] Second, "the Jewish canon exercised a profound influence on the Christian pursuit of the correct Old Testament."[71] The lists indicate that the issue of the correct OT—the Hebrew canon or the wider one—was not fully resolved in antiquity and continues to reverberate down to the present day. Nonetheless, their study emphasizes the primacy of the Hebrew canon.

Finally, Armin Lange has emphasized that the Christian OT, with its order of the Prophets at the end from early times through its permutations to its prominent final position in the Vulgate and other translations, represents a classic case of anti-Semitic supersessionism.[72] Such an arrangement emphasizes the prediction of a new covenant and a future deliverer, which provides an ideal segue into the NT. However, one could easily argue that the early HB structure, with its closure of Chronicles, is equally eschatological, looking forward to the end of exile, a Davidic scion, and a rebuilt temple—all features suggesting the end of an old covenant and the prospect of a new one. The allusion to Daniel's seventy weeks in the final verses of 2 Chronicles, reinterpreting Jeremiah's seventy years of exile, puts the exclamation point on this feature.[73]

Conclusion

A number of general points can also be made about OT canons:

1. The OT canons spring up as shoots from a tree whose large trunk is the HB. With rare exceptions, all the books in the HB appear in the earliest OT

68. Joseph Blenkinsopp, *Prophecy and Canon: A Contribution to the Study of Jewish Origins*, Studies in Judaism and Christianity (Notre Dame, IN: University of Notre Dame Press, 1977); Stephen B. Chapman, *The Law and the Prophets: A Study in Old Testament Canon Formation* (Tübingen: Mohr Siebeck, 2000).

69. John Sailhamer, *Introduction to Old Testament Theology: A Canonical Approach* (Grand Rapids: Zondervan, 1995); Erich Zenger, *Einleitung in das Alte Testament* (Stuttgart: Kohlhammer, 1995); Dempster, "Canons on the Right."

70. Gallagher and Meade, *Biblical Canon Lists*, 2.

71. Gallagher and Meade, *Biblical Canon Lists*, 29.

72. Armin Lange, "The History of the Christian Old Testament Canon," in *Textual History of the Bible*, vol. 1A, *The Hebrew Bible: Overview Articles*, ed. Armin Lange and Emmanuel Tov (Leiden: Brill, 2016), 48–81.

73. 2 Chron. 36:21; cf. Dan. 9:20–27; Jer. 25:1–11. If Luke 24:44 witnesses to a tripartite Jewish canon, the supersessionism charge is weak, at least for the first Christians.

lists. In sum, we can definitely say that without the HB, there would be no OT.

2. The general structure of the HB is reflected in all the OT canons. The Torah structure is universal, and the Former Prophets (without Ruth) follows.[74] The foundational role of the Torah can be blurred by the often-seamless transition to the succeeding historical books, which together form an Octateuch or a Heptateuch. There is no denying the importance of the so-called Primary History (Genesis–Kings) for all OT canons. Even when there is a major departure from the Hebrew sequence, major collections of books maintain their integrity, and the Latter Prophets are often united, as are the books in poetic verse.
3. The wider OT canons are best explained by the rapid growth of Christianity into the gentile world, its separation from its Jewish roots, and the growing use of other books for edification and instruction. Intermediate books were distinguished from canonical books, but over time and by dint of popular use, they sometimes lost their secondary status. The Protestant Reformation recovered the original distinction but still used the intermediate books for edification. Until relatively recently, these books were often found in Protestant Bibles.
4. While there are a few examples of manuscripts with NT books inserted into the OT,[75] the overwhelming number show the clear distinction and separation in Christian canons. The OT has its own integrity. Moreover, the OT could have been placed as an appendix to the NT, as desired by some,[76] or eliminated altogether.[77] At the same time, the NT is not an appendix to the OT but is viewed as its continuation.

74. This structure may have Jewish roots, as attested by Origen and Jerome, and perhaps Josephus before them.

75. See MSS 16, 71, and 125, in which the Gospels are placed within the OT. Berger, *Histoire de la Vulgate*, 331–39.

76. Friedrich Schleiermacher: "The proper sense of the matter [of relating the Testaments] would be better expressed if the Old Testament followed the New Testament as an appendix," in *Christian Faith: A New Translation and Critical Edition*, trans. Terrence N. Tice et al. (Louisville: Westminster John Knox, 2016), 1011.

77. Most notably these include Marcion in the 2nd cent. CE, Adolf von Harnack in the 20th cent., and some prominent evangelical voices in the 21st cent.

12

The Pentateuch

Samuel L. Boyd

Within the realm of research on the Bible, critical studies of the Pentateuch are deemed some of the most difficult to understand. Research on the history of the composition of these texts has generated entire libraries of scholarly tomes. This situation reflects the incredible intellectual efforts to explain why Genesis, Exodus, Leviticus, Numbers, and Deuteronomy look the way they do and the importance of the Pentateuch within the biblical corpus. In the following, I identify the major recent trends that account for the history and present state of the pentateuchal texts.

Divergence and Convergence in Current Research

All academic research entails some diversity of thought, and approaches to the composition of the Pentateuch are no exception. For example, some scholars agree that the Priestly material (P) existed as an independent source prior to its redaction into the Pentateuch. In this view, P was not composed as part of the editing process. Others maintain that the author of P was the final compiler of pre-Priestly materials, an editor of sorts using Priestly material as a supplement to literature that preexisted P.[1] Another debate concerns the original extent and

1. For P as a supplement, see Frank Moore Cross, *Canaanite Myth and Hebrew Epic* (Cambridge, MA: Harvard University Press, 1973), 294–321. See a rebuttal in Baruch J. Schwartz, "The Priestly Account of the Theophany and Lawgiving at Sinai," in *Texts, Temples, and*

growth of the source. Beginning in Gen. 1:1–2:4a (which is the start of P, though Bill Arnold, e.g., ascribes this section to the Holiness school [H], a later stratum of P), a number of original endings have been identified for P. Proposals include Exod. 29 (Otto), Exod. 40 (Kratz), Lev. 9 (Zenger), or Lev. 16 (Nihan), with other additions as part of a series of expansions.[2] Or does P end in Deut. 34 (Baden), or even in Joshua (Rofé and Feldman)?[3] Despite such debates, other elements of P are essentially agreed upon.[4]

Most scholars agree that the priestly circles responsible for P did not function as the final redactor of the Pentateuch as a whole.[5] The concept of a final redaction, as well as a redactor or compiler, is even questioned by some. Reinhard Müller, Reinhard Achenbach, and others posit that the Pentateuch went through a series of editions, with late postexilic Priestly (perhaps proto-Chronicles) versions focused on God as universal king. These editions are labeled "theocratic editions" or "theocratic reworkings."[6] Most argue that the latest editing occurred in the Persian period with subsequent additions.[7] The relationship between P and the Holiness Code (H) has gained general agreement, particularly since Israel Knohl's work demonstrating that H includes not only Lev. 17–26 (or, as others have argued, Lev. 17–27) but also other texts outside Leviticus as a later stratum added to P.[8]

The identification of the Deuteronomist source (D) has largely reached a consensus. Additionally, most posit a literary relationship between the legal collection

---

Traditions: A Tribute to Menahem Haran, ed. Michael V. Fox et al. (Winona Lake, IN: Eisenbrauns, 1996), 103–34.

2. Diana V. Edelman et al., *Opening the Books of Moses*, BibleWorld (London: Routledge, 2014), 47–50. See also Bill T. Arnold, "The Holiness Redaction of the Primeval History," *ZAW* 129, no. 4 (2017): 483–500.

3. Joel Baden, *The Composition of the Pentateuch: Renewing the Documentary Hypothesis*, AYBRL (New Haven: Yale University Press, 2012), 176; Alexander Rofé, "Joshua 20: Historico-Literary Criticism Illustrated," in *Empirical Models for Biblical Criticism*, ed. Jeffrey Tigay, Dove Studies in Bible, Language, and History (Eugene, OR: Wipf & Stock, 1985), 131–48; Liane M. Feldman, *The Biblical Priestly Narrative* (Berkeley: University of California Press, 2023).

4. For a recent review of the nature of P (as an independent document or supplement) and the ending of P (attesting to literary growth), see Friedhelm Hartenstein and Konrad Schmid, eds., *Farewell to the Priestly Writing? The Current State of the Debate*, AIL 38 (Atlanta: SBL Press, 2022).

5. For an argument that P and its later stratum the Holiness School functioned as the final redactor, see Israel Knohl, *The Sanctuary of Silence: The Priestly Torah and the Holiness School* (Winona Lake, IN: Eisenbrauns, 2017). For arguments against this thesis, see Baden, *The Composition of the Pentateuch*, 177–88; Edelman et al., *Opening the Books of Moses*, 47.

6. Reinhard Müller, *Jahwe als Wettergott: Studien zur althebräischen Kultlyrik anhand ausgewählter Psalmen*, BZAW 387 (Berlin: De Gruyter, 2008); Reinhard Achenbach, "Theocratic Reworking in the Pentateuch: Proto-Chronistic Features in the Late Priestly Layers of Numbers and Their Reception in Chronicles," in *Chronicles and the Priestly Literature of the Hebrew Bible*, ed. Jaeyoung Jeon and Louis C. Jonker, BZAW 528 (Berlin: De Gruyter, 2021), 53–78.

7. For a helpful discussion, see Jean-Louis Ska, *Introduction to Reading the Pentateuch* (Winona Lake, IN: Eisenbrauns, 2006), 217–29.

8. For a review of this issue, see Liane M. Feldman, *The Story of Sacrifice: Ritual and Narrative in the Priestly Source*, FAT 141 (Tübingen: Mohr Siebeck, 2020), 195–200.

in D and that found in Exod. 20:22–23:19, also called the "Covenant Code." Still debated is whether D exists as a supplement to the earlier legislation or as an independent composition replacing the material in Exodus though also engaging it.[9] Though scholars disagree on the history of composition of D, its general parameters (essentially Deut. 1:1–32:47) have been a matter of agreement for some time. Thus, a broad consensus about the literary material that belongs to P and D exists, even if other aspects (e.g., their character, history, and extent) remain debated.

Two Main Approaches

The topics discussed above bring to the fore the two main approaches in the study of the Pentateuch: non-Documentary approaches and Neo-Documentarianism. Each entails a certain diversity, as many non-Documentary scholars do not agree with one another, and many Neo-Documentarians likewise have areas of disagreement. Disagreement occurs largely about the non-P portions of the Tetrateuch (Genesis through Numbers) and the literary material traditionally assigned to the J and E sources. Moreover, other models continue to provide productive insights into the history and composition of the Torah as well.[10] Nonetheless, it is worth highlighting these two approaches as their methods, assumptions, and conclusions have become major topics of discussion in the field.

Non-Documentary Approaches

In 1977, Rolf Rendtorff published a seminal work arguing that smaller units identified through the tradition-historical work of Martin Noth and Gerhard von Rad could not be assembled literarily in a manner that resulted in the sources traditionally assigned as J or E.[11] Rendtorff's work was already presaged by a number of scholars in North America and Europe who had questioned some of the foundations of source criticism.[12] Consequently, an independent J and E source has been doubted by many, particularly (though not exclusively) European,

9. Jeffrey Stackert, *Deuteronomy and the Pentateuch*, AYBRL (New Haven: Yale University Press, 2022), 52–85.

10. For recent and comprehensive resources, see Jan C. Gertz et al., eds., *The Formation of the Pentateuch: Bridging the Academic Cultures of Europe, Israel, and North America*, FAT 111 (Tübingen: Mohr Siebeck, 2016); Joel S. Baden and Jeffrey Stackert, eds., *The Oxford Handbook of the Pentateuch* (New York: Oxford University Press, 2021).

11. See also the English translation published a few years later, Rolf Rendtorff, *The Problem of the Process of Transmission in the Pentateuch*, trans. John J. Scullion, JSOTSup 89 (Sheffield: Sheffield Academic, 1990).

12. For precursors to Rendtorff, such as Rainer Kessler's unpublished dissertation at Heidelberg, which Rendtorff read, and for the pitfalls of ascribing to Rendtorff too much influence in the change in source critical paradigms exclusive of other thinkers both in Germany and in Toronto (and elsewhere), see David M. Carr, "Changes in Pentateuchal Criticism," in *From*

scholars.[13] The Tetrateuch is considered to be the result of accretion, or the iterative addition of supplements over time (*Fortschreibung*), which were added to P and D to make up the Pentateuch.[14] Some supplements may contain Deuteronomist elements and even later, post-Priestly supplements.[15] These additions are based on the core of P, using its language and matrix of thought.[16]

One of the important issues is the idea of literary coherence. If the non-P material does not connect to an identifiable literary source more generally, then perhaps it would have existed as discrete units. For example, Konrad Schmid argues that non-P material in Genesis is distinct from non-P material in Exodus and the Moses story.[17] As such, the ancestral narratives and the Moses story compose two independent etiologies in non-P for the origin of Israel. This issue of literary continuity has become a major area of disagreement between these non-Documentary scholars and other approaches.[18]

Another key area of methodological discussion involves attempting to date texts based on their themes and theologies. Benjamin Sommer calls attention to the methodological problems in assigning a date to certain texts based on theological content, criticizing and labeling such approaches as "pseudo-historicism." In contrast, Schmid has argued that such a method is more rigorous than Sommer claims.[19]

Neo-Documentarianism

Arising from the influence of Yehezkel Kaufmann and Menahem Haran, the Neo-Documentary approach diverges from non-Documentary models in several key respects that center largely on the nature of the Pentateuch as literature.

Sources to Scrolls and Beyond: Essays on the Study of the Pentateuch, FAT (Tübingen: Mohr Siebeck, 2024).

13. Konrad Schmid, *The Old Testament: A Literary History*, trans. Linda M. Maloney (Minneapolis: Fortress, 2012), 120–25, 160–62. This approach has been termed "traditional historical." See, for non-Europeans, the works of Shimon Gesundheit, Thomas Dozeman, and David Carr. Further, see the term "transmission-historical" in Baden and Stackert, *Oxford Handbook of the Pentateuch*, 1–19.

14. Erhard Blum, *Studien zur Komposition des Pentateuch*, BZAW 189 (Berlin: De Gruyter, 1990).

15. Joel S. Baden, "The Deuteronomic Evidence for the Documentary Hypothesis," in *The Pentateuch: International Perspectives on Current Research*, ed. Thomas B. Dozeman, Konrad Schmid, and Baruch J. Schwartz, FAT 78 (Tübingen: Mohr Siebeck, 2011), 329n8.

16. Schmid, *Old Testament*, 156–57.

17. Konrad Schmid, *Genesis and the Moses Story: Israel's Dual Origins in the Hebrew Bible* (Winona Lake, IN: Eisenbrauns, 2010); Schmid, "Genesis and Exodus as Two Formerly Independent Traditions of Origins for Ancient Israel," *Bib* 93, no. 2 (2012): 187–208.

18. David Andrew Teeter and William A. Tooman, "Standards of (In)coherence in Ancient Jewish Literature," *HeBAI* 9, no. 2 (2020): 94–129.

19. Benjamin D. Sommer, "Dating Pentateuchal Texts and the Perils of Pseudo-Historicism," in Dozeman, Schmid, and Schwartz, *Pentateuch*, 85–108; Konrad Schmid, "How Old Is the Hebrew Bible? A Response to Ronald Hendel and Jan Joosten," *ZAW* 132, no. 4 (2020): 622–32.

Schmid describes the literary thrust of Neo-Documentarianism as "one of the most serious divergences in current Pentateuch research."[20] Schwartz argues that the tradition-historical approach that Rendtorff leverages to reconstruct the processes of growth from the smallest literary units to literary sources such as J, E, D, or P was never meant to be applied in such a manner.[21] For von Rad and Noth, the smallest components were oral units only and cannot be treated as literary precursors since they do not necessarily develop linearly toward the final literary documents.[22] Instead, the Documentary Hypothesis is a way to explain literary features of the final form of the Pentateuch. It assumes that only when the final form cannot be explained synchronically should a scholar revert to diachrony.[23] The sources J, E, D, and P are not meant to be literary documents that could be reconstructed from the smallest oral units but instead are always reconstructed from the final form as the stage immediately preceding the editing of the Pentateuch.

Neo-Documentarianism posits four sources, J, E, D, and P, underlying the compilation of the Pentateuch, but it is not a simple return to Julius Wellhausen's original theory. The methodological approaches of Hermann Hupfeld and August Dillmann are as influential, if not more so.[24] In line with Dillmann, Neo-Documentarians argue that all four sources were combined in a single, minimally invasive redactional event, unlike Wellhausen's argument that J and E were combined quite early.[25] This literary assemblage leads to other important distinctions in Neo-Documentarianism. There is no need to theorize an independently compiled JE-source prior to the editing of the Pentateuch. Both J and E are identified as distinct, each presenting its own perspective on the history of Israel and its religion.[26]

Moreover, the compiler, in maintaining contradictions, was not mindless. Rather, comprehensiveness is the primary value for editing the sources, similar to other ancient bodies of literature such as the Talmud.[27] The presence of literary seams, contradictions, or redundancies does not entail poor editing, and these features are not evaluated as good or bad to the degree that they conform

20. Konrad Schmid, "The Neo-Documentarian Manifesto: A Critical Reading," *JBL* 140, no. 3 (2021): 469.

21. Baruch J. Schwartz, "Does Recent Scholarship's Critique of the Documentary Hypothesis Constitute Grounds for Its Rejection?," in Dozeman, Schmid, and Schwartz, *Pentateuch*, 6–10.

22. Baden, *Composition of the Pentateuch*, 53–67, esp. 64.

23. Schwartz, "Recent Scholarship's Critique," 10.

24. Joel Baden, *J, E, and the Redaction of the Pentateuch*, FAT 68 (Tübingen: Mohr Siebeck, 2009), 13–19, 37–40.

25. Jeffrey Stackert, *A Prophet like Moses: Prophecy, Law, and Israelite Religion* (New York: Oxford University Press, 2014), 21.

26. Stackert, *Deuteronomy and the Pentateuch*, 56.

27. Baden, *Composition of the Pentateuch*, 224–25; Seth L. Sanders, "What If There Aren't Any Empirical Models for Pentateuchal Criticism?," in *Contextualizing Israel's Sacred Writings: Ancient Literacy, Orality, and Literary Production*, ed. Brian B. Schmidt, AIL 22 (Atlanta: SBL Press, 2015), 281–304.

to modern literature. In fact, many features of the text, such as different sources, are productively understood in the context of Jewish thought and theology.[28] Understanding these recent trends has encouraged constructive engagement with the distinct literary material in the Pentateuch.

Literary Criticism and/as Source Criticism

One example of constructive engagement is how a close reading of D reveals distinct strata in the Tetrateuch.[29] For instance, the narratives in Exod. 33–34 could be divided into two plots: (a) a story about Moses receiving the second set of commandments after he smashed the first, and (b) a story about Moses seeing the divine.[30] Neo-Documentary scholars assign the former story to E and the latter to J. Each fits with the broader narrative claims of E and J respectively. In Exod. 33–34, these two stories are intertwined, almost braided together in a double-helix fashion. In the corresponding narrative in Deut. 10:1–8, only the (a) story appears, with no trace of the interwoven (b) plot. One could likewise divide literary sources in Exod. 19 between the theophany on Horeb (E) and Sinai (J). Only the E account, however, appears in Deut. 4. This phenomenon is consistent throughout D and occurs in every known example of D's reuse of the Tetrateuch. While D knows J and E material, it uses them selectively and as distinct literary materials to rewrite the giving of the law, acknowledging the Ten Commandments (Deut. 5) but denying any additional laws given at Horeb to Israel (Deut. 5:22). The additional laws were, instead, given to Moses alone, who proclaimed them on the plains of Moab (so the distinction between the Ten Words in Deut. 4:13 as the covenant that Moses received on the mountain, and the rest of the laws in Deut. 4:14, which Moses was only then imparting to the Israelites).

The literary nature of the source-critical task can help obviate long-held perceived tensions between synchronic and diachronic readings. This approach is used productively in considering the ritual narratives in P.[31] Others have pointed out apparent conflicts between the two methods. Joshua Berman argues that source criticism cannot account for Gordon Wenham's proposed chiasmus and literary artistry of the flood account in Gen. 6–9.[32] Berman lists five specific issues where the standard division of P and non-P (or J) subverts the literary nature of the text (see table).[33]

28. Benjamin Sommer, *Revelation and Authority: Sinai in Jewish Scripture and Tradition* (New Haven: Yale University Press, 2015).

29. August Dillmann, *Die Bücher Numeri, Deuteronomium, und Josua*, Kurzgefasstes exegetisches Handbuch zum Alten Testament 13 (Leipzig: S. Hirzel, 1886), 609–11, 679.

30. Baden, "Deuteronomic Evidence," 336–42.

31. See, e.g., Feldman, *Story of Sacrifice*.

32. Joshua Berman, *Inconsistencies in the Torah: Ancient Literary Convention and the Limits of Source Criticism* (New York: Oxford University Press, 2017), 236–69.

33. Berman, *Inconsistencies in the Torah*, 260–64.

Structure[a]	Verse	Summary	Source Assignment
A	Gen. 6:13	Elohim pledges to Noah to destroy all flesh	P
A′	Gen. 9:17	Elohim pledges to Noah to preserve all flesh	non-P
B	Gen. 6:17	Flood to destroy all flesh	P
B′	Gen. 9:15	No flood will destroy flesh	non-P
C	Gen. 6:18–20	Covenant to sustain Noah and his animals	P
C′	Gen. 9:8–10	Covenant to sustain all flesh	non-P
E	Gen. 7:1–5	Command to enter the ark + fulfillment	non-P
E′	Gen. 8:15–19	Command to leave the ark + fulfillment	P
G	Gen. 7:8	Birds enter the ark	P
G′	Gen. 8:10b–12	Dove leaves the ark	non-P

[a]Steps D, F, and others are omitted from the table because they correspond to source alignment (so D and D′ are assigned to P, as are F and F′; H and H′ are non-P, and so on). Berman's focus is on a supposed chiastic structure and his claim that mismatched elements (A and A′) cannot explain this putative literary structure.

Berman does not indicate where the source division he presents comes from; none of the major schools would assign Gen. 9:8–17 to non-P.[34] This realignment resolves three of the five mismatches: A, B, and C align with A′, B′, and C′ as part of P. Further, Schwartz, attending to the literary issues in the final text as clues for the reconstruction of literary sources, assigns the entrance of the birds (Gen. 7:8) and the release of the doves (Gen. 8:10–12) to non-P (or J).[35] This eliminates another supposed mismatch of G and G′. The only mismatches remaining concern the command to enter the ark (Gen. 7:1–5) and the command to leave the ark (Gen. 8:15–19). This parallel forms part of a larger narrative in which a character enters and exits the flotation vessel. Since both P and non-P (or J) tell a story in which Noah enters the ark and exits, it would hardly be worth questioning the entire source-critical approach if these notices happen to derive, in the final text, from distinct sources.

Comparative Approaches and Empirical Models as Evidence

The flood accounts in J and P have occasioned interesting research recently in comparative studies as well as the history of each source.[36] For example, the

34. Gen. 9:8–17 is assigned to P in Richard E. Friedman, *The Bible with Sources Revealed* (San Francisco: HarperCollins, 2003), 42; Jean Louis Ska, "The Story of the Flood: A Priestly Writer and Some Later Editorial Fragments," in *The Exegesis of the Pentateuch: Exegetical Studies and Basic Questions*, FAT 66 (Tübingen: Mohr Siebeck, 2009), 1–22; Baruch J. Schwartz, "The Flood Narratives in the Torah and the Question of Where History Begins" (in Hebrew), in *Shai le-Sara Japhet: Studies in the Bible, Its Exegesis and Its Language*, ed. Moshe Bar-Asher et al. (Jerusalem: Bialik, 2007), 139–54; John Day, "The Source Analysis and Redaction of the Genesis Flood Story," in *From Creation to Abraham: Further Studies in Genesis 1–11*, LHBOTS 726 (New York: T&T Clark, 2022), 134.

35. Schwartz, "Flood Narratives," 143–47.

36. Irving Finkel, *The Ark before Noah: Decoding the Story of the Flood* (London: Houghton & Stodder, 2014); Samuel Boyd, "The Flood and the Problem of Being an Omnivore," *JSOT* 43, no. 2 (2019): 163–78.

flood episode in the Epic of Gilgamesh was added from the earlier flood story found in the Epic of Atrahasis. In two instances, the flood hero in Gilgamesh, Utnapishtim, is called Atrahasis, though even this nod to the source is interpreted as a meaningful feature of the Gilgamesh Epic. In a similar manner, the flood story in Gen. 6–9 can be understood as a secondary addition. In P, the original survivor of a flood may have been Enoch. In most other flood stories from the ANE, the flood survivor either lives forever (Utnapishtim) or goes to live with the gods (Ziusudra). Enoch fits this description and shares with Noah the peculiar phrasing of walking with God (Gen. 5:22, 24; 6:9). Also, some details from the pattern of genealogy (resumed in Gen. 10 from Gen. 5) suggests that the flood narrative was added to P's story.[37] Idan Dershowitz points to the phrasing of the Noah story in J that may have originally described a different account, one in which Noah survived a drought and not a flood.[38] In each case, the flood story becomes an essential feature of the source, at least in the immediately precompositional stage of the Pentateuch. For P, the flood is an essential event that changes humans from vegetarians (Gen. 1:29–30; 6:20–22) to meat eaters (Gen. 9). This change ultimately resolves in the sacrificial cult. For J, the flood is instigated by the episode in Gen. 6:1–4 as part of a number of infractions of the divine-human boundary in J's primeval history that led to catastrophe.[39] It is nonetheless noteworthy that if the flood narrative was added into P and J, then these observations about the composition history of these two sources would constitute a third example alongside Gilgamesh in which a deluge was added in the process of forming a larger, literary composition.

The focus on comparing the compilation of the Pentateuch to Mesopotamian literature is part of the search for "empirical models." Since the 1980s, led by Jeffrey Tigay's pioneering work, this comparative approach seeks to understand the compilation of the Pentateuch from documented manuscript and literary evidence in other ancient cultures, notably from the literature of Mesopotamia and Qumran.[40]

Even if comparative studies do not prove which kind of diachronic method best explains the final form of the Pentateuch, they do, at least, indicate that the Pentateuch is a composite text. For example, James Hoffmeier has appealed, in the legacy of George Mendenhall, to Hittite treaties to explain the features

37. Samuel Boyd, *Babel: The Political Rhetoric of a Confused Legacy* (Minneapolis: Fortress, 2023), 146–47.

38. Idan Dershowitz, "Man of the Land: Unearthing the Original Noah," *ZAW* 128, no. 3 (2016): 357–73.

39. For these aspects of P and J and their incorporation of the flood story, see Boyd, *Babel*, 147, 157.

40. Jeffrey Tigay, *The Evolution of the Gilgamesh Epic* (Philadelphia: University of Pennsylvania Press, 1982); Tigay, ed., *Empirical Models for Biblical Criticism*, Dove Studies in Bible, Language, and History (Eugene, OR: Wipf & Stock, 1985); Sanders, "Empirical Models?," 281–304; Raymond F. Person Jr. and Robert Rezetko, eds., *Empirical Models Challenging Biblical Criticism*, AIL 25 (Atlanta: SBL Press, 2016).

of Exod. 19–24. This comparison is intended to argue both for the unity of the text and for its historicity in the second millennium BCE.[41] Unity and history, however, go only so far and cannot account for a case like Exod. 25:22. In all other historical examples, treaty stipulations followed by ratification ceremonies (as in Exod. 24) would mark the end of the stipulations. No more laws or commands are expected. Yet laws appear in Leviticus and Numbers. John Sailhamer argues that the golden-calf narrative in Exod. 32 prompted another law, since Israel transgressed the first.[42] Critical scholars would respond that this explanation fails on multiple grounds to account for a unified text, particularly since in Exod. 25:22, chapters prior to the golden calf, God tells Moses that he will speak his law to Moses in the Tent of Meeting, as though he had not already done so. This arrangement is unexpected and unparalleled elsewhere in ancient texts, given that the ratification occurred immediately prior, in Exod. 20–24, which further indicates different sources.[43]

D as the Archimedean Point of Pentateuchal Studies

The study of D is related to another major facet of the current study of the Pentateuch: legal hermeneutics. The legal collection in D reuses previous source material from the Covenant Code. On a variety of grounds, it is argued to be Neo-Assyrian in origin (if not specifically late eighth or early 7th cent. BCE).[44] Why, how, and when this reuse happens are important areas of research. First, does D reuse legal material to supplement or replace the previous material? D presents a different context for the legal revelation at Horeb than does the Covenant Code. The Covenant Code identifies the legislation received *after* the Ten Commandments as the covenant ratified in Exod. 24. Yet Deut. 4:11–13 equates the covenant with the Ten Commandments and claims that only this material was delivered publicly to Israel at Horeb. (Moses privately received the rest of the statutes and rules, which, according to Deut. 4:14, he was instructed to deliver for living in the land, as in Deut. 12–26, which uses the same heading of "statutes and rules.") Deuteronomy 5:22 states that only the Ten Commandments were

41. James K. Hoffmeier, "'These Things Happened': Why a Historical Exodus Is Essential for Theology," in *Do Historical Matters Matter to Faith? A Critical Appraisal of Modern and Postmodern Approaches to Scripture*, ed. James K. Hoffmeier and Dennis R. Magary (Wheaton: Crossway, 2012), 113–15.

42. John Sailhamer, *The Meaning of the Pentateuch: Revelation, Composition and Interpretation* (Downers Grove, IL: InterVarsity, 2009), 362.

43. Julius Wellhausen, *Prolegomena zur Geschichte Israel* (Berlin: Georg Reimer, 1899), 357–58.

44. David P. Wright, *Inventing God's Law: How the Covenant Code of the Bible Used and Revised the Laws of Hammurabi* (New York: Oxford University Press, 2009), 343–44. For D's reuse of source material and for dating D, see Stackert, *Deuteronomy and the Pentateuch*, 52–109 and 134–58, respectively.

revealed to the congregation and nothing else. The subsequent legal material in Deut. 12–26 was received by Moses privately, only to be revealed thirty-eight years later to the Israelites immediately prior to their entrance into the land (4:13–14).[45] In this fashion, D denies any public revelation at Horeb of laws beyond the Ten Commandments in the Covenant Code, in order to make room for its own legal vision that focuses on centralization of a chosen place of worship (Deut. 12–26).

Does D treat its source materials, mostly from the Covenant Code, to replace or to supplement them? Similar phenomena exist elsewhere in the ancient world. Assyrian scribes replace Marduk's name with Assur in the Enuma Elish. The Temple Scroll likewise reworks its source material from the Torah.[46] In both cases the extent to which these texts intend to replace their older sources is debated. In the Enuma Elish, the Assyrian recension appears in only a few manuscripts, and none of the commentary texts show any awareness of its existence. As Stackert and Levinson argue, there is a functional analogue between D and the Vassal Treaty of Esarhaddon (VTE, also called Esarhaddon's Succession Treaty). In VTE, the Assyrian king Esarhaddon displays a concern for the succession of his son, Assurbanipal. In a similar manner, D demonstrates a concern for legal succession, recrafting the history of the Horeb event, echoing its authoritative source material, and removing the Covenant Code to make room for its own legal vision.

The questions why and when D might do such a thing are perhaps related. In several of its legislations, the Covenant Code either states or implies that there will be multiple altars or places to meet the deity and sacrifice (Exod. 20:22–26). D rewrites these prior legislations so that only one altar, designated as God's chosen place in the land, is recognized (Deut. 12). This shift is understandable in the wake of Sennacherib's invasion and destruction of forty-six towns surrounding Jerusalem in 701 BCE. Only one place was left standing. D could have capitalized on this situation to centralize religious worship (though the implications of the Tel Moẓa temple complicate this history).

Another piece of evidence connects the curse formulations in Deut. 28 to VTE. The exact connection is debated.[47] The curses could reflect broader ANE

45. Samuel Boyd, "What Were the Qualifications for Being a Leader in Ancient Israel? Revelation, Authority, and Philological Issues in Deut 1:13 and 1:15," *VT* 68, no. 2 (2018): 173–96.

46. Sidnie White Crawford, "Where Is Moses? The Temple Scroll's Claim to Authority," *HeBAI* 11, no. 1 (2022): 49–59.

47. K. Lawson Younger Jr. and Neal A. Huddleston correctly demonstrate some of the difficulties involved when using treaty traditions to date Deuteronomy, including issues with respect to both the Hittite and Neo-Assyrian comparisons. See their "Challenges to the Use of Ancient Near Eastern Treaty Forms for Dating and Interpreting Deuteronomy," in *Sefer Torath Moshe: Studies in the Composition and Interpretation of Deuteronomy*, ed. Daniel I. Block and Richard L. Schultz (Peabody, MA: Hendrickson, 2017), 78–109. It should be noted that Younger and Huddleston do not engage Spencer Allen's article (see below) and Eckart Otto's *Das Deuteronomium: Politische, Theologie und Rechtsreform in Juda und Assyrien* (Berlin: De Gruyter, 1999). These works would obviate some of Younger and Huddleston's criticisms, yet many of their observations about the complexities involved in such comparisons remain helpful.

treaty influence and not necessarily VTE specifically.[48] D and VTE, however, share several rhetorical strategies. Neo-Assyrian kings often reused Old and Middle Assyrian rhetoric, offering a sense of continuity with the past while innovating and creating new meanings and new idioms to aid in their governance.[49] The Taʿyinat exemplar of VTE contains three seals, from the Old, Middle, and Neo-Assyrian Empires.[50] The seals offer visual evidence of continuity. Likewise, D presents itself as narrating the past, creating a sense of continuity that makes its legal innovations more palatable.

The similar strategy in both D and VTE can also be seen in Deut. 13:2–6 and VTE (SAA 2 6:116–17).[51] In both passages, the authors show a concern that the audience makes known to the king or sanctioned authority (in D's case) any potential for subversion of the proper succession (VTE) or the legal-religious vision (D). This theme is significant, since the phrasing concerning the potential source of subversion in VTE (*šāʾili amāt ili*, "one who inquires for a divine message") is poorly attested elsewhere in Akkadian and unparalleled in other Assyrian treaty texts. Likewise, the Hebrew phrase חֹלֵם חֲלוֹם (*ḥōlēm ḥălôm*) does not occur elsewhere, and the construction דִּבֶּר־סָרָה (*dibber-sārâ*) in Deut. 13:6 could be an Akkadian loan. This unparalleled example of חֹלֵם חֲלוֹם could be linguistic evidence for a "blind motif" peculiarly related to VTE.[52] If this is the case, it would have been borrowed from a source text like VTE and incorporated into Deut. 13, where such phenomena of dream interpretation stand out uniquely.

Of further note is the relationship between Deut. 28:20–44 and the VTE curses. In the 1960s, Rintje Frankena and then Moshe Weinfeld examined the connections and argued for a direct relationship between VTE and Deut. 28.[53] The parallel entails a list of curses involving natural elements (sun, moon, sky, etc.). When those elements are translated into the corresponding deities from Mesopotamia, the list in Deut. 28:20–44 bears an uncanny resemblance to that in VTE. This correlation is particularly close in clusters such as Deut. 28:26–33 and VTE 39–42, but it is unknown in any other treaty or text from the ANE. Such a relationship

---

See Laura Quick's work cited below, published in 2017, which addresses futility curses and how they relate to Deut. 28 from West Semitic influence even as VTE influences the biblical text.

48. While Mario Liverani ("The Medes at Esarhaddon's Court," *JCS* 47 [1995]: 57–62) attempted to dislocate VTE from wider circulation, the discovery of the Taʿyinat exemplar of VTE clearly demonstrates that the Assyrian text was in the general orbit of, if not directly encountered in, Judah. See a rebuttal in Hans Ulrich Steymans, "Deuteronomy 28 and Tell Tayinat," *Verbum et Ecclesia* 32 (2013): 1–13.

49. Beate Pongratz-Leisten, *Religion and Ideology in Assyria*, Studies in Ancient Near Eastern Records 6 (Boston: De Gruyter, 2015).

50. Mark Lester, "The Material Transmission of Tradition in Deuteronomy" (PhD diss., Yale University, 2020), 116.

51. Stackert, *Deuteronomy and the Pentateuch*, 86–109, esp. 97–98.

52. Stackert, *Deuteronomy and the Pentateuch*, 97.

53. Rintje Frankena, "The Vassal-Treaties of Esarhaddon and the Dating of Deuteronomy," in כה*: 1940–1965*, ed. P. A. H. de Boer, OtSt 14 (Leiden: Brill, 1965), 122–54; Moshe Weinfeld, "Traces of Assyrian Treaty Formulae in Deuteronomy," *Bib* 46 (1965): 417–27.

is even more remarkable since the curses in VTE reflect an innovation on other curse formulas elsewhere in Neo-Assyrian texts and share features of this innovation with Deut. 28.[54] Laura Quick argues that this curse section reflects multiple venues of influence, and the futility curses in Deut. 28 ("maximal effort, minimal gain") likely originate in the sphere of West Semitic contact alongside the East Semitic influence of Neo-Assyrian treaties such as VTE.[55]

There has been a resurgence of arguments proposing connections between Deuteronomy and Hittite treaties from the second millennium BCE. One shared formal feature is a historical prologue. Robert Miller argues that there is a Neo-Assyrian treaty with such a prologue, though the evidence in this case is debated.[56] In many respects, however, Deuteronomy and second-millennium Hittite treaties are quite different. Hittite treaties frame their discourse in the first-person narrative, whereas Deuteronomy uses a third-person omniscient narrator. The evidence for the literary growth of D argues against recourse to a single Hittite treaty form.[57] It is possible that some literary forms as evidenced in Hittite treaties continued into the first millennium.[58] However, the Hittite historical prologues and D's historical prologue are not identical and do not necessitate the conclusion of direct borrowing. Instead, D's use of a prologue could be explained by its engagements with the literary material in the Tetrateuch. The more specific data puts D closer to the seventh century BCE than to the second millennium in terms of composition. Sennacherib's invasion, as well as influence from both the Covenant Code and VTE, appears to lie behind D's composition and growth.

Responding to Questions as a Way Forward

Current pentateuchal research can be summed up by the query "What sorts of literatures and genres are we reading when we read the text?" Recent source-critical approaches are keenly attuned to the literary features of the text. Neo-Documentarianism and non-Documentary approaches understand that the literary features of the text reveal its history and explain its final form. Each source, strand, strata, and supplement presents insights into distinct literary, ritual, and theological worlds, though, as theoreticians of religion remind us, historical and ritual texts are first and foremost texts and not necessarily reality.[59] As an example, Robert Alter observes that many of his analyses in *The Art of Biblical Narrative*

54. Spencer L. Allen, "Rearranging the Curses in Esarhaddon's Succession Treaty (SAA 2 6:414–65)," *WO* 43, no. 1 (2013): 1–24.

55. Laura Quick, *Deuteronomy 28 and the Aramaic Curse Tradition*, Oxford Theology and Religion Monographs (Oxford: Oxford University Press, 2018).

56. Robert D. Miller, "The Israelite Covenant in Ancient Near Eastern Context," *BN* 139 (2008): 5–18.

57. Stackert, *Deuteronomy and the Pentateuch*, 86–109.

58. Stackert, *Deuteronomy and the Pentateuch*, 87.

59. Feldman, *Story of Sacrifice*.

supported, rather than undermined, source-critical approaches, and he changed his framing from 1981 to 2011 to acknowledge the ways diachronic and source approaches may be constructively attuned to literary studies.[60]

So does the state of pentateuchal studies result in a "complexity that is difficult to sort out"?[61] The complexity can instead be explained as evidence of the vitality of the study of these texts and how history, theory, and religion relate in the human experience. Indeed, the materiality of the texts and how writing occurred in history have resulted in David Carr's call for more "scrolls-based approaches." While not confirming one critical school of thought or another, the focus on historically sensitive limits to writing technology certainly supports diachronic approaches and undermines the idea that the Pentateuch is an essentially unified composition.[62]

Is there a bias to see pervasive diachrony in the text?[63] Reading parts of Deuteronomy demonstrates the validity of diachronic interpretations. While some scholars may still claim implicit bias, many critical scholars explicitly state a preference for a unified text and employ sources and diachronic methods as an explanation only when compelled by difficulties in the text.[64] Future critiques should acknowledge this important starting point as part of the method of source criticism.

Disagreements remain, just as in any institution, field, or ecclesiological denomination. Some disagreements are greater than others, but there are also areas of significant overlap and agreement. And, as with all areas of humanistic or scientific inquiry, there is still much to learn.

60. Robert Alter, *The Art of Biblical Narrative*, rev. ed. (New York: Basic Books, 2011), xi.

61. Richard E. Averbeck, "The Exodus, Debt Slavery, and the Composition of the Pentateuch," in *Exploring the Composition of the Pentateuch*, ed. L. S. Baker et al., BBRSup 27 (University Park, PA: Eisenbrauns, 2020), 26.

62. David Carr, "Rethinking the Materiality of Biblical Texts: From Source, Tradition and Redaction to a Scroll Approach," *ZAW* 132, no. 4 (2020): 594–621.

63. So Richard E. Averbeck, "Pentateuchal Criticism and the Priestly Torah," in Hoffmeier and Magary, *Historical Matters?*, 151–80; T. Desmond Alexander, *From Paradise to Promised Land: An Introduction to the Pentateuch*, 4th ed. (Grand Rapids: Baker Academic, 2022), 297.

64. Schwartz, "Recent Scholarship's Critique," 3–16; Baden, *Composition of the Pentateuch*, 30, 248; Stackert, *Prophet like Moses*, 22; Stackert, *Deuteronomy and the Pentateuch*, 4.

13

Joshua, Judges, and Ruth

David T. Lamb

A unique feature of the books of Joshua, Judges, and Ruth is that, in English Bibles, the names together form a complete sentence, which was capitalized on by the gospel-blues singer Lyle Lovett in his 1992 album, cleverly titled *Joshua Judges Ruth*. The eponymous military leader of the book of Joshua, however, was long gone by the time Ruth arrived in Israel with her mother-in-law, Naomi, so Joshua never had a chance to judge, condemn, or in any way besmirch her character. And the judges of the book of Judges don't really do any judging either, at least in today's sense of adjudicating legal cases.

But Joshua does lead his nation in a series of military conquests enabling the wandering Israelite nomads to finally find a home in the promised land. And the charismatic judges of the book of Judges similarly defeat many of the same peoples, who had become not only Israel's neighbors but also their oppressors. And at some point, while Israel was ruled by these judges, a woman named Ruth immigrated to Israel from Moab, one of these oppressing nations, and eventually became the ancestor of two of Israel's most famous sons, David and Jesus.

Historical Issues

The book of Joshua records the Israelite people taking possession of the land of the Canaanites. A variety of historical issues arise related to the date and the nature of this "conquest." (On models for the conquest and settlement of Israel, see Ralph Hawkins's archaeology essay in the present volume as well as his book on the topic.)[1]

Date of the Exodus and Conquest

The date of the conquest as recorded in Joshua is integrally tied to the date of the exodus, as recorded in Exodus–Deuteronomy, after accounting for the older generation of Israelites that died in the wilderness. Scholars who believe that the exodus/conquest happened take one of two main positions: an early date in the fifteenth century BCE, or a late date in the thirteenth century BCE.[2]

The key text for the early-date proponents is 1 Kings 6:1, which states that Solomon began to build the temple 480 years after the Israelites came out of Exodus. Since Solomon's temple is dated to about 960 BCE, based on 1 Kings 6 the exodus could be set to about 1440 BCE. The problem with this date is that Egyptians controlled the land of Canaan during this time frame, but the books of Joshua and Judges mention no Egyptian engagements among their many conflicts in the land.

Scholars who date the conquest to the thirteenth century interpret 1 Kings 6:1 figuratively and focus on the comment in Exod. 1:11 that the Israelites built a storage city named Rameses, presumably named after Pharaoh Ramesses II (1279–1213 BCE), which would be more consistent with this later date.[3]

Both sides mention two ANE sources. The Merneptah stele is typically dated to about 1210 BCE. It was commissioned by Pharaoh Merneptah (1213–1203), the son of Ramesses II. This stele includes one of the oldest references to ancient Israel.[4] Listed among Merneptah's various military victories is one over Israel: "Israel is wasted, its seed is not" (*COS* 2:41). Early-date proponents believe this reference suggests that Israel had been established for an extended period, while late-date proponents believe it describes a more recent development.

The Amarna letters, a collection of correspondence between Canaanite rulers and several fourteenth-century Egyptian pharaohs, mention at least eleven cities that appear in the book of Joshua.[5] The Amarna tablets also refer to a group

1. Ralph Hawkins, *How Israel Became a People* (Nashville: Abingdon, 2013).

2. For summaries of the arguments, see Hélène Dallaire, *Joshua*, Expositor's Bible Commentary, vol. 2, rev. ed. (Grand Rapids: Zondervan, 2012), 825–28; Mark A. Leuchter and David T. Lamb, *The Historical Writings: Introducing Israel's Historical Literature* (Minneapolis: Fortress, 2016), 35–38.

3. See also Ralph K. Hawkins, "Propositions for Evangelical Acceptance of a Late-Date Exodus-Conquest: Biblical Data and the Royal Scarabs from Mt. Ebal," *JETS* 50, no. 1 (2007): 31–46.

4. Manfred Görg's view that an earlier reference to "Israel" appears in an inscription, ÄM 21687, has gained wide approval; see Wolfgang Zwickel and Pieter van der Veen, "The Earliest Reference to Israel and Its Possible Archaeological and Historical Background" *VT* 67, no. 1 (2017): 129–40.

5. On the Amarna letters, see Leuchter and Lamb, *Historical Writings*, 41–43; table 2.1 on p. 42 lists the eleven cities from the book of Joshua mentioned in the letters.

of people, the Habiru, which some scholars believe should be connected to the Hebrew people because of etymological similarities. If the names of these two peoples are synonymous, it provides evidence for the early conquest date, locating Israel in Canaan long before the thirteenth century. However, most scholars no longer make this connection since the term "Habiru" consistently has derogatory connotations of a marginalized people, equivalent to "outcast" and not applied to a nation as a whole.[6]

For much of the twentieth century, many evangelicals believed that the only option for dating the exodus/conquest was the early one. However, in 1990 Bruce Waltke stated, "Either date is an acceptable working hypothesis, and neither date should be held dogmatically."[7] But as late as 2013, Hawkins observed that scholars who did not subscribe to the early date were criticized, and questions were raised about their views on the reliability of Scripture.[8] More recently, an increasing number of Joshua commentaries written by evangelicals have not only expressed openness to the late date but have also concluded that it is the more reasonable one, based both on the text and archaeological evidence.[9]

Literary Issues

Deuteronomistic Redaction

For the latter half of the twentieth century, academic research on the Former Prophets (Joshua, Judges, 1–2 Samuel, and 1–2 Kings) focused on Deuteronomistic redaction. While interest in this topic has diminished since 2000, an understanding of the primary perspectives and the scholars who advocated for these views is important background for anyone doing academic work on these books.[10]

Since Martin Noth's seminal work *The Deuteronomistic History* (German original, 1943), scholars have theorized that redactors edited source material, both oral and written, using the language, terminology, and ideology from Deuteronomy to create a unified history of Israel from conquest of the land to the

6. Anson F. Rainey makes a compelling and definitive case against any connection between the Habiru and the Hebrews in Egypt in *The El-Amarna Correspondence: A New Edition of the Cuneiform Letters from the Site of El-Amarna Based on Collations of All Extant Tablets* (Leiden: Brill, 2014), 31–35.

7. Bruce Waltke, "The Date of the Conquest," *WTJ* 52, no. 2 (1990): 200.

8. Hawkins, *How Israel Became a People*, 50.

9. For example, see David G. Firth, *Joshua*, Evangelical Biblical Theology Commentary (Bellingham, WA: Lexham Academic, 2021), 22n41; Dallaire, *Joshua*, 828; Robert L. Hubbard, *Joshua*, NIVAC (Grand Rapids: Zondervan, 2009), 27.

10. On this topic, see Gilmour's essay on Samuel-Kings, chap. 14 of the present volume. For a summary of research on the Deuteronomistic History, see David T. Lamb, *Righteous Jehu and His Evil Heirs: The Deuteronomist's Negative Perspective on Dynastic Succession* (Oxford: Oxford University Press, 2007), 28.

downfall of the monarchy—the Deuteronomistic History (DH).[11] While Noth originally perceived a single redactor working during the exile, the number of redactors has gradually increased in the minds of subsequent scholars.

During the 1970s and 1980s, the idea of a "double redaction"—first theorized by Frank Cross and later developed by one of his students, Richard Nelson—became popular in American circles.[12] According to this view, the first Deuteronomist (Dtr1) was pro-monarchy and worked during the reign of King Josiah of Judah in the late seventh century BCE. The second Deuteronomist (Dtr2) was antimonarchy and revised the history in the sixth century BCE during the Babylonian exile.

Simultaneously with the work of Cross and Nelson, the theory of a "triple redaction" was developed by Rudolf Smend (German original, 1971), along with two of his students, Walter Dietrich (German original, 1972) and Timo Veijola (German original, 1975).[13] This perspective had more proponents in Europe. Smend originally perceived merely a primary historical redactor (DtrH), who was followed by a redactor with a concern for obedience to the law (DtrN; *nomos* is Greek for law). Dietrich added the third, prophetic redactor (DtrP), and he dated all three layers to the exile.

The lack of consensus regarding the number of possible layers of Deuteronomistic redaction has given rise to alternative theories, including a Deuteronomic school of scribal editors who may have worked on the history as well as on other books, such as Jeremiah. Critics of these theories argue that the process of separating one layer of Deuteronomistic redaction from another layer was overly esoteric and subjective. Of the three books that this chapter is focusing on, only Judges, with its cyclical framework, is perceived by redaction critics as having significant Deuteronomistic shaping.

Instead of focusing on distinct Deuteronomists, Susan Niditch discerns three distinct voices in Judges: the Epic-Bard, the Theologian, and the Humanist.[14] The Epic-Bardic voice recalls heroic exploits of the judge-deliverers who, with

11. Martin Noth, *The Deuteronomistic History*, JSOTSup 15 (Sheffield: Sheffield Academic, 1981).

12. Frank M. Cross, *Canaanite Myth and Hebrew Epic: Essays on the History of the Religion of Israel* (Cambridge, MA: Harvard University Press, 1973); Richard D. Nelson, *The Double Redaction of the Deuteronomistic History*, LHBOTS 18 (Sheffield: JSOT, 1981).

13. Rudolf Smend, "The Law and the Nations: A Contribution to Deuteronomistic Tradition History," in *Reconsidering Israel and Judah: Recent Studies on the Deuteronomistic History*, ed. Gary Knoppers and J. Gordon McConville, Sources for Biblical and Theological Study 8 (Winona Lake, IN: Eisenbrauns, 2000), 95–110; Walter Dietrich, "Deuteronomistic Historiography and Deuteronomic Law Exemplified in the Passage from the Period of the Judges to the Monarchical Period," in *Israel Constructs Its History: Deuteronomistic Historiography in Recent Research*, ed. Albert de Pury, Thomas Römer, and Jean-Daniel Macchi, LHBOTS 306 (Sheffield: Sheffield Academic, 2000), 315–42; Timo Veijola, *Die ewige Dynastie: David und die Entstehung seiner Dynastie nach der deuteronomistischen Darstellung* (Helsinki: Suomaleinen Tiedeakatemia, 1975).

14. Susan Niditch, *Judges*, OTL (Louisville: Westminster John Knox, 2008).

YHWH's assistance, defeated Israel's oppressive enemies, as seen in the Song of Deborah and the Samson narrative. The Theologian is concerned about covenant loyalty and obedience and is thus the voice that sounds the most like the Deuteronomist; it appears in Judg. 2 and the framing structure of the main body. The Humanist narrates less heroically than the Epic-Bard, wanting the stories to speak for themselves in a more understated manner, and this voice is found most clearly in the first and the final five chapters of the book.

Since roughly 2000, scholarly interest in the quest for the elusive Deuteronomist(s) has waned, but many scholars still speak of a Deuteronomist, or perhaps a school. Regardless of one's views on Deuteronomistic redaction, the Former Prophets, particularly Judges and Kings, include significant terminology and ideology that is reminiscent of Deuteronomy, with a strong concern for obedience and a harsh condemnation of idolatry.

Literary Approaches

Alter and Biblical Narrative

As interest in Deuteronomistic redaction has declined, it has been replaced, at least in part, with a concern for the literary analysis of these books. Robert Alter's *The Art of Biblical Narrative* served as a catalyst for a new interest in literary approaches.[15] In 1999, he published his translation and commentary on the life of David, and in 2013 he expanded this work to include all the Former Prophets.[16] Typical of Alter's work, it lacks the detailed exegesis or engagement with critical scholarship that one might expect to find in a traditional commentary, but it is filled with literary insights into the language and the narrative, making it a useful introduction when researching or teaching a narrative text.

Over the past thirty years, a variety of scholars have done literary and rhetorical work on the book of Judges. Barry Webb perceives a unifying theme in Judges, that of Israel's apostasy resulting in YHWH withholding his promise to give his people the land.[17] For Lillian Klein, the unifying element of the book is a literary device, that of irony, as the book eventually devolves into chaos.[18] In a rhetorical analysis of Judges, Robert O'Connell argues that the book is intended to set up a divinely elected king who would in turn set up a legitimate Davidic dynasty in contrast to the series of imperfect judges on whom the narrative focuses.[19] After

15. Robert Alter, *The Art of Biblical Narrative* (New York: Basic Books, 1981; rev. ed., 2011).

16. Robert Alter, *The David Story: A Translation with Commentary on 1 and 2 Samuel* (New York: Norton, 1999); Alter, *Ancient Israel: The Former Prophets; Joshua, Judges, Samuel, and Kings; A Translation with Commentary* (New York: Norton, 2013).

17. Barry Webb, *The Book of Judges: An Integrated Reading*, JSOTSup 46 (Sheffield: JSOT, 1987).

18. Lillian R. Klein, *The Triumph of Irony in the Book of Judges*, JSOTSup 68, Bible and Literature 14 (Sheffield: Almond, 1988).

19. Robert O'Connell, *The Rhetoric of the Book of Judges*, VTSup 63 (Leiden: Brill, 1996).

noting how various scholars have perceived unifying themes in Judges, Wong shows how these linkages are intentional and lead to the conclusion that a single author wrote the book in order to support the royal authority of YHWH.[20]

Trible and Feminist Approaches

While Alter was inspiring a new generation of literary scholars, Phyllis Trible was accomplishing similar things in the realm of feminist hermeneutics, specifically in narrative texts, with her classic work *Texts of Terror* (1984).[21] She unashamedly examines some of the most disturbing yet ignored, biblical stories. From Judges she discusses the rape of the Levite's concubine (Judg. 19) and the sacrifice of Jephthah's daughter (Judg. 11). Her close readings of the biblical text and her insights into its rhetorical aspects have helped a generation of scholars learn from these troubling texts. About the Levite's concubine, she states, "Captured, betrayed, raped, tortured, murdered, dismembered, and scattered—this woman is the most sinned against."[22] In some ways, she pioneered the way for much of the ethical work on violence and sexuality in the books of Joshua and Judges that has taken place since 2000.

Several scholars have taken up Trible's mantle, using a feminist hermeneutic in their studies of Judges. Athalya Brenner edited a collection of feminist essays on the women of Judges (e.g., Aksah/Achsah, Jephthah's daughter, Delilah, the Levite's concubine).[23] Brenner edited another volume in the same series, on the book of Ruth, that examines the stories of Ruth and Naomi in their roles as immigrants, wives, and mothers.[24] Susan Ackerman compares the fascinating women of Judges (Deborah, Jael, Sisera's mother, Manoah's wife, Delilah, and the daughters of Shiloh) to other biblical and ANE heroic women.[25] She offers fresh perspectives on each of these women and how they stood out in a patriarchal culture.

As should be the case for all biblical disciplines, the insights of feminist scholars into Scripture generally, and into the world of marginalized women specifically, desperately needs to be heard by scholars who use other approaches. As I was writing my book on nonideal sexual behavior in the OT, I found their discussions illuminating, particularly in my treatment of the Canaanite prostitute Rahab (Josh. 2; 6) and the rape of the Levite's concubine (Judg. 19).[26]

20. Gregory T. K. Wong, *Compositional Strategy of the Book of Judges: An Inductive, Rhetorical Study*, VTSup 111 (Boston: Brill, 2006).

21. Phyllis Trible, *Texts of Terror: Literary-Feminist Readings of Biblical Narratives* (Philadelphia: Fortress, 1984).

22. Trible, *Texts of Terror*, 81.

23. Athalya Brenner, ed., *Judges*, FCB 4 (Sheffield: Sheffield Academic, 1993).

24. Athalya Brenner, ed., *Ruth*, FCB 3 (Sheffield: Sheffield Academic, 1993).

25. Susan Ackerman, *Warrior, Dancer, Seductress, Queen: Women in Judges and Biblical Israel*, AYBRL (New York: Doubleday, 1998).

26. David T. Lamb, *Prostitutes and Polygamists: A Look at Love, Old Testament Style* (Grand Rapids: Zondervan, 2015).

Other Distinctive Approaches

While readers can easily find lists of the standard commentaries on each of the biblical books discussed in this chapter, I mention a few recent series that attempt to address gaps often left by more traditional approaches. The Eerdmans Two Horizons series combines theological exegesis and theological reflection, specifically focusing on how each book relates to the rest of Scripture and contributes to biblical theology.[27] The Brazos Theological Commentary series also approaches these books theologically.[28] The works in this series are written by theologians rather than biblical scholars, and they interpret the text not only alongside contemporary theologians but also in light of ancient commentators and creedal confessions.

Zondervan produced two series (NIVAC and Story of God) that attempt to help ministers not only understand and interpret the text but also apply it to our contemporary context.[29] The Story of God series is not only practical but also contextual as it examines how the story of the Bible is understood within its ANE context.[30]

Two other commentary series are quite recent and currently include volumes on only two of our three books. The Wisdom Commentary series examines books from a feminist perspective, helping readers and ministers appreciate and teach on texts emphasizing themes of justice, dignity, and equality.[31] The Asia Bible Commentary series is specifically aimed toward readers and pastors who live and work in Asian contexts, enabling them to better understand and apply Scripture.[32]

In Fortress's new collection of introductory textbooks on specific sections of the Bible, I coauthored, with Mark Leuchter, the textbook on the historical books, which includes chapters on Joshua and Judges (but not Ruth).[33] The book contains numerous tables and images, and each chapter includes a discussion of literary, historical, and theological issues for each book.

27. Gordon McConville and Stephen Williams, *Joshua*, THOTC (Grand Rapids: Eerdmans, 2010); David J. H. Beldman, *Judges*, THOTC (Grand Rapids: Eerdmans, 2020); James McKown, *Ruth*, THOTC (Grand Rapids: Eerdmans, 2015).

28. Paul R. Hinlicky, *Joshua*, Brazos Theological Commentary on the Bible (Grand Rapids: Brazos, 2021); Laura A. Smit and Stephen E. Fowl, *Judges & Ruth*, Brazos Theological Commentary on the Bible (Grand Rapids: Brazos, 2018).

29. Hubbard, *Joshua*; K. Lawson Younger, *Judges, Ruth*, NIVAC (Grand Rapids: Zondervan, 2002).

30. Lissa M. Wray Beal, *Joshua*, Story of God (Grand Rapids: Zondervan, 2009); Marion Ann Taylor, *Ruth, Esther*, Story of God (Grand Rapids: Zondervan, 2020); David T. Lamb, *1–2 Kings*, Story of God (Grand Rapids: Zondervan, 2021).

31. Alice L. Laffey and Mahri Leonard-Fleckman, *Ruth*, Wisdom Commentary (Collegeville, MN: Liturgical Press, 2017); Mercedes L. García Bachmann, *Judges*, Wisdom Commentary (Collegeville, MN: Liturgical Press, 2018).

32. Athena E. Gorospe, *Judges: A Pastoral and Contextual Commentary*, Asia Bible Commentary (Carlisle, UK: Langham Global Library, 2016); Havilah Dharamraj, *Ruth: A Pastoral and Contextual Commentary*, Asia Bible Commentary (Carlisle, UK: Langham Global Library, 2019).

33. Leuchter and Lamb, *Historical Writings*.

Theological and Ethical issues

Immigration

Immigration is a controversial topic in our politically charged context and, unfortunately, biblical texts such as Ruth that speak to the issue are often not examined to see how they might apply. In M. Daniel Caroll R.'s discussion of the story of Ruth, he uses assimilation theory, noting how Ruth assimilates following three mechanisms.[34] Ruth the Moabite first takes initiative in her commitment to Naomi the Israelite. Then she engages with the social networks in Bethlehem (the women, the reapers, the elders). Finally, she follows the appropriate laws (institutional avenues) related to gleaning and inheritance. Carroll R. acknowledges that while on some level her identity remains that of an immigrant (the descriptor "Moabite" appears throughout), she is nonetheless welcomed into Israel's story via her legacy as the ancestor of David and Jesus.

Violence

Violence in the OT has been one of the most active topics in biblical scholarship over the past few decades. Although many OT texts could be examined on the subject of biblical bloodshed, the book of Joshua receives much attention because it narrates what is arguably the most troubling example of divine violence, the conquest of the land of the Canaanites. This section discusses scholarship on OT violence, including works that are not focused exclusively on Joshua and Judges.

Precursors: Scholars Writing between 1990–2003 (Younger, Longman, Reid, Gundry)

In many respects the works surveyed in this section serve as precursors for the research on violence that has emerged since they were published. K. Lawson Younger examines Israel's conquest in light of other ANE conquest narratives and concludes that, while Joshua is unique in many aspects, it is also a product of its context.[35] The conquest reports of Joshua, comparable to the ANE parallels, show evidence of hyperbole and should not be interpreted hyperliterally. Texts that speak of complete destruction (e.g., Josh. 10:40; 11:12) not only lack details but also use language consistent with an ideological perspective designed for maximum rhetorical impact. Younger's thesis of hyperbole also helps reconcile the supposed conflict of Joshua's complete eradication of the Canaanites with the picture we see at the beginning of Judges, which clearly describes many foreign peoples still present in Canaan.

34. M. Daniel Carroll R., *The Bible and Borders: Hearing God's Word on Immigration* (Grand Rapids: Brazos, 2020), 72–76.

35. K. Lawson Younger, *Ancient Conquest Accounts: A Study in Ancient Near Eastern and Biblical History Writing*, JSOTSup 98 (Sheffield: Sheffield Academic, 1990).

In their treatment of divine warfare, Tremper Longman and Daniel Reid make only limited references to Joshua and Judges because their main thesis is that the image of God as a warrior is not limited to a few OT texts. Rather, it is a prominent theme that appears throughout the Bible.[36] Neither God nor the Bible is uncomfortable with this aspect of God's character.

Stanley Gundry edited a volume on four views of the Canaanite "genocide," in which the contributors seek to relate the OT idea of holy war to the NT ideal of loving our enemy.[37] C. S. Cowles argues for strong discontinuity between the two themes, Eugene Merrill for moderate discontinuity, Daniel Gard for eschatological continuity, and Longman for spiritual continuity.

Scholars Who Conclude That God Is Not Violent (Seibert, Boyd)

A few scholars address the problem by concluding that, despite what books like Joshua appear to say, God is not in fact violent. Some of the arguments that Cowles uses in the Gundry volume appear in longer works by Eric Seibert and Gregory Boyd. Seibert's *Disturbing Divine Behavior* boldly discusses some of the most troubling texts in Scripture. He argues convincingly that it is important to think rightly about God, since a person's view of God will shape not only their relationship with God, but also their behavior.[38] He concludes that the OT texts describing a violent God should be rejected because such behavior is not consistent with the divine character of Jesus, a man of nonviolence, as revealed in the Gospels. Seibert's Christocentric hermeneutic, while attractive because it makes the problem of a violent God go away, will not satisfy many evangelicals who are unwilling to reject large portions of Scripture because the God portrayed doesn't fit a perception of what he should be like. Seibert pushes back on some of these criticisms in a later book.[39]

Boyd's approach, while perhaps not as troubling to many evangelicals as Seibert's, comes to similar conclusions.[40] Using a cruciform hermeneutic, Boyd reframes the violent portrayal of God. According to Boyd, the Jesus we see on the cross is the fullest revelation of God's essence and character. When there is a conflict, the nonviolent crucified Christ must reinterpret (and essentially trump) the violent YHWH of the conquest of Joshua. He claims that God's original plan

36. Tremper Longman III and Daniel G. Reid, *God Is a Warrior*, Studies in Old Testament Biblical Theology (Grand Rapids: Zondervan, 1995).

37. Stanley N. Gundry, *Show Them No Mercy: 4 Views on God and Canaanite Genocide*, Counterpoints (Grand Rapids: Zondervan, 2003).

38. Eric A. Seibert, *Disturbing Divine Behavior: Troubling Old Testament Images of God* (Minneapolis: Fortress, 2009).

39. Eric A. Seibert, *The Violence of Scripture: Overcoming the Old Testament's Troubling Legacy* (Minneapolis: Fortress, 2012).

40. Gregory A. Boyd, *Crucifixion of the Warrior God: Interpreting the Old Testament's Violent Portraits of God in Light of the Cross* (Minneapolis: Fortress, 2017).

involved a nonviolent conquest. Where violence ensued, it was the result of God allowing it to take place by removing his hand of protection.

Because of their conclusions, Seibert and Boyd have been associated with Marcion, the early church heretic who rejected the OT because of the prevalence of disturbing divine behavior. Both Seibert and Boyd claim not to be Marcionites, and unlike Marcion, they do not reject the entire OT. But their rejection of major portions of the OT, wherever God appears to condone violence, still borders on Marcionism. The fact that the NT not only accepts wholesale the authority of the OT but also uses similar violent language to speak of judgment seriously undermines the conclusions of Seibert and Boyd.

Scholars Who Make Sense of a Violent God (Wright, Copan, Lamb)

Instead of denying the violent portrayal of God in the OT, other scholars attempt to make sense of it. These apologetic works tend to be more popular in tone, while the text-focused works of the next section are more academic and written primarily for scholars. This group is essentially asking, "How can we make sense of a violent God?" while the next group is asking, "How can we make sense of a violent Bible?"

In *The God I Don't Understand*, Christopher Wright specifically asks, "What about the Canaanites?"[41] While not claiming to have solved the problem, Wright offers many helpful perspectives on it. He begins by showing how two of the common methods to resolve the problem are "dead ends." First, the conflict was not just an OT problem, since both Testaments speak of a God of wrath and violence. Second, the Israelites were not confused, thinking that God wanted the conquest when he actually didn't, because the witness of Scripture is clear: God was behind the command. Discussing helpful frameworks for understanding the conquest, Wright emphasizes the importance of understanding the ancient context and the need to interpret hyperbolic language appropriately. He also works through the many texts that make clear that, because God is a righteous judge, he needed to condemn the wickedness of the Canaanites. Whether he is writing for a popular or academic audience, Wright consistently combines a strong focus on the text with a practical, ethical, and missional awareness.

On the topic of divine violence, Paul Copan followed up his book *Is God a Moral Monster?* with a coauthored book, *Did God Really Command Genocide?*[42]

41. Christopher J. H. Wright, *The God I Don't Understand: Reflections on Tough Questions of Faith* (Grand Rapids: Zondervan 2008).

42. Paul Copan, *Is God a Moral Monster? Making Sense of the Old Testament God* (Grand Rapids: Baker Academic, 2011); Paul Copan and Matthew Flannagan, *Did God Really Command Genocide? Coming to Terms with the Justice of God* (Grand Rapids: Baker Academic, 2014).

The first book is primarily a response to the critiques of the so-called New Atheists. The second book is longer, more academic, and focused specifically on the conquest of Joshua. In addition to acknowledging the hyperbolic nature of Joshua's conquest, Copan and Matthew Flannagan observe that the primary biblical mandate regarding the Canaanites was not destruction but driving them out of the land. Copan is a philosophy and ethics professor and so engages more actively with other philosophers than with biblical scholars. His engagement with the biblical text has occasionally left this Bible scholar somewhat disappointed (e.g., neither book has a Scripture index). At times his approach seems not to take the ethical problems seriously enough, brushing them aside too quickly, which may not trouble Christian readers but probably leaves serious skeptics unsatisfied.

In my book *God Behaving Badly*, I discuss the Canaanites in three chapters.[43] In chapter 2, I observe that God was slow to anger with the Canaanites since, after declaring their wickedness, he waited "four hundred years" (Gen. 15:13–16) before punishing them. In chapter 4, I point out that, in contrast to other ANE conquest narratives, Joshua has no glorification of bloody and violent details, merely an emphasis on the obedience of the Israelites. Furthermore, rather than conquering foreign lands to expand national boundaries, Israel was merely attempting to establish a homeland after experiencing hundreds of years of oppression as exiles in Egypt. The destruction of the Canaanites was viewed as an act of divine punishment against the Canaanites. To show that this destruction was not racially motivated, I point out that God also violently judged his own people, as demonstrated by the exiling of the Northern and Southern Kingdoms. I also observe that every Canaanite who showed hospitality to Israel was in turn shown hospitality (e.g., Rahab). In chapter 5, I point out that the primary biblical image for the conquest is not slaughter but "driving out" the people of the land.

My book has been criticized for lacking academic rigor, which I acknowledge. But I chose a more popular tone because many nonacademics struggle with the problematic portrayals of God they see in the Bible, and I was writing for them. I wrote on a related topic for an academic audience in a volume titled *Holy War in the Bible*, where I argue that compassion and wrath are the two primary motivations for divine warfare.[44] Throughout Scripture, God fights with compassion for the oppressed and with anger against the oppressor.[45]

43. David T. Lamb, *God Behaving Badly: Is the God of the Old Testament Angry, Sexist and Racist?* (Downers Grove, IL: InterVarsity, 2011; expanded ed., 2022).

44. David T. Lamb, "Compassion and Wrath as Motivations for Divine Warfare," in *Holy War in the Bible: Christian Morality and an Old Testament Problem*, ed. Heath A. Thomas, Jeremy Evans, and Paul Copan (Downers Grove, IL: IVP Academic, 2013), 133–51.

45. In Thomas, Evans, and Copan, *Holy War in the Bible*, see also Douglas A. Earl, "Joshua and the Crusades," 19–43.

Scholars Who Make Sense of a Violent Bible (Walton and Walton, Webb and Oeste)

As another installment of the Lost World series, John Walton and J. Harvey Walton cowrote *The Lost World of the Israelite Conquest*.[46] They show how crucial the ancient context is for understanding the problems of the Canaanite conquest. They argue that the חֵרֶם (*ḥērem*), typically translated "devoted to destruction" (e.g., Deut. 7:26 ESV), did not primarily involve killing people but destroying cultural identity, in this case that of the Canaanites. While their perspective on חֵרֶם is consistent with other scholars writing on the conquest, other conclusions are not. They argue that since the Canaanites were not under the covenant, they are not being judged for their wickedness but are being removed from the land because they represent disorder and chaos. This conclusion seems to go against much of the biblical witness (e.g., Gen. 15:16; Deut. 12:29–32) and many of the scholarly works discussed above.

Perhaps the most exhaustive recent treatment on violence in the OT comes from William Webb and Gordon Oeste.[47] In contrast to some of the apologetic works that may not take the problem of biblical violence seriously enough, Webb and Oeste go deeply into the problem, as evidenced not only by their bold title but also by their extended discussions of troubling texts. At points, however, they seem to exaggerate the problem, only to correct the overstatement in a later chapter. They commendably dedicate three chapters to the often-ignored topic of war rape, but one of their titles is overly problematic: "War Rape, Part Two: The Redemptive Side." While they discuss clear ANE examples of war rape, I don't think the OT text they examine (Deut. 21:10–14) describes war rape, although, as they point out, this law is clearly moving in a redemptive direction. Over the course of four chapters on hyperbole, they examine arguments for and against the hyperbole thesis first proposed by Younger. They conclude there is more textual evidence in favor of it, specifically in terms of the total-land conquest and total-kill language.

Scholars Who Summarize and Synthesize (Trimm, Longman)

Two recent books provide helpful perspective on the issues of divine violence and on the scholarship on this topic. Approximately one quarter of Longman's book on OT controversies focuses on the problem of divine violence.[48] Longman first shows how extensive the theme of divine violence is throughout Scripture, appearing not just in the conquest narrative but also in the OT more generally.

46. John H. Walton and J. Harvey Walton, *The Lost World of the Israelite Conquest: Covenant, Retribution, and the Fate of the Canaanites* (Downers Grove, IL: IVP Academic, 2017).

47. William J. Webb and Gordon K. Oeste, *Bloody, Brutal, and Barbaric: Wrestling with Troubling War Texts* (Downers Grove, IL: IVP Academic, 2019).

48. Tremper Longman III, *Confronting Old Testament Controversies: Pressing Questions about Evolution, Sexuality, History, and Violence* (Grand Rapids: Baker Books, 2019), 123–206.

Next, he discusses scholars (e.g., Seibert, Boyd) who differentiate between what God is really like and how he is portrayed in books like Joshua. Longman is not convinced by their views and concludes by calling them "Practical Marcionites."[49] He finds more agreement with scholars who "soften the blow" as they make sense of the problem (e.g., Copan, Lamb) but is not fully convinced by their arguments. He focuses on Copan, who has written the most on the topic, and points out various instances where Copan overstates his case by minimizing the violent aspects in a way that does not take the text seriously. (My own views on these subjects are closer to Longman than to Copan.) Longman concludes by presenting his perspective on biblical violence, that God consistently, in both the OT and NT, is portrayed as engaging in warfare against evil.

Like Longman's, Charlie Trimm's short book on the Canaanites summarizes research on violence, specifically the Canaanite conquest.[50] His first section includes general discussions of ANE warfare, genocide, and background on the Canaanites (chaps. 1–3). He then discusses the views of scholars who reevaluate either God (chap. 4), the OT (chap. 5), or the interpretation of violence in the OT (chaps. 6–7). In his discussions of these various scholars, Trimm observes some of the same weaknesses that Longman and others have noted. However, unlike Longman, Trimm does not lay out his own perspective; rather than trying to offer "the correct answer," he seeks to invite readers into the discussion. Longman and Trimm are great starting points for readers interested in gaining perspective on scholarship addressing OT violence and specifically the conquest of Joshua.

While scholars disagree over how to make sense of a violent God or a violent Bible, there is widespread consensus that the violence depicted in the books of Joshua and Judges should not be interpreted as normative for the people of God today as we engage with enemies.

Final Reflections

As I reflect on the state of research and future directions for study related to the books of Joshua, Judges, and Ruth, it seems likely that recent trends will continue. The historical debates regarding the dating and the nature of the conquest will persist and probably not reach a consensus. Interest in Deuteronomistic redaction will likely diminish, while literary work will expand. Possible areas for growth in literary approaches include character studies and research on intertextuality. More work could be done in the area of ANE contextual studies, particularly in light of how Younger's research on ancient conquest narratives has impacted subsequent discussions of biblical violence.

49. Longman, *Confronting Old Testament Controversies*, 164.

50. Charlie Trimm, *The Destruction of the Canaanites: God, Genocide, and Biblical Interpretation* (Grand Rapids: Eerdmans, 2022).

Most of the scholars working on the problem of biblical violence are men, while the majority of the scholars engaged in ethical problems related to sex and sexual abuse (e.g., rape, prostitution) are women. Perhaps this is not surprising, but both of these areas of research would greatly benefit from more diverse perspectives on these problematic issues. People of faith are going to continue to struggle with the bloodshed and sexual abuse found not only in the Bible but also in contemporary societies. Biblical scholarship on the books of Joshua, Judges, and Ruth should therefore continue to help make sense of these troubling texts.

14

Samuel-Kings

Rachelle Gilmour

> The stories that grow up around a king are strong vines with a fierce grip.
>
> *The Secret Chord*, Geraldine Brooks

The portrait of David and his royal descendants in Samuel and Kings has proved timeless in its capacity to grip the imagination of its readers. Retellings of its stories abound, stretching from the book of Chronicles in the biblical period to the contemporary Australian author Geraldine Brooks in the last decade. These stories have also allured scholars to analyze their narrative structures and features. This is particularly the case for the book of Samuel and the first two chapters of 1 Kings, where David's charismatic character and family drama are narrated.

The accounts of the heroes of the book of Kings—such as Solomon, Hezekiah, and Josiah—have gripped recent scholarship in a different way. These narratives offer tantalizing hints of how and when Kings was written, and indeed the whole so-called Deuteronomistic History, including Joshua, Judges, and Samuel. It is difficult to speak of authorship for such composite texts, but the history of composition and the relationship of the text to history are means by which the worlds of the authors can be explored.

Alongside the text and author, the reader is increasingly an object of critical reflection in scholarship on Samuel and Kings. As the voices of scholars outside traditional European and English-speaking universities and seminaries have become more accessible in the last twenty years, their perspectives have enriched appreciation, or suspicion, of these texts and prompted reexamination of presuppositions regarding theology, gender, and class.

Such reflection has led to the addition of a fourth category alongside history, text, and reader through which we can organize scholarship on Samuel and Kings: power.[1] Some of the most intriguing studies in Samuel and Kings have emerged on this topic, since deliberations about power are integral to the books' storylines, and politics is a fundamental factor in their composition. The categories of author, text, reader, and power are not unique to scholarship on Samuel and Kings, but they will guide our grouping of the diverse avenues of recent research on this corpus.

History of the Histories

The Deuteronomistic History Theory

In 2005, Thomas Römer published what might be called the standard work that overviews the Deuteronomistic History theory.[2] This theory has dominated scholarship on Samuel-Kings since it was first proposed by Martin Noth in 1943. It claims, in brief, that the books of Joshua, Judges, Samuel, and Kings underwent shared redaction(s) to produce one cohesive work to address the crisis of exile, influenced by the theology of Deuteronomy. Römer's work surveys the contemporary state of scholarship, outlining developments on Noth's theory and presenting his own. He gives an overview of Frank Cross's model from North America, which posits a Josianic first edition and exilic second edition of the history, and of the strata model, more influential in Europe, that posits at least three "Deuteronomists" (preexilic, exilic, and postexilic).

Two key points grow out of Römer's work: (1) Kings is integral to any study of the Deuteronomistic History, especially its accounts of Josiah and the exile, and (2) Samuel is largely peripheral. These observations are borne out in subsequent research that works with a Deuteronomistic History model.

Three trends are discernible in recent directions in scholarship: analysis of the ideology and theology of the Deuteronomistic historians, not just its redactional layers or editions, primarily in the book of Kings; focus on sources for the Deuteronomistic History rather than on the work of the Deuteronomistic historians, especially in Samuel; and movement toward alternative models for reconstructing the composition history of both Samuel and Kings.[3]

1. Gale A. Yee, "The Author/Text/Reader and Power: Suggestions for a Critical Framework for Biblical Studies," in *Reading from This Place*, vol. 1, *Social Location and Biblical Interpretation in the United States*, ed. Fernando F. Segovia and Mary Ann Tolbert (Minneapolis: Fortress, 1995), 109–18.

2. Thomas Römer, *The So-Called Deuteronomistic History: A Sociological, Historical, and Literary Introduction* (London: T&T Clark, 2005).

3. My survey is largely limited to English-language studies. European scholars have produced other studies on composition: e.g., Hannes Bezzel, *Saul: Israels König in Tradition, Redaktion und früher Rezeption*, FAT 97 (Tübingen: Mohr Siebeck, 2015) and the multivolume commentary by Walter Dietrich, *Samuel*, BKAT (Neukirchen-Vluyn: Neukirchener Theologie, 2010–). For other current approaches in Europe and Israel, see Joachim J. Krause, Omer Sergi, and

The Deuteronomistic Historians

Several recent works focus on the ideology and theology of the Deuteronomistic historian(s), especially in Kings. David Lamb examines Deuteronomistic disapproval of dynastic succession, particularly the Jehu narratives in 2 Kings 9–15.[4] Alison Joseph examines kingship in Kings, identifying David as the prototype for good kings, epitomized in the portrayal of Josiah, and Jeroboam as an antitype for bad kings.[5] Both Lamb and Joseph reflect on what these portrayals of kings suggest about the composition of the Deuteronomistic History, with Lamb rejecting and Joseph endorsing Cross's proposal of a Josianic edition.[6] These works offer compelling readings of Kings, but their contradictory conclusions point toward the present impasse in scholarship regarding the number and nature of Deuteronomistic editions and redactions.

Daewook Kim considers prophets, rather than kings, in so-called Deuteronomistic texts of Samuel and Kings and places their polemics against syncretism and idolatry in the postexilic period.[7] Kim sensitively reads prophetic critiques in 1 Sam. 28, 1 Kings 12, and 1 Kings 20–22 alongside archaeological evidence to highlight their concerns with syncretism and idolatry. By selecting a single theme dating to a later period in these books, Kim manages to illuminate connections between the texts and their contexts without entering the methodological quagmire of delineating every source or redaction.[8]

By contrast, David Janzen treats the Deuteronomistic History as a single authored whole and gives an account of its unevenness from the perspective of trauma.[9] Subversions of the history's "master narrative" are not a sign of multiple redactions but rather trauma's "non-memories." In his application of contemporary social-scientific theory, Janzen returns to Noth's original formulation of the

Kristin Weingart, eds., *Saul, Benjamin, and the Emergence of Monarchy in Israel: Biblical and Archaeological Perspectives,* AIL 40 (Atlanta: SBL Press, 2020).

4. David T. Lamb, *Righteous Jehu and His Evil Heirs: The Deuteronomist's Negative Perspective on Dynastic Succession* (Oxford: Oxford University Press, 2007).

5. Alison L. Joseph, *Portrait of the King: The Davidic Prototype in Deuteronomistic Poetics* (Minneapolis: Fortress, 2015).

6. Lauren A. S. Monroe rejects Cross's Josianic edition, advocates a Hezekian edition, and includes editing from the Holiness school in her model. See Monroe, *Josiah's Reform and the Dynamics of Defilement: Israelite Rites of Violence and the Making of a Biblical Text* (Oxford: Oxford University Press, 2011).

7. Daewook Kim, *Prophetic Conflicts in the Deuteronomistic History*, Beiträge zur Wissenschaft vom Alten und Neuen Testament 229 (Stuttgart: Kohlhammer, 2021).

8. Roy L. Heller, *The Characters of Elijah and Elisha and the Deuteronomic Evaluation of Prophecy: Miracles and Manipulation*, LHBOTS 671 (London: T&T Clark, 2018); Lissa M. Wray Beal, *The Deuteronomist's Prophet: Narrative Control of Approval and Disapproval in the Story of Jehu (2 Kings 9 and 10)*, LHBOTS 478 (New York: T&T Clark, 2007); James Donkor Afoakwah, *The Nathan-David Confrontation (2 Sam 12:1–15a): A Slap in the Face of the Deuteronomistic Hero?* (Frankfurt am Main: Peter Lang, 2015).

9. David Janzen, *The Violent Gift: Trauma's Subversion of the Deuteronomistic History's Narrative*, LHBOTS 561 (New York: T&T Clark, 2012).

Deuteronomistic History as a single continuous work in which a Deuteronomist interprets preexisting narratives.

Pre-Deuteronomistic Sources

Several recent studies focus on the constituent pre-Deuteronomistic sources of these books, rather than on the work of the Deuteronomist(s). This has been the case especially in the book of Samuel, where questions arise about whether Samuel should be considered Deuteronomistic at all. So-called Deuteronomistic redactions and material are identified in different studies through the occurrence of "Deuteronomic language,"[10] connections to Deuteronomic law, or material explaining the national disaster of the Babylonian exile.[11] Samuel contains little of this kind of evidence. Moreover, such broad parameters for "Deuteronomistic" puts its usefulness at risk. A consensus remains that there are Deuteronomistic touches on Samuel, but these are considered minimal.[12]

Some studies continue to engage deeply with the Deuteronomistic History theory, while also examining its sources. For example, Jeremy Hutton delivers a thorough and sophisticated reconstruction of Samuel's composition that considers a large proportion of the material to be pre-Deuteronomistic.[13]

Others focus on one document or tradition inserted into Samuel by the Deuteronomist or after the Deuteronomist. Andrew Knapp's work on the Succession Narrative (2 Sam. 9–1 Kings 2) reviews royal apology as a "mode" rather than a literary form. Knapp dates these apologetic texts close to Solomon's kingship, before the development of Deuteronomy or any so-called Deuteronomistic school.[14] Similarly, Sung-Hee Yoon focuses on a putative source, the "History of David's Rise."[15] If Samuel indeed has so little Deuteronomistic editing, further research on these earlier components of the book will ultimately develop a fuller picture of its composition and political and theological contexts.

10. Moshe Weinfeld, *Deuteronomy and the Deuteronomic School* (Oxford: Clarendon, 1972), 320–65.

11. Konrad Schmid, "Deuteronomy within the 'Deuteronomistic Histories' in Genesis–2 Kings," in *Deuteronomy in the Pentateuch, Hexateuch, and the Deuteronomistic History*, ed. Konrad Schmid and Raymond F. Person Jr. (Tübingen: Mohr Siebeck, 2012), 8–30.

12. Cynthia Edenburg and Juha Pakkala, eds., *Is Samuel among the Deuteronomists? Current Views on the Place of Samuel in a Deuteronomistic History*, AIL 16 (Atlanta: Society of Biblical Literature, 2013).

13. Jeremy M. Hutton, *The Transjordanian Palimpsest: The Overwritten Texts of Personal Exile and Transformation in the Deuteronomistic History*, BZAW 396 (Berlin: De Gruyter, 2009).

14. Andrew Knapp, *Royal Apologetic in the Ancient Near East*, WAWSup 4 (Atlanta: SBL Press, 2015).

15. Sung-Hee Yoon, *The Question of the Beginning and the Ending of the So-Called History of David's Rise: A Methodological Reflection and Its Implications*, BZAW 642 (Berlin: De Gruyter, 2014).

John Van Seters accounts for the minimal Deuteronomistic theology in the David story in a somewhat different way, positing a post-Deuteronomistic rewriting of the work in the Persian period.[16] This postexilic author introduced a satirical vein, parodying David as king. Van Seters suggests that the Deuteronomistic material in Samuel, though limited, cannot be rejected entirely, revising his earlier studies that posited a solely postexilic historiography.[17]

Alternative Models

Recent studies have sought to shift the paradigm of the Deuteronomistic History theory altogether. The Deuteronomistic History theory has been applied more productively as a lens to Kings than to Samuel, but the lack of substantial Deuteronomistic work in Samuel destabilizes the theory in its dominant form. Nevertheless, paradigms are not easy to shift, and an alternative has yet to fully take hold.

One of the most persistent and convincing opponents to standard formulations of the Deuteronomistic History theory is A. Graeme Auld. He is one of the few to offer a constructive alternate model.[18] Auld uses a comparison between Samuel-Kings and Chronicles as his starting point, arguing that there existed a "Book of Two Houses" largely consisting of their overlapping material. Samuel and Kings grew out of the development and elaboration of the Book of Two Houses. Auld also argues that Deuteronomy is more likely influenced by Samuel-Kings than vice versa. Indeed a more complicated relationship between Deuteronomy and redactions of the Deuteronomistic History has been averred in other studies.[19]

The methods of source and redaction criticism associated with the Deuteronomistic History theory have also been seriously challenged by empirical methodologies. Sara Milstein highlights the evidence of ANE scribal practices, including what she calls "revision through introduction," a practice where material is recast by reframing rather than substantial rewriting.[20] Another challenge from empirical methodologies comes from Raymond Person, who grounds his work in orality and textual plurality.[21] According to Person, Samuel-Kings and Chronicles are competing contemporary historiographies. Modern scholarship has reconstructed theological divergences where there were none for ancient audiences.

16. John Van Seters, *The Biblical Saga of King David* (Winona Lake, IN: Eisenbrauns, 2009).

17. John Van Seters, *In Search of History: Historiography in the Ancient World and the Origins of Biblical History* (New Haven: Yale University Press, 1983).

18. A. Graeme Auld, *Life in Kings: Reshaping the Royal Story in the Hebrew Bible*, AIL 30 (Atlanta: SBL Press, 2017).

19. Schmid, "Deuteronomy."

20. Sara J. Milstein, *Tracking the Master Scribe: Revision through Introduction in Biblical and Mesopotamian Literature* (New York: Oxford University Press, 2016).

21. Raymond F. Person Jr., *The Deuteronomic History and the Book of Chronicles: Scribal Works in an Oral World*, AIL 6 (Atlanta: Society of Biblical Literature, 2010).

Some have also moved to investigating the ideology and theology of Kings as an independent book. Nathan Lovell, although not rejecting the Deuteronomistic History theory, reads Kings as a self-contained exilic book.[22] Lovell utilizes an ethno-symbolic approach to national identity to demonstrate a southern-biased pan-Israelite national vision. Lovell's work demonstrates that the term "Deuteronomistic" and the underlying theory may not be needed in order to do productive work on the books' political contexts.

In summary, the Deuteronomistic History theory continues to be an important heuristic model for reading Kings and, to a lesser extent, Samuel. It is used as the foundation for dividing the books into sources and redactions and learning something of their composition history. Paradoxically, it is also used to assert a unified text, containing a discoverable theological and political purpose imposed by the Deuteronomists. Whether this composition history and theology will continue to be shared between Samuel and Kings remains to be seen. "Deuteronomistic" may increasingly become a shorthand reference to a final major redaction of Samuel and Kings at some point in the Persian period, or the theory may give way to the study of each text as an independent book.

Historiography, Memory, and the History of the Monarchy

Recent research on Samuel and Kings has been interested not only in the history *of* the texts, but also the history *in* the texts. In the past, the debate has been fierce between so-called *minimalists*, who assert little of historical value in these books, and *maximalists*, who champion the historical accuracy of the books. This debate has mellowed to a middle way that acknowledges that the books eschew modern categories of either fact or fiction.[23]

Recent research can be divided into two complementary categories: (1) studies that excavate texts for historical information, often in conjunction with archaeological findings and literary critical methods, and (2) studies that examine Samuel and Kings as works of historiography or memory that reveal more about the context in which the books were composed than about the historical period they recount.

Text as Source of Historical Data

Mahri Leonard-Fleckman focuses on the early monarchy. Considering the terminology of "House of David" in 2 Samuel and 1 Kings, she argues that it did not originally refer to a dynastic house of Judah.[24] The period of Jehu's dynasty

22. Nathan Lovell, *The Book of Kings and Exilic Identity: 1 and 2 Kings as a Work of Political Historiography*, LHBOTS 708 (London: T&T Clark, 2021).

23. Rachelle Gilmour, *Representing the Past: A Literary Approach to Narrative Historiography in the Book of Samuel*, VTSup 143 (Leiden: Brill, 2011).

24. Mahri Leonard-Fleckman, *The House of David: Between Political Formation and Literary Revision* (Minneapolis: Fortress, 2016).

has a greater wealth of extrabiblical sources, and Shuichi Hasegawa[25] and Jonathan Robker[26] have studies demonstrating that a more comprehensive historical reconstruction of this period can be fruitful.

Other studies investigate the economic and social history of ancient Israel either by relying primarily on the biblical text with assistance from extrabiblical material or by relying primarily on extrabiblical evidence to elucidate the text. Roger Nam examines the text for the primary source material to examine evidence of different economic systems in Kings, including reciprocity, redistribution, and market exchange.[27] Mercedes García Bachmann catalogs the types of work performed by women throughout the Deuteronomistic History.[28] These studies must contend with the difficulties of dating texts and questions around their historical value.

Matthew Suriano uses extrabiblical texts and archaeological evidence to elucidate the death notices in Kings.[29] Stephen Russell demonstrates the ways in which space, such as the city gate or the threshing floor, is used to construct power in selected texts in Samuel and Kings.[30] Both studies straddle historical studies with exegetical work, illuminating the text and social context in equal measure.

Text as Historiography or Memory

Jacob Wright compares memories in Samuel to war memorials and shown how the exploits of David might be exaggerated or remolded to suit changing interests during the monarchy and postexilic periods.[31] Essays in a volume edited by Diana Edelman and Ehud Ben Zvi examine the texts as social memory of the Persian-era literati of Yehud.[32] Using this approach, Ian Wilson examines memories of David in Samuel and Chronicles.[33] Different views of kingship, attributed to different

25. Shuichi Hasegawa, *Aram and Israel during the Jehuite Dynasty*, BZAW 434 (Berlin: De Gruyter, 2012).

26. Jonathan Miles Robker, *The Jehu Revolution: A Royal Tradition of the Northern Kingdom and Its Ramifications*, BZAW 435 (Berlin: De Gruyter, 2012).

27. Roger S. Nam, *Portrayals of Economic Exchange in the Book of Kings*, BibInt 112 (Leiden: Brill, 2012).

28. Mercedes L. García Bachmann, *Women at Work in the Deuteronomistic History*, IVBS 4 (Atlanta: Society of Biblical Literature, 2013).

29. Matthew J. Suriano, *The Politics of Dead Kings: Dynastic Ancestors in the Book of Kings and Ancient Israel*, FAT 2/48 (Tübingen: Mohr Siebeck, 2010).

30. Stephen C. Russell, *The King and the Land: A Geography of Royal Power in the Biblical World* (New York: Oxford University Press, 2017).

31. Jacob L. Wright, *David, King of Israel, and Caleb in Biblical Memory* (New York: Cambridge University Press, 2014).

32. Diana Vikander Edelman and Ehud Ben Zvi, eds., *Remembering Biblical Figures in the Late Persian and Early Hellenistic Periods: Social Memory and Imagination* (Oxford: Oxford University Press, 2013).

33. Ian D. Wilson, *Kingship and Memory in Ancient Judah* (New York: Oxford University Press, 2017).

sources since Julius Wellhausen, are examined in terms of multivocality within a group of elites in Yehud.

Although these scholars do not reject the proposal that the texts are made up of earlier sources and redactions, they focus on the texts as Persian-era literature and the ways in which they reflect interacting national histories and group identity. They have a great advantage over more traditional historical inquiry in that they deal with the received text tradition, rather than relying on proposed reconstructions of earlier composition and source history. Once again, as the discipline of biblical studies becomes increasingly conversant with developments in the social sciences, especially collective memory studies, this avenue for researching Samuel-Kings in relation to diverse historical contexts will expand.

The Text and Its Textures

The literary richness of Samuel has made it the subject of many groundbreaking literary studies on biblical narrative. Along with Genesis, its stories were central to the formulation of influential literary approaches such as those of Robert Alter and Meir Sternberg.[34] These narrative depths continue to place Samuel at the center of explorations of new theories in biblical studies and, to an increasing extent, Kings.

Characterization has long been a key focus in literary readings, and the wealth of characters across Samuel and Kings has allowed ever new perspectives. Two edited volumes by Keith Bodner and Benjamin Johnson on characterization in Samuel and Kings demonstrate how characterization can be an entry point to a broader literary reading of the books.[35] For example, characterization may be a way into ethics, through the evaluation of characters' actions. In this vein, Cephas Tushima revisits the question of David's characterization in Samuel, examining his treatment of Saul's heirs and concluding that David is calculating and unjust.[36] Virginia Miller argues that the Succession Narrative is a satirical work critiquing David.[37]

Bodner exemplifies the art of "close reading" in focusing on the stories of Absalom, Jeroboam, and Elisha.[38] His readings are compelling, and they tend

34. Robert Alter, *The Art of Biblical Narrative*, rev. ed. (New York: Basic Books, 2011); Meir Sternberg, *The Poetics of Biblical Narrative: Ideological Literature and the Drama of Reading* (Bloomington: Indiana University Press, 1985).

35. Keith Bodner and Benjamin J. M. Johnson, *Characters and Characterization in the Book of Samuel*, LHBOTS 669 (London: T&T Clark, 2019); Bodner and Johnson, *Characters and Characterization in the Book of Kings*, LHBOTS 670 (London: T&T Clark, 2019).

36. Cephas T. A. Tushima, *The Fate of Saul's Progeny in the Reign of David* (Cambridge: James Clarke, 2012).

37. Virginia Miller, *A King and a Fool? The Succession Narrative as a Satire*, BibInt 179 (Leiden: Brill, 2019).

38. Keith Bodner, *Jeroboam's Royal Drama*, Biblical Reconfigurations (Oxford: Oxford University Press, 2012); Bodner, *Elisha's Profile in the Book of Kings: The Double Agent* (Oxford: Oxford University Press, 2013); Bodner, *The Rebellion of Absalom* (London: Routledge, 2014).

toward opening the possibilities of the text's meanings rather than foreclosing any one interpretation or historical context for its composition. The open-ended nature of his readings has its roots in the theory of Mikhail Bakhtin, whose work is foundational for Bodner's earlier study of David in Samuel.[39]

Bakhtin's thought has been a productive interlocutor in other literary studies, including two on the Elijah and Elisha stories. Gilmour uses Bakhtinian dialogism as a guide to analyzing juxtaposition in the Elisha cycle, examining the ways in which adjacent episodes produce new meaning through contradiction, corroboration, and question and answer.[40] Helen Paynter applies Bakhtin's concept of the carnivalesque to the stories of Elijah and Elisha.[41]

Literary approaches examine a text, but there are many manuscript traditions of Samuel and Kings, and any literary approach requires some adjudication of these witnesses. Updated studies of Qumran and Septuagint scrolls and other text-critical studies provide the necessary critical studies for readings, whether literary or historical.[42] Scholars have been slower to offer literary readings of multiple texts. One innovative contribution comes from Johnson, who compares literary readings of 1 Sam. 17–18 in the MT and LXX.[43] These manuscript traditions may complicate literary readings, but Johnson shows that they can enrich the process further.

After the flurry of close readings of these texts in the late twentieth century, only the most skilled practitioners, such as Bodner, still successfully offer anything new. Most new research now integrates close engagement with literary theory, and literary approaches are increasingly a tool co-opted for pursuing questions other than an appreciation of the text's literary qualities. These approaches are often placed in conversation with the text's reception history or reader response, a category to which we now turn.

Receptive and Unreceptive Readers

Text-critical studies point to the textual fluidity of Samuel and Kings in the Second Temple period, the beginning of the afterlife of these books. In this section, we consider the ongoing reception of the books from ancient to modern times

39. Keith Bodner, *David Observed: A King in the Eyes of His Court*, HBM 5 (Sheffield: Sheffield Phoenix, 2005).

40. Rachelle Gilmour, *Juxtaposition and the Elisha Cycle*, LHBOTS 594 (London: T&T Clark, 2014).

41. Helen Paynter, *Reduced Laughter: Seriocomic Features and Their Functions in the Book of Kings*, BibInt 142 (Leiden: Brill, 2016).

42. Philippe Hugo and Adrian Schenker, *Archaeology of the Books of Samuel: The Entangling of the Textual and Literary History*, VTSup 132 (Leiden: Brill, 2010); Jason K. Driesbach, *4QSamuel[a] and the Text of Samuel*, VTSup 171 (Leiden: Brill, 2016); Julio Trebolle Barrera, *Textual and Literary Criticism of the Books of Kings*, VTSup 185 (Leiden: Brill, 2020).

43. Benjamin J. M. Johnson, *Reading David and Goliath in Greek and Hebrew: A Literary Approach*, FAT 2/82 (Tübingen: Mohr Siebeck, 2015).

as well as other contemporary readings. We can define reception as retelling and reworking. Other readings—such as theological, canonical, and contextual—engage with critical methods to read the text but do so with particular questions for specific audiences. All of these approaches share an emphasis on the reader: the reader's context, concerns, or theological constructs.

A study that illustrates the blurred boundaries between history and reader is Song-Mi Park's treatment of the composition history of the Hezekiah account in Kings and then the subsequent development and redaction of the account when incorporated into Chronicles and Isaiah.[44] She argues for a model of dialogue in which the text is placed in conversation with new concerns and reshaped accordingly.

Recent studies explore early retellings and reworkings of Samuel and Kings beyond the biblical corpus. Ariel Feldman's publication of Qumran texts 4Q160, 4Q382, 4Q481a, and 6Q9 with commentary is useful for inquiry into these texts and aiding biblical exegesis.[45] He finds the Qumran texts more interested in speeches, prayers, and psalms than in the "historical" narrative dimension of Samuel and Kings. Unlike Chronicles, which rewrites Samuel-Kings (or proto–Samuel-Kings) as part of a larger history, Feldman argues that these Qumran texts focus on Samuel and Kings as independent books. Michael Avioz's study of Josephus is similarly illuminating.[46] He contributes an evaluation of Josephus's method as first and foremost concerned with the *peshat* (plain sense) meaning. Here modern literary readings find encouragement as Josephus offers an ambiguous portrait of Saul and David. Modern suspicions about David's wielding of power and Saul's rejection find their roots in interpretations from antiquity.

A hermeneutic of suspicion is found in the much-later reception of Samuel in art, in fragments of a play by Bertolt Brecht. According to David Shepherd and Nicholas Johnson, Brecht imagines that David, not God, kills his newborn son in 2 Sam. 12.[47] Sara Koenig argues that the biblical text characterizes Bathsheba as generally positive and dynamic, but later traditions, beginning with Josephus, place blame on her for David's actions.[48] This trend continues in other contemporary scholarship. Harding considers the frequently asked question of whether David and Jonathan were gay lovers.[49] Rather than answer the question, he addresses why modern readers persistently ask it.

44. Song-Mi Suzie Park, *Hezekiah and the Dialogue of Memory*, Emerging Scholars (Minneapolis: Fortress, 2015).

45. Ariel Feldman, *The Dead Sea Scrolls Rewriting Samuel and Kings: Texts and Commentary*, BZAW 469 (Boston: De Gruyter, 2015).

46. Michael Avioz, *Josephus' Interpretation of the Books of Samuel*, LSTS 86 (London: T&T Clark, 2015).

47. David J. Shepherd and Nicholas E. Johnson, *Bertolt Brecht and the David Fragments (1919–1921): An Interdisciplinary Study* (London: T&T Clark, 2020).

48. Sara M. Koenig, *Isn't This Bathsheba? A Study in Characterization* (Eugene, OR: Pickwick, 2011).

49. James E. Harding, *The Love of David and Jonathan: Ideology, Text, Reception*, Bible World (London: Routledge, 2014).

Theological and canonical readings are guided by attentiveness to the reader, in this case the reader's theological positioning, even if critical methods are simultaneously employed.[50] Stephen B. Chapman's commentary on 1 Samuel is an example of an explicitly Christian reading of Samuel and Kings.[51] His reading of Saul's tragedy in conversation with the tragedy of Christ is a much-needed innovation on tendencies to limit Christian interest to David as a messianic-type figure. David Firth also challenges contemporary Christian readings in a study on foreigners in the Former Prophets.[52] Although the characterization of foreigners as enemies in these books is well known, he points to where Israel is a witness to foreigners or where the Israelites themselves are portrayed as foreigners. Daniel Stulac advances a "canonical agrarian" hermeneutic and applies it to the stories of Elijah in the book of Kings.[53]

Other readings place less emphasis on the reader's theological commitments and more on the particularity of the reader.[54] Most readings surveyed here do not consider themselves contextual, but Uriah Kim demonstrates that they do indeed derive from normative groups in scholarship, and compelling alternatives are possible.[55] He positions himself as a Korean American and employs postcolonial theory from Homi Bhabha and Yehouda Shenhav to develop a postcolonial reading of David. Using critical methods to examine the term חֵסֶד (*ḥēsed*) in the narrative, he defamiliarizes the term by using the Korean concept *jeong*, described as "the stickiness in people relations."

A project based at the Ujamaa Centre for Community Development and Research in South Africa uses contextual Bible study of 2 Sam. 13, the rape of Tamar, with women to discuss issues of violence against women. Access to these women's voices is given in a number of studies, including that of Charlene van der Walt.[56] Reflections that the story of Tamar might be empowering for women affected by violence are profound and suggestive for broader interpretations of this troubling text.

Throughout all these studies, critical reflections on the roles of the reader in interpretations of Samuel and Kings will play an increasing part in composition

50. For methodological reflections, see Paul Hedley Jones, *Anonymous Prophets and Archetypal Kings: Reading 1 Kings 13*, LHBOTS 704 (London: T&T Clark, 2020).

51. Stephen B. Chapman, *1 Samuel as Christian Scripture: A Theological Commentary* (Grand Rapids: Eerdmans, 2016).

52. David G. Firth, *Including the Stranger: Foreigners in the Former Prophets*, NSBT 50 (Downers Grove, IL: IVP Academic, 2019).

53. Daniel J. D. Stulac, *Life, Land, and Elijah in the Book of Kings*, SOTSMS (Cambridge: Cambridge University Press, 2020).

54. Harding, *Love of David and Jonathan.*

55. Uriah Y. Kim, *Identity and Loyalty in the David Story: A Postcolonial Reading*, HBM 22 (Sheffield: Sheffield Phoenix, 2008).

56. Charlene van der Walt, "Hearing Tamar's Voice—How the Margin Hears Differently: Contextual Readings of 2 Samuel 13.1–22," in *Samuel, Kings and Chronicles*, ed. Athalya Brenner-Idan and Archie C. C. Lee, Texts@Contexts 5 (London: T&T Clark, 2017), 1:2–23.

and text-oriented studies. Critical work on the text is not only a prelude to reader-oriented studies, but reader-oriented studies can in turn also contribute to larger questions of the Deuteronomistic History theory and the interpretation of specific texts.

Prying Open Power

Finally, a collection of studies can be categorized as concerned with power relations, whether found in the text, the composition of the text, or its reception. Several could be categorized elsewhere, but their grouping here highlights two points: (1) divine and human sovereignty are central to the content and composition of Samuel and Kings, so reflection on power relations inside and outside the text is crucial; and (2) attention to power provides a point of intersection for the integration of different methodologies.

One perspective on the question of power in Samuel and Kings considers the ethics of kingship as portrayed within the text.[57] Richard Smith examines David's execution of justice and righteousness in 2 Samuel, demonstrating the ways in which David attempts but fails to uphold this ANE monarchic ideal.[58] April Westbrook examines the "woman stories" in 1 and 2 Samuel.[59] She illuminates how David fails to bring monarchic justice through the misuse of his power and suggests that the narrative generates sympathy for those he has injured.

Marti Steussy and Rachelle Gilmour interrogate divine power and action in the book of Samuel. Steussy considers the portrayal of God in consultation with his prophet Samuel and points to their immoral action and God's so-called dark side.[60] She attributes this portrayal to a "pre-axial" way of thinking in the composition of Samuel. In contrast, Gilmour's work analyzes divine violence in Samuel in conversation with Immanuel Kant, Martha Nussbaum, and Walter Benjamin. She argues that divine action may indeed be recognizable to contemporary ethics, particularly when understood in the context of Judahite monarchic ideology.[61]

Other works interrogate the portrayal of gender and gender-related violence. Melissa Jackson explores the subversive dimension of comedy in a reading of

57. On ethics as shaping the reader, see Sung Min Chun, *Ethics and Biblical Narrative: A Literary and Discourse-Analytical Approach to the Story of Josiah* (Oxford: Oxford University Press, 2014).

58. Richard G. Smith, *The Fate of Justice and Righteousness during David's Reign*, LHBOTS 508 (New York: T&T Clark, 2009).

59. April D. Westbrook, *"And He Will Take Your Daughters . . .": Woman Story and the Ethical Evaluation of Monarchy in the David Narrative*, LHBOTS 610 (London: T&T Clark, 2015).

60. Marti J. Steussy, *Samuel and His God* (Columbia: University of South Carolina Press, 2010).

61. Rachelle Gilmour, *Divine Violence in the Book of Samuel* (New York: Oxford University Press, 2021).

Jezebel at the intersection of ethnicity and feminist concerns.[62] Reading against the grain, Jezebel stands out as a strong character, unwilling to subordinate her religious traditions to those of her husband. Rhiannon Graybill reconsiders stories about sexual violence in the HB, including a chapter on harm in the Bathsheba story.[63] Graybill advances discussions of sexual violence in 2 Samuel, which have struggled with how to apply the category of "rape" in 2 Sam. 11–12. Graybill demonstrates that "consent" is a problematic category and that Bathsheba's story is better read through a model of harm and the "limiting of future possibility" for Bathsheba.

Another topic is imperial power. The ambivalent attitude toward kings in these books is a possible response to empire, whether Assyrian, Babylonian, or Persian. However, because a large proportion of the so-called Deuteronomistic History has traditionally been dated to the reign of Josiah, a period in which the Assyrians were in decline and Babylon was not yet a menacing threat, broader studies on the impact of imperial royal ideology or power in the book are few. Kari Latvus explores how Solomon is portrayed as an imperial ruler, despite Solomon's "empire" being a matter of imagination rather than historical reality.[64] With scholarship on the ongoing composition of Samuel and Kings during the Persian period still developing, the responses and formulations of imperial power will undoubtedly be an area of future research.[65]

Reflections

Prying open power in Samuel and Kings draws us back to where this overview began: the Deuteronomistic History theory. What is the locus of divine authority in Samuel and Kings? The traditional formulation of the Deuteronomistic History theory suggests that divine sovereignty is represented by the Mosaic law of Deuteronomy and divine intervention enforces this law with retributive punishment. Yet written law has little place in Samuel, certainly nothing comparable to its place in the story of Josiah in Kings.

By contrast, prophetic authority is pervasive throughout both books. For example, the prophet Samuel presides over the institution of the monarchy in

62. Melissa A. Jackson, *Comedy and Feminist Interpretation of the Hebrew Bible: A Subversive Collaboration* (Oxford: Oxford University Press, 2012).

63. Rhiannon Graybill, *Texts after Terror: Rape, Sexual Violence, and the Hebrew Bible* (New York: Oxford University Press, 2021).

64. Kari Latvus, "The Empire of Solomon: An Analysis of Imperial Rhetoric in 1 Kings 3–11," in *Postcolonial Commentary and the Old Testament*, ed. Hemchand Gossai (London: T&T Clark, 2019), 161–74.

65. See Wilson, *Kingship and Memory*. See also Jon L. Berquist, "Identities and Empire: Historiographic Questions for the Deuteronomistic History in the Persian Period," in *Historiography and Identity (Re)formulation in Second Temple Historiographical Literature*, ed. Louis Jonker, LHBOTS 534 (New York: T&T Clark, 2010), 3–13.

1 Sam. 8–12. A prophetic redaction of these two books is thus widely accepted, but what then is the relationship of these books to Deuteronomy? Deuteronomy advocates discernment between true and false prophets in Deut. 18:20–22, but such discernment is of little concern in Samuel. Perhaps the dominance of the Deuteronomistic History theory has distracted scholars from other constructions of sovereignty throughout Samuel and Kings, such as the mediating role of elders, and from formulations of divine intervention and violence that do not follow a retributive principle for law transgression.[66]

Conclusion

The future of Samuel-Kings studies will answer these and other compositional, literary, and ethical questions most effectively through the integration of methodologies. Reception and contextual studies highlight the effects and oversights of dominating theories in normative European and English-speaking scholarship, prying open power in new and exciting ways. Solely text-oriented and composition-oriented studies have approached their limits, but fresh new developments continue to emerge as such studies increasingly interact with and are enriched by cross-disciplinary engagement with material culture, literary theory, and the social sciences.

66. Mark G. Brett, *Locations of God: Political Theology in the Hebrew Bible* (New York: Oxford University Press, 2019), 13–25; Gilmour, *Divine Violence*.

15

Chronicles

Kenneth Ristau

Biblical scholars sometimes assess and value texts, especially ostensibly historiographic texts like Chronicles, based on their perceived or demonstrated historical accuracy.[1] Based on that criterion, Chronicles has not fared well.[2] When compared to Samuel-Kings, a version of which it likely employs as a source (see below), and certainly when compared to inscriptions and other extrabiblical

1. I refer to the (implied) author of Chronicles, excluding Ezra-Nehemiah, as the Chronicler. Based on historical and cultural considerations, I assume that the author was male and, therefore, use the pronouns "he/him." On the so-called Chronicler's History, which treats Chronicles-Ezra-Nehemiah as a collection or unit similar to the so-called "Deuteronomistic History," see Ralph W. Klein, "The Rise and Fall of the So-Called Chronicler's History and the Current Study of the Composition of Chronicles, Ezra, and Nehemiah," in *The Oxford Handbook of the Historical Books of the Hebrew Bible*, ed. Brad E. Kelle and Brent A. Strawn (New York: Oxford University Press, 2020), 353–66.

2. Matt Patrick Graham, *The Utilization of 1 and 2 Chronicles in the Reconstruction of Israelite History in the Nineteenth Century*, SBLDS 116 (Atlanta: Scholars Press, 1990); Kai Peltonen, *History Debated: The Historical Reliability of Chronicles in Pre-critical and Critical Research*, 2 vols., Publications of the Finnish Exegetical Society 64 (Helsinki: Finnish Exegetical Society; Göttingen: Vandenhoeck & Ruprecht, 1996); Jean-Louis Ska, "The Book of Chronicles through the Ages: A Cinderella or a Sleeping Beauty?," in *Chronicles and the Priestly Literature of the Hebrew Bible*, ed. Jaeyoung Jeon and Louis C. Jonker, BZAW 528 (Berlin: De Gruyter, 2021), 15–50. For the most recent critical assessments of the Chronicler's historical and archaeological reliability, see Yigal Levin, *The Chronicles of the Kings of Judah: 2 Chronicles 10–36; A New Translation and Commentary* (London: T&T Clark, 2017); and Levin, "Chronicles as a Source for the History of Pre-exilic Israel: Between 'Negativism' and 'Positivism,'" *BN* 193 (2022): 29–44.

sources, Chronicles has been devalued as a late, tendentious, sanitized, and overly schematized text.[3] This negative opinion of the text has pervaded not only academic circles but even religious communities. Rabbis and Christian theologians, past and present, have criticized Chronicles for its perceived inaccuracies, its late production, its derivative nature, and its penchant for pedantry in genealogical records and lists.[4]

Despite this negative opinion, Chronicles has received considerable scholarly attention in the past four or five decades due to the narrativist turn in the study of historiography.[5] Almost thirty years after Martin Noth's monograph,[6] Thomas Willi played a formative role in reviving academic interest in the book, arguing that Chronicles was not a slavish borrowing of the so-called Deuteronomistic History but rather an innovative commentary on, or interpretation (*Auslegung*) of, it.[7] Peter Welten and Rudolf Mosis quickly followed. Welten continues a tradition of criticizing the historicity of Chronicles yet also provides new insight on the literary-ideological function of its war reports and building accounts.[8] Mosis presents the Chronicler as a theologian rather than historian or apologist.[9] This German-language scholarship inspired the groundbreaking work of Hugh Williamson in *Israel in the Book of Chronicles* and Sara Japhet in *The Ideology of the Book of Chronicles and Its Place in Biblical Thought*, which breathed new life into the study of the book through literary-ideological approaches.[10] Both scholars, whose subsequent commentaries remain influential,[11] place less emphasis on the historicity of the narrated events and greater attention on what the construction of the text reveals about its author and the community in which and for whom it was written.

3. Graham, *Utilization of 1 and 2 Chronicles*; Peltonen, *History Debated*; Ska, "Chronicles through the Ages."

4. Ska, "Chronicles through the Ages"; Blaire A. French, *Chronicles through the Centuries* (West Sussex: Wiley, 2017).

5. John W. Kleinig, "Recent Research in Chronicles," *CurBS* 2 (1994): 43–76; Rodney K. Duke, "Recent Research in Chronicles," *CurBR* 8, no. 1 (2009): 10–50; Steven J. Schweitzer, "Synthetic and Literary Readings of Chronicles and Ezra-Nehemiah," in Kelle and Strawn, *Oxford Handbook of the Historical Books*, 379–92; Ska, "Chronicles through the Ages"; Thomas Willi, "Zwei Jahrzehnte Forschung an Chronik und Esra-Nehemia," *Theologische Rundschau* 67, no. 1 (2002): 61–104.

6. Martin Noth, *Überlieferungsgeschichtliche Studien* (Tübingen: Niemeyer, 1943).

7. Thomas Willi, *Die Chronik als Auslegung* (Göttingen: Vandenhoeck & Ruprecht, 1972).

8. Peter Welten, *Geschichte und Geschichtsdarstellung in den Chronikbüchern* (Tübingen: Neukirchener, 1973).

9. Rudolf Mosis, *Untersuchungen zur Theologie des Chronistischen Geschichtswerkes* (Freiburg: Herder, 1973).

10. H. G. M. Williamson, *Israel in the Books of Chronicles* (New York: Cambridge University Press, 1977); Sara Japhet, *The Ideology of the Book of Chronicles and Its Place in Biblical Thought*, trans. A. Barber, BEATAJ 9 (Frankfurt: Peter Lang, 1979).

11. H. G. M. Williamson, *1 and 2 Chronicles* (Grand Rapids: Eerdmans; London: Marshall, Morgan & Scott, 1982); Sara Japhet, *I & II Chronicles: A Commentary*, OTL (Louisville: Westminster John Knox, 1993).

Excellent surveys by John Kleinig and Rodney Duke highlight studies and trends that have emerged in the years since Williamson and Japhet, specifically covering 1982–93 and 1994–2007, respectively.[12] For this chapter, I focus on the past twenty-five years, especially on scholarly debates that have emerged or substantially evolved since 2007. The emphasis is primarily on English-language scholarship, though a concerted effort is made to feature a diversity of scholars. Among many interesting trajectories and studies, this article highlights recent research into the Achaemenid imperial context, the relationship of Chronicles to its sources and other real or fictive texts, the compositional technique and reception of the text (including the role of memory), and some recent trends in literary-ideological readings.

The Achaemenid Context

A scholarly consensus reflected in leading commentaries is that Chronicles was initially written in the late Achaemenid or early Hellenistic period in the province of Yehud.[13] While advocates for later Hellenistic or even Hasmonean period dates persist,[14] a Hasmonean date has been persuasively rejected, not least because any such dating severely compresses or even makes impossible the time line within which to account for the textual history of Chronicles itself and that of later, related texts influenced by it.[15] Reflecting the accepted dating, a growing body of scholarship demonstrates the considerable influence of Achaemenid royal ideology on Chronicles.

In the past, the relative scarcity of a royal Achaemenid literary tradition has been an obstacle to comparative studies in Chronicles scholarship. However, Margaret Cool Root transformed Achaemenid studies through a careful and innovative illumination of royal ideology informed by material culture.[16] This approach is now helping biblical scholars to situate Chronicles and its unique presentation of

12. Kleinig, "Recent Research"; Duke, "Recent Research."

13. In addition to Japhet's commentary, see esp. Gary N. Knoppers, *I Chronicles 1–9: A New Translation with Introduction and Commentary*, AB (New York: Doubleday, 2003); Knoppers, *I Chronicles 10–29: A New Translation with Introduction and Commentary*, AB (New York: Doubleday, 2004); Ralph W. Klein, *1 Chronicles*, Hermeneia (Minneapolis: Fortress, 2006); Klein, *2 Chronicles*, Hermeneia (Minneapolis: Fortress, 2012).

14. Israel Finkelstein, "The Expansion of Judah in II Chronicles: Territorial Legitimation for the Hasmoneans?," *ZAW* 127, no. 4 (2015): 669–95. With earlier redactional layers, see Andreas Hilpert, *Die Komposition der Chronikbücher: Redaktionsgeschichtliche Studien zu 2 Chr 10–36*, BZAW 526 (Berlin: De Gruyter, 2022).

15. Gary N. Knoppers, "Israel or Judah? The Shifting Body Politic and Collective Identity in Chronicles," in *Rethinking Israel: Studies in the History and Archaeology of Ancient Israel in Honor of Israel Finkelstein*, ed. Oded Lipschits, Yuval Gadot, and Matthew J. Adams (Winona Lake, IN: Eisenbrauns, 2017), 173–88.

16. Margaret Cool Root, *The King and Kingship in Achaemenid Art: Essays on the Creation of an Iconography of Empire*, Acta Iranica 3/19, Textes et mémoires 9 (Leiden: Brill, 1979).

the Jerusalem temple and cultus within its likely historical milieu. Helen Dixon, for example, shows that Cool Root's elucidation of a paradigmatic Achaemenid iconographical theme, "The King on High," is imitated or reflected in the Chronicler's distinctive representation of Solomon, on a dais, before the people, at the temple's dedication (2 Chron. 6:13).[17] Evidence supporting the likelihood of her thesis has increased in light of broader research that highlights the imitation of Achaemenid political ceremony in religious ceremonies throughout Chronicles;[18] the apparent influence of Old Persian texts and Achaemenid ideology on key concepts of kingship and social order;[19] the influence of Achaemenid mythemes and anachronisms in the account of David's reign;[20] the importance of the theme of rest and peace, evoking the Pax Persica, in the Chronicler's account of Solomon's reign;[21] and the Chronicler's reconfiguration of the relationship between Solomon and Huram to reflect Achaemenid satrapal governance.[22]

In *Defining All-Israel in Chronicles*, the first comprehensive reinvestigation of the "all Israel" motif since Williamson's *Israel in the Book of Chronicles*, Louis Jonker considers the imperial context and its influence on the text.[23] Jonker's approach to the topic is grounded in identity and the sociological functioning of texts. He argues that the Persian-period community of the text experienced a multileveled sociohistorical existence; that is, they negotiated their identity within imperial, regional, and local contexts. For Jonker, the Chronicler co-opts Achaemenid Persian ideology for subversive political and religious messaging within these contexts. The Achaemenid concepts and ideas, as the most valuable ideological currency of the day, are reoriented or even undermined to convey the supremacy of Judean political and cultic institutions.

17. Helen Dixon, "Writing Persepolis in Judah: Achaemenid Kingship in Chronicles," in *Images and Prophecy in the Ancient Eastern Mediterranean*, ed. Charles E. Carter and Martti Nissinen, FRLANT 233 (Göttingen: Vandenhoeck & Ruprecht, 2009), 163–94.

18. Matthew J. Lynch, *Monotheism and Institutions in the Book of Chronicles: Temple, Priesthood, and Kingship in Post-exilic Perspective*, FAT 2/64 (Tübingen: Mohr Siebeck, 2014), 61–67.

19. Christine Mitchell, "The Testament of Darius (DNa/DNb) and Constructions of Kings and Kingship in 1–2 Chronicles," in *Political Memory in and after the Persian Empire*, ed. J. Silverman and C. Waerzeggers, ANEM 13 (Atlanta: SBL Press, 2015), 363–80.

20. Christine Mitchell, "David and Darics: Reconsidering an Anachronism in 1 Chronicles 29," *VT* 69, no. 4–5 (2019): 748–54; Mark Leuchter, "The Census 'Crisis Episode' and the Chronicler's Mythic Agenda in 1 Chronicles 21," *VT* 73 (2022): 1–29.

21. Louis C. Jonker, "The Chronicler's Portrayal of Solomon as the King of Peace within the Context of the International Peace Discourses of the Persian Era," *OTE* 21, no. 3 (2008): 653–69.

22. Gary N. Knoppers, "More than Friends? The Economic Relationship between Huram and Solomon Reconsidered," in *The Economy of Ancient Judah in Its Historical Context*, ed. Marvin Lloyd Miller, Ehud Ben Zvi, and Gary N. Knoppers (Winona Lake, IN: Eisenbrauns, 2015), 49–72.

23. Louis C. Jonker, *Defining All-Israel in Chronicles: Multi-levelled Identity Negotiation in Late Persian-Period Yehud*, FAT 106 (Tübingen: Mohr Siebeck, 2016). See also "Chronicles in an (Un)changing World: The 'Persian Context' in Biblical Studies," *JSOT* 42, no. 3 (2018): 267–83.

Within a multicultural and diverse imperial system, however, it seems unlikely that the adoption of imperial rhetoric was a subversive act. Applying the ideology of the Teispid and Achaemenid monarchs to YHWH and the Judean state did not undercut Ahura Mazda or the Great King. Instead, it argued for the political and cultic legitimacy of YHWH and the Judean state. It presented the Judean deity and institutions as forerunners or regional manifestations, proxies, or models of the imperial deity and institutions, sharing in their power and authority.[24] Encouraging this alignment between imperial and regional deities and institutions, and related ideologies and customs, was likely an intentional strategy of Achaemenid royal engagement with local elites. This policy promoted cohesion, affiliation, and loyalty. It could also substantially improve the prestige and fortunes of clients within the imperial system and reinforce and project power locally.[25]

The Relationship of Chronicles to Its Sources

Perhaps the most important axiom in textual and literary criticism of Chronicles is the priority of Samuel-Kings and its use as a source.[26] Two notable detractors of this theory, A. Graeme Auld and Raymond Person, argue that Chronicles and Samuel-Kings depend on a shared source.[27] While this challenge has been vigorously opposed by scholars,[28] Julio Trebolle Barrera has gained traction by arguing for a modified version of the hypothesis, especially in the shared material through 1 Kings 10.[29] He highlights how the available Hebrew manuscripts and Greek translations of both texts provide significant evidence for textual fluidity, which he correlates with the *kaige* and non-*kaige* sections of LXX Samuel-Kings. He

24. Thomas M. Bolin, "The Temple of יהו at Elephantine and Persian Religious Policy," in *The Triumph of Elohim: From Yahwisms to Judaisms*, ed. Diane V. Edelman, CBET 13 (Kampen: Kok Pharos, 1995), 127–42.

25. Jason M. Silverman, *Persian Royal-Judaean Elite Engagements in the Early Teispid and Achaemenid Empire: The King's Acolytes*, LHBOTS 690 (New York: T&T Clark, 2019).

26. Knoppers, *I Chronicles 1–9*, 66–71; Reinhard G. Kratz, *The Composition of the Narrative Books of the Old Testament*, trans. John Bowden (London: T&T Clark, 2005), 9–48.

27. A. Graeme Auld, *Kings without Privilege: David and Moses in the Story of the Bible's Kings* (Edinburgh: T&T Clark, 1994); Auld, *I & II Samuel*, OTL (Louisville: Westminster John Knox, 2011); Auld, *Life in Kings: Reshaping the Royal Story in the Hebrew Bible*, AIL 30 (Atlanta: SBL Press, 2017); Raymond F. Person Jr., *Deuteronomic History and the Book of Chronicles: Scribal Works in an Oral World*, AIL 6 (Atlanta: SBL Press, 2010).

28. Gary N. Knoppers, review of A. Graeme Auld, *Kings without Privilege*, *ATJ* 27 (1995): 118–21; Zipora Talshir, "The Reign of Solomon in the Making: Pseudo-Connections between 3 Kingdoms and Chronicles," *VT* 50, no. 2 (2000): 233–49.

29. Julio Trebolle Barrera, "Samuel/Kings and Chronicles: Book Divisions and Textual Composition," in *Studies in the Hebrew Bible, Qumran, and the Septuagint Presented to Eugene Ulrich*, ed. Peter W. Flint, Emanuel Tov, and James C. VanderKam (Leiden: Brill, 2006), 96–108; Trebolle Barrera, "Kings (MT/LXX) and Chronicles: The Double and Triple Textual Tradition," in *Reflection and Refraction: Studies in Biblical Historiography in Honour of A. Graeme Auld*, ed. Robert Rezetko, Timothy H. Lim, and W. Brian Aucker (Leiden: Brill, 2007), 483–501.

contends that, while Auld has taken an oversimplified approach, there are good reasons to posit the existence of a shorter shared source for some sections of the narrative that developed in two distinct ways, leading to the MT traditions of Samuel-Kings and Chronicles commonly accepted today.

One implication of Trebolle Barrera's work is that the relationship between the texts is far more complicated than typically assumed. In my recent research on the account of Rehoboam in Chronicles, I confronted a stark example of this textual complexity.[30] The LXX Kingdoms text attests significant pluses at 1 Kgdms. 11:43a and 12:24[a-z], the latter of which represents a substantial and especially creative reworking of material attested in 1 Kings 11–12, 14. These pluses present alternative timelines and motivations for Jeroboam's return to Israel after his flight to Egypt. They seem to depend, in part, on the version of the story in MT Chronicles rather than the one in MT Kings, while also pointing to a simpler, pre-MT source. At a very early point, it appears that scribes not only read, copied, and translated Chronicles in light of Samuel-Kings, as has long been recognized, but also Samuel-Kings in light of Chronicles.[31]

Chronicles not only shares a textual tradition with Samuel-Kings but also incorporates material attested in other biblical texts and demonstrates a masterful control over this material.[32] The Chronicler references stories and integrates genealogies attested in Genesis, Joshua, and Ruth (especially in his genealogical preamble),[33] resourcefully applies and even synthesizes Torah legislation,[34] alludes

30. Kenneth A. Ristau, "One Nation under David: An Ideological Innovation in Chronicles," in *The Formation of Biblical Texts: Chronicling the Legacy of Gary Knoppers*, ed. Deirdre N. Fulton et al. (Tübingen: Mohr Siebeck, 2024).

31. Uwe Becker and Hannes Bezzel, eds., *Rereading the Relecture? The Question of (Post)-chronistic Influence in the Latest Redactions of the Books of Samuel*, FAT 2/66 (Tübingen: Mohr Siebeck, 2014).

32. Knoppers, *I Chronicles 1–9*, 66–71, esp. 68.

33. In addition to James T. Sparks, *The Chronicler's Genealogies: Towards an Understanding of 1 Chronicles 1–9*, AcBib 28 (Atlanta: Society of Biblical Literature, 2008), recent articles on the Chronicler's use of genealogical material include Louis C. Jonker, "Reading the Pentateuch's Genealogies after the Exile: The Chronicler's Usage of Genesis 1–11 in Negotiating an All-Israelite Identity," *OTE* 25, no. 2 (2012): 316–33; David A. Glatt-Gilad, "Genealogy Lists as a Window to Historiographic Periodization in the Book of Chronicles," *Maarav* 21, nos. 1–2 (2014): 71–79; Neriah Klein, "Between Genealogy and Historiography: Er, Achar and Saul in the Book of Chronicles," *VT* 66, no. 2 (2016): 217–44; David Janzen, "A Monument and a Name: The Primary Purpose of Chronicles' Genealogies," *JSOT* 43, no. 1 (2018): 45–66; Joachim Schaper, "Genealogies as Tools: The Case of P and Chronicles," in Jeon and Jonker, *Chronicles and the Priestly Literature*, 307–21.

34. Louis C. Jonker, "Within Hearing Distance? Recent Developments in Pentateuch and Chronicles Research," *OTE* 27, no. 1 (2014): 123–46; Louis C. Jonker, "Numbers and Chronicles: False Friends or Close Relatives?," *HeBAI* 8, no. 3 (2019): 332–77; Lars Maskow, *Tora in der Chronik: Studien zur Rezeption des Pentateuchs in den Chronikbüchern*, FRLANT 274 (Göttingen: Vandenhoeck & Ruprecht, 2019); Jeon and Jonker, *Chronicles and the Priestly Literature*; Julia Rhyder, "The Reception of Ritual Laws in the Early Second Temple Period Evidence from Ezra-Nehemiah and Chronicles," in *Text and Ritual in the Pentateuch: A Systematic and*

to and quotes prophetic texts,[35] and creatively uses psalms or hymnic refrains.[36] Scholars continue to examine the significance of this reuse on the development of those texts, even in relation to the canonization of the HB and its associated problems,[37] and on the development of the ideas that those texts advance, such as cult centralization.[38] Furthermore, scholars remain interested in the Chronicler's possible use of extrabiblical sources and the function of the Chronicler's many citations and appeals to authority.[39]

Comparative Approach, ed. Christophe Nihan and Julia Rhyder (University Park, PA: Eisenbrauns, 2021), 255–79.

35. Pancratius C. Beentjes, "Isaiah in the Book of Chronicles," in *Isaiah in Context: Studies in Honour of Arie van der Kooij on the Occasion of His Sixty-Fifth Birthday*, ed. Michaël van der Meer et al., VTSup 138 (Leiden: Brill, 2010), 15–24; Louis C. Jonker, "The Chronicler and the Prophets: Who Were His Authoritative Sources?," in *What Was Authoritative for Chronicles?*, ed. Ehud Ben Zvi and Diana V. Edelman (Winona Lake, IN: Eisenbrauns, 2011), 145–64; Amber K. Warhurst, "The Chronicler's Use of the Prophets," in Ben Zvi and Edelman, *What Was Authoritative for Chronicles?*, 165–81; Mark Leuchter, "Remembering Jeremiah in the Persian Period," in *Remembering Biblical Figures in the Late Persian and Early Hellenistic Periods: Social Memory and Imagination*, ed. Ehud Ben Zvi and Diana V. Edelman (Oxford: Oxford University Press, 2013), 384–414.

36. Adele Berlin, "Psalms in the Book of Chronicles," in *Shai le-Sara Japhet: Studies in the Bible, Its Exegesis and Its Languages*, ed. Moshe Bar-Asher et al. (Jerusalem: Bialik Institute, 2007), 21*–36*; Pancratius C. Beentjes, "'Give Thanks to YHWH. Truly He Is Good': Psalms and Prayers in the Book of Chronicles," in *Tradition and Transformation in the Book of Chronicles*, SSN 52 (Leiden: Brill, 2008), 141–75. More specific issues are addressed in Susan Gillingham, "Psalms 105 and 106 and the Participation in History through Liturgy," *HeBAI* 4, no. 4 (2015): 450–75; Melody D. Knowles, "The Treatment of Ps 132 in 11QPsa (11Q5) and Chronicles: Politics and Religious Practices in the Second Temple Period," in Fulton et al., *Formation of Biblical Texts*.

37. Hilpert, *Komposition der Chronikbücher*; Hendrik J. Koorevaar, "Chronicles as the Intended Conclusion to the Old Testament Canon," in *The Shape of the Writings*, ed. Julius Steinberg and Timothy J. Strone, Siphrut 16 (Winona Lake, IN: Eisenbrauns, 2015), 207–35; cf. Edmon L. Gallagher, "The End of the Bible? The Position of Chronicles in the Canon," *TynBul* 65, no. 2 (2014): 181–99; Louis C. Jonker, "From Pentateuch to Chronicles: What Does the End (Chronicles) of the Hebrew Bible Canon Imply for the Understanding of Its Beginning (Pentateuch)?," *BZ* 59, no. 1 (2015): 39–53; Greg Goswell, "Putting the Book of Chronicles in Its Place," *JETS* 60, no. 2 (2017): 283–99.

38. Benjamin D. Giffone, "According to Which 'Law of Moses'? Cult Centralization in Samuel, Kings, and Chronicles," *VT* 67, no. 3 (2017): 432–47; Christophe Nihan, "Cult Centralization and the Torah Traditions in Chronicles," in *The Fall of Jerusalem and the Rise of the Torah*, ed. Peter Dubovský, Dominik Markl, and Jean-Pierre Sonnet, FAT 107 (Tübingen: Mohr Siebeck, 2016), 253–88.

39. Knoppers, *I Chronicles 1–9*, 118–28; Katherine M. Stott, *Why Did They Write This Way? Reflections on References to Written Documents in the Hebrew Bible and Ancient Literature*, LHBOTS 492 (New York: T&T Clark, 2008); Ehud Ben Zvi, "One Size Does Not Fit All: Observations on the Different Ways That Chronicles Dealt with the Authoritative Literature of Its Time," in Ben Zvi and Edelman, *What Was Authoritative for Chronicles?*, 13–36; Steven J. Schweitzer, "Judging a Book by Its Citations: Sources and Authority in Chronicles," in Ben Zvi and Edelman, *What Was Authoritative for Chronicles?*, 37–65; Michael Avioz, "The 'Spring of the Year' (2 Chronicles 36:10) and the Chronicler's Sources," *JHebS* 12 (2012): 1–9.

Composition, Memory, and Reception

Reflecting on the Chronicler's use and adaptation of texts, George Brooke suggests that Chronicles and Deuteronomy are biblical exemplars of "rewritten Bible," as attested at Qumran.[40] Although Chronicles scholars such as Ehud Ben Zvi and Gary Knoppers express reservations about such a genre, the similarities show how Chronicles and the Judean library developed through the constant interplay of texts and traditions. Some scribes copied older materials with little change, while others brought together divergent materials with novel interpolations, commentary, and rewriting.[41] Georg Steins helpfully likens Chronicles to recycled materials (*Rezyklat*), giving the discussion more nuance with respect to the relationship between the old and the new texts by emphasizing that the new text is not simply a copy of an older text but a completely new product that repurposes the old text.[42] However one conceptualizes it, Chronicles is widely recognized as an early exemplar of this synoptic mode of textual production, intralingual translation, and rewriting that becomes commonplace in Hellenistic and early Roman Jewish and Christian literature, from Jubilees to the Gospels of Matthew, Mark, and Luke.[43] This mode of production created libraries of interrelated texts, and any new text within the system impacted how the others were understood without necessarily supplanting the older texts.[44]

40. George Brooke, "Rewritten Bible," *Encyclopedia of the Dead Sea Scrolls*, ed. Lawrence H. Schiffman and James VanderKam (Oxford: Oxford University Press, 2000), 2:777–81. See also Emanuel Tov, "3 Kingdoms Compared with Similar Rewritten Compositions," in *Flores Florentino: Dead Sea Scrolls and Other Early Jewish Studies in Honour of Florentino García Martínez*, ed. Anthony Hilhorst, Émile Puech, and Eibert Tigchelaar, JSJSup 122 (Leiden: Brill, 2007), 345–66.

41. Ehud Ben Zvi, "In Conversation and Appreciation of the Recent Commentaries by S. L. McKenzie and G. N. Knoppers," in "New Studies in Chronicles: A Discussion of Two Recently-Published Commentaries," ed. M. D. Knowles, special issue, *JHebS* 5 (2005): 21–45; Gary N. Knoppers, "Of Rewritten Bibles, Archaeology, Peace, Kings, and Chronicles," in "New Studies in Chronicles: A Discussion of Two Recently-Published Commentaries," ed. M. D. Knowles, special issue, *JHebS* 5 (2005): 69–94. On terminological pitfalls, the many forms of rewriting, and discussion of their applicability to Chronicles, see Molly M. Zahn, *Genres of Rewriting in Second Temple Judaism: Scribal Composition and Transmission* (Cambridge: Cambridge University Press, 2020).

42. Georg Steins, "Noch einmal von vorn . . . Die Bücher der Chronik als Rezyklat," in *Figuren der Offenbarung: Biblisch–Religionsphilosophisch–Politisch*, ed. Joachim Negel and Margareta Gruber, Jerusalemer Theologisches Forum 24 (Münster: Aschendorff, 2012), 61–81. In the industrial process, the original product is broken down and ceases to exist, whereas in the literary process, the original product may continue to exist.

43. This mode of production is common to many texts of the HB. In the case of Chronicles and later literature, we have the benefit of access to its source material, or at least parallel material developed in alternate ways. See Zahn, *Genres of Rewriting*; Gary N. Knoppers, "The Synoptic Problem: An Old Testament Perspective," *BBR* 19, no. 1 (2009): 11–34; John Screnock, "Is Rewriting Translation? Chronicles and Jubilees in Light of Intralingual Translation," *VT* 68, no. 3 (2018): 475–504.

44. Ehud Ben Zvi, "Chronicles and Samuel-Kings: Two Interacting Aspects of One Memory System in the Late Persian/Early Hellenistic Period," in *Rereading the Relecture? The Question*

Especially interesting is how Chronicles selectively memorializes and impacts the Yahwistic mnemonic cultural system—that is, how the Chronicler reflects and refracts the texts and knowledge within the community, how its reuse changed the way texts were reread and rewritten, and how the community's self-understanding and identity evolved as a result. Ben Zvi attempts to answer such questions, applying insights from memory studies to show how texts create a malleable discursive space in which dialogical interactions between them generate new readings and new ideologies.[45] Steven Schweitzer's work on Chronicles as utopian literature emphasizes that these discussions do not necessarily attempt to reflect historical realities, whether the past they purport to describe or the period in which they were written down (i.e., projecting into the past, to justify the present). Rather, these discussions may reflect an alternate, desired history and promote future possibilities.[46] Both Ben Zvi and Schweitzer imagine the Chronicler engaged in a highly creative, complex, and intellectual process, primarily (if not exclusively) among the Judean literati who were involved in the exchange, reading, and rewriting of Chronicles and related texts.

In a study of Ezra-Nehemiah, Laura Carlson Hasler has argued for the importance of archiving for Second Temple texts. She observes that Ezra-Nehemiah explicitly refers to Achaemenid archival space (בֵּית גִּנְזַיָּא, *bêt ginzayyāʾ*; Ezra 5:17; cf. 6:1) and argues that Ezra-Nehemiah presents itself as a repository of important texts (e.g., edicts, letters, lists).[47] Interestingly, Chronicles conceptualizes archival space in the temple using similar language (גַּנְזַכָּיו, *ganzakkāyw*; 1 Chron. 28:11) and repeatedly cites the existence of archival texts (סֵפֶר, *sēper*; 1 Chron. 9:1; 2 Chron. 16:11; 20:34; 24:27; 27:7; 28:26; 32:32; 35:27; 36:8). Thinking of Chronicles as an archive potentially highlights preservation and commemoration of antecedent texts as an important motive for its development.[48] Indeed, Aubrey Buster examines how historical summaries such as those found or "archived" in Chronicles (esp. 1 Chron. 16:8–36) are an important, continually evolving literary form that signals oral performance in the Second

of (Post)chronistic Influence in the Latest Redactions of the Books of Samuel, ed. Uwe Becker and Hannes Bezzel, FAT 2/66 (Tübingen: Mohr Siebeck, 2014), 41–56.

45. Ehud Ben Zvi, *Social Memory among the Literati of Yehud*, BZAW 509 (Berlin: De Gruyter, 2019).

46. Steven J. Schweitzer, *Reading Utopia in Chronicles*, LHBOTS 442 (London: T&T Clark, 2007); Joseph Blenkinsopp, "Ideology and Utopia in 1–2 Chronicles," in Ben Zvi and Edelman, *What Was Authoritative for Chronicles?*, 89–103; Steven J. Schweitzer and Frauke Uhlenbruch, eds., *Worlds That Could Not Be: Utopia in Chronicles, Ezra and Nehemiah*, LHBOTS 620 (London: Bloomsbury T&T Clark, 2016).

47. Laura Carlson Hasler, *Archival Historiography in Jewish Antiquity* (New York: Oxford University Press, 2020).

48. For an example with cross-cultural significance, see Wai Ching Angela Wong, "The Politics of Remembrance: Genealogies of 1 Chronicles 1–9 and Haunting Memories in China," in *The Bible and Feminism: Remapping the Field*, ed. Yvonne Sherwood with Anna Fisk (Oxford: Oxford University Press, 2017), 371–89.

Temple period.[49] In contrast to the elite models of Ben Zvi and Schweitzer, Buster argues that the historical summaries, and their emplotment, point to communal, participatory engagement with the functional memory that texts such as Chronicles preserve and promulgate.[50] Carlson Hasler and Buster, therefore, offer a more practical view of the development of texts motivated by cultural preservation, which broadens the audience of Chronicles beyond the elites.[51] In this case, the intellectual complexities created by the reuse of texts and the recombination of cultural memory are perhaps more incidental than often assumed.

Naturally, the complex interrelationship of texts raises fascinating questions about their authority and reception. A study undertaken by Mika Pajunen and a commentary by Blaire French examine the impact of Chronicles within the Second Temple period and later mnemonic systems.[52] Both scholars provide evidence that Chronicles significantly shaped and altered cultural memory. For example, Samuel-Kings identifies David as the eighth son of Jesse, whereas Chronicles lists him as the seventh (1 Sam. 16:10–11; 17:12–14; 1 Chron. 2:13–15). Notably though, it is the tradition of Chronicles that is represented in the work of Josephus (*Ant.* 6.161) and in the Dura-Europos synagogue wall paintings (3rd cent. CE).

Literary Interpretation and Identity Studies

Amid these questions of the date, development, and reception of the text, the literary, thematic, and ideological interpretation of Chronicles continues. As in the past, the discrete regnal accounts are often the focal point of such study.[53]

49. Aubrey E. Buster, *Remembering the Story of Israel: Historical Summaries and Memory Formation in Second Temple Judaism* (Cambridge: Cambridge University Press, 2022).

50. Buster, *Remembering*, 121–53.

51. Similarly, see Yigal Levin, "Who Was the Chronicler's Audience? A Hint from His Genealogies," *JBL* 122, no. 2 (2003): 229–45.

52. Mika S. Pajunen, "The Saga of Judah's Kings Continues: The Reception of Chronicles in the Late Second Temple Period," *JBL* 136, no. 3 (2017): 565–84; French, *Chronicles through the Centuries.*

53. For recent examples, see Itzhak Amar, "Chaotic Writing as a Literary Element in the Story of Ahaz in 2 Chronicles 28," *VT* 66, no. 3 (2016): 349–64; Amar, "The Characterization of Rehoboam and Jeroboam as a Reflection of the Chronicler's View of the Schism," *JHebS* 17 (2017): 1–30; Amar, "Form and Content in the Story of Asa in 2 Chr 13:23b–16:14: A Diachronic-Synchronic Reading," *VT* 69, no. 3 (2019): 337–60; Nissim Amzallag, "The Subversive Dimension of the Story of Jehoshaphat's War against the Nations (2 Chron 20:1–30)," *BibInt* 24, no. 2 (2016): 178–202; Gary N. Knoppers, "Saint or Sinner? Manasseh in Chronicles," in *Rewriting Biblical History: Essays on Chronicles and Ben Sira in Honor of Pancratius C. Beentjes*, ed. Jeremy Corley and Harm van Grol (Berlin: De Gruyter, 2011), 211–29; Kenneth A. Ristau, "Reading and Rereading Josiah: The Chronicler's Representation of Josiah for the Postexilic Community," in *Community Identity in Judean Historiography: Biblical and Comparative Perspectives*, ed. Gary N. Knoppers and Kenneth A. Ristau (Winona Lake, IN: Eisenbrauns, 2009), 219–47; Ristau, "One Nation under David"; Gerrie Snyman, "Read as/with the

This research, by providing new readings and understandings, illustrates the Chronicler's creative storytelling abilities and identifies or reinforces thematic and ideological threads woven throughout the text. Three newer areas of dialogue and investigation are feminist interpretation, disability studies, and African(a) scholarship.

Compared to other biblical texts of comparable length, feminist scholarship on Chronicles is scarce, almost certainly because of the relative absence of women in the narrative.[54] Antje Labahn and Ben Zvi attempt to highlight some of the positive features of the presentation of women in the genealogies, despite the book's overarching and dominant patriarchal schema.[55] Their work has informed subsequent analysis by Ingeborg Löwisch, also on the genealogies, and Funlola Olojede, who provides a comprehensive overview of the Chronicler's relatively scant references to women.[56] Julie Kelso, Roland Boer, and Christine Mitchell are critical of such hermeneutics of recovery and instead critique and contemplate the implications of the monosexual reproductive vision of the genealogies and the text's silence on and erasing of women's history.[57]

Disability studies is a perspective that is relatively new to biblical studies and has only recently made a mark on the study of Chronicles. Saul Olyan's groundbreaking work contains little more than passing reference to Chronicles.[58] Rebecca Raphael provides the first substantive engagement with Chronicles from this perspective. She observes that Chronicles provides examples of both physical

---

Perpetrator: Manasseh's Vulnerability in 2 Kings 21:1–18 and 2 Chronicles 33:1–20," *Scriptura* 116, no. 2 (2017): 188–207; Yisca Zimran, "'The Covenant Made with David': The King and the Kingdom in 2 Chronicles 21," *VT* 64, no. 2 (2014): 305–25; Brendan G. Youngberg, "Identity Coherence in the Chronicler's Narrative: King Josiah as a Second David and a Second Saul," *JHebS* 17 (2017): 1–16.

54. Julie Kelso, "Reading Silence: The Books of Chronicles and Ezra-Nehemiah, and the Relative Absence of a Feminist Interpretive History," in *Feminist Interpretation of the Hebrew Bible in Retrospect*, vol. 1, *Biblical Books*, ed. Susanne Scholz (Sheffield: Sheffield Phoenix, 2013), 268–89.

55. Antje Labahn and Ehud Ben Zvi, "Observations on Women in the Genealogies of 1 Chronicles 1–9," *Bib* 84, no. 4 (2003): 457–78.

56. Ingeborg Löwisch, "Cracks in the Male Mirror: References to Women as Challenges to Patrilinear Authority in the Genealogies of Judah," in Ben Zvi and Edelman, *What Was Authoritative for Chronicles?*, 105–32; Funlola Olojede, "Chronicler's Women: A Holistic Appraisal," *AcT* 33, no. 1 (2013): 158–74.

57. Julie Kelso, *O Mother, Where Art Thou? An Irigarayan Reading of the Book of Chronicles* (London: Equinox, 2007); Kelso, "The Patrilineal Narrative Machinery of Chronicles," in *The Oxford Handbook of Biblical Narrative*, ed. Danna Nolan Fewell (New York: Oxford University Press, 2016), 286–95; Roland Boer, "Of Fine Wine, Incense and Spices: The Unstable Masculine Hegemony of the Books of Chronicles," *Journal of Men, Masculinities and Spirituality* 4, no. 1 (2010): 19–31; Christine Mitchell, "1–2 Chronicles," in *Women's Bible Commentary*, ed. Carol A. Newsom, Sharon H. Ringe, and Jacqueline E. Lapsley, 3rd ed. (Louisville: Westminster John Knox, 2012), 184–91.

58. Saul M. Olyan, *Disability in the Hebrew Bible: Interpreting Mental and Physical Differences* (Cambridge: Cambridge University Press, 2008), 187.

and social disabilities and that the stories associated with each serve to reinforce divine and, in the Uzziah story, priestly prerogatives and authority.[59] Disabilities, therefore, reflect the text's reward-and-punishment paradigm. By contrast, Kerry Wynn argues for greater etiological diversity in the Chronicler's account of disabilities, providing analysis and readings not only of references to disabilities in Chronicles but also of parallel accounts in which Chronicles omits references to disability in Samuel-Kings.[60] Isabel Cranz takes a reception-history approach to the story of Uzziah's disease, highlighting the Chronicler's significant place in the story's evolution.[61]

The influence of Black African(a) scholarship on Chronicles has grown in recent years. This scholarship has been made more accessible in North America through recent African(a) commentaries on the Bible, which naturally include sections on Chronicles.[62] As African(a) scholarship continues a process of decolonialization, a new generation of voices is integrating critical scholarship with open discussion about African(a) politics and societies, creating a vibrant and active public intellectualism not nearly so prevalent in North America or Europe.[63] This scholarship is characterized by a sophisticated blending of methods and approaches and ancient and contemporary insights, often engaging pressing issues within African(a) societies. Ezra Chitando, for example, examines the use of 2 Chron. 7:14 in Zimbabwean politics, while Ntozakhe Simon Cezula argues for Chronicles as a countertext to the promotion of Ezra-Nehemiah in an African theology of reconstruction.[64]

59. Rebecca Raphael, "Disability, Identity, and Otherness in Persian-Period Israelite Thought," in *Imagining the Other and Constructing Israelite Identity in the Early Second Temple Period*, ed. Ehud Ben Zvi and Diana V. Edelman, LHSOTS 456 (London: Bloomsbury T&T Clark, 2014), 277–96.

60. Kerry H. Wynn, "First and Second Chronicles–Esther," in *The Bible and Disability: A Commentary*, ed. Sarah J. Melcher, Mikeal C. Parsons, and Amos Yong (Waco: Baylor University Press, 2017), 121–58.

61. Isabel Cranz, "The Motif of Uzziah's צרעת in the Deuteronomistic History, Chronicles, and Beyond," *JSOT* 44, no. 2 (2019): 233–49.

62. Nupanga Weanzana, "1 and 2 Chronicles," in *Africa Bible Commentary*, ed. Tokunboh Adeyemo, 2nd ed. (Nairobi: WordAlive, 2010), 467–530; Renita J. Weems, "1–2 Chronicles," in *The Africana Bible: Reading Israel's Scriptures from Africa and the African Diaspora*, ed. Hugh R. Page Jr. and Randall C. Bailey (Minneapolis: Fortress, 2010), 286–90.

63. Hulisani Ramantswana, "Past the Glorious Age: Old Testament Scholarship in South Africa—Are We Moving Anywhere Close to Blackening Old Testament Scholarship?," *Scriptura* 119, no. 3 (2020): 1–19; Gerald O. West, "African Biblical Scholarship as Post-Colonial, Tri-Polar, and a Site-of-Struggle," in *Present and Future of Biblical Studies: Celebrating Twenty-Five Years of Brill's Biblical Interpretation*, ed. Tat-siong (Benny) Liew, BibInt 161 (Leiden: Brill, 2018), 240–73.

64. Ezra Chitando, "'If My People . . .': A Critical Analysis of the Deployment of 2 Chronicles 7:14 during the Zimbabwean Crisis," in *The Bible and Politics in Africa*, ed. Masiiwa Ragies Gunda and Joachim Kügler, Bible in Africa Studies 7 (Bamberg: University of Bamberg Press, 2012), 274–89; Ntozakhe Simon Cezula, "The Chronicler as a Biblical Paradigm for a Theology of Reconstruction in Africa: An Exploration of 2 Chronicles 6:32," *OTE* 29, no. 2 (2016): 277–96.

Conclusion

Despite its frequent neglect in religious communities, Chronicles is a canonical text for Jews and Christians today. Consequently, bringing to light the Chronicler's method and the text's significance in antiquity provides a hermeneutical framework to address pressures of harmonization and positivism. If the Chronicler could contest the interpretation of earlier authoritative texts, even influence and reshape those texts, how should the authority of those texts and the text of Chronicles be understood today? What might religious communities learn from the Chronicler's method of reading and interpreting now-canonical texts?

In *Revelation and Authority*, Benjamin Sommer argues that biblical texts present divine revelation that imposes a duty on readers but also problematize revelation as mediated or "collaborative and participatory."[65] This insight takes seriously what the Bible reveals and claims about its own authority, which, perhaps surprisingly to some, is often tentative and uncertain. Chronicles reflects such a participatory approach in antiquity, implicitly by its method and explicitly by its enigmatic ending and invitation to return to Jerusalem. Chronicles encourages readers to reread texts in light of its own rereading and to participate in the dialogue between texts. The abrupt invitation to go up to Jerusalem that ends the book is an invitation to continue the dialogue.

It is unlikely the author sought to erase other texts or their differences through the process of rewriting, and certainly neither early Jewish nor Christian communities did so during the process of preservation and canonization. Ignoring this evidence reinforces outdated models of textual production and sustains misconceptions about the authority of texts from antiquity to today. Research on Chronicles, therefore, not only helps academic audiences better understand the processes of rereading, rewriting, and translation in Persian-period and early Hellenistic Judaisms/Yahwisms, but it can also help religious audiences dialogue about differences and think about the authority of texts in new ways that respect canons of text, thought, and tradition. Current research is re-presenting Chronicles as a vital and important text, a text that changed "the Bible" and that invites a constant rethinking and reapplication of "the Bible" in new contexts.

65. Benjamin D. Sommer, *Revelation and Authority: Sinai in Jewish Scripture and Tradition* (New Haven: Yale University Press, 2015).

16

Ezra-Nehemiah and Esther

Aubrey E. Buster

At the turn of the twentieth century, Hugh Williamson observed that the postexilic period had emerged from a position of relative neglect to become "one of the liveliest fields in the whole discipline of Old Testament study."[1] This shift took place in part due to an increased interest in the postexilic period as a crucial time in the development of the HB and an increased analysis of its archaeological remains, which had previously been overshadowed by excavation of earlier Iron Age and later Hellenistic layers. In the past decade, these trends have continued. Ongoing excavation and publication of Persian-period sites in Judah have provided additional data for the historical reconstruction of the narrative setting of Ezra-Nehemiah.

Ezra-Nehemiah and Esther are very different stories: the former presents itself as a combination of historical narrative, first-person memoir, lists, and letters; the latter is an almost satirical tale of the travails of life in a foreign court. Both, however, testify to the struggle of the colonized to live under imperial rule. Methods and models from the social sciences—including postcolonial studies, social memory, identity, ethnicity, and intersectionality—offer particularly useful insights into these texts. The past decade has therefore witnessed the exciting dynamism of a moment in which the current of scholarly interest within the guild intersects with texts almost tailor-made for these particular analytical tools.

1. H. G. M. Williamson, "Exile and After: Historical Study," in *The Face of Old Testament Studies: A Survey of Contemporary Approaches*, ed. David W. Baker and Bill T. Arnold (Grand Rapids: Baker, 1999), 236.

These currents in the study of Ezra-Nehemiah and Esther will structure this essay. In the following discussion, I (1) provide a brief overview of archaeological research related to the social and economic status of Jerusalem within Persian-period Judah; (2) briefly describe the contributions of political studies, postcolonial theory, social memory, diaspora studies, and intersectionality to the study of these texts; and (3) offer brief case studies of the ways in which these methods have illumined major interpretive issues within these books—specifically, the authenticity of the documents embedded in Ezra, bilingualism in Ezra, the question of Esther's status as an icon of resistance or an imperial collaborator, and the prohibition of intermarriage in Ezra-Nehemiah.

Archaeology and History

While the archaeological finds from Persian-period Judah remain meager in comparison to Iron Age and Hellenistic sites, several sources of data contribute significantly to our understanding of the period. The significance of the analyses of Ramat Raḥel published in the last decade is hard to overstate.[2] Ramat Raḥel is the contemporary name for a site four kilometers south of Jerusalem, where the remains of a palatial administrative complex have been discovered. Based on the extravagance of the architecture, which includes the remains of a Persian royal garden (*pairidaeza*/*paradeisos*) containing water features and ornamental plants imported from Persia, Ramat Raḥel likely functioned as the administrative seat of the province for most of the Persian period.[3] Hundreds of jar handles discovered there, impressed with the Yehud stamp, further confirm its status as an economic center for production and tax collection.[4]

The profile of Ramat Raḥel has considerable implications for understanding the status of Jerusalem during the Persian period. Ramat Raḥel has been tentatively identified as בֵּית־הַכָּרֶם (*bêt-hakkārem*), referenced in passing in Jer. 6:1 and Neh. 3:14.[5] What is most notable, however, is the lack of references in the biblical text to such a significant location. Instead, the narrative of the return focuses on Jerusalem, which remained a sparsely populated and impoverished site throughout most of the Persian period. Current population estimates for Jerusalem during the Persian period range from a few hundred to fifteen hundred individuals.[6]

2. See summary in Oded Lipschits et al., *What Are the Stones Whispering? Ramat Raḥel: 3000 Years of Forgotten History* (Winona Lake, IN: Eisenbrauns, 2017).

3. Pierre Briant, *From Cyrus to Alexander: A History of the Persian Empire*, trans. Peter T. Daniels (Winona Lake, IN: Eisenbrauns, 2002), 78–86; Oded Lipschits, Yuval Gadot, and Dafna Langgut, "The Riddle of Ramat Raḥel: The Archaeology of a Royal Persian Period Edifice," *Transeuphratène* 41 (2012): 57–79.

4. Oded Lipschits and David S. Vanderhooft, "Yehud Stamp Impressions from Ramat-Raḥel: An Updated Tabulation," *BASOR* 384 (2020): 191–209.

5. Lipschits et al., *What Are the Stones Whispering?*, 15–18.

6. Israel Finkelstein ("Jerusalem in the Persian [and Early Hellenistic] Period and the Wall of Nehemiah," *JSOT* 32, no. 4 [2008]: 501–20) estimates a population of 400 to 500. Both

The distribution of Yehud jar stamp impressions, referenced above, confirms that Jerusalem played a secondary role to Ramat Raḥel in the administration of the province. In total, 647 Yehud stamp impressions have been discovered across twenty-four archaeological sites: of these, 372 come from Ramat Raḥel and 136 from Jerusalem. As we move from the sixth/fifth century to the second century, we see a marked increase in the percentage of stamp impressions found in Jerusalem, and by the second century, 60 percent of Yehud stamp impressions are found in Jerusalem, signaling its ascendency to the lead role in commodity production.[7]

Despite its apparently secondary administrative role until the Hellenistic period, Jerusalem functioned as a significant cultural and religious center during the Persian period. Besides the narratives in Ezra and Nehemiah, which present the rebuilding of the temple and city walls, documents from a Judean colony in Elephantine record correspondence between that diaspora Judean community and the high priest and Jerusalem community, in which Jerusalem appeals to the Elephantine community for aid in rebuilding their destroyed temple (*TAD* A 4.7/8). This demonstrates that for Jews living in diaspora, Jerusalem still functioned as a religious and cultural center, even as its economic and political role remained secondary.

Ezra-Nehemiah as Political Theology

The material remains from the Persian period provide a tantalizing yet frustratingly incomplete portrait of life in Judah under the Persian Empire. What they do reveal, however, is the remarkable challenge faced by the returnees to the land as they sought to recover from dispersion, reconstruct their communal identity, and rebuild what lay in ruins. Ezra-Nehemiah commemorates the challenges of communal reconstruction in these circumstances and has thus been analyzed in terms of political theology. A particularly significant work in this vein, and one that demonstrates the continued shift in Ezra-Nehemiah studies toward analyses informed by categories from the social sciences, is Tamara Cohn Eskenazi's recent commentary on Ezra.[8]

Eskenazi's 1988 volume *In an Age of Prose*, a narrative analysis of Ezra-Nehemiah, remains one of the most influential literary readings of Ezra-Nehemiah in the field.[9] Her commentary builds on the structure and themes presented in

C. E. Carter (*The Emergence of Yehud in the Persian Period: A Social and Demographic Study*, JSOTSup 294 [Sheffield: Sheffield Academic, 1999]) and Oded Lipschits ("Persian Period Finds from Jerusalem: Facts and Interpretations," *JHebS* 9 [2009]: 1–30, esp. 20) estimate 1,500.

7. Lipschits and Vanderhooft, "Yehud Stamp Impressions."

8. Tamara Cohn Eskenazi, *Ezra*, AB (New Haven: Yale University Press, 2023); see also Eskenazi, "The Political Theology of Ezra-Nehemiah," in *Political Theologies in the Hebrew Bible*, ed. Mark Brett and Rachelle Gilmour, JAJSup 35 (Paderborn: Brill Schöningh, 2023), 242–56.

9. Tamara Cohn Eskenazi, *In an Age of Prose: A Literary Approach to Ezra-Nehemiah*, SBLMS 36 (Atlanta: Scholars Press, 1988).

her earlier volume but adds significant attention to issues of social and political concern. According to Eskenazi, the book of Ezra-Nehemiah constructs a political theology for a "small, fragile community" that must both "accommodate and resist imperial domination."[10] In light of continued foreign domination, Ezra-Nehemiah constructs a distinctive political vision in which power is not concentrated in the figure of the king or another centralized political leader. Instead, the people are the primary agents of communal regulation.[11] This communal governance is founded on the principles of Torah, a foundation called for and approved by the community.

While Eskenazi presents Ezra-Nehemiah as a recovery of political agency *despite* and *within* imperial rule, several studies observe how the political vision of Ezra-Nehemiah imitates Achaemenid royal ideology. Lisbeth Fried presents the innovative thesis that Ezra and Nehemiah are Persian officials (though of Judean descent) working on behalf of the Persian king.[12] Though few others go so far, several argue for a model of political ideology in Ezra-Nehemiah that imitates Achaemenid royal ideology.[13] David Janzen observes that the community presents itself as the Achaemenids presented colonized peoples but also functions like colonizers, a group sent "from the center of the empire to its margins to do the divine will as mediated by Cyrus."[14] According to Janzen, Ezra 1–6 presents the narrative ideal, a royally sponsored troop of Judeans returning to the land, while Ezra 7–Neh. 13 describes the actions of a group sent by the king in order to correct a community that has gone astray. The book therefore presents Persian rule as both necessary and beneficial for the survival of the community. Mark Brett also argues that the returnees reflect a "colonial character," but that this is not assumed to support Persian interests. He argues instead that it functions as a "survival strategy" for a community that has experienced significant trauma.[15]

Related to the reconstruction of a shared polity is the reconstruction of a shared national memory. Ehud Ben Zvi, Katherine Southwood, and I each engage social-memory studies in order to demonstrate the way in which the community

10. Eskenazi, *Ezra*, 3.

11. Eskenazi notes Lisbeth S. Fried's claim that Ezra 1–6 is structured like an ANE building inscription but points out a key difference: the role of the king is played by the people. See Fried, *Ezra: A Commentary*, Critical Commentary (Sheffield: Sheffield Phoenix, 2015).

12. Fried, *Ezra*; Fried, *Nehemiah: A Commentary*, Critical Commentary (Sheffield: Sheffield Phoenix, 2021).

13. David Janzen, *The End of History and the Last King: Achaemenid Ideology and Community Identity in Ezra-Nehemiah*, LHBOTS 713 (London: T&T Clark, 2021). See also Herbert Marbury, *Imperial Dominion and Priestly Genius: Coercion, Accommodation, and Resistance in the Divorce Rhetoric of Ezra-Nehemiah* (Upland, CA: Sopher, 2012); Christopher M. Jones, "Embedded Written Documents as Colonial Mimicry in Ezra-Nehemiah," *BibInt* 26, no. 2 (2018): 158–81; Mark G. Brett, *Locations of God: Political Theology in the Hebrew Bible* (New York: Oxford University Press, 2019), 75–85.

14. Janzen, *End of History*, 46.

15. Brett, *Locations of God*, 75.

selectively engages models from Israel's past in order to construct an ideal vision of the community in the present. The past provides an authoritative model for historical analogy,[16] ethnic identity,[17] and models of leadership and communal boundaries.[18] This collective memory, of which Ezra-Nehemiah and Esther become a crucial part, enabled the people of Judah to construct a resilient communal identity capable of surviving not only the trauma of exile but also ongoing domination by successive gentile empires.

New Answers to Old Questions: The Authenticity of the Embedded Documents?

Although the rise of postcolonial theory in the academy stems primarily from an analysis of the impact of European colonial rule across the globe, its fundamental claims about the influence of imperialism on colonized peoples provide valuable tools to analyze the texts produced under imperial rule in the ancient world. The concept of imperial imitation drawn from postcolonial studies has also played a significant role in reevaluations of a classic *crux interpretum*: the authenticity of the embedded documents. The arguments both for and against their authenticity can be grouped into three debated areas: epistolary form (Persian or Hellenistic), linguistic character (Imperial or later Middle Aramaic), and ideology (whether the contents of the letter are historically probable). Lester Grabbe effectively summarizes the arguments for their inauthenticity: he argues that the letters demonstrate more affinity with early Hellenistic letters than with those from the Persian period; he points to examples of Middle Aramaic in the letters to justify their late date; and he argues that the extravagant financial support and tax relief promised to the local Judean temple and its personnel are historically unlikely.[19]

16. Aubrey E. Buster, *Remembering the Story of Israel: Historical Summaries and Memory Formation in Second Temple Judaism* (Cambridge: Cambridge University Press, 2022).

17. Katherine E. Southwood, "'But Now . . . Do Not Let All This Hardship Seem Insignificant before You': Ethnic History and Nehemiah 9," *SEÅ* 79 (2014): 1–23.

18. Ehud Ben Zvi, "Memory and Political Thought in the Late Persian / Early Hellenistic Yehud/Judah: Some Observations," in *Leadership, Social Memory, and Judean Discourse in the Fifth–Second Centuries BCE*, ed. Diana V. Edelman and Ehud Ben Zvi (Bristol: Equinox, 2016), 9–22; Ben Zvi, "Re-negotiating a Putative Utopia and the Stories of the Rejection of Foreign Wives in Ezra-Nehemiah," in *Worlds That Could Not Be: Utopia in Chronicles, Ezra, and Nehemiah*, ed. Steven J. Schweitzer and Frauke Uhlenbruch, LHBOTS 620 (London: T&T Clark, 2016), 105–28.

19. Lester L. Grabbe, "The 'Persian Documents' in the Book of Ezra: Are They Authentic?," in *Judah and the Judeans in the Persian Period*, ed. Oded Lipschits and Manfred Oeming (Winona Lake, IN: Eisenbrauns, 2006), 531–70. See also Dirk Schwiderski, *Handbuch des Nordwestsemitischen Briefformulars*, BZAW 295 (Berlin: De Gruyter, 2000); Sebastian Grätz, "The Literary and Ideological Character of the Letters in Ezra 4–7," in *Letters and Communities: Studies in the Socio-Political Dimensions of Ancient Epistolography*, ed. Paola Ceccarelli et al. (Oxford: Oxford University Press, 2018), 239–51.

While he allows that the editors might have edited and updated authentic letters, he views it as unlikely that they reflect authentic Persian communication in the form in which they are preserved in Ezra-Nehemiah.[20]

Nevertheless, the authenticity of the letters has continued to receive vigorous defense.[21] On the linguistic front, a recent reevaluation by Naʿama Pat-El and Noam Mizrahi has strengthened the argument that the documents date from the Persian period and are unlikely to be Hellenistic forgeries.[22] This, of course, does not solve the problem of whether they are authentic Persian documents or merely written during the Persian period. They do observe, however, that many of the linguistic features taken as incontrovertible evidence of lateness (as Grabbe states, "Early forms can occur in late texts, but late forms cannot occur in early texts")[23] are found in securely dated Achaemenid-period texts. These include the mixed features present in Ezra, such as the use of the relative marker דִּי (*dî*), usually held to be late, alongside spellings with ז and the presence of second- and third-person plural pronominal suffixes ending in both *-m*, the earlier form (see, e.g., לְהֹם, *ləhōm*; Ezra 5:3), and *-n*, which eventually replaces the early form (see, e.g., לְהוֹן, *ləhôn*; 5:2). They also observe linguistic features that do not show up as frequently in discussions to support an early date. For example, Ezra rarely uses the proleptic genitive, and when it does so, the referents are exclusively humans. This is in contrast to later texts (such as Daniel) that use the construction frequently and in relationship to inanimate objects. So too, prolepsis with prepositions is attested only without the relative marker in Ezra, unlike in Hellenistic-period dialects, in which the relative marker was frequently used.

In terms of epistolary format, Pat-El and Mizrahi argue that many of the features interpreted as Hellenistic by Grabbe, Dirk Schwiderski, and Sebastian Grätz find a closer parallel in Aramaisms already appearing in Neo-Assyrian letters, including the use of the preposition -לְ (*lə-*) instead of the expected עַל (*ʿal*). Neo-Assyrian letters demonstrate the frequent use of the preposition *ana* to mark the direct object, which is usually viewed as an Aramaic loan translation of -ל (*l-*) and therefore early.[24] One of the main arguments against the authenticity of the letters is the salutation in Ezra 4:17, which appears without an addressee. This form does not appear in Achaemenid letters, but it does appear in Hellenistic ones. Mizrahi and Pat-El point out, however, that this form occurs

20. See also Fried (*Ezra*, 222–28), who argues that the letters are composite.

21. Williamson, "Exile and After"; Williamson, "The Aramaic Documents in Ezra Revisited," *JTS* 59, no. 1 (2008): 41–62.

22. Naʿama Pat-El and Noam Mizrahi, "Revisiting the Language of the Aramaic Documents in Ezra" (paper presented at the Annual Meeting of the Society of Biblical Literature, San Antonio, TX, November 2021). Shared with the author and cited with permission.

23. Grabbe, "Persian Documents," 533.

24. See Olga Vinnichenko, "The Reassessment of the Influence of Aramaic on Assyrian Syntax" (PhD diss., Cambridge University, 2016), 59–60.

in Neo-Babylonian and Neo-Assyrian letters when the sender is of a higher status than the recipient. It is not a greeting, but a *report,* which can occur as a simple noun phrase.[25]

Pat-El and Mizrahi's argument is innovative in terms of the epistolary evidence marshaled and the historical linguistic evidence used, and future discussions of the Aramaic in Ezra (and Daniel) must take their argument into account. However, recent discussion has turned away from questions of authenticity toward the way in which the documents reveal a relationship between the community in Yehud and the Persian Empire. The most significant of these studies is Laura Carlson Hasler's *Archival Historiography in Jewish Antiquity*, which argues that Ezra-Nehemiah presents an innovative form of historiography that emphasizes textual collection in imitation of imperial archives. Unlike Pat-El and Mizrahi, Carlson Hasler does not compare texts on the basis of epistolary convention, linguistics, or ideology but instead interrogates the very form of document storing as an imperial activity.[26] She draws from postcolonial theorists who link the imperial appetite for territory acquisition to the corresponding activity of textual acquisition. She connects what Thomas Richards calls the "fantasy of knowledge collected and united" to the massive library of Alexandria and the vast collection of Assurbanipal and, to a lesser extent, Nabonidus.[27] Although she does not focus on traditional historical-critical questions concerning the document's authenticity, her inquiry remains fundamentally historical, as it engages a deep study of the development and purpose of imperial archives.

This presentation of the letters as acts of imperial imitation is also observed by Janzen and Christopher Jones.[28] Jones highlights the way in which the differing use of the letters in Ezra-Nehemiah demonstrates a tension between colonial mimicry (a term important in Homi Bhabha's presentation of colonial discourse)[29] on the one hand and resistance toward empire on the other. Jones argues that Ezra 7 mimics imperial discourse in order to present a royal endorsement of the Torah and temple in Yehud, while Neh. 10 claims to preserve a document that underlines the community's commitment to Torah above the empire. While Jones uses this difference in the books' ideologies to argue that the two books developed separately, the text as it stands also demonstrates the characteristic of hybridity and the tension between resistance and assimilation to colonial power commonly observed in postcolonial discourses.

25. See the phrase *šulmu adanniš*, "[everything] is very well" (SAA 01 177, r 9).

26. Laura Carlson Hasler, *Archival Historiography in Jewish Antiquity* (New York: Oxford University Press, 2020).

27. Thomas Richards, *The Imperial Archive: Knowledge and the Fantasy of Empire* (London: Verso, 1993), 6.

28. Janzen, *End of History*; Jones, "Embedded."

29. Homi K. Bhabha, *The Location of Culture*, Routledge Classics (London: Routledge, 2004), 3–4, 19–39.

Esther and Postcolonialism

The critical social sciences, most prominently postcolonial theory and intersectionality, also figure prominently in the recent study of Esther. Many analyses highlight the role of gender within the book.[30] Some readings have upheld her as a feminist icon, while others have denigrated her as complicit in the patriarchal structures of her Judean household (in relationship with Mordecai) and the empire (in her relationship with the king).[31] Recent studies, however, have begun to identify how various aspects of her identity—her ethnicity, gender, sexuality, and political status as well as the intersection of these traits in the surrounding characters—characterize her intersectional identity.

This recognition of intersectional identity has set the stage for a dynamic conversation concerning the ambivalence of Esther as a model of accommodation or resistance within the book. Most readings, both popular and academic, present her as an ideal character. Daniel Smith-Christopher, a primary contributor to postcolonial interpretations of the Bible, interrogates this popular idea of Esther through a postcolonial lens. He builds on Timothy Beal's intriguing suggestion that Esther might have been written to put its very protagonist on trial: Will Esther function as a collaborator with imperial power, or will she align herself with her people and defend their well-being? He uses the frame of "collaboration studies" to ask what it might mean if Esther (and Mordecai) do not fit the more "acceptable models of resistance that praise historical examples of acceptably patriotic and/or nationalist behavior," but are instead presented as collaborators with the Persian Empire.[32]

Continuing the conversation on whether Esther and Mordecai resist or accommodate the Persian rulers, several interpreters from the Asian diaspora identify the way in which Esther's marginalized identity nuances the nature of her resistance. They argue that the path of overt resistance is not available to Esther, who must remain "passive, submissive, obedient, and sexualized."[33] Ciin Sian Siam Hatzaw describes Esther as the "assimilated model minority of the Persian empire," an identity that she relates to her own experiences as a Burmese

30. David J. A. Clines, "Reading Esther from Left to Right: Contemporary Strategies for Reading a Biblical Text," in *The Bible in Three Dimensions*, ed. David J. A. Clines et al., JSOTSup 87 (Sheffield: Sheffield Academic, 1992), 31–52; Michael V. Fox, *Character and Ideology in the Book of Esther*, 2nd ed. (Grand Rapids: Eerdmans, 2001), 205–11; Anne-Mareike Wetter, *"On Her Account": Reconfiguring Israel in Ruth, Esther, and Judith*, LHBOTS 623 (London: T&T Clark, 2015), 138–52.

31. Esther Fuchs, "Status and Role of Female Heroines in the Biblical Narrative," *Mankind Quarterly* 23 (1982): 1419–60.

32. Daniel Smith-Christopher, "Esther on Trial: Resistance or 'Collaboration Horizontale,'" in *Postcolonial Commentary and the Old Testament*, ed. Hemchand Gossai (London: T&T Clark, 2019), 209–29. See further Timothy K. Beal, *The Book of Hiding: Gender, Ethnicity, Annihilation, and Esther*, Biblical Limits (London: Routledge, 1997), 72.

33. Ciin Sian Siam Hatzaw, "Reading Esther as a Postcolonial Feminist Icon for Asian Women in Diaspora," *Open Theology* 7, no. 1 (2021): 3.

immigrant living in England. Paul K.-K. Cho similarly identifies the ways in which Esther transforms her position of weakness within "three overlapping structures of power" (gender, politics, and the social world) to one of small advantage for the purpose of the salvation of her people.[34] Hyun Woo Kim and Eunil David Cho write with existential urgency in the aftermath of the racially motivated murder of Asian women in Atlanta, Georgia, in 2021. They identify in Esther a model of "segmented assimilation," a figure who is partially assimilated into the dominant culture but maintains ties to her Jewish identity through her intergenerational relationship with Mordecai.[35]

These contextualized readings of Esther, richly informed by the critical social sciences, illuminate the narrative through a deeper understanding of the experiences, actions, and speech of (formerly) colonized peoples or people from identity groups often underrepresented within the academy. So too, biblical scholars' engagement with the critical social sciences offers to these areas of study the insight of ancient literature that reflects on the experience of imperial rule.

The influence of the biblical story on academic theories is highlighted by Tsaurayi Kudakwashe Mapfeka's careful genealogy of the concept of "diaspora" and its relationship to the book of Esther.[36] The use of the term "diaspora" has become increasingly prevalent in the last decade, but Mapfeka's is the first sustained analysis of the term in relationship to Esther.[37] He identifies that the meaning of the term "diaspora" itself is historically related to the Jewish diaspora, which functions as the paradigm for the term. Esther is therefore one of the earliest examples of diaspora literature. His work demonstrates the theoretical nuance contributed by the interaction of biblical scholars with the social sciences but also shows how biblical texts themselves function as originating cultural models.

Ezra-Nehemiah-Esther and Identity

As seen above, these three postexilic books center on questions of identity.[38] How does one construct and demarcate one's identity, either as a displaced

34. Paul K.-K. Cho, "A House of Her Own: The Tactical Deployment of Strategy in Esther," *JBL* 140, no. 4 (2021): 663–82.

35. Hyun Woo Kim and Eunil David Cho, "Breaking the Asian American Silence at a Time Like This: Lessons from the Diasporic Jews in Exile" (paper presented at the Annual Meeting of the Society of Biblical Literature, San Antonio, TX, November 2021). Shared with author and cited with permission.

36. Tsaurayi Kudakwashe Mapfeka, *Esther in Diaspora: Toward an Alternative Interpretive Framework*, BibInt 178 (Leiden: Brill, 2019).

37. See, e.g., Elsie R. Stern, "Esther and the Politics of Diaspora," *JQR* 100, no. 1 (2010): 25–53; Anne-Mareike Wetter, "How Jewish Is Esther? Or How Is Esther Jewish? Tracing Ethnic and Religious Identity in a Diaspora Narrative," *ZAW* 123, no. 4 (2011): 596–603; Aaron J. Koller, *Esther in Ancient Jewish Thought* (New York: Cambridge University Press, 2014).

38. See Jacob Wright, "Ezra," in *New Interpreter's Bible: One Volume Commentary*, ed. Beverly Roberts Gaventa and David Petersen (Nashville: Abingdon, 2010), 263–70.

group resettling in a land under imperial power (Ezra-Nehemiah) or as an orphan woman from an ethnically and religiously minoritized group within the empire's capital (Esther)? The questions of identity and identity definition, so prevalent in the guild, unsurprisingly find rich material in books that are, in the words of Helena Zlotnick-Sivan, "fundamentally concerned with issues of identity and boundaries."[39] To provide two representative case studies, I examine the perennial issue of Ezra's bilingualism and the infamous crisis of foreign marriage.

Language

Ezra is one of two books in the HB, along with Daniel, that contains significant portions of Aramaic in addition to Hebrew. Timothy Hogue and Roger Nam identify the language alternation in Ezra as a form of "code-switching." Hogue argues that the shifts in language—from Hebrew to Official Aramaic to vernacular Aramaic—construct a linguistic narrative that traces the transition of the Jewish people from a diaspora community, through opposition, to a stabilized minority community in Jerusalem.[40] It is not only in the shift between Aramaic and Hebrew that language plays a significant role in the narrative. Several scholars have connected the way in which language becomes a particularly significant identity marker in the text with the contemporary experiences of migrant and returnee communities.

Nam identifies the switch in languages as an identity marker for an adaptive community willing to converse in the language of the Persian Empire while preserving their own cultural heritage.[41] He compares the bilingualism of Ezra-Nehemiah with that of the Korean-American community, particularly as second- and third-generation Korean Americans who are fluent in English also work to preserve a knowledge of the Korean language as a link to their heritage.

Scholars have also recognized the complexity of Nehemiah's critique of those who cannot speak the language of Judah (Neh. 13:23–31) in light of the experience of minority language groups. Katherine Southwood highlights how the preservation of language is part of the preservation of a distinctive ethnic identity threatened with the dissolution of communal boundaries and linguistic assimilation.[42] The loss of language that Nehemiah condemns signifies a threat to their culture,

39. Helena Zlotnick-Sivan, "The Silent Women of Yehud: Notes on Ezra 9–10," *JJS* 51, no. 1 (2000): 3.

40. Timothy Hogue, "Return from Exile: Diglossia and Literary Code-Switching in Ezra 1–7," *ZAW* 130, no. 1 (2018): 54–68.

41. Roger S. Nam, "Half Speak Ashdodite and None Can Speak Judean: Code-Switching in Ezra-Nehemiah as an Identity Marker for Repatriate Judeans and Koreans," in *Landscapes of Korean and Korean American Biblical Interpretation*, ed. John Ahn (Atlanta: SBL Press, 2019), 119–32.

42. Katherine E. Southwood, "'And They Could Not Understand Jewish Speech': Language, Ethnicity, and Nehemiah's Intermarriage Crisis," *JTS* 62, no. 1 (2011): 1–19.

their values, their survival as a recognizably distinct group, and their historical ties to the land of Judea. Jean-Pierre Ruiz, however, writes from the perspective of those *excluded* for their language use in the narrative. He sees an analogy between the way language fluency is used to exclude Latin American immigrants to the United States and the way the children of the "foreign women" in Neh. 13 are identified as outsiders because they speak Ashdodite rather than Hebrew.[43] As a significant component of ethnic identity, language can be used as a tool not only to preserve a threatened identity and reinforce ties to the community, but also to exclude those who do not possess this identity marker.

"Foreign Wives"

The challenge of community definition is nowhere more apparent in these books than in the proscription of intermarriage in Ezra 9–10 and Neh. 13. Both Ezra and Nehemiah condemn intermarriage with women who are described variously as the "daughters" of "the peoples of the lands" (Ezra 9:1–2), as "foreign women" (Ezra 10:2; Neh. 13:27), and as the "women of Ashdod, Ammon, and Moab" (Neh. 13:23). The narratives concerning intermarriage are of significant literary value in discerning the message of a book that centers on the identification and definition of the returnee community, but they are a source of significant concern for religious communities who find such scenes within sacred Scripture (justifiably) horrifying and offensive. Interpretations of the relevant passages can be heuristically divided into two general groups: (1) those that seek to understand how and why the community justifies the intermarriage prohibition, and (2) those that engage in ethical evaluation of the prohibition. An increasing number of studies also bring analogical contextual connections to bear as the authors write from communities that have themselves experienced intermarriage bans of some kind.

Ezra 9–10 and Neh. 13 clearly present a strict enforcement of community boundaries. The primary interpretive question (among many) is how these boundaries are defined. The first subset of interpreters understands the division between the returning community and the daughters of the "people of the lands" as one of physical descent or ethnicity defined in kinship terms.[44] From its beginning, Israelite identity is intertwined with ethnicity and with kinship relationships.

43. Jean-Pierre Ruiz, *Readings from the Edges: The Bible and People on the Move* (Maryknoll, NY: Orbis Books, 2011), 109.

44. Christine Hayes, *Gentile Impurities and Jewish Identities: Intermarriage and Conversion from the Bible to the Talmud* (Oxford: Oxford University Press, 2002); Csilla Saysell, *"According to the Law": Reading Ezra 9–10 as Christian Scripture*, JTISup 4 (Winona Lake, IN: Eisenbrauns, 2012); Katherine E. Southwood, *Ethnicity and the Mixed Marriage Crisis in Ezra 9–10: An Anthropological Approach*, Oxford Theological Monographs (Oxford: Oxford University Press, 2012); Bob Becking, *Ezra-Nehemiah*, HCOT (Leuven: Peeters, 2018), 97; Hannah K. Harrington, *The Purity and Sanctuary of the Body in Second Temple Judaism*, JAJSup 33 (Göttingen: Vandenhoeck & Ruprecht, 2019).

Ezra-Nehemiah, however, presents an intensification of these boundaries in which intermarriage with another group (whose definition I will come to shortly) is explicitly proscribed, and some of the unions are dissolved. Interpreters argue that the phrase זֶרַע הַקֹּדֶשׁ (*zeraʿ haqqōdeš*), which they translate "holy seed," and the description of the prohibited wives as "foreign" or as daughters of "the peoples of the lands" implies that holiness is conferred by descent (hence the children of these unions are also implicated).

One of the issues with this line of argumentation is the question of the identification of "the peoples of the lands." While Ezra 10 and Neh. 13 describe the women as foreign (נָשִׁים נָכְרִיּוֹת, *nāšîm nokrîyôt*), Ezra 9 introduces the mixed unions as between a Judean from the returnee community and one of the daughters of "the peoples of the lands." The consensus is that "the peoples of the lands" most likely includes Judeans and Israelites who remained in the land during the exile.[45] If this is the case, then there would be little "biological" or "ethnic" difference between these two groups, which leads some scholars to argue that the distinction is based not on ethnicity or biology but on the actions of these daughters of "the peoples of the lands."

Eskenazi, for example, argues that the issue with the foreign women is not their *ethnicity* but their *practices*, which align them with the practices of previous groups who inhabited the land.[46] Intimate relationships with wives who practice these abominations would then defile the community and desecrate the sancta. Eskenazi's position is bolstered by her argument regarding the translation of זֶרַע הַקֹּדֶשׁ. This phrase, used in Ezra 9:2 to describe the גּוֹלָה (*gôlâ*, diaspora) community, is usually translated "holy seed" or "holy race." Eskenazi points out that the translation "holy seed" incorrectly represents the term קֹדֶשׁ (*qōdeš*), which signifies a concept that is different from the corresponding adjectival form קָדוֹשׁ (*qādôš*). The adjective "imputes holiness to the object it describes," while the noun form "depicts a relationship to the holy by way of dedication to the holy."[47] The phrase signifies not an innate holiness derived from biological descent but a claim that they have been dedicated as holy to God, a status that they can lose if they disqualify themselves through contact with those who practice abominations. This argument does not deny that there is a genealogical basis for membership but insists that genealogy alone does not suffice to confirm membership in the group. It must also include a dedication to Torah.[48]

45. Dalit Rom-Shiloni, *Exclusive Identity: Identity Conflicts between the Exiles and the People Who Remained (6th–5th Centuries BCE)*, LHBOTS 543 (New York: Bloomsbury, 2013), 44; Tamara Cohn Eskenazi, "Conflict over Marriage and the Holy in Ezra 9–10," in *The Formation of Biblical Texts: Chronicling the Legacy of Gary N. Knoppers*, ed. Deirdre N. Fulton et al., FAT 176 (Tübingen: Mohr Siebeck, 2024).

46. Eskenazi, "Conflict"; Eskenazi, *Ezra*, 379–81.

47. Eskenazi, "Conflict."

48. Eskenazi, "Conflict"; Eskenazi, *Ezra*, 378–81.

Interpreters also engage the social sciences to better understand the motivation behind the strict redefinition of community boundaries, but a tension emerges here. Historical and archaeological records confirm how the community described in Ezra-Nehemiah was a small minority group living under a dominant empire, returning to an impoverished land in an attempt to rebuild their community after exile and amid ongoing diaspora. The communal anxiety that often undergirds endogamous practices, the intentional engagement of language preservation to maintain ties to a heritage culture, and the tightening of community boundaries over and against a fear of destruction or disappearance through assimilation, are experiences with which minority communities living within a majority dominant culture can identify. Models related to return migration and shared communal trauma illuminate the way in which communities engage endogamy as a strategy of survival against forces that would harm them.[49] Other interpreters focus on the fact that Ezra-Nehemiah preserves only one perspective on the matter. Though written by a small community struggling to survive, these books have become the dominant narrating voice of that period within Judah. Interpreters therefore perceive in Ezra-Nehemiah an analogy to colonizing voices who erase minority counternarratives, such as the voices and identity of "the peoples of the lands," their daughters with their children, and the so-called adversaries who desire to be included in the temple-building project. The strategies of endogamy and strictly enforced communal boundaries used by communities in crisis can also become strategies of exclusion wielded by those in power, as the narrative of Ezra-Nehemiah indicates.

Several studies seek to recover counter-voices in Ezra-Nehemiah. Nāsili Vaka'uta rereads the narrative of the marriage crisis from the perspective of the peoples of the lands.[50] As the text narrates a prohibition of intermarriage, it also preserves a record of it even between priestly families and the peoples of the lands. This record demonstrates that not all in the community agreed with the prohibition. Brett suggests that Ezra 1–6 itself, and most infamously Ezra 6:21, presents a more inclusive vision of the community than that presented in Ezra 7–Neh. 13.[51] Concerning other counter-voices within the narrative, Gafney elevates the text's brief witness to Noadiah (Ezra 8:33; Neh. 6:14) as a record of an "anti-colonial prophet of resistance" against a group that equated the imperial voice and the divine voice.[52] The prayer in Neh. 9:6–37, with its representation of life under Persian rule as "slavery," in analogy with the slavery in Egypt, also presents a potential counter-voice questioning the validity of Achaemenid rule by comparing it to slavery under Egyptian rule.[53]

49. Southwood, *Ethnicity*; Brett, *Locations of God*.

50. Nāsili Vaka'uta, *Reading Ezra 9–10* Tu'a-*Wise: Rethinking Biblical Interpretation in Oceania*, IVBS 3 (Atlanta: Society of Biblical Literature, 2011).

51. Brett, *Locations of God*, 75–85.

52. Wilda Gafney, "A Prophet-Terrorist(a) and an Imperial Sympathizer: An Empire-Critical, Postcolonial Reading of the Noʿadyah/Nechemyah Conflict," *BlTh* 9 (2011): 161–76.

53. Buster, *Remembering*, 154–98.

Conclusion

In the past decade, archaeological analyses and the social sciences (critical and otherwise) have offered particularly illuminating insights into Ezra-Nehemiah and Esther. This is in part because the books themselves present such rich material in their narration of the significant challenges of a community seeking to survive, both in terms of individual life and distinctive communal identity, amid imperial rule that threatens bodily safety and communal integrity. The disciplines of political theology, intersectionality, and postcolonial studies have inspired innovative theses to address old questions in both Ezra-Nehemiah and Esther, even while more traditional methods such as historical linguistics and careful historical-critical and literary analyses clarify aspects of the text and context. In my assessment, the most urgent and meaningful analyses of these texts will continue to combine historical reconstruction of the text with humanistic models that elevate topics of ongoing concern for peoples across the globe—questions of identity, forced and return migration, inclusion and exclusion, and the construction of community in the face of often horrific challenges.[54]

54. Special thanks to Megan Stidham for her valuable editorial assistance on this chapter.

17

The Psalms

JAMIE A. GRANT

For many years the book of Psalms was something of a problem child for the academy. In an era where theology was struggling to justify its place within the increasingly secular university, the psalms were something of an embarrassment. They do not sit particularly well within the methodological approaches of either source criticism or the history-of-religions school. The book is undeniably "spiritual": its content is focused on worship, and the poems are predominantly prayers. The study of them could not be easily couched in the quest for underlying sources reflecting competing visions of the ancient and pure religion of Israel. Accordingly, Psalms was for many years largely neglected by academic study. There were of course commentaries aplenty, but *study* was another matter entirely.[1] The rise of form criticism in the 1920s did much to restore a viable presence for psalmody in the academic study of the OT. However, even this was somewhat muted by a focus on putative historical *Sitze im Leben* and functions within the cult rather than on the rhetorical purposes of psalm genres. But Psalms studies have come a long way since the literary and canonical turns of the 1980s. From a position of relative neglect, the study of the Psalms has become a vibrant area of OT study, producing some of the most creative work in current biblical scholarship.

This brief historical sketch (arguably a caricature) of Psalms study in the modern era is necessary if we are to understand the present state of the field,

1. This chapter will not, by and large, discuss the many excellent commentaries on the Psalms that have been written over the last twenty years. It will instead concentrate on developments in Psalms studies.

since current debates and emphases developed from what went before. The questions that are being asked and answered today are rooted in the interpretative issues that were addressed or ignored in the past. The current trends in Psalms research could be divided into three main groupings, but I have also reserved a fourth, catchall category: (1) canonical readings, (2) Qumran texts, (3) studies of *Wirkungsgeschichte* (reception history), and (4) miscellanea. As can be seen throughout many years of form-critical studies, all classification is, to one degree or another, notional, if not spurious. Many of the works under consideration below could, legitimately, be placed in more than one of these four groups. Discussions of canon inevitably intersect with the evidence from Qumran. Studies of reception history delve into discussions of theology and hermeneutics. So the suggested groupings should be read not as strict boundaries but merely as a way to organize and survey the main currents in Psalms study.

Canonical Readings

The catalyst for the revival of Psalms studies within the academy was arguably the arrival of the canonical approach to the Psalter from the mid-1980s onward. The trigger was Brevard Childs's *Introduction to the Old Testament as Scripture*.[2] Childs's chapter on the Psalms may, superficially, be taken to indicate a degree of uncertainty regarding the application of his approach to an anthological collection. There is no "narrative" per se in a collection of poems or songs, and in a psalmic world dominated at that time by genre, discussions revolved around type and not order. The form-critical school viewed the canonical order of the Psalter as basically irrelevant. At the risk of overstatement, priority was given to the unitary nature of each composition. Psalm 1 could just as easily be moved to any other position in the book without any harm being done either to the individual composition or the book. As Claus Westermann observed, "How are we to explain the fact that form-critical research has not changed in any way or even raised doubts about the thesis dominant up to this point concerning the categorization of the Psalms according to purely formal considerations? The reason for this, it seems to me, lies simply in the fact that in laying the foundation for his interpretation of the Psalms, [Hermann] Gunkel above all had no interest in how the collection was handed down to us."[3] Without really applying his theory holistically to the book, Childs questioned this assumption by asking, Why is Ps. 1 the first composition in the book of Psalms? It is, after all, an unlikely candidate. In terms of genre, it is neither a praise psalm nor a lament, the two dominant psalm types. It is a wisdom psalm with a torah emphasis. The wisdom psalms are viewed as a rather minor type in form-critical terms, neither frequently

2. Brevard Childs, *Introduction to the Old Testament as Scripture* (London: SCM, 1979).

3. Claus Westermann, *Praise and Lament in the Psalms*, trans. Keith Crim and Richard Soulen (Atlanta: Westminster John Knox, 1981), 251.

occurring nor readily placeable within the cult. Nor is Ps. 1 given prominence because of its dearness to the hearts of the people, like Ps. 23, or its length and complex artistry, like Ps. 119.

Childs made two further observations about the canonical psalms that had far-reaching effects. First, he wondered, what is the significance of the rather obvious links connecting Ps. 1 and Ps. 2? These links include a shared lack of title, an inclusio rooted in אַשְׁרֵי (*ʾašrê*, happiness), and a multitude of lexical links.[4] To Childs's mind, this seemed more purposeful than accidental. Second, he asked whether there might be something also purposeful in placing a torah psalm at the beginning of a new canonical section. Pointing out the appearance of torah themes at the beginning of the Former Prophets (Josh. 1:7–8) and Major Prophets (Isa. 1:10) as well as at the end of the Minor Prophets (Mal. 4:4), he posited that the decision to place this short psalm at the beginning of both the Psalter and the Writings was a deliberate authority claim that these songs are every bit as much divine speech as are the Torah and the Nevi'im. These observations and questions seem innocuous enough and rather modest in their reach, but in asking them, a methodology began to develop.

Asking why Ps. 1 comes at the start of the Psalter and whether it was deliberately linked with Ps. 2 opened a world of possibilities for finding purposeful editorial activity in the ordering of the Psalms. The first to expand on the ramifications of Childs's musings was his doctoral student Gerald Wilson in his classic 1985 work *The Editing of the Hebrew Psalter*.[5] Wilson began with analysis of comparable ANE anthological collections to see if there were signs of deliberate collection, editing, and ordering. His research on the Sumerian Temple Hymns and Catalog of Hymnic Incipits led to the conclusion that both explicit and tacit signs of editing are present. Explicitly, they name editors who gathered groups of texts or include dedications to particular deities. Implicitly, they group texts by shared keywords or themes repeated in neighboring compositions (concatenation). The second part of Wilson's thesis focused on signs of editing in the Hebrew Psalter (e.g., the colophon at the end of Ps. 72). He developed this argument further by analyzing the placement of royal psalms at the seams of the Psalter, developing what he described as a "narrative" of the establishment (Ps. 2), continuation (Ps. 72), and fall of the Davidic monarchy (Ps. 89) in books 1–3 of the Psalter, which is replaced by a focus on the kingship of YHWH in books 4 and 5.

David Howard was working on similar ideas at the same time as Wilson, but his contribution is often overlooked because his 1986 doctoral dissertation was not published until some twelve years after Wilson's *Editing*.[6] Wilson's work focused

4. Pierre Auffret, *La Sagesse a Bâti Sa Maison: Études de Structures Littéraires dans l'Ancient Testament et Spécialement dans les Psaumes*, OBO 49 (Fribourg: Editions Universitaires, 1982).

5. Gerald H. Wilson, *The Editing of the Hebrew Psalter*, SBLDS 76 (Chico, CA: Scholars Press, 1985).

6. David M. Howard, *The Structure of Psalms 93–100*, BJS/UCSD 5 (Winona Lake, IN: Eisenbrauns, 1997).

on theory and questions of method in macro-level analysis of the Psalter, whereas Howard's was the first vital and extensive work on a micro-level, looking at the signs of connection between Pss. 93–100, the יהוה מָלָךְ (*YHWH mālak*, YHWH reigns) psalms. Based on detailed exegetical analysis, Howard arrived at methodological conclusions similar to Wilson's regarding signs of editing and canonical connection in the MT Psalter.[7]

The combined work of Wilson and Howard led to a vibrant study group at the annual meetings of the Society of Biblical Literature throughout the late 1980s and early 1990s. Wilson and Howard were prominent in this group, as were eminent scholars like J. Clinton McCann, Walter Brueggemann, James Mays, and Patrick Miller.[8] It would not be an overstatement to contend that this group revitalized the study of the Psalms from its somewhat moribund focus on the minutiae of form. Several highly significant works on the Psalms were published in this period by McCann,[9] Brueggemann,[10] Nancy deClaissé-Walford,[11] and David Mitchell.[12] These works set a new direction for the academic study of the Psalter that continues to offer vibrant scholarship almost forty years after the publication of Wilson's *Editing*.

Jerome Creach's study of the "refuge" word group and theme was one of the first monograph-length applications of the canonical approach within the Psalter, highlighting the significant placement of refuge psalms throughout the book, including the theme's foregrounding in Ps. 2.[13] Robert L. Cole was, arguably, the first to provide a systematic canonical study of a book of the Psalter. His study of the dialogic nature of book 3 (Pss. 73–89) presents the interplay between the human voices of lament and divine response, arguing that these provide a structure to the flow of the collection.[14] I examined the role of the torah psalms in the Psalter and their association with royal psalms, asking whether this association of the king with torah is a deliberate echo of the kingship law (Deut. 17:14–20), presenting the king as an idealized reader and practitioner

7. Wilson, *Editing of the Hebrew Psalter*, 199–200; and Howard, *Structure*, 99–102. See elsewhere Howard, "Editorial Activity in the Psalter: A State-of-the-Field Survey," in *The Shape and Shaping of the Psalter*, ed. J. Clinton McCann, JSOTSup 159 (Sheffield: JSOT Press, 1993); and Wilson, "The Shape of the Book of Psalms," *Int* 46, no. 2 (1992): 129–41.

8. See their respective articles in McCann, *Shape and Shaping*.

9. J. Clinton McCann, *A Theological Introduction to the Books of Psalms: The Psalms as Torah* (Nashville: Abingdon, 1993).

10. Walter Brueggemann, *The Psalms and the Life of Faith*, ed. Patrick D. Miller (Minneapolis: Fortress, 1995).

11. Nancy L. deClaissé-Walford, *Reading from the Beginning: The Shaping of the Hebrew Psalter* (Macon, GA: Mercer University Press, 1997).

12. David Mitchell, *The Message of the Psalter: An Eschatological Programme in the Book of Psalms*, JSOTSup 252 (Sheffield: Sheffield Academic, 1997).

13. Jerome Creach, *Yahweh as Refuge and the Editing of the Hebrew Psalter*, JSOTSup 217 (Sheffield: Sheffield Academic, 1996).

14. Robert L. Cole, *The Shape and Message of Book III: Psalms 73–89*, LHBOTS 308 (Sheffield: Sheffield Academic, 2000).

of the Psalms.[15] A spate of constructive canonical studies have asked how a contextual reading of individual songs in their canonical place impacts our understanding of both the individual compositions and the Psalter as a whole. As soon as a text is given a context, it is read differently.[16]

It is impossible to list all the canonical studies, but I must highlight several significant works in this field. Michael McKelvey's study of book 4 of the Psalms expands on the groundwork provided by Howard regarding the יהוה מָלַךְ psalms and gives deeper consideration to Wilson's presentation of book 4 as the "hermeneutical heart" of the Psalter by examining presentations of David, Moses, and YHWH.[17] Michael Snearly takes a somewhat similar approach in his study of book 5, arguing (contra Wilson) for a type of Davidic narrative being worked out across the final collection, which indicates a strengthening sense of messianic expectation in books 4 and 5.[18] Adam Hensley expands the discussion of covenant as an organizing structure within the Psalter beyond reflection on the Davidic covenant to include the influences of the Abrahamic and Mosaic covenants. He concludes that the editors viewed the three covenants as a theological whole and that they anticipated some sort of fulfillment of the covenant assurances in a royal eschatological figure.[19] Finally, we must mention Peter Ho's important work on the design of the Psalter and the various approaches to reading the book.[20] Ho's combination of macro-level and micro-level analyses advocates three different approaches—linear, concentric, and intertextual readings—all of which bring different but complementary insights to one's reading of an individual psalm or collection of poems.[21] Ho's encouragement to seek answers to different types of questions at different levels of reading is commendable because the indeterminacy of the psalms lends itself to a variety of analyses.[22] However, both the question of an overall Davidic narrative (macrostructure) to the Psalter and the encouragement to read the Davidic psalms intertextually in light of the historical superscriptions remain, to varying degrees, controversial and disputed.

15. Jamie A. Grant, *The King as Exemplar: The Function of Deuteronomy's Kingship Law in the Shaping of the Book of Psalms*, AcBib17 (Atlanta: SBL Press; Leiden: Brill, 2004).

16. James Mays, "The Question of Context in Psalm Interpretation," in McCann, *Shape and Shaping*, 14–20.

17. Michael McKelvey, *Moses, David and the High Kingship of Yahweh: A Canonical Study of Book IV of the Psalter*, GDBS 55 (Piscataway, NJ: Gorgias, 2010).

18. Michael Snearly, *The Return of the King: Messianic Expectation in Book V of the Psalter*, LHBOTS 608 (London: T&T Clark, 2015).

19. Adam Hensley, *Covenant Relationships and the Editing of the Hebrew Psalter*, LHBOTS 666 (London: T&T Clark, 2018), 9–10.

20. Peter C. Ho, *The Design of the Psalter: A Macrostructural Analysis* (Eugene, OR: Pickwick, 2019). See also O. Palmer Robertson, *The Flow of the Psalms: Discovering Their Structure and Theology* (Phillipsburg, NJ: P&R, 2015).

21. Ho, *Design of the Psalter*, 62–82.

22. Jamie A. Grant, "Determining the Indeterminate: Issues in Interpreting the Psalms," *Southeastern Theological Review* 1, no. 1 (2010): 3–14.

Further studies on various collections within the book of Psalms have appeared. These vary in focus, intent, and extent, but each in its own way brings light to the reader's understanding of various psalms, both individually and in their *Sitze im Psalter*.[23] Along with the English-language literature, which—following Childs—mainly focuses on synchronic readings of the MT Psalms, there is a strong train of German diachronic studies of the canonical *formation* of the Psalter, asking how the Psalter came into being as a book.[24] Much of the German commentary work on the Psalms of recent years blends the ideas of shape and shaping relatively seamlessly.[25]

Two schools of thought seem to have arisen within the canonical approach to the Psalter and, as with the analysis of biblical history, might be described as "maximalist" or "minimalist." The maximalists look for broad themes and complex structures across the books of the Psalter and the entire anthology. The assumption of the maximalist approach is that editors had a completely free hand to edit and arrange the collection as they pleased. Within this approach, one is most likely to come across the language of "narrative," the idea that some sort

23. For book 1, see Andrew Witt, *A Voice without End: The Role of David in Psalms 3–14*, JTISup 20 (University Park, PA: Eisenbrauns, 2021); Robert L. Cole, *Psalms 1–2: A Gateway to the Psalter*, HBM 37 (Sheffield: Sheffield Phoenix, 2013). On book 2, see Gianni Barbiero, *Perché, o Dio, ci hai rigettati? Salmi scelti dal secondoe terzo libro del Salteri*, AnBib 2 (Rome: Pontifical Biblical Institute, 2014); Stefan M. Attard, *The Implications of Davidic Repentance: A Synchronic Analysis of Book 2 of the Psalter (Psalms 42–72)*, AnBib 212 (Rome: Pontifical Biblical Institute, 2016). On book 3, see Cole, *Shape and Message*; Stephen J. Smith, *The Conflict between Faith and Experience and the Shape of Psalms 73–83*, LHBOTS 723 (London: T&T Clark, 2022). On book 4, see Howard and McKelvey mentioned above, as well as David A. Gundersen, "Davidic Hope in Book IV of the Psalter" (PhD diss., Louisville, Southern Baptist Theological Seminary, 2015). On book 5, see Snearly, *Return of the King*; W. Dennis Tucker, *Constructing and Deconstructing Power in Psalms 107–150*, AIL 19 (Atlanta: SBL Press, 2014); Ian Vaillancourt, *The Multifaceted Saviour of Psalms 110 and 118: A Canonical Exegesis* (Sheffield: Sheffield Phoenix, 2019); Jill Firth, "The Re-presentation of David in Psalms 140–143" (PhD diss., Melbourne, Ridley College, 2016).

24. Matthias Millard, *Die Komposition des Psalters: Ein Formgeschichtlicher Ansatz*, FAT 9 (Tübingen: Mohr Siebeck, 1994); Klaus Koch, "Der Psalter und seine Redaktionsgeschichte," in *Neue Wege der Psalmenforschung: Für Walter Beyerlin*, ed. Klaus Seybold and Erich Zenger, HBS 1 (Freiburg: Herder, 1994), 243–78. For a helpful survey of English and German Psalms scholarship, see Peter Flint and Patrick Miller, *The Book of Psalms: Composition and Reception*, VTSup 99 (London: Brill, 2004). See also Christoph Rösel, *Die messianische Redaktion des Psalters: Studien zu Entstehung und Theologie des Sammlung Psalm 2–89*, Calwer Theologische Monographien 19 (Stuttgart: Calwer, 1999); Claudia Süssenbach, *Der elohistische Psalter: Untersuchungen zu Komposition und Theologie von Ps 42–83*, FAT 2/7 (Tübingen: Mohr Siebeck, 2005); M. Leuenberger, *Konzeptionen des Königtums Gottes im Psalter: Untersuchungen zu Komposition und Redaktion der theokratischen Bücher IV–V im Psalter*, AThANT 83 (Zurich: Theologischer Verlag, 2004).

25. Frank-Lothar Hossfeld and Erich Zenger, *Psalms*, vol. 2, *A Commentary on Psalms 51–100*, trans. Linda Maloney, Hermeneia (Minneapolis: Fortress, 2005); Hossfeld and Zenger, *Psalms*, vol. 3, *A Commentary on Psalms 101–150*, trans. Linda Maloney, Hermeneia (Minneapolis: Fortress, 2011).

of story is being told in the ordering of the songs and books. This narrative tends to revolve around the figure of David, either as historically or eschatologically understood. The maximalist approach tends to prioritize each psalm's place and function within the book over the voice of the individual composition.

The minimalist approach, on the other hand, tends to focus more on the exegetical details of collocated psalms and the influences that result from reading a psalm in the light of near neighbors. Canonical minimalists reject the idea of narratives being told across the whole collection since this does not seem to be the way anthologies work in either ancient or modern realities. The voice of the individual composition remains primary for canonical minimalists, and the contextual influence of near neighbors, or of the collection, provides a form of rereading of the song. Minimalist interpreters of the Psalms seem happy to adopt the same approach Raymond Van Leeuwen applied to canonical readings of Prov. 10–29, in which he reads the individual aphorism as having "limited autonomy."[26] Similarly, the psalm as a composition must be read as autonomous but with the recognition that context does inevitably impact the reading of any text, even within an anthology, and so some reading strictures inevitably apply. The minimalist does not necessarily assume that the editors of the Psalter had an entirely free hand; instead, they were dealing with known and recognized collections that were added incrementally to the developing Psalter.

While there is diversity of approach in the adoption of their method, it would not be an exaggeration to state that the early work of Wilson and Howard has transformed the face of Psalms study. Almost forty years after the publication of Wilson's *Editing*, the study of the canonical shape of the Psalms continues to produce work that is rigorously exegetical and theologically creative.[27]

The Qumran Texts

Another area of study to flourish recently involves the Qumran Psalms scrolls. Several early Hebrew Psalms scrolls were recovered near Khirbet Qumran and elsewhere.[28] The number of Psalms texts found at Qumran indicates the popularity of the book and of this literary medium for these communities, as seems to be the case with all generations of believers, Jewish and Christian.[29] Psalms

26. Raymond Van Leeuwen, *Context and Meaning in Proverbs 25–27*, SBLDS 96 (Atlanta: Scholars Press, 1988).

27. David Howard and Michael Snearly, "Reading the Psalter as a Unified Book: Recent Trends," in *Reading the Psalms Theologically*, ed. David Howard and Andrew Schmutzer, Studies in Scripture and Biblical Theology (Bellingham, WA: Lexham, 2023).

28. Masada Psalms[a] contains most of Pss. 81:1–85:6, Masada Psalms[b] contains Ps. 150, and the Naḥal Ḥever Psalms scroll contains Pss. 7–31 in canonical order.

29. James VanderKam (*The Dead Sea Scrolls Today* [Grand Rapids: Eerdmans, 2010], 48) lists 36 biblical Psalms scrolls or fragments. The number rises to 45 with *pesher* and noncanonical psalms (www.deadseascrolls.org.il).

fragments have been found broadly across the Judean caves, but the largest and most complete texts were found in caves 4 and 11, most importantly, the Great Psalms Scroll (i.e., 11Q5 or 11QPs[a]).[30]

Most discussion regarding the Qumran scrolls focuses on text-critical questions, but the Psalms scrolls have also provoked vibrant debate regarding canon criticism. From the early work of James Sanders on the Qumran Psalms scrolls has arisen an argument that books 1–3 of the Psalter (Pss. 1–89 or 3–89) were fixed in the first century BCE, whereas the canonical shape of books 4 and 5 was still in flux and open to local variation.[31] This view has obvious bearing on how the canonical method is applied to the book of Psalms and efforts to find meaning in the order and arrangement of the 150 psalms of the Masoretic Text (MT). The coherence of the collection is vital to the argument that it has been, to greater or lesser degree, deliberately put together in this manner by editors.

Good work has continued along this line through the efforts of Peter Flint and, more recently, David Willgren.[32] Flint expands on Sanders's observations, calling into question an early date for the closure of the Psalms canon and questioning the language of "canon" and "book" as a singular reference to the MT's 150.[33] He suggests that, in fact, the Qumran scrolls, the Masada Psalms texts, and the diverse LXX traditions reflect various Psalter traditions active in the period extending from the first century BCE to the first century CE.[34] Wilson holds a similar view, arguing for early stability to books 1–3 and relative flux in the formation of books 4 and 5 until the end of the first century CE.[35] The Septuagint challenges this view by broadly reflecting the canonical Psalms sequence, and that perhaps as early as the third century BCE. As Klaus Seybold and others point out, in all likelihood a more centralized, Jerusalem-based tradition viewed the MT's 150 as the standard and authoritative text of the Psalter.[36] This argu-

30. Peter Flint, "Five Surprises in the Qumran Psalms Scrolls," in *Flores Florentino: Dead Sea Scrolls and Other Early Jewish Studies in Honour of Florentino García Martínez*, ed. A. T. Hilhorst, E. Puech, and E. J. C. Tigchelaar (Leiden: Brill, 2007), 183–95.

31. James Sanders, "Cave 11 Surprises and the Question of Canon," *McCormick Quarterly* 21 (1968): 284–98; Sanders, *The Dead Sea Psalms Scroll* (Ithaca, NY: Cornell University Press, 1967).

32. Peter Flint, *The Dead Sea Psalms Scrolls and the Book of Psalms* (Leiden: Brill, 1997); David Willgren, *The Formation of the "Book" of Psalms: Reconsidering the Transmission and Canonization of Psalmody in the Light of the Material Culture and the Poetics of Anthologies*, FAT 2/88 (Tübingen: Mohr Siebeck, 2016).

33. Flint, *Dead Sea Psalms Scrolls*, 24–26.

34. Flint argues, "11QPs[a] represents the latter part of a Psalter that was viewed and used as Scripture at Qumran and is not a secondary collection dependent upon Pss 1–150 as found in the Masoretic Text" ("Five Surprises," 184).

35. Wilson, *Editing*, 63–92; "The Qumran Psalms Scroll (11QPsa) and the Canonical Psalter: Comparison of Editorial Shaping," *CBQ* 59, no. 3 (1997): 448–64.

36. Klaus Seybold, "The Psalter as a Book," in *Jewish and Christian Approaches to the Psalms: Conflict and Convergence*, ed. Susan Gillingham (Oxford: Oxford University Press, 2013), 168–81.

ment is further sustained by Psalms[b] from Masada, where the text of Ps. 150 is followed by a section of blank scroll, normally indicating a major division, such as the end of a book.

Willgren develops the arguments of Flint and others that the Great Psalms Scroll reflects an alternative canonical structure to the MT's 150. He critiques the idea of intentional editorial ordering within the Psalter, arguing instead that anthologies unfold organically rather than under the purposeful hand of editors/compilers.[37] Willgren unfolds an extended metaphor throughout his study, suggesting that the "'Book' of Psalms" should be seen as a "garden" rather than a "garland."[38] The former suggests something broad and diverse, an entity to be wandered through, with elements that can be either admired or passed by. The "garland," on the other hand, is curated for the observer by the choices of others. Willgren concludes, "An anthology is a compilation of independent texts, actively selected and organized in relation to some present needs, inviting readers to a platform of continuous dialogue."[39] The psalm sequence in 11Q5, therefore, is another valid arrangement and should not be viewed as a departure from an established Psalms canon represented by the MT's 150.[40]

There is much that is helpful in Willgren's work. In particular, he asks the process questions that tend to be ignored by most synchronic interpreters. He reflects on the practicalities of accumulation within an anthology in a milieu that was awash with psalmic literature. His discussion of the dynamics of "selection" and "preservation" is pertinent and worth consideration. In a religious setting where psalms were clearly common currency, as reflected in the additional compositions found in 11Q5 or in the (so-called) pseudepigraphal literature, why did the editors, regardless of their setting, choose *these* psalms? Why were these psalms considered worth preserving as, in some sense, authoritative or significant, while others were not? This gives rise to significant ancillary questions regarding the prior existence of smaller collections or groupings and their later inclusion into growing anthologies. Did editors have a free hand to cut and paste as they pleased, or could a prior collection be included only as a set? Were

37. More recently, Willgren questions if editors have a particular purpose or aim in the arrangement of Psalms, arguing instead that a varied array of factors led to the incremental development of the Psalter as an anthology. See David Willgren, "A Teleological Fallacy in Psalms Studies? Decentralizing the 'Masoretic' Psalms Sequence in the Formation of the 'Book' of Psalms," in *Intertextualität und die Entstehung des Psalters*, ed. A. Brodersen, F. Neumann, and D. Willgren, FAT 2/114 (Tübingen: Mohr Siebeck, 2020), 33–50.

38. Willgren, *"Book" of Psalms*, 28.

39. Willgren, *"Book" of Psalms*, 25.

40. Alma Brodersen, *The End of the Psalter: Psalms 146–150 in the Masoretic Text, the Dead Sea Scrolls, and the Septuagint*, BZAW 505 (Berlin: De Gruyter, 2017); Eva Mroczek, *The Literary Imagination in Jewish Antiquity* (Oxford: Oxford University Press, 2016); William Yarchin, "Is There an Authoritative Shape of the Book of Psalms? Profiling the Manuscripts of the Hebrew Psalter," *RB* 122, no. 3 (2015): 355–70.

there social expectations that impacted the incremental addition of texts? For example, could the Egyptian Hallel psalms (Pss. 113–118) or the Songs of Ascent (Pss. 120–134) be included in the growing whole only as sets? These texts were potentially known as collections, so social expectations may have required that they be included *as a collection* in the anthology. If so, the editors did not have an *entirely* free hand in their organization and arrangement of poems within the collection.

Another valuable contribution from Willgren's work is his reflection on anthologies and how they work. The tension between the autonomy of the individual text and its belonging to a collection will always lie somewhere on a continuum for the reader. At times, the individual voice will dominate. At others, the relationship between compositions becomes more apparent and significantly impacts the reading of the individual voices. However, Willgren's work casts significant doubt on the idea that "narratives" can be read from anthologies of poetic works, which challenges the maximalist approach.

It could be argued, however, that certain brute facts present challenges to aspects of Willgren's careful work. First, the insistence that 11Q5 represents an alternative canon to the MT's 150 is simply unprovable. The Essenes may have viewed this scroll in its entirety as "biblical" and authoritative. However, Qumran had a wide variety of community texts, meaning that 11Q5 may have fulfilled a function in liturgical worship practices. Second, even if 11Q5 did reflect the authoritative psalms canon of this remote and sectarian Judean desert community, it in no way invalidates the existence of a centralized and more widely accepted psalms canon based on the MT, an arrangement also reflected with only minor variations by the material culture drawn from Masada and the Septuagint. Third, Willgren's rejection of the language of the "book" of psalms runs counter to the reading traditions of generations of Jewish and Christian communities. Ultimately, Psalms is more than a songbook and more than *just* an anthology. Its existence as a book is an observable reality.[41] Clearly, anthologies are different from prose narratives, yet they remain books, and this was as true in antiquity as it is today. The rejection of the language of "book" elevates the individual composition over its location within the collection. However, both must have a role in the reading of any anthology. Fourth, if for the sake of argument we reject the idea of purposeful editorial intervention in the collection and ordering of the Psalter, then we forced to explain an array of seemingly fortuitous coincidences. The lexical and thematic connections between Pss. 1 and 2 *are* numerous. The cry of dereliction in Ps. 22:1 *is* followed by the assurance that "the Lord is my Shepherd" in the psalm that follows. Psalms numbered in the 90s *do* share the language and ideology of YHWH's universal reign. These and many other connections appear to be reasonable and observable facts within the text of the Psalter. The reader is left to decide whether it is more likely that these connections are accidental or purposeful.

41. McCann, *Theological Introduction*, esp. 9–14.

Wirkungsgeschichte Studies

No presentation of the current state of Psalms scholarship can fail to mention the outstanding work of Susan Gillingham on the history of interpretation and the cultural locatedness of Psalms across the centuries. Gillingham has provided three works of note in recent years. The Blackwell Bible Commentary was followed by two reception-history commentaries on Psalms in the same series.[42] These works have added a fascinating layer of discussion to Psalms studies.[43]

Of particular note is her analysis of the pervasive influence of Psalms and psalmody on the arts. The three-volume Wiley-Blackwell series contains many reproductions of visual art linked to the Psalms—from illuminations in early editions of Jewish and Christian Bibles and stained glass representations of psalms to twentieth- and twenty-first-century visual representations of psalmic images of praise, lament, and comfort. Alongside these helpful reflections, Gillingham charts the pervasive influence of the psalms in music and song (liturgical and "secular"), poetry (again, of every type), and literature. This is one of the great contributions of these *Wirkungsgeschichte* reflections: one quickly comes to realize the pervasive impact and influence of psalmody on Western culture. It is broadly acknowledged that Psalms has always had a special place in the hearts of communities of faith throughout all generations. Gillingham's work documents this by showing how much the arts owe to the Psalms. She provides a key voice in documenting and recording both Jewish and Christian liturgical uses of the Psalms as well as approaches to interpretation, whereas most publications tend to focus on the communities to which they are writing. This deliberately bifocal approach highlights the continuing vitality of the songs in a wide variety of settings and the similar yet different interpretive traditions within the Jewish and Christian reading communities.[44]

Miscellanea

Although interest in canonical criticism, Qumran Psalms scrolls, and *Wirkungsgeschichte* has predominated in Psalms studies over the past twenty years, various

42. Susan E. Gillingham, *Psalms through the Centuries*, vol. 1, Blackwell Bible Commentaries (Oxford: Blackwell, 2008); Gillingham, *Psalms through the Centuries: A Reception History Commentary on Psalms 1–72*, Wiley Blackwell Bible Commentaries (London: Wiley, 2018); Gillingham, *Psalms through the Centuries: A Reception History Commentary on Psalms 73–151*, Wiley Blackwell Bible Commentaries (London: Wiley, 2022).

43. See also Gillingham, *A Journey of Two Psalms: The Reception of Psalms 1 and 2 in Jewish and Christian Tradition* (Oxford: Oxford University Press, 2013); Gillingham, *Jewish and Christian Approaches to the Psalms: Conflict and Convergence* (Oxford: Oxford University Press, 2013).

44. For other important *Wirkungsgeschichte* works, see the IVP Ancient Christian Commentary Series and the Bloomsbury International Theological Commentary Series. See the analysis of Calvin on the Psalms by Herman Selderhuis, *Calvin's Theology of the Psalms*, Texts and Studies in Reformation and Post-Reformation Thought (Grand Rapids: Baker Academic, 2007). Also see Luther's approach by Brian German, *Psalms of the Faithful: Luther's Early Reading of the Psalter in Canonical Context*, Studies in Historical and Systematic Theology (Bellingham, WA: Lexham, 2017).

works that do not fit neatly into these three categories deserve mention. This section focuses on individual publications that I have found to be particularly useful or significant in my own study of the Psalms.

Many psalms are naturally delightful. Others move our souls or give voice to our pain. But some psalms include troubling texts that are, at first sight, profoundly disturbing. The imprecatory psalms call for blindness to fall upon an enemy (69:23), destitution upon his family (109:9–10), or the brutal death of Babylonian babies (137:9)—troubling indeed. A few key works respond to the challenge presented by these cursing psalms, and in turn make an important contribution to hermeneutical questions and how the Psalms should be read, interpreted, and adopted. David Firth's work sets out the rhetorical dynamics of the imprecatory psalms, making clear that these are not visceral, instinctual responses to harm but are instead carefully structured responses to violence.[45] Erich Zenger's reflection on the "psalms of divine wrath" powerfully challenges Western readers to step out of their comfortable slumber and to turn their minds to the world's blatant injustices as they pray.[46] He brings a profound challenge to contemporary faith communities regarding both a lackadaisical acceptance of evil and a privatist approach to faith that no longer believes in an interventionist God. Kit Barker picks up on these themes and examines the imprecations as speech-acts.[47] He points to the divine illocutions that affirm the voice of the psalmist as right and appropriate and yet also remind the reader of his all-encompassing love, even when this does not appear to be the case. He further points to Jesus's adoption of imprecation in John's Gospel and shows that this psalmic voice does not "misfire" in the NT. Along with ably addressing this awkward genre, these studies shed light on the question of how the psalms should be read, understood, and preached today.

The word "magisterial" can be overused, but Bernd Janowski's *Arguing with God* merits the adjective.[48] This work is an important study of biblical anthropology, as much as it is a valuable reflection on themes and texts from the Psalms. Janowski considers many of the main psalmic foci: divine forsakenness, human enmity, social injustice, and sickness. Each of the main chapters ends with reflection on an "anthropological keyword" (e.g., "seeing and hearing," "revenge," "hearts and kidneys," "vitality"). The book is replete with fascinating excurses into matters such as the biblical worldview, light and darkness, and closeness to God. These reflections paint a masterful, overarching

45. David G. Firth, *Surrendering Retribution in the Psalms: Responses to Violence in the Individual Complaints*, Paternoster Biblical Monographs (Milton Keynes: Paternoster, 2005).

46. Erich Zenger, *A God of Vengeance? Understanding the Psalms of Divine Wrath* (Louisville: Westminster John Knox, 1996).

47. Kit Barker, *Imprecation as Divine Discourse: Speech Act Theory, Dual Authorship, and Theological Interpretation*, JTISup 16 (Winona Lake, IN: Eisenbrauns, 2016).

48. Bernd Janowski, *Arguing with God: A Theological Anthropology of the Psalms*, trans. Armin Siedlecki (Louisville: Westminster John Knox, 2013).

picture of the Psalms, of their theology, and of the human experience. It is an unignorable work.[49]

I have also found great edification and delight from reading Robert Alter's translation of the Psalms.[50] Although ostensibly a commentary, the comments are few, leaving the focus on the translation of the original texts into English. It is well worth reading, both for research purposes and also to warm the heart, as the Psalms always should.

49. Other such works include: William Brown, *Seeing the Psalms: A Theology of Metaphor* (Louisville: Westminster John Knox, 2002); Brueggemann, *Life of Faith*, with the seminal article "The Costly Loss of Lament"; John Eaton, *Kingship and the Psalms*, 2nd ed., Studies in Biblical Theology, 2/32 (London: SCM Press, 1986); Hans-Joachim Kraus, *Theology of the Psalms*, trans. K. Crim (Minneapolis: Augsburg, 1986); Klaus Seybold, *Introducing the Psalms*, trans. R. G. Dunphy (Edinburgh: T&T Clark, 1990); Westermann, *Praise and Lament*. In the "delightful and worth reading" category, I commend: Christoph F. Barth, *Introduction to the Psalms*, trans. R. A. Wilson (New York: Charles Scribner's, 1966); Geoffrey Grogan, *Prayer, Praise and Prophecy: A Theology of Psalms*, Mentor (Fearn: CFP, 2001); Tremper Longman, *How to Read the Psalms* (Downers Grove, IL: InterVarsity, 1988); James Mays, *The Lord Reigns: A Theological Handbook to the Psalms* (Louisville: Westminster John Knox, 1994); McCann, *Theological Introduction*; Nahum M. Sarna, *On the Book of Psalms: Exploring the Prayers of Ancient Israel* (New York: Schocken, 1993); Gordon J. Wenham, *Psalms as Torah: Reading Biblical Song Ethically*, STI (Grand Rapids: Baker Academic, 2012); Wenham, *The Psalter Reclaimed: Praying and Praising with the Psalms* (Wheaton: Crossway, 2013).

50. Robert Alter, *The Book of Psalms: A Translation with Commentary* (New York: Norton, 2007).

18

Wisdom Literature

Will Kynes

This chapter should not be in this volume, but the influence of the "Wisdom literature" category in biblical scholarship over the past century and a half justifies its inclusion, as does the significance of both the concept of wisdom and the books traditionally associated with this category: Job, Proverbs, Ecclesiastes, and the Deuterocanonical books Sirach and Wisdom of Solomon. However, biblical interpretation would be better off if the increasingly questioned "Wisdom literature" classification were abandoned altogether. Rather than illuminating our understanding of biblical wisdom or the texts traditionally included in this category, the label obscures significant features of these books and their meaning and casts long shadows across the broader landscape of the canon, its social setting, and its theology. It is merely a heuristic category, something post-Enlightenment scholars invented to aid their biblical interpretation. Yet this heuristic category has outlived its interpretive benefit, if it ever provided any. Its protracted usage hinders interpretation as it fashions the Bible into its post-Enlightenment image. "Wisdom literature" is dead.[1]

Some might say that the very existence of this chapter in this survey of current OT research proves that, to adapt Mark Twain's quip, rumors of the demise of "Wisdom literature" have been greatly exaggerated. However, "Wisdom literature" cannot joke about its own death. Its existence depends on us. Having made sense out of the chaos of infinite potential textual meaning, heuristic categories

1. I use "Wisdom literature" with scare quotes to indicate its status as a scholarly construct. Other derivative constructs, such as the "Wisdom tradition" and "Wisdom theology," are prefaced with capitalized "Wisdom." The *concept* of wisdom is spelled with a lowercase letter.

are tenacious. Their loss, like any other bereavement, inspires denial. Sometimes, though, reading an obituary of the deceased will move a mourner from denial to acceptance.[2] My ultimate aim is to bring life. I propose an alternative approach to wisdom in the Bible and the so-called Wisdom books, one that pries them free from the distorting constraints of "Wisdom literature" to bring new life to their meaning within the broader canon.

The Attraction of "Wisdom Literature"

The "Wisdom literature" label emerged in biblical studies and continues to be employed by some biblical interpreters because it captures something of what is going on in the books it includes, and it enables broader conclusions to be drawn about their meaning, purpose, and setting. However, is that capturing a captivity, and are those conclusions more limiting than liberating?

Interest in Wisdom

The Hebrew word for "wisdom" (חָכְמָה, *ḥokmâ*) refers broadly to "a high-degree of knowledge and skill in any domain." It appears across the HB, extending from women spinning goats' hair into linen (Exod. 35:25–26; cf. Prov. 31:24) to God creating the world (Jer. 10:12; Prov. 3:19).[3] Its semantic range includes "skill," "learning," "perceptiveness," "cleverness," "prudence," and "sagacity."[4] Ultimately, "wisdom aims at a successful life and proves itself to be a life skill."[5] However, the nature of this wisdom, including how it defines success and the skills it advocates in pursuit of that end, is determined by which texts shape our understanding and how we allow them to do so.

Proverbs, Ecclesiastes, and Job undoubtedly show an interest in the subject matter of wisdom. The word חָכְמָה and its cognates appear in these books more than in any others in the HB, and the term is joined by a range of other related vocabulary.[6] To read these books well and to understand wisdom, interpreters must closely attend to the texts' reflections on this concept.

Proverbs indicates its interest in wisdom early and often, mentioning חָכְמָה more than any other biblical book. After the attribution to Solomon, the king

2. Will Kynes, *An Obituary for "Wisdom Literature": The Birth, Death, and Intertextual Reintegration of a Biblical Corpus* (Oxford: Oxford University Press, 2019).

3. Michael V. Fox, *Proverbs 1–9*, AB 18A (New York: Doubleday, 2000), 32.

4. Fox, *Proverbs 1–9*, 33.

5. Markus Witte, "Literary Genres of Old Testament Wisdom," in *The Oxford Handbook of Wisdom and the Bible*, ed. Will Kynes (New York: Oxford University Press, 2021), 359. For extensive analysis of the concept of wisdom, see chaps. 1–19 of *The Oxford Handbook of Wisdom and the Bible*, hereafter *Handbook of Wisdom*.

6. R. N. Whybray, *The Intellectual Tradition in the Old Testament*, BZAW 135 (Berlin: De Gruyter, 1974), 15–31.

renowned for his wisdom (Prov. 1:1; cf. 1 Kings 4:30), the prologue (Prov. 1:2–7) expresses the book's purpose, beginning with providing wisdom (v. 2). The personification of wisdom develops across Prov. 1–9 (1:20–33; 3:13–18; 4:5–9; 7:4; 8:1–36; 9:1–6) and shapes the perception of the sentence literature in the remainder of the book, making each wise choice an embrace of personified wisdom rather than personified folly (9:1–6, 13–18).[7]

Ecclesiastes uses חָכְמָה and its cognates fifty-two times in twelve chapters, but its depiction of wisdom is more fraught than that of Proverbs. Though wisdom is a key concept for Qoheleth, he denigrates it as הֶבֶל (*hebel*, "vanity"; 2:15) and criticizes a fundamental thesis of the "Wisdom movement": that wisdom, not wickedness, leads to life (Eccles. 8:12; cf. Prov. 8:35).[8] Yet the epilogue praises Qoheleth's wisdom (Eccles. 12:9–11).

Job and his friends debate who is wise (11:6; 12:2, 12; 13:5; 15:8; 26:3; 32:9), though none but arrogant Elihu (33:33) claims wisdom for himself. Following the breakdown of their dialogue, a majestic poem (Job 28) declares wisdom to be a divine possession (vv. 23–27), inaccessible to humans (vv. 13, 21), which the divine speeches implicitly reinforce (38:36–37). The poem concludes by associating wisdom with fearing the Lord and turning away from evil (28:28), two traits in the book's superlative description of Job's character (1:1) echoed by God (1:8).

Canonical Distinctions

Proverbs, Ecclesiastes, and Job, then, are united in their interest in wisdom. The label "Wisdom literature" also responds to their apparent lack of interest in Israel's history, law, and covenants. These texts have an international flavor that many consider unparalleled in other biblical texts. The comparison of Solomon's wisdom (1 Kings 4:30 [5:10 MT]) to that of the people of the east and Egypt gives the latter an implicit value difficult to imagine being offered to foreign priests or prophets.[9] Proverbs explicitly incorporates the wisdom of two foreigners, Agur and King Lemuel (30:1; 31:1), and likely draws directly on the Egyptian Instruction of Amenemope (22:17–24:22).[10] Job and his friends are foreigners from the east (Job 1:3), reflecting that area's reputation for wisdom. Ecclesiastes and the dialogue section of Job avoid the divine name of Israel's God (apart from Job 12:9), instead preferring more general terminology, such as אֱלֹהִים (*'ĕlōhîm*, God) or שַׁדַּי (*šadday*, the Almighty).

7. William P. Brown, *Wisdom's Wonder: Character, Creation, and Crisis in the Bible's Wisdom Literature* (Grand Rapids: Eerdmans, 2014), 64–66.

8. The verse from Ecclesiastes claims that sinners prolong their lives, which contradicts a major tenet of wisdom as demonstrated in Prov. 8:35. See Hans Wilhelm Hertzberg, *Der Prediger*, Kommentar zum Alten Testament 17/4–5 (Gütersloh: Mohn, 1963), 233–34.

9. Tremper Longman III, "Theology of Wisdom," in Kynes, *Handbook of Wisdom*, 390.

10. Michael V. Fox, *Proverbs 10–31*, AYB 18B (New Haven: Yale University Press, 2009), 707–33, 753–69.

Shared Traits

This canonical distinction associates the "Wisdom literature" with a broader discourse surrounding wisdom in the ancient world. The nature of this intercultural discourse, many argue, prevents its orientation around the distinctive features of Israelite belief and practice. Instead, it relates to common beliefs, frequently characterized by traits such as humanism, internationalism, secularism, empiricism, and general (rather than special) revelation. For example, Douglas Miller echoes many of those traits in his attempt to uncover the attributes inspiring the widespread "intuition" that Job, Proverbs, and Ecclesiastes are "acknowledged 'prototypes'" of a "Wisdom" category. He proposes three shared traits: instructive rhetoric, realized eschatology that advocates for a successful life in the present, and experiential epistemology.[11]

Modern readers are not alone in recognizing similar shared traits among the "Wisdom" books. For example, Theodore of Mopsuestia (d. 428 CE) was condemned by the Fifth General Council (act 4.72) for believing Proverbs and Ecclesiastes were the products of Solomon's human experience, not divine inspiration, and a passage in the Tosefta (Yadayim 2.14) appears to agree regarding Ecclesiastes, proclaiming, "Ecclesiastes does not make the hands unclean because it is [merely] Solomon's wisdom." This anticipates those who define "Wisdom literature" by its humanistic "non-revelatory speech."[12]

Even Zoltán Schwáb's canonical and theological reading of Proverbs can only qualify, not fully reject, the book's secularism, universalism, eudaemonism, and individualism.[13] He even employs the distinctiveness of "Wisdom literature" as a "mode of discourse," with its interests in the individual and "abstract level of discussion," to explain apparent theological contrasts between Proverbs and the rest of the canon, such as its minimal interest in Israel's history.[14]

Instructional intent, the trait most said to unite the "Wisdom literature," is less controversial. Clearly, these books intend to teach. But which do not? Are Job or Ecclesiastes more oriented toward instruction than Deuteronomy? A didacticism defined broadly enough to include these books would also apply to every biblical book.[15]

11. Douglas B. Miller, "Wisdom in the Canon: Discerning the Early Intuition," in *Was There a Wisdom Tradition? New Prospects in Israelite Wisdom Studies*, ed. Mark Sneed, AIL 23 (Atlanta: SBL Press, 2015), 90–95, 109; cf. James L. Crenshaw, *Old Testament Wisdom: An Introduction*, 3rd ed. (Louisville: Westminster John Knox, 2010), 50–51, 207–28.

12. James L. Crenshaw, "Wisdom," in *Old Testament Form Criticism*, ed. J. Hayes (San Antonio: Trinity University Press, 1974), 226. See Kynes, *Obituary for "Wisdom Literature,"* 73–75.

13. Zoltán S. Schwáb, *Toward an Interpretation of the Book of Proverbs: Selfishness and Secularity Reconsidered*, JTISup 7 (Winona Lake, IN: Eisenbrauns, 2013), see, e.g., 66–67, 176, 209, 241.

14. Schwáb, *Book of Proverbs*, 67.

15. John J. Collins, "Epilogue: Genre Analysis and the Dead Sea Scrolls," *DSD* 17, no. 3 (2010): 429.

Comparisons within the Category

Grouping Proverbs, Ecclesiastes, and Job together has inspired valuable comparisons. For example, Job and Ecclesiastes challenge the confidence that Proverbs displays in the blessings of wise living,[16] and Ecclesiastes combines the didactically oriented form of Proverbs with the reflective, problem-oriented content of Job.[17]

However, comparison within the category also exposes cracks in the category's foundations. Wisdom may be fundamental in these books, but scholarly reflection on Job and Ecclesiastes as "Wisdom literature" challenges their definitions of wisdom and thus the category's coherence. Job "questions the wisdom tradition to such an extent that it breaks outside its bounds."[18] The "uninhibited parade of all that negates" the "Wisdom movement" in Job[19] makes the book, at most, "anti-wisdom wisdom."[20] Ecclesiastes, similarly, "strikes at the foundation of the sages' universe."[21] It may be "wisdom at its limits,"[22] but readers who consider it "instructive wisdom literature" are "systematically disappointed."[23] The book is arguably the "reverse of 'wisdom'"[24] and perhaps the "end" of the movement.[25] Since Job and Ecclesiastes reside at the borderland of the purported "Wisdom tradition," questioning or rejecting many of its tenants, the "Wisdom" classification provides limited interpretive guidance.

Literary Form

Katharine Dell argues that the proverb form is "the mainspring of the biblical wisdom enterprise."[26] This form is prevalent in Proverbs and appears through-

16. Johannes Marböck, "Zwischen Erfahrung, Systematik und Bekenntnis: Zu Eigenart und Bedeutung der alttestamentlichen Weisheitsliteratur," in *Weisheit und Frömmigkeit: Studien zur alttestamentlichen Literatur der Spätzeit*, ed. Johannes Marböck, Österreichische biblische Studien (Frankfurt: Peter Lang, 2006), 201–14.

17. Thomas Krüger, *Qoheleth: A Commentary*, trans. O. C. Dean, Hermeneia (Minneapolis: Fortress, 2004), 11.

18. Katharine J. Dell, *The Book of Job as Sceptical Literature*, BZAW 197 (Berlin: De Gruyter, 1991), 83.

19. David Wolfers, *Deep Things out of Darkness: The Book of Job—Essays and a New Translation* (Kampen: Kok Pharos, 1995), 49.

20. Marvin H. Pope, *Job*, 3rd ed., AB 15 (Garden City, NY: Doubleday, 1973), lxviii.

21. James L. Crenshaw, *Ecclesiastes: A Commentary*, OTL (Philadelphia: Westminster, 1987), 23.

22. Katharine J. Dell, *Interpreting Ecclesiastes: Readers Old and New* (Winona Lake, IN: Eisenbrauns, 2013), 11–12.

23. Krüger, *Qoheleth*, 11.

24. Svend Holm-Nielsen, "The Book of Ecclesiastes and the Interpretation of It in Jewish and Christian Theology," *ASTI* 10 (1975–76): 51.

25. Martin A. Shields, *The End of Wisdom: A Reappraisal of the Historical and Canonical Function of Ecclesiastes* (Winona Lake, IN: Eisenbrauns, 2006), 6.

26. Katharine J. Dell, "Deciding the Boundaries of 'Wisdom': Applying the Concept of Family Resemblance," in Sneed, *Was There a Wisdom Tradition?*, 146. Given the diverse usage of the term מָשָׁל (*māšāl*), from Balaam's "oracle" (Num. 23:7) to Isaiah's "taunt" against the king of Babylon (Isa. 14:4) and Ezekiel's eagle "allegory" (Ezek. 17:2), it cannot simply be

out Ecclesiastes and Job, though all three books also incorporate other forms. Therefore, in his oft-cited attempt to define "Wisdom literature," James Crenshaw claims, "Formally, wisdom consists of proverbial sentence or instruction, debate, intellectual reflection."[27] This just restates the problem as Crenshaw merely enumerates the diverse literary forms employed by the "Wisdom" books.[28]

Social Setting

This circular building of the defining features of the "Wisdom" category on the assumption of the category's existence extends to arguments regarding its social setting. One of the category's attractions is its facilitation of historical conjecture about this subject. "Wisdom literature" is considered the product of a distinct class of "the wise" (חָכָם, *ḥākām*), as reconstructed from Jer. 18:18.[29] This verse supports theories regarding "wisdom schools" and scribal activity.[30] Ecclesiastes and Job are then considered to be the result of a purported "crisis of wisdom" as sages reflected on the failure of wisdom to guarantee success.[31]

This offers a satisfying historical explanation for the traits the "Wisdom" books share and the internecine debate between them. However, more explanatory weight is put on both this verse from Jeremiah and this "Wisdom tradition" than either can bear. Jeremiah 18:18 does not tell us which, if any, texts "the wise" composed or their theological views. The parallel construction in Ezek. 7:26 replaces "the wise" (חָכָם) with "elders" (זְקֵנִים, *zəqēnîm*), suggesting that the term may not have a technical sense.[32] Further, "the wise" are never mentioned among lists of officials or other groups (e.g., 1 Kings 4:1–6; 2 Kings 24:10–16; 1 Chron. 28:1), and Israelite royal counselors are never called wise.[33] Recent studies reveal a more integrated scribal setting, in which scribes produced various genres and even mixed them.[34] Stuart Weeks, followed by Mark Sneed, argues that evidence

translated as "proverb" or considered central to Proverbs or "Wisdom literature" more broadly. See Jacqueline Vayntrub, *Beyond Orality: Biblical Poetry on Its Own Terms* (London: Routledge, 2019). However, whether there was a distinct Hebrew term or not, the sentence literature in Prov. 10–29 does primarily consist of proverbs or aphorisms in two-line parallel form.

27. Crenshaw, *Old Testament Wisdom*, 12.

28. Stuart Weeks, *An Introduction to the Study of Wisdom Literature* (New York: T&T Clark, 2010), 142–43.

29. R. B. Y. Scott, "Priesthood, Prophecy, Wisdom, and the Knowledge of God," *JBL* 80, no. 1 (1961): 5.

30. André Lemaire, "The Sage in School and Temple," in *The Sage in Israel and the Ancient Near East*, ed. John G. Gammie and Leo G. Perdue (Winona Lake, IN: Eisenbrauns, 1990), 165–81.

31. Hans Heinrich Schmid, *Wesen und Geschichte der Weisheit: Eine Untersuchung zur altorientalischen und israelitischen Weisheitsliteratur*, BZAW 101 (Berlin: Töpelmann, 1966), 186–96.

32. Kynes, *Obituary for "Wisdom Literature,"* 76–77.

33. Whybray, *Intellectual Tradition*, 17.

34. Mark Sneed, *The Social World of the Sages: An Introduction to Israelite and Jewish Wisdom Literature* (Minneapolis: Fortress, 2015), 67–182.

is lacking for a purported class of "wise men" participating in an international "Wisdom movement."[35]

The Problem

The problem with the "Wisdom literature" category is not that its generalizations are not true to some degree. Rather, like all generalizations, they overshadow the complexities of each text and their conceptions of wisdom. The "Wisdom literature" label is particularly pernicious because its generalizations associate these texts with traits that accord closely with what modern interpreters value. As Crenshaw says, "Wisdom literature" has "stood largely as a mirror image of the scholar painting her portrait."[36] If anything, "Wisdom literature" is too attractive. To encompass its diverse contents, scholars move to a level of abstraction that leaves ample room for their own views. This appeal derives from the category's origins.

The Origins of "Wisdom Literature"

The "Wisdom" category does not go back to ancient Jewish and Christian interpretation. Early readers grouped these books in various ways for different reasons, but no grouping directly parallels the modern "Wisdom" category. Three early examples are the Solomonic corpus (Proverbs, Ecclesiastes, and Song of Songs), the Greek canon's poetry section (which adds Job, Psalms, and frequently Sirach and Wisdom of Solomon), and the Jewish Sifrei Emet collection (Psalms, Job, and Proverbs).[37] These different collections reflect diverse criteria of inclusion, categories that are quantitatively and qualitatively different from "Wisdom literature."

A distinct "Wisdom literature" corpus (which included Job but not Song of Songs and Psalms) does not appear until 1851 in Johann Friedrich Bruch's *Wisdom Teaching of the Hebrews: A Contribution to the History of Philosophy*.[38] Understanding why Bruch developed this category reveals why it continues to be so influential, and so damaging, in biblical scholarship. In nineteenth-century Germany, many Christians held a low view of the OT. Kant claimed that it was characterized by dogmatic faith, theocratic institutions, legal coercion, and exclusion. He argued that Judaism prepared the way for Christianity as "a purely

35. Stuart Weeks, *Early Israelite Wisdom*, Oxford Theological Monographs (Oxford: Oxford University Press, 1994); Mark Sneed, "Is the 'Wisdom Tradition' a Tradition?," *CBQ* 73, no. 1 (2011): 50–71; Sneed, *Was There a Wisdom Tradition?*

36. James L. Crenshaw, "Prolegomenon," in *Studies in Ancient Israelite Wisdom*, ed. James L. Crenshaw, The Library of Biblical Studies (New York: Ktav, 1976), 3.

37. Kynes, *Obituary*, 60–81.

38. Johann Friedrich Bruch, *Weisheits-Lehre der Hebräer: Ein Beitrag zur Geschichte der Philosophie* (Strasbourg: Treuttel & Würtz, 1851).

moral religion" only after it had been enlightened by Greek thought.[39] Bruch, however, attempted to find enlightenment within the OT. He writes, "It seemed to me that the breath of the non-theocratic spirit, present in the Old Testament's multiple texts, ought to have made one aware that—even among the Hebrews—there was no lack of men who found no satisfaction in the religious institutions of their nation. These men therefore sought other ways—namely, the way of free thinking—to gain answers about the questions that moved them and to seek their spirit's rest."[40]

Developing "Wisdom literature" as the "universalistic, humanistic, philosophical" collection, as Franz Delitzsch characterized it at the time,[41] was Bruch's attempt to resolve Christianity's struggle with its Jewish roots. Delitzsch adopted the category from Bruch, whom he claimed was the first to call attention to it. However, Delitzsch says that Bruch was "mistaken in placing [Wisdom] in an indifferent and even hostile relation to the national law and the national cultus, which [Bruch] compares to the relation of Christian philosophy to orthodox theology."[42] Yet still today independence from Israel's law, cult, and history continues to be a defining feature of "Wisdom literature." As Roland Murphy observes, the "most striking characteristic" uniting current definitions of "Wisdom literature" is "the absence of what one normally considers as typically Israelite and Jewish."[43] Why was a category built around the absence of Israelite religion? Might this focus have blinded us to evidence of Israel's law, covenants, history, and revelation in these texts?

The traits commonly associated with "Wisdom literature"—universalism, humanism, rationalism, secularism, individualism, and skepticism—bear a suspicious resemblance to the post-Enlightenment context from which the category emerged. This appears to be another example of scholars looking down into the well and seeing their own reflections. The anti-Jewish perspectives shimmering at the bottom of that well are concerning. While scholars do not adopt the "Wisdom" category for those reasons today, the early influence remains. Interpreters have long struggled to integrate the "Wisdom literature" with the theology of the HB.[44] In fact, in the first volume of Gerhard von Rad's *Old Testament Theology*, "Wisdom literature" is simply tacked on as "Israel's answer" to YHWH.[45] This

39. Immanuel Kant, *Religion within the Limits of Reason Alone*, trans. Theodore M. Greene and Hoyt H. Hudson, 2nd ed. (New York: Harper & Row, 1960), 116–18. A translation of *Die Religion innerhalb der Grenzen der blossen Vernunft* (Königsberg: Nicolovius, 1793).

40. Bruch, *Weisheits-Lehre*, ix–x (my trans.).

41. Franz Delitzsch, *Das Buch Iob* (Leipzig: Dörfling & Franke, 1864), 5.

42. Franz Delitzsch, *Biblical Commentary on the Proverbs of Solomon*, trans. M. G. Easton, 2 vols., Clark's Foreign Theological Library 43, 47 (Edinburgh: T&T Clark, 1874), 1:46.

43. Roland E. Murphy, *The Tree of Life: An Exploration of Biblical Wisdom Literature*, 3rd ed. (Grand Rapids: Eerdmans, 2002), 1.

44. R. B. Y. Scott, "The Study of Wisdom Literature," *Int* 24, no. 1 (1970): 39.

45. Gerhard von Rad, *Old Testament Theology*, 2 vols., OTL (Louisville: Westminster John Knox, 2001), 1:355, 418–59.

tension was baked into the category from the beginning, since apparent disregard for theology was the category's primary defining criterion.

The "Wisdom" category was created to fulfill post-Enlightenment scholarly desires, which it has since perpetuated and magnified. Since its inception, interpreters have demonstrated a tendency to apply the "Wisdom" label to "any form of knowledge that is recognized as good" by modern academics rather than ancient Israelites.[46] A century later, John Rylaarsdam, for example, echoes Bruch's sentiments without indicating any knowledge of his work, imagining the "Wisdom movement" beginning "as a 'revolt' of a free-thinking, empirically minded element of 'scientists' against the tribalistic and irrational ideas of religion characteristic of pre-Exilic Hebrews."[47]

The Effects of "Wisdom Literature" on the Interpretation of Biblical Books

To make things worse, the "Wisdom literature" category limits our understanding of Proverbs, Ecclesiastes, and Job to this philosophical conception of wisdom and obscures their important connections with other texts and ideas across the canon. In a vicious cycle, this limited understanding then reinforces a limited grasp of the concept of wisdom.

Though comparing Proverbs, Ecclesiastes, and Job to one another within "Wisdom literature" has illuminated various features of these books and the concept of wisdom, exclusively classifying them this way distorts their interpretation. In other words, the comparison can be helpful when considered as just one of the multiple genre groupings that may illuminate certain features of texts, but it becomes a hindrance when it is treated as an exclusive taxonomic category that defines what these texts *are*.[48] After discussing this interpretive approach's detrimental effects, I suggest alternative avenues for interpretation that have emerged in recent scholarship as the influence of "Wisdom literature" wanes.

Canonical Separation

The "Wisdom" category leads to canonical separation. Craig Bartholomew explicitly states the problematic working assumption of current scholarship: "Since Ecclesiastes is an OT wisdom text, Proverbs and Job provide the immediate intertextual context for reading it."[49] If the interpretation of these books starts from the

46. John J. Collins, "Response to George Nickelsburg" (paper presented at the annual meeting of the Society of Biblical Literature, Chicago, 1994), 2.

47. John Coert Rylaarsdam, *Revelation in Jewish Wisdom Literature* (Chicago: University of Chicago Press, 1946), viii–ix.

48. Kynes, *Obituary for "Wisdom Literature,"* 12–15.

49. Craig G. Bartholomew, *Ecclesiastes*, Baker Commentary on the Old Testament Wisdom and Psalms (Grand Rapids: Baker Academic, 2009), 84.

presupposition that "Wisdom" is a "third strand of Hebrew culture" next to Torah and Prophecy,[50] it inevitably (and circularly) reinforces that presupposition, as the interplay of those three books circumscribes and determines their meaning while fortifying their perceived distinctiveness. Thus, Michael Fox claims that "Wisdom literature" is "human in its particulars and in its workings" and "offers itself as a complete and self-contained moral system." Accordingly, he claims that Proverbs "shows no interest in Yahweh's revealed Torah" and little regard for prophetic revelation.[51] Yet Bernd Schipper demonstrates the significance of the Torah in the book.[52] Similarly, before the "Wisdom" category's interpretive dominance, Job's airing of the doctrine of retribution drew it into conversation with texts across the HB.[53] David Clines, however, acknowledges Deuteronomy as the preeminent exponent of retribution but takes Job's questioning of the doctrine as solely a confrontation of "the ideology of Proverbs."[54] Thus the category cordons off its contents from the broader canonical discourse.

Theological Abstraction

Canonical separation contributes to theological abstraction. The diverse contents of the "Wisdom" corpus consistently produce vague, abstract, and potentially all-encompassing definitions of its distinctive features. Alastair Hunter, for example, acknowledges the "glaring omission" of Job from his efforts to identify "Wisdom literature" on formal linguistic grounds but attempts to satisfy the scholarly consensus that it belongs in the category by considering "the underlying perspectives which emerge from a consideration in broader terms of what these books are concerned with."[55] These perspectives, he claims, are the universalism, humanism, naturalism, and intellectualism the books share. This list well summarizes the post-Enlightenment approach to reality when Job was first associated with the constructed category of "Wisdom literature."

When applied to Job, this approach directs attention to abstract philosophical reflections on the nature of suffering rather than to existential questions such as "Why must I suffer?"[56] Many associate Ecclesiastes with philosophy or, at

50. Robert Gordis, *Koheleth, the Man and His World: A Study of Ecclesiastes*, 3rd ed. (New York: Schocken, 1968), 16.

51. Fox, *Proverbs 10–31*, 946, 947.

52. Bernd Schipper, "When Wisdom Is Not Enough! The Discourse on Wisdom and Torah and the Composition of the Book of Proverbs," in *Wisdom and Torah: The Reception of "Torah" in the Wisdom Literature of the Second Temple Period*, ed. Bernd U. Schipper and D. Andrew Teeter, JSJSup 163 (Leiden: Brill, 2013), 55–80.

53. W. T. Davison, *The Wisdom-Literature of the Old Testament* (London: Kelly, 1894), 79; Edouard Dhorme, *A Commentary on the Book of Job*, trans. Harold Knight (London: Nelson, 1967), cxxxvii, cxxxix.

54. David J. A. Clines, *Job*, 3 vols., WBC 17, 18A, 18B (Nashville: Nelson, 1989), 1:lxi–lxii.

55. Alastair Hunter, *Wisdom Literature* (London: SCM, 2006), 23.

56. Claus Westermann, *The Structure of the Book of Job: A Form-Critical Analysis*, trans. Charles A. Muenchow (Philadelphia: Fortress, 1981), 1–2.

least, an analytical methodology that trusts in experience and observation.[57] Taking this theological abstraction to its extreme, Hans-Peter Müller claims that Qoheleth operates according to a different religion with a distinct, impersonal God.[58] Finally, in contrast to the "crisis of wisdom" in Job and Ecclesiastes, scholars characterize the sages of Proverbs as "dogmatic, rigid, or removed from the human condition," presenting "a wisdom that is removed from reality and is more theoretical than practical."[59] This "more abstract, theoretical level," as Schwáb claims, "has some parallels with the nineteenth century understanding of wisdom as 'philosophical.'"[60] In each case, "Wisdom literature" encourages an abstraction that associates the books with the philosophical interests of the interpreters, raising questions about how accurately these interpretations reflect the original authors' interests.

Hermeneutical Limitation

Theological abstraction combined with canonical separation leads to hermeneutical limitation. The book of Job participates in multiple genres—including "wisdom, prophecy, psalm, drama, contest, lament, theodicy, history, and allegory"—and so strains most obviously against the constraints of the "Wisdom" category, which has "hedged in" and "unduly restricted" its interpretation.[61] Jacques Ellul similarly warns of how reading Qoheleth as a philosopher within the "Wisdom" genre can strip the book of "the essential distinctives of Israel's belief."[62] This includes an inability to reconcile Qoheleth's reflections with the epilogue's endorsement of obeying God's commands.[63] Even single words may be misunderstood. When interpreting the word אֶרֶץ (*'ereṣ*, land) in Prov. 2:21–22, Fox demonstrates the category's interpretive sway by arguing that, despite the context's Deuteronomic resonance, the word refers to "this world" and not to the land of Israel, supporting his conclusion with the circular argument that "concern for the Land of Israel is absent from biblical Wisdom literature."[64] According to Bartholomew, the assumptions that "Wisdom literature" develops

57. Roland E. Murphy, *Ecclesiastes*, WBC 23A (Dallas: Word, 1992), lxiii; C. L. Seow, *Ecclesiastes*, AB 18C (New York: Doubleday, 1997), 54.

58. Hans-Peter Müller, "Neige der althebräishcen 'Weisheit': Zum Denken Qohäläts," *ZAW* 90, no. 2 (1978): 238–64.

59. Anne W. Stewart, "Wisdom's Imagination: Moral Reasoning and the Book of Proverbs," *JSOT* 40, no. 3 (2016): 352–53.

60. Schwáb, *Book of Proverbs*, 241.

61. Wolfers, *Deep Things*, 50–51; Timothy Jay Johnson, *Now My Eye Sees You: Unveiling an Apocalyptic Job*, HBM 24 (Sheffield: Sheffield Phoenix, 2009), 77; James Edward Harding, "The Book of Job as Metaprophecy," *Studies in Religion/Sciences religieuses* 39, no. 4 (2010): 525.

62. Jacques Ellul, *The Reason for Being: A Meditation on Ecclesiastes*, trans. Joyce M. Hanks (Grand Rapids: Eerdmans, 1990), 25, 27.

63. Michael V. Fox, *A Time to Tear Down and a Time to Build Up: A Rereading of Ecclesiastes* (Grand Rapids: Eerdmans, 1999), 374–75.

64. Fox, *Proverbs 1–9*, 123.

from secular to religious and is separated from the Torah and Prophets have obscured the moral and religious significance of terms in Ecclesiastes such as מִשְׁפָּט (*mišpāṭ*, judgment; 11:9; cf. 3:17) and חטא (*ḥṭʾ*, to sin; 5:6 [5:5 MT]; cf. 2:26; 7:26; 8:12).[65] The single perspective of "Wisdom literature" limits and therefore distorts interpretation.

An Alternative to "Wisdom Literature": Broadening Hermeneutical Horizons

Rather than reading the "Wisdom" books solely through this lens, incorporating the various reading approaches throughout reception history better reflects the depth and complexity of these books.[66] We can imagine texts as stars forming different genre constellations from various perspectives in three-dimensional space rather than from a two-dimensional earthly vantage point.[67] This multiperspectival approach would benefit the reading of any text in the canon and beyond because no genre fully comprehends the texts associated with it. "Wisdom literature" particularly needs this type of reevaluation due to the lingering ideological influences from its origin.

Ecclesiastes beyond "Wisdom Literature"

Before Bruch's seminal work, W. M. L. de Wette highlighted Ecclesiastes's agonized search for meaning in response to life's *Unglück* (misfortune), a search shared with Job and the lament psalms.[68] Earlier, the ancient Solomonic collection responded to the royal garb of the book's reflections,[69] while the poetry collection recognized its formal characteristics.[70] Interpreters, both ancient and modern, have noted the features it shares with other texts and genres.[71] Interpreting the book more fully requires that these constellations be blended together, along with others, such as Torah, history, apocalyptic, diatribe, and frame narrative. The abundance of genres that contribute to the book's meaning has even led to Qoheleth being

65. Bartholomew, *Ecclesiastes*, 90.

66. Will Kynes, "Genre as Reception: A Multidimensional Network Approach," *JBR* 10, no. 1 (2023): 93–121.

67. Kynes, *An Obituary for "Wisdom Literature,"* 107–46.

68. W. M. L. de Wette, "Beytrag zur Charakteristik des Hebraismus," in *Studien*, ed. Carl Daub and Friedrich Creuzer (Heidelberg: Mohr & Zimmer, 1807), 3:241–312.

69. Y. V. Koh, *Royal Autobiography in the Book of Qoheleth*, BZAW 369 (Berlin: De Gruyter, 2006).

70. Oswald Loretz, "Poetry and Prose in the Book of Qoheleth (1:1–3:22; 7:23–8:1; 9:6–10; 12:8–14)," in *Verse in Ancient Near Eastern Prose*, ed. Johannes C. de Moor and Wilfred G. E. Watson (Neukirchen-Vluyn: Neukirchener, 1993), 155–89.

71. Kynes, *Obituary for "Wisdom Literature,"* 190–217; Katharine Dell and Will Kynes, eds., *Reading Ecclesiastes Intertextually*, LHBOTS 587 (London: Bloomsbury T&T Clark, 2014).

characterized as an "assembler," not merely of wise sayings (Eccles. 12:9–10) but of genres.[72] The book's meaning is more than any single grouping can encompass. It cannot be comprehended without these genres since each illuminates significant features of the book.

Job beyond "Wisdom Literature"

In premodern interpretation, Job was grouped not merely with the Sifrei Emet and poetry collections but also with Torah, history, prophecy, and dramatic and epic texts in the canon and beyond. Modern interpretation has resurrected a number of those genre proposals and suggested that the book's author adapted other genres, including dramatizing lament[73] and lawsuit,[74] or transformed prophecy into "metaprophecy."[75] For some, the author's manipulation of genre becomes a genre itself, a meta-genre, such as parody[76] or polyphonic dialogue.[77] "Wisdom literature" is increasingly questioned as the book's genre.[78] Instead, many categorize it as sui generis.[79] If Job is sui generis, however, this is due not to the book's isolation but to its dense textual interconnections, which reveal its theological depth and poetic complexity.[80]

Proverbs beyond "Wisdom Literature"

The emphasis on wisdom in Proverbs guarantees this topic a prominent role in any interpretation of the book. However, other texts included in that interpretation will affect how the nuance and complexity of Proverbs and its depiction of wisdom are understood.[81] For example, Sifrei Emet highlights the book's emphasis on righteousness.[82] The poetry collection underscores the contribution

72. T. Anthony Perry, *The Book of Ecclesiastes (Qohelet) and the Path to Joyous Living* (Cambridge: Cambridge University Press, 2015), 203–4.

73. Westermann, *Book of Job*.

74. S. H. Scholnick, "Lawsuit Drama in the Book of Job" (PhD diss., Brandeis University, 1975); cf. F. Rachel Magdalene, *On the Scales of Righteousness: Neo-Babylonian Trial Law and the Book of Job*, BJS 348 (Providence: Brown University, 2007).

75. Harding, "Metaprophecy."

76. Dell, *Book of Job*, 109–57.

77. Carol A. Newsom, *The Book of Job: A Contest of Moral Imaginations* (Oxford: Oxford University Press, 2003).

78. Dell, *Book of Job*, 63–88; Wolfers, *Deep Things*, 47–51; Johnson, *Now My Eye Sees You*, 15–23.

79. Pope, *Job*, xxx; C. L. Seow, *Job 1–21: Interpretation and Commentary*, Illuminations (Grand Rapids: Eerdmans, 2013), 61.

80. Kynes, *Obituary for "Wisdom Literature,"* 190–217; Katharine Dell and Will Kynes, eds., *Reading Job Intertextually*, LHBOTS 574 (New York: Bloomsbury, 2013).

81. Peter T. H. Hatton, *Contradiction in the Book of Proverbs: The Deep Waters of Counsel* (Aldershot: Ashgate, 2008), 17–45.

82. Sun Myung Lyu, *Righteousness in the Book of Proverbs*, FAT 2/55 (Tübingen: Mohr Siebeck, 2012), 115–33, 135.

of its poetic form to its message.[83] And the Solomonic collection ties it with Song of Songs.[84] Further, the association with Solomon invites the variegated description of his wisdom in 1 Kings 1–11 into our reading of Proverbs, intertwining wisdom with political, legal, and cultic acumen and creating a more intricate intertextual network. Scholars have explored this network by grouping Proverbs with political narratives, legal texts conveying ethical paraenesis, and texts depicting the construction of cultic spaces with their psalmic liturgies.[85] As Alice Ogden Bellis concludes her recent survey of Proverbs scholarship, "Paradigms are on the verge of shifting. And Proverbs is being viewed as much more central to the Hebrew Bible."[86] The rest of the HB is now being viewed as more central to Proverbs as well.

Other Texts: "Wisdom Influence"?

Those familiar with "Wisdom" scholarship are likely to object that interpreters have long noted similarities between Proverbs, Ecclesiastes, and Job and other texts ranging from Genesis to Esther,[87] including a distinct category of "Wisdom psalms,"[88] and even NT texts such as James.[89] Here the "Wisdom literature" category's effect may be most pernicious. More and more texts are pulled into its sway, enabled by its abstract definition and motivated by its attractive post-Enlightenment traits. As the term "Wisdom influence" suggests, when those texts are compared to Proverbs, Ecclesiastes, and Job, it is not to explore the literary or theological depth and complexity of the "Wisdom" books but to conform other books throughout the Bible and the ANE to the universalism, humanism, rationalism, and so forth of "Wisdom literature." That leads to statements such as "Wisdom thinking was in the main stream of biblical literary production from whence its style and ideas radiated throughout biblical writings."[90] It inspires Sneed to claim that "scribal scholars" were responsible not only for producing the

83. Anne W. Stewart, *Poetic Ethics in Proverbs: Wisdom Literature and the Shaping of the Moral Self* (Cambridge: Cambridge University Press, 2016).

84. Kathryn Imray, "Love Is (Strong as) Death: Reading the Song of Songs through Proverbs 1–9," *CBQ* 75, no. 4 (2013): 649–65; Martin Ravndal Hauge, *Solomon the Lover and the Shape of the Song of Songs*, HBM 77 (Sheffield: Sheffield Phoenix, 2015), 166–73.

85. Kynes, *Obituary for "Wisdom Literature,"* 222–43. See also Katharine Dell and Will Kynes, eds., *Reading Proverbs Intertextually*, LHBOTS 629 (New York: Bloomsbury, 2019).

86. Alice Ogden Bellis, "Proverbs in Recent Research," *CurBR* 20, no. 2 (2022): 145.

87. Gerhard von Rad, "Josephsgeschichte und ältere Chokma," in *Congress Volume: Copenhagen 1953*, VTSup 1 (Leiden: Brill, 1953), 120–27; Shemaryahu Talmon, "'Wisdom' in the Book of Esther," *VT* 13, no. 4 (1963): 419–55.

88. Kynes, *Obituary for "Wisdom Literature,"* 44–47.

89. See Mariam Kamell Kovalishyn, "Wisdom in the New Testament," in Kynes, *Handbook of Wisdom*, 173–86.

90. Richard J. Clifford, "Introduction to the Wisdom Literature," in *The New Interpreter's Bible*, vol. 5, *Introduction to Wisdom Literature, Proverbs, Ecclesiastes, Song of Songs, Book of Wisdom, Sirach* (Nashville: Abingdon, 1997), 1.

"Wisdom literature" but also for "the preservation, composition, utilization, and instruction of the other literary genres of our Hebrew Bible."[91] Yoram Hazony even "look[s] forward to a time when most of the Hebrew Bible, if not all of it, will be recognized as 'wisdom literature.'"[92] Though our interpretive desires inevitably tint our reading, the "Wisdom literature" lens fits a modern mindset so well that it can be difficult to resist viewing the entire Bible through it.

A Third Way

This pan-sapiential expansion of "Wisdom literature" is one response to the recent challenges posed to the category. Others have responded with efforts to defend the traditional category.[93] Whether or not the appeal to its continued value for interpretation is convincing, arguing that an idea is alive and well hardly makes a strong case for its vitality.

I argue for a third option, which questions fundamental features of "Wisdom" study—such as its separate tradition, social setting, and theology—and proposes dispensing with the category entirely in order to better appreciate both the individuality and the broader intertextual network of the so-called "Wisdom" texts.[94] Comparison of texts based on a shared interest in wisdom may continue (particularly if other texts that share this interest, such as 1 Kings 1–11, are included), but texts should not be categorized as "Wisdom literature" with all its associated ideological interests and historical conjecture. The field is experiencing a paradigm shift. Old paradigms and long-held assumptions are being questioned, and new methods and theories are being proposed and debated.[95] It remains to be seen whether future chapters on "Wisdom literature" will be justified or necessary.

91. Sneed, "'Wisdom Tradition'?," 62–64.

92. Yoram Hazony, *The Philosophy of Hebrew Scripture* (Cambridge: Cambridge University Press, 2012), 284–85n26.

93. Annette Schellenberg, "Don't Throw the Baby Out with the Bathwater: On the Distinctness of the Sapiential Understanding of the World," in Mark Sneed, *Was There a Wisdom Tradition?*, 115–43; Matthew Goff, "The Pursuit of Wisdom at Qumran: Assessing the Classification 'Wisdom Literature' and Its Application to the Dead Sea Scrolls," in Kynes, *Handbook of Wisdom*, 617–34.

94. See also, e.g., Sneed, "'Wisdom Tradition'?"; Stuart Weeks, "Is 'Wisdom Literature' a Useful Category?," in *Tracing Sapiential Traditions in Ancient Judaism*, ed. Hindy Najman, Jean-Sébastien Rey, and Eibert J. C. Tigchelaar, JSJSup 174 (Leiden: Brill, 2016), 3–23; Katharine J. Dell, *The Solomonic Corpus of "Wisdom" and Its Influence* (Oxford: Oxford University Press, 2020).

95. Will Kynes, "Wisdom and Wisdom Literature: Past, Present, and Future," in Kynes, *Handbook of Wisdom*, 1–14. See Thomas S. Kuhn, *The Structure of Scientific Revolutions*, 2nd ed. (Chicago: University of Chicago Press, 1970).

19

Prophetic Literature

Major Prophets

Brad E. Kelle

The current study of Isaiah, Jeremiah, and Ezekiel blends long-established approaches with emerging perspectives. What began with predominantly historical-critical norms has flourished into multifaceted fields of study that include historical, cultural, social, literary, ideological, ethical, and theological approaches, with increasingly diverse readers foregrounding different contexts and convictions.[1] Some interpreters challenge older approaches, others reconfigure them, and still others introduce new directions, especially through the use of critical theory and interdisciplinary perspectives. The following survey will first sketch the trends

1. Carolyn J. Sharp, ed., *The Oxford Handbook of the Prophets* (Oxford: Oxford University Press, 2016); Mark J. Boda and J. Gordon McConville, eds., *Dictionary of the Old Testament: Prophets* (Downers Grove, IL: InterVarsity, 2012); Lena-Sofia Tiemeyer, ed., *The Oxford Handbook of Isaiah* (Oxford: Oxford University Press, 2020); Louis Stulman and Edward Silver, eds., *The Oxford Handbook of Jeremiah* (Oxford: Oxford University Press, 2021); Corrine Carvalho, ed., *The Oxford Handbook of Ezekiel* (Oxford: Oxford University Press, 2023); Jacob Stromberg, *An Introduction to the Study of Isaiah*, T&T Clark Approaches to Biblical Studies (London: Bloomsbury, 2011); C. L. Crouch, *An Introduction to the Study of Jeremiah*, T&T Clark Approaches to Biblical Studies (London: Bloomsbury T&T Clark, 2017); Michael A. Lyons, *An Introduction to the Study of Ezekiel*, T&T Clark Approaches to Biblical Studies (London: Bloomsbury T&T Clark, 2015); C. L. Crouch and Christopher B. Hays, *Isaiah: A Paradigmatic Prophet and His Interpreters; An Introduction and Study Guide*, T&T Clark Study Guides to the Old Testament (London: T&T Clark, 2022).

since the early 2000s in the study of the prophetic literature generally and the Major Prophets specifically.[2] Subsequent sections will provide highlights from two categories (allowing for some artificial division and overlap): (1) traditional approaches receiving new formulations and (2) new lines of inquiry, especially in conversation with interdisciplinary perspectives. The survey will not detail scholarship on Isaiah, Jeremiah, and Ezekiel individually but will identify approaches that cut across the study of these compositions.

Of Prophets and Paradigm Shifts

Major changes in methodological norms and interpretive approaches to the prophetic texts have occurred over the last two decades. It is common to hear talk of a paradigm shift, meaning especially a movement away from an older focus on the historical prophets as individuals and the reconstruction of their words and contexts to a focus on the prophetic books as literary compositions and the dynamics of readers and reading.[3] Earlier historical-critical interpretation featured the study of ANE prophecy and other comparative materials. Form and redaction criticisms were used to distinguish original oral units from later material. Scholarship concentrated on the orality of the prophetic messages and minimized the final literary compositions. Interests in the 1980s and 1990s began to move toward literary analysis, rhetorical criticism, intertextuality, and metaphor theory. By the early 2000s, the shift was noticeable, with a new focus on the prophetic books as complex but unified works of literature. Scholars gave special attention to the books' literary elements, the relationship between the final forms and the individual texts within them, and the ways these books function within larger canonical collections.[4]

2. For surveys extending further back, see Mary Chilton Callaway, *Jeremiah through the Centuries*, Wiley Blackwell Bible Commentaries (Hoboken, NJ: Wiley-Blackwell, 2020); John F. A. Sawyer, *Isaiah through the Centuries*, Wiley Blackwell Bible Commentaries (Hoboken, NJ: Wiley-Blackwell, 2018).

3. Reinhard G. Kratz, *The Prophets of Israel*, Critical Studies on the Hebrew Bible (Winona Lake, IN: Eisenbrauns, 2015), 110, 115. For summaries, see Carolyn J. Sharp, "Introduction," in Sharp, *Handbook of the Prophets*, xxi–xxxv; Robert P. Gordon, "A Story of Two Paradigm Shifts," in *The Place Is Too Small for Us: The Israelite Prophets in Recent Scholarship*, ed. Robert P. Gordon, Sources for Biblical and Theological Study 5 (Winona Lake, IN: Eisenbrauns, 1995), 3–26; Alan J. Hauser, ed., *Recent Research on the Major Prophets*, RRBS 1 (Sheffield: Sheffield Phoenix, 2008); John Day, ed., *Prophecy and the Prophets in Ancient Israel*, LHBOTS 531 (New York: T&T Clark, 2010); Mark McEntire, *A Chorus of Prophetic Voices: Introducing the Prophetic Literature of Ancient Israel* (Louisville: Westminster John Knox, 2015); Dalit Rom-Shiloni, "From Prophetic Words to Prophetic Literature: Challenging Paradigms That Control Our Academic Thought on Jeremiah and Ezekiel," *JBL* 138, no. 3 (2019): 565–86.

4. David L. Petersen, *The Prophetic Literature: An Introduction* (Louisville: Westminster John Knox, 2002); James D. Nogalski, *An Introduction to the Hebrew Prophets* (Nashville: Abingdon, 2018).

The attempt to take the prophetic literature more seriously has moved in two directions. Especially in German scholarship, interpreters have concentrated on reconstructing the literary history of the books as intentional scribal compositions. Instead of distinguishing the original words of the prophets from later additions, they hypothesize the ongoing editorial work of scribes that produced the final forms.[5] This effort is unavoidably speculative, resulting in multiple compositional models without consensus. Partially in response, others (especially in English-language scholarship) have concentrated on the present canonical form of the books. Without denying a prehistory of scribal composition, the emphasis is on synchronic readings that consider literary and thematic elements, the coherence of the whole, the theology found across the book, and the canonical location and function. Although the nature of research into literacy within ancient Israel is fluid, the shift toward studying the prophetic books as literature has also entailed an emphasis on the role of readers and the ways diverse reading communities—both ancient and modern—have received, understood, and performed these texts.

One example of these changes has been the creation of new models of the book of Isaiah that explore the interrelationship of the parts in earlier and final stages of composition and how editorial activity reflects the ongoing theological tradition captured by the canonical book.[6] Similarly, today's interpreters often distinguish the literary characters of Isaiah, Jeremiah, and Ezekiel from the historical figures that may stand behind them, looking first and foremost to how these prophetic figures function in and are constructed by the books themselves. For example, throughout the twentieth century, a focus on the composition of Jeremiah led to efforts to reconstruct the life of the historical prophet and divide between poetic, prose, and other sources to find his original words. Initial challenges emerged in the 1980s and 1990s, arguing that the book of Jeremiah, including its central character, is a literary creation with little connection to the historical realities in monarchical Judah.[7] Interpreters now increasingly consider the reading communities involved in the book's production and how various reading strategies illuminate the book's polyphonic voices and multiple perspectives.

In sum, today's study of the Major Prophets moves beyond a focus on historical approaches. It emphasizes the meaning of these books in their literary and canonical forms; engages theological, cultural, and ideological realities of the past and present; and responds to diverse interpretive methodologies.

5. On scribal practice, see Christopher A. Rollston, *Writing and Literacy in the World of Ancient Israel: Epigraphic Evidence from the Iron Age*, ABS 11 (Atlanta: SBL Press, 2010); David Carr, *Writing on the Tablet of the Heart: Origins of Scripture and Literature* (Oxford: Oxford University Press, 2005).

6. Ulrich Berges, "Isaiah: Structure, Themes, and Contested Issues," in Sharp, *Handbook of the Prophets*, 153–70; H. G. M. Williamson, "Isaiah, Book of," in Boda and McConville, *Prophets*, 364–78; Bo H. Lim, "Isaiah: History of Interpretation," in Boda and McConville, *Prophets*, 378–91.

7. Surveys appear in Louis Stulman and Edward Silver, "A Critical Introduction," in Stulman and Silver, *Handbook of Jeremiah*, 1–21; Crouch, *Study of Jeremiah*.

Traditional Approaches and Their New Formulations

Scholars today reconfigure many of the traditional questions from new angles, often informed by interdisciplinary insights and critical theory. The following serve as illustrative examples.

One traditional approach generating new ideas is research into the phenomenon of ancient prophecy as the backdrop for the study of Isaiah, Jeremiah, and Ezekiel.[8] Already by the year 2000, scholars considered prophecy a widespread religious and cultural phenomenon (as a type of intermediation and divination) throughout the ANE. Today's scholarship features ongoing examination of the comparative data, with increased attention to how ANE texts illuminate both the characteristics and compositional process of specific books such as Isaiah.[9] Additionally, researchers have broadened the phenomenological and sociological comparisons to consider evidence from Assyrian texts and beyond that reveal the entire prophetic experience from inception to literary development and collection, with a textualization process that involved the production of the prophetic messages with readers and communities as the social context.[10]

New work in this area examines female prophets in ancient Israel. The majority of named prophets in Neo-Assyrian texts are female, and female prophets were known in several other ANE cultures. Recent research has attempted to show that female prophecy was prevalent and significant in ancient Israel.[11] Key is a broader definition of "prophetic" activities. Female prophecy may have included healthcare, musical activities, funerary rites, and scribal practices. References within the Major Prophets play a role in this discussion. Four named women in the OT are identified as prophets (Miriam, Deborah, Huldah, Noadiah), and Isa. 8:3 also refers to an unnamed woman as a prophet. It is unclear whether this woman was Isaiah's wife, but she was a public figure recognizable as a prophet within monarchic Judah. Similarly, Ezek. 13:17–23 describes a group of female prophets among Ezekiel's exilic community

8. Brad E. Kelle, "The Phenomenon of Israelite Prophecy in Contemporary Scholarship," *CurBR* 12 (2014): 275–320; Christopher A. Rollston, ed., *Enemies and Friends of the State: Ancient Prophecy in Context* (University Park, PA: Eisenbrauns, 2018); Martti Nissinen, *Ancient Prophecy: Near Eastern, Biblical, and Greek Perspectives* (Oxford: Oxford University Press, 2017); Jonathan Stökl, *Prophecy in the Ancient Near East: A Philological and Sociological Comparison*, CHANE 56 (Leiden: Brill, 2012).

9. Michaël N. van der Meer et al., eds., *Isaiah in Context: Studies in Honour of Arie van der Kooij on the Occasion of His Sixty-Fifth Birthday*, VTSup 138 (Leiden: Brill, 2010); Matthijs de Jong, *Isaiah among the Ancient Near Eastern Prophets: A Comparative Study of the Earliest Stages of the Isaiah Tradition and the Neo-Assyrian Prophecies*, VTSup 117 (Leiden: Brill, 2007).

10. Robert R. Wilson, "Prophecy," in *The Wiley Blackwell Companion to Ancient Israel*, ed. Susan Niditch (Malden, MA: Wiley-Blackwell, 2016), 317–32, esp. 319.

11. H. G. M. Williamson, "Prophetesses in the Hebrew Bible," in Day, *Prophecy and the Prophets*, 65–80; Jonathan Stökl, "Female Prophets in the Ancient Near East," in Day, *Prophecy and the Prophets*, 47–61; Wilda C. Gafney, *Daughters of Miriam: Women Prophets in Ancient Israel* (Minneapolis: Fortress, 2008).

performing intercessory practices. This research helps interpreters recognize the overwhelmingly male cast of prophecy in the biblical texts (including many of the metaphors that appear as a result), while also attending to overlooked dimensions of the prophetic experience that stand behind books such as Isaiah, Jeremiah, and Ezekiel.

As noted above, the study of the compositional history of the Major Prophets has seen the most substantial reformulation in recent scholarship. Redaction criticism no longer focuses on oral speech forms and on separating (and often dismissing) material thought to be later additions. Instead, it resists the label "secondary" and operates in terms of literary insertions, expansions, and frameworks added to an original layer of tradition to produce a whole prophetic composition. This approach has a "much higher regard for the work of the scribes and tradents who collected, shaped, and transmitted the scrolls" and sees the interpretation of the final form as the "task of redaction criticism."[12] Current redactional analysis attends to a multistage process in which small collections were linked together over time and older portions were deliberately, creatively, and sometimes systematically reworked with an eye to the whole.

Among the Major Prophets, Isaiah has been at the center of these new redactional approaches. Already in the 1990s and early 2000s, interpreters were moving away from a focus on discrete parts developing in isolated settings and toward synchronic readings of the whole, arguing that the different parts of the book developed in relationship with one another and that material from the later exilic and postexilic periods appears throughout the entire collection.[13] Some interpreters conclude that Isaiah's unity results from later editorial work that conjoined originally independent compositions (e.g., Isa. 1–33 and 40–55) by placing links and expansions within each. Others assert that the later parts of the book, such as so-called Deutero-Isaiah (chaps. 40–55), were written specifically to be literary continuations of the earlier material in First Isaiah (chaps. 1–39) and never existed independently. The debate about Isa. 56–66 (so-called Third Isaiah) is similar, and the general conversation about the book as a whole now includes several important evangelical perspectives.[14]

Earlier theories of Jeremiah's sources and their development have likewise given way to a new emphasis on editorial shaping in the exile and the book's remaining

12. James D. Nogalski, "Redaction Criticism and the Prophets," in Sharp, *Handbook of the Prophets*, 277.

13. H. G. M. Williamson, *The Book Called Isaiah: Deutero-Isaiah's Role in Composition and Redaction* (Oxford: Clarendon, 1994); Ulrich Berges, *The Book of Isaiah: Its Composition and Final Form*, HBM 46 (Sheffield: Sheffield Phoenix, 2012); Brevard S. Childs, *Isaiah*, OTL (Louisville: Westminster John Knox, 2000).

14. Tiemeyer, *Handbook of Isaiah*; Hyun Chul Paul Kim, "Recent Scholarship on Isaiah 1–39," in Hauser, *Major Prophets*, 118–41. For evangelical perspectives, see Daniel L. Block and Richard L. Schultz, eds., *Bind Up the Testimony: Explorations in the Genesis of the Book of Isaiah* (Peabody, MA: Hendrickson Academic, 2015); David G. Firth and H. G. M. Williamson, eds., *Interpreting Isaiah: Issues and Approaches* (Leicester: IVP Academic, 2009).

internal complexity and incongruities.[15] Although Ezekiel's apparent structure and consistent style have resulted in fewer compositional hypotheses, today's scholarship features a spectrum of opinions. Some see the book as essentially an original unity from the sixth century BCE, while others hypothesize numerous redactional expansions of earlier units extending into the fourth century BCE. Some also propose thematic distinctions between exile-oriented and diaspora-oriented redactions.[16] Recent work also entertains the possibility that the book originated as a written work and that the extensive priestly material should be taken seriously (not discounted as later, inauthentic impositions) for the book's origins and meaning.

Redactional work on the Major Prophets today is breaking down the dichotomy between oral and written origins. Maximally, this move has led to the conclusion that the prophetic books, at least in their ultimate (and perhaps penultimate or even originary) forms, are entirely scribal compositions from literati in the postmonarchic period. At the very least, however, the move suggests that "prophecy" could include scribal work.[17]

Building on literary methods established in the 1980s and 1990s, the study of metaphors in the Major Prophets remains a central focus today.[18] Often at the forefront now are female and sexualized metaphors. Interpreters continue to use feminist and other perspectives to engage the misogyny, patriarchy, violence, and hierarchy present in these tropes and images. They focus on the portrayal of God as a husband and the female personification of Israel (its people, elites, or cities) as God's promiscuous/adulterous wife who is subjected to violent punishments described in graphic language and images (e.g., Ezek. 16; 23).[19] They engage the gendered metaphors in ways both emic and etic: *emic* by explaining the historical and cultural meaning among ancient metaphorical commonplaces, and *etic* by interpreting the images from the viewpoint of modern readers and their responses.[20]

15. See the critique of traditional models in Joseph M. Henderson, *Jeremiah under the Shadow of Duhm: A Critique of the Use of Prophetic Form as a Criterion of Authenticity*, T&T Clark Biblical Studies (London: T&T Clark, 2019). See also Jack R. Lundbom, Craig A. Evans, and Bradford A. Anderson, eds., *The Book of Jeremiah: Composition, Reception, and Interpretation*, VTSup 178 (Leiden: Brill, 2018); Peter Diamond, "The Jeremiah Guild in the Twenty-First Century: Variety Reigns Supreme," in Hauser, *Major Prophets*, 232–48.

16. Andrew Mein, "Ezekiel: Structure, Themes, and Contested Issues," in Sharp, *Handbook of the Prophets*, 190–206; Lyons, *Study of Ezekiel*, 52–70.

17. Rom-Shiloni, "From Prophetic Words to Prophetic Literature," 565–86; Diana V. Edelman and Ehud Ben Zvi, eds., *The Production of Prophecy: Constructing Prophecy and Prophets in Yehud*, BibleWorld (London: Equinox, 2009).

18. Mason D. Lancaster, "Metaphor Research and the Hebrew Bible," *CurBR* 19 (2021): 235–85. On Isaiah, see Göran Eidevall, "The Use of Metaphors," in Tiemeyer, *Handbook of Isaiah*, 409–25.

19. Christl M. Maier, "Feminist Interpretation of the Prophets," in Sharp, *Handbook of the Prophets*, 467–82.

20. Sharon Moughtin-Mumby, *Sexual and Marital Metaphors in Hosea, Jeremiah, Isaiah, and Ezekiel*, Oxford Theological Monographs (Oxford: Oxford University Press, 2008); Gerlinde

Some constructive approaches balance these negative portrayals by highlighting prophetic texts that use female imagery in positive ways, especially in portrayals of YHWH. Isaiah contains a comparatively high number of such portrayals, depicting YHWH as a mother (49:15; 66:13), midwife (66:9), and woman in labor (42:14).[21] Similarly, interpreters now reread the prophetic condemnations in order to recover women's religious practices in ancient Israel (often deemed illegitimate and labeled as "fornication" or "adultery" in the prophetic metaphors). Practices such as the worship of the "Queen of Heaven" condemned in Jeremiah (7:18; 44:17–19, 25) may indicate that the cultic practices of women were not relegated to domestic settings outside of Israel's official cult.

Fresh engagements with the theology of Isaiah, Jeremiah, and Ezekiel are making creative contributions to the long-standing theological interpretation of these books. Some of these offer specific formulations of the importance of canonical form and function from Christian perspectives, attending to how the canonical prophetic collection works in unity to bear witness to the character of God and depict history as the unfolding accomplishment of God's word (through Christ) throughout time.[22] At a broader level, an increasing number of evangelical works, representing a variety of perspectives, are now engaging the Major Prophets as formative, enduring, and presently speaking theological voices that call for a response, especially from the church amid the realities of its world.[23]

Finally, reception history of the Major Prophets (previously defined more strictly as the "history of interpretation" within Jewish and Christian traditions) has become an expansive category that considers not only formal interpretation within Jewish and Christian literature and tradition but also the use of the prophets by diverse readers and communities within art, music, literature, architecture, liturgy, politics, and other cultural expressions that were once seen as largely inconsequential for the texts' meanings.[24] The goal is not merely description but critical

---

Baumann, *Love and Violence: Marriage as a Metaphor for the Relationship between Yahweh and Israel in the Prophetic Books*, trans. L. M. Maloney (Collegeville, MN: Liturgical Press, 2003).

21. Sharon Moughtin-Mumby, "Feminist/Womanist Readings of Isaiah," in Tiemeyer, *Handbook of Isaiah*, 601–20.

22. Christopher R. Seitz, *Essays on Prophecy and Canon: The Rise of a New Model for Interpretation*, FAT 149 (Tübingen: Mohr Siebeck, 2021).

23. John Goldingay, *The Theology of Jeremiah: The Book, the Man, the Message* (Downers Grove, IL: IVP Academic, 2021); Andrew T. Abernethy, *Discovering Isaiah: Content, Interpretation, Reception* (Grand Rapids: Eerdmans, 2021); Abernethy, *The Book of Isaiah and God's Kingdom: A Thematic-Theological Approach*, NSBT 40 (Downers Grove, IL: IVP Academic, 2016); Hyun Chul Paul Kim, *Reading Isaiah: A Literary and Theological Commentary* (Macon, GA: Smyth & Helwys, 2016).

24. H. J. Klauck et al., eds., *Encyclopedia of the Bible and Its Reception*, 30 vols. (Berlin: De Gruyter, 2009–); Michael Lieb, Emma Mason, and Jonathan Roberts, eds., *The Oxford Handbook to the Reception History of the Bible* (Oxford: Oxford University Press, 2011); Sawyer, *Isaiah through the Centuries*; Callaway, *Jeremiah through the Centuries*; Paul M. Joyce and Andrew Mein, eds., *After Ezekiel: Essays on the Reception of a Difficult Prophet*, LHBOTS 535 (New York: T&T Clark, 2011).

analysis of interpretive practices in different contexts that reveal how readers have adapted the prophetic books to face new challenges and how new readers might be stimulated to do the same.

New Lines of Inquiry

Conversation with interdisciplinary perspectives has opened new lines of inquiry into the Major Prophets. Space permits only highlights that cut across all three books and show the most generative energy for present and future study. Many of these perspectives reflect how the prophetic texts intersect with the lived experiences of diverse readers and communities past and present.

The use of gender studies to engage Isaiah, Jeremiah, and Ezekiel has created new and broader paths. Earlier feminist readings came from white, Western, middle-class, heterosexual women. More recent "womanist" approaches focus on the marginalized, oppressed, and silenced women in the texts and among their modern-day readers, especially those from nonwhite, poor, and underserved communities. These approaches employ historical, literary, and theory-based reading strategies but with a concentration on ethics and liberation that asks how marginalized women are understood within, and as a result of, the biblical texts. They consider how the interlocking elements of gender, race, ethnicity, and class created systems and portrayals of privilege and oppression that appear in the prophets and their depictions of women, children, poverty, and more. But they also consider the ethical impact of the prophetic texts on vulnerable people and communities today, especially how the texts may be used to harm and how persons in those communities may need to name and even resist some of the ethical claims made in the prophetic utterances.[25]

Similarly, the portrayals of masculinity within the Major Prophets are receiving increased attention, especially in connection with the depictions of God, Israel, and the prophets themselves. Recognizing masculinity as a social construct represented in texts, but one that permeated multiple aspects of ancient societies, recent studies focus on what ideals are associated with masculinity (what it means to "be a man"), how masculinity is performed (what it means to "act like a man"), and what effects the portrayals of masculinity in the prophetic texts might have on male readers past and present. Cultures like ancient Israel typically had a dominant form of masculinity that was culturally enshrined, yet multiple notions of masculinity were simultaneously operative in cultures and texts. For Israel's world, the dominant masculinity was connected to power and involved military might, violence, control, and sexual virility. Attention to the construction and use of such masculinity sheds light not only on portrayals of God, Israel, and the prophets but also on how those portrayals may reflect

25. Valerie Bridgeman, "Womanist Approaches to the Prophets," in Sharp, *Handbook of the Prophets*, 483–90; Moughtin-Mumby, "Feminist/Womanist Readings."

the unsettling experiences of war, violence, trauma, and defeat. The marriage imagery used for God and Israel in Jeremiah and Ezekiel, for instance, relies on certain understandings of masculinity to reassert divine authority and renegotiate the relationship between God and the people.[26] Ezekiel's depictions of divine sovereignty and control, especially through gendered metaphors in chapters 16 and 23 or the portrayals of bodies and their fate throughout the book, may serve to reassert God's power in response to Jerusalem's destruction and exile.[27] Although our analysis of social and textual constructions of masculinity is chronologically and culturally removed and necessarily hypothetical, it may reveal cracks in the portrayals of God and the prophets that reflect the dilemmas and fractured masculinity created by Israel's experiences of defeat, subordination, and marginalization.[28]

Perhaps the most expansive new line of inquiry involves reading these books against the background of exile, with special attention to its attendant realities of violence, imperialism, and trauma. Isaiah noticeably lacks explicit and detailed representations of the exile (containing mostly indirect and metaphorical depictions), but the exile and its experiences stand at the heart of Jeremiah and Ezekiel, even shaping the primary physical, psychological, and emotional realities of the prophetic figures themselves. At the general level, this interpretive approach focuses on the poetry, metaphors, and images related to exile (e.g., metaphors connecting death and exile in Isaiah; rebirth imagery used with exile in Jeremiah and Ezekiel). Some studies look at specific passages, and others compare elements and themes across texts.[29] The emphasis on exile has also generated interdisciplinary conversations with studies of forced migration,[30] which emphasize that types of migration and displacement vary and that one should expect differing intellectual and theological responses. Hence, Stephen Cook proposes that Deutero-Isaiah's response to the exile differs from those in Jeremiah and Ezekiel by using priestly material and theology from the Pentateuch with a special emphasis on a theology of reverence before divine otherness.[31]

With this focus on exile, interpreters increasingly approach the violence described in Isaiah, Jeremiah, and Ezekiel (especially depictions of war and killing) as reflecting the violence experienced by Israelites and Judeans through their encounters with

26. Moughtin-Mumby, *Sexual and Marital Metaphors*.

27. Amy Kalmonofsky, "Ezekiel and Gender," in Carvalho, *Handbook of Ezekiel*, 402–17; Rhiannon Graybill, *Are We Not Men? Unstable Masculinity in the Hebrew Prophets* (Oxford: Oxford University Press, 2017).

28. Susanna Asikainen, "The Masculinity of Jeremiah," *BibInt* 28, no. 1 (2020): 34–55.

29. Jesper Høgenhaven, Frederik Poulsen, and Cian Power, eds., *Images of Exile in the Prophetic Literature*, FAT 2/103 (Tübingen: Mohr Siebeck, 2019); Dalit Rom-Shiloni, "Exile in the Book of Isaiah," in Tiemeyer, *Handbook of Isaiah*, 293–317.

30. Mark J. Boda et al., eds., *The Prophets Speak on Forced Migration*, AIL 21 (Atlanta: SBL Press, 2015).

31. Stephen L. Cook, "Second Isaiah and the Aaronide Response to Judah's Forced Migrations," in Boda et al., *Forced Migration*, 47–62.

the Assyrian and Babylonian Empires.[32] This connection allows new hermeneutical insights into how and why the prophetic books blame the people for their exile and assert that God was justified in enacting retributive violence. We see that these were rhetorical maneuvers born out of a struggle with theodicy, an attempt to make sense of tragedy by clinging to faith in a powerful God (e.g., Isa. 5:8–30; 63:1–6; Jer. 13:15–27). Images of sexual violence and mutilation in texts such as Ezek. 16 and 23 may represent the experiences of the Judean community during invasion, war, and displacement, and the abused female figures in those and similar texts may represent the humiliation and emasculation of Jerusalem's male ruling elite.

Reading Isaiah, Jeremiah, and Ezekiel against the backdrop of the exile invites reconsideration of the prophets' denunciations of structural violence (e.g., socioeconomic inequality and oppression; racial and ethnic hostility) and cultural violence (the use of religion, ideology, and language to justify harmful structures and practices).[33] Connecting prophetic violence with the exile moves readers to seek strategies of ethical interpretation that might include resistance to the texts, awareness of how the texts might be used today to blame victims of forced migration for their own suffering, or the search for alternative and more life-giving metaphors for God within the prophetic books.

Along these lines, new approaches read the Major Prophets with an eye toward ancient empires and the social, religious, and ideological dimensions of their imperialism. Postcolonial criticism considers how the prophets reflect varying social engagements with power, especially imperial power, and how those engagements may be relevant for today's realities of imperialism, nationalism, and authoritarianism.[34] The focus is on the discourse modes and social practices related to empire and resistance in the prophetic books. For example, Gregory Lee Cuéllar has correlated the representations of exile in the poems of Isa. 40–55 with the experiences of contemporary Mexican immigrants in the United States as expressed in their *corridos* (ballads), particularly the realities of economic exploitation, forced displacement, and the notion of return.[35] At the same time, however, scholars recognize that the biblical prophetic texts have a complex relationship to empire because, while they at times critique imperial power, they remain inescapably connected to and sometimes reinscribe imperial attitudes and violence. Books such as Jeremiah announce the dismantling of imperial powers and the coming of a new world but retain the language and logic of empire with calls for hegemony,

32. L. Juliana Claassens, "God and Violence in the Prophets," in Sharp, *Handbook of the Prophets*, 334–49.

33. Tamar S. Kamionkowski, "The 'Problem' of Violence in the Prophetic Literature: Definitions as the Real Problem," in *Religion and Violence: The Biblical Heritage*, ed. David A. Bernat and Jonathan Klawans (Sheffield: Sheffield Phoenix, 2007), 38–46.

34. Steed Vernyl Davidson, "Postcolonial Readings of the Prophets," in Sharp, *Handbook of the Prophets*, 507–26.

35. Gregory Lee Cuéllar, *Voices of Marginality: Exile and Return in Second Isaiah 40–55 and the Mexican Immigrant Experience*, AUS 7/271 (New York: Peter Lang, 2008).

vengeance, and new kings and kingdoms (e.g., the Oracles against the Nations in Jer. 46–51), all of which have allowed the books to become tools of imperial oppression in later contexts.[36]

Attention to empires and imperialism has been especially fruitful for the recent study of Isaiah. Efforts to explore both its reflections of imperial influence and its elements of resistance or anti-imperial rhetoric have produced fresh engagements with topics such as the imagery of eating and death, the rhetoric of sovereignty, and the depictions of "Daughter Zion" and the city of Jerusalem. One can come to hear especially First Isaiah as the voice of a "colonized poet" whose message was shaped by the struggle between submission and resistance to the Assyrian Empire, and who shares some of the ideologies, circumstances, and literary methods also found in colonized authors from modern Africa.[37] Shawn Zelig Aster rereads passages throughout First Isaiah in dialogue with Assyrian imperial propaganda and ideology (e.g., 6:1–8 with visual imperial propaganda; 10:5–34 with Assyrian royal rhetoric). Isaiah's arguments, ideology, language, and imagery rework Assyrian imperial motifs and often polemicize and subvert Assyrian royal propaganda, especially claims to universal dominion.[38] The prophets spoke as the subjugated in an imperial setting and may aid in the work of challenging imperialist elements within the texts and imperialist interpretations drawn from them.

The focus on exile has especially involved the interdisciplinary application of trauma theory to the Major Prophets. The trauma hermeneutic brings the interpretation of the books into touch with experiences of disaster and survival known by many of their readers in today's global contexts. Through the lens of trauma, the prophetic texts are disaster-and-survival literature meant to help communities make meaning and build resilience in the wake of destruction and loss. The books of Jeremiah and Ezekiel have received the most attention in this regard since the early 2000s. These approaches go beyond treating the prophets themselves as traumatized persons (or their audiences as traumatized people), which was the emphasis of much of the earliest trauma interpretations. Instead, they now focus on the prophetic *books* as trauma *literature*, which allows for multiple voices to form a complex response to realities of war, captivity, death, and deportation.[39] The prophetic books are literary efforts at survival that tell

36. Steed Vernyl Davidson, *Empire and Exile: Postcolonial Readings in the Book of Jeremiah*, LHBOTS 542 (New York: T&T Clark, 2011); Christl M. Maier and Carolyn J. Sharp, eds., *Prophecy and Power: Jeremiah in Feminist and Postcolonial Perspective*, LHBOTS 577 (London: Bloomsbury, 2013).

37. Andrew T. Abernethy et al., eds., *Isaiah and Imperial Context: The Book of Isaiah in the Times of Empire* (Eugene, OR: Pickwick 2013), esp. Christopher B. Hays, "Isaiah as a Colonized Poet: His Rhetoric of Death in Conversation with African Postcolonial Writers," 51–70.

38. Shawn Zelig Aster, *Reflections of Empire in Isaiah 1–39: Responses to Assyrian Ideology*, ANEM 19 (Atlanta: SBL Press, 2017).

39. Louis Stulman, "Prophetic Words and Acts as Survival Literature," in Sharp, *Handbook of the Prophets*, 319–33; Louis Stulman and Hyun Chul Paul Kim, *You Are My People: An Introduction to the Prophetic Literature* (Nashville: Abingdon, 2010).

the truth about traumatic pain, seek meaning within it, and imagine new futures for the defeated.

Especially for Jeremiah, the trauma lens explains the numerous references to violence, pain, and terror throughout both the book's depictions of the people and the prophet's expressions of his own feelings and experiences. For Kathleen O'Connor, these elements reflect the wounds suffered by the prophet and his community in the realities of war and devastation at the hands of the Babylonians.[40] Others engage the book of Jeremiah as a literary and cultural expression of suffering and loss composed specifically for surviving Judean communities. The trauma lens shows the book to be resilience literature meant to keep the memory of trauma alive, grieve over it, and create meaning in its wake. This conjoining of the themes of disaster and survival may even account for the book's literary complexities that were often explained through source division. These literary fissures may be "refractions of the lived chaos of war, the impenetrability of trauma."[41] The use of trauma hermeneutics with Ezekiel has received even more attention since the early 2000s.[42] The book's focus on events surrounding Jerusalem's destruction and its description of Ezekiel as an exile living among a community of Judean deportees in Babylonia invite consideration of the book as trauma literature meant to address generations of those who lived in the wake of destruction and exile. Today's interpreters increasingly understand the book's arguments, priestly language and themes (holiness, defilement, abomination, temple), visions and repetitions, and overall movement from destruction to restoration as attempts to interpret the trauma of exile and provide hope for a new future.[43]

A Multidirectional and Polyphonic Future

Today's study of the Major Prophets expresses an energy, variety, and creativity that has proven generative for new insights and new voices. Future study will likely proceed along the two trajectories of reformulations of traditional approaches and the pursuit of new lines of inquiry. This study should continue to feature diversity in methods, approaches, and conclusions, especially through interdisciplinary engagements with other fields and critical theories.

Given the long dominance of historical modes of interpretation, those taking up Isaiah, Jeremiah, and Ezekiel in present and future moments may feel especially compelled toward theological interpretation, one of the traditional

40. Kathleen M. O'Connor, *Jeremiah: Pain and Promise* (Minneapolis: Fortress, 2011).

41. Stulman and Silver, "Critical Introduction," 6. See also L. Juliana Claassens, "Jeremiah: The Traumatized Prophet," in Stulman and Silver, *Handbook of Jeremiah*, 358–73.

42. Brad E. Kelle, *Ezekiel: A Commentary in the Wesleyan Tradition*, New Beacon Bible Commentary (Kansas City: Beacon Hill, 2013); Nancy R. Bowen, *Ezekiel*, Abingdon Old Testament Commentaries (Nashville: Abingdon, 2010).

43. Ruth Poser, "Ezekiel as Trauma Literature," in Carvalho, *Handbook of Ezekiel*, 437–54; Dalit Rom-Shiloni, "Ezekiel among the Exiles," in Carvalho, *Handbook of Ezekiel*, 187–217.

areas receiving creative new formulations. Walter Brueggemann advocates for this "post-critical" future of prophetic study in which interpreters can encounter the texts as presently speaking voices that demand to be dialogically engaged.[44] Future study needs more (and multifaceted) attempts to hear the texts as appeals that call for a response amid complex social realities. Theological interpretations need not be set over against historical analyses. Rather, all readers aware of their readerly location can seek to explore the lasting significance of these books, and an interdisciplinary and multidirectional future will allow the Major Prophets to contribute to discussion of the ever-present issues of racism, sexism, war, violence, poverty, ecojustice, and more.

The future also lies in welcoming new interpretive voices. The new lines of inquiry now emerging continue to be dominated by North American and European scholars. The differentials of access and power in the field of biblical scholarship provide platforms of visibility (e.g., academic journals, monographs, handbooks) for some voices more easily than others. More attention to readings of Isaiah, Jeremiah, and Ezekiel from racial-, ethnic-, and social-minority voices is needed. Creative works that feature authors from a variety of contexts with diverse approaches and aims are burgeoning.[45] Future research will flourish if and when these voices are seen as more than just contextual readings that augment some objective interpretive tradition and instead come to represent an integral part of the meaning-making work being done with Isaiah, Jeremiah, and Ezekiel.

44. Walter Brueggemann, "Futures in Prophetic Studies," in Sharp, *Handbook of the Prophets*, 655–65.

45. Bungishabaku Katho, *Reading Jeremiah in Africa: Biblical Essays in Sociopolitical Imagination* (Cave Creek, AZ: Langham Partnership International, 2021); Hugh R. Page Jr. et al., *The Africana Bible: Reading Israel's Scriptures from Africa and the African Diaspora* (Minneapolis: Fortress, 2010); Tokunboh Adeyemo, ed., *Africa Bible Commentary: A One-Volume Commentary Written by 70 African Scholars* (Grand Rapids: Zondervan, 2006).

20

Prophetic Literature

Minor Prophets

DANIEL C. TIMMER

Sustained study of the Minor Prophets as a self-defined unity began in the 1990s. The foundational stage of research was largely guided by historical-critical perspectives that analyzed these books' diachronic formation and focused on correlating their redaction histories with a developmental history of ancient Israelite religion.[1] More recently, scholars working outside the historical-critical paradigm have diversified and broadened research on the Twelve, challenging that paradigm's premises while also formulating new questions. This chapter surveys and evaluates these two phases in the study of the Twelve before proposing ways in which future scholarship might clarify persistent questions or draw attention to issues that have not yet been adequately explored.[2]

The Birth of Study of the Book of the Twelve

The Book of the Twelve is a recent creation. Only since the 1990s has the corpus of the Minor Prophets been widely studied as a discrete entity, unified primarily

1. Due to the predominance of interest in the Twelve as a collection, this chapter gives limited attention to individual books in the Minor Prophets corpus.

2. Online bibliographies by Aaron Schart (https://www.zotero.org/groups/248047/twelve prophets/library) and C. J. Conroy (www.cjconroy.net/bib/twelve-studies.htm) facilitate access to the relevant literature.

by compositional (diachronic) features, redaction in particular. Over the past two centuries, interpreters occasionally observed that the Minor Prophets shared formal or material features that might be evidence of their gradual formation as an independent group of writings, including catchwords linking adjacent books (F. Delitzsch) and formally similar superscriptions (H. Ewald).[3] This research remained intermittent, however, until James Nogalski consolidated and surpassed these scattered contributions, launching the first phase of continuous exploration of the Twelve.[4]

The Redacted-Corpus Approach

Nogalski begins his study by affirming that "incontrovertible evidence," including references to "the Twelve Prophets" in Sir. 49:10 and their being counted as one in 4 Ezra/2 Esd. 14:45 and Josephus (*Ag. Ap.* 1.37–45), leaves no doubt that "the twelve Minor Prophets were . . . considered as a single book."[5] The core of Nogalski's argument begins with his identification of catchwords and related redactional processes that link adjacent books in the Twelve.[6] These additions, identifiable because of the literary tensions Nogalski sees between them and their contexts, used catchwords, thematic elements, and other features to knit the collection together as it grew, a process that began after Jerusalem's fall and ended after 332 BCE.[7] This literary connectedness exists alongside the different emphases and claims of these redactions, which preserve significant discord at the level of content.

In his 1998 monograph, Aaron Schart accepted much of Nogalski's hypothesis, especially the belief that the Twelve forms a single book. Schart's contribution included the proposal that a hymnic layer unites Nahum and Habakkuk; a reduced emphasis on Deuteronomy's influence on Hosea, Amos, Micah, and Zephaniah; and a larger role for Amos in the final formation of the corpus.[8] Schart too found that the integrating effects of his proposed redactional layers exist alongside "a certain incompleteness and tension in the text."[9] Almost a decade later, Jakob Wöhrle offered a rather different account of the Twelve's formation, arguing that the redaction histories of the Book of the Four (Hosea, Amos, Micah, Zephaniah)

3. For more detail, see Aaron Schart, "Twelve, Book of the: History of Interpretation," in *Dictionary of the Old Testament: Prophets*, ed. Mark J. Boda and J. Gordon McConville (Downers Grove, IL: IVP Academic, 2012), 806–17, esp. 813.

4. James D. Nogalski, *Literary Precursors to the Book of the Twelve*, BZAW 217 (Berlin: De Gruyter, 1993); Nogalski, *Redactional Processes in the Book of the Twelve*, BZAW 218 (Berlin: De Gruyter, 1993).

5. Nogalski, *Literary Precursors*, 1, 12.

6. Nogalski, *Literary Precursors*, 13–14.

7. Nogalski, *Redactional Processes*, 279–80.

8. Aaron Schart, *Die Entstehung des Zwölfprophetenbuchs: Neubearbeitungen von Amos im Rahmen schriftenübergreifender Redaktionsprozesse*, BZAW 260 (Berlin: De Gruyter, 1998).

9. Schart, *Die Entstehung des Zwölfprophetenbuchs*, 313 (my trans.).

and of 2 Kings 17–25 are interrelated and simultaneous, although each has a different intention.[10] He identified redactional activity across the Twelve that is tied to foci or emphases such as condemnations of individual nations versus condemnations of all nations, the Davidic covenant, and the grace formula of Exod. 34:6–7.

Complements, Challenges, and Alternatives to Redactional Approaches

During this first phase of study of the Twelve as a unified collection, several assumptions or conclusions that underlie the redactional theories surveyed above were supplemented or challenged. Barry Jones questioned the presumption that the MT order was either original or normative. He concluded, "It is better to speak not so much of any 'original' arrangement of the Twelve, but rather of an original *diversity* of arrangements . . . before the Common Era."[11] Marvin Sweeney contended that the LXX order gives prominence to the Northern Kingdom as an example for Judah, while the MT order focuses on Jerusalem. He further observed that the logic behind the LXX arrangement draws into question redactional arguments that depend on the Masoretic order of the Twelve.[12] Sweeney claimed, "When the individual books are read in relation to each other, their communicative functions and outlooks change."[13] This draws attention to the hermeneutical significance of the collection's order in many approaches to the Twelve.

Paul House's choice of a synchronic (holistic) approach to Zephaniah (1989) and to the Book of the Twelve (1990) offered an alternative to redactional approaches. Observing that recent study of the OT prophetic books had almost done away with "a unified prophetic canon," House insisted that the interpreter should move beyond the historical circumstances in which a particular passage or book may have arisen—which is often where historical-critical interpretation ends—to consider "every aspect of the final, written form of biblical texts." He concluded that the Twelve constitute a unified whole, with a point of view that "strives to match the intentions of the Lord, . . . the person behind the whole book."[14]

10. Jakob Wöhrle, *Die frühen Sammlungen des Zwölfprophetenbuches: Entstehung und Komposition*, BZAW 360 (Berlin: De Gruyter, 2006); Wöhrle, *Der Abschluss des Zwölfprophetenbuches: Buchübergreifende Redaktionsprozesse in den späten Sammlungen*, BZAW 389 (Berlin: De Gruyter, 2008).

11. Barry Jones, "The Book of the Twelve as a Witness to Ancient Biblical Interpretation," in *Reading and Hearing the Book of the Twelve*, ed. James D. Nogalski and Marvin A. Sweeney, SBLSS 15 (Atlanta: Scholars Press, 2000), 69.

12. Marvin A. Sweeney, "Sequence and Interpretation in the Book of the Twelve," in Nogalski and Sweeney, *Reading and Hearing*, 63–64.

13. Sweeney, "Sequence and Interpretation," 56.

14. Paul R. House, *The Unity of the Twelve*, JSOTSup 97, Bible and Literature 27 (Sheffield: Almond, 1990), 12, 20, 240.

Rolf Rendtorff was also unsatisfied with the limited unity that compositional or redactional approaches found in the Twelve and its constituent books. Espousing the view that one should "try to understand the texts in their given form and to find out what intention and message they would have had," Rendtorff concluded that the Twelve includes significant thematic complementarity as well as "controversies, and even contradictions." Notably, he appealed to the books' explicit or implicit dates as the most relevant "diachronic features" for understanding their diversity.[15] Insofar as these and similar studies demonstrate significant degrees of unity within the collection or its constituent books, they diminish or eliminate the necessity of compositional or redactional explanations of their origins.[16]

Shortly after Nogalski's 1993 study appeared, Ehud Ben Zvi developed an extensive critique of his approach and of much work that followed in its wake. Ben Zvi argued that although the Twelve was viewed as a collection as early as the second century BCE, the data mustered by Nogalski and others do not make clear whether that collection was a *unity*.[17] Even if those sources made this claim, Ben Zvi countered that they are significantly later than the Twelve and so have limited weight. He was also not convinced that catchwords bind the Twelve together since Nogalski did not demonstrate that those words are "substantially" more prominent within the Twelve than outside it. Similarly, the thematic links Nogalski highlighted can be found elsewhere in the OT, and so do not favor seeing the Twelve as a self-defined unity. Perhaps most significantly, Ben Zvi argued that because every book of the Twelve has a superscription, they are clearly "separate prophetic books," so any attempt to blend them into a composite work is untenable.[18]

Although the studies by Kenneth H. Cuffey (1987) and Mignon Jacobs (2001) were limited to Micah, their discussions of the different kinds and degrees of coherence that literary works can exhibit challenged important features of redactional proposals.[19] Jacobs saliently observed that "the coherence of the whole cannot be determined by the observation of only parts of that whole," which problematized the integration of incompatible redactions in a genuinely unified

15. Rolf Rendtorff, "How to Read the Book of the Twelve as a Theological Unity," in Nogalski and Sweeney, *Reading and Hearing*, 75, 87.

16. Paul Noble, "Synchronic and Diachronic Approaches to Biblical Interpretation," *Journal of Literature & Theology* 7 (1993): 130–48.

17. Ehud Ben Zvi, "Twelve Prophetic Books or 'The Twelve': A Few Preliminary Considerations," in *Forming Prophetic Literature: Essays on Isaiah and the Twelve in Honor of John D. W. Watts*, ed. James W. Watts and Paul R. House, JSOTSup 235 (Sheffield: Sheffield Academic, 1996), 131–33.

18. Ben Zvi, "Twelve Prophetic Books," 135–37.

19. Kenneth H. Cuffey, "The Coherence of Micah: A Review of the Proposals and a New Interpretation" (PhD diss., Drew University, 1987); Mignon R. Jacobs, *The Conceptual Coherence of the Book of Micah*, JSOTSup 322 (Sheffield: Sheffield Academic, 2001). See the representative enumeration of redactional traces in Odil H. Steck, *Old Testament Exegesis: A Guide to the Methodology*, trans. James D. Nogalski, 2nd ed. (Atlanta: Scholars Press, 1998), 54, 85, 87, 90–91.

or primitive whole.[20] Similarly, Edgar Conrad and others argued that in some examples of historical-critical interpretation, "the texts are beaten into new shapes" that dispense with the intentional and canonical nature of the texts themselves.[21]

By the (gradual) end of this first phase of research, the discussion of what the Twelve is and what kind(s) of unity it possesses had become quite diverse. The different kinds of unity attributed to the collection involve distinct views on authorship, the nature of literary texts, and the role and limitations of the reader. Interplay between these different perspectives continued in the second phase, further diversified by postmodern and ideological approaches.

The Development of Study of the Book of the Twelve

The second phase of scholarly study of the Twelve shows no sharp discontinuity with what came before. Publications and presentations in the SBL Book of the Twelve program unit in the 2000s show the continued participation of historical-critical scholars with a strong commitment to redactional analysis of the Twelve. At the same time, some of these scholars and a number of new ones exhibited growing interest in the collection's thematic, inner-biblical, and rhetorical dimensions.[22] However, whereas Paul Redditt could write in 2003 that "the principal issue" in research on the Twelve was "whether to read the text diachronically or synchronically,"[23] ideological and other approaches introduced quite different interests and methods in subsequent years. The following survey traces some of these currents and their significance for the present status of research in the Twelve.

Methodological Diversification

The Synchronic/Diachronic Dichotomy and the Unity-Diversity Spectrum

Biblical scholars typically use the terms synchronic and diachronic, common in linguistics, to refer respectively to approaches that treat the text as primarily unified in its present form (i.e., as a whole) or as an artificial assemblage of disparate units composed in different historical circumstances and promoting competing

20. Jacobs, *Conceptual Coherence*, 194. On varieties of holism, see Francis J. Pelletier, "Holism and Compositionality," in *The Oxford Handbook of Compositionality*, ed. Markus Werning, Wolfram Hinzen, and Edouard Machery (Oxford: Oxford University Press, 2012), 149–74.

21. Edgar Conrad, *Reading the Latter Prophets: Toward a New Canonical Criticism*, LHBOTS 376 (London: T&T Clark, 2003).

22. E.g., Martin Roth, *Israel und die Völker im Zwölfprophetenbuch: Eine Untersuchung zu den Büchern Joel, Jona, Micha und Nahum*, FRLANT 210 (Göttingen: Vandenhoeck & Ruprecht, 2005).

23. Paul Redditt, "The Formation of the Book of the Twelve: A Review of Research," in *Thematic Threads in the Book of the Twelve*, ed. Paul L. Redditt and Aaron Schart, BZAW 325 (Berlin: De Gruyter, 2003), 23.

perspectives and claims. The relationship between these two approaches is complex and potentially confusing.[24] On the one hand, these approaches offer mutually exclusive explanations of diversity within texts: if changes in perspective, theological complexity, and tensions can be attributed to a single author's (or several authors') complex but coherent thought, then there is no need to propose different sources for each facet of that complexity.[25] On the other hand, some degree of complexity is inevitably present in all texts, and textual production and the text's references to circumstances outside it oblige the interpreter to reckon with its multifaceted relationship to history.[26] Francis Landy, like many linguists, argues that a text is coherent as long as the features and structures that hold it together prevail over those that push in the opposite direction, and similar logic lies behind many holistic (nonredactional) approaches to the Twelve.[27] Replacing the synchronic/diachronic polarity with a *spectrum* bounded by the poles of incoherence and coherence allows interpreters to avoid a binary approach to textual unity in favor of a continuum that accommodates more nuanced interpretation of consistency and coherence. To emphasize this point in what follows, the terms "holistic" and "compositional/redactional" will be used instead of synchronic and diachronic.[28]

The Rapprochement of Unity and Diversity in Interpretation of the Twelve

Due at least in part to this theoretical and methodological reflection, recent interpretation of the Twelve shows increased sensitivity to the delicate interplay of unity and diversity in individual books and in the collection. The ongoing disagreement between Ben Zvi and Nogalski regarding the nature of the collection crystallizes attention to this issue, and subsequent thematic, anthological, and other studies continue to develop this trend.[29]

24. See J. C. de Moor, ed., *Synchronic or Diachronic? A Debate on Method in Old Testament Exegesis*, OtSt 34 (Leiden: Brill, 1995).

25. Noble, "Synchronic and Diachronic Approaches."

26. William A. Tooman, "Literary Unity, Empirical Models, and the Compatibility of Synchronic and Diachronic Reading," in *Ezekiel: Current Debates and Future Directions*, ed. William A. Tooman and Penelope Barter, FAT 112 (Tübingen: Mohr Siebeck, 2017), 497–512; Daniel C. Timmer, "Observations linguistiques en lien avec le débat entre approches synchroniques et diachronique dans le livre d'Ésaïe," *Théologie Évangélique* 20 (2021): 19–45.

27. Francis Landy, "Three Sides of a Coin: In Conversation with Ben Zvi and Nogalski, *Two Sides of a Coin*," *JHebS* 10 (2010): article 11, https://doi.org/10.5508/jhs.2010.v10.a11. Representative is Dieter Viehweger, "Coherence—Interaction of Modules," in *Connexity and Coherence: Analysis of Text and Discourse*, ed. Wolfgang Heydrich et al. (Berlin: De Gruyter, 1989), 256–74.

28. Following the suggestion of Jacob Hoftijzer, "Holistic or Compositional Approach: Linguistic Remarks to the Problem," in de Moor, *Synchronic or Diachronic*, 98–114.

29. Ehud Ben Zvi and James D. Nogalski, *Two Sides of a Coin: Juxtaposing Views on Interpreting the Book of the Twelve / Twelve Prophetic Books*, ed. Thomas Römer, Analecta Gorgiana 201 (Piscataway: Gorgias, 2009); see Landy's discussion of this volume in "Three Sides."

Jason LeCureux, seeking to balance "the individuality of the [twelve] writings and the unity of the Book," adopts a thematic reading grounded in the Twelve's "self-referencing or intertextuality."[30] His study is a cogent argument for the unity of the Twelve that neither ignores significant differences between the books nor reads them as one.[31] I follow Rolf Knierim's groundbreaking work on conceptual coherence in an attempt to demonstrate the compatibility of the different viewpoints on non-Israelites that appear in the Twelve.[32] Emphasizing the different ways that each book characterizes non-Israelites and the different historical settings in which they are placed, I contend that this diversity reflects a coherent logic that accounts for the different present and future identities, statuses, and experiences of non-Israelites.[33]

A similar turn to unifying approaches is evident in many of the essays in a 2015 volume dedicated to New Form Criticism.[34] This approach shifts attention from the text's "preliterary past" (i.e., its composition) to "the particular work as a whole in order to see how its parts relate to the whole and communicate its message."[35] Many of these essays explore diverse literary genres, tensions, and themes but integrate that diversity with an interpretation of the final form of the text that finds its coherence to be predominant. A research group of the Institute for Biblical Research begun in 2014 also focuses more on holistic interpretations of the Twelve and its books than on compositional approaches. This line of research continues in a published collection of these thematically focused essays integrating the themes of theodicy and hope with their overall contribution to the message of the book(s) in which they appear.[36]

Scholars who hold that the Twelve is an anthology are also less likely to propose diachronic explanations of its diversity, and they sometimes see substantial unity in the individual books.[37] Heiko Wenzel argues that the Twelve is "something between an anthology and a unified book," and he promotes a narrative reading

30. Jason T. LeCureux, *The Thematic Unity of the Book of the Twelve*, HBM 41 (Sheffield: Sheffield Phoenix, 2012), 16, 26.

31. LeCureux, *Thematic Unity*, 26–31, 37–39.

32. Daniel C. Timmer, *The Non-Israelite Nations in the Book of the Twelve: Thematic Coherence and the Diachronic-Synchronic Relationship in the Minor Prophets*, BibInt 135 (Leiden: Brill, 2015).

33. Timmer, *Non-Israelite Nations*, 221–44.

34. Mark J. Boda, Michael H. Floyd, and Colin M. Toffelmire, eds., *The Book of the Twelve and the New Form Criticism*, ANEM 10 (Atlanta: Society of Biblical Literature, 2015).

35. Antony F. Campbell, "Form Criticism's Future," in *The Changing Face of Form Criticism for the Twenty-First Century*, ed. Marvin A. Sweeney and Ehud Ben Zvi (Grand Rapids: Eerdmans, 2003), 16, 23.

36. George Athas et al., eds., *Theodicy and Hope in the Book of the Twelve*, LHBOTS 705 (London: T&T Clark, 2021).

37. For the former, see Martin Beck, "Das Dodekapropheton als Anthologie," *ZAW* 118, no. 4 (2006): 576–77; for the latter, see Tchavdar S. Hadjiev, "A Prophetic Anthology Rather than a Book of the Twelve," in *The Book of the Twelve: Composition, Reception, and Interpretation*, ed. Lena-Sofia Tiemeyer and Jakob Wöhrle, VTSup 184 (Leiden: Brill, 2020), 90–108, esp. 103–4.

of the Twelve based on the opening lines of each of the books, such that each contributes to the message of the whole.[38] Christopher R. Seitz likewise affirms that we should "take the [twelve] books as having their own literary significance," but he finds the placement of Mic. 3:12 at the center of the collection to be crucial for its interpretation: "Later witnesses diachronically understood have been placed" before this fulcrum verse "*in order precisely to correlate typologically events whose significance cannot be understood by plotting them on the one-after-another model of secular historiography*."[39] Similarly, Christophe L. Nihan concludes that although Malachi has links to earlier texts in the Twelve, it uses those texts in such a way that the collection's coherence is "that of a dialogue between writings that preserve distinct perspectives."[40] Donatella Scaiola's canonical reading of the Twelve similarly interrelates (1) the historical dynamics of war, exile, and return in the history of Israel/Judah and their fluctuating conformity/nonconformity to (2) Torah, with YHWH's consistently just and merciful character, so that the dynamic relationship of YHWH with his people is at the heart of the Twelve and unites its individual books.[41] Despite their differences, these studies reflect growing interest in the macro-level unity in the Twelve—whether literary, theological, or conceptual—in contrast to the relatively weak and diachronically isolated unity offered by many redactional interpretations.

Variations of and Challenges to Redactional Approaches

At the same time, interest in redactional and other predominantly historical-critical approaches continues, although they are increasingly used together with other interpretative optics. For example, Anselm Hagedorn examines the non-Israelite nations in Nahum, Zephaniah, Obadiah, and Joel in relation to each book's redactional histories, although he considers any significant inter-book redaction unlikely.[42] His conclusion that each book reflects a different appraisal of the nations integrates the books' literary, historical, theological, and anthropological features with relevant sociological insights.[43] For detailed overviews of

38. Heiko Wenzel, "One or Twelve? Hermeneutics, Expectations, and a Framework for Reading the Twelve," in *The Book of the Twelve: An Anthology of Prophetic Books or The Result of Complex Redactional Processes?*, ed. H. Wenzel, Osnabrücker Studien zur Jüdischen und Christlichen Bibel 4 (Göttingen: Vandenhoeck & Ruprecht, 2017), 105–7, 108.

39. Christopher R. Seitz, "The Unique Achievement of the Book of the Twelve: Neither Redactional Unity nor Anthology," in Wenzel, *Book of the Twelve*, 41, 48 (emphasis original).

40. Christophe L. Nihan, "Remarques sur la question de l'unité' des XII," in *The Book of the Twelve—One Book or Many?*, ed. Elena Di Pede and Donatella Scaiola, FAT 91 (Tübingen: Mohr Siebeck, 2016), 165.

41. Donatella Scaiola, "The Twelve, One or Many Books? A Theological Proposal," in Di Pede and Scaiola, *Book of the Twelve*, esp. 192–93.

42. Anselm C. Hagedorn, *Die Anderen im Spiegel: Israels Auseinandersetzung mit den Völkern in den Büchern Nahum, Zefanja, Obadja und Joel*, BZAW 414 (Berlin: De Gruyter, 2011), 1–24.

43. Hagedorn, *Die Anderen*, 269–97.

recent discussion of diachronic approaches to the Twelve, see Wöhrle's essays on the Book of the Four (variously defined),[44] Lena-Sofia Tiemeyer's on the Haggai-Zech. 1–8 corpus, and Nogalski's on the final stages of the Twelve's formation.[45]

Significantly for the study of the Twelve, recent OT research has formulated serious methodological challenges to redaction criticism. Benjamin Ziemer contends that redaction-critical reconstructions of nonextant *Vorlagen* as commonly practiced in OT studies—that is, as hypotheses of textual development—are in principle impossible. His reasons for this assertion include the fact that the proposed earlier forms of the texts do not exist and that the criteria used to detect a redactor's work are not reliable: "The fundamental problem is the expectation that one is generally able to recognize 'source and redaction layers' within a literary work. Critical use of historical linguistics can serve to dampen these expectations and to reckon instead with the possibility that older sources were used that are not suggested by the literary form of the text."[46] The absence of earlier editions of the text being analyzed; the paradoxical idea of a redactor both preserving *and* significantly modifying the text he is editing; and contrary evidence suggesting that "not growth, but selection, is characteristic of the production of texts" lead Ziemer to urge that redactional analysis of the OT be abandoned.[47] Similar notes are struck in a collection of studies edited by Raymond F. Person and Robert Rezetko, in which the authors find a mix of confirming and contrary evidence that should chasten scholarly confidence in redaction-critical reconstructions of textual development.[48] A significant discussion of textual criticism also calls for more caution in reconstructing textual development in the absence of empirical evidence.[49]

These considerations reinforce methodological reservations on the part of scholars working in the Twelve. Hervé Tremblay argues, "A 'redactional unity' is an oxymoron, a contradiction. If it is redactional, it cannot be a unity. . . . One does not create unity by adding material. One cannot 'decide' to make a unity that was not there from the outset."[50] Much like Ziemer, Karl Möller observes that

44. Note Christoph Levin's pessimism regarding the viability of this corpus in "Das 'Vierprophetenbuch': Ein exegetischer Nachruf," *ZAW* 123 (2011): 221–35.

45. Jakob Wöhrle, "The Book of the Four"; Lena-Sofia Tiemeyer, "The Haggai-Zechariah 1–8 Corpus"; and James D. Nogalski, "The Compilation of the Book of the Twelve," all in Tiemeyer and Wöhrle, *Book of the Twelve*, 15–37, 38–64, 65–89, respectively.

46. Benjamin Ziemer, *Kritik der Wachstumsmodells: Die Grenzen alttestamentlicher Redaktionsgeschichte im Licht empirischer Evidenz*, VTSup 182 (Leiden: Brill, 2019), 120 (my trans.).

47. Ziemer, *Kritik der Wachstumsmodells*, 697, 24.

48. Raymond F. Person Jr. and Robert Rezetko, eds., *Empirical Models Challenging Biblical Criticism*, AIL 25 (Atlanta: SBL Press, 2016), 35.

49. See Reinhard Müller and Juha Pakkala, *Editorial Techniques in the Hebrew Bible: Toward a Refined Literary Criticism*, RBS 97 (Atlanta: SBL Press, 2022), esp. 545–49.

50. Hervé Tremblay, "*Vox clamantis in deserto?* L'enseignement d'Amos sur la justice sociale dans le contexte de la théorie de l'unité des douze," in Di Pede and Scaiola, *Book of the Twelve*, 114 (my trans.).

the criteria used to identify textual problems presumably indicating diachronic development are rarely justified on literary or theoretical grounds.[51] This lack of definition or precision gives rise to redaction-critical analyses of the Twelve that propose different or even contradictory conclusions, which in turn reduces their plausibility.[52] Whichever approach carries the day—Ziemer's rejection of predominant redaction-critical method and practice *or* a chastened use of such reconstructions driven by methodological refinements—this discussion promises to lead to more nuanced evaluations of textual unity and diversity and to more plausible reconstructions of textual composition.

Hermeneutical Diversification

Ideological Approaches

Ideological or perspectival approaches offer a different sort of challenge to the historical-critical tradition of interpretation by prioritizing contemporary perspectives and dealing with the biblical books in their final form. Yet they also resist holistic, coherent readings by critiquing prominent elements of the text's message or assumptions. For example, Suzanne Scholz contends that "gendered or sexualized scripts" are "often invisibly embedded in readers' interpretations."[53] Her "framework of inscription and erasure" relativizes historical-critical concerns and finds a unity of perspective in the text's multifaceted use or avoidance of gender and sexuality.[54] Stacy Davis's survey of race and intersectionality in the Twelve explores ethnicity and negative portrayals of non-Israelites as ancient manifestations of "identity politics and ethnic bias." Because this approach foregrounds textual content relevant to this optic, it partially bypasses reconstructions of the text's development and suggests that these discourses might be rooted in the author's general "ancient Near Eastern environment" rather than in particular circumstances.[55] The suitability of postcolonial approaches to the Twelve is indicated by the overlap between the imperialism of Assyria, Babylon, and Persia and the conquest-and-occupation dynamic of more recent colonialism.[56] However, some postcolonial perspectives militate against theological features in the Twelve, as when Jeremiah Cataldo insists that Yahwism must be interpreted purely on a

51. Karl Möller, "Reconstructing and Interpreting Amos's Literary Prehistory: A Dialogue with Redaction Criticism," in *"Behind" the Text: History and Biblical Interpretation*, ed. Craig Bartholomew et al., SHS 4 (Grand Rapids: Zondervan, 2003), 413.

52. Möller, "Reconstructing," 415–20.

53. Suzanne Scholz, "Reading the Minor Prophets for Gender and Sexuality," in *The Oxford Handbook of the Minor Prophets*, ed. Julia M. O'Brien (Oxford: Oxford University Press, 2021), 299.

54. Scholz, "Reading the Minor Prophets," 300.

55. Stacy Davis, "Race and Intersectionality in the Study of the Minor Prophets," in O'Brien, *Handbook of the Minor Prophets*, 313, 316.

56. Jeremiah Cataldo, "Postcolonial Approaches to the Minor Prophets," in O'Brien, *Handbook of the Minor Prophets*, 344.

"historically contingent, *political* level" if one is to avoid "any ideological influence of monotheism" in ancient Israel.[57] James L. Crenshaw helpfully outlines how other perspectives, including political, economic, and pedagogical, might be explored in harmony with concerns that are indigenous to the Twelve.[58]

The Twelve's Relation to the Old Testament and Beyond

Interpreters of the Minor Prophets have long recognized the diverse ways in which they echo or otherwise draw upon other parts of the OT. Recent studies have focused on these phenomena, aided by methodological refinements in intertextuality and inner-biblical interpretation.[59] These findings reveal numerous connections, some as subtle as they are substantive, between the Twelve and other OT texts. Notably, because these studies typically focus on the *semantics* of the source and receiving texts, they reveal more meaningful connections between the Twelve and the rest of the canon than do merely lexical links such as catchwords.

Thomas Renz's study of the Torah in the Twelve concludes that its authors linked "the cultic and the ethical" and made "loyalty to Yahweh . . . the wellspring of all true conformity to Torah."[60] Similarly, Rannfrid Thelle argues that the Twelve "read *with* and interactively complement" the Torah and the Former Prophets.[61] Steed Davidson finds variegated but strong continuity between the messages of the Twelve and the Major Prophets, and a number of studies explore the complex relation of the Twelve to Isaiah.[62] Researchers have also given attention to the theme of wisdom in relation to the Twelve, and their findings reinforce the renewed appreciation for Wisdom literature's organic relationship to the rest of the OT.[63] More broadly, Richard Schultz highlights the array of inner-biblical

57. Cataldo, "Postcolonial Approaches," 346, 345 (emphasis original).

58. James L. Crenshaw, "Latter Prophets: The Minor Prophets," in *The Blackwell Companion to the Hebrew Bible*, ed. Leo G. Perdue (Oxford: Blackwell, 2001), 371–73.

59. See the survey by Michael R. Stead, "Intertextuality and Innerbiblical Interpretation," in Boda and McConville, *Prophets*, 355–64.

60. Thomas Renz, "Torah in the Minor Prophets," in *Reading the Law: Studies in Honour of Gordon J. Wenham*, ed. J. Gordan McConville and Karl Möller, LHBOTS 461 (London: T&T Clark, 2007), 93–94.

61. Rannfrid I. Thelle, "The Minor Prophets' Relation to the Torah and Former Prophets," in O'Brien, *Handbook of the Minor Prophets*, 197 (emphasis original).

62. Steed V. Davidson, "The Relationship of the Minor Prophets to the Major Prophets," in O'Brien, *Handbook of the Minor Prophets*, 201–12. On Isaiah, see Richard J. Bautch, Joachim Eck, and Burkard M. Zapff, eds., *Isaiah and the Twelve: Parallels, Similarities and Differences*, BZAW 527 (Berlin: De Gruyter, 2020).

63. Mark J. Boda, Russell L. Meek, and William R. Osborne, eds., *Riddles and Revelations: Explorations into the Relationship between Wisdom and Prophecy in the Hebrew Bible*, LHBOTS 634 (London: T&T Clark, 2018); Jutta Krispenz, "Das Zwölfprophetenbuch und die alttestamentliche Weisheit," in *The Books of the Twelve Prophets: Minor Prophets, Major Theologies*, ed. Heinz-Josef Fabry, BETL 295 (Leuven: Leuven University Press, 2018), 183–212.

connections that tie the Twelve to the rest of the OT,[64] a phenomenon that Seitz explains on the basis of "internal editorial and canonical features."[65] Studies of intertextuality or inner-biblical interpretation focused on particular books are too numerous to canvas here but are conveniently gathered in many of the discussions in Herder's Theologischer Kommentar zum Alten Testament.[66] Others that merit mention include a collection of essays edited by Mark J. Boda and Michael H. Floyd on inner-biblical allusion in Zech. 9–14, Ruth Scoralick's study of Exod. 34:6–7 in the Twelve, and a collection of essays on the Twelve in the NT.[67]

Future Prospects for the Study of the Book of the Twelve

Many issues noted in this survey invite further exploration. This final section summarizes some of the most important among them.

The Nature of the Twelve

Recent research has shown that attributing the books that make up the Twelve to the prophets named in their incipits requires interpreters to situate them in their uniquely Levantine context, where prophecy was "scribal and public as soon as we see it" and claimed unparalleled authority.[68] The respect for "the connection between prophets and the texts that bear their names," attested across the ANE over more than a millennium, demonstrates the importance of such attributions and also makes the modification of prophetic messages unlikely.[69] Consequently, readers must reckon with these books' self-presentation as YHWH's speech

64. Richard Schultz, "The Ties That Bind: Intertextuality, the Identification of Verbal Parallels, and Reading Strategies in the Book of the Twelve," in Redditt and Schart, *Thematic Threads*, 27–47.

65. Christopher R. Seitz, *The Goodly Fellowship of the Prophets: The Achievement of Association in Canon Formation*, Acadia Studies in Bible and Theology (Grand Rapids: Baker Academic, 2009), 43.

66. E.g., Heinz-Josef Fabry, *Nahum*, HThKAT (Freiburg im Breisgau: Herder, 2006), 94–104. Note also Richard J. Coggins and Jin H. Han, *Six Minor Prophets through the Centuries*, Blackwell Bible Commentaries (Chichester: Wiley-Blackwell, 2011), and the discussions of each of the Minor Prophets in Gregory K. Beale et al., eds., *Dictionary of the New Testament Use of the Old Testament* (Grand Rapids: Baker Academic, 2023).

67. Mark J. Boda and Michael H. Floyd, eds., with Rex Mason, *Bringing Out the Treasure: Inner Biblical Allusion in Zechariah 9–14*, JSOTSup 370 (Sheffield: Sheffield Academic, 2003); Ruth Scoralick, *Gottes Güte und Gottes Zorn: Die Gottesprädikationen in Exodus 34,6f und ihre intertextuellen Beziehungen zum Zwölfprophetenbuch*, HBS 33 (Freiburg: Herder, 2002); Maarten J. J. Menken and Steve Moyise, eds., *The Minor Prophets in the New Testament*, Library of New Testament Studies 377 (Bloomsbury T&T Clark, 2009).

68. Seth L. Sanders, "Why Prophecy Became a Biblical Genre," *HeBAI* 6, no. 1 (2017): 32–35.

69. John Hilber, "The Culture of Prophecy and Writing in the Ancient Near East," in *Do Historical Matters Matter to Faith? A Critical Appraisal of Modern and Postmodern Approaches to Scripture*, ed. Dennis R. Magary and James K. Hoffmeier (Wheaton: Crossway, 2012), 241.

transmitted through designated spokespersons. Alongside this fundamental characteristic of prophecy as mediated divine speech, the importance of the human author/prophet is a helpful corrective to tendencies that marginalize the author and textually rooted meaning.[70]

Meaning and the Twelve

Although the historical-critical tradition has rightly insisted on the historical situatedness of the biblical writings, "any act of meaning . . . must involve both reference and sense."[71] The text's references to realities outside itself must therefore be understood as such, and textual meaning cannot be reduced to the historical circumstances in which the text was ostensibly produced, nor should meaning be located "behind the text." The related problem of "pseudo-historicism," which presumes that "if an idea or text is especially relevant to a particular historical period, then the idea or text must have originated in that period,"[72] must also be avoided, as should naively synchronic approaches that undervalue the text's historical setting, circumstances of production, and extratextual reference. Interpreters should also consider whether paratextual features such as the order(s) of the books are material to the text's meaning or merely facilitate the reader's understanding of linguistically expressed meaning.[73]

Diversity and the Twelve

The interface of unity and diversity is central to interpretation and must be patiently explored rather than eliminated by parceling out the alleged antecedents of complex concepts or perspectives among different *Sitze im Leben* and redactors. Wrestling with the text's complexity preserves the possibility of it being understood in its extant form, and such efforts are part of the reader's responsibility to learn "the ways of the text" in order to read it well.[74] The linguistic concept of coherence, referring essentially to the "conceptual unity" of a text, offers a helpful corrective to the tendency in some biblical interpretation to atomize complex phenomena.[75] The attendant realization that ancient and contemporary

70. See Kevin Vanhoozer, "Scripture and Tradition," in *The Cambridge Companion to Postmodern Theology*, ed. Kevin Vanhoozer (Cambridge: Cambridge University Press, 2003), 157.

71. D. J. Cunningham, "Meaning, Sense, Reference," in *Concise Encyclopedia of Semantics*, ed. Keith Allan (Amsterdam: Elsevier, 2009), 531.

72. Benjamin D. Sommer, "Dating Pentateuchal Texts and the Perils of Pseudo-Historicism," in *The Pentateuch: International Perspectives on Current Research*, ed. Thomas B. Dozeman, Konrad Schmid, and Baruch J. Schwartz, FAT 78 (Tübingen: Mohr Siebeck, 2011), 94.

73. See Greg Goswell, "The Order of the Books in the Greek Old Testament," *JETS* 52, no. 3 (2009): 449–66.

74. David A. Teeter and William A. Tooman, "Standards of (In)coherence in Ancient Jewish Literature," *HeBAI* 9, no. 2 (2020): 127, adopting a phrase of Alexander Samely.

75. Valuable insights on this point can be found in Teeter and Tooman, "Standards"; Alexander Samely, "How Coherence Works: Reading, Re-reading and Inner-Biblical Exegesis," *HeBAI* 9,

standards for coherence and unity may differ substantially signals the danger of anachronism and the consequent failure to appreciate "the complexities of biblical literature."[76] In the same vein, the often divergent conclusions of redactional and similar analyses show the need for clearer, linguistically validated criteria for identifying textual incohesion.[77] Still more importantly, the studies of Ziemer and of Müller and Pakkala challenge the field to radically reevaluate its readiness to grant probative value to hypothetical reconstructions of textual development.[78]

The Message and Function of the Twelve

Finally, readers who recognize Scripture as God's Word must ensure that their methods and hermeneutical approaches are consistent with or authorized (practiced) by Scripture, since "strategies of interpretation will be maladroit unless fitting to the actual nature of the text which they seek to unfold."[79] The one divine Author who speaks through the authors of the Twelve ensures that it possesses a unity far stronger and a diversity far richer than a historical-critical approach can yield or than an overweening holistic interpretation can accommodate. In contrast to "naturalistic accounts of Scripture and its interpretation," which "exclude from the beginning the actual conditions under which God's revelation makes itself present,"[80] the inspiration of Scripture provides an organic link between the Twelve and the rest of the OT (for Jewish and Christian readers) and the NT (for Christian readers).

The message of the Twelve so understood is accessible via canonically validated hermeneutical structures and methods, which reckon with the unity and discontinuity that underlie the NT's claims that the themes and promises of the Twelve find their culmination and fulfillment in Jesus Christ.[81] God's grace and

no. 2 (2020): 130–82; Michael A. Lyons, "Standards of Coherence and Incoherence: Evidence from Early Readers," *HeBAI* 9, no. 2 (2020): 183–208; and Daniel C. Timmer, "Reconsidering Textual Coherence: Complexity, Unity, and the Historical-Critical Task," *VT* (forthcoming).

76. Tooman, "Literary Unity," 509. On coherence, see Ted J. M. Sanders and H. L. W. Pander Maat, "Cohesion and Coherence," in Allan, *Concise Encyclopedia of Semantics*, 92–96.

77. Timmer, "Observations linguistiques."

78. Ziemer, *Kritik der Wachstumsmodells*; Müller and Pakkala, *Editorial Techniques in the Hebrew Bible*.

79. John Webster, *The Domain of the Word: Scripture and Theological Reason* (London: T&T Clark, 2012), viii. For helpful reflections on which interpretative perspectives and procedures are consistent with Scripture, see J. I. Packer, "Infallible Scripture and the Role of Hermeneutics," in *Scripture and Truth*, ed. D. A. Carson and John D. Woodbridge (Grand Rapids: Baker, 1992), 321–56.

80. Webster, *Domain of the Word*, 9.

81. See the illuminating discussion of reference in Kevin J. Vanhoozer, "Toward a Theological Old Testament Theology? A Systematic Theologian's Take on Reading the Old Testament Theologically," in *Interpreting the Old Testament Theologically: Essays in Honor of Willem A. VanGemeren*, ed. Andrew Abernethy (Grand Rapids: Zondervan, 2018), 293–317. For an example, see Aaron W. White, *The Prophets Agree: The Function of the Book of the Twelve Prophets in Acts*, BibInt 184 (Leiden: Brill, 2020).

justice, Israel's spiritually defined "remnant" and its role as a channel of blessing to the nations, and the call to live in faithful fellowship with God all reach their full expression in Christ, "the climax of the story of Israel."[82] As Paul House argued when study of the Twelve had just begun, a method that is "God-centered, intertextually oriented, authority-conscious, historically sensitive, and devoted to the wholeness of the Old Testament message"[83] promises to animate and guide continued exploration of the Twelve that is faithful to the text, open to correction and enrichment, and able to speak transformingly to the reader.

82. Heath Thomas, "Hearing the Minor Prophets: The Book of the Twelve and God's Address," in *Hearing the Old Testament: Listening for God's Address*, ed. Craig G. Bartholomew and David J. H. Beldman (Grand Rapids: Eerdmans, 2012), 373. I have attempted such an interpretation with several of the Twelve in Daniel C. Timmer, *The Theology of the Books of Nahum, Habakkuk, and Zephaniah*, OTT (Cambridge: Cambridge University Press, 2024).

83. Paul R. House, "The Character of God in the Book of the Twelve," in Nogalski and Sweeney, *Reading and Hearing*, 127.

21

Apocalyptic Literature

Stephen L. Cook

Taxonomy and Definitions

Disagreements about definitions and persisting negative value judgments continue to hamper the study of OT apocalyptic literature. A consensus accepts that the best starting point for study is the definition devised in the 1970s by a working group within the Society of Biblical Literature.[1] The definition, however, pertains to a defined body of Jewish and Christian apocalypses that includes only one OT text, Daniel. By beginning with the 1979 definition, one commits to working backward in examining other OT literature that shares some, but not all, of the traits of a later corpus.

Most researchers agree that the apocalyptic literature discloses "a transcendent reality which is both temporal, insofar as it envisages eschatological salvation, and spatial insofar as it involves another, supernatural world."[2] Daniel fares well in this approach; at least chapters 7–12 do. Scholars can elucidate many features of these chapters through comparison with other apocalypses. Earlier texts such as Ezek. 38–39 and Zech. 1–8, however, are orphaned. Their genre and worldview remain contested.

An interpretive positivism that narrows the rubric "apocalypticism" so that it applies to only one OT text (Dan. 7–12) is unfortunate for several reasons, not

1. John J. Collins, "Introduction: Towards the Morphology of a Genre," in *Apocalypse: The Morphology of a Genre*, ed. J. J. Collins, *Semeia* 14 (Decatur, GA: Scholars Press, 1979), 1–20.
2. Collins, "Introduction," 9.

least that full-blown apocalypses conceived themselves to be in continuity with pre-Daniel apocalyptic prophecy. The author of Revelation, for example, had no doubt that Ezekiel's Gog was an end-time fiend (Rev. 20:7–8), that Joel's locusts were a doomsday threat (9:1–12), and that Zechariah's lampstand vision looked forward to the end of days (11:3–4). Likewise, in Dan. 7:24–25 a blasphemous horn puts down three other horns. The imagery alludes to God's summoning of a fourth terrible, ruthless "shepherd" in Zech. 11:8, 15–17. It also reuses a vision of four doomed altar horns in Zech. 1:18–21.

Since the Jewish and Christian canons exclude most of the full-blown apocalypses of antiquity, contextualizing Daniel mostly within this late corpus risks downplaying its inner-biblical ties. A false impression of stark discontinuity between OT texts and mostly extracanonical apocalypses can arise. In 2003, for example, John Collins famously theorized that what discriminates apocalyptic thought from other eschatological expectations is belief in a postmortem judgment of individuals.[3] Such a position drives a wedge between Daniel (see 12:2) and earlier biblical wisdom and prophetic works thought to lack such a belief. It also risks underplaying the psychic, visionary, and spiritual experiences that brought the content to expression.

Intertextuality and Culmination

When scholars emphasize the discontinuity between apocalyptic and other biblical literature, some begin searching for logical, social, or historical etiologies to account for apocalypticism's dawn. Some etiologies are quite sophisticated. Amy C. Merrill Willis's 2010 study of the dissonance behind Daniel's composition traces its origins to a felt dissonance between faith in God's sovereignty and the people's experience of foreign subordination in second-century BCE Judea.[4] While etiological theories from the social sciences remain popular, so do theories of foreign influence. Some scholars have begun taking more seriously Zoroastrian influence in apocalypticism's development. Prominent works expanding this field of study include those of Jason M. Silverman and Vincente Dobroruka.[5] Likewise, C. D. Elledge finds Zoroastrianism to be instrumental in the rise of early-Jewish apocalyptic ideas, such as belief in the resurrection. Persian influence, he argues, made it plausible for early

3. John J. Collins, "Prophecy, Apocalypse and Eschatology: Reflections on the Proposals of Lester Grabbe," in *Knowing the End from the Beginning: The Prophetic, the Apocalyptic, and Their Relationships*, ed. Lester L. Grabbe and Robert D. Haak, JSPSup 46 (London: T&T Clark, 2003), 44–52.

4. Amy C. Merrill Willis, *Dissonance and the Drama of Divine Sovereignty in the Book of Daniel*, LHBOTS 520 (London: T&T Clark, 2010).

5. Jason M. Silverman, *Persepolis and Jerusalem: Iranian Influence on the Apocalyptic Hermeneutic*, LHBOTS 558 (New York: T&T Clark, 2012); Vincente Dobroruka, *Persian Influence on Daniel and Jewish Apocalyptic Literature*, Jewish and Christian Texts in Context and Related Studies 19 (London: Bloomsbury T&T Clark, 2022).

Judaism to start taking literally imagery like that of Ezekiel's resuscitation of dry bones.[6]

Jon D. Levenson rightly cautions that while Zoroastrianism has striking connections with Israelite apocalypticism, its influence on Jewish apocalyptic was mostly late and indirect.[7] It likely impacted beliefs at Qumran, but since its influence came through Hellenism, it offers little insight into the rise of Persian apocalyptic literature.

Since Lester Grabbe's foundational study, many scholars increasingly believe that Persian-era apocalyptic literature preceding Daniel is better illuminated through anthropological and other social-scientific comparisons than by comparisons with Hellenistic apocalypses.[8] Deadlock over terminology related to "apocalypse" and "apocalyptic" might be overcome by using the social-scientific nomenclature of millenarian groups. Such groups, whose worldviews center on a literal imminent judgment and deliverance of the world, occur across history and cultures. Examples include the Ghost Dance, cargo cults, and the Millerites.

Native American Ghost Dance rituals provide particularly helpful comparisons. Body painting within older Sun Dance ceremonies was a prime source for the Ghost Dance symbol system. The imagery on garments of the Ghost Dance reuses traditional mythological symbols, such as those preserved on older shields. Whereas the symbolic system of Plains shields orients itself toward raiding, trading, and hunting, the Ghost Dance garments focus on eschatology, on ushering in a new world. An emphasis on select motifs and a new use of colors betrays an apocalyptic shift in orientation toward regeneration, re-creation, and world renewal.[9]

Like the millennial Ghost Dance religion, the dawn of biblical apocalypticism drew heavy inspiration from autochthonous (indigenous), inner-biblical material, especially cosmogonic mythic patterns and images. Marvin Sweeney, among others, has shown the patent use of earlier pentateuchal and prophetic material in texts such as Joel, Ezek. 38–39, and Zechariah to define core sacramental perspectives and to teach and elevate the core ideals of the Torah.[10] The OT apocalyptic literature was highly intertextual and allusive from its start and remained so through the composition of Daniel.

6. C. D. Elledge, *Resurrection of the Dead in Early Judaism, 200 BCE–CE 200* (Oxford: Oxford University Press, 2017), 52–53.

7. Jon D. Levenson, *Resurrection and the Restoration of Israel* (New Haven: Yale University Press, 2008), 215–16, 218.

8. Lester L. Grabbe, "The Social Setting of Early Jewish Apocalypticism," *JSP* 2, no. 4 (1989): 27–47; Stephen L. Cook, *Prophecy and Apocalypticism: The Postexilic Social Setting* (Minneapolis: Fortress, 1995).

9. Trudy Carter Thomas, "Crisis and Creativity: Visual Symbolism of the Ghost Dance Tradition" (PhD diss., Columbia University, 1988), 18, 123, 148, 155.

10. Marvin A. Sweeney, "The Priesthood and the Proto-Apocalyptic Reading of Prophetic and Pentateuchal Texts," in Grabbe and Haak, *Knowing the End*, 167–78.

Daniel arose as Israel experienced the inner-biblical ripening of sacral ideals, of cosmogonic themes, and of prophecies now received and read as farsighted visions. Mythic archetypes gathered steam, such as aqueous chaos churning floodwaters as amniotic agents and the girding of the divine warrior's loins. Walter Wink grasps the dynamic well: "Something new was constellating, some unprecedented God-hunger was manifesting. There was a desire to make good on the ancient prophecies."[11] The canon was solidifying, its hopes, dreams, and eschatological trajectories beginning to push out from the biblical texts into live expectations among "peoples of the book." Simultaneously, as forced migrants and refugees, God's people faced the psychic challenge of renegotiating their self-identity.[12]

Validating the Experiential Dimensions of Apocalypticism

Apocalypses such as Daniel arose in a time of expectancy, a time of swells and crests in what Hans Urs von Balthasar calls "the dramatic rhythm" of God's economy of salvation.[13] Apocalypticism's visions reveal the denouement and telos of this intensifying rhythm, this "continual raising of the stakes." The rhythm's ever-impactful prolepses anticipate God's coming reign. The visions of denouement reveal how the legacy of the past, especially the sequence of empires in Dan. 2 and 7, represents a trajectory of oppression, chaos, and dissolution. The crests of the rhythm, at the same time, brush up against God's transcendent reality and climactic intervention in history.

Salvation history experiences crests, micro-effulgences of God's reign, at the exodus, again in the era of Elijah and Elisha, and once more in the prophetic visions of Isa. 40–55. Daniel's authors understood themselves to be living in such a time of effulgence. The appearance of the figure riding the clouds in Dan. 7:13–14 recalls God's guidance by a cloud at the exodus (Exod. 13:21–22; 14:19–20, 24; Num. 9:15–22; Neh. 9:12; Ps. 78:14). The phrase "everlasting righteousness" in Dan. 9:24 rings with the diction of Isa. 40–55 and its theme of the eschatological exodus and the final consolation of Israel. The verse's language is especially close to Isa. 51:6, 8 and embodies the Isaian vision of a homecoming of victory and righteousness. The resurrection of the dead in Dan. 12:2 recalls Elijah's and Elisha's miracles of bringing the dead to life (1 Kings 17:22; 2 Kings 4:33–35; 13:21), as well as Elijah's ascension to heaven without dying (2 Kings 2:11–12).

Through Daniel's storyline, the book's authors, living in the second century BCE, let slip their own transcendental, spiritual experience of wrestling with

11. Walter Wink, *The Human Being: Jesus and the Enigma of the Son of Man* (Minneapolis: Fortress, 2002), 57.

12. For an insightful treatment of the challenge from a Latino perspective, see M. Daniel Carroll R., "Processing the Processes of Migration: Insights from Book of Daniel," *Apuntes* 41, no. 1 (2021): article 6, https://scholar.smu.edu/apuntes/vol41/iss1/6.

13. Hans Urs von Balthasar, *Theo-Drama*, vol. 4, *The Action* (San Francisco: Ignatius, 1994), 56–58.

apocalyptic psychic content. Like Pharaoh and Nebuchadnezzar of old, their psyches tossed and turned with inner experiences of imminent miracles that their senses had yet to perceive. Visionary contents impinge on Daniel's ego-consciousness from *outside it*, causing emotional and physiological effects. He states: "I, Daniel, was overcome and lay sick for some days. . . . I was dismayed by the vision and did not understand it" (Dan. 8:27 NRSV; cf. 7:15, 28; 12:8). Daniel awakens from his visions shaking. His mind cannot apprehend their content, which represents far more than mere coded symbolism of historical reality.

Biblical scholars need metaphysical and psychological terms and models to help elucidate apocalyptic content. Carl Jung is helpful in his insistence that such content is not invented but enters inner perception spontaneously. It is not subject to our will but exhibits a certain autonomy. We should regard the contents of visions not only as objects but as subjects with their own laws. Jung admits that we "can, of course, describe them as objects, and even explain them . . . in the same measure as we can describe and explain a living human being. But then we must disregard their obvious autonomy."[14]

The book of Daniel bears witness to a surging crest in divine salvation's economy, a submission to psychoid, transcendental spiritual evidence conveyed in dreams and visions. The fact that revelation impelled its writing rather than *outer*, empirical etiologies has confused historical criticism. Michael Stone points out scholars' discomfort with explicit claims by seers about actual revelatory experience.[15] From the nineteenth century, critics have disparaged postexilic apocalyptic literature. Samuel Davidson found apocalyptic visions to be "a mark of decay" in the faith of "the later Jews." Such revelations are an "imitation of real visions."[16] Davidson's views partake of the prejudices of his time, including a romantic elevation of preexilic oral poetic prophecy and a suspicion of scribal mantic revelation.[17] With those prejudices now behind us, it is harder to excuse recent scholarship that often still assumes apocalyptic vision accounts to be fictional.[18]

Stone dismantles the historicist argument that the texts' literary conventions and stock elements contradict the reality of the experiences reported, even when

14. Carl Gustav Jung, *Answer to Job*, trans. R. F. C. Hull, Bollingen Series (Princeton: Princeton University Press, 1973), xiv.

15. Michael E. Stone, "A Reconsideration of Apocalyptic Visions," *HTR* 96, no. 2 (2003): 167–80; cf. Lorenzo DiTommaso, "Apocalypses and Apocalypticism in Antiquity (Part I)," *CurBR* 5, no. 2 (2007), 235–86, esp. 264–65.

16. Samuel Davidson, *An Introduction to the Old Testament: Critical, Historical, and Theological* (Covent Garden, London: Williams & Norgate, 1863), 3:175. With the dawn of apocalypticism, "independent prophecy was forsaking Israel."

17. It is unacceptable, we now recognize, that Davidson (*Introduction*, 177) labeled the apocalyptic literature of Judaism's earliest dawn as "degenerate Judaism."

18. E.g., Martha Himmelfarb, "The Practice of Ascent in the Ancient Mediterranean World," in *Death, Ecstasy, and Otherworldly Journeys*, ed. John J. Collins and Michael Fishbane, Suny Series in Religious Studies (New York: State University of New York Press, 1995), 123–37. See Stone, "Reconsideration."

real, not-invented apocalyptic content must be communicated in culture-specific forms since "there is no other language . . . to use." Millennial groups can receive and validate only those vision reports of seers employing recognizable generic conventions and diction.[19]

The *ex eventu* (after the event) approach of historicists reads Daniel's confessions of disorientation at his visions *obliquely* as a literary ploy of the second-century BCE authors. The protagonist Daniel must experience disorientation, for he "supposedly" peers into a distant and alien future.[20] (He does not so peer, since his foreknowledge of centuries of world history is prophecy after the fact, *vaticinium ex eventu*.) His visions are portrayed as outrageously miraculous in the mind of a Babylonian exile. A literary and canonical approach, by contrast, reads the confessions of perturbation *straightforwardly* as a witness to the struggle of finite human consciousness with transcendent content. Thus, in chapter 10, Daniel experiences his finite humanity not in a vision of a distant future but of an angel (Dan. 10:8–9, 16–17; also see 8:17–18). This is a common pattern in apocalypses.

In the Similitudes, Enoch sees God enthroned. A great trembling and fear seizes him, and his loins lose control (1 En. 60.3–4; cf. 39.14). Nebuchadnezzar, in Dan. 4, dreams not of the far future but of his own glory and judgment. Still, the revelation profoundly disorients him (Dan. 4:5). John R. Markley aptly states, "When confronted with *revelation generally* . . . humanity is vividly portrayed through . . . fear, weakness, inability to speak, and the enduring effects of these revelatory episodes."[21]

Major Scholarly Disagreements

The rise of modernist criticism of the OT represents a break with classical Jewish and Christian conceptions of prophecy. Historical critics contest classical notions that prophecy concerned the eschatological goal of history and the coming of the Messiah. Julius Wellhausen conflated prophetic eschatology with apocalypticism and associated both with later Judaism, not with Israelite prophecy.[22] Sigmund Mowinckel's foundational work on eschatology and messianism determined that both were generally foreign to Israel's preexilic prophets.[23] Such views commanded

19. Stone, "Reconsideration," 179.

20. John J. Collins, *A Commentary on the Book of Daniel*, Hermeneia (Minneapolis: Fortress, 1993), 341–42.

21. John R. Markley, *Peter—Apocalyptic Seer: The Influence of the Apocalypse Genre on Matthew's Portrayal of Peter*, WUNT 2/34 (Tübingen: Mohr Siebeck, 2013), 82 (emphasis added). See also Wink, *Human Being*, 53.

22. Julius Wellhausen, *Prolegomena to the History of Israel*, trans. J. Sutherland Black and Alan Menzies (Atlanta: Scholars Press, 1994), 502–88; cf. Julius Wellhausen, *Israelitische und Jüdische Geschichte*, 9th ed. (Berlin: De Gruyter, 1958), 109–47, 151–61, 206.

23. Sigmund Mowinckel, *He That Cometh: The Messianic Concept in the Old Testament and Later Judaism*, trans. G. W. Anderson (New York: Abingdon, 1954), 460; Johannes Lindblom, *Prophecy in Ancient Israel* (Oxford: Blackwell, 1963), 360–75.

a virtual consensus at SBL's 2021 program unit "Apocalypse Now: Apocalyptic Reception and Impact throughout History Section." Not only did the unit broadly agree that the OT (including postexilic prophecy) lacked any messianism, but also a common view understood the antichrist as a post-NT conception based on an illegitimate harmonization of disparate NT texts. I push back against these developing convictions.

Messianic Expectation

Apocalyptic literature often anticipates the imminent advent of a messianic age, ushered in by a messiah, a divinely anointed ideal deliverer. One current trend in critical scholarship relegates messianism to a late development, arising only in early Judaism. I contend that messianism has a deeper, preexilic pedigree. Apocalyptic messianism is far from discontinuous with canonical expectations of a messiah. Through the Succession Narrative and the Deuteronomistic History, Scripture attests to a stark tension between the Davidic line's sacral kingship and the deep failures of both Judah's and Israel's royal leadership. As Bill Arnold recognizes, "By sustaining and prolonging the antinomy between ideal promises and unfulfilled reality, the [Deuteronomistic History] outlines the contours of an eschatological messianism that emerges in the prophets (Isa. 11:1–2; Jer. 23:5; Amos 9:11–15)."[24] Prophetic scrolls, such as Isaiah, projected into an ideal future the divine promises to the Davidic line.

The OT term מָשִׁיחַ (*māšîaḥ*, anointed) is most often not a technical term for "Messiah" nor is it the most common designation for the coming royal figure. Other terms include "the Branch" (Isa. 11:1; Jer. 23:5; 33:15; Zech. 3:8; 6:12), "Immanuel" (Isa. 7:14; 8:8; 8:10), and the "signal" (11:10; 49:22). Nevertheless, Walter C. Kaiser Jr. correctly asserts that out of thirty-nine usages, many or all of the following nine refer to a coming Davidide of promise: 1 Sam. 2:10, 35; Pss. 2:2; 20:6; 28:8; 84:9; Hab. 3:13; Dan. 9:25, 26.[25] To this list I would add 2 Sam. 22:51; 23:1; Pss. 89:51; 132:17–18.

Two texts, one using מָשִׁיחַ and the second using חוֹתָם (*ḥôtām*, signet ring) may be sampled as typical messianic passages. First Samuel 2:10 contains the lexical pair מָשִׁיחַ and קֶרֶן (*qeren*, horn, power), which occurs elsewhere only in Ps. 132:17, a messianic psalm also employing the allusive diction of the Davidic lamp (see 1 Sam. 3:3; 2 Sam. 21:17; 22:29). The psalm verse also contains the verb צמח (*ṣmḥ*, sprout, branch), a verbal root with strong messianic connotations (2 Sam. 23:5; Jer. 33:15; Ezek. 29:21; Zech. 6:12). It is fair to assert that 1 Sam. 2:10 is messianic when read in its intertextual matrix—that is, in its holistic, canonical context.

24. Bill T. Arnold, "Old Testament Eschatology and the Rise of Apocalypticism," in *The Oxford Handbook of Eschatology*, ed. Jerry L. Walls (New York: Oxford University Press, 2008), 26.

25. Walter C. Kaiser Jr., *The Messiah in the Old Testament* (Grand Rapids: Zondervan, 1995), 16.

The second text, Hag. 2:23, lacks the term מָשִׁיחַ but is clearly messianic when read dialogically in its canonical context. In one of the prophet Jeremiah's remarkable images, God metaphorically "wears" Israel's anointed ruler like a signet ring. Dramatically, when the people go into exile, that ring, signaling God's commitment, is torn off (Jer. 22:24). In Song 8:6 and Hag. 2:23, however, a new setting of a seal of commitment signals that now is the time for God to put on a new signet, a revival of the messianic promise. Considering the finality of Jer. 22:30, the reversal in Haggai must indicate a radical, apocalyptic re-creation of Israel's monarchy, which God earlier terminated.

Is Hag. 2:23 mistaken in applying the term "signet ring" to Zerubbabel, a historical governor of Yehud circa 520 BCE? Hermeneutical reflection suggests not. Consider the biblical pattern noted above of periodic effulgences of God's reign. Given this pattern, Haggai's message to Zerubbabel is necessarily provisional. Haggai declares him a messianic candidate, or *at least* a prefiguration, finding in him an ideal Davidic leader reestablishing Zion. Other partial messianic fulfillments include King Josiah, who died prematurely, and Jesus, whose "coming with the clouds" (Mark 14:62 NRSV) is delayed.

The Haggai-Zech. 1–8 corpus, in its present literary and theological shape, does not treat Hag. 2:23 as false prophecy. Rather, texts such as Zech. 6:15, which are canonical reflections on the earlier words of Haggai and Zechariah, understand divine messianic promises like Hag. 2:23 as flexible. Embedding contingency, they are susceptible to being delayed due to factors such as unfaithfulness. Thus, Robert Kashow aptly renders Zech. 6:15 as follows: "[Messianic epiphany] will take place, if you completely obey the Lord."[26]

Transcendent, Otherworldly Messianism

Many scholars suppose that notions of transcendent, supernatural messianism are foreign to the OT canon and appear in early Christianity only after Jesus's lifetime on earth. The strong monotheistic convictions of Judaism always resisted such ideas, and Jesus's followers began to consider him a divine savior only retrospectively, after his earthly career had ended. Notions of a divine savior, many hold, are implausible before Christianity expanded within the Hellenistic culture of the Roman Empire. Is this view correct?

In the Similitudes (1 En. 45.3; 62.3, 5), an apocalypse from the middle of the first century CE, the Son of Man figure from the vision of Dan. 7 is a future figure of glory. Likewise, in Qumran's "Daniel Apocryphon" (4Q246 II, 1) from the end of the first century BCE, the same figure from Daniel is a transcendent being alongside the Most High, one called "Son of God" (the very diction of Luke

26. Robert C. Kashow, "Zechariah 1–8 as a Theological Explanation for the Failure of Prophecy in Haggai 2:20–23," *JTS* 64, no. 2 (2013): 398. Later, Zech. 8:15–17 again ties God's eschatological promises together with what Israel needs to do if promises are to be realized (Kashow, "Theological Explanation," 402).

1:32, 35!). Peter Schäfer, among several others, understands the apocryphon's "Son of God" as a "second divine figure," who "will judge the earth."[27] Israelite apocalyptic texts describe God or a messianic figure, not God's people on earth, presiding over an end-time judgment.

The lively apocalyptic interest in Daniel's Son of Man within early Second Temple Judaism and the NT indicates that the excitement may well have roots in the Aramaic text of Dan. 7 itself. Indeed, upon inspection, the figure of that text bears clear marks of transcendence and even divinity. The diction in Dan. 7:14 parallels that of 4:3 (3:33 MT) and 6:26 and associates his dominion directly with God's own. Likewise, the reverence paid him (לֵהּ יִפְלְחוּן, *lēh yiplәḥûn*, they should serve him) pertains to deity (Dan. 3:17–18, 28; 6:16, 20 [6:17, 21 MT]). Above all, deities, not humans or angels, arrive on clouds.[28] The fourth-century CE Iranian church father Aphrahat aptly proclaims: "Have the children of Israel received the kingdom of the Most High? God forbid! Or has that people come on the clouds of heaven?"[29] No! In the Son of Man, the archetype of the divine warrior constellates, taking bodily form.

Peter Schäfer, John Collins, and others equate the Son of Man figure of Dan. 7 with the angel Michael (see Dan. 10:13, 21; 12:1), but this is highly unlikely. The one "like a son of man" (כְּבַר אֱנָשׁ, *kәbar ʾĕnāš*) is decidedly human, as seen in his distinct appellation and his ties to Ps. 8's "son of man" (בֶּן־אָדָם, *ben-ʾādām*)[30] and in his links with the people of the holy ones in Dan. 7:27. The figure is a new apocalyptic hybrid, a novel synthesis of human consciousness and transcendence. Is not Dan. 7:13–14 in dialogue with Ps. 8:4–7 and Gen. 1:26, "Let us make humanity in our image to resemble us so that they may take charge" (CEB)?

Israel Knohl sums up the biblical background of the hybridization. After surveying the biblical evidence, he concludes: "In several psalms and . . . prophets . . . the King-Messiah is a kind of hybrid of the human and the divine. In these sources, there is a glorification of the position of the king to the point where he attains a superhuman status. . . . The king is glorified in several ways: through a description of the king as the son of God, by giving the king divine names, or when the king is given eternal life."[31]

Daniel 7 passes the baton of leadership from angels to a new Adam, who renews the *imago Dei* and bridges the painful gulf between heaven and earth in

27. Peter Schäfer, *Two Gods in Heaven: Jewish Concepts of God in Antiquity*, trans. Allison Brown (Princeton: Princeton University Press, 2020), 41–44.

28. J. A. Emerton states incisively: "If Dan. vii. 13 does not refer to a divine being, then it is the only exception out of about seventy passages in the OT." Emerton, "The Origin of the Son of Man Imagery," *JTS* 9, no. 2 (1958): 232. The OG of Dan. 7:13 is especially interesting since the figure is clearly on, not with, the clouds, and a literal reading of the Greek has him coming "as a son of man" and "as the Ancient of Days."

29. Aphrahat, *Demonstration* 5.21.

30. The term *ʾĕnoš* that appears in the Aramaic phrase "son of man" in Dan. 7 is also used of the primordial human in the Aramaic targum on Gen. 1:26.

31. Israel Knohl, "The Messianic Controversy," in *Congress Volume: Aberdeen 2019*, ed. Grant Macaskill, Christl M. Maier, and Joachim Schaper, VTSup 192 (Leiden: Brill, 2022), 157.

place since Gen. 3. Like the "son of man" in Ps. 8:4–7, he is elevated just beneath God and subdues beasts. Whatever else the Son of Man represents, he is God's chosen viceroy who replaces imperial savagery with humane rule. In him is restored our reflection of God.[32]

The expectation of a coming sacral vicar of God to preside over earthly life on God's behalf is hardly Dan. 7's innovation. Hebrew prophecy had previously projected as an eschatological promise the archetypal and mythic ideal of sacral kingship, known since ancient Ugarit and amply attested in ancient Egypt. Several of the messianic texts pinpointed by Kaiser attest to this development. For present purposes, it must suffice to mention Isa. 9:6 as a straightforward example. Despite the verse's well-known contribution to Handel's *Messiah*, modern critics often raise serious objections to the traditional view of divine kingship in the text.

Isaiah 9:6 [5 MT] reads, "For a child has been born for us, a son given to us; authority rests upon his shoulders; and he is named Wonderful Counselor, Mighty God, Everlasting Father, Prince of Peace" (my trans.). A popular critical approach takes the royal title אֵל גִּבּוֹר (*ʾēl gibbôr*, Mighty God) as a *theophoric name*—that is, a human's name that includes a reference to God's activity.[33] "Nathan," meaning "[YHWH] has given [this child]," would be a parallel. The new king and his name signal God's might: "Mighty indeed is God!" This view is problematic.

Whatever the first prophetic author, or authors, understood by Isa. 9's prophecy of the righteous reign of a coming king, the text's present literary and canonical context gives it an eschatological trajectory extending far beyond its first Assyrian-era setting. It now arcs forward into the postexilic era of consolation described in Isa. 40–66. By placing the messianic promise after Isa. 8:22, the canonical context makes clear that the new era of light will come only in the far future, after the darkness of the exile to come.

The light of messianic consolation (Isa. 9:2) will appear only after the אֲפֵלָה (*ʾăpēlâ*, thick darkness) of 8:22. This darkness, in the rare diction of the verse, resonates with the hopes of 58:10 and 59:9 for postexilic salvation. What is more, consolation comes to people forced from the land. The verbal root used in 8:22 is נדח (*ndḥ*, thrust out) as in 56:8 ("those driven out," REB). This is a distant liberation from an extended diaspora.

As for the startling title "Mighty God" (Isa. 9:6), it rings with connotations of divine sonship. As suspected since Albrecht Alt's work, ancient Egyptian royal titulary conventions are comparable.[34] Isaiah 10:21 shows that the name אֵל גִּבּוֹר

32. See Wink, *Human Being*, 53–54. Wink notes that the Son of Man is "archetypally human," something akin to Adam's humanness as such. The figure is able to "draw nearer to God, to realize the divine likeness of the image of God, to transcend the bestiality of the Domination System."

33. Andrew Abernethy, *The Book of Isaiah and God's Kingdom: A Thematic-Theological Approach*, NSBT 40 (London: Apollos; Downers Grove, IL: InterVarsity, 2016), 128–31.

34. Knohl, "Messianic Controversy," 137–39. Knohl believes it more likely that Isaiah's language expresses hope for a future wonderous birth than, as Alt supposed, a liturgical elevation

is a divine name, not a theophoric one. As if to banish all doubt, Isa. 9:4 alludes to Judg. 6, where the appellation "mighty warrior" in 6:12, comparable to "Mighty God," describes Gideon's own identity, not God's work. Again, a theophoric name is not in play.

How do we explain the audacity of using titles such as "Mighty God" and "Eternal Father" of a human king? It is a projection, Knohl asserts, of existing biblical traditions of divine kingship as eschatology. Psalms 21:3–4, 45:6, and 61:7 all speak of Israel's ideal king as transcendent and enthroned forever beside God.[35] This is the idiom that funds Isa. 9:6 and, crucially, Dan. 7's vision of the Son of Man's enthronement.

Radical Evil

Apocalyptic literature characteristically wrestles with the problem of radical impurity and evil, recognizing anti-God powers at work in creation. A commonplace critical view consigns notions of transpersonal cosmic evil and demonic hosts to the status of late intrusions appearing in Israelite tradition only in the second and first centuries BCE (e.g., 1 En. 15.8–16.1; Jub. 5; 10; 23.29; 1Q27 1 I, 2, 7; 4Q416 1 10–13). In this analysis, apocalyptic ideas of evil represent an ungrounded paradigm shift, perhaps a result of Persian influence on early Judaism. Yet it is doubtful that Persian religion effected such a fundamental change in the tradition. I argue that the threat of preternatural defilement and evil is authentic to biblical tradition.

As Arnold notes, the preexilic prophetic literature is intimately familiar with the "radical wrongness of the present world and the conviction that radical changes, to make things right, will indeed occur 'in that day'"—that is, the eschatological day of YHWH.[36] A glance at Ezekiel's eschatology prior to Jerusalem's fall in 586 BCE suffices to illustrate how creation's "radical wrongness" may be attributed to real anti-God forces. For Ezekiel, the impure, evil front opposing holiness cannot be domesticated. Like a preternatural ether, it can leak out of corpses to infect people (Ezek. 44:25–27; Num. 19:11 [Holiness school]). It can even enter containers not covered with lids (see the treatment of corpse contagion in Num. 19:15). Uncanny in character, it has built up in Jerusalem like encrusted gunk in a pot (Ezek. 24:6). The antithesis of holiness has spatial, territorial dimensions. In Ezek. 4:12, 15, an image of excrement describes the filthy repulsion of territorial space outside God's land. The image reappears later in Zech. 3:3–4. The Aramaic punning in Dan. 5:6, where Babylon's last king soils his pants (cf. 1 En. 60.3–4), satirically associates his desecrating profanation of the temple vessels with a release of excrement.

---

of an actual adult king at a coronation ceremony. Cf. Brevard S. Childs, *Isaiah*, OTL (Louisville: Westminster John Knox, 2001), 80.

35. See Knohl, "Messianic Controversy," 140–42.

36. Arnold, "Old Testament Eschatology," 25.

In Zech. 5:5–11 a personification of impurity departs Israel to receive its own shrine in Babylonia. Here, archetypal evil has constellated in apocalyptic form as something realistic and embodied. Earlier, in Ezek. 38–39, archetypal evil similarly invades history, incarnate as Gog of Magog, chaos constellated and focused as God's end-time foe. Ezekiel hardly fashions Gog of Magog from scratch. His inner-biblical referencing reveals that he considered transcendent hubris and terror to be embedded in earlier prophecy. Ezekiel 38:17 reads, "[Gog,] are you the one of whom I spoke in former days?" (NASB). The primary reference is to the transcendent being of Isa. 14:4b–21, the tyrant called the Shining One.[37]

In Ezek. 28:11–19 the prophet describes a cherub's fall from Mount Eden. Cherubim mostly appear in Ezekiel's book as lightning-fast beings who interact with mirrored partners. The cherubim underneath God's throne-chariot (e.g., Ezek. 1:5–14) dart here and there in synchronized steps to contain unspeakable power and to resist its enormous pull. Ezekiel 28 reveals that sometimes a fatal misstep happens. Jung's description of the archetype of the quaternity helps us conceptualize cherubim figures, and their heraldic arrays, as innately associated with a guarded cosmic center.[38]

A widespread transpersonal and psychoid object, the quaternity archetype consists of a four-point or fourfold arrangement of objects or symbols associated with the cosmic center, with Mount Eden. According to Jung, the quaternity paradigm of mythology can sometimes fail at one of its four points.[39] One point can lose its angelic character, while the other three remain morally positive. Jung notes that the fallen point becomes "demonic." Ezekiel 28 depicts only one of four cherubim becoming corrupt, which fits the mythological pattern of one point of the cosmic array undergoing a fall.

Postexilic apocalyptic prophecy in Isa. 65:17–25 refers to a confrontation of good and evil on Mount Eden. As the section concludes in verse 25, language of a changed reality in a new creation appears. The first two poetic lines of verse 25 describe the disappearance of predator and prey, a fundamental category of postdiluvian existence. With the advent of God's reign, wolves' and lions' metabolisms transform to make them herbivores. Eden's vegetarianism (Gen. 1:29–30) returns. The final colon of Isa. 65:25a shifts to a new theme: "As for the serpent, its food will be dust" (REB). The English equivalent would be to proclaim that the serpent "bites the dust." This is the metaphor of defeat that Gen. 3:14 applies when God curses the primordial Eden serpent.

37. Stephen L. Cook, "Isaiah 14: The Birth of a Zombie Apocalypse?," *Int* 73, no. 2 (2019): 130–42.

38. See Stephen L. Cook, "Cosmos, Kabod, and Cherub: Ontological and Epistemological Hierarchy in Ezekiel," in *Ezekiel's Hierarchical World: Wrestling with a Tiered Reality*, ed. Stephen L. Cook and Corrine L. Patton, SBLSS 31 (Atlanta: Society of Biblical Literature, 2004), 181.

39. See Cook, "Cosmos, Kabod, and Cherub," 194.

An echo of Gen. 3:14 is heard, especially given the textual context that already recalls Eden. It is apparent that both the Septuagint and the targum consider the pericope to point in this direction, since they introduce Eden's tree of life in Isa. 65:22. The pericope encourages this move with its general intertextual, allusive style and with Edenic longevity specifically promised by the text in verses 20–22. As Childs observes, "The line 'dust will be the serpent's food' is a play on Genesis 3:14, which describes the curse of the serpent at the Fall."[40] Here the curse of the serpent mounts to a denouement, a permanent defanging. The snake of the first creation returns and is neutralized.

Incarnation of Transcendent Reality

In Isa. 65:25 wolves' and lions' metabolisms transform to make them herbivores again, as on Mount Eden. With the advent of God's reign, God's curse of the primordial serpent is fulfilled in human experience. In Dan. 7 a new Adam finally appears to renew the *imago Dei* and reverse the spiral into bestial human tyranny begun in Gen. 3, embodied in Nebuchadnezzar's boanthropy in Dan. 4, and climaxing in the horrors of Dan. 7's four beasts. This new sacral son of God takes a throne beside God as divine vicar par excellence, a role of sacral dominion with contours glimpsed in Dan. 4:22.

As a second Adam appears with the clouds, archetypal reality unfolds in embodied form in the world. With the grand enthronement of the Son of Man figure, the Divine Warrior archetype has penetrated the veil hiding transcendence. He has materialized on earth. This is more than an elusive manifestation, more than a simple theophany. The transcendent itself here interrupts history. As André Lacocque puts it, Daniel transformed mythology such that "no longer were there two levels or layers, one above the other. The two became one, *thus revealing the truth of their unity from the beginning*."[41]

Jung elucidates the dynamics of such a *symbolum* as a merging of heterogenous natures, archetypal and embodied. In *Answer to Job*, Jung opens up about his metaphysics. He outlines his views on how a psychoid archetype could fulfill itself in a radically climactic manner akin to an apocalyptic unfolding.

Jung is well known for his descriptions of how the collective unconscious and its powerfully real archetypes can possess humans and determine their fates. This happened to Nebuchadnezzar in Dan. 4 when his dream became his lived reality. Less widely accepted is Jung's theory of synchronicity, which accounts for the occurrence of experiences in the physical world that represent the unconscious

40. Childs, *Isaiah*, 538; cf. Joseph Blenkinsopp, *Isaiah 56–66: A New Translation with Introduction and Commentary*, AB 19B (New Haven: Yale University Press, 2003), 284–85, 290.

41. André Lacocque, *The Book of Daniel*, 2nd ed. (Eugene, OR: Cascade, 2018), 159–60 (emphasis original). In n. 61 Lacocque adds that this constitutes a rejoinder to many modern scholars who abuse the expression "apocalyptic dualism."

and the archetypes. Pharaoh dreamed of seven lean cows (Gen. 41:27), and seven years later, with no causal connection to the dream, seven years of famine began (41:54). "The archetype," Jung states, "fulfils itself not only psychically in the individual, but objectively outside the individual."[42] What would happen if archetypes began not merely intervening in the world but merging with it, fully overcoming dualism? Cosmogenesis would be the operative rubric!

For Jung, the transcendental realm (psyche) is always intervening in the existing natural order. Such intervention is fundamental and necessary if the universe is to have any serious purpose and direction. No one can say with certainty where this divine intervention will end.[43] Perhaps it ends in a "supreme moment" that entails a "bringing together of heterogeneous natures," a "*peripeteia* charged with affect."[44]

Such a supreme moment, Jung insists, is eschatological, for eschatology is the interpenetration of two natures, the transcendent and the humanly conscious. That the transcendent realm can interpenetrate our world at all means that archetypes are irreducibly real.[45] They are supraordinate and preexistent to all phenomena of human experience. Here Jung inverts the thinking of materialism, which views the physical world as what is truly real and considers mind, psyche, and spirit to be epiphenomenal and ephemeral. Jung would sooner say that experiential states create organic regularities than the reverse. Ultimately, it is the psychic function that creates physical structures.

Future Directions

By embracing interdisciplinary methods, respecting the complexity of the texts, and recognizing the rich connections between apocalyptic literature and the wider scriptural tradition, ongoing research continues to uncover the nuances and insights that these texts have to offer. This approach allows for a more comprehensive interpretation of texts, circumventing the red herring of debating the semantics of the term "apocalyptic." Avoiding the pitfalls of reductionism and domestication of the literature, researchers must be cautious not to dismiss the texts' symbolic, psychoanalytic, and metaphysical dimensions in favor of political or ideological interpretations. Historicizing and psychologizing approaches provide unsatisfying etiologies for apocalyticism's rise.

The origins of Scripture's apocalyptic imagination lie in the deep structure of a biblical canon emerging after the exile. Within this theological substrate,

42. Jung, *Answer to Job*, 47. See Bernardo Kastrup, *Decoding Jung's Metaphysics: The Archetypal Semantics of an Experiential Universe* (Winchester, UK: IFF, 2021), 46–70.

43. C. G. Jung, *On the Nature of the Psyche* (London: Routledge, 2001), 151.

44. Jung, *Answer to Job*, 44, 46.

45. As Kastrup (*Decoding Jung's Metaphysics*, 86) puts it, the psyche for Jung is neither illusory nor reducible to something else. It is a fundamental aspect of reality, existing in and by itself. In fact, the substrate of all reality is essentially experiential (100).

unresolved antitheses, deep paradoxes, unrealized ideals, and unfulfilled promises percolated, straining for resolution and integration. New eschatological and apocalyptic syntheses emerged, including a new heterogeneous *imago Dei*, the reversal of the Genesis spiral into bestial human tyranny, and the blossoming of ancient ideals of sacral kingship.

By appreciating the complexities and nuances of the OT apocalyptic literature, researchers will be better equipped to understand the rich tapestry of the biblical tradition and the ways that apocalyptic texts synthesize and resolve the dualities, antipodes, and antinomies within the deep structures of canon consciousness. By embracing a multidisciplinary approach and resisting reductionism, scholars can contribute to a deeper understanding of the diverse dimensions of the apocalyptic texts, enhancing our comprehension of the OT.

PART 3

Interpretive Approaches

22

Studies of Ideology

Mark G. Brett

Antoine Destutt de Tracy (1754–1836) first coined the term *idéologie* in 1796 when speaking about his "science of ideas," meaning in this context positivist ideas developed during the French Enlightenment. Within the space of five years, however, Napoleon could complain in a manifestly negative tone about "windbags and ideologues who have always fought the existence of authority."[1] Napoleon's lament is echoed today by those who use the term as a byword for tendentious cant.

Competing concepts of ideology overlap and intersect with each other in such controversial ways that biblical scholars have often chosen to avoid the relevant social-scientific debates and to adopt this terminology simply as a label for disagreeable views, both ancient and modern.[2] One might imagine that there is safer ground to be found where scholars narrow their focus on historical criticism, ancient semantics, literary genre, the intentions of biblical authors, and so on. Alas, all of these concepts have attracted the attention of critics who are unafraid of the term "ideology," to the extent that some scholars have begun to fret over the demise of critical historical studies.[3] For example, the idea that great individuals

1. Emmet Kennedy, "'Ideology' from Destutt De Tracy to Marx," *Journal of the History of Ideas* 40 (1979): 358.

2. James Barr, *History and Ideology in the Old Testament: Biblical Studies at the End of a Millennium* (Oxford: Oxford University Press, 2000), 102–40.

3. In this connection, William G. Dever (*The Lives of Ordinary People in Ancient Israel: Where Archaeology and the Bible Intersect* [Grand Rapids: Eerdmans, 2012], 28) refers to Keith

like Isaiah, Jeremiah, "J," or "P" should be the focus of critical historical attention is an intellectual assumption much more indebted to nineteenth-century Romanticism than to ancient understandings of authorship.[4] The present chapter is a modest attempt to identify some of the key issues at stake in these controversies.

We can begin with some lesser-known prophets who provided something of a catalyst for the French Enlightenment. In particular, Mi'kmaq and Wendat leaders encountered in the North American colonies were reportedly skeptical about the hierarchical ethics advanced under the banner of civilization. A Wendat leader named Kandiaronk (ca. 1649–1701) debated the French views on social and economic ethics with officials in Montreal in the 1690s, and on some accounts, the essential elements of his arguments were represented under the name "Adario" by Baron de Lahontan in *Dialogues curieux entre l'auteur et un sauvage de bon sens qui a voyagé* (1703).[5] This indigenous critique then fed into Jean-Jacques Rousseau's discussions of inequality and the social contract later in the eighteenth century.[6] Importantly, Rousseau's construction of the "noble savage" showed that utopias may belong just as much to the past as to the future, as Karl Mannheim also suggests in his classic sociological work *Ideology and Utopia*.[7] Thus, well in advance of Marxist accounts of ideology, colonial encounters had evidently provoked a radical questioning of social hierarchy that played out in eighteenth-century French history.[8]

Windschuttle, *The Killing of History: How Literary Critics and Social Theorists Are Murdering Our Past* (New York: Free Press, 1996). Citing Windschuttle as an opponent of ideological historical studies is ironic in the extreme, however, since he has become notorious for obfuscating Aboriginal history in my home country of Australia. See, for example, Robert Manne, ed., *Whitewash: On Keith Windschuttle's Fabrication of Aboriginal History* (Melbourne: Black, 2003).

4. Hindy Najman, *Seconding Sinai: The Development of Mosaic Discourse in Second Temple Judaism*, Supplements to the Journal for the Study of Judaism 77 (Leiden: Brill, 2003), 1–40; Dalit Rom-Shiloni, "From Prophetic Words to Prophetic Literature: Challenging Paradigms That Control Our Academic Thought on Jeremiah and Ezekiel," *JBL* 138, no. 3 (2019): 565–86; Mark G. Brett, "Authors, Imaginaries and the Ethics of Interpretation," *Political Trauma and Healing: Biblical Ethics for a Postcolonial World* (Grand Rapids: Eerdmans, 2016), 55–74.

5. Barbara Alice Mann, "Are You Delusional? Kandiaronk on Christianity," in *Native American Speakers of the Eastern Woodlands: Selected Speeches and Critical Analyses*, ed. Barbara A. Mann (Westport, CT: Greenwood, 2001), 35–82.

6. See the illuminating account in David Graeber and David Wengrow, *The Dawn of Everything: A New History of Humanity* (London: Allen Lane, 2021), chap. 2.

7. Karl Mannheim, "The Third Form of the Utopian Idea: The Conservative Idea," in *Ideology and Utopia: An Introduction to the Sociology of Knowledge*, trans. Louis Wirth and Edward Shils (London: Routledge & Kegan Paul, 1936), 206–15; cf. the exemplary discussions of utopia in Steven J. Schweitzer and Frauke Uhlenbruch, eds., *Worlds That Could Not Be: Utopia in Chronicles, Ezra and Nehemiah*, LHBOTS 620 (London: Bloomsbury, 2016).

8. In the 17th century, a critique of political ideology had been advanced by Protestant thinkers like John Milton, using in particular 1 Sam. 8:10–18 and Deut. 17:14–20 to undermine the supposed divine right of kings. See Eric Nelson, *The Hebrew Republic: Jewish Sources and the Transformation of European Political Thought* (Cambridge, MA: Harvard University Press, 2010).

Faced with the myriad theories that could potentially demand our attention, it is necessary to select only indicative works that illustrate a spectrum of research questions, concepts, and methodologies. The analysis briefly evaluates the strengths and weaknesses of various approaches, stretching from the most reductive explanations of ancient texts to proposals that purport to be merely descriptive.

Marxist and Class Analyses

In the mid-nineteenth century, Karl Marx and Friedrich Engels famously argued, first, that human consciousness arises from its material conditions and, second, that ruling classes control the world of ideas in ways that seek to protect their dominant social interests. These two theses have energized Marxist thought ever since, although the precise relationship between the two is fraught. A number of key studies have emphasized the material conditions of thought, beginning with the landmark volume of Norman Gottwald, *The Tribes of Yahweh* (1979), and extending to the recent work of Joachim Schaper, *Media and Monotheism* (2019).[9] Sweeping analyses of ancient economic systems—whether of rural subsistence, palatine estates, or imperial regimes of extraction—properly embrace the *longue durée* in historical studies, but they are accordingly not designed to explain the intricacies of the diverse textual repertoire in the HB.[10] Initially framed in a confrontation with modern capitalism, Marxist theories require multiple modifications when scholars turn to ancient economies.[11]

The idea that dominant classes can effectively control or incorporate subaltern groups is questioned by sociologists who doubt whether dominant classes in ancient times actually had the communicative means to incorporate lower classes, even presuming a monopoly of force. The question comes into sharp focus if one acknowledges that "the Hebrew Bible is primarily a corpus written by elites to elites."[12] It is difficult to see how scribal productions could incorporate subaltern

9. Norman K. Gottwald, *The Tribes of Yahweh: A Sociology of the Religion of Liberated Israel, 1250–1050 B.C.E.* (Maryknoll, NY: Orbis Books, 1979); Joachim Schaper, *Media and Monotheism: Presence, Representation, and Abstraction in Ancient Judea*, Orientalische Religionen in der Antike 33 (Tübingen: Mohr Siebeck, 2019).

10. Roland Boer, *Marxist Criticism of the Bible*, 2nd ed. (London: Bloomsbury, 2014), is helpful in this respect, since he takes key concepts from a range of thinkers and applies them in textual studies.

11. Philippe Guillaume, *Land, Credit and Crisis: Agrarian Finance in the Hebrew Bible*, BibleWorld (Sheffield: Equinox, 2012); Marvin Lloyd Miller, Ehud Ben Zvi, and Gary N. Knoppers, eds., *The Economy of Ancient Judah in Its Historical Context* (Winona Lake, IN: Eisenbrauns, 2015); Thomas Piketty, *Capital and Ideology* (Cambridge, MA: Belknap, 2020); Walter Houston, "'Justice and Right': Biblical Ethics and the Regulation of Capitalism," *De Ethica* 2, no. 3 (2015): 7–21.

12. Christopher A. Rollston, *Writing and Literacy in the World of Ancient Israel*, ABS 11 (Atlanta: SBL Press, 2010), 127. Regarding the "dominant ideology thesis," see Mark G. Brett,

groups unless the communicative gaps were bridged in some way by forms of oral performance and commemorative ritual.[13]

Such key questions about the means and effectiveness of communication are difficult to resolve, especially when one considers the remarkable diversity of the HB. Many of the prophetic and skeptical wisdom traditions, for example, wield critiques of royal or legal theologies found elsewhere in the HB. The book of Jeremiah is quite willing to assert that "the lying pen of the scribes" has distorted the law of YHWH (Jer. 8:8 NIV), and Deuteronomy can oppose royal-Zion ideology.[14] Ancient hermeneutics of suspicion ironically permeate the literature.

The obvious gaps between social classes in ancient Israel have provoked some biblical critics to wonder whether the exploitation of the poor explicitly spoken about in the prophetic books can be taken at face value.[15] Scholarly methodologies dig below the surface to identify evidence for subaltern voices, which often entails the use of redaction criticism. According to Itumeleng Mosala, a good example comes from the earliest layer of Micah, which likely stems from a rural Judean context in the eighth century BCE.[16] Micah's vision of each family enjoying their own "vine and fig tree" reflects the aspirations of a humble subsistence economy (Mic. 4:4) but also rejects the exploitative system of palatine estates (cf. the royal ideology of vine and fig tree in 1 Kings 4:25).[17]

"Literacy and Domination: G. A. Herion's Sociology of History Writing," in *Social Scientific Old Testament Criticism: A Sheffield Reader*, ed. David J. Chalcraft, The Biblical Seminar 47 (Sheffield: JSOT Press, 1997), 109–34.

13. Aubrey Buster, *Remembering the Story of Israel: Historical Summaries and Memory Formation in Second Temple Judaism* (Cambridge: Cambridge University Press, 2022), 39–71.

14. Even when arguing explicitly for a conservative approach, J. Gordon McConville presents Deuteronomy as a critique of royal and Zion ideologies. E.g., McConville, "Law and Monarchy in the Old Testament," in *A Royal Priesthood? A Dialogue with Oliver O'Donovan*, ed. Craig Bartholomew et al., Scripture and Hermeneutics 3 (Carlisle, UK: Paternoster, 2002), 69–88. A classic overview of inner-biblical critiques is provided in Walter Brueggemann, *Theology of the Old Testament: Testimony, Dispute, Advocacy* (Minneapolis: Fortress, 1997).

15. Steed V. Davidson, "Prophets Postcolonially: Initial Insights for a Postcolonial Reading of Prophetic Literature," *The Bible and Critical Theory* 6, no. 2 (2010): 8, citing Gayatri Chakravorty Spivak, *A Critique of Postcolonial Reason: Toward a History of the Vanishing Present* (Cambridge, MA: Harvard University Press, 1999). Similarly, regarding the language of "the poor" in the book of Amos, see Walter Houston, *Contending for Justice: Ideologies and Theologies of Social Justice in the Old Testament*, rev. ed., LBHOTS 428 (London: T&T Clark, 2008), 52–75; David J. A. Clines, "Metacommentating Amos," in *Interested Parties: The Ideology of Writers and Readers of the Hebrew Bible*, JSOTSup 205; Gender, Culture, Theory 1 (Sheffield: Sheffield Academic, 1995), 76–93.

16. Itumeleng J. Mosala, *Biblical Hermeneutics and Black Theology in South Africa* (Grand Rapids: Eerdmans, 1989), 101–53, argues that only the earliest layer of texts in Micah transmits an ancient critique of economic oppression. Cf. Jorge Pixley, "Liberation Criticism," in *Methods for Exodus*, ed. Thomas B. Dozeman, Methods in Biblical Interpretation (Cambridge: Cambridge University Press, 2010), 131–62.

17. Daniel L. Smith-Christopher, *Micah: A Commentary*, OTL (Louisville: Westminster John Knox, 2015), 21, 139–45. See further, Erin Runions, *Changing Subjects: Gender, Nation and Future in Micah*, Playing the Texts 7 (Sheffield: Sheffield Academic, 2001).

Employing a class analysis, Jakob Wöhrle's account of the so-called Book of the Four (Hosea, Amos, Micah, and Zephaniah) reconstructs a unified redaction across these four prophetic books. On Wöhrle's view, this redaction condemns the upper class as those who are primarily responsible for the fall of Judah and finds hope precisely in the poor who were left behind in the land. In contrast to the Deuteronomistic History, this prophetic theology highlights economic matters and holds no expectation of a restoration of the Davidic royal house.[18] Strikingly, Wöhrle never uses the word "ideology" in this class analysis, and a question arises here as to whether some notions of ideology may be largely interchangeable with concepts of political theology,[19] theological geography,[20] or worldview.

Ideology as Worldview

In contrast with the Marxist lines of inquiry and critique, some biblical scholars propose descriptive approaches such as those advanced by the influential anthropologist Clifford Geertz. If ideology is taken in this broader sense, it becomes largely synonymous with notions of culture, mindscape, worldview, or social imaginary.[21] Whether an ideology is dominant or subaltern, conscious or unconscious, it can be seen as an assemblage of ideas through which, as Charles Taylor puts it, people "imagine their social existence, how they fit together with

18. Jakob Wöhrle, "'No Future for the Proud and Exultant Ones': The Exilic Book of the Four Prophets (Hos., Am., Mic., Zeph.) as a Concept Opposed to the Deuteronomistic History," *VT* 58, no. 4 (2008): 608–27. Regarding the occlusion of economic matters in the Deuteronomistic theology and an exception that proves the rule, see Gerald O. West, "In Search of an Economic Remnant of Resistance: 3 Reigns 12:24p–t," *HTS Theological Studies* 78, no.1 (2022), https://doi.org/10.4102/hts.v78i1.7440.

19. See the indicative studies in Eckart Otto, *Das Deuteronomium: Politische Theologie und Rechtsreform in Juda und Assyrien*, BZAW 284 (Berlin: De Gruyter, 1999); Anathea Portier-Young, *Apocalypse against Empire: Theologies of Resistance in Early Judaism* (Grand Rapids: Eerdmans, 2011); Mark G. Brett, *Locations of God: Political Theology in the Hebrew Bible* (New York: Oxford University Press, 2019), responding critically to Jan Assmann, *Politische Theologie zwischen Ägypten und Israel*, ed. Heinrich Meier, 3rd ed. (Munich: Carl Friedrich von Siemens, 2006), 23–114. Norman C. Habel advances a distinction between "theology" as God-talk and "ideology" as essentially sociological, without feeling any need to reconstruct the social history of Israel and Judah. Habel, *The Land Is Mine: Six Biblical Land Ideologies*, OBT (Minneapolis: Augsburg Fortress, 1995).

20. Joachim J. Krause, "Im Licht des Spatial Turn: Theologische Geographien der Hebräischen Bibel," *TQ* 201, no. 1 (2021): 6–19, makes the point that his understanding of theological geography is often termed "ideology" in English-language works (8). See, e.g., Nili Wazana, *All the Boundaries of the Land: The Promised Land in Biblical Thought in Light of the Ancient Near East*, trans. Liat Qeren (Winona Lake, IN: Eisenbrauns, 2013); Stephen C. Russell, *Space, Land, Territory, and the Study of the Bible*, Brill Research Perspectives on Biblical Interpretation (Leiden: Brill, 2017).

21. Clifford Geertz, "Ideology as a Cultural System," in *Ideology and Discontent*, ed. David E. Apter (New York: Free Press, 1964), 47–76; cf. Eviatar Zerubavel, *Social Mindscapes: An Invitation to Cognitive Sociology* (Cambridge, MA: Harvard University Press, 1997).

others, how things go on between them and their fellows, the expectations that are normally met, and the deeper normative notions and images that underlie these expectations."[22] The question of how people relate to "others"[23] emerges also in environmental[24] and animal studies.[25]

Descriptive understandings of social imagination can be aligned, for example, with the broader account of ideology developed by David Janzen in *The Social Meanings of Sacrifice in the Hebrew Bible*, where he regards ideology and worldview as essentially synonymous.[26] He finds it necessary to reject Marxist approaches on the ground that "rituals do not intend to communicate ideologies (or worldviews) that distort or obscure social reality" and instead associates his descriptive account with Martin Rose's broad definition of ideology as "an assemblage of ideas, beliefs and doctrines specific to an epoch, to a society or class."[27] With this starting point, Rose is thus enabled to interpret the ideology/ worldview of the so-called Deuteronomistic historians. Janzen notes that "the question of whether or not this is a good interpretation of history is one for other social groups to raise."[28]

Unfortunately, this is precisely the question at issue elsewhere in the biblical canon, notably in the wholesale rewriting of history in Chronicles where the political imaginary shifts from national models to a kind of imperial mimicry.[29] Chronicles no longer accepts "the blackballing of Manasseh" in 2 Kings,

22. Charles Taylor, *Modern Social Imaginaries* (Durham, NC: Duke University Press, 2004), 23. Regarding Taylor's influential contrast between modern and ancient social imaginaries, see Carol A. Newsom, *The Spirit within Me: Self and Agency in Ancient Israel and Second Temple Judaism* (New Haven: Yale University Press, 2021), 1–14, with an overview of the relevant biblical studies.

23. Ehud Ben Zvi and Diana V. Edelman, *Imagining the Other and Constructing Israelite Identity in the Early Second Temple Period*, LHBOTS 456 (London: Bloomsbury, 2014).

24. Ellen Davis, *Scripture, Culture, and Agriculture: An Agrarian Reading of the Bible* (Cambridge: Cambridge University Press, 2009); Mari Joerstad, *The Hebrew Bible and Environmental Ethics: Humans, Nonhumans, and the Living Landscape* (Cambridge: Cambridge University Press, 2019); Hilary Marlow and Mark Harris, eds., *The Oxford Handbook of the Bible and Ecology* (New York: Oxford University Press, 2022).

25. Ken Stone, *Reading the Hebrew Bible with Animal Studies* (Stanford, CA: Stanford University Press, 2018); Arthur Walker-Jones and Suzanna R. Millar, eds., *Exploring Animal Hermeneutics* (Atlanta: SBL Press, 2022).

26. David Janzen, *The Social Meanings of Sacrifice in the Hebrew Bible: A Study of Four Writings*, BZAW 344 (Berlin: De Gruyter, 2004), 57–63.

27. Martin Rose, "Deuteronomistic Ideology and Theology of the Old Testament," in *Israel Constructs Its History: Deuteronomistic Historiography in Recent Research*, ed. Albert de Pury, Thomas Römer, and Jean-Daniel Macchi, JSOTSup 306 (Sheffield: Sheffield Academic, 2000), 425. Rose adopts the wording of the French dictionary *Le Petit Robert* (Paris: Le Robert, 1984) instead of the pejorative German definition of "Ideologie" in *Der grosse Duden* (Leipzig: Bibliographisches Institut, 1938).

28. Janzen, *Social Meanings*, 63.

29. Jonathan E. Dyck, *The Theocratic Ideology of the Chronicler*, BibInt 33 (Leiden: Brill, 1998); Louis C. Jonker, "Being Both on the Periphery and in the Centre: The Jerusalem Temple

as Francesca Stavrakopoulou memorably puts it.[30] Any broader definitions of ideology—such as those proposed by Geertz, Rose, or Janzen—eventually provoke the question of how such a worldview/imaginary/mindscape relates to the alternatives available in successive periods of history. The critical thinking in Chronicles is even analogous in some respects to modern worries about the coherence between law and narrative in the so-called Deuteronomistic History. The rewriting in Chronicles establishes more alignment with the legal traditions in the Pentateuch, while the older narratives in Samuel and Kings are left open to deconstructive readings, such as those offered by Rachelle Gilmour.[31]

From Ideology to Hegemony

Attempts to link each identifiable ideology with only one social group are notoriously fraught with difficulties. Ideologies are often reproduced in complex ways across a range of social institutions, rather than being self-interested strategies in the hands of particular groups.[32] When significant intersections and overlaps have been sustained across generations, other conceptual tools may be necessary, such as those provided by Antonio Gramsci in his notion of hegemony. In their own interpretation of Gramsci, for example, Jean and John Comaroff distinguish between a conscious ideology—"an articulated system of meanings, values, and beliefs"—and hegemony defined as "that part of a dominant worldview which has been naturalized and, having hidden itself in orthodoxy, no more appears as ideology at all."[33] The assemblage of meanings, values, and beliefs in an ideology are overtly articulated in some way, whereas hegemony can work even in unconscious ways across multiple groups and generations.

The achievements of the Jerusalem literati during the late Persian and early Hellenistic periods could in this sense be seen as hegemonic; the privilege afforded to Jerusalem was so thoroughly interwoven across a wide range of biblical

in Late Persian Period Yehud from Postcolonial Perspective," in *Centres and Peripheries in the Early Second Temple Period*, ed. Ehud Ben Zvi and Christoph Levin, FAT 108 (Tübingen: Mohr Siebeck, 2016), 243–67.

30. Francesca Stavrakopoulou, "The Blackballing of Manasseh," in *Good Kings and Bad Kings: The Kingdom of Judah in the Seventh Century BCE*, ed. Lester L. Grabbe, LHBOTS 393; ESHM 5 (London: T&T Clark, 2007), 248–63; Konrad Schmid, "Manasse und der Untergang Judas: 'Golaorientierte' Theologie in den Königsbüchern?," *Bib* 78, no. 1 (1997): 87–99.

31. Rachelle Gilmour, "Saul's Rejection and the Obscene Underside of the Law," *The Bible and Critical Theory* 15.1 (2019): 34–45; cf. Louis C. Jonker, "Was the Chronicler More Deuteronomic than the Deuteronomist?," *SJOT* 27, no. 2 (2013): 185–97.

32. Boer, *Marxist Criticism of the Bible*, 24–26; Louis Althusser, *Lenin and Philosophy and Other Essays*, trans. Ben Brewster (London: New Left Books, 1971).

33. Jean Comaroff and John L. Comaroff, *Of Revelation and Revolution*, vol. 1, *Christianity, Colonialism, and Consciousness in South Africa* (Chicago: University of Chicago Press, 1991), 24–25. Antonio Gramsci, *Selections from the Prison Notebooks of Antonio Gramsci*, trans. Quinton Hoare and Geoffrey Nowell-Smith (New York: International Publishers, 1971).

genres and traditions, mediated from earlier centuries, that this may not have been consciously ideological in any narrow sense.[34] Indeed, the Pentateuch and Chronicles seem to have addressed the southern bias that is evident in the earlier traditions of Ezra-Nehemiah,[35] providing different versions of pan-Israelite imagination instead. Nevertheless, it was still possible for the Samarians to resist this hegemony while nurturing substantially the same Torah of Moses. Indeed, the complex shaping of the Pentateuch embraces two possible paradigms for interpreting the geography of promised land, with Mount Gerizim and Mount Zion each claiming sacred centrality.[36]

Within the Pentateuch itself, matters of ethnicity, class, and gender were all subject to lively rethinking and rewriting. Cheryl Anderson has demonstrated how the laws in Exodus and Deuteronomy construct multiple and shifting identities, establishing an ethnic or national solidarity at one level while discriminating at the levels of gender and class.[37] The wives of priests are awarded a higher status than wives among the laity, as has been illuminated by Sarah Shectman.[38] The narratives of Genesis reveal particularly complex relationships between families and ethnic groups that are under negotiation, whether forging alliances or denigrating some people on the basis of class or ethnicity.[39] The narratives concerning Hagar and Sarah have, in particular, been a fruitful focus in recent

34. Diana Vikander Edelman and Ehud Ben Zvi, eds., *Remembering Biblical Figures in the Late Persian and Early Hellenistic Periods: Social Memory and Imagination* (Oxford: Oxford University Press, 2013); Ehud Ben Zvi, *Social Memory among the Literati of Yehud*, BZAW 509 (Berlin: De Gruyter, 2019).

35. Dalit Rom-Shiloni, *Exclusive Inclusivity: Identity Conflicts between the Exiles and the People Who Remained (6th–5th Centuries BCE)*, LHBOTS 543 (London: Bloomsbury, 2013).

36. Julia Rhyder, *Centralizing the Cult: The Holiness Legislation in Leviticus 17–26*, FAT 134 (Tübingen: Mohr Siebeck, 2019), 398–407; Mark G. Brett, "The Imperial Context of the Pentateuch," in *The Oxford Handbook of the Pentateuch*, ed. Joel S. Baden and Jeffrey Stackert (New York: Oxford University Press, 2021), 443–62; Benedikt Hensel, "Debating Temple and Torah in the Second Temple Period: Theological and Political Aspects of the Final Redaction(s) of the Pentateuch," in *Torah, Temple, Land: Constructions of Judaism in Antiquity*, ed. Markus Witte, Jens Schröter, and Verena M. Lepper, TSAJ 184 (Tübingen: Mohr Siebeck, 2021), 27–47.

37. Cheryl B. Anderson, *Women, Ideology, and Violence: Critical Theory and the Construction of Gender in the Book of the Covenant and the Deuteronomic Law* (New York: T&T Clark, 2004). See also Barbara Deutschmann, *Creating Gender in the Garden: The Inconstant Partnership of Eve and Adam*, LHBOTS 729 (London: Bloomsbury, 2022); and more generally, Yvonne Sherwood, ed., *The Bible and Feminism: Remapping the Field* (Oxford: Oxford University Press, 2017).

38. Sarah Shectman, "The Social Status of Priestly and Levite Women," in *Levites and Priests in History and Tradition*, ed. Mark A. Leuchter and Jeremy M. Hutton, AIL 9 (Atlanta: SBL Press, 2011), 82–89.

39. Sarah Shectman, "Israel's Matriarchs: Political Pawns or Powerbrokers?," in *The Politics of the Ancestors: Exegetical and Historical Perspectives on Genesis 12–36*, ed. Mark G. Brett and Jakob Wöhrle, FAT 124 (Tübingen: Mohr Siebeck, 2018), 151–65; Brian Rainey, *Religion, Ethnicity and Xenophobia in the Bible: A Theoretical, Exegetical and Theological Survey*, Routledge Studies in the Biblical World (London: Routledge, 2019).

research.[40] Hegemonic patterns of social rank were obviously sustained over the centuries.

Racialized Reception Histories

It would be anachronistic to interpret ancient ethnic antagonism in terms of race, although it is still possible to foreground the anachronism when reading biblical texts with contemporary analogies in mind.[41] Modern readers seized on the difference between enslaved persons emancipated in the seventh year (Deut. 15:12–17) and foreigners who could remain inheritable property under the jubilee legislation (Lev. 25).[42] Nationalized and racialized hermeneutics have beset the question of how to read analogies between modern migrants and ancient גֵּרִים (*gērîm*, strangers).[43] When it comes to modern uses of the Bible, Exodus is notorious for its vast range of influences, for better and for worse.[44] Nehemiah has been pulled in opposite directions in South Africa,[45] as has Deuteronomy in Aotearoa/New Zealand.[46]

40. Vanessa L. Lovelace, "'This Woman's Son Shall Not Inherit with My Son': Towards a Womanist Politics of Belonging in the Sarah-Hagar Narratives," *Journal of the International Theological Centre* 41, no. 1 (2015): 63–82; Nyasha Junior, *Reimagining Hagar: Blackness and Bible* (New York: Oxford University Press, 2019); Rhiannon Graybill, "Rape and Other Ways of Reading: Hagar and Sarah in the Company of Women," in *Texts after Terror: Rape, Sexual Violence, and the Hebrew Bible* (New York: Oxford University Press, 2021), 85–112.

41. Denise Kimber Buell, "Anachronistic Whiteness and the Ethics of Interpretation," in *Ethnicity, Race, Religion: Identities and Ideologies in Early Jewish and Christian Texts, and in Modern Biblical Interpretation*, ed. Katherine M. Hockey and David G. Horrell (New York: Bloomsbury T&T Clark, 2018), 149–67.

42. Mignon Jacobs, "Parameters of Justice: Ideological Challenges regarding Persons and Practices in Leviticus 25:25–55," *ExAud* 22 (2006): 133–58; John W. Watts, "Drawing Lines: A Suggestion for Addressing the Moral Problem of Reproducing Immoral Biblical Texts in Commentaries and Bibles," in *Writing a Commentary on Leviticus: Hermeneutics–Methodology–Themes*, ed. Thomas Hieke and Christian A. Eberhart, FRLANT 276 (Göttingen: Vandenhoeck & Ruprecht, 2019), 235–52.

43. M. Daniel Carroll R., *The Bible and Borders: Hearing God's Word on Immigration* (Grand Rapids: Brazos, 2020); Mark R. Glanville and Luke Glanville, *Refuge Reimagined: Biblical Kinship in Global Politics* (Downers Grove, IL: InterVarsity, 2021); Markus Zehnder, *The Bible and Immigration: A Critical and Empirical Reassessment* (Eugene, OR: Pickwick, 2021).

44. John Coffey, *Exodus and Liberation: Deliverance Politics from John Calvin to Martin Luther King Jr.* (Oxford: Oxford University Press, 2014); Allison Paige Sellers, "The 'Black Man's Bible': The Holy Piby, Garveyism, and Black Supremacy in the Interwar Years," *Journal of Africana Religions* 3, no. 3 (2015): 325–42; Kenneth N. Ngwa, *Let My People Live: An Africana Reading of Exodus* (Louisville: Westminster John Knox, 2022).

45. Ntozakhe Cezula, "A Comment on Ehud Ben Zvi's 'Total Exile, Empty Land and the General Intellectual Discourse in Yehud,'" *OTE* 30, no. 3 (2017): 592–608. Cf. the broader overviews in Janneke Stegeman, "The Bible and the Dutch Empire," in *The Oxford Handbook of Postcolonial Biblical Criticism*, ed. R. S. Sugirtharajah (Oxford: Oxford University Press, 2021), https://doi.org/10.1093/oxfordhb/9780190888459.013.13; Gerald O. West, *The Stolen Bible: From Tool of Imperialism to African Icon* (Leiden: Brill; Pietermaritzburg: Cluster, 2016).

46. Brett, *Locations of God*, 137–39, highlighting Wiremu Tāmihana's biblical interpretation.

The construction of blackness has an older history than the invention of whiteness. Earlier expressions of ethnic hierarchy were not crystalized into an explicit ideology of whiteness before the late seventeenth and eighteenth century.[47] While antecedents can be found in the fifteenth-century Spanish idea of "purity of blood" (*limpieza de sangre*),[48] this was not linked to the tortuous legal defenses of the imperial doctrine of discovery at the time.[49] In the eighteenth and nineteenth centuries, an imagined community of whiteness provided a new lens for reinterpreting the older Curse of Ham traditions.[50] The hegemony of whiteness in European and settler colonial contexts remains embedded until today in church, society, and academy.

Pluralizing the Academy

The pressing need to pluralize the voices of the academy is now self-evident to all scholars of goodwill. According to Wongi Park, one constructive way forward would be to name historical criticism as hegemonic in biblical studies ("whiteness as method") and to turn away from it.[51] The suggestion would be, I suspect, music to the ears of many conservative evangelicals who have never accepted historical criticism in the first place.

There is also no doubt that Protestant and anti-Jewish assumptions have permeated the elite university departments of biblical studies since the nineteenth century.[52] Gerhard von Rad's influential contributions illustrate some of the complexities at

47. Theodore Allen, *The Invention of the White Race*, vol. 1, *Racial Oppression and Social Control* (London: Verso, 1994); Colin Kidd, *The Forging of Races: Race and Scripture in the Protestant Atlantic World, 1600–2000* (Cambridge: Cambridge University Press, 2006); Rebecca Goetz, *The Baptism of Early Virginia: How Christianity Created Race* (Baltimore: Johns Hopkins University Press, 2012).

48. María Elena Martínes, *Genealogical Fictions: Limpieza de Sangre, Religion and Gender in Colonial Mexico* (Stanford: Stanford University Press, 2008).

49. Christiane Birr, "*Dominium* in the Indies: Juan López de Palacios Rubios' *Libellus de insulis oceanis quas vulgus indias appelat* (1512–1516)," *Rechtsgeschichte—Legal History* 26 (2018): 264–83; Yvonne Sherwood, "Francisco de Vitoria's More Excellent Way: How the Bible of Empire Discovered the Tricks of [the Argument from] Trade," *BibInt* 21, no. 2 (2013): 215–75.

50. Marilyn Lake and Henry Reynolds, *Drawing the Global Colour Line: White Men's Countries and the Question of Racial Equality* (Cambridge: Cambridge University Press, 2008); David M. Goldenberg, *Black and Slave: The Origins and History of the Curse of Ham*, Studies of the Bible and Its Reception 10 (Berlin: De Gruyter, 2017).

51. Wongi Park, "Multiracial Biblical Studies," *JBL* 140, no. 3 (2021): 445–48. For earlier efforts in a similar vein, see R. S. Sugirtharajah, ed., *Voices from the Margin: Interpreting the Bible in the Third World*, 25th anniversary ed. (Maryknoll, NY: Orbis Books, 2016); Randall C. Bailey, Tat-siong Benny Liew, and Fernando F. Segovia, eds., *They Were All Together in One Place: Toward Minority Biblical Criticism*, SemeiaSt 57 (Atlanta: SBL Press, 2009); Jione Havea, David J. Neville, and Elaine M. Wainwright, eds., *Bible, Borders, Belonging(s): Engaging Readings from Oceania* (Atlanta: SBL Press, 2014).

52. Anders Gerdmar, *Roots of Theological Anti-Semitism: German Biblical Interpretation and the Jews, from Herder and Semler to Kittel and Bultmann*, Studies in Jewish History and Culture 20 (Leiden: Brill, 2009).

issue here, since he mediated the Romantic historicism of his predecessors while simultaneously doing intellectual battle with the Nazi ideology that overtook the German universities. His work on the Priestly material, for example, betrays a legacy of anti-Judaism, as demonstrated by Bernard Levinson.[53] But the older presumptions of Protestant scholarship, whether stemming from Julius Wellhausen or moderated by von Rad, can hardly be determining the current research on Priestly tradition that is promoted by Jewish scholars.[54] Precisely because historical criticism is not one thing, we need more research on its contradictory methods and motivations.[55]

A helpful approach has been taken in South Africa by Madipoane Masenya and Hulisani Ramantswana, who are mindful of the biases that have infected the dominant Western traditions of research but see value in historical disciplines that seek to illuminate ancient cultures and languages. When undoing those biases, they see the lenses provided by African knowledge systems and communal interpretation as essential in their own context.[56]

The imperative to decolonize knowledge is associated with a number of methodological questions. Nāsili Vaka'uta, for example, resists the terminology of "vernacular hermeneutics" on the grounds that he reserves the right to criticize his own Oceanic culture. He suggests that every culture has the potential to assert its own hegemonies, and anticolonial discourses should not veil the need for such internal critique.[57]

53. Bernard M. Levinson, "Reading the Bible in Nazi Germany: Gerhard von Rad's Attempt to Reclaim the Old Testament for the Church," *Int* 62, no. 3 (2008): 238–54. On Romantic historicism, see Georg G. Iggers, *The German Conception of History: The National Tradition of Historical Thought from Herder to the Present* (Middletown: Wesleyan University Press, 1968). Romantic historicism reacted against the various forms of Enlightenment rationalism, and accordingly, condemnations of "the Enlightenment Bible" sometimes miss their mark. The dominant tropes of historicism stem from Romantic rather than Enlightenment philosophy. As shown by Gerdmar (*Roots*, 77–94), W. M. L. de Wette sits at the intersection of the two intellectual currents.

54. Sarah Shectman and Joel S. Baden, eds., *The Strata of the Priestly Writings: Contemporary Debate and Future Directions*, AThANT 95 (Zurich: TVZ, 2009).

55. Gregory L. Cuéllar, e.g., notes that S. R. Driver's own views on race derive from the anthropology of his day, but Driver explicitly argued that these views could not be found in the text of Genesis. See Cuéllar, "S. R. Driver and Higher Criticism: Mapping 'The Differences of Race' in Genesis," in Hockey and Horrell, *Ethnicity, Race, Religion*, 75–91. See also Maurice Olender, *The Languages of Paradise: Race, Religion, and Philology in the Nineteenth Century*, trans. Arthur Goldhammer (Cambridge, MA: Harvard University Press, 2008); Paul Michael Kurtz, *Kaiser, Christ, and Canaan: The Religion of Israel in Protestant Germany, 1871–1918*, FAT 122 (Tübingen: Mohr Siebeck, 2018).

56. Madipoane Masenya (ngwan'a Mphahlele) and Hulisani Ramantswana, "*Lupfumo lu Mavuni* (Wealth Is in the Land): In Search of the Promised Land (cf. Exod. 3–4) in the Post-Colonial Post-Apartheid South Africa," *JTSA* 151 (2015): 96–116. See further, Elivered Nasambu-Mulongo, "*Bosadi*: Madipoane (ngwan'a Mphahlele) Masenya's Contribution to Women's Biblical Hermeneutics," in *Postcolonial Perspectives in African Biblical Interpretations*, ed. Musa W. Dube, Andrew M. Mbuvi, and Dora Mbuwayesango, GPBS 13 (Atlanta: SBL Press, 2012), 43–61; Hulisani Ramantswana, "Decolonising Biblical Hermeneutics in the (South) African Context," *AcT* 36, suppl. 24 (2016): 178–203.

57. Nāsili Vaka'uta, *Reading Ezra 9–10 Tu'a Wise: Rethinking Biblical Interpretation in Oceania*, SBLIVBS (Atlanta: SBL Press, 2011), 3–8. Similarly, see Sarojini Nadar, "Beyond

Reflecting on her own cultural location, Grace Tsoi questions a return to Chinese classical literature as a marker of authentic contextualizing. Instead, she provides a postcolonial critique of the dominant Chinese translation of Judg. 19, drawing attention to the intersecting anti-concubinage agendas of the missionary translators and the Republican administrators at the beginning of the twentieth century. In this context, the Chinese translation of Judg. 19 inflated the guilt of the concubine and ignored the anti-Levite rhetoric in the text, which can be brought to light in dialogue with masculinity studies.[58] While various forms of "ethnocentrism from below" are ethically justifiable,[59] there are dangers in postcolonial tribalization that have been highlighted by Amartya Sen and Mahmood Mamdani, among others.[60] Politics of identity deserve attention precisely because they present both complexities and opportunities to society and to the academy.

Conclusion

Ideology, as Terry Eagleton puts it, is "less a matter of the inherent linguistic properties of a pronouncement than a question of who is saying what to whom for what purposes."[61] Ideologies were not inert substances in biblical texts, as if written in stone rather than on manifestly mutable scrolls. Biblical discourses were always alive and argumentative—taking ironic twists and turns, often mimicking imperial ideologies while simultaneously resisting them. The dominant hermeneutics of Christendom appear decidedly unbiblical in this respect, and with the benefit of hindsight, we can be confident that Kandiaronk was well justified in disputing the colonial ideas that were promoted to him under the banner of civilizational progress. Among the most pressing questions for future research is how to recover from the imaginary of progress.[62] The protean mutations of coloniality endure in the heart of professional biblical studies in the twenty-first century.

---

the 'Ordinary Reader' and the 'Invisible Intellectual': Shifting Contextual Bible Study from Liberation Discourse to Liberation Pedagogy," *OTE* 22, no. 2 (2009): 397–98.

58. Grace Kwan Sik Tsoi, *Who Is to Blame for Judges 19? Interplay between the Text and a Chinese Context* (Eugene, OR: Pickwick, 2022). Cf. Susan E. Haddox, "Masculinity Studies of the Hebrew Bible: The First Two Decades," *CurBR* 14, no. 2 (2016): 176–206.

59. Daniel Boyarin, *A Radical Jew: Paul and the Politics of Identity* (Berkeley: University of California Press, 1994), 252–58; Mark G. Brett, "Interpreting Ethnicity: Method, Hermeneutics, Ethics," in *Ethnicity and the Bible*, ed. Mark G. Brett (Leiden: Brill, 1996), 3–22.

60. Amartya Sen, *Identity and Violence: The Illusion of Destiny* (London: Allen Lane, 2006); Mahmood Mamdani, *Neither Settler nor Native: The Making and Unmaking of Permanent Minorities* (Johannesburg: Wits University Press, 2021).

61. Terry Eagleton, *Ideology: An Introduction* (London: Verso, 1991), 9.

62. Priya Satia, *Time's Monster: How History Makes History* (Cambridge, MA: Belknap, 2020), 289.

23

Environmental Approaches

Sandra L. Richter

The last several decades have witnessed an explosion of literature regarding ecology and the Bible. Although the discussion and legislation of environmental ethics may be traced back to the earliest ANE law codes, and generations of commentators have attempted to link their sacred texts to particular mandated actions toward land, flora, and fauna, the current surge of interest in the ecotheology of the Old (and New) Testament is unprecedented. Most commentators concur that this surge has been spurred by an equally unparalleled escalation in societal concern for the state of our global environment and the less-than-complimentary perception of the church's role in that crisis.

What Is Ecotheology?

Ecotheology—or "creation care,"[1] as some prefer—describes theological discourse that engages the sovereignty of God, the creatureliness of humanity, and the world of nature as an interrelated system. Some speak of it as a "liberative" theology in that it is "first and foremost concerned with guiding and stimulating right action."[2] Since the final destiny of the created order figures prominently in this conversation, eschatology is an essential partner, as are biblical declarations regarding

1. Douglas J. Moo and Jonathan A. Moo, *Creation Care: A Biblical Theology of the Natural World*, Biblical Theology for Life (Grand Rapids: Zondervan, 2018), 24–26.

2. Kiara Jorgenson and Alan Padgett, "For the Love of the World: A Dialogue on Ecotheology," in *Ecotheology: A Christian Conversation*, ed. Kiara Jorgenson and Alan Padgett (Grand Rapids: Eerdmans, 2020), 1.

human dominion *over* and stewardship *of* creation in a fallen world. Issues such as appropriate land use, care for the wild creature and its habitat, humane animal husbandry, the impact of environmental degradation on the marginalized, environmental terrorism, global warming, and the role of the church amid these societal ills are all addressed within this subphylum of theological discourse.

Where Did It Begin?

As David Kinsley rehearses in his *Ecology and Religion*, some early Christian theologians can be credited with laying the foundations of contemporary ecotheology.[3] Church fathers Irenaeus and Augustine deserve mention as early voices of celebration and concern for the created order, as does Francis of Assisi, named the patron saint of ecology by Pope John Paul II.[4] Daniel Swartz highlights like-minded early Jewish commentary, stating that the Mishnah and Talmud unequivocally affirm that "God owns everything in the world; we are but tenants in the garden, meant to till and to tend, to serve and to guard."[5] The Jewish signers of the 1999 Cornwall Declaration on Environmental Stewardship concur, stating that a "Torah-based" approach to the environment must recognize that "tenants do not have the same rights as owners" and that the "golden mean" of the Torah chastises humanity into moderation.[6]

In the modern era, early prophetic voices include Joseph Sittler,[7] Richard Baer Jr.[8] and Paul Santmire.[9] But it was the convergence of works by Rachel Carson,[10]

3. David Kinsley, *Ecology and Religion: Ecological Spirituality in Cross-Cultural Perspective* (Englewood Cliffs, NJ: Prentice Hall, 1994), 103–23; cf. John Doody, Kim Paffenroth, and Mark Smillie, eds., *Augustine and the Environment* (Lanham, MD: Lexington, 2016).

4. Francis of Assisi is known for his "Canticle of the Creatures" and saintly tales of rescuing and taming wild doves, negotiating peace between a small Italian village and a man-eating wolf, and preaching to wild animals. Cf. Brother Ugolino, *The Little Flowers of St. Francis of Assisi* (Grand Rapids: Christian Classics Ethereal Library, n.d.), 38, 48–49, 50.

5. Daniel Swartz, *To Till and to Tend: A Guide to Jewish Environmental Study and Action* (Scranton, PA: Coalition on the Environment and Jewish Life, 1994), 90.

6. Kenneth B. Fradkin et al., "A Comprehensive Torah-Based Approach to the Environment," in *Environmental Stewardship in the Judeo-Christian Tradition: Jewish, Catholic, and Protestant Wisdom on the Environment*, ed. Jay W. Richards (Grand Rapids: Acton Institute, 2007), https://www.acton.org/public-policy/environmental-stewardship/theology-e/comprehensive-torah-based-approach-environment.

7. Joseph Sittler, "A Theology for Earth," *The Christian Scholar* 37 (1954): 367–74; cf. Steven Bouma-Prediger and Peter Bakken, eds., *Evocations of Grace: The Writings of Joseph Sittler on Ecology, Theology, and Ethics* (Grand Rapids: Eerdmans, 2000).

8. In "Land Misuse: A Theological Concern" (*ChrCent* 88, no. 41 [1966]: 1239–41), Richard Baer Jr. strikes the reader as a modern-day Jeremiah pouring out his soul to a crowd of besieged and complacent consumers. Also see Baer, "The Ethical Quality of Life: Ecology, Religion, and the American Dream," *American Ecclesiastical Review* 165, no. 1 (1971): 43–59; Baer, "Conservation: An Arena for the Church's Action," *ChrCent* 86, no. 2 (1969): 40–43.

9. H. Paul Santmire, *Brother Earth: Nature, God, and Ecology in Time of Crisis* (New York: Nelson, 1970).

10. Rachel Carson, *Silent Spring* (Boston: Houghton Mifflin, 1962).

Lynn White,[11] and Francis Schaeffer[12]—all amplified by the tragic 1969 Santa Barbara oil spill[13]—that brought the emerging field of "ecology"[14] into the crosshairs of theological discourse. These were the days of President Richard Nixon's National Environmental Policy Act (that birthed the Environmental Protection Agency) and the first "Earth Day" (April 22, 1970). The proliferation of voices that followed is rehearsed in Roderick Nash's *The Rights of Nature: A History of Environmental Ethics* (1989) and catalogued in *Christianity Today*'s collection of published essays on the topic in *Stewards of the Earth: Christianity and Creation Care* (2022).

The contemporary surge of publications, however, has overwhelmed all that has come before.[15] Important points of entry include: James A. Nash, *Loving Nature: Ecological Integrity and Christian Responsibility* (1991); Norman Wirzba, *The Paradise of God: Renewing Religion in an Ecological Age* (2003); R. S. Gottlieb, *A Greener Faith: Religious Environmentalism and Our Planet's Future* (2006); Ellen Davis, *Scripture, Culture, and Agriculture: An Agrarian Reading of the Bible* (2009); Douglas and Jonathan Moo, *Creation Care* (2018); and Kiara A. Jorgenson and Alan G. Padgett, *Ecotheology* (2020). These contemporary Christian ecotheologians represent an array of perspectives regarding the relationship between the OT and the environment. These perspectives may be organized under three broadly defined headings: (1) biocentrism; (2) stewardship; and (3) sacramental environmentalism.

Biocentrism

Biocentrism, or as some prefer, "ecojustice,"[16] affirms nature's membership in God's world and thereby attributes to its members ethical rights. Embracing

11. Lynn White, "The Historical Roots of Our Ecological Crisis," *Science* 155, no. 3767 (1967): 1203–7. White assesses Christianity as "the most anthropocentric religion the world has seen . . . bearing a huge burden of guilt" for the philosophical and ethical framework that has fueled the modern technological exploitation of nature (1205). White's critique has been repeated, clarified, and contested many times.

12. Francis A. Schaeffer, *Pollution and the Death of Man: The Christian View of Ecology* (Carol Stream, IL: Tyndale, 1970).

13. Jon Hamilton, "How California's Worst Oil Spill Turned Beaches Black and the Nation Green," NPR, January 28, 2019, https://www.npr.org/2019/01/28/688219307; Emily Martin, "How the First Earth Day Ushered in a Golden Age of Activism," *National Geographic*, https://www.nationalgeographic.com/history/article/how-the-first-earth-day-ushered-in-a-golden-age-of-activism.

14. Ernst Haeckel was the first to use the term "ecology" in his *General Morphology of Organisms* in 1866. Eugenius Warming furthered the recognition of the subdiscipline. See R. P. McIntosh, *The Background of Ecology: Concept and Theory* (Cambridge: Cambridge University Press, 1985).

15. More than 7,000 titles on Christianity and ecology have been published in the past 15 years (Jorgenson and Padgett, "Love of the World," 3).

16. Jorgenson and Padgett, "Love of the World," 6–12.

an array of approaches, including ecofeminism and animal rights groups, each shares the common belief that nature itself and all its species have intrinsic value. "And if they have intrinsic value . . . they have rights."[17] As James Nash defines it, "Biotic rights are an effort to redefine responsible human relationships with the rest of the planet's beleaguered biota, and to ground these responsibilities not simply in human generosity and utility but in the moral claims inherent in the conation for appropriate treatment."[18]

Steven Bouma-Prediger's "Ecological Virtue Theory" likely fits best in this category.[19] The essential idea is that humanity is a member of the *community* of creation, with moral responsibility to nurture the virtues of humility, self-control, and compassion in our relationship with the flora and fauna of this planet. "When we recognize that we're part of a larger community of creation, we can more easily overcome the power hierarchy humans have typically embraced with respect to our fellow creatures" and thereby produce a just global environment.[20] Richard Bauckham is an important voice for this approach.[21]

A related position, ecofeminism, names the subjugation of women as an analogue to the subjugation of nature. "Male domination of women and domination of nature are interconnected, both in cultural ideology and in social structures. . . . The hatred of women and the hatred of nature are intimately connected and mutually reinforcing."[22] Put more stridently, it is the "masculine consciousness" that "seeks to gain control over women [and] over nature,"[23] and it is the "patriarchy" that produces the oppression of both the natural world and the bodies of women.[24] Thus, if the goal is a real solution to the oppression of nature, we must first resolve the oppression of women. The belief is that an egalitarian and collaborative society in which no group is dominant will produce environmental justice. Rosemary Radford Ruether, Carolyn Merchant, and Ynestra King are representative of this line of thought.

A significant theological challenge, particularly to this last line of thought, is the tenet that all power hierarchies are sinful and must be eradicated, particularly in light of Gen. 1. The great *practical* dilemma for each is how to adjudicate the

17. Thomas Sieger Derr, with James A. Nash and Richard John Neuhaus, *Environmental Ethics and Christian Humanism*, Abingdon Press Studies in Christian Ethics and Economic Life (Nashville: Abingdon, 1996), 24.

18. James A. Nash, "In Flagrant Dissent," in Derr, *Environmental Ethics*, 111.

19. Steven Bouma-Prediger, "The Character of Earthkeeping: A Christian Ecological Virtue Ethic," in Jorgenson and Padgett, *Ecotheology*, 119–52.

20. Jorgenson and Padgett, "Love of the World," 8.

21. Richard Bauckham, *The Bible and Ecology: Rediscovering the Community of Creation*, Sarum Theological Lectures (London: Darton, Longman & Todd, 2010).

22. Rosemary Radford Ruether, *Gaia and God: An Ecofeminist Theology of Earth Healing* (San Francisco: Harper, 1992), 2; cf. Francoise d'Eaubonne, *La féminisme ou la mort* (Paris: Horay, 1974).

23. Derr, *Environmental Ethics*, 50.

24. Jorgenson and Padgett, "Love of the World," 6.

competing rights of the natural world. To quote Holmes Rolston III: "Wilderness is a gigantic food pyramid, and this sets value in a grim deathbound jungle."[25] How might one adjudicate the rights of a hungry lion versus an herbivore zebra, or the moral standing of a human being needing a cure for cancer versus an animal in a laboratory needing its freedom, or perhaps closer to home, the moral standing of the Montana wilderness versus the fossil-fuel needs of a petroleum-dependent nation?

Stewardship

Stewardship takes as its core principle that "the earth is the LORD's, and all it contains" (Ps. 24:1 NASB). Therefore, humanity has been entrusted as stewards, not empowered as kings. The bedrock of this paradigm is the creation narratives: Gen. 1 identifies humanity as God's representative within the realms of the created order and as rulers of it, and Gen. 2:15 commands humanity to "tend" (לְעָבְדָהּ, *lə'obdāh*) and "protect" (לְשָׁמְרָהּ, *ləšomrāh*) the garden. At issue here, however, is one's definition of "stewardship." To quote James Nash, does "stewardship" mean "loving care and service for the sake of both humans and other lifeforms, or the technical management of the biosphere as nothing more than a 'resource base' for human needs and wants"?[26] Students of historical theology will recognize that the posture of "serve and protect" stands in some contrast to the Enlightenment imperative that humanity must become "rulers of nature,"[27] and critics of the stewardship model "rightfully note how the concept borders on management, reinforcing harmful anthropocentric emphases."[28] Bauckham, for example, holds that the hierarchical relationship between creation and humanity implied by the term "stewardship" echoes the ecological errors of modernity, and that "we urgently need to recover a biblical view of our solidarity with the rest of God's creatures . . . to locate ourselves once again where we belong—within creation."[29] Bouma-Prediger agrees, arguing that the term should be "retired" and replaced with "earthkeepers," a more appropriate expression of God's imperative

25. Holmes Rolston III, *Environmental Ethics: Duties to and Values in the Natural World*, Ethics and Action (Philadelphia: Temple University Press, 1988), 218.

26. Nash, "Flagrant Dissent," 107; cf. Douglas John Hall, *Imagining God: Dominion as Stewardship* (Grand Rapids: Eerdmans, 1986), 76–87; Loren Wilkinson, ed., *Earthkeeping: Christian Stewardship of Natural Resources* (Grand Rapids: Eerdmans, 1980), 214–16.

27. Francis Bacon understood human dominion as a mandate for the progressive exploitation of nature for the improvement of human life. In Bacon's mind, science and technology would be how humans would recover their God-given control of the earth. See Richard Bauckham, "Being Human in the Community of Creation: A Biblical Perspective," in Jorgenson and Padgett, *Ecotheology*, 17–18.

28. Jorgenson and Padgett ("Love of the World," 10) are referring to Lynn White's infamous essay. It is important to realize that White himself was a Christian and was calling for a Christian ecotheology that would emphasize right *relationship*, not simply right management. See Francis Schaeffer's response in *Death of Man*, 93.

29. Bauckham, "Being Human," 20.

to humanity.[30] Contemporary scholars who embrace the stewardship model include Daniel Block, Raymond Van Leeuwen, and Douglas and Jonathan Moo.

Sacramental Environmentalism

Sacramental environmentalism sees the earth as sacred, "the bearer of the Holy."[31] The view is best represented by Niels Gregersen's notion of "deep incarnation." Gregersen argues that "the incarnation of God in Christ can be understood as a radical or 'deep' incarnation, that is, an incarnation into the very tissue of biological existence . . . and system of nature."[32] Here the "enfleshment of God" becomes an "analogy for God's being in the all of creation,"[33] and the crucifixion becomes a microcosm in which God suffers with his creation, bearing "the costs of evolution, the price involved in the hardship of natural selection."[34] Similarly, Elizabeth Johnson speaks of the animal kingdom as the "the flesh of the World," which the Word of God has joined via incarnation.[35] For the Christian, then, environmentally responsible behavior becomes a spiritual practice whereby the believer works *with* God, participating *in* "God's ongoing act of creation and renewal."[36] As John F. Haught states, "To lose nature, then, would be to lose God."[37] Essential questions for the Christian theologian are (1) Where might we locate the fall in this paradigm? and (2) Where are the lines between "deep incarnation" and pantheism?

Each of the scholars named above, despite their significant differences, has a shared ambition, to give voice to the Bible regarding humanity's right relationship with nature. Whereas many contemporary commentators have chosen to jettison biblical faith as irrelevant or obsolete (or in some cases, the *cause* of global ecological degradation),[38] others have chosen instead to engage the church's ancient rule of faith and praxis to seek solutions. As a result, each shares a sense

30. Bouma-Prediger, "Earthkeeping," 119–52; cf. H. Paul Santmire, *Nature Reborn: The Ecological and Cosmic Promise of Christian Theology*, Theology and the Sciences (Minneapolis: Fortress, 2000), 120; Wilkinson, *Earthkeeping*.

31. Nash, "Flagrant Dissent," 108–9.

32. Niels Henrik Gregersen, "The Cross of Christ in an Evolutionary World," *Dialog* 40 (2001): 205, esp. 192–207; cf. Gregersen, "*Cur Deus Caro*: Jesus and the Cosmos Story," *Theology and Science* 11 (2013): 370–93.

33. Jorgenson and Padgett, "Love of the World," 9.

34. Gregersen, "Cross of Christ," 205; cf. Denis Edwards, *Deep Incarnation: God's Redemptive Suffering with Creatures* (Maryknoll, NY: Orbis Books, 2019).

35. Elizabeth A. Johnson, *Ask the Beasts: Darwin and the God of Love* (London: Bloomsbury, 2014), 212, 219, 224, 226.

36. Jorgenson and Padgett, "Love of the World," 9.

37. John F. Haught, "The Unfinished Sacrament of Creation," in Jorgenson and Padgett, *Ecotheology*, 180.

38. Sandra L. Richter, "Religion and the Environment," in *Handbook of Religion: A Christian Engagement with Traditions, Teachings, and Practices*, ed. Terry C. Muck et al. (Grand Rapids: Baker Academic, 2014), 746–55.

of urgency and a common data pool, the Bible. In the remaining pages, I sketch out what I believe a biblical-theological framework on this topic might be. Aspects of each paradigm named above will find some representation and some critique.

Ecotheology in the Old Testament

The Garden

The biblical message of humanity's relationship with the natural world begins as it ought, at the *beginning*. In Gen. 1, God announces his plan for the cosmos: a perfect and perfectly interdependent biosphere described via the literary framework of an equally perfect "week." Six days of creative activity are crowned by the Sabbath. In figure 23.1, days 1–3 report the creation of three habitats: day and night, sea and sky, and dry land. These are paralleled by days 4–6 in which three sets of inhabitants are fashioned to fill and bless those domains: sun and moon, fish and birds, and the creatures of the יַבָּשָׁה (*yabbāšâ*, dry ground). All creatures great and small are animated and placed in their proper domain, and so it is "good."

A close reading of the text demonstrates that this design is not simply about *order*; it is also about *authority* and *responsibility*. The sun and moon will

Figure 23.1. The Seven Days of Creation (Gen. 1:1–2:2)

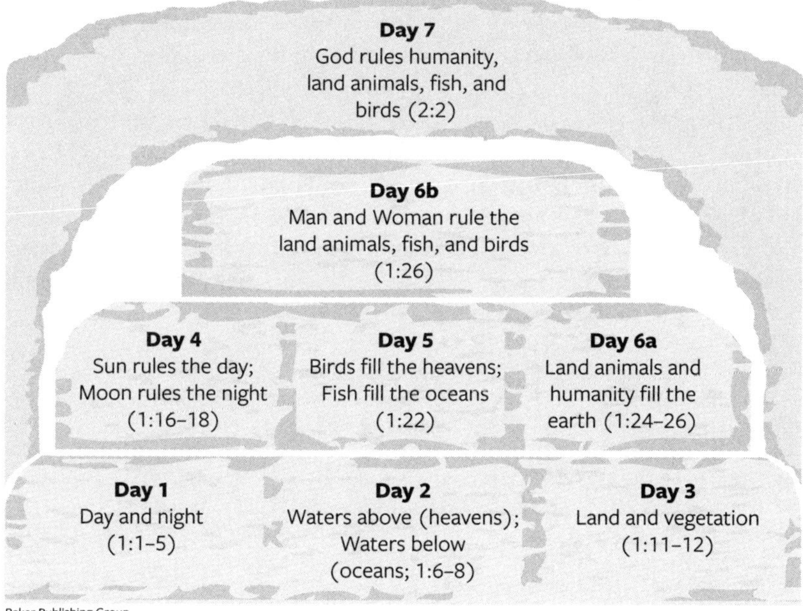

Baker Publishing Group

משׁל (*mšl*, govern) the day and night (Gen. 1:16, 18), the fish and birds and land animals are commanded to פרה (*prh*, fill) their domains (1:22), and YHWH is enthroned over all on the seventh day—communicating that the perfect balance of this splendid and synergetic system is dependent on the sovereignty of the Creator.

At the sixth day, the lyrical pattern of the piece shifts dramatically, drawing the reader's attention to the penultimate climax—the installation of God's steward, under the Creator but over the creation.

> Then God said, "Let us make אָדָם [*ʾādām*, humanity] in our image [צֶלֶם, *ṣelem*], according to our likeness; and let them rule . . ." (1:26)[39]

The implications of humanity being fashioned and animated as God's צֶלֶם are profound.[40] As ANE analogues make clear, woman and man are here depicted as the physical representatives of God's presence and sovereignty within the created order. Humans as אָדָם are vassals, custodians, and stewards *because* they are YHWH's royal representatives. Like the fish and birds, humanity is commanded to "be fruitful, multiply, and fill" their habitat. But because they are the image bearers of the Almighty, they are also commanded to כבשׁ (*kbš*, take possession of,[41] Gen. 1:28) and רדה (*rdh*, rule) all of the habitats and creatures of the previous six days.

In the language of covenant, YHWH is suzerain, אָדָם his vassal, and Eden the land grant. The garden *belongs* to YHWH, but humanity has been given the privilege to rule and the responsibility to care for this garden under the sovereignty of their divine lord. The "earthkeepers" are commissioned to their task. And although this hierarchy is indeed collaborative, it is a hierarchy all the same.

Thus, when humanity violates the covenant, their rebellion casts the entire cosmos into chaos. As אָדָם has rebelled against God (Gen. 3:6), the אֲדָמָה (*ʾădāmâ*, earth) rebels against humanity (3:17), and "not enough" becomes the legacy of their choice (3:18–19).[42] Humankind and animal kind are transformed into predator and prey (9:2–4). Creation itself is subjected to futility, "unable to attain the purpose for which it was created"[43] (Rom. 8:20), and the epic tale of redemption for both אָדָם and the garden begins.

39. Unless otherwise indicated, all Scripture quotations are the author's translation.

40. Catherine McDowell, *The Image of God in the Garden of Eden: The Creation of Humankind in Genesis 2:5–3:24 in Light of the* mīs pî pīt pî *and* wpt-r *Rituals of Mesopotamia and Ancient Egypt*, Siphrut 15 (Winona Lake, IN: Eisenbrauns, 2015).

41. *HALOT*, s.v. כבשׁ. This term is used when a new people group has taken possession of new territory (e.g., Num. 32:22, 29; Josh. 18:1; 2 Sam. 8:11; 1 Chron. 22:18).

42. Sandra L. Richter, *The Epic of Eden: A Christian Entry into the Old Testament* (Downers Grove, IL: IVP Academic, 2008), 102–16.

43. Douglas Moo, "Nature in the New Creation: New Testament Eschatology and the Environment," *JETS* 49, no. 3 (2006): 461; cf. Moo and Moo, *Creation Care*, 147–52.

Israel

Yet even in this "fallen" state of affairs, God's expectation that his people responsibly steward God's property remains. Thus, the law codes of ancient Israel are replete with regulations regarding sustainable agriculture, humane animal husbandry, care for the wild creature, and environmentally sensitive boundaries in warfare.[44] We are repeatedly told that YHWH owns this land, having appointed each of the tribes to their particular, inalienable patrimony. As a result, the only legal means of permanent land transfer in Israel is inheritance (Lev. 25:8–17, 23). Moreover, Deuteronomy is expressly clear that YHWH retains the right to reclaim his land and evict his people "in fury and in great wrath, and cast them into another land," if they fail to keep his covenant (Deut. 29:28 NASB 1995; cf. 28:15–68). As it was in the garden, so it is in the land of Israel: the land *belongs* to God, and it is his people's *privilege* to live upon it.

Sustainable Land Use

In concert with Israel's understanding that YHWH owns the land of Canaan, a number of laws address the longevity of the land's fertility. The core of these is the Sabbath rest, a command to regularly cease production so that the land might replenish itself:

> You shall sow your land for six years and gather in its yield, but the seventh year you shall let it rest and lie fallow. (Exod. 23:10–11a NASB 1995; cf. Lev. 25:4)

The fallowing described here not only aided in the recovery of fertility but also broke the natural cycle of noxious plant pests and diseases. Then as now, such farming practices limit short-term yield, but they help to ensure long-term fecundity. A critical ideological principle is communicated here: In Israel, it was not acceptable to take from the land everything that the populace *could*. Rather, God's people were commanded to operate with the long-term well-being of the land as their ultimate goal. The rationale for this long-term perspective? "Because I am YHWH" (Lev. 25:17), and "the land is mine" (25:23). The sovereign Lord of the nation of Israel had future harvests and future generations to think about. Indeed, Israel's *failure* to fallow is named as a reason for the exile (Lev. 26:34; 2 Chron. 36:21).[45]

44. Israel's identity as "tenant" is most evident in the laws of the tithe, firstfruits, and the firstborn. Cf. Deut. 14:22–23; 15:19–20; 18:3–5. See Sandra L. Richter, "Environmental Law in Deuteronomy: One Lens on a Biblical Theology of Creation Care," *BBR* 20, no. 3 (2010): 358–61; Richter, "Environmental Law: Wisdom from the Ancients," *BBR* 24, no. 3 (2014): 307–29, esp. 313–19.

45. Sandra L. Richter, *Stewards of Eden: What Scripture Has to Say about the Environment and Why It Matters* (Downers Grove, IL: InterVarsity, 2020), 21–28.

The Widow and the Orphan

Because the land ultimately belongs to YHWH, its produce does as well. Thus, although cereal, olive oil, and viticulture were essential to domestic and commercial survival,[46] Deut. 24:19–22 commands the Israelite farmer to refrain from fully harvesting these dietary anchors in order to leave enough for the widow, the orphan, and the *gēr* (cf. Lev. 19:9–10; 23:22). Knowing that the typical Iron Age village experienced an annual shortfall of fifteen million calories, which translates into a sixty-day hunger season for the typical family of five,[47] we recognize that the command to leave food in the field required the Israelite farmer to surrender a portion of his household's *essential* food supply. Here we find another critical biblical principle: the people of God are to restrict their own access to the resources of the land in order to guarantee that the marginalized have access as well. It has been broadly demonstrated that environmental degradation strikes those on the margins first[48] and that there is a perennial link between unsustainable land use and forced relocation.[49] Israelite law provides us fertile soil for reassessing land use in light of the command to care for the widow and the orphan.[50]

Warfare

If there was ever an appropriate time to sacrifice the long-term fecundity of the land for short-term gain, surely it would be during the crisis of warfare. War zones from the days of Hazael's destruction at Tell es-Ṣafi to World War I's No Man's Land and the ongoing legacy of Vietnam's "Operation Ranch Hand" testify to this broadly held belief.[51] In Israel's world, the Babylonians, Assyrians, Hittites, and Egyptians were notorious for environmental terrorism—specifically, the calculated decimation of an enemy's vineyards and orchards in time of siege. The

46. Sandra L. Richter, "The Question of Provenance and the Economics of Deuteronomy," *JSOT* 42, no. 1 (2017): 23–50; cf. Richter, *Stewards of Eden*, 68–78.

47. Baruch Rosen, "Subsistence Economy in Iron Age I," in *From Nomadism to Monarchy: Archaeological and Historical Aspects of Early Israel*, ed. I. Finkelstein and N. Na'aman (Jerusalem: Israel Exploration Society, 1994), 348–49; cf. Richter, "Environmental Law in Deuteronomy," 371–72.

48. Norman Wirzba, "The Grace of Good Food and the Call to Good Farming," *Review and Expositor* 108, no. 1 (2011): 61–71; Wirzba, *The Paradise of God: Renewing Religion in an Ecological Age* (New York: Oxford University Press, 2003); Pavan Sukhdev, "The Economics of Ecosystems and Biodiversity—TEEB," *EurekAlert!*, May 29, 2008, https://www.eurekalert.org/news-releases/653906.

49. Scott Sabin, "Environmental Emigration: The World on Our Doorstep," *Creation Care* 37 (2008): 37–38.

50. See Richter, *Stewards of Eden*, 78–90, for discussion and case studies.

51. Aren M. Maeir, Oren Ackermann, and Hendrik J. Bruins, "The Ecological Consequences of a Siege: A Marginal Note on Deuteronomy 20:19–20," in *Confronting the Past: Archaeological and Historical Essays on Ancient Israel in Honor of William G. Dever*, ed. Seymour Gitin, J. Edward Wright, and J. P. Dessel (Winona Lake, IN: Eisenbrauns, 2006), 239–43; cf. Richter, "Wisdom from the Ancients," 319–20.

goal was to speed victory and/or economically cripple the opponent for decades beyond the battle.[52] Yet in Deut. 20:19b–20 YHWH forbids such practices: "For is the tree of the field a man that it should be besieged by you? Only a tree that you know does not produce food may you destroy and cut down, and you may build your siege works against the city with which you are at war until it falls." Why? As Michael Hasel states, "It would not be in Israel's interest to destroy the very resources that would later sustain them."[53] Thus, although environmental terrorism delivers an instant military advantage, Israelite law teaches that the long-term lethal impact on the enemy's life-support systems is ultimately *self*-destructive.[54]

Wild Creatures and Their Habitat

What of the creatures that inhabited the land with God's people? Throughout the OT we read that even in a fallen world, God rejoices in the beauty and balance of his creation. Psalm 104 states that God "sends forth the springs into the wadis; between the mountains they flow, giving drink to each of his wild creatures" (vv. 10–11). It is YHWH who "sent out the wild donkey free" and "gave to him the wilderness for a home" (Job 39:5–6). In the flood narrative, although God judges humanity, he rescues animal kind, and the re-creational covenant of Gen. 9:10–11 is with "every living creature." The politeia of ancient Israel recognizes and reinforces this value system. "If you happen upon a bird's nest in front of you in the road, or in a tree, or upon the ground, with young ones or eggs, and the mother sitting upon the young or on the eggs, do not take the mother [who is sitting] upon the young. Rather, you will surely shoo the mother away, and the young you may take for yourself, in order that it may be well with you and that you may prolong your days" (Deut. 22:6–7). In concert with 20:19–20, sparing fruit trees during siege warfare, a common idea is communicated: if Israel takes both tree and fruit, mother and offspring, the means of life would be exterminated. So again, in contrast to the practice of their larger culture, the citizenry of Israel was instructed to preserve the wild animals with whom they shared the promised land, "so that it may go well with you and your children after you and that you may live long in the land" (Deut. 4:40 NIV).[55]

Humane Animal Husbandry

As is true today, livestock were maintained in Israel for the well-being of humankind. Yet the Sabbath ordinance commands Israel to honor their God by allowing their beasts to rest: "But the seventh day is a Sabbath belonging to YHWH your God; you shall not do any work, not you or your son or your daughter or your

52. Richter, "Environmental Law in Deuteronomy," 365–68.

53. Michael Hasel, *Military Practice and Polemic: Israel's Laws of Warfare in Near Eastern Perspective* (Berrien Springs, MI: Andrews University Press, 2005), 102–13.

54. See Richter, *Stewards of Eden*, 61–67.

55. Richter, "Environmental Law in Deuteronomy," 365–68.

male servant or your female servant or your ox or your donkey or any of your domesticated beasts" (Deut. 5:14). Deuteronomic law further commands that the Israelite not muzzle his ox while threshing the grain (25:4). In the small farms of the central hill country, the Iron Age farmer leaned heavily on the strength of his animal for the labor required to plant, harvest, and thresh grain. And in Israel's subsistence economy, the three to four kilos (five to seven quarts) of grain that an ox might consume over the course of a day of threshing made a difference.[56] Yet the Israelite farmer is commanded to treat his animal with generosity and compassion, even when doing so compromised the farmer's *essential* food supply. This ancient law offers a pointed critique of a current norm: the widespread and profoundly inhumane practice of mass-confinement animal husbandry (also known as "factory farming").[57] In contrast to current practices, in Israelite society, the humane treatment of domestic animals was a divine ordinance, not an economic option.[58]

In sum, we find that in Israel the all-too-human drive for economic and military security was circumscribed by charity, long-term stewardship of the land, and the active protection of wild and domestic creatures. It was Israel's privilege to live on the land and utilize its resources, but covenant law made it expressly clear that Israel was steward not king, lessee not lessor. Moreover, the Sabbath ordinance made it equally clear that production and consumption must have limits.[59] Would a biocentrist find here the sort of boundaries necessary to a "biotic justice [that] imposes obligations on the human community to limit production and consumption in order to prevent the excessive exploitation and toxication of wildlife and wild land"?[60] I believe so. But the biocentrist would be hard-pressed to demonstrate that the source of those boundaries was the elevation of rock and tree and creature to "intrinsic moral value." Rather, these biblical restraints emerge from the proper positioning of humanity over the creation, but *under* the Creator.

Ecotheology in the New Testament

Although this volume focuses on the state of *Old Testament* studies, the fact that the fate (and therefore value) of this planet finds its resolution in the NT demands that we engage it, at least briefly. But in doing so, we quickly encounter a problem: although there is ample material in the OT for the formation of a Christian ecotheology, this is less true in the NT. Rather, the largely urban audience of the NT, the post-theocratic economic and political identity of God's people in the first century, and the corpus's singular focus on making plain the character of the new אָדָם seem to have pushed issues of creation care, so evident in the OT,

56. Richter, "Environmental Law in Deuteronomy," 368–74.
57. Richter, *Stewards of Eden*, 35–47.
58. Richter, "Environmental Law in Deuteronomy," 374–75; Richter, *Stewards of Eden*, 42–46.
59. See Richter, *Stewards of Eden*, 45–47.
60. Nash, "Flagrant Dissent," 112.

to the periphery.[61] As a result, more than one NT interpreter has concluded that there is no ecotheology to be found in the New Covenant, and some that the NT is actually *opposed* to environmental concerns.[62]

Passages such as 2 Pet. 3:10–13, 1 Thess. 5:2–3, and Rev. 6:12–17 seem to say that the created order is destined for annihilation, belying any divine expectation of human conservation. Here we find the echo of Lynn White's indictment that Christianity posits a dichotomy between people and nature: "man and nature are two things, and man is master, and therefore, whereas the exploitation of people would be ethically evil, the exploitation of creation was right and good."[63] But in reality these NT passages are connecting the great and fearsome OT "Day of YHWH"[64] with the parousia of Christ.[65] Thus, as in the OT, the fantastic and sometimes bizarre apocalyptic imagery that populates these NT passages is actually the language of judgment, *not* of annihilation.[66] When this imagery is translated according to its OT lexicon, signs in heaven and earth, earthquakes, fire, and thunder become hallmarks of the Second Coming, not the eradication of the cosmos.

When these same passages are juxtaposed with God's ultimate purposes for the created order rehearsed in Rom. 8, an entirely new picture emerges. "For the creation waits with eager longing for the revealing of the sons of God; for the creation was subjected to futility, not of its own will, but because of him who subjected it, in hope that the creation itself also will be set free from its bondage to decay into the freedom of the glory of the children of God" (8:19–21). Here not only humanity awaits "the revealing of the sons of God" but the entire created order as well. For with the return of the Last Adam, creation itself is finally freed from the chaos of the rebellion of אָדָם. Moreover, the iconography of Rev. 22:1–5 makes clear that the inheritance of the redeemed children of the fall is Eden restored, this very earth healed of its scars and washed clean of its diseases.

Colin Gunton describes the nature of this resurrected planet as "transformation within continuity."[67] Greg Beale speaks of the "new heavens and the new earth" as "an identifiable counterpart to the old cosmos and a renewal of it, just as the body will be raised without losing its former identity."[68]Although "the

61. Moo and Moo, *Creation Care*, 130–34.

62. Richter, *Stewards of Eden*, 91–105; cf. Al Truesdale, "Last Things First: The Impact of Eschatology on Ecology," *Perspectives on Science and Christian Faith* 46 (1994): 116–20.

63. White, "Ecological Crisis," 1205.

64. E.g., Isa. 13:2–13; Jer. 46:10; Ezek. 7:10; 13:5; 30:3; Joel 1:15; 2:1, 11.

65. Douglas Moo, "Eschatology and Environmental Ethics," in *Keeping God's Earth: The Global Environment in Biblical Perspective*, ed. Noah Toly and Daniel Block (Downers Grove, IL: IVP Academic, 2010), 36–38.

66. Richter, *Stewards of Eden*, 95–100.

67. Colin E. Gunton, *Christ and Creation: The Didsbury Lectures 1990* (Eugene, OR: Wipf & Stock, 2005), 31.

68. G. K. Beale, *The Book of Revelation*, NIGTC (Grand Rapids: Eerdmans, 1999), 1040–41; cf. Beale, "The Eschatological Concept of New Testament Theology," in *"The Reader Must*

continuity between this world and the next one is difficult to determine,"[69] Paul's association of the final destiny of the planet with the ultimate expression of a believer's identity as God's redeemed child and heir speaks volumes about the profound value that God places on the earth and its creatures.

In short, in the new covenant, the garden still belongs to God, and God still intends that it be used for his purposes. Here the trajectory of redemptive history is fully coherent. Genesis 1 offers us a perfectly balanced ecosphere, animated by the creative will of God, stewarded by an allied and obedient humanity. Revelation 22 offers us the same.

Conclusion

As each scholar cited in this essay recounts, the OT provides fertile soil for a robust Christian ecotheology, and as our current situation on this earth is perilous, I am grateful for the urgency that echoes in every voice. In the beginning "YHWH Elohim took the human and put him into the garden of Eden to tend it and protect it" (Gen. 2:15). May this generation of the heirs of the kingdom rise up, reflect on the task, and do the same.

Understand": Eschatology in Bible and Theology, ed. K. E. Brower and M. W. Elliott (Leicester, UK: InterVarsity, 1997), 11–52.

69. Moo, "Nature in the New Creation," 464.

24

Old Testament Ethics

M. Daniel Carroll R.

There was no substantial interest in OT ethics before 1980.[1] The few full-length treatments that appeared before that time tended to follow a moral-development or history-of-religions model dependent on the reigning critical theories that saw the OT's ethics progressing over time to culminate with Jesus and the NT. Some of the more significant works in English early in the twentieth century include those by Archibald Duff, W. S. Bruce, and Hinckley Mitchell.[2] At midcentury, important studies in German appeared by Johannes Hempel and Hendrik van Oyen.[3] James Muilenburg's English volume and J. García Trapiello's Spanish volume also deserve mention.[4] Since 1980, interest in OT ethics as a whole has exploded, as has specialized

1. For surveys, see Eckart Otto, *Theologische Ethik des Alten Testaments*, Theologsiche Wissenschaft 3/2 (Stuttgart: W. Kohlhammer, 1994), 9–17; Christopher J. H. Wright, *Old Testament Ethics for the People of God* (Downers Grove, IL: InterVarsity, 2004), 387–440; Rainer Kessler, *Der Weg zum Leben: Ethik des Alten Testaments* (Munich: Gütersloher, 2017), 35–50. Regarding my use of the term "Old Testament" instead of "Hebrew Bible" in this essay, please see the editors' preface.

2. Archibald Duff, *The Theology and the Ethics of the Hebrews* (London: John C. Nimmo, 1902); W. S. Bruce, *The Ethics of the Old Testament*, 2nd ed. (Edinburgh: T&T Clark, 1909); Hinckley G. Mitchell, *The Ethics of the Old Testament* (Chicago: University of Chicago Press, 1912).

3. Johannes Hempel, *Das Ethos de Alten Testaments*, 2nd ed., BZAW 67 (Berlin: Töpelmann, 1964); Hendrik van Oyen, *Die Ethik des Alten Testaments* (Güttersloh: Gerd Mohn, 1967).

4. James Muilenburg, *The Way of Israel: Biblical Faith and Ethics* (New York: Harper & Row, 1961); J. García Trapiello, *El problema moral en el Antiguo Testamento* (Barcelona: Herder, 1977).

research into ethics within specific OT sections, genres, books, and topics.[5] The field of OT ethics has grown complex and requires preliminary, interconnected decisions on several introductory matters.[6] These are the focus of this essay, and the massive and growing bibliography demands that this treatment be selective.

Authority of the Old Testament for Ethics

In heuristic terms, the authority of the OT for ethics can be understood in three ways. The first argues that its authority be defined functionally; it is not an inherent property of the text.[7] In this view, the enduring significance of the OT over the centuries in moral matters testifies to its value for shaping and guiding the people of God. The Bible is a repository of reflections about God and life by ancient faith communities who sought to discern God's will in their time and place; hence, its pages include many different, contrasting, and even contradictory ethical viewpoints. Today's world and its moral issues are different from ancient times. Therefore, the OT's perspective, though still instructive, must be supplemented by and coordinated with insights from other sources (e.g., archaeology, the social sciences, philosophy) and evaluated as to its ethical appropriateness for modern contexts. Communities of faith should authorize the OT as a primary, although not the sole, source for their ethics.

A second position holds a more ontological perspective of biblical authority, which is grounded in the conviction of the text's divine inspiration (although this is defined in diverse ways).[8] This approach considers the functional aspect of biblical authority to be a phenomenological given and recognizes the wide swath of voices within the OT, but it believes the OT is timeless revelation in ways that

5. For the ethics of each OT book and other issues, see Joel B. Green, ed., *Dictionary of Scripture and Ethics* (Grand Rapids: Baker Academic, 2011). For a Jewish orientation, see Elaine Adler Goodfriend, "Ethical Theory and Practice in the Hebrew Bible," in *The Oxford Handbook of Jewish Ethics and Morality*, ed. Elliot N. Dorff and Jonathan K. Crane (New York: Oxford University Press, 2012), 35–49.

6. Works on OT ethics generally discuss these matters. A helpful introduction is C. L. Crouch, "Ethics," in *The Hebrew Bible: A Critical Companion*, ed. John Barton (Princeton: Princeton University Press, 2016), 338–55. For my own earlier treatments, see M. Daniel Carroll R., "Old Testament Ethics," in Green, *Scripture and Ethics*, 561–65; Carroll R., "Ethics and Old Testament Interpretation," in *Hearing the Old Testament: Listening for God's Address*, ed. Craig G. Bartholomew and David J. H. Beldman (Grand Rapids: Eerdmans, 2012), 204–27.

7. Bruce C. Birch, *Let Justice Roll Down: The Old Testament, Ethics, and Christian Life* (Louisville: Westminster John Knox, 1991), 29–50; Birch, "Scripture in Ethics: Methodological Issues," in Green, *Scripture and Ethics*, 27–34; William P. Brown, *Deep Calls to Deep: The Psalms in Dialogue and Disruption* (Nashville: Abingdon, 2021), 421–33.

8. See esp. Wright, *Old Testament Ethics*, 445–71; Wright, *The Mission of God: Unlocking the Bible's Grand Narrative* (Downers Grove, IL: IVP Academic, 2006), 48–69; cf. John Goldingay, *Models for Scripture* (Grand Rapids: Eerdmans, 1994). These approaches can include apologetic responses to critiques of the OT, such as Walter C. Kaiser Jr., *Toward Old Testament Ethics* (Grand Rapids: Zondervan, 1983), 247–314.

the first option does not. This second position stands in stronger continuity with the historic positions of the synagogue and church.

Both of these first two options operate with what might be called a hermeneutic of trust, even if the functional and ontological views qualify this differently. A third approach works from more of a hermeneutic of suspicion to argue that the OT has little or no moral authority today.[9] It reads "against the grain," questioning what it considers to be the OT's prejudices and damaging ideologies. The OT's worldview is considered outdated and foreign, its ethical insights exaggerated and misunderstood, and its moral vision unacceptable and even irredeemable.

Troublesome aspects of the OT necessarily surface in discussions about its authority, the most prominent of which is the violence of God.[10] Resistance to this textual feature appears as early as the second century CE with Marcion of Sinope, who famously rejected the OT (and much of the NT) as presenting a deity alien to the person and teachings of Jesus. The conquest account in Joshua is a special target, but other texts—even those that heretofore have been taken as central to OT ethics, such as the Ten Commandments, the exodus narrative, the charity laws, and the prophetic literature—have also been deemed objectionable.[11] In addition, the history of interpretation presents multiple instances where the OT has been used in discriminatory ways against women[12] and marginalized peoples[13] or to sanction colonial projects.[14] Bringing this negative record to light

9. E.g., Cyril S. Rodd, *Glimpses of a Strange Land: Studies in Old Testament Ethics*, OTS (London: T&T Clark, 2001), 322–29.

10. See Eric A. Seibert, "Recent Research on Divine Violence in the Old Testament (with Special Attention to Christian Theological Perspectives)," *CurBR* 15, no. 1 (2016): 8–40; and the bibliography in Amy C. Cottrill, *Uncovering Violence: Reading Biblical Narratives as an Ethical Project* (Louisville: Westminster John Knox, 2021). For different approaches, see Eryl W. Davies, *The Immoral Bible: Approaches to Biblical Ethics* (London: T&T Clark, 2010); M. Daniel Carroll R. and J. Blair Wilgus, eds., *Wrestling with the Violence of God: Soundings in Old Testament Texts*, BBRSup 10 (Winona Lake, IN: Eisenbrauns, 2015). Note also David Lamb's essay in the present volume (chap. 13, "Joshua, Judges, and Ruth").

11. E.g., Harold V. Bennett, *Injustice Made Legal: Deuteronomic Law and the Plight of Widows, Strangers, and Orphans in Ancient Israel* (Grand Rapids: Eerdmans, 2002); Cheryl B. Anderson, *Ancient Laws and Contemporary Controversies: The Need for Inclusive Biblical Interpretation* (Oxford: Oxford University Press, 2009); Carol J. Dempsey, *Hope amid the Ruins: The Ethics of Israel's Prophets* (St. Louis: Chalice, 2000); Julia M. O'Brien, *Challenging Prophetic Metaphor: Theology and Ideology in the Prophets* (Louisville: Westminster John Knox, 2008).

12. Feminist, womanist, and *mujerista* literature speak to this issue. See, e.g., Yvonne Sherwood, ed., *The Bible and Feminism: Remapping the Field* (Oxford: Oxford University Press, 2017).

13. See essays in, e.g., Cain Hope Felder, ed., *Stony the Road We Trod: African American Biblical Interpretation*, 30th anniversary ed. (Minneapolis: Fortress, 2021); Francisco Lozada Jr. and Fernando F. Segovia, eds., *Latino/a Theology and the Bible: Ethnic-Racial Reflections on Interpretation* (Lanham, MD: Lexington/Fortress Academic, 2021); Uriah Y. Kim and Seung Ai Yang, eds., *T&T Clark Handbook of Asian American Biblical Hermeneutics* (London: T&T Clark, 2019).

14. Mark G. Brett, *Decolonizing God: The Bible in the Tides of Empire*, Bible in the Modern World 16 (Sheffield: Sheffield Phoenix, 2008); R. S. Sugirtharajah, ed., *Voices from the Margin:*

has had constructive results, such as recovery of ignored or silenced OT voices, reinterpretation of key texts, and putting problematic passages into conversation with other parts of the canon to complement, develop, or correct them. Whatever one's stance vis-à-vis the OT, these recent approaches call for readers to engage its ethical content more self-consciously and responsibly.[15]

The Subject and Task of Old Testament Ethics

To what does "Old Testament ethics" actually refer? It is helpful to distinguish (a) what ancient Israelites may have thought about a moral issue at different moments in their history, (b) what OT authors may have believed, and (c) what the OT canon as a whole might suggest to faith communities for engaging current ethical matters.[16]

The first two items (a and b) are descriptive. Moving from the biblical text to appropriation for life today is not their primary purpose. John Barton makes this distinction clear: "I am concerned with the Hebrew Bible or Old Testament not as the Scriptures of Judaism or Christianity, but as evidence for the thinking of ancient Israelites and Jews."[17] Descriptive approaches can be of several kinds. One of the most basic is to survey pertinent OT vocabulary, such as the various terms for the poor (e.g., אֶבְיוֹן, *ʾebyôn*; דַּל, *dal*; עָנִי, *ʿānî*) and justice (e.g., מִשְׁפָּט, *mišpāṭ*; צֶדֶק/צְדָקָה, *ṣedeq*/*ṣədāqâ*).[18] Some try to ascertain the ethical stances of those who may have produced the strata that now compose the OT. This can also involve reconstructions of social settings and ideologies that may have generated these OT ethical concerns.[19] Others explore the ethics and moral behavior of ancient

Interpreting the Bible in the Third World, 25th anniversary ed. (Maryknoll, NY: Orbis Books, 2016). The literature on the so-called doctrine of discovery is relevant here, as are certain ideological approaches, such as Roland Boer, *Marxist Criticism of the Bible*, 2nd ed. (London: Bloomsbury, 2015).

15. In addition to the matters mentioned earlier in this paragraph, pertinent here are approaches to OT ethics that focus on a specific area of concern, such as gender, ecology, disability, trauma, migration, and more. To these can be added insights into OT ethics arising from Latin America, Africa, and Asia, but this material lies beyond this essay's constraints.

16. John Barton, *Understanding Old Testament Ethics: Approaches and Explanations* (Louisville: Westminster John Knox, 2003), 15–16; Wright, *Old Testament Ethics*, 441–45.

17. John Barton, *Ethics in Ancient Israel* (Oxford: Oxford University Press, 2014), 4.

18. See the lexicons, theological dictionaries, and book-length works, such as Jacques Pons, *L'oppression dans l'Ancien Testament* (Paris: Letouzey et Ané, 1981); Jože Krašovec, *God's Righteousness and Justice in the Old Testament* (Grand Rapids: Eerdmans, 2022). More focused studies include Hemchand Gossai, *Justice, Righteousness, and the Social Critique of the Eighth-Century Prophets*, American University Studies 141 (New York: Peter Lang, 1993); William Robert Domeris, *Touching the Heart of God: The Social Construction of Poverty among Biblical Peasants*, LHBOTS 466 (London: T&T Clark, 2007).

19. E.g., J. David Pleins, *The Social Visions of the Hebrew Bible: A Theological Introduction* (Louisville: Westminster John Knox, 2001); Norman K. Gottwald, *The Politics of Ancient Israel*, LAI (Louisville: Westminster John Knox, 2001); Douglas A. Knight, *Law, Power, and*

Israel and OT texts in relation to those of the surrounding cultures to discover differences and similarities. This comparative work has been done particularly in relationship to the law codes, whether in broad perspective or with a focus on specific topics, such as the poor or slavery.[20] Others turn their attention from hypothetical reconstructions to the received text.[21] A growing number of literary approaches explore the morality of biblical scenes, characters, and institutions (such as the monarchy). These have concentrated especially on the narratives in Genesis, Joshua, Judges, 1–2 Samuel, and 1–2 Kings.[22]

The third item (c) seeks to appropriate the OT for today. This can begin with a descriptive foundation within ancient Israel's historical contexts and in dialogue with its surrounding cultures as an initial step toward trying to ascertain how the OT might be normative for us today.[23] The contemporary use of the OT is quite varied, as we will see later in this chapter.

Determining the Source Material for Old Testament Ethics

Appropriating the OT requires a decision regarding the form of the text to which one should appeal. Some studies are based on a canonical form and read it synchronically. This choice can be based on theological convictions about its ontology, but it also may be for practical or pastoral reasons. That is, a faith community's canon is the only text that it knows and uses.[24] To construct OT ethics on critical hypotheses, it is felt, essentially takes the Bible out of the community's hands and makes its application dependent on academic circles. Even scholars with critical

Justice in Ancient Israel, LAI (Louisville: Westminster John Knox, 2011); Roland Boer, *The Sacred Economy of Ancient Israel*, LAI (Louisville: Westminster John Knox, 2015). For surveys, see Walter J. Houston, *Contending for Justice: Ideologies and Theologies of Social Justice in the Old Testament* (London: T&T Clark, 2008), 18–51; M. Daniel Carroll R., *Amos*, NICOT (Grand Rapids: Eerdmans, 2020), 20–25.

20. E.g., Léon Epsztein, *Social Justice in the Ancient Near East and the People of the Bible*, trans. John Bowden (London: SCM, 1986); Moshe Weinfeld, *Social Justice in Ancient Israel and in the Ancient Near East* (Jerusalem: Magnes; Minneapolis: Fortress, 1995); cf. n. 23 below.

21. Barton, *Ethics in Ancient Israel*, 1–13; R. Norman Whybray, *The Good Life in the Old Testament* (Edinburgh: T&T Clark, 2002); cf. Michael Walzer, *In God's Shadow: Politics in the Hebrew Bible* (New Haven: Yale University Press, 2012).

22. E.g., Keith Bodner and Benjamin J. M. Johnson, eds., *Character and Characterization in the Books of Kings*, LHBOTS 670 (London: T&T Clark, 2020).

23. This has often been done with OT law. E.g., David L. Baker, *Tight Fists or Open Hands? Wealth and Poverty in Old Testament Law* (Grand Rapids: Eerdmans, 2009); Roy E. Gane, *Old Testament Law for Christians: Original Context and Enduring Application* (Grand Rapids: Baker Academic, 2017), 126–33. From a Jewish perspective, note Joshua A. Berman, *Created Equal: How the Bible Broke with Ancient Political Thought* (New York: Oxford University Press, 2008); Jeremiah Unterman, *Justice for All: How the Jewish Bible Revolutionized Ethics*, JPS Essential Judaism Series (Philadelphia: Jewish Publication Society, 2017).

24. A good example is Wright's *Old Testament Ethics*.

convictions are aware of this potentiality and typically do not foreground such matters.[25]

Others, in contrast, make critical reconstructions central to their discussions. Because OT ethical issues arose in response to particular contexts, these scholars seek to specify the original sociohistorical and ideological seedbeds of the texts' ethical reflections as an indispensable foundation for determining their relevance.[26] Mark Brett has done this in sophisticated fashion by coordinating critical results with other disciplines (such as anthropology, history, postcolonial studies, and political theologies past and present) to demonstrate that issues faced by ancient Israel echo across time, as do its theological insights for real-world challenges.[27]

Another determination pertaining to OT texts is the choice of genre. While some studies work with the entire corpus for their ethics, others concentrate on certain canonical sections.[28] The Law, especially the Ten Commandments, has long commanded the attention of theologians, ethicists, and biblical scholars as primary for understanding the OT's ethical values.[29] The imperatives of the Decalogue, it is argued, were applied across the OT to all kinds of topics in the larger legal corpus, fleshed out in narratives, and reaffirmed in the poetic and prophetic literature. They continue to find relevance today.

Increasingly, and for several reasons, narrative is being appreciated as a valuable resource for OT ethics.[30] Principally, is the power of sacred stories. Their plots and

25. E.g., Birch, *Let Justice Roll Down*; Johanna W. H. van Wijk-Bos, *Making Wise the Simple: The Torah in Christian Faith and Practice* (Grand Rapids: Eerdmans, 2005); John Goldingay, *Old Testament Theology*, vol. 3, *Israel's Life* (Downers Grove, IL: IVP Academic, 2009).

26. This is the stated aim of C. L. Crouch, ed., *The Cambridge Companion to the Hebrew Bible and Ethics* (Cambridge: Cambridge University Press, 2021); cf. Otto, *Theologische Ethik*; John Rogerson, *Theory and Practice in Old Testament Ethics*, ed. and with an introduction by M. Daniel Carroll R., JSOTSup 405 (London: Continuum T&T Clark, 2004); Houston, *Contending for Justice*; Houston, *Justice for the Poor? Social Justice in the Old Testament in Concept and Practice* (Eugene, OR: Cascade, 2020).

27. Mark G. Brett, *Political Trauma and Healing: Biblical Texts for a Postcolonial World* (Grand Rapids: Eerdmans, 2016); Brett, *Locations of God: Political Theology in the Hebrew Bible* (Oxford: Oxford University Press, 2019).

28. Some volumes offer studies across the genres. See, e.g., Katherine Dell, ed., *Ethical and Unethical in the Old Testament: God and Humans in Dialogue*, LHBOTS 528 (London: T&T Clark, 2010); Crouch, *Hebrew Bible and Ethics*. From a Jewish perspective, see Susan Niditch, *Ethics in the Hebrew Bible and Beyond* (Oxford: Oxford University Press, 2023).

29. For historical viewpoints and contemporary reflections, see William P. Brown, ed., *The Ten Commandments: The Reciprocity of Faithfulness*, Library of Theological Ethics (Louisville: Westminster John Knox, 2004). In addition to the studies cited in an earlier note, see Kaiser, *Toward Old Testament Ethics*; Otto, *Theologische Ethik*; Patrick D. Miller, *The Ten Commandments*, Interpretation (Louisville: Westminster John Knox, 2009).

30. Birch, *Let Justice Roll Down*; Barton, "Reading for Life: The Use of the Bible in Ethics," in *Understanding Old Testament Ethics*, 55–64; Gordon J. Wenham, *Story as Torah: Reading the Old Testament Ethically*, OTS (Edinburgh: T&T Clark, 2000); Mary E. Mills, *Biblical Morality: Moral Perspectives in Old Testament Narratives*, Heythrop Studies in Contemporary Philosophy, Religion and Theology (Aldershot: Ashgate, 2001); Sung Min Chun, *Ethics*

characters draw the community of faith into these textual worlds to provide a lens into reality different from that of their cultural contexts. The characters' moral quandaries may shed light on readers' own complex ethical questions. Narratives can promote character formation in individuals and communities, leading them to live a certain kind of life and, in turn, be better readers of the text for ethics.[31] The growing interest in virtue ethics buttresses this turn to biblical narrative.[32]

Wisdom and poetic literature also offer fruitful ground for the study of ethics.[33] Patricia Vesely works within the framework of Aristotelian virtue ethics to evaluate the relationships between Job and his friends in order to consider the moral responsibilities of friendship.[34] Others apply virtue ethics to Proverbs, which stresses the importance of shaping the individual through observation and life choices.[35] William Pohl examines Job's character through his prayers of protest and argues that the book commends such God-talk from innocent sufferers.[36] Gordon Wenham laments the lack of attention paid in contemporary worship to the ethical concerns of the Psalms.[37] William Brown argues for a "hermeneutics of dialogue," a "deep reading" that puts individual psalms in relationship with other psalms and other passages across the OT. This exercise of "canonical inclusivity" reflects the complexity of ethical discourse, decision-making, and moral life in the ancient world and today.[38]

---

and Biblical Narrative: A Literary and Discourse-Analytical Approach to the Story of Josiah, Oxford Theology and Religion Monographs (Oxford: Oxford University Press, 2014); Shira Weiss, *Ethical Ambiguity in the Hebrew Bible: Philosophical Analysis of Scriptural Narrative* (Cambridge: Cambridge University Press, 2018).

31. Richard S. Briggs, *The Virtuous Reader: Old Testament Narratives and Interpretive Virtue*, STI (Grand Rapids: Baker Academic, 2010). He includes implied and actual readers.

32. See, e.g., M. Daniel Carroll R. and Jacqueline E. Lapsley, eds., *Character Ethics and the Old Testament: Moral Dimensions of Scripture* (Louisville: Westminster John Knox, 2007). John Barton is less sanguine; see Barton, "Virtue in the Bible," in *Understanding Old Testament Ethics*, 65–74; Barton, *Ethics in Ancient Israel*, 157–74. Appropriation of virtue ethics raises the issue of the use of philosophical ethics (the other two classic approaches are deontological ethics and teleological ethics). Rogerson appeals to discourse ethics in *Theory and Practice*, 60–79. This topic lies beyond the purview of this essay.

33. William P. Brown, *Wisdom's Wonder: Character, Creation, and Crisis in the Bible's Wisdom Literature* (Grand Rapids: Eerdmans, 2014).

34. Patricia Vesely, *Friendship and Virtue Ethics in the Book of Job* (Cambridge: Cambridge University Press, 2019).

35. Anne W. Stewart, *Poetic Ethics in Proverbs: Wisdom Literature and the Shaping of the Moral Self* (Cambridge: Cambridge University Press, 2016); Arthur Jan Keefer, *The Book of Proverbs and Virtue Ethics: Integrating the Biblical and Philosophical Traditions* (Cambridge: Cambridge University Press, 2021).

36. William C. Pohl IV, *Ethical God-Talk in the Book of Job: Speaking to the Almighty*, LHBOTS 698 (London: T&T Clark, 2020).

37. Gordon J. Wenham, *Psalms as Torah: Reading Biblical Song Ethically*, STI (Grand Rapids: Baker Academic, 2012). Although he surveys the use of the psalms in both Jewish and Christian worship, his primary interest is in the latter. Cf. Daniel C. Owens, *Portraits of the Righteous in the Psalms: An Exploration of the Ethics of Book I* (Eugene, OR: Pickwick, 2013).

38. Brown, *Deep Calls to Deep*. "Hermeneutics of dialogue," "deep reading," and "canonical inclusivity" are his terms.

Many portray the prophetic books as advocating for social justice on behalf of the vulnerable,[39] and virtue-ethics approaches also have been applied to this literature.[40] The scholar most associated with championing their impact on the modern context is Walter Brueggemann. Ever since his groundbreaking work *The Prophetic Imagination*, he has been prolific in expounding the power of prophetic language.[41] Brueggemann says that the prophetic ministry has a twofold task: "prophetic criticizing" and "prophetic energizing." The former confronts the unquestioned reigning ideologies of a culture (the "royal consciousness"), especially its theological legitimations, and denounces their destructive vision of the world. The latter offers hope for a different reality beyond the present evils and for future judgment on this unacceptable state of affairs. This prophetic imagination can move the people of God from anger and lament ultimately to doxology.

The Rationale for Old Testament Ethics

While works on OT ethics usually represent the breadth of its theological themes without necessarily arguing for the priority of any particular theme, some claim a specific theological orientation as fundamental.[42] Three of the most prominent approaches, all with biblical support, are (1) divine command, (2) *imitatio Dei*, and (3) natural law.[43] Each perspective has been criticized as reductionistic, but each highlights key elements of OT ethics. Although it might seem like an attempt to synthesize or temper the OT's ethical diversity under a single rubric, the true intent of each approach is to elucidate what is felt to be the core or fountainhead of OT ethics. They all contribute to a fuller picture of the OT's ethics.

39. For a survey, see M. Daniel Carroll R., "Ethics," in *Dictionary of the Old Testament: The Prophets*, ed. Mark J. Boda and J. Gordon McConville (Downers Grove, IL: InterVarsity, 2012), 185–93.

40. E.g., Jacqueline E. Lapsley, *Can These Bones Live? The Problem of the Moral Self in the Book of Ezekiel*, BZAW 301 (Berlin: De Gruyter, 2000); M. Daniel Carroll R., "Seeking the Virtues among the Prophets: The Book of Amos as a Test Case," *ExAud* 17 (2001): 77–96; Carroll R., "'He Has Told You What Is Good': Moral Formation in Micah," in Carroll R. and Lapsley, *Character Ethics and the Old Testament*, 103–18.

41. Walter Brueggemann, *The Prophetic Imagination*, 40th anniversary ed. (Minneapolis: Fortress, 2018). In addition to his many works on the prophetic literature, see Brueggemann, *Theology of the Old Testament: Testimony, Dispute, Advocacy* (Minneapolis: Fortress, 1997), 622–49; cf. M. Daniel Carroll R., *The Lord Roars: Recovering the Prophetic Voice for Today*, Theological Explorations for the Church Catholic (Grand Rapids: Baker Academic, 2022).

42. Interestingly, not all OT theologies engage ethics. See M. Daniel Carroll R., "Ethics in Old Testament Theologies: Theological Significance and Modern Relevance," in *Interpreting the Old Testament Theologically: Essays in Honor of Willem A. VanGemeren*, ed. Andrew T. Abernethy (Grand Rapids: Zondervan, 2018), 239–51.

43. Barton (*Ethics in Ancient Israel*, 127–37, 261–72, and 94–126) discusses each in turn. For divine command, cf. Walther Eichrodt, *Theology of the Old Testament*, vol. 2, trans. J. A. Baker (Philadelphia: Westminster, 1967), 316–79; for natural law, cf. Barton, *Understanding Old Testament Ethics*, 32–44, 77–153.

Divine-command ethics contends that all morality ultimately derives from God, who has revealed ethical imperatives to humanity.[44] It resonates with the prominence of OT narratives about the giving of the law and of the law codes themselves. God has communicated God's moral will and moral imperatives. This presupposes a relationship (covenant) between the sovereign God and the people of God. The OT witnesses to this revelation and to Israel's responses to the demand of obedience, and it continues to make its claim on communities of faith today.

Imitatio Dei defines ethics as the imitation of God.[45] Ethics is not just about doing the right thing or making correct decisions. Because humans are made in God's image (affinity) and because God's people have been redeemed with a purpose (relationship), the expectation is that they reflect divine qualities declared in certain OT texts (e.g., Exod. 34:6–7) and portrayed in the various genres. These would include holiness, compassion, faithfulness, patience, righteous anger, and more.

Natural law, the third option, turns to the natural order. God has embedded a moral order within creation, all peoples can perceive it, and all are therefore held accountable to it. There are inevitable consequences inherent in the flow of life and history that correspond to the morality of human behavior.[46] This divinely established natural law differs from customary ethics, or "natural morality," which refers to the generally accepted moral norms in any given context.

Appropriating the Old Testament for Ethics

Clearly, the OT offers an immense and diverse fund of ethical material as well as multiple ways of engaging it as an ethical resource. What is not well defined in the text, however, is *how* to make the move from the OT to contemporary issues. There is no one authoritative way to appropriate the OT for moral life and ethical decisions.[47]

Some obvious obstacles make applying the OT challenging, including the contextual distance of time, place, and cultural settings between the ancient text

44. Brevard S. Childs, *Biblical Theology of the Old and New Testaments: Theological Reflection on the Christian Bible* (Minneapolis: Fortress, 1992), 676–78, 712–15; cf. Miller, *Ten Commandments*, 415–32. In theological ethics this view is connected especially to Karl Barth. From a different framework, see Kaiser, *Toward Old Testament Ethics*, 139–244.

45. Birch, *Let Justice Roll Down*, 125–26; Goldingay, *Old Testament Theology*, 3:586–607.

46. Terence Fretheim, *God and World in the Old Testament* (Nashville: Abingdon, 2005); H. G. M. Williamson, *He Has Shown You What Is Good: Old Testament Justice Here and Now* (Eugene, OR: Wipf & Stock, 2012).

47. For case studies, see Charles H. Cosgrove, "Scripture in Ethics: A History," in Green, *Scripture and Ethics*, 13–25; John Rogerson, *According to the Scriptures? The Challenge of Using the Bible in Social, Moral and Political Questions* (London: Equinox, 2007); Carroll R., *The Lord Roars*, 5–9, 53–62, 87–92, 108–12.

and the modern world. How can one extrapolate or universalize, as it were, the particularity of the OT to audiences across the centuries and around the globe? The OT is not a treatise on moral philosophy or a systematic presentation of ethical topics, even as it contains ethical material of all kinds. Is there sufficient coherence or compatibility amid this complex mixture to propose an OT ethics that can speak to today? That all this is housed together in the canon, however, demonstrates that its compilers (and faith communities since then) embraced it as encompassing the will of God. For Christians there is the added complexity of coordinating the OT with the NT and Christian theologies, which evaluate and appeal to the OT in differing ways.[48]

Many ways of bringing OT ethics to bear on life today have been proposed, only a few of which are summarized here as illustrative. Several biblical ethicists contend that what is to be gleaned from the text is a general orientation about God and living as the community of faith in the world. It is more about discerning fundamental values and a moral vision than seeking explicit guidelines for life today.[49] They claim that this perspective arises from continuities across the Testaments both in the person and work of God and in what is expected from the community of faith. Others speak of a prophetic vision of reality that schools the people of God in criticizing the injustices of society and revitalizing faith in those contexts with the hope of a different tomorrow.[50]

Other works in OT ethics seek to glean ethical principles, particularly from the Pentateuch. Jewish and Christian approaches differ here. For instance, working from features of Jewish ethics gleaned from the Torah, Rabbi Jonathan Sacks offers reflections on the scriptural texts of the weekly parashah (portion) of the Torah.[51] These are insights and lessons—principles, if you will—for understanding and living out the Torah's moral vision.[52] From a Christian perspective, Patrick Miller expounds each of the Ten Commandments in great detail and explores trajectories within the OT and into the NT, concluding each discussion with broad considerations for Christian life today.[53]

In contrast, some from conservative Christian persuasions have developed methodologies for extracting transcendent principles from OT law codes to derive

48. Debates about the levels of continuity and discontinuity between the Testaments lie beyond the purview of this essay.

49. Birch, *Let Justice Roll Down*; van Wijk-Bos, *Making Wise the Simple*.

50. Brueggemann, *Prophetic Imagination*; Brueggemann, *Theology of the Old Testament*, 622–49; Carroll R., *The Lord Roars*.

51. Rabbi Jonathan Sacks, *Essays on Ethics: A Weekly Reading of the Jewish Bible* (New Milford, CT: Maggid, 2016). The features are the dignity of the individual, human freedom, the sanctity of life, guilt not shame, loyalty and love, the ethics of covenant (social responsibility), and the dual covenant (Noah and universal obligations along with Abraham and particular demands on the Jewish people).

52. Jewish approaches are another field of study. See Dorff and Crane, *Handbook of Jewish Ethics*.

53. Miller, *Ten Commandments*.

concrete applications for Christians individually and the church corporately. These proposals can be articulated within certain theological frameworks (e.g., Reformed, Lutheran, Anabaptist, dispensational), but all go into detail as to how the OT law should be understood in light of the life and ministry of Jesus and of what the NT has to say about the Law.

To draw viable principles from the OT, Walter Kaiser proposes a "ladder of abstraction," which he defines as "a continuous sequence of categorizations from a low level of specificity up to a high point of generality in a principle and down again to a specific application in the contemporary culture."[54] Roy Gane offers a "progressive moral wisdom" approach.[55] First, he tries to relate OT laws, which are connected to the ancient world with its limitations of context and human sin, to creation and new-creation ideals. He then explores possible trajectories of moral growth in the OT and into the NT as a basis for viable applications.

Waldemar Janzen and Christopher Wright develop distinct paradigm approaches. Janzen focuses on "ethical model stories" of imperfect individuals who act in certain moments in commendable ways.[56] He cites familial (regarded as primary), priestly, wisdom, royal, and prophetic narratives; even the legal material is embedded in stories. Key facets across these paradigms are life, land, and hospitality. These facets are interconnected and constitutive of the family paradigm, which Janzen considers fundamental. This framework culminates in Jesus, who embodies the paradigms and foreshadows the familial realities of the kingdom.

Wright presents several superimposed triangles that represent levels of applying the OT. The apex of all the triangles is God (the theological angle); the two other angles are the social and economic. For biblical Israel, the two angles are Israel as a society and the land. The God-Israel-land triangle was to be paradigmatic for God's relationship with humanity and the earth. This OT triangle connects typologically to the NT triangle of God-church-koinonia (fellowship), and this scheme projects out eschatologically to a triangle consisting of God, redeemed humanity, and new creation. Israel's beliefs and social structures were a concrete, contextualized paradigm. The NT community and humanity in general must work out analogous social models that reflect those core values.

John Rogerson's model is quite different.[57] He perceives a pattern of ethical discernment in the text. Rogerson starts with what he calls "natural morality," the moral consensus of any society, ancient or modern. In this can be found some

54. Kaiser, "A Principlizing Model," in *Four Views of Moving beyond the Bible to Theology*, Counterpoints, ed. Gary T. Meadors (Grand Rapids: Zondervan Academic, 2009), 24; cf. Kaiser, *Toward Old Testament Ethics*, 64–67.

55. Gane, *Old Testament Law*, 163–218. For another detailed approach, see Richard E. Averbeck, *The Old Testament Law for the Life of the Church: Reading the Torah in the Light of Christ* (Downers Grove, IL: IVP Academic, 2022).

56. Waldemar Janzen, *Old Testament Ethics: A Paradigmatic Approach* (Louisville: Westminster John Knox, 1994). For Janzen, these flawed individuals are not themselves paradigmatic.

57. Rogerson, *Theory and Practice*, 13–28.

enduring ethical principles that echo Israel's moral ideals. The difference is that Israel should have been motivated by its "imperatives of redemption" grounded in the character and acts of God.[58] These would yield what Rogerson calls "structures of grace," tangible social arrangements appropriate to Israel within the broader context. This creative dynamic shows how Christians can partner with the natural morality of their context and support social structures and legislation that mirror their moral convictions and thereby promote the common good.

Finally, John Goldingay offers three hermeneutical criteria for Christians when appropriating the OT for ethics, each of which is based on a scriptural passage. Appropriation may require "bringing out the inherent implications of some injunction" (Matt. 5:17–20), "asking how an injunction may be an expression of love for God or for one's neighbor" (Deut. 6:5; Lev. 19:18; Matt. 23:34–40), or "asking where an injunction stands on the axis that runs between God's creation will and God's making allowance for human stubbornness" (Matt. 19:3–12).[59] Goldingay explicitly argues for the importance of appreciating the significance of the OT for ethics vis-à-vis the NT. Because of its size and breadth, the OT wrestles with some topics more than the NT does and is the foundation of much of what the NT presents for the moral life of the community of faith.[60]

Conclusion

There is much to consider when using the OT for ethics. This essay has introduced foundational issues that require decisions: the nature of the OT's authority, the descriptive versus prescriptive nature of the discipline, the form and genre of text, potential rationales, and ways to appropriate OT ethical material. Establishing a method beforehand can make the appeal to the OT for ethical topics clearer and more viable. There is still much work to be done. The potential impact of this rich field extends beyond the academy into communities of faith within a needy world.

58. As is evident in the motive clauses, this imperative would come especially from the exodus (e.g., Exod. 22:21 [22:20 MT]; Lev. 19:34; Deut. 24:18, 22). For Christians, it is found in the person of Jesus and the cross.

59. John Goldingay, *Do We Need the New Testament? Letting the Old Testament Speak for Itself* (Downers Grove, IL: IVP Academic, 2015), 147. Cf. Goldingay, *Old Testament Ethics: A Guided Tour* (Downers Grove, IL: IVP Academic, 2019), 1–5.

60. Goldingay, *Do We Need the New Testament?*, 139–56; Goldingay, *Reading Jesus's Bible: How the New Testament Helps Us to Understand the Old Testament* (Grand Rapids: Eerdmans, 2017), 227–47.

25

Gender and Sexuality

Katherine Davis

The last three decades have witnessed major shifts in cultural thinking about gender and sexuality in the Western world. Mirroring these cultural shifts, gender and sexuality approaches to the OT have formed distinctive interpretive lenses for viewing the text of the HB. The purpose of this essay is to tell the story of the present state of these approaches within OT studies. In particular, this essay surveys feminist studies, masculist studies, and queer biblical criticism.[1] I acknowledge that these perspectives are rooted in personal convictions about identity and what it means to be human, so I appreciate the need for a generous sensitivity in narrating the state of play in gender and sexuality approaches to the OT.

Feminist Interpretations

Walter Brueggemann offered the following reflection in 1997 about the state of feminist interpretation: "The gains in feminist interpretation in recent years are immense. Indeed, since the publication of *God and the Rhetoric of Sexuality* by Phyllis Trible in Overtures in 1978, feminist practices in Scripture interpretation have become well established as inescapable and welcome perspectives."[2] This

1. For a resource surveying theological issues in gender and sexuality, see Adrian Thatcher, ed., *The Oxford Handbook of Theology, Sexuality, and Gender* (Oxford: Oxford University Press, 2015).

2. Walter Brueggemann, "Preface," in *Missing Persons and Mistaken Identities: Women and Gender in Ancient Israel*, ed. Phyllis A. Bird, OBT (Minneapolis: Fortress, 1997), vii.

momentum was not solely an outcome of Trible's work.[3] The first generation of feminist approaches included the works of Mieke Bal,[4] Alice Ogden Bellis,[5] Phyllis A. Bird,[6] Athalya Brenner,[7] Peggy L. Day,[8] Cheryl Exum,[9] Carol Meyers,[10] Letty M. Russell,[11] and Katharine Doob Sakenfeld.[12] Inspired by this first generation, a flurry of works have been published over the past two decades. This survey begins with two notable examples, Claudia Camp's *Wise, Strange and Holy*[13] and Susanne Scholz's *Rape Plots*.[14]

3. See Phyllis Trible, "Depatriarchalizing in Biblical Interpretation," *JAAR* 40 (1973): 30–48; Trible, *God and the Rhetoric of Sexuality*, OBT (Philadelphia: Fortress, 1978); Trible, *Texts of Terror: Literary-Feminist Readings of Biblical Narratives*, OBT (Philadelphia: Fortress, 1984).

4. E.g., Mieke Bal, *Anti-Covenant: Counter-Reading Women's Lives in the Hebrew Bible*, BLS 22 (Sheffield: Almond, 1989); Bal, *Lethal Love: Feminist Literary Readings of Biblical Love Stories*, Indiana Studies in Biblical Literature (Bloomington: Indiana University Press, 1997).

5. Alice Ogden Bellis, *Helpmates, Harlots, and Heroes: Women's Stories in the Hebrew Bible* (Louisville: Westminster John Knox, 1994).

6. See Bird's compiled essays from 1981–94 in *Missing Persons*.

7. E.g., Athalya Brenner, *A Feminist Companion to Genesis* (Sheffield: Sheffield Academic, 1998); Brenner, *A Feminist Companion to the Latter Prophets* (Sheffield: Sheffield Academic, 1995); Brenner, *I Am: Biblical Women Tell Their Own Stories* (Minneapolis: Fortress, 2005); Brenner, *Are We Amused? Humour about Women in the Biblical Worlds* (New York: T&T Clark, 2003); Athalya Brenner and Fokkelien van Dijk Hemmes, *On Gendering Texts: Female and Male Voices in the Hebrew Bible*, BibInt 1 (Leiden: Brill, 1993).

8. E.g., Peggy L. Day, ed., *Gender and Difference in Ancient Israel* (Minneapolis: Fortress, 1989); Day, "The Bitch Had It Coming to Her: Rhetoric and Interpretation in Ezekiel 16," *BibInt* 8 (2000): 231–54; Day, "'Until I Come and Take You Away to a Land Like Your Own': A Gendered Look at Siege Warfare and Mass Deportation," in *Women in Antiquity: Real Women across the Ancient World*, ed. Stephanie Budin and Jean Turfa, Rewriting Antiquity (New York: Routledge, 2016), 521–32.

9. E.g., Cheryl Exum, *Fragmented Women: Feminist (Sub)versions of Biblical Narratives*, JSOTSup 163 (Sheffield: JSOT Press, 1993); Exum, *Plotted, Shot, and Painted: Cultural Representations of Biblical Women*, JSOTSup 215 (Sheffield: Sheffield Academic, 1996).

10. Carol Meyers, *Discovering Eve: Ancient Israelite Women in Context* (New York: Oxford University Press, 1991), revised as Meyers, *Rediscovering Eve: Ancient Israelite Women in Context* (New York: Oxford University Press, 2013). For a recent work adopting Meyers's approach, see Celina Durgin and Dru Johnson, eds., *The Biblical World of Gender: The Daily Lives of Ancient Men and Women* (Eugene, OR: Cascade, 2022).

11. Letty M. Russell, *Feminist Interpretation of the Bible* (Oxford: Blackwell, 1985).

12. Katharine Doob Sakenfeld, "Feminist Biblical Interpretation," *ThTo* 46, no. 2 (1989): 154–68; Sakenfeld, "Feminist Theology and Biblical Interpretation," in *Biblical Theology Problems and Perspectives in Honor of J. Christiaan Beker*, ed. Steven Kraftchick, Charles Myers, and Ben C. Ollenburger (Nashville: Abingdon, 1995), 247–59.

13. Claudia V. Camp, *Wise, Strange and Holy: The Strange Woman and the Making of the Bible*, JSOTSup 320 (Sheffield: Sheffield Academic, 2000). Her other works include "Over Her Dead Body: The Estranged Woman and the Price of the Promised Land," *JNSL* 29, no. 2 (2003): 1–13; *Wisdom and the Feminine in the Book of Proverbs*, JSOTSup 58 (Sheffield: Almond, 1985).

14. Susanne Scholz, *Rape Plots: A Feminist Cultural Study of Genesis 34*, StBibLit 13 (New York: Peter Lang, 2000).

In *Wise, Strange and Holy*, Camp argues from Prov. 1–9 that the Strange Woman is an "outsider to the family household" and is "symbolic of the forces deemed destructive of patriarchal control."[15] As an "embodiment of defilement," the Strange Woman is a polemical "expression of male anxiety as one generation attempts to pass its ideology of control to the next."[16] She also observes a blurring of distinctions to the point of unity between the Wise Woman and the Strange Woman in Proverbs and that other "biblical imagery for women points in this same direction."[17] Camp then explores the subversion of the polarity between wisdom and strangeness in wider OT texts. She uses her analysis of "the rhetoric of strangeness, sexuality, and religion" to "construct the national/ethnic identity of postexilic Judaism."[18]

Very different from Camp's work, Susanne Scholz's *Rape Plots* adopts "feminist standpoint theory" that "analyzes the causes for women's conditions and debates how to change those conditions in conjunction with other oppressive structures."[19] She analyzes "Genesis 34 and selected interpretations from the perspective of the subjugated, the one who is raped rather than from the perspective of the powerful."[20] Scholz's study was the second volume-length work from a feminist approach that sheds light on how cultural conditioning affects our reading of texts where there is sexual violence.[21]

Katharine Doob Sakenfeld's *Just Wives* tells the stories of eleven women from the OT. Sakenfeld describes her method as a "culturally cued literary approach," where she brings together sociocultural background with a rhetorical approach to the text. While Sakenfeld does not describe her work as an explicitly "feminist approach," she refers to her 1989 article, "Feminist Biblical Interpretation," in which she outlines the usefulness of a "culturally cued literary approach" for feminist biblical criticism, which *Just Wives* exemplifies.[22] Following the same trajectory, Jacqueline E. Lapsley published *Whispering the Word* with the view to modeling "*how* to read women's stories *faithfully*, as a word from God to us" by examining four case studies: Rachel, Judg. 19–21, Exod. 1–4, and Ruth. She describes her goal as follows: "My driving motivation is to offer to both feminist biblical scholarship and the church an alternative voice to those dominating the field, many of which claim that the patriarchal character of the Bible is its *defining* characteristic. According to this dominant perspective, no reading of the Bible

15. Camp, *Wise, Strange and Holy*, 61.
16. Camp, *Wise, Strange and Holy*, 64.
17. Camp, *Wise, Strange and Holy*, 76.
18. Camp, *Wise, Strange and Holy*, 42.
19. Scholz, *Rape Plots*, 10.
20. Scholz, *Rape Plots*, 12.
21. See also Frank M. Yamada, *Configurations of Rape in the Hebrew Bible: A Literary Analysis of Three Rape Narratives*, StBibLit 109 (New York: Peter Lang, 2008), 10–14, for a helpful overview from Trible to Scholz.
22. Katharine Doob Sakenfeld, *Just Wives? Stories of Power and Survival in the Old Testament and Today* (Louisville: Westminster John Knox, 2003), 5n1.

may proceed until this central feature is addressed."[23] Instead of a hermeneutic of suspicion, Lapsley proposes a hermeneutic of trust, because "trust functions relationally and reciprocally: we are trusted to read, and we trust the reading in return."[24] For example, Lapsley finds that Rachel's voice "confronts, resists, and ultimately subverts the dominant discourse. . . . We can hear an implicit critique of a juridical process that excludes women."[25] We are "invited to understand this exclusion as a *theological issue*."[26] Both Sakenfeld's and Lapsley's works are emblematic of a trend in feminist approaches that hear the stories of women, as minority characters, in OT texts.

So far, this overview suggests that feminist interpretations vary from historical reconstructions (Camp) to the rhetorical-critical in the service of hearing the stories of women (Sakenfeld) or bringing to light sexual violence in the text (Scholz). In 2007, Scholz published *Introducing the Women's Hebrew Bible*, in which she acknowledges the varied avenues of research under the feminist umbrella.[27] This volume seeks to help the "process of forging a path through the maze of feminist work on the Hebrew Bible" by offering "an overview on the historical, social, and academic developments of reading the Hebrew Bible as the 'Women's Hebrew Bible' during the past 40 years."[28] Scholz also identifies and discusses critical questions about the development of feminist approaches, such as, "Is the Hebrew Bible thoroughly patriarchal and is its androcentrism 'redeemable'?" and "What makes a reading of the Bible 'feminist'?"[29] After a brief survey of views, Scholz finds Elisabeth Schüssler Fiorenza's stance persuasive, describing feminist hermeneutics as "every woman's struggles to transform patriarchal structures, both in biblical and in our own times, rather than focusing its gaze solely on the androcentric biblical text and its authority."[30]

Scholz's observation about feminist interpretations taking "varied avenues of research" is an apt description of the continued trajectory of feminist approaches from 2007 to the present day.[31] Three examples of this trajectory are works by Sarah Shectman, a more recent book by Suzanne Scholz, and a study by Rhiannon Graybill.

23. Jacqueline E. Lapsley, *Whispering the Word: Hearing Women's Stories in the Old Testament* (Louisville: Westminster John Knox, 2005), 4.

24. Lapsley, *Whispering the Word*, 18, 113n50.

25. Lapsley, *Whispering the Word*, 30.

26. Lapsley, *Whispering the Word*, 34 (emphasis original).

27. Susanne Scholz, *Introducing the Women's Hebrew Bible: Feminism, Gender Justice, and the Study of the Old Testament* (New York: T&T Clark, 2007), 4–5, 25–28; cf. rev. ed., 2017.

28. Scholz, *Women's Hebrew Bible* (2007), 5–6, 25–31.

29. Scholz, *Women's Hebrew Bible* (2007), 6.

30. Scholz, *Women's Hebrew Bible* (2007), 31. See Elisabeth Schüssler Fiorenza, "Transforming the Legacy of the Woman's Bible," in *Searching the Scriptures: A Feminist Introduction*, ed. Elisabeth Schüssler Fiorenza, Shelly Matthews, and Ann Graham Brock (London: SCM, 1994), 20.

31. Scholz, *Women's Hebrew Bible* (2007), 5–6.

Shectman's *Women in the Pentateuch* was motivated by her curiosity about "what a feminist source-critical analysis would look like."[32] Her volume examines how priestly and non-priestly threads in the Pentateuch differ "in their treatments of and attitudes towards women."[33]

Scholz's *Sacred Witness* continues to build on her earlier work of wrestling with rape texts in the HB. Her goal is "to provide readings of biblical rape texts that endorse a hermeneutics of meaning and present the HB as a 'sacred witness' to rape in the lives of women, children, and men."[34] The exception to rape texts being a "sacred witness" are texts where God is portrayed as a rapist. In this instance, she states, "the biblical rape metaphor should not be classified as a 'sacred' witness."[35] She argues that rape texts are not prescriptive but rather descriptive, and their function in the HB is to "strengthen our ability to confront sexual violence."[36]

Graybill's *Texts after Terror* is "an effort to imagine feminist biblical reading after Phyllis Trible's *Texts of Terror* and other similar approaches."[37] Her goal is "to expand the range of ways we think about and understand sexual violence, including biblical rape stories. In this way, reading with literature complements and augments the hermeneutic insights that the other three tactics—refusing innocence, resisting paranoia, and following the sticky affect—all instigate."[38] When examining various rape stories, Graybill states that "there is no single story or script," "there is no one way of framing harm," "the *after* of rape stories takes multiple forms," and "the work of feminist criticism is about finding ways to read and live with biblical rape stories."[39] She concludes, "To do feminist work is, instead, to stay with the fuzzy, messy, and icky even or especially when such readings seem difficult."[40]

These three contributions demonstrate the breadth of research avenues in which feminist studies continue to advance, and numerous other studies could be mentioned.[41] During the last two decades, significant contributions to OT studies

32. Sarah Shectman, *Women in the Pentateuch: A Feminist and Source-Critical Analysis*, HBM 23 (Sheffield: Sheffield Phoenix, 2009), ix.

33. Shectman, *Women in the Pentateuch*, 1.

34. Susanne Scholz, *Sacred Witness: Rape in the Hebrew Bible* (Minneapolis: Fortress, 2010), 23. For Scholz's explanation of her "hermeneutic of meaning" as it relates to a "hermeneutic of suspicion," see 21–23.

35. Scholz, *Sacred Witness*, 208.

36. Scholz, *Sacred Witness*, 7.

37. Rhiannon Graybill, *Texts after Terror: Rape, Sexual Violence, and the Hebrew Bible* (New York: Oxford University Press, 2021), 1–2.

38. Graybill, *Texts after Terror*, 173.

39. Graybill, *Texts after Terror*, 174, 175.

40. Graybill, *Texts after Terror*, 176.

41. See, e.g., Deryn Guest, *Beyond Feminist Biblical Studies*, Bible in the Modern World (Sheffield: Sheffield Phoenix, 2012), x (though included here, Guest does not find feminist interpretation a comfortable home and prefers the category "gender criticism"); Elisabeth Schüssler Fiorenza, ed., *Feminist Biblical Studies in the Twentieth Century: Scholarship and*

have also emerged from womanist approaches[42] and from feminist perspectives in Arab,[43] Asian,[44] Asian-American,[45] and Latina[46] social locations.

Masculist Interpretations

A year after the publication of Howard Eilberg-Schwartz's *God's Phallus* (1994), David Clines published "David the Man," which has been described as "one of the most influential works for the early stages of masculist interpretation of the Hebrew Bible."[47] Clines's essay had three goals: to understand what it means to be a man in Western culture, to examine what it was like being a man in the biblical world through the David story, and to ask whether the biblical portrait has been colored by Western cultural norms.[48] He observes that masculinity is a "social construction" and that "different societies write different scripts for their

---

Movement, The Bible and Women 9.1 (Atlanta: Society of Biblical Literature, 2014); Susanne Scholz, *The Bible as Political Artifact: On the Feminist Study of the Hebrew Bible* (Minneapolis: Fortress, 2017); Yvonne Sherwood and Anna Fisk, eds., *The Bible and Feminism: Remapping the Field* (Oxford: Oxford University Press, 2017); Susanne Scholz, ed., *The Oxford Handbook of Feminist Approaches to the Hebrew Bible* (New York: Oxford University Press, 2020).

42. E.g., Wilda C. Gafney, "A Black Feminist Approach to Biblical Studies," *Encounter* 67 (2006): 391–403; Gafney, *Womanist Midrash: A Reintroduction to the Women of the Torah and the Throne* (Louisville: Westminster John Knox, 2017).

43. E.g., Viola Raheb, "Women in Contemporary Palestinian Society: A Contextual Reading of the Book of Ruth," in *Feminist Interpretation of the Bible and the Hermeneutics of Liberation*, ed. Silvia Schroer and Sophia Bietenhard, LHBOTS 374 (London: Sheffield Academic, 2003), 88–93; Niveen Sarras, "A Palestinian Feminist Reading of the Book of Jonah," *Journal of Lutheran Ethics* 15, no. 8 (2015): https://www.elca.org/JLE/Articles/1112.

44. E.g., Monica J. Melanchthon, "Engaging Women's Experiences in the Struggle for Justice, Dignity, and Humanity: Hebrew Bible Readings by South Asian Women," in *Feminist Interpretation of the Hebrew Bible in Retrospect*, vol. 2, *Social Locations*, ed. Susanne Scholz (Sheffield: Sheffield Phoenix, 2017), 51–69.

45. E.g., Gale A. Yee, "'She Stood in Tears amid the Alien Corn': Ruth, the Perpetual Foreigner and Model Minority," in *They Were All Together in One Place? Toward Minority Biblical Criticism*, ed. Randall C. Bailey, Tat-siong Benny Liew, and Fernando F. Segovia, SemeiaSt 57 (Atlanta: Society of Biblical Studies, 2009), 119–40.

46. E.g., Mercedes L. García Bachmann, "A Foolish King, Women, and Wine: A Dangerous Cocktail from Lemuel's Mother," in Sherwood, *Bible and Feminism*, 315–27; Mónica Isabel Rey, "Reexamination of the Foreign Female Captive: Deuteronomy 21:10–14 as a Case of Genocidal Rape," *Journal of Feminist Studies in Religion* 32 (2016): 37–53.

47. Howard Eilberg-Schwartz, *God's Phallus and Other Problems for Men and Monotheism* (Boston: Beacon, 1994); David J. A. Clines, "David the Man: The Construction of Masculinity in the Hebrew Bible," in Clines, *Interested Parties: The Ideology of Writers and Readers of the Hebrew Bible*, JSOTSup 205, Gender, Culture, Theory 1 (Sheffield: Sheffield Academic, 1995), 212–41; Susan E. Haddox, "Masculinity Studies of the Hebrew Bible: The First Two Decades," *CurBR* 14 (2016): 188. Another foundational essay is John Goldingay, "Hosea 1–3, Genesis 1–4 and Masculist Interpretation," in Brenner, *Latter Prophets*, 161–68.

48. Clines, "David the Man," 212.

men."[49] He avers, "I am quite sure that the construction of masculinity in the David story was not invented by its author—or by some historical David—but reflects the cultural norms of men of the author's time."[50] He then argues that the characteristics of being male in the David story are having the strength to be capable of violence, possessing a persuasive intelligence, being admired, loyal friendship with other men, being "casual about women," and having a mastery of particular musical instruments.[51]

Building on this first essay, Clines published "He-Prophets," where he sought "to isolate in the prophets elements that are characteristic of masculinity."[52] He observes that the metaphor commonly used for prophets is "messengers," which is a gendered metaphor.[53] Clines argues that "masculine strength" is portrayed by the prophets for "salvific purposes," as well as "for fighting with other males, and for killing them," and for the "sadism of verbal violence against women."[54] Moreover, Clines observes that honor is "essential for male identity" as "males *need* and *seek* honour, the social esteem awarded to males both human and divine."[55]

Dennis T. Olson's essay "Untying the Knot?" represents a contrast to the trajectory of Clines's masculist approach. Olson aims to read Gen. 2–4 as "one interrelated story" to understand the depiction of "male images and masculinities that we encounter in the book of Genesis."[56] Based on his reading of Gen. 2, Olson observes, "We see hints of multiple and complex masculinities—humble, subservient, and passive, as well as lifted up, active, and empowered. The man is created to be . . . a human embedded in a community of intimate companionship. The relationship between the man and the woman is one of mutual help and interdependence."[57] From Gen. 3 he argues that the shattering of relationships as depicted in Gen. 2 replaced the "previous relationship of mutuality and interdependence between the man and the woman" with a "relationship of one 'ruling over' the other."[58] The fact that the woman "is alone in speaking and debating

49. Clines, "David the Man," 214, 215.
50. Clines, "David the Man," 216.
51. Clines, "David the Man," 216–28.
52. David J. A. Clines, "He-Prophets: Masculinity as a Problem for the Hebrew Prophets and Their Interpreters," in *Sense and Sensitivity: Essays on Reading the Bible in Memory of Robert Carroll*, ed. Philip R. Davies and Alastair G. Hunter, JSOTSup 348 (Sheffield: Sheffield Academic, 2002), 311. See also Clines, "Being a Man in the Book of the Covenant," in *Reading the Law: Studies in Honour of Gordon J. Wenham*, ed. J. G. McConville and Karl Möller, LHBOTS 461 (London: T&T Clark, 2007), 3–9.
53. Clines, "He-Prophets," 311–12.
54. Clines, "He-Prophets," 314; see also 312–13.
55. Clines, "He-Prophets," 316, 317.
56. Dennis T. Olson, "Untying the Knot? Masculinity, Violence, and the Creation-Fall Story of Genesis 2–4," in *Engaging the Bible in a Gendered World: An Introduction to Feminist Biblical Interpretation in Honor of Katharine Doob Sakenfeld*, ed. Linda Day and Carol Pressler (Louisville: Westminster John Knox, 2006), 74.
57. Olson, "Untying the Knot?," 78.
58. Olson, "Untying the Knot?," 78–79.

with the serpent in Gen 3" shows that "the *woman* needs a mutually supportive and active helper as her partner to speak up and join her in resisting the serpent."[59] He concludes from Gen. 2–3 that "men and women also need regularly to be with each other in community in order to discover the fullness of what it means to be male and female as faithful people of God."[60] Olson then reads Gen. 4 as part of this narrative: "But the pairing of Gen 4 as necessary to understand Gen 3 means that the story in the end tilts even more toward a condemnation of specifically male sin and the violence that flows from it."[61]

In 2010 Ovidiu Creangă published the first of his edited works, *Men and Masculinity in the Hebrew Bible and Beyond*.[62] This collection of twelve essays covers a range of topics from various OT books as well as rabbinic midrash. For example, Susan Haddox's essay examines "the way the masculinity of the characters is constructed" in Genesis's depiction of relationships and rivalries and the role masculinity "plays in the selection of the favored sons."[63] She focuses on "Abraham's masculinity" and then turns to "two pairs of brothers, Isaac and Ishmael and Jacob and Esau."[64] Based on Clines's argument about the characteristics of masculinity, Haddox approaches "the selected men from Genesis" through the lens of four attributes: "avoidance of being feminized," "potency," "honor," and "persuasiveness."[65] Haddox concludes, "The masculinities portrayed in the book of Genesis, like the men themselves, have multiple significations. While men may strive toward performing the norms of hegemonic masculinity, these are constantly in tension with various subordinate masculinities. These tensions help define the emerging identity of Israel. . . . Genesis favors those patriarchs expressing subordinate masculinities as the best choice for the emerging nation of Israel, both as a political entity and as a people in relationship with God."[66] Haddox builds on Clines's study of masculinity, furthering his approach by introducing the nuances of hegemonic and subordinate masculinities.

Creangă published two additional edited works, *Biblical Masculinities Foregrounded* and *Hebrew Masculinities Anew*.[67] In the latter, a couple of essays extend the boundaries of masculist studies to address queer masculinities in the

59. Olson, "Untying the Knot?," 79.

60. Olson, "Untying the Knot?," 80.

61. Olson, "Untying the Knot?," 82–83.

62. Ovidiu Creangă, ed., *Men and Masculinity in the Hebrew Bible and Beyond*, Bible in the Modern World 33 (Sheffield: Sheffield Phoenix, 2010).

63. Susan Haddox, "Favoured Sons and Subordinate Masculinities," in Creangă, *Men and Masculinity*, 2.

64. Haddox, "Favoured Sons," 2.

65. Haddox, "Favoured Sons," 6–7.

66. Haddox, "Favoured Sons," 16.

67. Ovidiu Creangă and Peter-Ben Smit, eds., *Biblical Masculinities Foregrounded*, HBM 62 (Sheffield: Sheffield Phoenix, 2014); Ovidiu Creangă, ed., *Hebrew Masculinities Anew*, HBM 79 (Sheffield: Sheffield Phoenix, 2019).

HB and to explore the application of queer and drag theory by examining "gender ambiguity in prophetic rhetoric."[68]

From 2011 to 2017 four contributions were published that represent emerging themes within masculist studies. First, Stephen M. Wilson's *Making Men* addressed an absence of studies exploring the theme of "male coming to age."[69] His goal was "to read a select group of biblical narratives in light of the coming-of-age theme." Wilson examined the characteristics of hegemonic masculinity Clines had identified in Hebrew texts, so that markers of "what is meant by the designations 'man' and 'boy' in biblical literature" could be identified.[70] He observed that the narratives either "tell the tale of a boy becoming a man, or failing to make that transition in two cases."[71] Wilson found that "the kind of man that the main characters of these stories become (or attempt to become) . . . is not the same in each story," and he points to Samuel in 1 Sam. 3 and Solomon in 1 Kings 3 as an exemplar comparison.[72]

Second, Rhiannon Graybill's *Are We Not Men?* represents a trend in examining the *whole* textual body.[73] Her interest is in the experience of "male bodies and body parts" of the Hebrew prophets, where often "these experiences are peculiar, troubling, painful, or otherwise out of the ordinary."[74] Graybill explores how the variety of experiences of the male body relates to gender categories and gender performances.[75] She argues that there is "no single norm of the prophetic body, no ideal exemplar." Moreover, the experience of the male body is often "queer" in two senses, as "oblique trajectory" and "nonnormative sexuality."[76] This queerness represents the instability of masculinity in the prophets' experiences.[77]

68. Susan Haddox, "The Queenmakers: Transformational Rhetoric of Gender in the Prophets," in Creangă, *Hebrew Masculinities Anew*, 190.

69. Stephen M. Wilson, *Making Men: The Male Coming-of-Age Theme in the Hebrew Bible* (New York: Oxford University Press, 2015), 1–2. See also Stephen M. Wilson, "Why Hebrew Bible Masculinity Studies and Childhood Studies Have Not Connected, and Why They Should," in *Children and Methods: Listening to and Learning from Children in the Biblical World*, ed. Kristine Henriksen Garroway and John W. Martens, Brill's Series in Jewish Studies 67 (Leiden: Brill, 2020), 35–52.

70. Wilson, *Making Men*, 29.

71. Wilson, *Making Men*, 148.

72. Wilson, *Making Men*, 148.

73. Rhiannon Graybill, *Are We Not Men? Unstable Masculinity in the Hebrew Prophets* (New York: Oxford University Press, 2016). For other examples of masculist studies focusing on the textual body but with a focus on the sexual organs, see Roland Boer, *The Earthy Nature of the Bible: Fleshly Readings of Sex, Masculinity, and Carnality* (Basingstoke: Palgrave Macmillan, 2012); Eilberg-Schwartz, *God's Phallus*; Alan Hooker, "'Show Me Your Glory': The *Kabod* of Yahweh as Phallic Manifestation?," in Creangă and Smit, *Biblical Masculinities Foregrounded*, 17–34.

74. Graybill, *Are We Not Men?*, 1.

75. For an in-depth study on gender performance that integrates feminist, masculist, and queer studies, see Amy Kalmonofsky, *Gender-Play in the Hebrew Bible: The Ways the Bible Challenges Its Gender Norms*, Routledge Interdisciplinary Perspectives on Biblical Criticism (New York: Routledge, 2017).

76. Graybill, *Are We Not Men?*, 5.

77. Graybill, *Are We Not Men?*, 5.

Third, Will Briggs's article "A Man's Gotta Do What a Man's Gotta Do?" returns to the trajectory of masculinity studies established by Clines in a reading of Judg. 19:1–20:7.[78] Briggs summarizes his argument, "A thorough study of Judg. 19.1–20.7 reveals that this text deconstructs the HB's conception of hegemonic masculinity by pitting various expectations for the behavior of a hegemonic male against one another through the actions and characterization of the Levite."[79] He concludes, "The narrative critiques hegemonic masculinity by illustrating both its competing demands, which result in death and chaos, and its vile consequences even when it functions properly."[80] Clines identified the characteristics of masculinity in Hebrew texts, and Haddox used Clines's approach to explore the dynamic between hegemonic and subordinate masculinities. Briggs takes a further step by examining how a text like Judg. 19:1–20:7 critiques the "defining characteristics" of "hegemonic masculinity."[81]

The fourth contribution is Kelly J. Murphy's *Rewriting Masculinity*, in which Murphy "considers why Judg 6–8 is so ambiguous when it comes to Gideon's masculinity alongside how later readers and interpreters have understood this ambiguity."[82] The motivation for Murphy's study is a tension between Clines's approach that identifies hegemonic and subordinate male characteristics and the observation that "gender is performative, something that individuals do."[83] Murphy's study raises a critical question for masculist studies: What is the relationship between male characteristics observed in a text and gender performance?

Queer Biblical Criticism

In the 2000 introduction to *Take Back the Word*, Robert E. Goss and Mona West noted that the "relationship queers have had with the Bible has been defensive."[84] An overview of queer biblical criticism over the two decades since then reveals a major shift from this defensive posture. A theme permeating the overview below is the common goal to "disrupt" heteronormative readings of the OT.

78. Will Briggs, "'A Man's Gotta Do What a Man's Gotta Do?': The Criticism of Hegemonic Masculinity in Judges 19.1–20.7," *JSOT* 42, no. 1 (2017): 58–60. For another example following this methodological trajectory, see Jon-Michael Carman, "Abimelech the Manly Man? Judges 9.1–57 and the Performance of Hegemonic Masculinity," *JSOT* 43, no. 3 (2019): 301–16.

79. Briggs, "A Man's Gotta Do?," 52.

80. Briggs, "A Man's Gotta Do?," 52.

81. Briggs, "A Man's Gotta Do?," 70.

82. Kelly J. Murphy, *Rewriting Masculinity: Gideon, Men, and Might* (Oxford: Oxford University Press, 2019), 6.

83. Murphy, *Rewriting Masculinity*, 8.

84. Robert E. Goss and Mona West, eds., *Take Back the Word: A Queer Reading of the Bible* (Cleveland: Pilgrim, 2000), 3.

Take Back the Word applies a "queer biblical hermeneutic that engages the entire Bible and its message."[85] Nine essays are devoted to the OT, such as Mona West's "Outsiders, Aliens, and Boundary Crossers."[86] West's essay is "a queer reading of the Hebrew Exodus," approaching the text as "a coming-out story."[87] She observes, "For those who identify with the Israelites, at the core of these readings of revolution, deliverance, and liberation is the realization that Exodus is ultimately a story of transformation."[88] She then states, "The themes of enslavement, exodus, wilderness wanderings, promised land, and exile parallel stories of queer Christians who risk the security of their closets to find wholeness in relation to God and the believing community."[89] She concludes, "The Exodus tradition reminds the queer community that indeed silence equals death and to claim the power of their stories makes a way for life."[90]

The publication of *The Queer Bible Commentary* in 2006 marked a pivotal development intended to "demonstrate . . . that these texts will not be bound but, rather, have the ever-surprising capacity to be disruptive, unsettling, and unexpectedly but delightfully *queer*."[91] For example, in Michael Carden's commentary on Genesis, he describes his reading of Genesis: "I want first of all to render it alien, strange, to defamiliarize it."[92] In reading 25:19–28:9, for instance, he avers, "I believe Isaac and Rebecca can be read as representing two types of queer experience involving heterosexual marriage. Isaac is the closet case who marries to conform to hetero-patriarchal norms, to escape from, suppress or cure his minority sexuality. Rebecca's choice, however, demonstrates that not all queer people rely on marriage to secure the regime of the closet."[93] He concludes, "What I have attempted is a queer turning and turning of many threads that make up the meta-tapestry that is Genesis. . . . I hope . . . to invite, if not provoke, a multiplicity of queer readings across all the traditions and beyond."[94]

Continuing this theme of disruption, Erin Runions's journal article "From Disgust to Humor" is an examination of the use of humor in the Rahab story of Josh. 2 by using queer theory and cultural analysis.[95] She examines "how the biblical text continues to generate disgust through the racialization of non-heteronormativity, and at the same time might be deployed to disrupt that affect.

85. Goss and West, *Take Back the Word*, 4.

86. West, "Outsiders, Aliens, and Boundary Crossers," in Goss and West, *Take Back the Word*, 71–81.

87. West, "Outsiders, Aliens, and Boundary Crossers," 72.

88. West, "Outsiders, Aliens, and Boundary Crossers," 72.

89. West, "Outsiders, Aliens, and Boundary Crossers," 73.

90. West, "Outsiders, Aliens, and Boundary Crossers," 80.

91. Deryn Guest et al., eds., *The Queer Bible Commentary* (London: SCM, 2015), xii.

92. Michael Carden, "Genesis/Bereshit," in Guest, *Queer Bible Commentary*, 25.

93. Carden, "Genesis/Bereshit," 45.

94. Carden, "Genesis/Bereshit," 60.

95. Erin Runions, "From Disgust to Humor: Rahab's Queer Affect," *Postscripts: A Journal of Sacred Texts and Contemporary Worlds* 4 (2008): 41–69.

My purpose is to consider how another biblically produced affect—laughter—can be put to work against the Bible's generation of disgust over racialized sexuality."[96] Runions suggests that "the best designation for Rahab is trickster," since she is "well positioned to make the jokes that upset the status quo, even while perhaps seeming uncomfortably to maintain it."[97] She argues that "the story of Rahab revalues the usual affect that buttresses depictions of the Canaanites in the Tanakh: it uses humor to represent the racialized nonheteronormative subject positively, and it undercuts the positive aura surrounding the Israelites' conquest."[98] She concludes, "It is as a trickster that Rahab brings the queer hilarity that can move affect in another direction, away from the disgust that guards the promise of the hope, inclusion, and safety of white heteronormative citizenship."[99]

Queer studies progressed slowly in the first decade of the twenty-first century. In the preface to *Bible Trouble*, Teresa Hornsby and Ken Stone observe, "Queer readings of biblical texts not only remain . . . 'experimental.' They also remain remarkably rare."[100] This rarity provided motivation for Hornsby and Stone to publish *Bible Trouble*. They define queer approaches as "interrogating boundaries and categories that structure discourses of sexuality and gender," as well as bringing "a critical lens to bear on the intersection of sexual dynamics with other dynamics such as race, class, nation, or culture."[101] Three essays focus on reading OT texts, one of which is Deryn Guest's "From Gender Reversal to Genderfuck." Guest observes that the "confrontational, uncompromising stance of queer theory is one of resistance to such binaries: subverting, undoing, deconstructing the normalcy of sex/gender regimes, cracking them open, focusing on the fissures that expose their constructedness."[102] Through a feminist-queer lens, Guest reads Judg. 4–5 as an illustration of the "troubled" boundaries between biblical scholarship and the approaches of feminism, masculist studies, and queer theory.[103]

Gil Rosenberg's 2019 *Ancestral Queerness* asks a critical question: "How can queerness be recognized, particularly in an ancient text with its own set of norms and deviances?"[104] To answer this question, he uses Jonathan Z. Smith's four-step method of description, comparison, redescription, and rectification to examine

96. Reunions, "From Disgust to Humor," 42.

97. Reunions, "From Disgust to Humor," 65.

98. Reunions, "From Disgust to Humor," 43.

99. Reunions, "From Disgust to Humor," 70.

100. Teresa J. Hornsby and Ken Stone, "Already Queer: A Preface," in *Bible Trouble: Queer Reading at the Boundaries of Biblical Scholarship*, ed. Hornsby and Stone, SemeiaSt 67 (Atlanta: Society of Biblical Literature, 2011), ix.

101. Hornsby and Stone, "Already Queer," ix.

102. Deryn Guest, "From Gender Reversal to Genderfuck: Reading Jael through a Lesbian Lens," in Hornsby and Stone, *Bible Trouble*, 9.

103. Guest, "Gender Reversal," 10.

104. Gil Rosenberg, *Ancestral Queerness: The Normal and the Deviant in the Abraham and Sarah Narratives*, HBM 80 (Sheffield: Sheffield Phoenix, 2019), 3.

the narratives of "Abraham, Sarah, and cross-cultural queerness."[105] Rosenberg's conclusion is simple: "Abraham and Sarah are Queer." He then clarifies, "To say that Abraham and Sarah are Queer is to say that they share very specific characteristics with contemporary queer families, but they are different enough from those families that a new, more inclusive term seems warranted."[106] These five characteristics are (1) non-normativity that is often hidden;[107] (2) "deviations from familial norms"; (3) "resistance to norms of reproduction"; (4) presence of "inverted tragedy"; and (5) "ethnic and/or class privilege" used "to achieve greater inclusion into normativity."[108] Rosenberg argues, "These characteristics are sufficient to justify Abraham and Sarah's inclusion in the category. Moreover, I propose these characteristics as a starting point for further elaboration and definition of Queer as a tool for cross-cultural reflection on Queerness."[109]

Queer biblical criticism in OT scholarship continues to progress predominantly through edited works, although some significant monographs have been published that ask critical questions, such as Rosenberg's *Ancestral Queerness*. Studies applying trans theory and intersex theory are also beginning to emerge as a subfield of queer biblical criticism, such as Hornsby and Guest's *Transgender, Intersex, and Biblical Interpretation*.[110] In this volume, Hornsby and Guest argue that "biblical narratives have been read and continue to be read through a gender-binary lens with heteronormative bias."[111] Hornsby outlines their goal: "In each chapter, we offer an example of how paradigmatic narratives are radically transformed when we read without the assumptions that go along with that binary [i.e., male and female] and acknowledge the presence of ambiguously gendered subjectivities."[112] She continues, "In short, we are trying to undo the heteronormative way in which biblical texts have been read and used; we are . . . using the lens of trans theory to interpret texts in new and illuminating ways."[113]

Conclusion

As feminist interpretive approaches forged ahead over the past two decades, masculist and queer interpretative approaches formed distinctive hermeneutical lenses.

105. Rosenberg, *Ancestral Queerness*, 4–8, 9.
106. Rosenberg, *Ancestral Queerness*, 173–74.
107. Rosenberg, *Ancestral Queerness*, 174.
108. Rosenberg, *Ancestral Queerness*, 174.
109. Rosenberg, *Ancestral Queerness*, 174; see 174–77 for Rosenberg's final descriptions in support of her argument.
110. Teresa J. Hornsby and Deryn Guest, *Transgender, Intersex, and Biblical Interpretation*, SemeiaSt 83 (Atlanta: Society of Biblical Literature, 2016). Another example is Jo Henderson-Merrygold, "Gendering Sarai," *Open Theology* 6 (2020): 496–509.
111. Hornsby, "Introduction: The Body as Decoy," in Hornsby and Guest, *Transgender*, 11.
112. Hornsby, "Introduction: The Body as Decoy," 11.
113. Hornsby, "Introduction: The Body as Decoy," 11.

As each has evolved, key issues have emerged. Feminist hermeneutics has as many feminist approaches as there are studies. There is not just one feminist approach; nor is there only one feminist hermeneutic. The above narrative describes diverse hermeneutical approaches—from a hermeneutic of suspicion to a hermeneutic of trust to a hermeneutic of meaning. Furthermore, there are disagreements about how texts can be understood as Holy Scripture when they seem contradictory to female experience or portray God as a perpetrator of sexual violence. At the crux of this issue lies another: In what sense is a text theological? A final question that this survey has highlighted is whether the OT text is patriarchal, patrilineal, or something else and whether this should impact women's reception of the OT text. These issues could be catalysts for fruitful research.

There is an emerging disagreement in masculist studies about the nature of gender and the relationship between "being" male (i.e., hegemonic and subordinate characteristics) and gender performance. Related to this is the question of how a text functions to critique hegemonic and subordinate masculinities. In queer hermeneutics, methodological clarity is still needed for the exploration of gender ambiguity in the text. Both masculist studies and queer biblical criticism are by nature integrative with other approaches. Where this integration is yet to be considered fully is with social identity theory, trauma theory (particularly moral injury theory), and speech act theory. As with feminist studies, integration with these approaches may provide masculist studies and queer biblical criticism with future avenues of research.

26

Inner-Biblical Exegesis

Katharine J. Dell

When one gets to know the text of the Bible, it quickly becomes apparent that certain texts echo or even cite other texts, which immediately raises the questions: What purpose does such citation have, and what function does it fulfill? This brings us to the authors and redactors of texts and their purposes, and it showcases the literary connections between texts. It also takes us forward to the formation of a canon of Scripture and to the Bible's authority and power to generate ever-new translations, reinterpretations, and applications. It takes us even further forward to a modern appropriation and interpretation of ancient texts through the lenses of both religious tradition and literary development. Interconnections are visible on the levels of words and phrases, including apparent glosses and arrangements of material, as well as between similar concepts and themes. The Bible likes to cite itself, correct itself, and reapply its own material, which is the basic meaning of the concept of inner-biblical exegesis.

The concept of inner-biblical exegesis has ancient roots in the methodologies of early Jewish and Christian interpreters, but the phrase "inner-biblical exegesis" was not coined until Nahum Sarna suggested the expression in 1963.[1] Sarna's predominant interest was limited to one exemplary psalm, but through it he introduced the idea of inner-biblical technique, writing, "The past is drawn upon to give sanction to the present, and the ancient words, precisely because they are invested with authority, are reinterpreted to make them applicable to

1. Nahum Sarna, "Psalm 89: A Study in Inner Biblical Exegesis," in *Biblical and Other Studies*, ed. Alexander Altmann (Cambridge, MA: Harvard University Press, 1963), 29–46.

the contemporary scene."[2] In *Biblical Interpretation in Ancient Israel*, Michael Fishbane gave the concept fuller expression, and his name is now most associated with the idea.[3]

Since then, advocates of the method and its critics have had their say, comparing inner-biblical exegesis with its close relative "intertextuality" and sometimes confusing the two. The similarity of these concepts adds to the debate and merits acknowledgment, but this chapter is more interested in the nature of inner-biblical exegesis as originally conceived and its usefulness now, how it has become one method in a larger scholarly toolbox, and whether this status is faithful to its roots as a means of understanding the growth of texts.

Sarna's Pioneering Observations

It is interesting that Sarna's initial observations sprang from the study of a single text instead of first formulating a methodology and then applying it to a variety of texts. Inner-biblical exegesis tends to be defined by looking at the way texts interrelate and work together, proceeding from the text upward rather than from the methodology downward.

This is a strength of the method, as it showcases how the Bible inherently functions and how therefore to get to the heart of its composition and dissemination. Psalm 89 is an interesting example because it naturally divides into three main parts (vv. 1–18, 19–37, 38–51 [2–19, 20–38, 39–52 MT]). The close relationship of verses 19–37 to Nathan's oracle to David in 2 Sam. 7:4–17, in which an everlasting dynasty is promised, has long been noticed.[4] Sarna seeks to draw out the authorial/redactorial techniques (e.g., associations of words, phrases, and ideas) used to unify this psalm. He also explores the nature of verses 19–37 in light of the 2 Samuel parallel and its further parallel in 1 Chron. 17:3–15. Sarna comes from a historical angle, interested in context and date as well as literary composition, and seeks to isolate the three genres of oracle, hymn, and lament within the psalm. He describes a process of gradual homogenization of the psalm through repetition of key words and phrases and through transitional verses, ascribing authorship to a final compiler.

Sarna's work on the reinterpretation of the Nathan oracle in this psalm is key. He notes how both the exegesis and the exposition of texts relate "the idea of authority and immutability and, ultimately, of sanctity."[5] This is not entirely

2. Sarna, "Psalm 89," 34.

3. Michael Fishbane, *Biblical Interpretation in Ancient Israel* (Oxford: Oxford University Press, 1988). See also his earlier article: Fishbane, "Revelation and Tradition: Aspects of Inner-Biblical Exegesis," *JBL* 99, no. 3 (1980): 343–61.

4. Hermann Gunkel, *The Psalms: A Form-Critical Introduction*, trans. Thomas Horner (Philadelphia: Fortress, 1967), classified this as a royal psalm.

5. Sarna, "Psalm 89," 33.

an Israelite phenomenon (Sarna draws on ANE parallels), but biblical evidence suggests a sanctity to "the word," given by divine command, which cannot be added to or subtracted from (Deut. 4:2), and an authority in the words of "earlier prophets" (Zech. 1:4–6; 7:7).

Change is built into this procedure of finalizing texts because a twofold process is necessary in order to make ancient texts relevant to the present. First is preservation of past texts, and second is reinterpretation in order to make them applicable. Sarna finds examples from early Jewish midrash and Christian "prophetic" exegesis of the HB to back up his claim. He also points out that it is a biblical phenomenon, an inner-biblical one. This kind of exegesis is clearest in postexilic texts such as Daniel and Chronicles, but it was also happening in preexilic times (e.g., when the literary prophets cite prophetic predecessors). It thus was a continuous process. Fishbane explores these kinds of examples in greater depth.[6]

For Sarna, Ps. 89 is at the center of interest for recognizing "this early phenomenon of inner Biblical exegesis."[7] Rather than focus on which tradition came first and whether poetry precedes prose or vice versa, as older scholars had done, Sarna draws attention to the psalmist's fresh exegesis in adapting an ancient oracle.[8] This involved omission as well as reinterpretation: the omission, for example, of any reference to the temple (unlike parallel passages that were contextualized by reference to it) or to Solomon or other kingly successors and reinterpretation of the promise of a Davidic dynasty, a promise now threatened by the present reality described in the final lament section. Sarna does try to isolate the historical circumstance that gave rise to the completed and unified psalm, placing it in 735–734 BCE, the invasion at the time of King Ahaz (Isa. 7:5–6), and thus before the exile in 586 BCE, but this attempt to date precisely is perhaps less convincing. The key idea for inner-biblical analysis is his argument that Ps. 89 is a midrash on the Nathan oracle.

Fishbane's Seminal Article

Fishbane's "Revelation and Tradition" does not mention Sarna's work, but as his title suggests, he is interested in the relationship between revelation and tradition (i.e., how established biblical revelations, such as the law given at Sinai, could be reapplied and updated in the light of more recent contexts and needs). While this is a well-known postbiblical phenomenon, Fishbane wishes to draw attention to the process before the formation of the canon and the fixed body of texts that ensued.

6. Fishbane (*Biblical Interpretation*, 91–277) discusses the prophetic reworking not only of former prophecies but of other genres too, predominantly legal ones.

7. Sarna, "Psalm 89," 36.

8. Sarna, "Psalm 89," 37–39.

Fishbane sees a "tension" between revelation and tradition that needs resolution in the areas of law, homily, and prophecy. He cites the revealed and authoritative Sinai revelation, in a sense fixed yet in another sense unable to deal with new situations, for which adjustments within the tradition were made. He finds evidence in Num. 27:1–5, for example, of a problem that needed a solution. The daughters of Zelophehad argue that their father's patrimony should not be lost because he had only daughters and no son. This was not covered in the existing law, and so Moses asked God for an oracle (Num. 27:6–7). The outcome is a new contingency designed to protect the clans (27:9–11), formulated in abstract terms to designate daughters and also covering the situation of a leader dying with no offspring.

But even this new addendum did not go far enough: it did not protect the clan if a daughter married into another clan, for the patrimony would again be lost. In Num. 36:1–4 Moses must respond again. This time the divine response overturns the principle of female inheritance since it limits transfer of property to just males. Both supplements legislate new regulations. Revealed laws from God to Moses on Sinai are extended to include other laws that become revealed laws, a process that authorizes what are essentially addenda. The essential point is that comparison between texts—the noting of inner-biblical exegesis at work—enables us to see how tradents ("redrafters, or reformulators of older laws")[9] interact and ultimately how the material has been made to cohere within the legal tradition.

Fishbane also considers the Covenant Code (Exod. 20–24) and the Deuteronomic legislation. For example, Exod. 23:4 addresses the duty of returning an enemy's ox, but in Deut. 22:1–3 the owner is responsible to collect lost property. The original command still holds for the one in possession of the ox. This addition helps to make the law more comprehensive, and again both are presented as divine laws. Legal expansions are incorporated into the legitimizing framework of the revelation at Sinai, whether the reason is juridical, scribal, or liturgical.

Prophetic contexts can also add small revisions to the law. For example, Jer. 17:21–22 reworks the Deuteronomic version of the Decalogue (Deut. 5) to add restrictions to activity on the Sabbath, again presenting them as the word of God from Sinai. Another technique is to combine texts to create a new divinely sanctioned law, such as the combining of laws from Exod. 22:31 on not eating ripped carcasses and from Exod. 23:19 on cultic prescriptions at festivals, notably a prohibition against boiling a kid in its mother's milk when offering the firstfruits. These two laws are combined in Deut. 14:21 and related to other themes (giving gifts to strangers and the holiness of Israel as a nation), and they become food laws rather than cultic prescriptions.

Fishbane notes how later biblical sources increasingly cite earlier ones such that a notion of scriptural study starts to become, in itself, a form of relationship with God. His example here is Ps. 119:42, 66 in relation to Torah as an object

9. Fishbane, "Revelation and Tradition," 360.

of devotion and even as a means of inquiry as to the divine will (cf. Ezra 7:10), replacing an older notion of consulting God directly (as in 1 Kings 22:8).

Fishbane goes on to explore similar examples in what he calls the "homiletical tradition," notably the prophetic expansion of law and its reinvigoration through reuse of material. One example is Mic. 7:18–20's reuse and expansion of Exod. 34:6–7a about the nature of God as compassionate and forgiving and then the subsequent additions to the Decalogue account in Exod. 20:5b–7. This is seen as a two-stage process: the commandments themselves are supplemented by homiletical remarks that both reflect and individualize those expansions (cf. Deut. 7, where this aspect is reinforced). This, of course, rests on disputed views about the relative dating of passages, leading to a circularity that modern study has tried to avoid.[10] Scholars today would probably be more cautious in their assessment of the direction of dependence and the development of ideas.[11]

Fishbane also explores how historical paradigms such as the exodus are reused as recurring patterns. One example is Exod. 3–11 and its reuse in Isa. 19:19–25. In Exodus, the beleaguered Pharaoh of Egypt occasionally asks Moses to pray for him, but the request is never granted. This notion is transformed in Isa. 19. The Egyptians have oppressors crying to God and they build an altar specifically to YHWH in Egypt, which serves as a sign that a deliverer is coming. Through this, Egyptians will come to know God and sacrifice to him and, despite God's plagues, will ultimately become his people. Fishbane describes this transformation as "an audacious theological counterpoint."[12]

Reinterpretation also occurs in prophetic oracles. Old oracles were sometimes unfulfilled or occasionally failed and so needed a divine "update." New situations require new authoritative oracles. Instead of replacing the old ones that are authoritative in their own right, the divine word that comes through the prophet redirects or reinspires them. Fishbane uses examples from Deutero- and Trito-Isaiah. Isaiah 58:14 recontextualizes Deut. 32:13 and 32:9 (Moses's Song, which was not originally an oracle) and transforms these texts into an unfulfilled oracle on the need for obedience on the Sabbath that will lead to the gift of land. Postexilic concerns with the restoration of the people to the land come through here. Fishbane concludes, "In the Hebrew Bible, exegetical tradition is the handmaiden of revelation—and so conceals its own paradoxical processes.

10. Interest in the final form of texts and how they were grouped in the final stages has in many ways replaced attention to how texts were originally formed in their oral and literary genre stages. Noticeably, in the study of the Psalms, interest now focuses on links between psalms, their arrangement, and interrelationships in light of the structuring of the Psalter. See Nancy deClaissé-Walford, ed., *The Shape and Shaping of the Book of Psalms: The Current State of Scholarship*, AIL 20 (Atlanta: SBL Press, 2014).

11. The belief that sources and key ideas developed across time but not in the way the HB describes them canonically goes back to Julius Wellhausen, *Prolegomena to the History of Israel*, trans. J. Sutherland Black and Allan Menzies (Edinburgh: A&C Black, 1885).

12. Fishbane, "Revelation and Tradition," 354.

By concealing its capacity to construct new worlds of meaning in older materials, it thereby preserves the viability of ancient revelations."[13]

Fishbane's Monograph on Biblical Interpretation

Fishbane's article is detailed and nuanced but nowhere near as detailed as the monograph! Here I highlight places in the monograph where Fishbane expands on what he already explored in the article. One distinction that he develops is between *traditum* (the inherited/received tradition) and *traditio* (the scribal/exegetical annotations that shape tradition[s]). In this context, he also clarifies the scope of inner-biblical exegesis within the HB, which incorporates "textual comments and clarifications, scribal remarks and interpolations and theological reactions and revisions."[14] He explains the link between these Latin terms and the inner-biblical method thus: "In these latter cases [the great majority of examples of inner-biblical exegesis] a nexus between the *traditum* and its *traditio* exists but must be analytically recovered and demonstrated in every instance."[15]

Inner-biblical exegesis can be scribal, legal, haggadic, or mantological, to use his categories. It is also varied, with one biblical example differing from the next, thus making formulation of general principles quite difficult. He remarks that the *traditio* can revitalize the *traditum*, but it can also undermine it, and at every stage divine revelation is invoked.

As in the article, Fishbane sees the legal tradition as an inner-biblical process of outgrowth and extensions as new situations arise, but he also sees the prophetic outworkings and expansions as more challenging and in tension with older tradition, reflecting rivalries between groups and ideologies. These processes ostensibly ended at the time of the canonization of the Scriptures.[16] Yet they continue both in the variation of translations and in the midrashic efforts of the postbiblical communities that find these Scriptures authoritative.[17] In that sense the process goes well beyond the confines of the HB, or even the Bible as a whole, into the history of interpretation and beyond. Fishbane writes, "Each solidification of the *traditum* was the canon in process of its formation; and each stage of canon-formation was a new achievement in *Gemeindebildung*, in the formation of an integrated, book-centred culture."[18]

13. Fishbane, "Revelation and Tradition," 361.

14. Fishbane, *Biblical Interpretation*, 10.

15. Fishbane, *Biblical Interpretation*, 12.

16. Fishbane is influenced by Brevard Childs on canonical criticism. Brevard S. Childs, *Introduction to the Old Testament as Scripture* (Minneapolis: Fortress, 1979).

17. Jacob Neusner, *What Is Midrash?*, GBS (Philadelphia: Fortress, 1987), suggests, "Since all Midrash begins in Scripture, we start with an account of what all later exegetes in Judaism learned *through* Scripture about correct interpretation *of* Scripture" (16, emphasis original).

18. Fishbane, *Biblical Interpretation*, 18.

He points to scribes as custodians of the *traditum*, who copied, transmitted, and reinterpreted texts and traditions, groups of which go back to the preexilic period but come to more prominence after the exile in Chronicles and Ezra-Nehemiah. Their annotations, however, end up forming the tradition; they not only copied and glossed but also interpreted. They dealt with parallel literary strands and textual variants but rarely left material out, preferring instead to conflate readings, to add brief explanations juxtaposed to what was already there, or to unify texts. Their comments are unsystematic and piecemeal, and sometimes the line between author and scribe is hard to draw. Fishbane comments, "Many scribes saw themselves as the cultural allies of the composers—teachers of their meanings and reporters of their teachings—and so composers in a derivative sense."[19]

Repetition, genre variations, additions, expansions, and clarification of obscure or problematic dimensions of texts are probably their main signatures. They form a shadowy group, their scribal activity usually unmarked in texts, and yet we find some passages indicating their existence. For example, Eccles. 12:9–12 describes a process of teaching, weighing, studying, and arranging many proverbs by a teacher who "sought to find pleasing words" and "wrote words of truth plainly" (12:10 NRSV). Fishbane writes, "Israelite scribes did not simply transcribe textual materials believed to be divinely revealed or otherwise authoritative; they intensively studied them and left us a record of their *traditio* in the received *traditum*." Ironically, "*traditum* exists by virtue of *traditio*."[20] From this scribal starting point, Fishbane divides his book into three main sections based on genre: law, haggadah, and mantology.

Fishbane argues that gaps in the *traditum* of ancient Israel led to the rise of a *traditio*. A lack of comprehensiveness required that new rules and laws be crafted for the new legal situations that arose; where there was not enough detail, processes of supplementation, amendment, and clarification appeared. The body of laws that gradually came together as authoritative law from Sinai was in fact a living body in that it had changed over time. For inner-biblical interpretation, the focus is on "where the exegesis of incomprehensive or incomprehensible legal formulations is expressly and explicitly preserved in the Hebrew Bible."[21] He maintains that because of the centrality of legal material for all other types of material in the HB, it is the richest source of inner-biblical exegetical examples, turning up not only in other legal material but also in prophetic discourse, in narratives about history, and in priestly formulations.

He uses Max Weber[22] to describe stages of law that often proceed from irrational to rational—that is, from revelation of law (as from God to Moses on

19. Fishbane, *Biblical Interpretation*, 85.

20. Fishbane, *Biblical Interpretation*, 88.

21. Fishbane, *Biblical Interpretation*, 232.

22. Max Weber, *Law in Economy and Society*, ed. M. Rheinstein, trans. Edward Shils and Max Rheinstein (Cambridge, MA: Harvard University Press, 1954).

Sinai) to social adaptions of it, imposition and systematization of law, and finally to elaboration. Fishbane further nuances the relationship between irrational and rational. "Formally irrational" gives way to "formally rational," and "substantially irrational" to "substantively rational." This categorization is unnecessarily complicated, but he fits various examples from the HB into each category, again reinforcing that it is the variety of texts and subtlety of variation that leads to the need for ever-more categories. This tendency to overcategorize is perhaps the primary flaw of Fishbane's work.

Fishbane further pursues the relationship between revelation and tradition in the mantic oracles—that is, intuitive oracles largely from the prophets that can be in tension with earlier legal patterns and lead to competing claims regarding the divine authority of what is being said. This challenges the *traditum* and yet inspires and ultimately forms a fresh *traditio*.

Fishbane looks at a wider range of genres under his haggadic exegesis, including epic narratives, historiographies, oratory, and liturgy, as well as prophetic oracles. New life-settings and new voices lead to revisions to the *traditum*. Yet old paradigms and traditions, such as Sinai or covenant, remain relevant and are transferred from one historical epoch to another with subtle changes. So books like Deuteronomy both preserve and revise desert and Sinai traditions from Exodus and Numbers, while historical books such as Chronicles preserve and revise older historical traditions from Samuel through Kings.

Fishbane's section on mantological exegesis is interested in the reinterpretation of oracles in texts such as Daniel. The roles of dream interpretation and understanding omens, visions, and so on are explored, as well as reinterpretation of old oracles in new situations and fulfillment of oracles that previously seemed to be false or unfulfilled. Fishbane speaks of a "1,000-year-long spectrum of exegetical proliferation and development"[23] and has given us a magisterial overview of such processes.

He asks the more difficult question of the motivations of those who did this work. Did they write back into the material to give it an authority it did not originally have? Pseudepigraphical exegesis might be an example of this, where attributing material to a person or voice from the past, such as Moses in Deuteronomy or the Chronicles, elevates its claims. Alternatively, in attributive exegesis, some "historical" source is cited as authoritative, as in 2 Chron. 30:16, for example, where Levite practices of blood sprinkling are ascribed to the "torah of Moses," even though this practice is not known in Pentateuch law.

Did these exegetes manipulate sources of authority or validate after the fact, or did they simply amend and elaborate traditions in a non-manipulative, rather pious way? Was the move toward revealed exegesis in the form of dreams and angelic mediators and the increased emphasis on the mysterious nature of wisdom and Torah a way of avoiding challenges to the authority of these readings or

23. Fishbane, *Biblical Interpretation*, 527.

simply the way the tradition developed? Fishbane takes the view that we cannot be sure of the motivation, so it is best to focus on what we find in the HB: that is, "complex blends of *traditum* and *traditio* in dynamic interaction, and dynamic interdependence" accompanied by many varied exegetical voices.[24]

Thus far, I have concentrated on scholars who introduced and defined the method of inner-biblical interpretation. But where have scholars taken these insights, and how has the field progressed? For an answer, we turn to two scholars who critique Fishbane and ask new questions of categorization and terminology: Lyle Eslinger and Russell Meek.

Eslinger on Inner-Biblical Exegesis and Allusion

Lyle Eslinger describes the Bible as an "interconnected compendium" on which inner-biblical exegesis hopes to shed light.[25] However, he has problems with the term "exegesis" in the description of this method, as it implies "an authorial intent at exposition or interpretation."[26] He holds that most instances of literary interconnection in the Bible only touch on a literary antecedent and that this may even be an unconscious process for the author.

He feels that Fishbane's scheme of genre categorization (scribal, legal, haggadic, and mantological) is open to challenge. I would add that within those four categories, the scribal is fairly brief, describing only a process of gathering together rather than the material that might have been penned by the wise or their scribal successors. This is perceived as a rabbinic model, which, according to James Kugel, "betrays a desire (perhaps only subconscious) to say: exegesis in biblical times was not terribly different from what we know in postbiblical times; indeed, it was really rather proto-rabbinic."[27]

Perhaps the greater criticism of Fishbane's model of inner-biblical exegesis is that it is a historical or diachronic approach along traditional literary-historical exegetical lines, which many scholars today have abandoned. According to Eslinger, Fishbane assumes (1) that texts are temporally distant from one another and have distinct authors and (2) that some texts precede others. Neither assumption is provable.

Do asides or expository comments in a text necessitate another hand? For Eslinger, the narrator's voice has "diverse modalities,"[28] and an author can correct or clarify himself. Does the literary unity of a passage simply rest with the hand that made a few modifications, or does it rest with the author? Eslinger also criticizes

24. Fishbane, *Biblical Interpretation*, 543.

25. Lyle Eslinger, "Inner-Biblical Exegesis and Inner-Biblical Allusion: The Question of Category," *VT* 42, no. 1 (1992): 47–58.

26. Eslinger, "Inner-Biblical Exegesis," 47n2.

27. James Kugel, "The Bible's Earliest Interpreters," *Proof* 7 (1987): 275–76.

28. Eslinger, "Inner-Biblical Exegesis," 49–50.

the assumption that texts precede others and that there is a diachronic framework within a reconstructed literary-history: "Such an approach to [inner-biblical allusion] can only be as good, as reliable, and as useful as the literary history on which it is based. If the model of the Bible's literary history is wrong, the analyses of inner-biblical exegeses can only compound the fallacy."[29] Eslinger abandons the term "inner-biblical exegesis" in favor of "inner-biblical allusion," which he feels is less problematic since it is less tied to literary-historical ideas about the precedence of biblical texts. For inner-biblical allusion, he speaks of the "vector of allusion" and the need to look at where each set of related texts points.[30]

Along with "inner-biblical allusion," Eslinger uses the term "biblical intertextuality." He differentiates the two terms as follows: inner-biblical allusion implies "a vector of dependence," but in biblical intertextuality there is none. This assumes that biblical intertextuality is always synchronic, a conclusion challenged in most circles today.[31]

Eslinger also critiques Fishbane's assumption of the historical precedence of the Pentateuch over prophetic books. Questions about priority of texts muddy the inner-biblical exegetical waters. In departing from literary-historical reconstructions of the Bible's development, Eslinger promotes a grounded focus, following the canon itself rather than some construct of what might have happened historically. He writes, "In the study of [inner-biblical allusion] we can turn again to the sequence of events actually described or implied in much of biblical literature and follow the chain of reverse trajectory allusions through from creation to apocalypse."[32]

Eslinger provides an interesting critique of Fishbane and shows the limitations of the diachronic, literary-historical approach.[33] His suggestion of "allusion" is helpful, although he does not take the idea far enough in this article, and its distinction from biblical intertextuality is false (especially since allusion is one of its major categories).[34] He describes "allusion" as a more literary analysis of textual interconnections in biblical literature.[35]

29. Eslinger, "Inner-Biblical Exegesis," 52.

30. Eslinger, "Inner-Biblical Exegesis," 53.

31. For how intertextual method combines diachronic and synchronic today, see John Barton, "Déjà Lu: Intertextuality, Method or Theory?," in *Reading Job Intertextually*, ed. Katharine Dell and Will Kynes, LHBOTS 574 (London: Bloomsbury 2013), 1–18.

32. Eslinger, "Inner-Biblical Exegesis," 58.

33. Diachronic and synchronic are commonly used together in exegetical analysis; see, e.g., Odil Hannes Steck, *Studien zu Tritojesaja*, BZAW 203 (Berlin: De Gruyter, 1991). So Eslinger is wrong to dismiss inner-biblical exegesis on these grounds.

34. Richard B. Hays proposes seven criteria for finding intertexts: availability, volume, recurrence, thematic coherence, historical plausibility, history of interpretation, and satisfaction. See Hays, *Echoes of Scripture in the Letters of Paul* (New Haven: Yale University Press 1989), 29–32.

35. For a rejection of Eslinger's terminology, see Benjamin Sommer, "Exegesis, Allusion and Intertextuality in the Hebrew Bible: A Response to Lyle Eslinger," *VT* 46, no. 4 (1996): 479–89. Sommer holds that allusion is part of the diachronic scene and that intertextuality is

Meek on Three Methods, Including Intertextuality

In his influential article,[36] Russell Meek begins with "intertextuality," a word avoided by Fishbane, describing it as a helpful term but actually used too generally to denote all kinds of literary relationships between texts of all types.[37] He calls for a clearer definition of what has become a catchall term defined in many ways. Meek notes that intertextuality can be problematic for scholars wishing to speak in terms of authorial intent. For this, the term inner-biblical exegesis is more satisfactory since it includes revisions of original texts, application of texts from one situation to another, and the unifying of texts and the drawing together of latent meanings.[38] Parody (e.g., Job 7:17–18's use of Ps. 8:4, also cited by Eslinger)[39] is a good example of a technique that depends on there being earlier texts on which to draw, and dream interpretation is another, as in Fishbane's analysis of Daniel.[40] Meek writes that "diachrony matters" in this paradigm,[41] as does "authorial intention."[42] He considers the term "inner-biblical allusion" to be similar to inner-biblical exegesis but with a greater interest in shared vocabulary and ideas. He writes, "Inner-biblical allusion sets out to determine whether a receptor text has in some way referred to a source text, but the goal is not to demonstrate that the receptor text has modified the source text."[43] Meek is mainly trying to draw comparisons between the methods and to clarify where inner-biblical exegesis stands in this lineup of methods.

---

substantially different in its focus "on manifold linkages among texts or on connections between text and commonplace phrases from the cultural systems in which the text exists" (486) and in its move away from the author to text and reader. He defends Fishbane's method and argues that Eslinger muddies the methodological waters by mixing terminology.

36. Russell Meek, "Intertextuality, Inner-Biblical Exegesis and Inner-Biblical Allusion: The Ethics of a Methodology," *Bib* 9, no. 2 (2014): 280–91.

37. Paul R. Noble, "Esau, Tamar, and Joseph: Criteria for Identifying Inner-Biblical Allusions," *VT* 52, no. 2 (2002): 219–52, uses the term broadly for "the interpretative relationships that pertain between texts" (219) but does not focus on "inner-biblical allusion" as a subcategory.

38. Benjamin Sommer agrees that inner-biblical exegesis is essentially an authorial approach. He suggests patterns of diachronic inner-biblical exegesis and allusion from Jeremiah to Deutero-Isaiah, such as explicit citation, implicit reference, inclusion, exegesis, influence, revision, polemic, reversal, re-prediction, fulfillment of earlier prophecies, typological linkages, wordplay, word order, and more. See Sommer, *A Prophet Reads Scripture: Allusion in Isaiah 40–66*, Contraversions (Stanford, CA: Stanford University Press, 1998).

39. Eslinger, "Inner-Biblical Exegesis," 55.

40. Fishbane argues that the book of Daniel reinterprets Jeremiah's "seventy years" (Jer. 25:9–12; already reinterpreted in Jer. 29:10) to refer to seventy sabbatical cycles or Jubilees (Dan. 9:24–27; cf. Lev. 25:1–24), probably influenced by 2 Chron. 36:21. Fishbane, "Revelation and Tradition," 357–59.

41. Meek, "Intertextuality," 287.

42. Meek, "Intertextuality," 288.

43. Meek, "Intertextuality," 289.

Recent Scholarship on Inner-Biblical and Intertextual Relationships

Having sprung out of a detailed analysis of individual texts from which methodology was wrought, inner-biblical exegesis now stands alongside its intertextual and inner-biblical allusion bedfellows. This marks its transition to a tool in the scholarly toolbox rather than a complex explanation of the growth and outworkings of texts, as Fishbane originally conceived it. In a new book titled *Second Wave Intertextuality and the Hebrew Bible*, for example, the editors elide these methods when they write, "Now at the turn of this century, more and more scholarly works in biblical scholarship either explicitly or implicitly (as 'inner-biblical exegesis or allusion') specify the method or issue of intertextuality."[44] Inner-biblical exegesis is a bit more than an implicit intertextuality! However, it is increasingly used as a synonym of intertextuality but without the "baggage" of intertextuality and its French origins[45] and limiting itself to the Bible. Marianne Grohmann and Hyun Chul Paul Kim coin the term "inner-biblical intertextuality" as a hybrid of the two methods and limited, as inner-biblical exegesis is, to the canonical corpus of the HB.[46]

The remaining question is whether it will be useful in today's biblical studies climate. Grohmann and Kim argue that various methods are increasingly in dialogue, largely due to growing interest not only in canonization but also in adaptations of biblical texts at Qumran and in other Second Temple literature.[47] Jewish exegetical traditions put biblical texts in dialogue with rabbinic literature, as Fishbane himself pioneered. Final-form readings of previously dissected books and sections of books have also enabled a process of reunifying texts.[48] However, it seems that the main contribution of "inner-biblical exegesis" is to add to a wider picture of intertextual relationships across texts, and scholars are increasingly

44. Marianne Grohmann and Hyun Chul Paul Kim, eds., *Second Wave Intertextuality and the Hebrew Bible*, RBS 93 (Atlanta: SBL, 2019), 1. They suggest that Fishbane might have known of this method but acknowledged a debt only to Martin Buber and Sarna's article on Ps. 89 (Fishbane, *Biblical Interpretation*, viii).

45. Julia Kristeva, *Desire in Language: A Semiotic Approach to Literature and Art*, ed. Leon Rodriguez, trans. Thomas Gora, Alice Jardin, and Leon Rodriguez (New York: Columbia University Press, 1980).

46. Many use the phrase "inner-biblical interpretation," which is also a hybrid term: e.g, Barton, "Déjà Lu," 4; with explicit application to Genesis, see Yair Zakovitch, "Inner-Biblical Interpretation," in *Reading Genesis: Ten Methods*, ed. Ron Hendel (New York: Cambridge University Press, 2010), 92–118.

47. James A. Sanders, *From Sacred Story to Sacred Text* (Philadelphia: Fortress, 1987).

48. E.g., for the book of Isaiah, a study of catchwords, signposts, and markers has inspired interest in its unity and continuities. For a summary, see Roy F. Melugin, "Isaiah 40–66 in Recent Research on the Major Prophets: The 'Unity' Movement," in *Recent Research on the Major Prophets*, ed. Alan J. Hauser, RRBS 1 (Sheffield: Sheffield Phoenix, 2008), 142–94. Much of this was inspired by Hugh Williamson, *The Book Called Isaiah: Deutero-Isaiah's Role in Composition and Redaction* (Oxford: Clarendon, 1994); and Jacob Stromberg, *Isaiah after Exile: The Author of Third Isaiah as Reader and Redactor of the Book* (Oxford: Oxford University Press, 2011).

using these methods together.[49] For example, Marvin Sweeney looks at texts on the dedication of the firstborn, primarily Exod. 22:29b–30 [28–29 MT] and 23:14–19, as forerunners of Exod. 13:1–16 and 34:10–27, all of which develop into the motif of the Levites replacing the firstborns in Num. 3:11–13, 40–43, 44–51 and 8:13–19. Each text has its own themes and functions but is noticeably an outworking of what came before.[50] This sounds like one of Fishbane's examples, but Sweeney is juxtaposing methods of redaction-criticism (with the isolation of strata) and of intertextuality in conjunction with this brand of inner-biblical exegesis.

A Final Mention of Scribalism

A final area when considering modern developments in the field is scribalism, as addressed by Fishbane.[51] Fishbane's "scribes" have much in common with what Philip Davies discusses as the final shapers and compilers of the biblical canon.[52] Davies argues that they shaped the text to such a degree that the historicity of much of the material is open to severe doubt. However, the processes of inner-biblical exegesis actually mitigate against this conclusion, suggesting that development took place in piecemeal ways over a long period of time and with a sense of the authority of older texts and tradition, which acted as a brake on changing or deleting material.

The scribes wielded power over the texts that they produced and were the experts. Indeed, Mark Sneed argues that "sages" are just one type of scribe and that scribalism is a wider phenomenon than simply the writing of texts.[53] Using insights from anthropology, he shows that the scribe had a much broader social role, encompassing anything to do with writing, teaching, education, foreign affairs, archives and libraries, and administration at all levels. This is a helpful corrective to the literary approach of inner-biblical exegesis, which focuses on the text alone.[54] We need to ask, as Fishbane in fact does at the end of his book, what the motivation for the inner-biblical method was and how it might have evolved within society as well as within the texts themselves. At the end of the

49. Karl Weyde, "Inner-Biblical Interpretation: Methodological Reflections on the Relationship between Texts in the Hebrew Bible," *SEÅ* 70 (2005): 287–300, argues that a sharp division between terms such as intertextuality, inner-biblical allusion, and inner-biblical exegesis is not helpful. But some of the original spirit and intent of "inner-biblical exegesis" (Fishbane's precise term) is lost.

50. Marvin A. Sweeney, "The Literary-Historical Dimensions of Intertextuality in Exodus–Numbers," in Grohmann and Kim, *Second Wave Intertextuality*, 41–52.

51. Fishbane, *Biblical Interpretation*, chaps. 1–4.

52. Philip R. Davies, *Scribes and Schools: The Canonization of the Hebrew Scriptures*, LAI (Louisville: Westminster John Knox, 1998).

53. Mark R. Sneed, *The Social World of the Sages: An Introduction to Israelite and Jewish Wisdom Literature* (Minneapolis: Fortress, 2015).

54. See also an influential work by David M. Carr, *Writing on the Tablet of the Heart: Origins of Scripture and Literature* (Oxford: Oxford University Press, 2005).

day, those who compiled and updated biblical texts over many millennia were real people, even if their identities are lost to us now. They left a huge compendium of texts to uncover and rediscover. Inner-biblical exegesis as a method has certainly opened our eyes to the wondrous complexity of our biblical heritage and will continue to do so.

27

Literary Approaches

Tremper Longman III

Over the past forty-plus years, the interface between the study of the OT and literary theory and practice has, at times, been intense. More recently, relations have been, at best, subdued. This chapter narrates the progression of the recognition within OT studies of the literary quality of the OT in order to understand the present state of the relationship. We start with the literary turn in OT study, which began in earnest in the early 1980s. Then we will look at four topics to describe the current state of the field of literary approaches to the OT: literary theory, literary practice, genre, and intertextuality.[1]

Paradigm Shift: From History to Literature

Old Testament scholarship focused on questions of history from the early nineteenth century through the end of the 1970s. Interest surrounded questions connected to referentiality (e.g., Did the exodus happen and, if so, when?) and history of composition (e.g., What are the potential sources of the Pentateuch?).[2]

In 1981, Robert Alter, a literary scholar, published a watershed book, *The Art of Biblical Narrative*, in which he explores the conventions of Hebrew narrative.[3]

1. For a more extensive and detailed treatment of these topics, see Tremper Longman III, *The Old Testament as Literature* (Grand Rapids: Baker Academic, 2024).

2. J. W. Rogerson, *Old Testament Criticism in the Nineteenth Century: England and Germany* (Philadelphia: Fortress, 1985).

3. Robert Alter, *The Art of Biblical Narrative* (New York: Basic Books, 1981).

He describes how Hebrew storytellers develop their plots, present characters, utilize the narrator, and more. The results shifted the focus from historical questions to literary ones so dramatically that some believed the field was experiencing a decisive paradigm change.

Alter was not the first person to suggest a literary approach to the OT. As Stephen Prickett has pointed out, until the turn of the nineteenth century, biblical studies engaged in literary analysis of biblical texts along with questions of history. He argues that the founding of the first modern university in Berlin in 1809 erected a "glacial-moraine . . . between biblical studies and the study of other literatures, both classical and modern."[4] Indeed, early church theologians like Augustine applied contemporary Roman literary categories to their study of Hebrew poetry. Prickett's argument suggests that what many experienced as radically new in Alter's literary study was really a recovery of a perspective lost with the Enlightenment.

We should also qualify Alter's role by noting important precursors of *The Art of Biblical Narrative*. Most importantly, James Muilenburg delivered an important SBL presidential address published as "Form Criticism and Beyond." As the title suggests, he felt it was time to move beyond the diachronic study of biblical texts represented by the type of form criticism (*Gattungsgeschichte*) formulated by Hermann Gunkel to a study of the final form of the text.[5] Other precursors include J. P. Fokkelman and Michael Fishbane.[6]

Still, Alter had an influence that went far beyond these precursors. His work inspired further studies of the literary quality of biblical texts. Biblical and literary scholars produced scores of studies signaling an interest in literary issues.[7] As mentioned above, some felt that a paradigm shift was underway, as many bracketed interest in historical questions to focus on close readings of the text. In terms of poetry, we might say that scholarship never completely lost sight of its literary quality, but before 1980, mainline historical criticism spent less time pondering poetic artistry and more effort trying to establish, say, a psalm's prehistory and original setting in life. At this transitional time, Alter and James Kugel made seminal contributions to our understanding of biblical poetics, particularly parallelism.[8]

4. Stephen Prickett, *Words and the Word: Language, Poetics and Biblical Interpretation* (Cambridge: Cambridge University Press, 1986), 1.

5. James Muilenburg, "Form Criticism and Beyond," *JBL* 88, no. 1 (1969): 1–18.

6. J. P. Fokkelman, *Narrative Art in Genesis: Specimens of Stylistic and Structural Analysis* (Assen, Netherlands: Van Gorcum, 1975); Michael Fishbane, *Biblical Text and Texture: A Literary Reading of Selected Texts* (New York: Schocken, 1979).

7. Representative collections of essays include Robert Alter and Frank Kermode, eds., *The Literary Guide to the Bible* (Cambridge, MA: Harvard University Press, 1987); Leland Ryken and Tremper Longman III, eds., *A Complete Literary Guide to the Bible* (Grand Rapids: Zondervan, 1993).

8. Robert Alter, *The Art of Biblical Poetry* (New York: Basic Books, 1983); James Kugel, *The Idea of Biblical Poetry: Parallelism and Its History* (New Haven: Yale University Press, 1981).

Biblical narrative benefited from this literary turn. Many studies zeroed in on Genesis and Samuel, soon recognized as the most literarily sophisticated of OT narratives. These books, which had been the subject of diachronic analysis for over a century, now were examined from the perspective of literary coherence. For instance, gaps within the text of Genesis that were once considered indications of clumsy editing of previously existing sources were now thought to be productive of meaning, with the narrative inviting the reader to fill in the gaps. Although Alter did not reject the composite nature of the biblical text, he and others felt that the final form of the text had a literary coherence often ignored by a historical approach.

One cannot be dogmatic about why Alter's work generated approval among many biblical scholars.[9] Perhaps it was felt that historical-critical approaches to biblical narrative had come to an impasse. Perhaps there was a sense that, even though acknowledging a history of composition, it was useful to consider its final form. Or maybe scholars simply found close readings of texts, mindful of the conventions of their producers, led to illuminating and compelling results. Alter paid little if any attention to theory, choosing instead to concentrate on practice. Theory asks meta questions about whether and how a text generates meaning; practice exposits the text.

Alter's practice arose out of a certain understanding of how literature works and how it is to be read. His close reading practice resonates with Russian formalism and Anglo-American New Criticism, which was developed in the 1920s and beyond. These movements insisted that reading needed to focus on the text and its conventions rather than, as previous generations of literary scholars held, on the biography of the author. Indeed, one of the most well-known doctrines of formalism, put forward by William Wimsatt and Monroe Beardsley, is the danger of the "intentional fallacy."[10] They warned against reading as if one could actually get into the author's mind. Like the formalists, Alter and others kept their attention on the text.

Once biblical scholars turned to their colleagues in literary fields for insight into the text, they discovered literary theory and developments in theory and practice that were newer than the kind of close reading offered by formalists. Soon, for instance, scholars adopted structuralist theories and applied them to the study of biblical texts. Structuralism arose from the thought of the linguist Ferdinand de Saussure (1857–1913).[11] Saussure described language in terms of signs composed of two parts, a signifier and a signified. The signifier is, say, a word that points toward the signifier, which is a concept of something. The signifier "dog," for instance, evokes the concept of a certain domesticated mammal that has four

9. James Kugel, "On the Bible and Literary Criticism," *Proof* 1 (1981): 99–104.

10. W. K. Wimsatt Jr. and M. Beardsley, "The Intentional Fallacy," in *The Verbal Icon: Studies in the Meaning of Poetry* (Lexington: University of Kentucky Press, 1954), 3–18.

11. Ferdinand de Saussure, *Course in General Linguistics*, ed. C. Bally and A. Sechehaye (New York: McGraw-Hill, 1959).

legs, claws, a good sense of smell, and barks. Significantly, Saussure points to the arbitrary nature of the relationship between a signifier and the signified. There is nothing necessary about the relationship between the word "dog" and the concept of a dog, since other languages have different words (e.g., *Hund*, *chien*, *keleb* in German, French, and Hebrew, respectively). Though arbitrary, agreement within a language group allows for communication. Later poststructuralist thinkers made much of this arbitrary relationship.

Another important structuralist distinction is between *langue*, the grammatical/syntactical rules of a language, and *parole*, the actual sentences produced by these linguistic conventions. To be competent in a language, one must know not every actual sentence but the *langue* that produces the *parole*.

After Saussure, literary scholars applied these linguistic concepts to literature. These classical structuralist thinkers speak of a grammar of literature; to be a competent reader, one must know the conventions (the *langue*: genre, plot structures, a story's manipulation through a narrator of time and space, etc.) to be able to read specific texts (*parole*). Structuralism was a quasi-scientific approach to literature that focused on the text and its conventions. Early structuralist thinkers include Vladmir Propp,[12] A. J. Greimas,[13] Claude Levi-Strauss,[14] Tzvetan Todorov,[15] Gerald Genette,[16] and the early Roland Barthes, whose essay titled "The Death of the Author" indicates the continued focus on the text to the neglect of authorial intention.[17]

Daniel Patte, a NT scholar who works within structuralist theory, admits that "structural exegetical studies are often unduly theoretical and methodological, and use a quite technical vocabulary."[18] His description is particularly true for studies inspired by Propp, Greimas, and Levi-Strauss. This obscurantist tendency is illustrated in Robert Polzin's study of Job, which reduces its message to a quasi-mathematical formula.[19] Structuralist narratology, in the line of Todorov and Genette, has had a more enduring legacy in its influence on the actual analysis of narratives as well as on present-day postclassical narratologists.

12. Vladmir Propp, *Morphology of the Folktale*, 2nd ed. (Austin: Texas University Press, 1968).

13. A. J. Greimas, *Structural Semantics: An Attempt at a Method* (Lincoln: University of Nebraska Press, 1966).

14. Claude Levi-Strauss, "The Structural Study of Myth," in *Myth*, ed. Thomas A. Sebeok (Bloomington: Indiana University Press, 1958).

15. Tzvetan Todorov, *The Fantastic: A Structural Approach to a Literary Genre* (Ithaca, NY: Cornell University Press, 1981).

16. Gerald Genette, *Narrative Discourse: An Essay in Method* (Ithaca, NY: Cornell University Press, 1980).

17. Roland Barthes, "The Death of the Author," in *Image/Music/Text*, trans. Stephen Heath (New York: Hill & Wang, 1977), 142–48.

18. Daniel Patte, "Structural Criticism," in *To Each Its Own Meaning: An Introduction to Biblical Criticisms and Their Application*, ed. Steve L. McKenzie and Stephen R. Haynes (Louisville: Westminster John Knox, 1999), 186.

19. Robert M. Polzin, *Biblical Structuralism: Method and Subjectivity in the Study of Ancient Texts*, SemeiaSup (Philadelphia: Fortress; Missoula, MT: Scholars Press, 1977), 75.

As the name implies, poststructuralism emerged from structuralism. Starting in the 1980s, the former exerted a major influence of debated benefit on biblical hermeneutics, particularly in the form of deconstruction. In the area of comparative literature, the origins of deconstruction are found in the thought of Jacques Derrida.[20] He exploited the idea of the arbitrary relationship between a signifier and what it signified to argue that there was unending slippage between the two, resulting in meaning always being deferred and never achieved. Since no absolute signifier can assure communication, Derrida declared determinate meaning unachievable. The idea that signs function by difference and always defer meaning led to the neologism *différance*. Deconstructive analysis involves no exposition as such but rather an uncovering of a text's aporia, a literary blackhole indicating interpretive undecidability. Much of Derrida's interaction with texts, whether literary or texts of his critics, involved punning and playing with the words of the text.

As applied to biblical texts, the results were sometimes simplistic. For instance, Peter Miscall finds an irreconcilable conflict in the David-and-Goliath story between the idea that God would win the victory for David and the fact that he used his sling. Rather than seeing this story as illustrating human agency *and* divine sovereignty, Miscall concludes that the story turned in on itself.[21]

Many took a deconstructive approach to the OT during this time, but no one more intelligently than David Clines. In one essay, he describes the task of the professional biblical scholar as that of a "bespoke tailor." The client buys cloth and then asks the tailor to cut it according to the client's specifications. Since, Clines believes, the text has no determinant meaning, the person paid to interpret the text (an academic or clergy) should cut the textual cloth according to the expectations of the paying customer.[22] He illustrates his approach in his three-volume Job commentary. The commentary provides an excellent traditional historical-critical/grammatical interpretation of the book. He explains that he wrote the commentary in this way because that was what the series and its audience expected. He goes on to say that, if he wanted to, he could have written from a feminist, Marxist, or even vegetarian perspective.[23]

Deconstruction, both inside and outside biblical scholarship, was the rage until the turn of the century. Starting about the turn of the millennium, such playful approaches to the text pretty much disappeared. By 2007, Robert Alter

20. Jacques Derrida, *Of Grammatology* (Baltimore: Johns Hopkins University Press, 1976).

21. Peter J. Miscall, *The Workings of Old Testament Narrative* (Philadelphia: Fortress, 1983), 57–83.

22. David J. A. Clines, "A World Established on Water (Psalm 24): Reader-Response, Deconstruction, and Bespoke Interpretation," in *The New Literary Criticism and the Hebrew Bible*, ed. J. C. Exum and D. J. A. Clines, JSOTSup 143 (Sheffield: Sheffield Academic, 1993), 79–90.

23. David J. A. Clines, *Job 1–20*, WBC (Dallas: Word, 1989), xlvii–lvi.

could say, "Who reads Paul de Man today? Derrida is on his way to becoming a dinosaur, and even Roland Barthes, once the *dernier cri* of literature studies, is looking increasingly dated."[24]

Sara Upstone suggests that a couple of factors brought deconstruction into disfavor.[25] First, critics of deconstruction felt that to argue that a text has no determinate meaning is inherently dangerous. To put it another way, if the text has no determinate meaning, then why not confer a fascist interpretation, or allow for one? (The revelation that a leading deconstructionist, Paul de Man, had suppressed information about his youthful fascist writing career was damaging to deconstruction.) Second, there was 9/11. How could deconstruction come to grips with horrific evil that resulted in the death of thousands?

In spite of recent attempts to reinvigorate this type of poststructuralist thought and defend it against the charge of interpretive anarchy, the field has largely left deconstruction behind.[26] That said, deconstruction is not the only approach that goes by the name poststructuralist. We now turn our attention to ideological approaches, prefacing our exploration by speaking more broadly of reader-response approaches. While ideological approaches are not all alike, all are instances of reader-response.

Whereas formalism and structuralism moved attention away from the author to the text for the construction of meaning, reader-response theorists drew attention to the role of the reader in the interpretive process. Three theorists in particular had an influence on biblical studies; their views are similar in focusing on the reader but slightly different from each other. Wolfgang Iser argues that the reader generates the meaning of a text but, importantly, believes that the text itself constrains interpretation. The practical effect is that the reader has to justify understanding from the text itself. Still, the text has "gaps," leaving it incomplete until filled by the reader.[27] Hans-Robert Jauss holds similar views. His influence on biblical studies is most felt in the development of *Rezeptionsgeschichte*, which asserts the importance of the history of the interpretation of biblical texts.[28] Finally, Stanley Fish differs from Iser's and Jauss's opinion that the text constrains interpretation, though he later came to emphasize the importance of "interpretive communities" as incubators of a text's meaning.[29] The influence of reader-response theories, and particularly *Rezeptionsgeschichte*, may be seen

24. Robert Alter, "Response," *Proof* 27 (2007): 368.

25. Sara Upstone, *Literary Theory: A Complete Introduction* (London: John Murray Learning, 2017), 226–32.

26. In NT studies, see Michal Beth Dinkler, *Literary Theory and the New Testament*, AYBRL (New Haven: Yale University Press, 2019), 103–36.

27. Wolfgang Iser, *The Act of Reading: A Theory of Aesthetic Response* (London: Routledge & Kegan Paul, 1978).

28. Hans-Robert Jauss, *Toward an Aesthetic of Reception*, trans. Timothy Bahti, Theory and History of Literature 2 (Minneapolis: University of Minnesota Press, 1982).

29. Stanley Fish, *Is There a Text in This Class? The Authority of Interpretive Communities* (Cambridge, MA: Harvard University Press, 1980).

in the projects that highlight what in English is called the history of reception of biblical texts.[30]

Reader-response theory and poststructuralism, however, have their largest imprint in various forms of ideological interpretation. Ideological readings are literary approaches to the Bible and grow out of literary theory, but they are also significantly impacted by other academic disciplines, including anthropology, sociology, and more. As with reader-response theory, ideological readings sometimes allow the text to constrain interpretation. At other times, practitioners read the text "against the grain," counter to the ideology of the text itself. We might also see these ideological interpretive approaches as growing out of the types of interpretive communities described by Fish.

Space does not permit detailed development of the plethora of current ideological readings, which includes feminist, Marxist, postcolonial, queer, and ecocritical approaches, but several of these are dealt with in more detail elsewhere in this volume. The names of these schools of thought indicate the perspectives from which biblical texts are being read. Feminist scholarship offers new interpretations of a wide range of texts when read through a lens that promotes woman-friendly texts and critiques patriarchal ones. Queer interpretation highlights texts that might be LGBTQ+ friendly and seeks to undermine those that have been used to discourage same-sex practice, while also arguing for new interpretations of other texts from that perspective. Postcolonial interpretation undermines texts that might be used or have been used for one group to dominate another. Some ecocritical studies endorse biblical texts that are planet and animal friendly; others critique interpretations that lead to mistreatment of the environment. Marxist interpretation begins with the understanding that texts themselves are bound up with economic, political, and social forces.

The underlying motivation of ideological interpretation is the awareness that the production of literature, as well as the development and practice of literary theory, has largely been the work of white, economically well-off, heteronormal males, at least in the West. Thus, literature and literary criticism, which often operate as if they are expressing universal values, are actually supportive of patriarchy and various forms of privilege. Regarding the goal of feminist interpretation, Robyn Warhol, a leading literary critic, puts it this way: "A feminist narrative critic will implicitly or explicitly evaluate a text according to its relation to patriarchy: the important question about a text's value is whether on the whole it operates to support patriarchal social and cultural arrangements or subverts them."[31]

30. E.g., the Blackwell Bible Commentary series or the *Encyclopedia of the Bible and Its Reception*. See Brennan W. Breed, *Nomadic Text: A Theory of Biblical Reception Theory* (Bloomington: Indiana University Press, 2014).

31. Robyn Warhol, "Narrative Values, Aesthetic Values," in *Narrative Theory: Core Concepts and Critical Debates*, ed. David Herman et al., Theory and Interpretation of Narrative (Columbus: Ohio State University Press, 2012), 165.

The other ideological approaches are suspicious of other types of assumptions in the text and in interpretation. Marxist interpretation asks questions of a socioeconomic type, typically against capitalism and in support of the oppressed classes.[32] Queer interpretation examines the assumption of heterosexuality in a text, and so forth. More recently, ideological interpreters, who often work in isolation from one another, have recognized a common cause. Warhol, again from a feminist perspective, gives voice to an intersectional approach to literature when she says: "In the wake of the third-wave critique of white-liberal feminism and in opposition to the postfeminist assumptions that prevail in the US mainstream, 'feminism' denotes the conviction that dominant culture and society are organized to the disadvantage of everyone who does not fit a white, masculine, middle- or upper-class, Euro-American, not-yet-disabled, heterosexual norm."[33]

Finally, I briefly mention New Historicism, whose emergence is most often associated with Stephen Greenblatt.[34] Often presented as a perspective rather than a method or theory, the central premise is that literature has a historical context and history is a literary construction. This view is reacting to formalism (New Criticism), which wants to study the text without context, and historicism, which aspires to the recovery of historical facts by a neutral interpreter.

The lines between a literary (fictional) text and a historical one are, in this perspective, blurred. New Historicism is poststructural in its belief that a stable, coherent historical narrative is unachievable. Since history is unstable, it is best treated in small chunks or anecdotes. Such anecdotes try to capture lived experience—not like a short story, but rather as something more eccentric that would again destabilize our understanding of history. An anecdote arises from the close study of a literary fragment, which reveals something about the culture in which it is embedded.[35] Another feature that characterizes New Historicism in contrast to the Old is that New Historicism understands the subjective nature of our knowledge of the past, whereas the Enlightenment perspective of Old Historicism argues for an objective knowledge.[36]

32. Roland Boer, *Marxist Criticism of the Bible* (London: Sheffield Academic, 2003).

33. Warhol, "A Feminist Approach to Narrative," in Herman et al., *Narrative Theory*, 9.

34. The term "New Historicism" was first used in Stephen Greenblatt, *Renaissance Self-Fashioning: From More to Shakespeare* (Chicago: University of Chicago Press, 1980).

35. John Drakakis and Monika Fludernick, "Introduction: Beyond New Historicism?," *Poetics Today* 35, no. 4 (2014): 495–513.

36. New Historicist treatments include Harold C. Washington, "Violence and the Construction of Gender in the Hebrew Bible: A New Historicist Perspective," *BibInt* 5, no. 4 (1997): 324–63; Yvonne Sherwood, "Rocking the Boat: Jonah and the New Historicism," *BibInt* 5, no. 4 (1997): 364–402.

Literary Approaches Today

Literary Theory

Literary theory asks how texts produce meaning, which also raises the question of the goal of interpretation. As biblical scholars engaged literary theory in the last decades of the twentieth century, they encountered various answers to the question of the locus of literary meaning.

We begin by describing the act of literary communication, which at its most simple begins with an author who writes a text for readers. The most natural understanding of this process would be that interpreters read the text to hear the author's voice. In other words, the meaning of the text is located in the author's intention. Such was the goal of interpretation at least from the end of the nineteenth century through the mid-twentieth century, when readers began a move away from the author to the text itself. Earlier we remarked on the "intentional fallacy." However, the "intentional fallacy" was never intended to dismiss the importance of the author; rather, it sought to correct problems with using the author's biography to try to get into the author's mind.[37]

Even so, the schools of literary theory that followed formalism ignored the role of the author in the production of meaning and denigrated the idea that the goal of interpretation was to hear the author's voice. Structuralism continued formalism's text-oriented approach to the point that Barthes could talk about the "death of the author." Reader response theories, including ideological readers, were invested in the idea that readers are active in the construction of meaning, whereas deconstruction denied that there was such a thing as meaning in a text.

The fervor that characterized these discussions in the late twentieth century is no longer evident today in biblical studies. Most biblical scholarship operates as if there is a meaning to the text. The idea of authorial meaning has received important defense from theology as well as literary theory. The works of E. D. Hirsch and Geoffrey Strickland indicate that authorial intention was never completely abandoned, even in literary theory at the end of the twentieth century, but these voices were seen as reactionary.[38] Among narratologists today, it is not uncommon to find literary theorists who critique the anti-intentionalist past of their field. One of the most interesting is David Herman, a postclassical structuralist narratologist influenced by cognitive theory. Herman critiques "anti-intentionalist assumptions" and states that "characterizing narration as a form of communicative

37. Meir Sternberg, *The Poetics of Biblical Narrative: Ideological Literature and the Drama of Reading*, Indiana Studies in Biblical Literature (Bloomington: Indiana University Press, 1987), 7–9.

38. E. D. Hirsch Jr., *Validity in Interpretation* (New Haven: Yale University Press, 1967); Hirsch, *The Aims of Interpretation* (Chicago: Chicago University Press, 1976); Geoffrey Strickland, *Structuralism or Criticism? Thoughts on How We Read* (Cambridge: Cambridge University Press, 1981).

action whose interpretation involves—indeed, requires—ascriptions of reasons for acting is a manifestly intentionalist line of inquiry."[39]

It seems wrong-minded to discount the author or, for that matter, the fact that the text has a meaning generated by the author. Of course, particularly in the case of biblical literature, there is no independent access to the author except through the text. Thus, interpretation should focus on the text and should study conventions, including genre, in order to make hypotheses about the author's intended meaning. Interpreters should also be mindful that they come to the text with questions and issues shaped by their own particular cultural and existential locations. Readers do not create the meaning of the text out of whole cloth, but still their limited perspective may shape that meaning. Self-awareness should lead, not to fear of relativism, but rather to the need to read in community, with similar-thinking individuals as well as with people who are different.

Literary Practice

Literary theory asks how texts construct meaning. Literary practice develops strategies for elucidating that meaning. The literary theories with which biblical scholars have engaged over the past few decades have led to different practices. Some, like deconstruction, seem not to be really interested in elucidating the text, concluding that texts have no stable meaning. Ideological interpretations focus on identifying texts that they find toxic to their ideology and promoting those friendly to it. Reader-response approaches attend to how past and present readers of the text appropriate the text to their own experiences and situations. Formalist and structuralist approaches, which focus on the text, work at understanding literary conventions in order to interpret them. Author-centered approaches that speak of authorial performance rather than authorial psychology are on a practical level also text centered, because the only way to get to the author's intention is through the text.

As mentioned, the literary turn in OT scholarship was initiated by the enthusiasm that Alter generated in 1980. His work is based on the principle that "every culture, even every era in a particular culture, develops distinctive and sometimes intricate codes for telling its stories."[40] In his work on narrative and on poetry, he explores the various ways in which Hebrew writers told their stories and wrote their poems.

In a 2007 retrospective, Steven Weitzman commented on the decline of interest in such work.[41] He was correct that the intense focus on literary approaches evi-

39. David Herman, "Authors, Narrators, Narration," in Herman et al., *Narrative Theory*, 47. For a similar view from a theologian, see Kevin Vanhoozer, *Is There a Meaning in This Text? The Bible, the Reader, and the Morality of Literary Knowledge* (Grand Rapids: Zondervan, 1998).

40. Robert Alter, "How Convention Helps Us Read: The Case of the Bible's Annunciation Type-Scene," *Proof* 3 (1983): 115.

41. Steven Weitzman, "Before and after *The Art of Biblical Narrative*," *Proof* 27 (2007): 191–210.

dent in the last couple decades of the twentieth century was on the wane. Rather, scholars of the HB had begun turning back to historical or diachronic questions.[42]

Nevertheless, there are reasons to push back against Weitzman's evaluation. First, literary analysis continues apace embedded within interpretation. The excitement of a paradigm shift has given way to a more balanced appreciation of the Bible as literature, along with the Bible as history and theology. Second, even historical studies are taking into account the Bible's literary quality.[43]

It may be time for biblical scholarship to reengage the work of their colleagues in literary studies, particularly to refine the tools and categories that we use in the study of biblical texts. Interesting work is being done among postclassical structuralists that portends to have usefulness for the study of biblical narratives. While these tools and categories are developed with the modern novel in mind, the work of scholars like David Herman, James Phelan, and others should be explored.[44]

Genre

Genre is a key literary concept and a good example of how interaction with literary disciplines can refine OT studies. Interactions with genre at the present time again temper Weitzman's claim that biblical scholars today have lost interest in literary issues.

Defined simply, a genre of literature is a collection of similar texts. To use structuralist terms, a genre is part of the *langue* of a literary culture. The particular texts are the *parole*. To be a competent reader, one must understand the *langue*, in this case genre, in order to interpret the *parole*. Genre triggers reading strategy: authors embed signals in a text that cue readers on how to understand their words.

Biblical scholars have long recognized the importance of genre, but for much of the twentieth century, they thought about genre as a sociological tool rather than as a literary category. The thought of Hermann Gunkel, often considered the father of form criticism, reigned supreme within historical criticism.[45] Gunkel applied an understanding of genre to OT texts that was already antiquated by the time Gunkel appropriated it, since his main inspiration came from the folklorists Jacob and Wilhelm Grimm, who were active in the early to mid-1800s.

Gunkel and those who followed him had an idea that genres were pure, with an ideal form. Genres could be recognized by similarities in content, theme, and

42. J. A. Emerton, "An Examination of Some Attempts to Defend the Unity of the Flood Narrative, Part II," *VT* 38, no. 1 (1988): 1–21.

43. David Carr, *Reading the Fractures of Genesis: Historical and Literary Approaches* (Louisville: Westminster John Knox, 1996).

44. Herman et al., *Narrative Theory*.

45. Hermann Gunkel, *The Psalms: A Form-Critical Introduction*, trans. Thomas M. Horner (Philadelphia: Fortress, 1967).

structure. Each genre had one and only one sociological setting in life (*Sitz im Leben*). Gunkel believed that biblical texts were largely the result of accretions to an original pre-literary form. In his conception, genre was a diachronic tool, a way to get behind the literary text to the presumed original oral form. Gunkel operated with a rigid conception of genre that was hierarchical/taxonomic and prescriptive.

During the last few decades of the twentieth century, when biblical studies was in conversation with literary disciplines, OT researchers appropriated a more flexible understanding of genre. Muilenburg,[46] Rolf Knierim,[47] and I[48] (as well as others) all advocated a theory of genre that recognized that genres have fuzzy boundaries and that texts can participate in more than one genre. Furthermore, genres can have more than one setting in life, and it may not be sociological. This view of genre is more in keeping with the insights of genre theorists in literary circles. In a mid-twentieth-century work, René Wellek and Austin Warren talk about genres as institutions, like a church that one joins and then follows its rules.[49] Todorov speaks of genres as codes that readers need to understand in order to decipher a literary text.[50] Roger Abrahams thinks of genres as "patterns of expression."[51] More recently, Katharine Dell and others have talked about how texts within a genre share a family resemblance.[52] No two family members look exactly alike, but certain similarities indicate that they are related.

Perhaps the most helpful and complex analogy is presented by Will Kynes. He likens a genre of texts to a constellation of stars.[53] The same stars can be grouped into different constellations, depending on the viewpoint of the observer. For example, some stars that form the Big Dipper are also part of Ursa Major. Stars can also be grouped together in different categories based on size or brightness. When the analogy is applied to genre, Kynes is careful to point out that this does not lead to relativism. It is possible to mischaracterize texts by suggesting that they participate in an incorrect genre. After all, he says, "any genre grouping is constrained by the actual features of the text."[54]

46. Muilenburg, "Form Criticism and Beyond."

47. Rolf Knierim, "Old Testament Form Criticism Reconsidered," *Int* 27, no. 4 (1973): 435–68.

48. Tremper Longman III, "Form Criticism, Recent Developments in Genre Theory, and the Evangelical," *WTJ* 47, no. 1 (1985): 46–67; Longman, *Fictional Akkadian Autobiography: A Generic and Comparative Study* (Winona Lake, IN: Eisenbrauns, 1991).

49. René Wellek and Austin Warren, *Theory of Literature* (New York: Harcourt Brace Jovanovich, 1965), 226.

50. Todorov, *Fantastic*, 11–12, 37.

51. Roger D. Abrahams, "The Complex Relations of Simple Forms," *Genre* 2, no. 2 (1969), 104–28.

52. Katharine J. Dell, "Deciding the Boundaries of 'Wisdom Literature': Applying the Concept of Family Resemblance," in *Was There a Wisdom Tradition? New Prospects in Israelite Wisdom Studies*, ed. Mark R. Sneed, AIL 23 (Atlanta: Society of Biblical Literature, 2015), 145–60.

53. Will Kynes, *An Obituary for "Wisdom Literature": The Birth, Death, and Intertextual Reintegration of a Biblical Corpus* (Oxford: Oxford University Press, 2019).

54. Kynes, *Obituary*, 139.

Intertextuality

The study of intertextuality of OT texts continues to be a productive avenue of study. As practiced in the field of OT studies, intertextuality is a literary phenomenon. Julia Kristeva, a literary critic, is often credited with starting the discussion in the 1960s. As Kynes describes it, she articulated "the belief that all texts, all of life even, are composed of words that have already been said."[55] Kynes points out how such a view contributes to the death-of-the-author thesis of that era. If a literary text is a pastiche of previous texts, then what significance does an author have? But the theory as developed by Kristeva and applied to literary texts is that the later text resonates with previous texts.

When we speak of intertextuality as a method, we distinguish two main approaches: diachronic and synchronic. The basic difference between the two is that the diachronic approach looks at how later texts allude to, quote, echo, and resonate with earlier texts; the synchronic approach considers two texts in light of each other, unconcerned with their relative dates. Most biblical scholars are comfortable with diachronic intertextuality because the author of the later text would be aware of the earlier text (though there could be a common third text). However, sometimes the relative dates of texts are uncertain, leading to speculation about their relative chronological order and the direction of influence.[56]

Conclusion

The literary study of the OT has been something of a roller-coaster ride over the past forty to fifty years. In the 1980s and early 1990s, many biblical scholars turned their attention to literary theory and analysis after a long century and a half of attention to historical matters. This literary turn required the biblical guild to learn from their scholarly colleagues in comparative literature and English departments. The most notable impact was in the study of biblical narrative. Since poetry is so obviously literary, attention has always been given to the conventions of Hebrew poetry (parallelism, imagery, acrostics, and other secondary poetical devices). The pendulum eventually began to swing back to historical issues starting in the mid-1990s. After the turn of the millennium, debates over literary theory declined and lost the interest of many in the field.

Still, literary and historical (and theological) study of biblical texts can and should work hand in hand. As suggested at the beginning of this essay, the literary approach, while not front and center, is still practiced by many biblical scholars as

55. Will Kynes, "Intertextuality: Method and Theory in Job and Psalm 119:1," in *Biblical Interpretation and Method: Essays in Honor of John Barton*, ed. Katharine J. Dell and Paul M. Joyce (Oxford: Oxford University Press, 2013), 201.

56. For an overview of intertextuality, see John Leonard, "Inner-Biblical Interpretation and Intertextuality," in *Literary Approaches to the Bible*, ed. Douglas Mangum and Douglas Estes, Lexham Methods Series 4 (Bellingham, WA: Lexham, 2017), 97–142.

they write commentaries and other scholarly interpretations. It may be time for biblical scholars to reconnect with their counterparts in literature. New work is being done among postclassical structuralist scholars—particularly among those who study narrative as rhetoric or narrative in the context of cognitive theory—that holds promise for further insight into the working of Hebrew stories.[57]

57. As represented by Herman, Rabinowitz, and Phelan in Herman et.al., *Narrative Theory*.

28

Migration Studies

C. A. Strine

Migration has always influenced interpretations of the texts known now as the Hebrew Bible (HB). The central role of both the exodus narrative and the so-called Babylonian exile in this anthology means that one can see this reflection happening already within the corpus. Ezekiel, for instance, reflects on the story of the exodus in enigmatic fashion (e.g., Ezek. 20, often known as the *Unheilsgeschichte,* the undoing of salvation history). Likewise, Jeremiah predicts seventy years of captivity for those Judahites forcibly displaced to Babylonia (Jer. 29:10), which motivates Daniel's prayer of lamentation and repentance in which he pleads for the Lord to return the people to Judah (Dan. 9). Far more recently, migration was influential during the rise of historical-critical scholarship. Julius Wellhausen, for instance, constructs his categories for reading the HB around a period that ends "with the Babylonian exile as certainly as it begins with the exodus from Egypt."[1]

To contextualize the role of migration in HB studies, I first review some key scholarly developments since the 1960s. Next follows a discussion of the ways migration currently appears in study of the HB through five foci. This essay concludes by imagining how this hermeneutical approach may develop in the coming decades.

1. Julius Wellhausen, *Prolegomena to the History of Ancient Israel*, trans. J. Sutherland Black and W. Robertson Smith (Charleston, SC: Bibliobazaar, 1885), 16.

Where Have We Come From?

One could touch on a large number of books and articles from the past fifty years to contextualize current work. For brevity, three noteworthy contributions (from the 1960s, 1970s, and 1980s) are featured here, with brief reflection on how each work anticipates a wider trend in more recent scholarship.

Historical-critical scholarship reigned in the 1960s. Scholars of this period were synthesizing the findings of the prior century, especially concerning the importance of the so-called exilic period. Peter Ackroyd's *Exile and Restoration* represents this stream of thinking.[2] Ackroyd synthesizes his own ideas gathered from a study of the Minor Prophets with more prominent findings on the exile drawn from Isaiah and Jeremiah, among other texts. The resulting two-part framework continues to dominate much scholarship on the HB.

Ackroyd's dominant idea is front and center in the title of his work: the experience of Jerusalem's destruction and the forced displacement of so many people to Babylonia created a paradigm in which this history of defeat requires an acceptance of responsibility. This must call forth "not merely a repentant attitude . . . because the disaster is not simply judgment . . . but also a stage within the working out of a larger purpose."[3] That purpose is restoration, so that "the more effectively the disaster is appreciated, the more evident it becomes that only in divine action can there be hope."[4] If the bipartite exile-and-restoration paradigm sounds familiar, it is because Ackroyd's formulation so deeply imbedded itself in the study of the HB that it appears in almost every introductory Bible course.

Ackroyd sets three further insights on this foundation, each of which anticipates later scholarly work. First, Ackroyd argues that this schema allows for a new controlling narrative to blossom from the sixth century onward: a new exodus. Appearing in confessional statements in Jeremiah (i.e., 16:14–15; 23:7–8) and the imagery of Deutero-Isaiah, the idea of a new exodus becomes "the central element in the faith as now re-experienced," one that "is an act of mercy, a restoration brought about by the willingness of God to have his people again in their own land."[5] Second, Ackroyd observes that this hope is delayed beyond its original term of seventy years, with Dan. 9 extending the seventy years between the exile and restoration into a period of 490 years. This is hardly new—rabbinic interpreters noted it—but Ackroyd observes how this approach to the "exile came to be of paramount importance, a great divide between the earlier and later stages" so that "only those who had gone through the exile—whether actually or spiritually—could be thought of as belonging."[6] Experience of exile rises to the level of an

2. Peter R. Ackroyd, *Exile and Restoration: A Study of Hebrew Thought of the Sixth Century BC*, OTL (London: SCM, 1968).

3. Ackroyd, *Exile and Restoration*, 234.

4. Ackroyd, *Exile and Restoration*, 234.

5. Ackroyd, *Exile and Restoration*, 239.

6. Ackroyd, *Exile and Restoration*, 243.

identity marker, a definitional aspect of belonging to those whom God calls God's own. This insight exerts influence not only on a great deal of HB scholarship but also on NT scholarship in the way the Gospels construct their depictions of Jesus of Nazareth as promised messiah.[7] Third, with this governing role for exile and restoration in mind, Ackroyd speculates on the way this experience of involuntary migration might have shaped texts seemingly as far afield as Jonah and Job.[8]

In both its synthesis of historical-critical scholarship and methodological instincts, Ackroyd anticipated future developments, some of which appear in the next section. And yet, it would take some thirty years for this process of development to begin in earnest.

Meanwhile, as the 1970s came to a close, a crucial contribution was made, not from biblical studies but from Assyriology. In 1979 Bustenay Oded published *Mass Deportations and Deportees in the Neo-Assyrian Empire*, offering a systematic evaluation of how the dominant power in the ANE from the tenth century BCE to the seventh employed forced displacement as "the most important means of its domination of other peoples, with far-reaching political, demographic and cultural consequences."[9]

Oded uses royal annals, administrative and legal texts, onomastic evidence, and iconographic remains to estimate how many people the Assyrians forcibly displaced. He estimates that over 150 state-directed displacements impacted more than 1.2 million people. This remains an influential attempt to reconstruct the imperial program of displacement, though scholars have justifiably challenged Oded's estimates.[10] Even if one disregards this numerical estimate, Oded's analysis of the program's contours marked an immense step forward in understanding how imperial powers employed the threat and reality of forced displacement in the ANE.

Oded observed that "the deportation of men together with their families" was a way "to prevent deportees from escaping to their homeland" and improved "the prospects of the deportees settling down and striking root in the new place."[11] This incentivized the forcibly displaced to contribute positively to Assyrian society, which supported their aim to build new settlements and strengthen Assyrian society. It may also explain why some involuntary migrant groups dissolved into Assyrian culture, functionally becoming "Assyrian" over a few generations and subsequently disappearing from history as identifiable groups.

7. See, e.g., the treatment of the theme in N. T. Wright's Christian Origins and the Question of God series. The best place to start may be Wright's *Jesus and the Victory of God*, Christian Origins and the Question of God 2 (Minneapolis: Fortress, 1996).

8. Ackroyd, *Exile and Restoration*, 244–45.

9. Bustenay Oded, *Mass Deportations and Deportees in the Neo-Assyrian Empire* (Wiesbaden: Ludwig Reichert, 1979), 2.

10. For an updated treatment, see Katsuji Sano, *Die Deportationspraxis in neuassyrischer Zeit*, AOAT 466 (Münster: Ugarit, 2020).

11. Oded, *Mass Deportations*, 24–25.

Oded also highlighted the role of two-way deportations, wherein people were brought from the frontiers of the empire to its heartland, while those causing issues within the heartland were removed to the frontier. Yet Oded demonstrates, largely from the iconographic evidence, that most forcibly displaced persons were not treated as dangerous prisoners but given a modicum of freedom and material support both during their journey to Assyria and at least initially upon arrival.

Oded culminates his analysis by offering seven reasons the Assyrians undertook these displacements. Reasons range from punishment for rebellion to military conscription but include Oded's influential argument that these people were selected for their skilled labor that they could bring to the massive building programs occurring in the urban centers at the heartland of this expanding empire. To support this urban growth, others were taken for their agricultural skill, which enabled them to increase the amount of arable land to ensure the economic stability and food security of the imperial elite.[12] Oded's work reveals how much can be gleaned from material from the Neo-Assyrian Empire, the society that bequeathed the greatest amount of textual and iconographic material for reconstructing the social and political context for the forced displacements depicted in the HB.

The epistemological developments of the 1970s created fertile ground for the development of new hermeneutical approaches in biblical studies. Though feminist readings, new literary approaches, and postcolonial exegesis outpaced work on migration, this began to change in the 1980s. The catalyst here was a new discipline outside the purview of biblical studies or even ancient history. Dawn Chatty explains how refugee studies coalesced around concerns for influencing policy in the 1980s, then emerged as an academic discipline with the creation of the Refugee Studies Centre in Oxford in 1982.[13] Elizabeth Colson observes that the discipline quickly reached a tipping point, having "acquired an ethnographic base sufficiently large so that we ought to be able to generalize about likely consequences of forced uprooting and resettlement."[14]

It is hardly a coincidence that a scholar based in Oxford soon thereafter applied insights from refugee studies to the HB. Daniel Smith (later Smith-Christopher) developed new questions for investigating the HB based on this contemporary sociological research, resulting in his 1989 volume *Religion of the Landless*.[15] In one sense, the book is a sibling to Ackroyd's *Exile and Restoration*, covering the same time frame and texts. In another sense, it is a child of Ackroyd, with a methodological underpinning from the next generation of scholarship. No longer

12. Oded, *Mass Deportations*, 54–74.

13. Dawn Chatty, "Anthropology and Forced Migration," in *The Oxford Handbook of Refugee and Forced Migration Studies*, ed. Elena Fiddian-Qasmiyeh et al. (Oxford: Oxford University Press, 2014), 77–80.

14. Elizabeth Colson, "Forced Migration and the Anthropological Response," *Journal of Refugee Studies* 16, no. 1 (2003): 3.

15. Daniel L. Smith, *The Religion of the Landless: The Social Context of the Babylonian Exile* (Bloomington, IN: Meyer-Stone, 1989).

is the exile Daniel a figure who offers a step along the way to restoration; now he is a figure of present hope for those in the diaspora. Jeremiah is no longer a pointer toward the promise of future restoration; now the prophet is a model for nonviolent resistance against the imperial overlord.

All this might be encapsulated in Smith-Christopher's view that his work comes from a "fourth-world" perspective, which he characterizes as "those 'migrants' and 'refugees' who choose to live without power, yet as a people."[16] No longer is exile a prelude to restoration, engendering a focus on reclaiming status, autonomy, and power. Now these texts outline how to survive as an involuntary migrant, whatever may come. By engaging with social-scientific research on migration, Smith sees these texts in the HB as manifestos for how to endure, perhaps even thrive, during the disorienting experience of involuntary migration.[17]

Where Are We Now?

Although it took time, in the period since 1990, migration studies has expanded into nearly every area of HB studies. Initially the focus remained on the so-called exilic period of the sixth century BCE, but with greater interdisciplinarity. This topic is, therefore, addressed first. Scholarship expanded quickly, and the other four areas overview that territory.

The Sixth Century BCE

Engagement with the social-scientific study of migration generally, and refugee studies more narrowly, gained influence among scholars through the 1990s and early 2000s, epitomized by Smith-Christopher's contribution. The approach came into the foreground in 2011 with John Ahn's *Exile as Forced Migrations*.[18] Ahn thrust ideas into scholarly dialogue from the cutting edge of refugee studies, such as development-induced displacement and internally displaced persons. Ahn demonstrated ways the study of migration offered new categories for analyzing ancient migration. The core of his work employs a schema that shows how subsequent generations of migrants process and respond to the experience differently. Ahn uses this schema to guide his exegesis of Ps. 137 (first-generation involuntary migrants), Jer. 29 (the 1.5 generation), Isa. 43 (second generation), and Num. 32 (third generation), revealing responses that mirror those of contemporary migrants of similar profile.

Ahn also questions whether "exile" accurately describes the sixth-century experience or whether more targeted language reflecting recent scholarship on

16. Smith, *Religion of the Landless*, 9.

17. Smith-Christopher revisits many of these questions in Daniel Smith-Christopher, *A Biblical Theology of Exile*, OBT (Minneapolis: Fortress, 2002).

18. John J. Ahn, *Exile as Forced Migrations: A Sociological, Literary, and Theological Approach on the Displacement and Resettlement of the Southern Kingdom of Judah*, BZAW 417 (Berlin: De Gruyter, 2011).

deportations and displacement should be used.[19] It is now commonplace to use the term "forced migration" rather than "exile." Indeed, the shift in nomenclature can be seen in the titles of some relevant volumes about the period: *The Prophets Speak on Forced Migrations*[20] and *Interpreting Exile: Displacement and Deportation in Biblical and Modern Contexts*.[21]

Work expanded quickly beyond Ahn's focus, largely on economic issues. One fruitful area has been the analysis of differences between Jeremiah and Ezekiel, two texts concentrated on the sixth century that share many features and yet depart sharply on their ideas about how involuntary migrants in Babylonia should live. A special issue of *Hebrew Bible and Ancient Israel* on Jeremiah, Ezekiel, and the social-scientific study of involuntary migration addressed the topic.[22] In that issue, I ask whether the term "exile" remains a legitimate summary of the diverse experiences of sixth-century BCE migration depicted in the HB. I conclude negatively, like Ahn, but also argue that there is now language even better than "forced migration" to distinguish the divergent ways hosts and migrants experience these events. I do this by highlighting clear references to at least three displaced communities: those forcibly displaced to the city of Babylon (Jer. 29), those settled in Babylonia's rural areas (Ezek. 1–3), and those forced to migrate within Judah in the wake of Jerusalem's destruction. This view is expanded and developed by C. L. Crouch in *Israel and Judah Redefined*.[23]

These arguments build upon important new texts from Assyriology that offer substantially better sociopolitical context for Jeremiah and Ezekiel. Texts from āl-Yāhūdu, ālu šam Našar, and the archive of Zababa-šar-uṣur, known together as the āl-Yāhūdu corpus, have recently appeared.[24] They go beyond what Oded had available for his reconstruction and have enabled advances on his analysis.

19. "Displacement" is the preferred term among social scientists, since "deportation" has connections to border regimes, the need for legal documentation, and associations with people labeled "illegal immigrants," itself an immensely problematic term. See John Ahn, "Exile," in *Dictionary of the Old Testament: Prophets*, ed. Mark J. Boda and J. Gordon McConville (Grand Rapids: IVP Academic, 2013), 198, for comments on the topic.

20. Mark Boda et al., eds., *The Prophets Speak on Forced Migration*, AIL 21 (Atlanta: SBL Press, 2015).

21. Brad E. Kelle, Frank Ritchel Ames, and Jacob L. Wright, eds., *Interpreting Exile: Displacement and Deportation in Biblical and Modern Contexts*, AIL 10 (Atlanta: Society of Biblical Literature, 2011). Also note John J. Ahn and Jill Middlemas, eds., *By the Irrigation Canals of Babylon: Approaches to the Study of the Exile*, LHBOTS 526 (London: T&T Clark, 2012).

22. C. L. Crouch and C. A. Strine, eds., "Jeremiah, Ezekiel, and the Social Scientific Study of Involuntary Migration," *HeBAI* 7, no. 3 (2018).

23. C. L. Crouch, *Israel and Judah Redefined: Migration, Trauma, and Empire in the Sixth Century BCE* (Cambridge: Cambridge University Press, 2021).

24. On the provenance and features of the corpus, see Tero Alstola, *Judeans in Babylonia: A Study of Deportees in the Sixth and Fifth Centuries BCE*, CHANE 109 (Leiden: Brill, 2020), 37–46. For a collection of the published texts, see Laurie E. Pearce and Cornelia Wunsch, *Documents of Judean Exiles and West Semites in Babylonia in the Collection of David Sofer*, CUSAS 28 (Bethesda, MD: CDL, 2014).

Laurie Pearce observes that within these texts one perceives "an urban-rural divide . . . among the Judeans from the inception of the exile"[25] in which a "physical distance separated the urban Judean elite situated in Babylon from a segment of the population relocated in the countryside."[26] Communities in these rural locations lived as "groups of 'ethnically' homogenous state dependents, concentrated in a town named for their place of origin,"[27] such as the "town of the Judeans" and shortly thereafter "Judahtown." They were either indentured to work on state-organized building projects or compelled to farm state-provided lands,[28] which they maintained in order to pay a substantial amount of rent and tax, thereby enriching the imperial apparatus of Babylonia.[29] Pearce's urban-rural divide points to a distinct form of involuntary migration in which formerly elite, cosmopolitan people ended up in camp-like settings, isolated from the host population and opportunities to engage with them. This maps well onto evidence from Ezekiel and contrasts with Jeremiah.[30] It indicates that the āl-Yāhūdu corpus may hold further insights on the migrations of the sixth century BCE.

Eric Trinka has invoked other ideas about mobility and explored the figure of Jeremiah as a "religiously motivated nonmover," someone who due to religious convictions refuses to migrate even when all circumstances encourage that decision.[31] His work shows how yet further categories can illuminate the lives of those who remain in Judah during the sixth century. This area of study, unraveling the myth of the empty land,[32] is surely a frontier where further work will occur.

25. Laurie Pearce, "Continuity and Normality in Sources Relating to the Judean Exile," *HeBAI* 3, no. 2 (2014): 179.

26. Pearce, "Continuity and Normality," 180.

27. Laurie E. Pearce, "'Judean': A Special Status in Neo-Babylonian and Achemenid Babylonia?," in *Judah and the Judeans in the Achaemenid Period: Negotiating Identity in an International Context*, ed. Oded Lipschits, Gary N. Knoppers, and Manfred Oeming (Winona Lake, IN: Eisenbrauns, 2014), 271; cf. Cornelia Wunsch, "Glimpses on the Lives of Deportees in Rural Babylonia," in *Arameans, Chaldeans, and Arabs in Babylonia and Palestine in the First Millennium B.C.*, ed. Angelika Berlejung and Michael P. Streck, Leipziger altorientalische Studien 3 (Wiesbaden: Harrassowitz, 2013), 248–49; F. Rachel Magdalene and Cornelia Wunsch, "Slavery between Judah and Babylon: The Exilic Experience," in *Slaves and Households in the Near East*, ed. Laura Culbertson, OIS 7 (Chicago: Oriental Institute of the University of Chicago, 2011), 127.

28. Oded, *Mass Deportations*, 98–99; cf. Michael Jursa, "On Aspects of Taxation in Achaemenid Babylon: New Evidence from Borsippa," in *Organisation des pouvoirs et contacts culturels dans les pays de l'empire Achéménide*, ed. Pierre Briant and Michel Chauveau, Persika 14 (Paris: de Boccard, 2009), 239; Magdalene and Wunsch, "Slavery," 126–28.

29. Wunsch, "Glimpses on the Lives," 25–27. See a similar analysis in Alstola, *Judeans in Babylonia*, 252–76.

30. See Crouch and Strine, "Jeremiah, Ezekiel."

31. Eric Trinka, "'If You Will Only Remain in This Land': Migration Decision-Making and Jeremiah as a Religiously Motivated Nonmover," *CBQ* 80, no. 4 (2018): 580–96.

32. The phrase is well known through the title of Hans Barstad, *The Myth of the Empty Land: A Study in the History and Archaeology of Judah during the "Exilic" Period*, Symbolae Osloensis Fasc. Suppl. 28 (Oslo: Scandinavian University Press, 1996), though it grew out of a

Intersections with Trauma and Postcolonial Studies

Biblical scholars have applied postcolonial theory and trauma studies too. This work ranges far beyond the sixth century BCE, but the so-called "exilic period" has been a particular focus. David Carr claims that trauma motivated the writing of many texts in the HB. His volume *Holy Resilience* has a chapter on "Jerusalem's Destruction and Babylonian Exile," with other chapters on many texts he thinks were written during this period. Carr compares the experience of these ancient Judahite communities to contemporary Palestinians in occupied territories.[33] His work helpfully illustrates that attending to migration need not preclude productive engagement with other strands of interpretation, but actually promotes such interaction.

Louis Stulman and Hyun Chul Paul Kim likewise demonstrate how trauma studies and migration enhance one another. Their *You Are My People* takes this approach to the book of Ezekiel, which they interpret as both "disaster literature" and "survival literature." Stulman and Kim contend that "forced resettlement exacts an enormous toll on Ezekiel's implied audience; it results in profound sadness, vulnerability, fear, and a protracted sense of disconnection to self, community, the world, and God."[34] This produces a text "fraught with overt signs of danger as well as covert subnarratives of trauma."[35] Stulman and Kim identify this elsewhere, remarking that "it is no coincidence Second Isaiah repeatedly uses the language and metaphor of the wilderness," which "captures the austere experience of forced deportation and internment."[36]

Postcolonial interpretation has also enhanced work foregrounding migration. One can see this in the writing of Smith-Christopher. He reads Jer. 27–29 as advocating nonviolent resistance against the Babylonian Empire among involuntary migrants.[37] Isaiah's suffering servant suggests to Smith-Christopher a diaspora hero that cannot be "properly understood apart from its exilic roots in a captive, powerless, 'low status' minority and the hope and resistance that the existence of the hero as social type persistently encourages."[38] Daniel is a forcibly

---

collected effort among historians, including Barstad, Thomas Thompson, Niels Lemche, and Philip Davies. See a different approach, building on the recognition of activity in Judah during the sixth century, in Dalit Rom-Shiloni, *Exclusive Inclusivity: Identity Conflicts between the Exiles and the People Who Remained (6th–5th Centuries BCE)*, LHBOTS 543 (London: Bloomsbury, 2013).

33. David M. Carr, *The Formation of the Hebrew Bible: A New Reconstruction* (Oxford: Oxford University Press, 2011), 225–303 (quote on 253). Carr references Julie Peteet, *Landscape of Hope and Despair: Palestinian Refugee Camps* (Philadelphia: University of Pennsylvania Press, 2005).

34. Louis Stulman and Hyun Chul Paul Kim, *You Are My People: An Introduction to the Prophetic Literature* (Nashville: Abingdon, 2010), 153.

35. Stulman and Kim, *You Are My People*, 153.

36. Stulman and Kim, *You Are My People*, 58.

37. Smith, *Religion of the Landless*, 132–37.

38. Smith, *Religion of the Landless*, 170.

displaced "wisdom warrior," who "defeats his enemies by means of wisdom,"[39] not violence.

I explore this dynamic in Ezekiel, arguing that the experience of forced displacement motivates a sustained polemic against Babylonian imperial hegemony. In *Sworn Enemies*, I maintain that Ezekiel contains a "hidden transcript," a concept borrowed from the work of James C. Scott to explain how subaltern communities resist imperial powers.[40] Their status as involuntary migrants under Babylonian rule prevented Ezekiel from openly expressing animosity for Judah's captors. Rather, a series of veiled images and coded language expresses anger and encourages resistance,[41] to the extent of even reimagining the Babylonian creation narrative in Ezekiel's vision of a return to Jerusalem (Ezek. 40–48).[42]

Return Migration

Speaking of return, Ezra-Nehemiah and Chronicles address just this concern. In the past, these two texts featured in studies of the accuracy of names and numbers of returnees and their connections to the political elites of the Persian Empire, but Smith-Christopher once again catalyzed change here. In *Religion of the Landless*, he explores how Haggai and Ezra-Nehemiah were expressions of "group solidarity and survival of minorities" generated by living through forced displacement.[43] The exclusivism of these texts operates as a "mechanism for survival during the Exile and led to conflicts after the return to Palestine."[44] Smith-Christopher foregrounds the concept of ethnicity, contending that this category illuminates the ways people who are forcibly displaced from their ancestral land seek to preserve their communal identity under duress.

Katherine Southwood puts this approach into dialogue with the best social-scientific work on return migration, carrying Smith-Christopher's ideas to their logical conclusion. Southwood explores the role of language preservation among migrants, explaining how this commitment motivates Neh. 13's concern for Hebrew language. "Those whose language is not an exilic ossification of the language preserved by those who went into exile and their children," she shows, "are not permitted to self-ascribe any claims to legitimate Yahwism."[45] Southwood later expands her analysis to the mixed-marriage "crisis" in Ezra 9–10. She argues that

39. Smith-Christopher, *Biblical Theology of Exile*, 186.

40. C. A. Strine, *Sworn Enemies: The Divine Oath, the Book of Ezekiel, and the Polemics of Exile*, BZAW 436 (Berlin: De Gruyter, 2013).

41. Strine, *Sworn Enemies*, 228–68.

42. C. A. Strine, "*Chaoskampf* against Empire: YHWH's Battle against Gog (Ezek 38–39) as Resistance Literature," in *Divination, Politics, and Ancient Near Eastern Empires*, ed. Alan Lenzi and Jonathan Stökl, ANEM 7 (Atlanta: Society of Biblical Literature, 2014), 87–108.

43. Smith, *Religion of the Landless*, 197.

44. Smith, *Religion of the Landless*, 197.

45. Katherine Southwood, "'And They Could Not Understand Jewish Speech': Language, Ethnicity, and Nehemiah's Intermarriage Crisis," *JTS* 62, no. 1 (2011): 1–19.

the strategies for maintaining group identity upon return to Judah are replications of those that successfully maintained group identity in Babylonia. In short, she concludes that the returning community redeploys those strategies because they are familiar and have succeeded before, regardless of whether they really suit the new context.

Scholars are now recognizing that return migration is relevant for many other texts. I apply it to the patriarch Jacob and King David. Jacob behaves as a return migrant with Esau (Gen. 32–33): Jacob's continued fear of Esau after their reconciliation (Gen. 33:12–20) arises directly from the persistent dishonesty and trickery of Laban, his host when he was a refugee.[46] Esau appears to Jacob as a second Laban, whom Jacob cannot trust even after promises to the contrary, so upon his return to Canaan, he redeploys strategies from his time as a refugee. Likewise, I contend that David's desire to build a house for YHWH, thus making the previously mobile deity sedentary (2 Sam. 7), reflects his experience as an involuntary migrant fleeing Saul, which he now wants to reverse completely.[47]

Origin Stories

Migration studies have also opened new possibilities for the origin stories preserved in the HB. This has taken various forms, from comparative analysis to the application of recent findings from refugee studies.

Guy Darshan compares the two major origin traditions—the migration of an ancestor to a new land (Genesis) and the migration of a group that ends in conquest (the exodus tradition)—to ancient Greek sources.[48] Darshan argues that the Israelites and Greeks, along with several other small kingdoms in the Mediterranean Basin, produced these stories as a result of "cultural exchange" that "familiarized the peoples of the region" with this sort of foundation narrative. Darshan's work highlights just how prevalent migration is among the origin stories of the first millennium BCE.

I explore the ancestral narratives in Genesis (chaps. 12–50) and maintain that they are indelibly linked to the experience of involuntary migration. My initial case is Jacob, who lives as a refugee (Gen. 29:14–32:1) and then as a return migrant.[49] But others also fit a similar pattern: Abraham and Sarah flee

46. C. A. Strine, "Your Name Shall No Longer Be Jacob, but Refugee: Insights into Gen 25:19–33:20 from Involuntary Migration Studies," in *Scripture in Social Discourse: Social Scientific Perspectives on Early Jewish and Christian Writings*, ed. Jessica M. Keady, Todd Klutz, and C. A. Strine (London: T&T Clark, 2018), 59–60; see also Strine, "Migrant Ethics in the Jacob Narrative," in *The Cambridge Companion to the Ethics of the Hebrew Bible*, ed. C. L. Crouch (Cambridge: Cambridge University Press, 2021), 101–16.

47. C. A. Strine, "On the Road Again: King David as Involuntary Migrant," *Open Theology* 7, no. 1 (2021): 407–9.

48. Guy Darshan, "The Origins of the Foundation Stories in the Hebrew Bible and the Ancient Eastern Mediterranean," *JBL* 133, no. 4 (2014): 689–709.

49. Strine, "No Longer," 51–69.

famine (Gen. 12, 20), as do Isaac and Rebekah (Gen. 26); Joseph is a trafficked person, sold into slavery, later reunited with his brothers, who are fleeing a famine (Gen. 37–47). I advance a particularly challenging reading for the three matriarch-sister stories in Gen. 12, 20, and 26: these stories evoke evidence that involuntary migrant women frequently must engage in sex work in order to provide for their families among host communities where the male head of household will not be allowed to work.[50] To exegete the Joseph narrative, I deploy a range of insights on trafficked people, involuntary migrants who live in cosmopolitan contexts and integrate with their foreign hosts, and the experience of environmentally induced involuntary migrants.[51] I conclude that Jacob and Joseph offer counterbalancing examples: Jacob exemplifies an immigrant who refuses any form of integration with outsiders; his son Joseph, on the contrary, embodies an attitude of open engagement with outsiders that provides for upward social mobility.[52]

Yet another approach to origin traditions appears in Eric Trinka's *Cultures of Mobility, Migration, and Religion in Ancient Israel and Its World*.[53] Highlighting mobility in religious practice, Trinka attempts to reconstruct early ideas about YHWH. "Biblical authors," he writes, "narrate Israel's history as one in which Yahweh's people come to know who their god is, how he acts, and who they are in relation to him, through migration."[54] He also revisits the questions of "Israel's emergence amid the changing demographic and political landscapes of the Late Bronze and Early Iron Ages"—a way of attempting to address the intensely debated question of whether or not Israel was originally a migrant community from outside the Levant.

Lived Experience of Migration and the Hebrew Bible

In an entirely different approach, scholars consider how the HB's depictions of involuntary migration relate to present lived experience.

Gerald West was one of the first scholars to work in this area. His approach, contextual biblical studies, seeks to read parts of the biblical texts with those who have experienced marginalization in various ways. West has not explicitly engaged with migration in his work, but it is a theme relevant to the largely African communities in which he works.

50. C. A. Strine, "Sister Save Us: The Matriarchs as Breadwinners and Their Threat to Patriarchy," in *Women and Exilic Identity in the Hebrew Bible*, ed. Katherine E. Southwood and Martien A. Halvorson-Taylor, LHBOTS 631 (London: T&T Clark, 2018), 53–66.

51. C. A. Strine, "The Famine in the Land Was Severe: Environmentally Induced Involuntary Migration and the Joseph Narrative (Gen 37–50)," *HS* 60 (2019): 55–69.

52. For this analysis, see C. A. Strine, "Genesis," in *The Oxford Bible Commentary*, ed. Katharine J. Dell and David Lincicum (Oxford: Oxford University Press, forthcoming).

53. Eric M. Trinka, *Cultures of Mobility, Migration, and Religion in Ancient Israel and Its World*, Routledge Studies in the Biblical World (London: Routledge, 2022).

54. Trinka, *Cultures of Mobility*, 176.

In *Christians at the Border*, M. Daniel Carroll R. engages more explicitly with the lived experience of migration, particularly Latin Americans migrating to the United States. He examines the biblical background to the sociopolitical issues around the lives of those coming to America.[55] Carroll R. presents a theological argument for offering a more generous welcome than has typically been given to those entering the United States, certainly in the past twenty years.

Similarly, Gregory Cuéllar's *Voices of Marginality* discusses ways the Judahite experience of forced displacement in the sixth century BCE parallels the experience of Mexican migrants under the imperial hegemony of the United States of America in the twentieth and twenty-first centuries.[56] Cuéllar zeroes in on the role of return in Second Isaiah, comparing it to Mexican immigrant *corridos* (ballads) that aim "to recover a distinct Mexican immigrant identity amid various forces of imperial domination."[57]

Outside the anglophone sphere, Johann Hinrich Claussen explores forty stories from the Bible about migration through photos and personal accounts. His perspective as a German, conscious of his postwar and post-Holocaust context, creates a fresh and often testing approach to the topic. *Das Buch der Flucht* asks the reader and viewer of its photos to think afresh about both the biblical text and the topic of migration.[58]

I offer yet another approach through working with artist and art therapist Emilie Taylor. Together, we facilitate responses to the stories of migration in the ancestral narrative from six people seeking asylum or living as refugees. Their insights, especially on Jacob, open up new vistas. The creative combination of contextual reading (drawing on the approach of Gerald West) and art therapy (contributed by Taylor) offers a "close engagement with the book of Genesis," demonstrating "beyond all doubt that involuntary migrants have an enormous amount to teach those without that experience about how to read [Genesis]."[59] "The image," I conclude, "has the capacity to initiate a chain reaction that invigorates our exegesis" and leads to fresh insights on both ancient texts and contemporary life.

55. M. Daniel Carroll R., *Christians at the Border: Immigration, the Church, and the Bible* (Grand Rapids: Baker Academic, 2008). See his updated thoughts in Carroll R., *The Bible and Borders: Hearing God's Word on Immigration* (Grand Rapids: Brazos, 2020). Mark W. Hamilton offers a similar analysis, minus the personal experience and focus on Latin America, in *Jesus, King of Strangers: What the Bible Really Says about Migration* (Grand Rapids: Eerdmans, 2019). Despite its title, Hamilton's focus is largely the HB/OT.

56. Gregory Lee Cuéllar, *Voices of Marginality: Exile and Return in Second Isaiah 40–55 and the Mexican Immigrant Experience*, AUS 7/271 (New York: Peter Lang, 2008).

57. Cuéllar, *Voices of Marginality*, 82.

58. Johann Hinrich Claussen, *Das Buch der Flucht: Die Bibel in 40 Stationen* (Munich: Beck, 2018).

59. C. A. Strine, "The Catalytic Image: Migration, Image, and Exegetical Imagination in the Jacob Narrative (Genesis 25–33)," in *Image as Theology: The Power of Art in Shaping Christian Thought, Devotion, and Imagination*, ed. C. A. Strine, Mark McInroy, and Alexis Torrance (Turnhout, Belgium: Brepols, 2021), 125–41, quote on 139.

Mark and Luke Glanville have attempted to integrate their expertise in the HB and international relations to offer a theological rationale for addressing policy issues related to migration. In *Refuge Reimagined*, they argue for an ethic of kinship, in which people are called to extend a version of welcome and hospitality to nonrelatives by treating them as if they are related.[60] The book engages more directly with the political realities of the current migration regime than many others and suggests ways that biblical scholarship can and should engage with those working in and with governments on this issue.

Where Are We Going?

This essay has shown how the social-scientific study of migration shapes the work of HB scholars. What has occurred over the past thirty years is the first phase of a process, and more is yet to come. But where is the field going? One can never know entirely, but some areas of development seem inevitable.

The social-scientific study of migration is still in its relative infancy and will continue to grow and offer findings that can be applied to the HB in various ways. No doubt some of its current findings will be revised, and thus biblical scholars will need to revisit their own application of that research. Scholars must aim for a virtuous interdisciplinary circle, a spiral, returning to familiar territory but further forward than where they began.

Attention should extend to an ever-widening set of texts in the HB and those outside it. The Deuteronomistic History is ripe for investigation, highlighted by work on David's rise.[61] The exodus tradition requires more analysis,[62] and important elements of the legal material within this tradition, along with comparative texts from Mesopotamia, remain underexplored.[63] Studies on less-obvious texts such as Esther, Lamentations, and even Job seem to be needed. All this work will test the limits of what interdisciplinary engagement with the social-scientific study of migration can produce.

Perhaps above all, the academic community should work toward the inclusion of more diverse voices, and the training and publishing of more scholars with different perspectives and varied lived experiences of migration must be encouraged. This expansion should also go far beyond the ivory towers. Further innovative collaborations with those who have experienced involuntary migration will give

60. Mark R. Glanville and Luke Glanville, *Refuge Reimagined: Biblical Kinship in Global Politics* (Downers Grove, IL: IVP Academic, 2021.

61. Strine, "On the Road Again."

62. E.g., Tchavadar S. Hadjiev, "'I Have Become a Stranger in a Foreign Land': Reading the Exodus Narrative as the Villain," *BibInt* 26, nos. 4–5 (2018): 515–27.

63. For examples of what is possible, see Mark Awabdy, *Immigrants and Innovative Law: Deuteronomy's Theological and Social Vision for the* גר, FAT 2/67 (Tübingen: Mohr Siebeck, 2014); and Mark Glanville, *Adopting the Stranger as Kindred in Deuteronomy* (Atlanta: SBL Press, 2018).

voice to the embodied knowledge resident among those with lived experience but no advanced training in biblical studies.

Like Abraham in Gen. 13, scholarship will in this way lift its eyes to the metaphorical four points of the scholarly compass, exploring all the possible ways the study of migration might reveal a varied and bountiful landscape.

29

Reading in Context

Bo H. Lim

Today, "contextual biblical interpretation" typically refers to interpreting the Bible in light of one's own social cultural location. Admittedly, the terminology has its weaknesses, since oftentimes it is associated with nontraditional forms of biblical scholarship, and therefore historical, literary, and theological interpretation are not labeled "contextual" even though they reflect particular social cultural contexts. Conversely, some may assume that because womanist, African, and Native American studies are considered "contextual," or given another unhelpful title, "global interpretation," they do not make historical, literary, and theological claims. Thankfully, scholars of the dominant culture in academic biblical studies have also begun to reflect on how their own social cultural location affects their work. For example, Daniel Patte has examined the contextual nature of male, European-American, and critical scholarship.[1]

Hopefully, better terminology will prevail over time, but for now I am content to continue to use the verbiage of "contextual biblical interpretation." This essay focuses on the HB, but it will also engage NT scholars and theologians, since oftentimes the discussion pertains to biblical and theological studies as a whole. Given that other essays in this volume address the topics of gender, sex, and

1. Daniel Patte, "Acknowledging the Contextual Character of Male, European-American Critical Exegesis: An Androcritical Perspective," in *Readings from This Place*, vol. 1, *Social Location and Biblical Interpretation in the United States*, ed. Fernando R. Segovia and Mary Ann Tolbert (Minneapolis: Fortress, 1995), 35–55; Patte, "The Guarded Personal Voice of a Male European-American Biblical Scholar," in *The Personal Voice in Biblical Interpretation*, ed. Ingrid Rosa Kitzberger (London: Routledge, 1998), 12–24.

ideology, I focus my attention on multicultural readings of the Bible, recognizing that there is much overlap with those other categories. Surveys of the various forms of contextual interpretation and their key figures and works already exist and need not be repeated here.[2]

I write as an Asian-American OT professor and ordained clergyperson teaching in a Christian liberal arts college and seminary in Seattle, Washington. These social and institutional contexts impact my scholarly interests and commitments. This essay would no doubt look different if it were written by someone with vocational aims and an institutional context different from mine. For example, someone teaching Christian ministers in Asia would engage interpretive questions different from someone teaching the Bible as part of a liberal arts curriculum to undergraduates in the United States.[3] However, global concerns are local concerns for cities like Seattle, where immigrants from the Global South and East have settled in the past several decades.[4] My students include African American and African, fourth-generation Japanese and recent immigrants from Asia, documented and undocumented Latinos and Latinas, Native Americans, Roman Catholics, Pentecostals, Eastern Orthodox, evangelicals, Muslims, Buddhists, atheists, and so forth. Although not all readers will share my context, I believe that the concerns I raise will align with many who engage biblical scholarship as an academic discipline and ecclesial resource. The purpose of this essay is to catalog broad trends in OT studies today so that students and teachers might better understand OT scholarship and make informed decisions for ongoing study. My aim is to provide some *context* to understand contextual biblical interpretation.

After the Collapse of History and the Text

When Ronald Clements's *A Century of Old Testament Study* was published in 1976, the geographical and cultural center of OT study was in Northern Europe. The Germans Julius Wellhausen and Hermann Gunkel, the Scotsman William Robertson Smith, and the Norwegian Sigmund Mowinckel were its towering figures. Clements recognizes the increasing influence of the American Brevard Childs, so perhaps the United States could also be included. He observes that early on, "history was elevated to become the queen of the Old Testament sciences,"[5] and throughout the mid- to late twentieth century, OT studies vacillated between

2. See, e.g., Michael J. Gorman, ed., *Scripture and Its Interpretation: A Global Ecumenical Introduction to the Bible* (Grand Rapids: Baker Academic, 2017).

3. See the recent work by Jerry Hwang, *Contextualization and the Old Testament: Between Asian and Western Perspectives*, Logia (Carlisle, UK: Langham Global Library, 2022).

4. See Mark R. Gornik, *Word Made Global: Stories of African Christianity in New York City* (Grand Rapids: Eerdmans, 2011). Gornik observes 150 African churches in New York City alone.

5. Ronald E. Clements, *A Century of Old Testament Study* (Cambridge: Lutterworth, 1976), 175.

historical and religious interests. As Clements looked to the future, he assumed that new methods would arise but that history and theology would continue to remain its foci. Whatever its future, he believed, "there can be no going back to seek a return to some kind of theological, or hermeneutical, approach which ignores the demands of proper historical method. The roots of the OT in real history reach down too far for this to be possible."[6]

As the title of Leo Perdue's 1994 work *The Collapse of History: Reconstructing Old Testament Theology* indicates, Clements was clearly mistaken.[7] While historical concerns continue to remain important to OT scholars, one might characterize the years following Clements's work as a movement away from history to "text as text." In Perdue's work, literary approaches dominate OT theology, but for the two reader-oriented methodologies he mentions, the readers remained largely Euro-American. While he acknowledges feminist interpretation and liberation theology's roots in Latin America, Perdue focuses on the Marxist interpretation of the US scholar Norman Gottwald.

When Perdue reworked his own book only a decade later, he maintained his thesis that historical studies had been decentered in OT study, but he shifted his attention away from text to readers.[8] This more recent work expands its attention to diverse and marginalized readers: entire chapters are devoted to liberation theology and ethnic readings, feminist interpretation, *mujerista* and womanist theologies, Jewish readings, postmodernism, and postcolonial interpretation. These theologies, which Perdue labeled "radical theology" in his 1994 work, were considered mainstream only a decade later. The Latino American Fernando Segovia and African American Vincent Wimbush are introduced as representative of liberation perspectives, and Gottwald is nowhere to be found. The 2005 edition of Perdue's book is not a simple revision of the previous work; it is an altogether complete re-narration of the trajectory of OT theology. Perdue's work focuses on OT theology, so it is not representative of the entire discipline of OT studies, but the trends he observes pertain broadly to biblical studies. After 2000, introductory works on biblical studies or interpretation almost uniformly include chapters on contextual interpretation.

Old Testament studies continue to prioritize historical and literary matters, but the sea change has been the increasing focus on diverse and marginalized readers. Clements understood the social, religious, and political influences in OT scholarship, so the recognition that one's cultural context impacts biblical study is not new. Significant scholarship on contextual interpretation has been taking place since the 1970s, but it was largely ignored by the wider academy until the last two decades. The question that has most dramatically shaped

6. Clements, *Century of Old Testament Study*, 179.

7. Leo G. Perdue, *The Collapse of History: Reconstructing Old Testament Theology*, OBT (Minneapolis: Fortress, 1994).

8. Leo G. Perdue, *Reconstructing Old Testament Theology: After the Collapse of History*, OBT (Minneapolis: Fortress, 2005).

biblical scholarship concerns not what the Bible is or how one reads it but rather *who* reads the Bible. It is not that white male Germans, Brits, Norwegians, or Americans are no longer the majority; it is that their *interests* no longer dominate OT study. Given the diverse readership of the Bible, those in the majority realize that they can no longer focus solely on Euro-American perspectives and concerns.

The Impact of Interdisciplinary Approaches on Diverse Readings

Whereas historical interests dominated biblical scholarship in the twentieth century, whether by the promoters of historical criticism or its detractors, today its hegemonic influence has certainly been chastened. Its current role within the discipline is contested, and its future standing remains to be determined. In addition to the diverse interpretive approaches Perdue described, a proliferation of studies have come from scholars who do not read the Bible for its theology or its history. One need only look at the program units of the Society of Biblical Literature to recognize the vast array of topics and approaches to the study of the Bible. For example, the annual meeting in 2022 included "Minoritized Criticism and Biblical Interpretation," "Cognitive Science Approaches to the Biblical World," "The Use, Influence, and Impact of the Bible," "Bible and Film," and "Biblical Literature and the Hermeneutics of Trauma."

Because of Christianity's ongoing influence in the West, for much of the twentieth century a consensus existed among those inside and outside the church on the importance of biblical history. In such an environment, it was not difficult to establish biblical studies as a legitimate academic discipline. For biblical studies to maintain its scholarly standing, it had to meet the standards and interests of academic institutions in the manner of other disciplines. It needed to be open to public scrutiny, avoid sectarianism, and value analytical innovation. In the West, where no one could dispute that the Bible was a cultural classic, universities offered courses on "The Bible as Literature" or "New Testament History," where students examined the Bible as they might study Shakespeare or as a way to better understand first-century Palestine.

The modern university in the twentieth and twenty-first centuries has both contributed to and been impacted by dramatic social-cultural changes. In the twentieth century, scholars shifted their focus away from the historical and philological study of ancient texts to a plethora of other critical engagements. In addition to engaging newer literary methods, students read Homer through the lens of psychology, or Shakespeare through the lens of postcolonial criticism. In the 1960s and 1970s, two social movements and trends transformed higher education in the United States. Michael Harris observes, "The student counterculture movement expanded student access and participation and the idea of what fields higher education should study. Enrollment among female and minority students continued to increase, as well as the need to include gender and ethnic studies as part of an expanding curriculum."[9] Diversity and the inclusion of marginalized perspectives in pedagogy, curricula, texts, faculty, and scholarship became a priority for all universities, academic societies, and academic publishers. These trends are no different in Christian higher education and are especially pertinent to seminaries, given the growing diversity of the church.[10]

With the study of the Bible housed in the academy, it was inevitable that the same intellectual and cultural shifts across higher education would occur within biblical scholarship. The modern university's concerns extend not only to diverse populations but also to engagement between academic disciplines. In interdisciplinary study, the Bible may not be granted a privileged place of authority, and the reader's contemporary context may be viewed as important as the Bible's ancient context. The topics, approaches, and interests in vogue in biblical scholarship mirror those of the wider academy, and therefore the Bible is studied not only from a nonreligious perspective but also for its nonreligious impact, both positive and negative. Religion departments are often housed within a college of arts and sciences, and therefore the context for reading the Bible may not be worship, prayer, and evangelism but rather be political discourse, the arts, popular culture, and psychology. Postcolonial biblical interpretation researches how the Bible is used to extend the political, economic, and religious interests of nations and people groups. Reception history, which traces the nonreligious impact of the Bible, has blossomed into a robust discipline. Both postcolonial interpretation and reception history possess their own reference works, commentaries, monograph series, and journals. Scholars are cataloging the history of biblical interpretation in countries across the globe, and so all peoples who have been impacted by the Bible may soon possess a record of the heritage of biblical interpretation in their own culture.

Given that *who* reads the Bible dramatically impacts the direction and research interests of biblical studies, with populations in the Global South and East far exceeding those of the North and West and with ongoing migration, globalization, and cultural diversity increasing in Western countries, contextual biblical scholarship will continue to grow. With the increasing influence of cultural studies on the curricula of Western universities, those who teach in this context may be required to be conversant with methods and disciplines traditionally considered outside the realm of biblical studies. Biblical studies has always been engaged with ancillary disciplines such as ANE studies, classics, Western literature, and Western philosophy, so interdisciplinary study is nothing new. What has changed are the disciplines of engagement. Now biblical scholars are reading the Bible in conversation with not only William Blake and Charles Peirce but also with Toni

9. Michael S. Harris, *Understanding Institutional Diversity in American Higher Education*, ASHE Higher Education Report 39, no. 3 (Hoboken, NJ: Wiley Periodicals, 2013), 32–33.

10. Five out of the seven volumes of the new series Theological Education between the Times (Grand Rapids: Eerdmans) directly address theological education for Christians of color.

Morrison and Frantz Fanon. As long as universities and seminaries value diversity, works in biblical studies will be written for marginalized populations through the use of interdisciplinary methods.

Mapping Contextual Interpretations

For half a century, contextual biblical scholarship existed at the margins, but within the past twenty-five years it has been recognized by mainstream biblical scholarship. It has grown due to social trends in higher education, but the growth of the church in the Global South and East, the growing diversity of the church in the Global West, and the church's increasing concern for marginalized peoples has most dramatically impacted the discipline. This new readership of the Bible was not satisfied with what biblical scholarship had to offer when their concerns were at the periphery, but this is no longer the case.

Because biblical scholarship has been based in the West, its scholarly traditions and canons are shaped by Western interests. Consequently, even the multicultural context and contributions of non-Western figures like Augustine were not explored until recently.[11] Missiologists, not biblical scholars or theologians, were among the few scholars interested in biblical interpretation in non-Western ecclesiastical contexts.

Contextual interpretation is a massive and diverse discipline. Any attempt to summarize it will inevitably be reductionistic and exclude important contributors. I cautiously proceed to do so because presently the field is so fragmented and diffuse that many scholars find the discipline inaccessible. Contextual interpretation is most often categorized according to race, ethnicity, or geography. Doing so has its merits, but also its weaknesses. For example, within Black, Chinese, or Latin American interpretation one will find vast divergences in ideological and theological commitments, so the taxonomy may be unhelpful and even misleading.[12] Similarly, any summary of White, Spanish, or North American interpretation would also fail to capture its diversity and provide meaningful coherence. Scholarship's consumers are largely in the West and therefore, whether from the West or not, academics write for the interests of the Western academy. This has sometimes resulted in the misrepresentation of contextual theologies and the failure to recognize the contributions of theologians in the Global South. For example, Simon Chan sharply criticizes academic Asian theology for misrepresenting

11. J. Kameron Carter, *Race: A Theological Account* (New York: Oxford University Press, 2008); Justo L. González, *The Mestizo Augustine: A Theologian between Two Cultures* (Downers Grove, IL: IVP Academic, 2013).

12. E.g., Philip Jenkins excludes Latin American interpretation in his summary of biblical interpretation in the Global South and East because he finds it too diffuse to generalize. See Philip Jenkins, *The New Faces of Christianity: Believing the Bible in the Global South* (New York: Oxford University Press, 2006), ix. The same could be said of Asia and possibly Africa too.

Asian theology, and Daniel Salinas argues that academics' conflation of Latin American theology with liberation theology has led to the erasure of the global impact of Latin American evangelical theology.[13]

Based on my reading of the literature, I have chosen to organize contextual interpretation into two categories: *liberationist* and *intercultural*.[14] Though not mutually exclusive categories—more like the overlapping circles of a Venn diagram rather than existing as separate columns—they are distinguished by their differing interpretive goals in, or between, various cultures. The goal of liberationist interpretation is ethical, seeking to empower and advocate for marginalized peoples and decenter the power of hegemonic forces.[15] The goal of intercultural interpretation is educational; it is to read the Bible in indigenous forms and across cultures, while often seeking to affirm common theological commitments. Both liberationist and intercultural readings of the Bible are practiced by communities in the Global South and East, possess important cultural and intellectual ties and influences with the West, and have impacted mainstream biblical scholarship. By the term "liberation," I include Latin American liberation theology but also postcolonial, African and African American, Latino/a American, Asian and Asian American, aboriginal, feminist, womanist, *mujerista*, queer, and other forms of interpretation that "see the Bible as a key resource in their emancipatory struggles."[16] These are the forms of interpretation that Perdue views as the future of OT theology and that largely dominate academic contextual biblical studies in North America and Europe.

The goal of intercultural interpretation is to gain greater insight into the Bible and other cultures through cross-cultural engagement by reading the Bible "through a particular *conceptual frame of reference* derived from the worldview and sociocultural context of a particular cultural community."[17] It is certainly not at odds with the goals of liberation interpretation, but it may not prioritize them in the same manner. This form of interpretation is found in missiology, intercultural studies, the study of World Christianity, Majority World theology, non-Western

13. Simon Chan, *Grassroots Asian Theology: Thinking the Faith from the Ground Up* (Downers Grove, IL: InterVarsity, 2014), 7; Daniel Salinas, *Latin American Evangelical Theology in the 1970's: The Golden Decade* (Leiden: Brill, 2009), 12–13.

14. According to Stephen B. Bevan's taxonomy of contextual theologies, his anthropological and praxis models would fall under Liberationist, and his translation, synthetic, transcendental, and countercultural models would reside under Intercultural. See Stephen B. Bevans, *Models of Contextual Theology*, rev. and expanded ed. (Maryknoll, NY: Orbis Books, 2002).

15. David Janzen in *The Liberation of Method: The Ethics of Emancipatory Biblical Interpretation* (Minneapolis: Fortress, 2021) proposes that due to the struggles of marginalized readers, biblical studies ought to be judged not on the basis of any method but rather on an ethic of liberation.

16. Janzen, *Liberation of Method*, 2.

17. Justin Ukpong, "Inculturation Hermeneutics: An African Approach to Biblical Interpretation," in *The Bible in a World Context: An Experiment in Contextual Hermeneutics*, ed. Walter Dietrich and Ulrich Luz (Grand Rapids: Eerdmans, 2002), 27 (emphasis original).

Christian scholarship, and missional hermeneutics. Henning Wrogemann subsumes mission studies under the broader term intercultural theology and hermeneutics, since the latter studies Christianity in areas of both growth and decline, engages non-theological issues, and is concerned for intercultural ecumenism.[18] Intercultural interpretation also includes African and African American, Latino/a and Latino/a American, Asian and Asian American, female perspectives, and other forms, in much the same categories as the liberationist models except for theologies that are considered incompatible with its interests. Not surprisingly, this form of interpretation is found more within ecclesial bodies and may not impact the academy in the West to the same extent as liberationist interpretations.

Scholars may write with both liberationist and intercultural aims, since the goals are interrelated and not mutually exclusive. Intercultural education may empower communities for liberation, and both forms of study aim to decenter traditional forms of biblical scholarship.

Liberationist Interpretations

Liberationist interpretations are united by their shared struggle against injustice and oppression of the poor and marginalized and therefore share many common characteristics, but the methodologies and foci vary, depending on the needs and concerns of particular social-cultural groups. Context is foundational to the interpretive task, so great attention is typically given to the author's social-cultural background. Since texts are never understood in abstraction, readers also ought to be examined in similar terms, as Fernando Segovia argues:

> I believe that the time has come to introduce the real reader, the flesh-and-blood reader, fully and explicitly, into the theory and practice of biblical criticism; to acknowledge that no reading, informed or uninformed, takes place in a social vacuum or desert; to allow fully for contextualization, for culture and experience, not only with regard to texts but also with regard to readers of texts, with a view of all readings as constructs proceeding from, dependent upon, and addressing a particular social location, however circumscribed.[19]

Segovia's definition is nothing short of a redefinition and reorientation of the discipline of biblical studies. Now sociology, psychology, cultural studies, gender studies, postcolonial studies, ethnic studies, and other disciplines would not only be applied to the Bible but also to authors, readers, and interpretive traditions. The *Ideologiekritik* of the Marxist Antonio Gramsci undergirds the method of many liberationist scholars: "The starting-point of critical elaboration is the

18. Henning Wrogemann, *Intercultural Theology*, vol. 1, *Intercultural Hermeneutics*, trans. Karl E. Böhmer (Downers Grove, IL: IVP Academic, 2016), 15–27.

19. Fernando R. Segovia, "Toward a Hermeneutics of Diaspora: A Hermeneutics of Otherness and Engagement," in Segovia and Tolbert, *Social Location*, 57.

consciousness of what one really is, and is 'knowing thyself' as a product of the historical process to date, which has deposited in you an infinity of traces, without leaving an inventory."[20] The liberationist scholar attempts to catalog and expose this "infinity of traces," and critical studies are required tools because these traces were deposited "without leaving an inventory." Many liberationist scholars received their academic training in Europe, so rather than being grassroots theologians, R. S. Sugirtharajah describes them as "transplanted or uprooted professionals who return to their community after learning their craft and Western theories of oppression."[21]

Liberationist interpreters lie on a continuum between those who criticize the Bible for its oppressive ideologies and those who believe that the message of liberation is intrinsic to the Bible. The oft-cited words of Nancy Ambrose, grandmother of Howard Thurman, demonstrate the need for marginalized groups to critique biblical teaching:

> During the days of slavery, the master's minister would occasionally hold services for the slaves. Old man McGhee was so mean that he would not let a Negro minister preach to his slaves. Always the white minister used as his text something from Paul. At least three or four times a year he used as a text: "Slaves, be obedient to them that are your masters, as unto Christ." Then he would go on to show how it was God's will that we were slaves, and how, if we were good and happy slaves, God would bless us. I promised my Maker that if I ever learned to read and if freedom ever came, I would not read that part of the Bible.[22]

This quote demonstrates that even for those who have been oppressed by the words of the Bible, it continues to be viewed as possessing special significance or authority. The *Dalit Bible Commentary* is based on the correspondence between two parallel narratives of enslavement and liberation, one Judeo-Christian and the other Indic, but it also probes the question "How is it that interpreters, practitioners and propagators of Christian Scripture in India engaged in their task, without confronting the caste system and its practice in India, though they were aware of the slavery-liberation story in the Bible?"[23] Liberationist scholars observe that among the poor and marginalized, the Bible remains one of the few accessible resources for social change. If the Bible is respected across all strata of

20. Antonio Gramsci, *Selections from the Prison Notebooks of Antonio Gramsci*, ed. Quintin Hoare and Geoffrey Nowell-Smith (New York: International Publishers, 1973), 324, as quoted in Robert P. Carroll, "An Infinity of Traces: On Making an Inventory of Our Ideological Holdings; An Introduction to *Ideologiekritik* in Biblical Studies," *JNSL* 21, no. 2 (1995): 25.

21. R. S. Sugirtharajah, *Asian Biblical Hermeneutics and Postcolonialism: Contesting the Interpretations* (Maryknoll, NY: Orbis Books, 1998), 129.

22. Howard Thurman, *Jesus and the Disinherited* (Boston: Beacon, 1996), 31.

23. T. K. John, "Two Narratives: Judeo-Christian and Indic Enslavement and Liberation," in *One Volume Dalit Bible Commentary: Old Testament*, ed. James Massey (New Delhi: Centre for Dalit Subaltern Studies, 2015), xxiii.

society, liberative readings of the Bible offer the poor and marginalized a resource to affect social change when they have few other options. Texts focused on the exodus and the exile have often been used for the sake of liberation, but texts such as the conquest narratives and the anti-miscegenation teachings of Ezra-Nehemiah are often found to be problematic.

Liberationist scholars are aware that liberation and revolutionary movements can lead to new regimes that go on to oppress people just as ruthlessly if not more so. For this reason, many scholars seek to be "organic intellectuals" in the manner described by Gramsci: they not only seek to be in solidarity with marginalized peoples but also read the Bible with them so that their scholarship reflects the concerns and interpretations of the oppressed rather than those of elite intellectuals. The dialogical method of reading the Bible with the poor captured in *El Evangelio en Solentiname* by the Nicaraguan priest Ernesto Cardenal would prove to be a model for liberationist contextual interpretation.[24] Other influential forms include African American slave narratives that demonstrate how black slaves, through reading the very Bible of their colonial masters, would resist their oppression and fuel their own emancipation.[25] Institutes for the study of the Bible among the poor would be established where academics did not teach per se, but rather facilitated study of the Bible so that interpretation was an act of the people. In this form of contextual study, the interpretations of "ordinary readers" rather than those of biblical scholars constitute scholarship.[26] Typically this form of interpretation occurs more in the Global South and East, and even though most scholars in Europe and North America may not be facilitating Bible studies among base communities, many still consider solidarity with marginalized people as vital to their hermeneutic. The womanist scholar Renita Weems states, "Like feminist biblical hermeneutics, womanist biblical hermeneutical reflections do not begin with the Bible. Rather, womanist hermeneutics of liberation begin with African American women's will to survive and thrive as human beings and as the female half of a race of people who live a threatened existence within North American borders."[27]

Intercultural Interpretations

Recent studies in reception history continue to make accessible to a wider audience the rich traditions of biblical interpretation from differing contexts, and

24. Ernesto Cardenal, *Love in Practice: The Gospel in Solentiname*, trans. Donald D. Walsh (London: Search, 1977).

25. Emerson B. Powery and Rodney Steven Sadler, *The Genesis of Liberation: Biblical Interpretation in the Antebellum Narratives of the Enslaved* (Louisville: Westminster John Knox, 2016).

26. See Gerald O. West, ed., *Reading Other-Wise: Socially Engaged Biblical Scholars Reading with Their Local Communities*, SemeiaSt 62 (Atlanta: Society of Biblical Literature, 2007).

27. Renita J. Weems, "Re-reading for Liberation: African American Women and the Bible," in *Voices from the Margin: Interpreting the Bible in the Third World*, ed. R. S. Sugirtharajah, 25th anniversary ed. (Maryknoll, NY: Orbis Books, 2016), 24.

various cultures have influenced the field of contextual biblical interpretation. These include interpretations influenced by missionaries. Mapping contextual biblical interpretation involves engaging missiology, intercultural studies, and postcolonial studies. I have already commented on postcolonial studies, so now I address the first two. Bible translation, cross-cultural ministry, and contextual theology are key concerns for missionaries, but their insights rarely impact biblical studies. For some time, missionaries have applied insights from cultural anthropology to compare and contrast what they conceive of as the assumptions between the cultures of the Bible and those of Western and other cultures.[28]

The sea change in contextual biblical interpretation corresponds with the growth of Christians in the Global South and East and Christians of color in the West within the last half century. No longer would Euro-American scholars be at the forefront of contextual biblical interpretation, but Christians of color would write for their own communities. Liberationist scholars sometimes appeal to the growth of Christianity among immigrant populations in the United States and the spread of Christianity in the Global South and East as justification for liberationist interpretive approaches,[29] but the majority of growth is among evangelical and Pentecostal congregations. For example, at the height of liberation theology's popularity in Nicaragua in the 1970s and 1980s, active members of base communities numbered less than 1 percent of the total population.[30] The dominant role of liberationist approaches in academic biblical interpretation represents the interests of Euro-American scholars rather than the majority of the world's poor or Bible readers in the Global South or East.[31]

Philip Jenkins has chronicled the exponential growth of indigenous forms of Christianity in Asia, Latin America, and Africa, and he describes the important role of the Bible within these congregations. He observes that the African and Asian churches show great respect for the authority of the Bible, an appreciation of the OT, an emphasis on supernatural and spiritual realities, and belief in the Bible's relevance for real-world concerns like poverty, famine, oppression, spiritual warfare, and persecution.[32] Jenkins popularizes what Lamin Sanneh and Andrew Walls had been describing for some time. They argue that once the

28. Jacob A. Loewen, *The Bible in Cross-Cultural Perspective* (Pasadena, CA: William Carey Library, 2000).

29. Fernando R. Segovia, "Interpreting beyond Borders: Postcolonial Studies and Diasporic Studies in Biblical Criticism," in *Interpreting beyond Borders*, ed. Fernando R. Segovia, The Bible and Postcolonialism 3 (Sheffield: Sheffield Academic, 2000), 22–23.

30. Phillip Berryman, *Stubborn Hope: Religion, Politics, and Revolution in Central America* (Maryknoll, NY: Orbis Books, 1994), 203; Jean-Pierre Reed, "The Bible, Religious Storytelling, and Revolution: The Case of Solentiname, Nicaragua," *Critical Research on Religion* 5, no. 3 (2017): 235.

31. Marcella María Althaus-Reid, "Gustavo Gutiérrez Goes to Disneyland: Theme Park Theologies and the Discourse of the Popular Theologian in Liberation Theology," in Segovia, *Interpreting beyond Borders*, 36–58.

32. Jenkins, *New Faces of Christianity*.

Bible was translated into the vernacular, it became indigenized and embodied, and subsequent interpretations would reflect the faith of the host culture.[33] The scales have tipped. Since most Christians live outside the West, their indigenous forms of biblical interpretation and theology are no longer marginal but the majority.

Scholars use the word "global" in multiple ways, not always to refer to the global church. In his introductory essay to the *Global Bible Commentary*, Patte appeals to the growth of the global church as warrant for such a work.[34] Yet he also makes clear that the readings follow liberationist and postcolonial methodologies and that the volume serves his pedagogical context, teaching diverse undergraduate and seminary students at Vanderbilt University. Indigenous evangelical scholars have gone on to produce commentaries for the church in Africa, South Asia, and Latin America to meet their own needs. Evangelical and Pentecostal scholars describe their work as representative of "World Christianity" or "Majority World theology," and liberationist scholars describe their writing as addressing "global perspectives" or "global concerns."

In light of these recent developments, studies have been aimed at creating dialogue between Western and non-Western scholars. An early example is *Conflict and Context: Hermeneutics in the Americas*, which published not only the papers presented by North American and Latin American evangelical biblical scholars but also their dialogue over a range of topics.[35] In a more recent volume, scholars from Europe and Africa present different approaches to biblical interpretation followed by respondents to answer the question "What does Africa have to say to Europe and Europe to Africa about the Bible?"[36] The exchange includes both "exegesis" and "actualization"—that is, exploring meanings found within the world of the text as well as the application and recontextualization of those meanings. Another form of contextual scholarship is Europeans or North Americans gathering scholars from Africa, Latin America, and Asia and each presenting their interpretation of the same biblical passage for the sake of comparison and learning between cultures.[37]

By far, the most prolific contextual biblical scholarship from an intercultural perspective is from evangelical Christians in the Global South and East. Much

33. Lamin Sanneh, *Translating the Message: The Missionary Impact on Culture* (Maryknoll, NY: Orbis Books, 1989); Andrew F. Walls, *The Missionary Movement in Christian History: Studies in the Transmission of Faith* (Maryknoll, NY: Orbis Books; Edinburgh: T&T Clark, 1996).

34. Daniel Patte, "Introduction," in *Global Bible Commentary*, ed. Daniel Patte et al. (Nashville: Abingdon, 1994), 34.

35. Mark Lau Branson and C. René Padilla, eds., *Conflict and Context: Hermeneutics in the Americas* (Grand Rapids: Eerdmans, 1986).

36. Hans de Wit, Hans Snoek, and Gerald O. West, "Introduction," in *African and European Readers of the Bible in Dialogue: In Quest of a Shared Meaning*, ed. Hans de Wit and Gerald O. West (Leiden: Brill, 2008), ix.

37. E.g., Walter Dietrich and Ulrich Luz, eds., *The Bible in a World Context: An Experiment in Contextual Hermeneutics* (Grand Rapids: Eerdmans, 2002); Priscilla Pope-Levison and John R. Levison, eds., *Return to Babel: Global Perspectives on the Bible* (Louisville: Westminster John Knox, 1999).

of this research is published by Langham Partnership, a ministry begun by John Stott dedicated to resourcing the majority world church. Thus far seventy-two theological monographs have been published, and one-volume commentaries on the entire Bible have been written for audiences in Africa, South Asia, Eastern Europe, Latin America, and the Middle East. To date, two volumes on OT books have been written in the Africa Bible Commentary Series and fourteen OT volumes in the Asia Bible Commentary series. Works on African biblical hermeneutics, OT biblical interpretation in Asian contexts, Bible translation, preaching, contextual theology, and contextual ethics have been published. Latin American evangelicals have long wrestled with contextual matters of theology and biblical interpretation and have played pivotal roles in shaping the social ethics of global evangelicalism.[38] In North America, evangelical theologians and biblical scholars have referred to these interpretations representative of the Majority World as a critique of both liberal and conservative Western Christianity.[39] Evangelical biblical scholars of color in the West are navigating their bicultural status alongside their transnational ties so their context includes global concerns as well as the struggles of being racial minorities in the West. Several works by these scholars are currently in production, so their theological contribution will only continue to grow.

Conclusion

All forms of contextual interpretation, whether liberationist or intercultural, no longer view biblical interpretation as an objective method to determine historical meanings. Historical criticism, or the historical-grammatical method, has been chastened and sometimes displaced altogether. Rather than striving for critical distance between reader and text throughout the process of exegesis and concluding with reflections on one's own context, contextual interpretation reverses the order. Now interpreters identify, reflect on, and possibly critique their own context as the first step in biblical interpretation. How one reflects on one's context differs based on the goals of interpretation. Liberationist interpreters typically use social-scientific and postcolonial methods to understand their context and then go on to apply these methods to biblical interpretation. Evangelical interpreters in non-Western contexts are increasingly using indigenous contextual theologies and cultural resources to understand themselves as well as interpret the Bible.

38. Sharon E. Heaney, *Contextual Theology for Latin America: Liberation Themes in Evangelical Perspective* (Milton Keynes, UK: Paternoster, 2008); David C. Kirkpatrick, *A Gospel for the Poor: Global Social Christianity and the Latin American Evangelical Left* (Philadelphia: University of Pennsylvania Press, 2019).

39. Gene L. Green, Stephen T. Pardue, and K. K. Yeo, eds., *Majority World Theology: Christian Doctrine in Global Context* (Downers Grove, IL: IVP Academic, 2020); Allen Yeh and Tite Tiénou, eds., *Majority World Theologies: Theologizing from Africa, Asia, Latin America, and the Ends of the Earth* (Pasadena, CA: William Carey, 2018).

30

Social-Scientific Approaches

Matthew J. M. Coomber

Social-scientific approaches to the study of the OT have produced an array of heuristic tools for probing the texts of the Bible in order to draw insights from the social, economic, and psychological realities that shaped them. In addition to developing new insights into texts' origins, social-scientific interpretations can enhance readers' understandings of how OT passages might resonate with the challenges and questions pertinent to the modern world.

John Elliot emphasizes that social-scientific interpretation is not a stand-alone strategy for interpretation but one phase of the exegetical process in which a text's social and cultural dimensions are analyzed through harnessing social-scientific perspectives, theories, and models.[1] The interdisciplinary nature of this approach makes it a particularly dynamic area of study. As theories and models arise, develop, and are discarded within the social sciences, those biblical-interpretive methods to which they are attached must also be revisited, augmented, or let go. Therefore, in addition to staying current in biblical studies, practitioners of social-scientific interpretation must also keep up to date in the social-scientific

1. John Elliot, *What Is Social-Scientific Criticism?*, GBS (Minneapolis: Fortress, 1993), 7. For more overviews, see Thomas Overholt, *Cultural Anthropology and the Old Testament*, GBS (Minneapolis: Fortress, 1992); John W. Rogerson, *Anthropology and the Old Testament*, Growing Points in Theology (Atlanta: John Knox, 1979); M. Daniel Carroll R., David J. A. Clines, and Philip R. Davies, eds., *The Bible in Human Society: Essays in Honour of John Rogerson*, JSOTSup 200 (Sheffield: Sheffield Academic, 1995); John F. A. Sawyer, ed., *The Blackwell Companion to the Bible and Culture* (Oxford: Wiley-Blackwell, 2006).

fields to which their work is connected. While an onerous pursuit, engaging in social-scientific interpretations can hone our interpretive methods, raise new questions pertaining to ancient texts, and offer fresh insights into how the Bible might relate to the lives and concerns of modern readers.

Some Limitations and Hazards

While the social sciences have produced valuable works, their interpretive fruits should not be thought of as evidence. Social-scientific methods of interpretation can create heuristic tools for developing better questions to ask biblical texts, but they do not produce definitive answers. Insights gained from the social sciences—such as expected societal behaviors, common economic cycles, or neurological responses to trauma—offer numerous lenses through which to consider biblical texts, but they do not create evidence. To assume that the ancient Hebrews or their contemporaries would follow societal paths or respond to similar circumstances in ways that are common or expected is to fail to appreciate the uniqueness and diversity of human individuals and groups when faced with challenges and change. Humans are too unpredictable to be tethered to societal or psychological patterns. Therefore, social-scientific methods are most effective when employed for the purpose of developing theories to be tested against extant literary and physical evidence.

When applying the social sciences to biblical studies, neither literary evidence nor archaeological artifacts are disinterested items. Much of the OT originated through oral tradition and, once written, was edited and added to for generations. Each OT text is best thought of as a historical product that was brought into being by a historical society, through a particular kind of individual or set of individuals within that society, and at a particular moment. Failure to consider these sociohistorical complexities opens the door to anachronistic and ethnocentric interpretations. In addition to the dangers that anachronism and ethnocentrism pose by imprinting false images onto the past, Vernon Robbins warns that they rob the Bible's readers of the basic social and cultural meanings that the texts evoke.[2]

Sociological and Anthropological Approaches

Benefits of Sociological and Anthropological Interpretation

Sociological and anthropological approaches to reading the Bible are wide-ranging in both methodology and purpose. To understand current trends in this

2. Vernon K. Robbins, "Social-Scientific Criticism and Literary Studies: Prospects for Cooperation in Biblical Interpretation," in *Modeling Early Christianity: Social-Scientific Studies of the New Testament in Its Context*, ed. Philip F. Esler (New York: Routledge, 1995), 278.

area of social-scientific criticism, an understanding of the roots of both sociological and anthropological approaches is helpful.

As the dawn of the Enlightenment led to new examinations of the natural world, religious systems and ideologies were also reassessed. Julia O'Brien notes that with the advent of scientific challenges to religious accounts of the natural world, social-scientific interpretation was born. An important early figure was Baruch Spinoza, a seventeenth-century Dutch-Jewish rationalist philosopher who recognized scriptural contradictions.[3] His call for empirical approaches to reading the Bible helped pave a path for future sociological interpretation.

Early attempts at anthropological interpretation can be understood through E. E. Evans-Pritchard's three stages of anthropological development, which he divides into the eighteenth to mid-nineteenth centuries, mid-nineteenth to the early twentieth centuries, and the early to mid-twentieth century. The first stage focused on natural systems based on notions of human nature. With a belief that societies follow predictable trajectories of advancement, terms like "natural morality," "natural religion," and "natural jurisprudence" were frequently employed.[4] Unfortunately, these early anthropologists tended to use facts to illustrate or corroborate speculative theories, rather than allowing the facts to speak for themselves. With European society as their benchmark for societal development, racist and xenophobic conclusions were often reached, as illustrated in Lewis Morgan's *Ancient Society: Or, Researches in the Lines of Human Progress from Savagery through Barbarism to Civilization* (1877). The second stage turned to systematic studies of social institutions by harvesting empirical data for comparative analysis. While researchers drew data from numerous societies, Philip Esler and Anselm Hagedorn note that it was often applied in fragmented ways that removed the data from their original contexts.[5] The final stage focused on classifications of societies based on social structures rather than ethnography. Evans-Pritchard calls this separation of anthropology and ethnography, which had been considered synonymous, "a first essential step towards making comparative studies profitable."[6] It was during this period that Julius Wellhausen dated the Prophets earlier than Torah and Louis Wallis explored social stratification and competing interests as factors that shaped OT authorship.[7]

The past few decades have witnessed a flurry of development in sociological and anthropological approaches in OT studies. Perhaps the most significant

3. Julia O'Brien, *Challenging Prophetic Metaphor: Theology and Ideology in the Prophets* (Louisville: Westminster John Knox, 2008), 11–12.

4. E. E. Evans-Pritchard, *Social Anthropology* (London: Cohen & West, 1951), 22–23.

5. Philip F. Esler and Anselm C. Hagedorn, "Social-Scientific Analysis of the Old Testament: A Brief History and Overview," in *Ancient Israel: The Old Testament in Its Social Context*, ed. Philip F. Esler (London: SCM, 2005), 16.

6. Evans-Pritchard, *Social Anthropology*, 40.

7. Julius Wellhausen, *Prolegomena to the History of Israel*, trans. J. Sutherland Black and Allan Menzies (Edinburgh: Adam & Charles Black, 1885), 2–3; Louis Wallis, "Sociological Significance of the Bible," *American Journal of Sociology* 12, no. 4 (1907).

catalyst for this growth has been Norman Gottwald's *The Tribes of Yahweh* (1979), in which he framed Israel's origin story as one of class conflict, culminating in a peasant revolt.[8] Understanding the Pentateuch's primary function as a set of narratives to remind a society of who they were as a people, Gottwald ignited numerous interpretive possibilities. Walter Brueggemann, who considers Gottwald the most important twentieth-century OT scholar in the United States, writes that Gottwald presents YHWH as "inescapably and integrally linked to economic fairness."[9] Gottwald's socioeconomically oriented image of the Hebrew movement and its religious frameworks shaped not only his exegetical works but also his view that the OT's anti-imperial messages continue to be relevant today. This idea is reflected in his 1992 presidential address to the Society of Biblical Literature, which championed social class as an analytic and hermeneutic category of its own.[10] Gottwald's many works over his long career, ending with his passing at age 95, have inspired generations of biblical scholars who continue to engage with his theories and models.

As with any use of the social sciences in biblical studies, the primary benefits of sociological and anthropological interpretations are found in developing new questions to ask of texts and archaeological data. As Hans Gerth and Don Martindale explain in the preface to their translation of Max Weber's *Ancient Judaism*, the value of Weber's sociological perspectives was in how they enabled him to bring new theories and perceptions to old facts.[11] In addition to shedding new light on existing literary and archaeological data, reading the OT through sociological and anthropological lenses can work to dislodge faulty interpretive assumptions that have been passed on for millennia, such as judgments about Eve's guilt in Gen. 3 or Jonah's silence in Jon. 4.[12] Discoveries in the fields of sociology and anthropology also help interpreters to see past paradigms that did not exist in the worlds of the OT, such as the economic systems of capitalism or socialism.

Current Sociological and Anthropological Approaches

Archaeology

Archaeology draws upon numerous anthropological approaches to understand the societies and cultures out of which OT texts arose. Archaeologists have

8. Norman K. Gottwald, *The Tribes of Yahweh: A Sociology of Liberated Israel, 1250–1050 BCE* (Sheffield: Sheffield Academic, 1999), 210–19.

9. Walter Brueggemann, "The Most Important American Old Testament Scholar of the Last Century Is Norman Gottwald," *ChrCent* 139, no. 11 (2022), https://www.christiancentury.org/article/features/most-important-american-old-testament-scholar-last-century-norman-gottwald.

10. Norman K. Gottwald, "Social Class as an Analytic and Hermeneutical Category in Biblical Studies," *JBL* 112, no. 1 (1993): 3–22.

11. Max Weber, *Ancient Judaism* (New York: Free Press, 1952), ix.

12. Gale A. Yee, *Poor Banished Children of Eve: Woman as Evil in the Hebrew Bible* (Minneapolis: Fortress, 2003). Chesung Justin Ryu, "Silence as Resistance: A Postcolonial Reading of the Silence of Jonah in Jonah 4:1–11," *JSOT* 34, no. 2 (2009): 195–218.

effectively applied anthropological data to socioeconomic cycles, gender relations, and the evolution and development of religions and their rituals. These areas of research have been utilized for interpreting excavations of ancient walled communities, temple complexes, processing centers, and rural settlements. Addressing the important role that the social sciences play in archaeology, Philip Davies writes, "Archaeology is a social science: hence the history of ancient *Israels* must be grounded in a social scientific enterprise."[13] Similar to how archaeological sites are composed of layers compiled over different periods of time, Davies argues that OT texts contain strata. Rather than representing a single and datable moment, biblical texts present interpreters with layers that are made up of their times of authorship and subsequent periods of addition and revision.[14] Collaboration between social-scientific analysis and archaeology help to expose those layers to develop a more reliable picture of the social, political, and religious history of each layer.[15] Because of this collaboration, Davies regarded archaeology as more a branch of anthropology than of history.[16]

Among the numerous archaeologists working to better understand sociopolitical aspects of ancient Hebrew societies, Israel Finkelstein is well known both within and outside the academy. He and Neil Asher Silberman published an article drawing on evidence of massive societal changes in late eighth-century Judah to offer insights into the centralization of the Jerusalem cult, motivations for committing the early days of the Davidic dynasty to writing, and the societal effects of economic change.[17] From this and other of Finkelstein's and Silberman's works, much biblical scholarship has been created on ninth- and eighth-century macroeconomics and political life in the region. This later dating of Israel has inspired significant pushback, including the work of Katharina Streit and Felix Höflmayer, which questions dating techniques that have been used in archaeology pertaining to Iron Age II sites.[18]

On the microeconomic level, Cynthia Shafer-Elliot's archaeological findings and interpretations have engaged the social sciences to better understand domestic life in Hebrew communities. Employing ethnoarchaeological approaches to various aspects of daily life, ranging from dietary customs to gender roles, she

13. Philip R. Davies, "Literary-Historical Exegesis as a Social Science," in *Scripture as Social Discourse: Social-Scientific Perspectives on Early Jewish and Christian Writings*, ed. Jessica M. Keady, Todd E. Klutz, and C. A. Strine (New York: T&T Clark, 2018), 29. Davies uses italics and the plural form to emphasize his view that there was not just one ancient Israel as portrayed in the biblical accounts.

14. Davies, "Literary-Historical Exegesis," 33.

15. Davies, "Literary-Historical Exegesis," 34.

16. Davies, "Literary-Historical Exegesis," 31.

17. Israel Finkelstein and Neil Asher Silberman, "Temple and Dynasty: Hezekiah, the Remaking of Judah and the Rise of the Pan-Israelite Ideology," *JSOT* 30, no. 3 (2006): 259–85.

18. Katharina Streit and Felix Höflmayer, "Archaeomagnetism, Radiocarbon Dating, and the Problem of Circular Reasoning in Chronological Debates: A Reply to Stillinger et al. 2016," *NEA* 79, no. 4 (2016): 233–35.

uses Jack Goody's comparative sociological studies on food preparation to offer new insights into Iron Age dietary habits. Assessing variances between cooking techniques and equipment in walled communities and rural settlements, Shafer-Elliot found evidence of higher meat consumption in urban homes. Her work gives readers and interpreters a more nuanced picture of the differences between urban and rural life in ancient Palestine.[19] Carol Meyers,[20] Oded Borowski,[21] Lawrence Stager,[22] and numerous other archaeologists have also employed sociological and anthropological approaches to understanding their findings. In addition to aiding archaeologists, the publications of their findings—ranging from domestic life to economic strategies and defense construction—have inspired scholars from across the field of OT studies.

Study of Ancient Hebrew Societies

Drawing on discoveries made by archaeologists, studies of the legal, political, and economic environments out of which Hebrew Scriptures arose flourished in recent decades. In addition to Norman Gottwald's aforementioned works, Robert Coote and Keith Whitelam, David Hopkins, Ellen Davis, Douglas Knight, Mario Liverani, Lester Grabbe, Walter Houston, Diana Edelman, and C. L. Crouch are but a few of the biblical scholars engaging in anthropological and sociological approaches to understanding the political and economic dynamics that shaped ancient Palestine.[23] Through interpreting archaeological data in light of anthropological and sociological methods and models, much light has been shed on agricultural strategies, modes of political coercion, and

19. Cynthia Shafer-Elliott, *Food in Ancient Judah: Domestic Cooking in the Time of the Hebrew Bible* (London: Acumen, 2013), 73, and 112–13.

20. Carol Meyers, "Terracottas without Texts: Judean Pillar Figurines in Anthropological Perspective," in *To Break Every Yoke: Essays in Honor of Marvin L. Chaney*, ed. Robert B. Coote and Norman K. Gottwald, SWBA 2.3 (Sheffield: Sheffield Phoenix, 2007), 115–30.

21. Oded Borowski, *Daily Life in Biblical Times*, ABS 5 (Atlanta: Society of Biblical Literature, 2003).

22. Lawrence E. Stager, "The Archaeology of the Family in Ancient Israel," *BASOR* 260 (1985): 1–35.

23. Robert B. Coote and Keith W. Whitelam, *The Emergence of Early Israel in Historical Perspective*, SWBA 5 (Sheffield: Almond, 1987); David C. Hopkins, *The Highlands of Canaan: Agricultural Life in the Early Iron Age*, SWBA 3 (Sheffield: Almond, 1985); Ellen F. Davis, *Scripture, Culture, and Agriculture: An Agrarian Reading of the Bible* (Cambridge: Cambridge University Press, 2009); Douglas A. Knight, *Law, Power, and Justice in Ancient Israel*, LAI (Louisville: Westminster John Knox, 2011); Mario Liverani, *Israel's History and the History of Israel*, BibleWorld (New York: Routledge, 2007); Lester L. Grabbe, *Ancient Israel: What Do We Know and How Do We Know It?*, rev. ed. (New York: T&T Clark, 2017); Walter J. Houston, *Contending for Justice: Ideologies and Theologies of Social Justice in the Old Testament* (London: T&T Clark, 2006); Diana Edelman, *The Origins of the "Second" Temple: Persian Imperial Policies and the Rebuilding of Jerusalem*, BibleWorld (New York: Routledge, 2005); C. L. Crouch, *The Making of Israel: Cultural Diversity in the Southern Levant and the Formation of Ethnic Identity in Deuteronomy*, VTSup 162 (Boston: Brill, 2014).

anti-imperial subversion. At times these studies have produced rather contentious conclusions, such as Herman Niemann's late dating of the state of Israel (to the time of King Omri) or proposals questioning Israel's history as a state altogether.[24]

Two members of the Copenhagen School, Philip Davies and Keith Whitelam, published books arguing that the state of ancient Israel is a literary construct rather than a historical political entity.[25] Associated with the so-called minimalist camp (a label given to those who look at biblical evidence with a greater degree of skepticism), Davies and Whitelam argue that the state of Israel was developed to bolster postexilic Jewish communities in their struggles to form collective identity and autonomy. Disillusioned with what he sees as blind acceptance of biblical narratives of Israel's history, Davies writes, "So long as there was 'no reason to doubt [a biblical account]' there appeared to be every reason to believe and no obligation to argue, much less prove."[26] Works by other minimalists, such as Thomas Thompson and Niels Peter Lemche, sparked responses from so-called maximalists (those who give greater credence to the historical authenticity of biblical narratives), including Kenneth Kitchen and William Dever, who pushed back against their questioning of traditional understandings of the early Davidic kingdom.[27]

Biblical economics is another subfield of OT studies that relies on sociological, anthropological, and economic research. In the past few decades, numerous publications have explored the diverse economic environments that shaped Hebrew texts, including those by Marvin Chaney, Ellen Davis, Walter Brueggemann, Richard Horsley, Samuel Adams, Roger Nam, Kelly Murphy, Brennan Breed, and Davis Hankins. Particularly influential have been Chaney's works on the economic realities of eighth-century Judah before, during, and after the Assyrian invasion. Drawing on archaeological discoveries in concert with the work of sociologists such as Gerhard Lenski, Chaney challenges traditional understandings of eighth-century prophetic oracles against injustice. Earlier interpretations tended to see these oracles as attacks on a few venal actors subverting a healthy economic order; Chaney argues that the attacks were on the order itself, which had been transformed by local and imperial elites in order to control producers' lands and

24. Herman M. Niemann, "The Socio-Political Shadow Cast by the Biblical Solomon," in *The Age of Solomon: Scholarship at the Turn of the Millennium*, ed. Lowell K. Handy, SHANE 11 (New York: Brill, 1997), 265–69.

25. Philip R. Davies, *In Search of "Ancient Israel": A Study in Biblical Origins*, LHBOTS 148 (Sheffield: Sheffield Academic, 1992); Keith W. Whitelam, *The Invention of Ancient Israel: The Silencing of Palestinian History* (London: Routledge, 1996).

26. Davies, *In Search of "Ancient Israel,"* 25.

27. Kenneth A. Kitchen, *On the Reliability of the Old Testament* (Grand Rapids: Eerdmans, 2003); William G. Dever, "Israelite Origins and the 'Nomadic Ideal': Can Archaeology Separate Fact from Fiction?," in *Mediterranean Peoples in Transition: Thirteenth to Early Tenth Centuries BCE, in Honor of Professor Trude Dothan*, ed. Seymour Gitin et al. (Jerusalem: Israel Exploration Society, 1998), 416–37.

extract their goods and labor.[28] In addition to "opening [Norman Gottwald's] eyes to the rich potential for comparative sociology to shed light on ancient Israel,"[29] Chaney's hypotheses have influenced current discussions on Judean economics, as found in the works of many scholars, including Richard Horsley, Avraham Faust, and D. N. Premnath.[30] They have also sparked hermeneutical explorations into how biblical economics might relate to modern concerns over extraction and resource allocation, as found in publications by Gale Yee and me.[31]

Roland Boer's *The Sacred Economy of Ancient Israel* has also sparked much discussion. The work explores systems of extraction and plunder through world-systems theory, Soviet-era Marxism, and regulation theory. By contrasting credit systems favoring the economically vulnerable over against debt systems favoring powerful economic interests, Boer traces the rise of estates and rulers to help frame economic concerns as expressed through numerous OT texts (Lev. 25:35–37; Deut. 15:7–8; Job 24:9; Ps. 112:5–6; Isa. 24:2).[32] *Sacred Economy* also examines the role of economic crises that arose out of extractive systems, which Boer argues were the norm rather than anomalous. Boer highlights that, as crises led to decline, the exploited found opportunities to benefit by hastening societal collapse, as reflected in the Habiru of the Amarna letters and the antimonarchical sentiments of Judg. 17:6 and 1 Sam. 8, to list two examples. Such events would mean that "no longer do the young men and women have to work periodically or permanently on palatine estates; no longer does the despised usurer-merchant-tax-collector call with his thugs to collect a debt slave."[33]

Another pursuit blending biblical scholarship with anthropological and sociological research is the recovery of marginalized voices. In addition to her important contributions to postcolonial and gender studies, Gale Yee draws on anthropology and sociology to highlight marginalized voices more generally. Emphasizing that a major segment of society was marginalized during the monarchical period rather than a minority of unfortunates, Yee seeks to recover aspects of lives beyond those of "the biblical triad" of foreigner, widow, and orphan. Seeking perspectives of

28. Marvin L. Chaney, "Bitter Bounty: The Dynamics of Political Economy Critiqued by the Eighth-Century Prophets," in *Reformed Faith and Economics*, ed. Robert L. Stivers (Lanham, MD: University Press of America, 1989), 16.

29. Norman K. Gottwald, "Marvin L. Chaney: A Tribute," in Coote and Gottwald, *To Break Every Yoke*, 3.

30. Richard A. Horsley, *Covenant Economics: A Biblical Vision of Justice for All* (Louisville: Westminster John Knox, 2009); Avraham Faust, *The Archaeology of Israelite Society in Iron Age II* (Winona Lake, IN: Eisenbrauns, 2012); D. N. Premnath, *Eighth Century Prophets: A Social Analysis* (St. Louis: Chalice, 2003).

31. Gale A. Yee, "Recovering Marginalized Groups in Ancient Israel: Methodological Considerations," in Coote and Gottwald, *To Break Every Yoke*, 10–27; Matthew J. M. Coomber, *Re-reading the Prophets through Corporate Globalization: A Cultural-Evolutionary Approach to Economic Injustice in the Hebrew Bible* (Eugene, OR: Cascade Books, 2022).

32. Roland Boer, *The Sacred Economy of Ancient Israel*, LAI (Louisville: Westminster John Knox, 2015), 156–63.

33. Boer, *Sacred Economy*, 196–97.

peasants, corvée laborers, foreign women, slaves, and other impoverished peoples,[34] Yee works to uncover voices of marginalization and resistance in the space between public and hidden transcript: public transcripts represent how elites wanted to be presented, and hidden transcripts are those discourses that took place beneath the view of primary powerholders.[35] In this space between, she finds vibrant oral cultures, folk stories and songs of resistance, and communal histories of opposition, which enable explorations of how these subversive traditions found expression within the OT's final written forms. Examples Yee points to include the deceptions of Shiphrah and Puah in Exod. 1, Rahab in Josh. 2–3, and acts of resistance against ruling elites as found in 1 Kings 12.

Psychological Approaches

Psychological research has had a profound influence on biblical scholarship in recent decades, but the relationship between the two fields was not always amicable. Although Franz Delitzsch, in the mid-1800s, employed psychology in his research on the Hebrew prophets, psychology was pushed to the margins of biblical studies for much of the twentieth century. In an article on the apostle Paul and Sigmund Freud, Robin Scroggs alludes to negative attitudes that had developed toward psychology: "Bultmann taught us years ago to be suspicious of psychology."[36] Wayne Rollins traces this break to attempts to psychologize Jesus in the late nineteenth century, which Albert Schweitzer disparaged as "psychological conjecture" and a "patch-work of opinions" produced by "mediocre minds."[37] Moves toward reductionist theories and the rise of psychoanalysis in early twentieth-century psychology, which tended to view religion as a neurosis, did not help relations. However, late twentieth-century developments in both psychology and biblical studies created new opportunities for collaboration.

The rise of humanistic, cognitive, and developmental psychology—which challenged earlier reductionist, materialist, and positivist approaches—created useful tools for biblical scholars. Psychology's expansion into such areas as interactive and relations theories, group psychology, and universal psychological traits have aided biblical scholars engaged in various areas of exegesis and research pertaining to how larger groups often act and respond to various circumstances.[38] Another important factor was popular culture's late twentieth-century embrace of psychology. Rollins and J. Harrold Ellens note that terms like "Freudian slip"

34. Yee, "Recovering Marginalized Groups," 11.

35. Yee, "Recovering Marginalized Groups," 16–18.

36. Robin Scroggs, "Psychology as a Tool to Interpret the Text," *ChrCent* 99, no. 10 (1982): 335.

37. Wayne G. Rollins, "The Bible and Psychology: New Directions in Biblical Scholarship," *Pastoral Psychology* 45, no. 3 (1997): 165.

38. D. Andrew Kille, "Psychology and the Bible: Three Worlds of the Text," *Pastoral Psychology* 51, no. 2 (2002): 127.

and "unconscious motives" entered into everyday use and thereby flowed more naturally into conversations pertaining to biblical research.[39]

As with any interpretive method, psychological interpretation presents challenges. In addition to the dangers of anachronism and ethnocentrism, it is easy to treat biblical characters as individuals rather than the literary constructs that they are. Despite such hazards, Joanna Collicutt finds a natural fit between psychology and biblical studies, especially considering psychology's interest in accounts of observed behavior, therapy diaries, and interview transcripts. The field has developed strategies for engaging texts in addition to individuals and groups. Furthermore, certain areas of psychological research naturally connect to biblical studies, including explorations into how authors' mental states affect writing. For example, research on how depressive states tend to cause victims to internalize trauma, rather than acknowledging the external forces that created it, are particularly fruitful for approaching texts that portray the Babylonian exile as divine punishment rather than a culmination of geopolitical factors. Collicutt also finds this research to be useful in interpreting biblical texts that couple affirmative statements with judgmental ones (e.g., Jer. 3:12; Hosea 14:1–7; Rom. 3:23–24).[40]

Considering that biblical texts were composed and collected by psychological beings, David Halperin sees the failure to consider these texts' psychological dimensions as a silencing of the ancient writers' perspectives and responses to human existence and behavior.[41] Similarly, David Clines argues that biblical texts exist because there was a psychological need to create them. While some texts were likely written under physical or financial duress, he states that we can presume most exist because writing them met their authors' psychological needs.[42]

Application of Psychology in Old Testament Studies

Social Memory and Notions of Self

Research on how the mind continually changes and reorganizes memories has aided biblical scholars who specialize in the formation and retention of self and group identities. Applying this phenomenon to identity formation in the OT, Ian Wilson considers how humans create and alter identities in concert. Due to humans' social nature, Wilson notes that we engage in these mnemonic processes collaboratively and, thereby, our social and collective memories function as an interplay of

39. J. Harold Ellens and Wayne G. Rollins, "Introduction," in *Psychology and the Bible: A New Way to Read the Scriptures*, vol. 1, *From Freud to Kohut*, ed. J. Harold Ellens and Wayne G. Rollins (Westport, CT: Praeger Perspectives, 2004), 2–3.

40. Joanna Collicutt, "Bringing the Academic Discipline of Psychology to Bear," *JTS* 63, no. 1 (2012): 31.

41. David J. Halperin, "Methodological Reflections on Psychoanalysis and Judaic Studies: A Response to Mortimer Ostow," in *Ultimate Intimacy: The Psychodynamics of Jewish Mysticism*, ed. Mortimer Ostow (New York: Routledge, 1995), 184.

42. David J. A. Clines, *Interested Parties: The Ideology of Writers and Readers of the Hebrew Bible*, JSOTSup 205; Gender, Culture, Theory 1 (Sheffield: Sheffield Academic, 1995), 133.

present and past sociocultural contexts.[43] Such interplay enables people to reshape past historical facts to the spiritual and ideological needs of their present. While Wilson cautions against engaging in notions of "mystical group mind," he draws upon Astrid Erll's observation that shared-past reconstructions hold some resemblance to individual-memory processes. Erll writes, "Societies do not remember literally; but much of what is done to reconstruct a shared past bears some resemblance to the processes of individual memory, such as the selectivity and perspectivity inherent in the creation of versions of the past according to present knowledge and needs."[44] Such observations have been used to consider the creation and preservation of Hebrew identity before, during, and after such significant events as the exile.

Ehud Ben Zvi engages social memory to explore authorship in the Persian period. Exploring why Chronicles might have been written as a second national history, Ben Zvi turns to memory's crucial role in group-identity formation to understand how a mnemonic community was born from authors who developed their sense of group identity "as a 'text'-centered-community."[45] Ideas of text-centered memory have also been employed by Edelman in her work on how Persian-era writers and audiences processed the many disparate accounts of King David, the Davidic dynasty, and the Babylonian exile.[46]

In the area of hermeneutics, Kenneth Ngwa has drawn upon memory studies to address the challenges of creating a unified national identity among Cameroonian citizens. In Ngwa's postwar reading of the identity of Gershom (Moses and Zipporah's son), he develops tools to help resolve the disparate linguistic and colonial histories of Cameroonians. Reading Exod. 2 as a text shaped by violence, Ngwa sees how five disparate areas of Cameroonian consciousness (national, regional, ethnic, religious, and gendered) can be approached through the three stages that led to Gershom's birth: construction (Exod. 2:1–10), deconstruction (2:11–15), and reconstruction (2:16–22).[47] Writing on "the narrative trope and communal embodiment that transforms the traumas of alienation to hopes of survival and integration,"[48] Ngwa argues that by combining the conjunctive memory of the cultural alien and political adoptee (Moses), the disjunctive memory of those who remained under forced labor (Hebrews in Egypt), and the adjunctive memory

43. Ian D. Wilson, "History and the Hebrew Bible: Culture, Narrative, and Memory," *Brill Research Perspectives in Biblical Interpretation* 3, no. 2 (2018): 22.

44. As quoted in Wilson, "History and the Hebrew Bible," 22. See Astrid Erll, "Cultural Memory Studies: An Introduction," in *A Companion to Cultural Memory Studies*, ed. Astrid Erll and Ansgar Nünning (Berlin: De Gruyter, 2010), 5.

45. Ehud Ben Zvi, "Chronicles and Social Memory," *Nordic Journal of Theology* 71, no. 1 (2017): 5.

46. Diana V. Edelman, "David in Israelite Social Memory," in *Remembering Biblical Figures in the Late Persian and Early Hellenistic Periods*, ed. Diana V. Edelman and Ehud Ben Zvi (Oxford: Oxford University Press, 2013).

47. Kenneth Ngwa, "The Making of Gershom's Story: A Cameroonian Postwar Hermeneutics Reading of Exodus 2," *JBL* 134, no. 4 (2015): 871.

48. Ngwa, "Making of Gershom's Story," 875.

of the returnee-remainee community (Moses and the Hebrews together), the Cameroonian community can find hope for survival and regeneration together.[49]

Considering how Hebrew communities saw themselves as moral actors, Carol Newsom employs neuroscience and cross-cultural-agency models. She argues that recent neuroscience research on the self "provides a context in which one can see how the particular formulations of the moral self in biblical and extrabiblical texts provide the necessary elements required for the development of an executive self, configuring and reconfiguring the basic options for constructing agency."[50] Her approach considers three ways of thinking about moral agency in relation to Second Temple Judaism:

1. Moral agency is affirmed: humans are entirely capable of making and executing moral decisions.
2. Moral agency is internally impaired—due either to a flaw within the individual or to outside forces, such as demonic interference—but the impairment can be overcome.
3. Moral agency is denied, with certain exceptions: most humans are not capable of moral agency (e.g., Gen. 1–3).[51]

Through this process, Newsom seeks to uncover the subjective experience of the self among Jewish groups in antiquity.

Another approach to understanding notions of self in the OT is found in Robert Carroll's work on dissonance theory and prophetic responses to failed prophecies. Using the social-psychological theory of cognitive dissonance, Carroll detects the use of hermeneutical coping mechanisms for resolving prophetic failure. Acknowledging dissonance theory's limitations in addressing this problem (e.g., prophetic authors' motivation to "explain away" failures),[52] Carroll argues that the theory helps reveal how the prophetic tradition "became the repository of [prophetic] insights, corrections, reinterpretations, adaptions and the whole range of hermeneutic activities that were necessary to ward off the triumph of dissonance over hope."[53]

Trauma and Recovery

Given Hebrew communities' sufferings under invasion, occupation, exile, and other stories of abuse, it is not surprising that trauma studies have found a home in psychological interpretations of OT texts.

49. Ngwa, "Making of Gershom's Story," 875.

50. Carol A. Newsom, "Models of the Moral Self: Hebrew Bible and Second Temple Judaism," *JBL* 131, no. 1 (2012): 25.

51. Newsom, "Models of the Moral Self," 15.

52. Robert P. Carroll, *When Prophecy Failed: Reactions and Responses to Failure in the Old Testament Prophetic Traditions* (London: SCM, 1979), 121.

53. Carroll, *When Prophecy Failed*, 183.

In the context of the diaspora, Dereck Daschke considers trauma in relation to Hebrew displacement with a view toward transforming trauma into hope for mending a broken world and creating new community.[54] Drawing on the traumatic experiences of homelessness and displacement as reflected in Ps. 137, Ezekiel, and Lamentations, he understands the core of the OT to be an extended response to the distress suffered during the Babylonian exile.[55] Viewing these compositions as outlets for grief and solutions to suffering, he writes that they simultaneously laid the groundwork for making a new home in exile: "the 'home' of the Law."[56]

Writing from a perspective of trauma experienced through Korea's colonial history, Chesung Justin Ryu argues that audiences from colonizing populations misread Jon. 4:9 when interpreting the prophet's anger as unjustified. Ryu asserts that the authors would not have used the Assyrian Empire (the quintessential villain of their age) as the enemy if they had not believed that Jonah was right to be angry. Rather, Ryu sees Jonah's silence as an act of "resistance on the part of the weak over against the rhetoric of the strong, which ignores unbalanced power structures in human relationships in the name of universalism."[57] Elizabeth Boase and Sarah Agnew also consider Jonah's flight, anger, and silence. Exploring various responses to trauma as psychological reactions to inexpressible horrors, they hypothesize that Jonah's reactions were his only viable responses to the situation in which he was placed. They write, "For Jonah and Jonah's community, silence speaks. There are no words to explain the flight, the anger and the final silence, for trauma itself cannot be spoken."[58]

Drawing upon Cheryl Exum's use of tragedy as a heuristic tool,[59] F. W. Dobbs-Allsopp explores common features between Lamentations and other tragedies in literature. Considering features such as struggling with the problem of evil and the centrality of a tragic hero, Dobbs-Allsopp finds that "healing-through-language" can be accomplished, including the processes of giving voice to a community's pain[60] and articulating divine compassion as a response to human suffering.[61]

Noting how those who struggle with past violent experiences frequently suffer from feelings of isolation and shame, Christopher Frechette considers a healing-

54. Dereck Daschke, "'How Deserted Lies the City': Politics and the Trauma of Homelessness in the Hebrew Bible," in *Next Year in Jerusalem: Exile and Return in Jewish History*, ed. Leonard J. Greenspoon, Studies in Jewish Civilization 30 (West Lafayette, IN: Purdue University Press, 2019), 45.

55. Daschke, "'How Deserted Lies the City,'" 32.

56. Daschke, "'How Deserted Lies the City,'" 33.

57. Ryu, "Silence as Resistance," 198.

58. Elizabeth Boase and Sarah Agnew, "Whispered in the Sound of Silence," *The Bible & Critical Theory* 12, no. 1 (2016): 20.

59. J. Cheryl Exum, *Tragedy and Biblical Narrative: Arrows of the Almighty* (Cambridge: Cambridge University Press, 1992), 5.

60. F. W. Dobbs-Allsopp, "Tragedy, Tradition, and Theology in the Book of Lamentations," *JSOT* 22, no. 74 (1997): 41–42.

61. Dobbs-Allsopp, "Tragedy, Tradition, and Theology," 56.

through-language approach to the book of Jeremiah. Acknowledging that trauma recovery involves fostering group solidarity and identity, Frechette concludes that narratives of collective trauma served the biblical authors' communities and have an ability to connect with modern audiences who face similar struggles.[62] In this modern application, Frechette finds Jeremiah to be an effective starting point for constructing sermons to assist the traumatized.

Conclusion

Biblical scholars have engaged the social sciences for many years, and each new generation develops novel methods for asking new questions of the OT's ancient texts. The social-scientific approaches to the OT considered above represent but a glimpse of the richness offered by this interpretive area of biblical studies, but they will hopefully serve as a springboard for those who wish to learn more about this area of biblical interpretation.

62. Christopher G. Frechette, "The Old Testament as Controlled Substance: How Insights from Trauma Studies Reveal Healing Capacities in Potentially Harmful Tests," *Int* 69, no. 1 (2014): 28–29.

31

Theological Interpretation

Heath A. Thomas

> At the heart of the hermeneutic advocated in this book is the belief that our love for the Old Testament and our desire for God will come together only when we make the goal of our interpretation to *listen for God's address*. If Scripture is God's Word, then any other goal is inadequate.
>
> David J. H. Beldman and Craig G. Bartholomew[1]

In the past twenty-five years, theological interpretation has grown as an approach to reading the corpus from Genesis to Malachi as Christian Scripture.[2] In a general sense, such interpretation is "teleologically oriented toward knowledge and love of God—however partial that knowledge and love might be on this side of the veil—and reaching out toward knowledge and love of neighbor. Thus understood,

1. David J. H. Beldman and Craig G. Bartholomew, "Preface: The Love of the Old Testament and the Desire for God," in *Hearing the Old Testament: Listening for God's Address*, ed. Craig G. Bartholomew and David J. H. Beldman (Grand Rapids: Eerdmans, 2012), xv.

2. See Craig G. Bartholomew and Heath A. Thomas, "A Manifesto for Theological Interpretation," in *A Manifesto for Theological Interpretation*, ed. Craig G. Bartholomew and Heath A. Thomas (Grand Rapids: Baker Academic, 2016), 1–3; Angus Paddison, "The History and Reemergence of Theological Interpretation," in *Manifesto for Theological Interpretation*, ed. Bartholomew and Thomas, 27–47; Bartholomew and Beldman, *Hearing the Old Testament*; Kevin J. Vanhoozer, ed., *Theological Interpretation of the Old Testament: A Book-by-Book Survey* (Grand Rapids: Baker Academic, 2008); cf. Andrea D. Saner, "Theological Interpretation of Scripture," in *The New Cambridge Companion to Christian Doctrine*, ed. Michael Allen (Cambridge: Cambridge University Press, 2022), 194–211.

theological interpretation is a task not restricted historically or geographically; it is as old as the church and as global as Christians' reading of the Bible, when their reading is oriented toward participation in the divine life."[3] Theological interpretation is interested not only in what God has done in the past but also in what God is doing in the present and how those realities correlate with God's Word. Thus, theological interpretation of the OT may be distinguished from biblical theology, which focuses on the theological content of the biblical text and less on its reception history or the ways in which the biblical text opens onto modern horizons ethically, ecclesially, politically, sociologically, and so on. Theological interpretation is ancient and modern, reinvigorated today by scholars returning to theological readings learned from the church's ancient past and by systematic theologians returning to sustained engagement with the biblical text.[4]

The moniker "Old Testament" conveys this corpus's necessary association with the later texts identified as the "New Testament," and together these texts constitute the content of the Christian Scripture. Recent scholarship employs the name "Hebrew Bible," but R. W. L. Moberly is right to identify "Old Testament" as a particularly Christian designation for the text. Theological interpretation reads the OT as Christian Scripture.[5] Christopher Seitz and John Goldingay prefer different terminology for this corpus ("Elder Testament" and "First Testament," respectively), but their point is the same: the Old/Elder/First Testament always and ever stands in relationship with the NT as Christian Scripture.[6] Theological interpretation requires that the discrete witness of the OT be heard in its own "voice" and then heard in the chorus of the Old and New together as they proclaim Israel's God, who is also Jesus Christ.[7]

Richard Briggs highlights the hermeneutical significance of reading the OT *as* Christian Scripture, which is different from proclaiming that the OT *is* Christian Scripture. Reading it *as* Christian Scripture is an interpretative strategy that is especially important for reading the text with others in a pluralistic context. Theological interpretation is "any interpretation which will make sure that

3. Saner, "Theological Interpretation," 194.

4. Saner, "Theological Interpretation," 194.

5. R. W. L. Moberly, "Theological Interpretation, Second Naiveté, and the Rediscovery of the Old Testament," *Anglican Theological Review* 99, no. 4 (2017): 654–65. For this terminology, see Moberly, *The God of the Old Testament: Encountering the Divine in Christian Scripture* (Grand Rapids: Baker Academic, 2020), 1–12; Moberly, *Old Testament Theology: Reading the Hebrew Bible as Christian Scripture* (Grand Rapids: Baker Academic, 2013), 1–4.

6. Christopher R. Seitz, *The Elder Testament: Canon, Theology, Trinity* (Waco: Baylor University Press, 2018), 13–50; John Goldingay, *The First Testament: A New Translation* (Downers Grove, IL: IVP Academic, 2018); Goldingay, *Old Testament Theology*, vol. 1, *Israel's Gospel* (Downers Grove, IL: IVP Academic, 2003).

7. Seitz, *Elder Testament*, 13–70; Seitz, *The Character of Christian Scripture: The Significance of a Two-Testament Bible*, STI (Grand Rapids: Baker Academic, 2011); Stephen G. Dempster, "The Canon and Theological Interpretation," in Bartholomew and Thomas, *Manifesto*, 131–48.

theological construals are among those explicitly considered" in the marketplace of ideas.[8] Briggs then identifies four key markers of appropriate theological wrestling with Scripture: (1) recognition of the two-Testament canon; (2) embrace of fundamental theological tensions (e.g., law-gospel, judgment-promise, divine sovereignty–human responsibility, etc.); (3) acceptance of Scripture as a means of grace (i.e., God engages a needy humanity through Scripture); and (4) affirmation that the diverse forms of the OT and NT come to us providentially as God's Word in human words.[9] Moberly shares Briggs's concern and believes reading *as* will open avenues for dialogue on the HB/OT, particularly between Christian and Jewish readers.[10] Their concern for reading *as* is especially successful in a contested hermeneutical landscape where dialogue and light "sans heat" is needed.

But reading *as* may not fully reckon with the reality of what the OT *is*—namely, its "ontology" or "metaphysical reality," as Mark Gignilliat maintains.[11] The ontology of the OT is vital for proper theological interpretation, which affirms that God, who has given the text of the OT through myriad ways and processes over time, discloses divine identity, purpose, and mission in and through its presentation. The OT *is* the Word of God. This commitment is not a hermeneutical but an ontological necessity: the triune God is the necessary cause of the material presence of the OT qua text.[12] As John Webster maintains, "To say 'Scripture' is to say 'revelation'—not just in the sense that these texts are to be handled *as if* they were bearers of divine revelation, but in the sense that revelation is fundamental to the texts' *being*."[13]

Theological interpretation oriented to hear God's address is not simple. Many tenets orient one toward such reading.[14] Nonetheless, theological interpretation begins and ends with the audacious claim that the OT ontologically constitutes and instrumentally conveys the very Word of God. So *what counts as theological interpretation of the OT is, at its most basic calculation, interpretation with a*

8. Richard S. Briggs, "Biblical Hermeneutics and Scriptural Responsibility," in *The Future of Biblical Interpretation: Responsible Plurality in Biblical Hermeneutics*, ed. Matthew R. Malcolm and Stanley E. Porter (Downers Grove, IL: IVP Academic, 2013), 64.

9. Briggs, "Biblical Hermeneutics," 65–69.

10. Moberly, *Old Testament Theology*, 2–3.

11. Mark S. Gignilliat, *Reading Scripture Canonically: Theological Instincts for Old Testament Interpretation* (Grand Rapids: Baker Academic, 2019), 83–98. Briggs and Moberly take the reality of the OT as Scripture as a given. Briggs, "Biblical Hermeneutics," 55; Moberly, *Old Testament Theology*, 2–4.

12. Heath A. Thomas, "Old Testament," in *The Trinity in the Canon: A Biblical, Theological, Historical, and Practical Proposal*, ed. Brandon D. Smith (Nashville: B&H Academic, 2023), 68.

13. John Webster, "Resurrection and Scripture," in *Christology and Scripture: Interdisciplinary Perspectives*, ed. Andrew T. Lincoln and Angus Paddison (London: T&T Clark, 2008), 144 (emphasis original).

14. Bartholomew and Thomas, "A Manifesto for Theological Interpretation," 1–25. Twelve facets of theological interpretation are explained in chapter-length treatments.

focus on the triune God (theology) and God's address (theological disclosure) for communion with God in all of life.

Complications in Theological Interpretation of the Old Testament

In this essay, we explore complications emerging from the definition offered above. These explorations are meant to clarify the face of OT theological interpretation for today.

Is the Old Testament "Theological"?

In the next chapter of this volume, Stephen Chapman considers a possibility that would be devastating for theological interpretation: perhaps there is no theology in the OT![15] This would be the case if one reduces the formation or content of the OT merely to brute politics, social forces, or the like. In such a configuration, the "whatness" of the OT is not theology but the politics of power.

Such reductionism diminishes the primacy and agency of Israel's God in the affairs depicted in the OT. Ancient Israel, like other cultures of the ANE, envisioned their world imbued with the divine. Israel deploys its theological vision distinctively in this ancient environment, and one can affirm this distinction without denying similarities with ANE cultures.[16] The OT is theological in that it fundamentally reveals Israel's God. The focus of OT theological interpretation derives from the primary subject matter of the text: Israel's God, who is also the God and Father of the Lord Jesus Christ. Other foci for biblical material (history, material culture, social forces, scribal forces, geopolitics, ideologies, economic interests, political forces, etc.) stand as secondary to the primary subject that imbues the OT: Who is the God of whom the text speaks? Or better, who speaks through the text?

Brevard Childs argued that the subject matter of the OT is God rather than any secondary focus, and he used several terms in support of his claim: the "reality," "content," "substance," "*res*," or "*Sache*" of the biblical text.[17] For Childs, the reality (*res* or *Sache*) of which the OT speaks is none other than God, particularly the triune God. Childs's theological focus did not go unchallenged. Criticism

15. See the engagement of Stephen Chapman (chap. 32 of the present volume) and Konrad Schmid, *Is There Theology in the Hebrew Bible?*, trans. Peter Altmann, Critical Studies in the Hebrew Bible 4 (Winona Lake, IN: Eisenbrauns, 2015).

16. E.g., Craig G. Bartholomew, *The Old Testament and God*, Old Testament Origins and the Question of God 1 (Grand Rapids: Baker Academic, 2022), 179–393; cf. Craig G. Bartholomew and Heath A. Thomas, *The Minor Prophets: A Theological Introduction* (Downers Grove, IL: IVP Academic, 2023), 27–39.

17. For Childs's conceptuality of the subject matter of the OT, see Daniel R. Driver, *Brevard Childs, Biblical Theologian*, FAT 2/46 (Tübingen: Mohr Siebeck, 2010); Philip Sumpter, *The Substance of Psalm 24: An Attempt to Read Scripture after Brevard S. Childs*, LHBOTS 600 (London: T&T Clark, 2015), 7–58.

appeared in several explorations of the predominantly continental volumes of *Jahrbuch für biblische Theologie* and was reexpressed in the analysis of Bernd Janowski.[18] In agreement with Childs, theological interpretation of the OT attests and witnesses to this divine reality.[19]

Is Theological Interpretation of the Old Testament Dogmatic and Conformist?

One could argue that theological interpretation is an apologetic for Christian systematic theology instead of a close and free investigation of the OT on its own terms. After all, because it is later than the OT, Christian systematic theology with its theological categories does not cohere with the OT, ancient and culturally disparate as it is. Or so the thinking goes.

Such a view supposes theological concepts about God from systematic theology are impositions *from the outside* (especially historically) onto the OT. Goldingay expresses this view: "The vocation of theological interpretation is to encourage that process [of widening theological thinking] and not let it be constrained by christocentrism, trinitarianism or an unqualified submission to the Christian tradition."[20] Goldingay's insistence on the autonomy of the OT apart from Christian categories derives from a desire that the OT be allowed to freely express its own theological concerns about, for instance, God, Israel, and life, some of which may be unrelated to dogmatic categories of Christian theology such as divine persons and the economic and immanent Trinity.[21] The goal is to encourage theological interpretation to be properly *theological*—that is, oriented toward divine disclosure—recognizing that theological disclosure evinces a grammar all its own, distinctively displayed in discrete texts of the OT. This disclosure is neither narrowly focused nor doctrinally conformist but emerges from the ancient historical contexts out of which the OT originates. Goldingay wants the freight of theological witness from the OT to inform the categories of doctrine itself.[22]

18. Bernd Janowski, "Biblische Theologie heute: Formale und materiale Aspekte," in *Biblical Interpretation: History, Context, and Reality*, ed. Christine Helmer, with Taylor G. Petrey, SBLSS 26 (Atlanta: SBL Press, 2005), 17–22; Bernd Janowski, Irmtraud Fischer, and Martin Ebner, eds., *Wie biblische ist Theologie?*, JBTh 25 (Neukirchen-Vluyn: Neukirchener, 2010); Bernd Janowski and Norbert Lohfink, eds., *Religionsgeschichte Israels oder Theologie des Alten Testaments?*, JBTh 10 (Neukirchen-Vluyn: Neukirchener, 1995).

19. Brevard Childs, *Biblical Theology of the Old and New Testaments: Theological Reflection on the Christian Bible* (Minneapolis: Fortress, 1993), 55–94, 86–87; Childs, *Old Testament Theology in a Canonical Context* (Philadelphia: Fortress, 1986), 20–27. Cf. Stephen E. Fowl, *Engaging Scripture*, Challenges in Contemporary Theology (Oxford: Blackwell, 1998), 97–127.

20. John Goldingay, *Do We Need the New Testament? Letting the Old Testament Speak for Itself* (Grand Rapids: Zondervan, 2015), 176.

21. Goldingay, *Do We Need the New Testament?*, 159.

22. Ironically, Thomas Andrew Bennett finds Goldingay's theological analysis of the OT properly Christian. See Bennett, "Ruled, Creedal, and Located: The Theological Interpretation of John Goldingay," *HBT* 35 (2013): 1–20; cf. Gignilliat, *Reading Scripture Canonically*, 83–89.

Goldingay's argument for the OT to speak freely in theological construction is preceded by Christian theologian Colin Gunton and followed by the recent work of Craig Bartholomew.[23] Bartholomew, superficially akin to Goldingay but following the logic of Gunton, desires that the conceptualities, language, and grammar of the OT (and the NT, for that matter) fund theological vision, reforming theological discourse, rather than permitting extrinsic properties to inform systematic or dogmatic Christian theology.[24] To allow the full scope of the OT to inform Christian theology, to say nothing of theological interpretation, one must understand the OT witness itself: what it says about God, the world, and divine action. One must understand the pressures that the OT itself exerts on theological presentation. Secondarily, one must recognize the freight of the OT in shaping and forming categories of Christian thought and teaching. The OT must be allowed to set the terms of divine realities and divine agency. Gunton summarizes: "It is one of the tragedies—one could almost say crimes—of Christian theological history that the Old Testament was effectively displaced by Greek philosophy as the theological basis of the doctrine of God, certainly so far as the doctrine of the divine attributes is concerned."[25]

More diplomatic than Gunton, recent interpreters reveal how Christian theology can be applied productively when reading the OT theologically. Gary A. Anderson uses Christian theology as a way to properly understand OT texts, relating apophatic theology with Lev. 10, divine impassibility with Moses's and Jonah's prayers, creation doctrine (*creatio ex nihilo*) with Gen. 1, and so on. In this way, Christian theology serves OT interpretation as a generative resource rather than a hurdle to overcome or an imposition from the outside.[26] Rather than being conformist, doctrine becomes a helpful way to approach the aporias in the OT or to clarify how the OT witness pressures toward Christian theology.

Don Collett reveals how the ontology of the OT, as it pressures toward Christian theology, productively reveals God's providential ordering of the two-Testament canon. Collett exposes the deficiency in historicist readings that divorce the ontology of the OT from its authorship, its content, and the diverse ways the OT figurally speaks to (and envelops) reality. For instance, he posits the impossibility of reading the OT qua the OT without recognizing its figural character. That is, the OT ultimately depicts theological realities that exceed historical moments in the past. Using the traditional Christian categories of figural interpretation that embrace the ontology of the OT, Collett reveals how the OT is trinitarian and

23. Colin E. Gunton, *Act and Being: Toward a Theology of the Divine Attributes* (Grand Rapids: Eerdmans, 2002); Bartholomew, *Old Testament and God*.

24. See, e.g., the account of divine action of the triune God in the divine economy discussed by Craig G. Bartholomew, *The God Who Acts in History: The Significance of Sinai* (Grand Rapids: Eerdmans, 2020).

25. Gunton, *Act and Being*, 3.

26. Gary A. Anderson, *Christian Doctrine and the Old Testament: Theology in the Service of Biblical Exegesis* (Grand Rapids: Baker Academic, 2017).

Christocentric, true to form and properly historical.[27] For Collett, Christian tradition does not distort the voice of the OT. Rather, Christian tradition and theology lead to a more faithful and true understanding of the substance of the OT witness without the distorting effects of historicism. "The Bible not only speaks figurally through its literal sense but also *must* speak figurally—not simply because Christians wish to do so but because its subject matter is theological. Stated more plainly, the Bible must speak figurally because it is a book *about* God."[28]

Somewhat differently, Chapman avers that Christian doctrine need not pressure theological reading for such reading to be properly theological. He argues for a communal approach to biblical interpretation that pushes against individualistic approaches; that is, he appeals for the "traditional craft" of theological reading. Chapman believes that Christian theology has much to offer theological reading and that this reading tradition instructs both theology and ethics.[29] But Christian theology should not run roughshod over the text. He states, "As much as there is a valuable, even essential, role in Christian theological interpretation for doctrinal reflection, the creeds, the Trinity, and Christology, biblical interpretation can still be theological without them—or at least without making them the explicit and exclusive starting points in theological reflection."[30] He negotiates how theological interpretation can be traditional without conforming to Christian theology.

What can be said of the charge of theological conformity in theological interpretation? First, general worries about the relationship (perceived gap?) between biblical and systematic theology, explored previously in *Jahrbuch für biblische Theologie*, still apply to theological interpretation today. Scholars engage the question variously. Recent commentary series attempt to overcome or bridge the gap between Christian theology and the OT, with greater or lesser degrees of success. I have in mind here the Two Horizons Old Testament Commentary Series (Eerdmans), the Brazos Theological Commentary Series (Brazos), and the International Theological Commentary Series (T&T Clark). Individual volumes are judged successful (or not) based on varying criteria.[31] The most fruitful of these theological interpretations of the OT express interrelated commitments: (a) embrace of the ontology of the OT and its theological witness; (b) sustained evaluation of the OT text (Hebrew and/or Greek traditions) in its canonical and cultural contexts; (c) embrace of the OT witness within the full testimony of a

27. Don C. Collett, *Figural Reading and the Old Testament: Theology and Practice* (Grand Rapids: Baker Academic, 2020); Collett, "Reading Forward: The Old Testament and Retrospective Stance," *ProEccl* 24, no. 2 (2015): 178–96.

28. Collett, *Figural Reading*, 55.

29. Stephen B. Chapman, "Theological Interpretation as a Traditional Craft," in *Interpreting the Old Testament Theologically: Essays in Honor of Willem A. VanGemeren*, ed. Andrew T. Abernethy (Grand Rapids: Zondervan, 2018), 118–19.

30. Chapman, "Traditional Craft," 119.

31. E.g., Heath A. Thomas, *Habakkuk*, THOTC (Grand Rapids: Eerdmans, 2018); Mark S. Gignilliat, *Micah*, International Theological Commentary (London: T&T Clark, 2019); Paul R. Hinlicky, *Joshua*, Brazos Theological Commentary (Grand Rapids: Brazos, 2021).

two-Testament canon; (d) a focus upon God's address to be heard for the present day (often described as "ethics"); and (e) attention to readings of Christian tradition throughout the past two millennia as they relate to OT texts, precisely because of their embrace of the ontology of the OT and attentiveness to God's address for today. These commentaries are anything but theologically conformist.

Second, one notes a hermeneutical complexity that speaks against theological interpretation being conformist to the interests of Christian theology. Although these scholars read theologically, one witnesses diversity and complexity in their readings. Further, the Scripture and Hermeneutics Seminar (SAHS) has, for the past twenty-five years, employed academic rigor to explore what it might mean for the OT (and NT) to be received and interpreted as the "living Word of God."[32] Bartholomew insists that it is possible, and hermeneutically and philosophically responsible, to read the OT as God's Word in which God speaks, and for today.[33] Such an affirmation of the ontology of the OT does not *necessarily* diminish intellectual creativity, historical investigation, socio-historical inquiry, philosophical precision, or literary sensitivity. The efforts of SAHS (to mention only one set of works) counters such prejudice against the ontology of the OT.[34] Thus, theological interpretation of the OT that is oriented to hear God's address and engages Christian theology can be creative, rigorous, surprising, and compelling. Moreover, it can challenge Christian theology even while dialoguing within the tradition.

Does Theological Interpretation Flatten the Old Testament's Diverse Theological Vision?

Another complication with the definition offered above emerges from both the diversity of material in the OT and the diversity of interpreters engaging the OT. Erhard Gerstenberger expresses this concern for OT theology, but it applies equally to theological interpretation: Does theological interpretation of the OT require a unitary or unified "theology," or can this approach acknowledge diverse theological voices within the text? Gerstenberger also alerts us to the diverse worlds engaging the OT that defy reductionism: contextual theological engagements with the OT preclude a unitary theology. Whether from within or from without, theology cannot mean only one thing![35]

However, theological interpretation of the OT does not imply that the theological terrain of the OT is smooth or that it emerged all at once. Rather, the

32. Craig G. Bartholomew, "On Not Refusing—Indeed Welcoming!—the One Who Is Speaking: The History of the Scripture and Hermeneutics Seminar," in *The Scripture and Hermeneutics Seminar: Retrospect and Prospect*, ed. Craig G. Bartholomew et al., Scripture Collective Series (Grand Rapids: Zondervan Academic, 2022), 3–23.

33. Bartholomew, *Old Testament and God*; Bartholomew, *God Who Acts*.

34. For a listing of the seminar volumes, see Bartholomew et al., *Scripture and Hermeneutics Seminar*, 27–60.

35. Erhard S. Gerstenberger, *Theologies in the Old Testament*, trans. John Bowden (London: T&T Clark, 2002), esp. 1–12.

divine substance of the OT affirms its composite nature as a text emerging from hundreds of years (and hands) of textual production. Moreover, close theological reading enables rich and multifaceted presentation of the one triune God, as Brown reveals in his reading of Genesis, wherein a "manifest diversity" of theological presentation regarding divine presence and action emerges from the text.[36] Social, political, economic, or historical realities that impact the production of the OT text are not discounted but recalibrated (or adumbrated) within the theological focus of the OT.

Seitz clarifies how textual production is a theological, rather than merely sociological, affair.[37] He applies considerable insight to canonical and theological readings of the OT, wherein the complex canonical shaping of the OT serves as indices for the divine action and revelation of Israel's God. In his analysis, historical criticism (broadly construed), or *any* kind of biblical criticism (literary, ideological, or the like), is not discounted as anti-theological but recognized as partial and generative, opening understanding. This legitimate aperture opened by any critical "ism," properly understood, enables interpreters "to recognize what is the brilliant achievement of the canonical form and shape of the biblical presentation."[38] The OT in its canonical form (Torah, Prophets, and Writings) gives rise to diverse (and sometimes surprising) theological visions, which can be propagative and nuanced. The canonical form of the OT, in concert with the NT, presents the text's primary function: to witness to Israel's God and to disclose this God to needy hearers.

Is Theological Interpretation of the Old Testament Simply a Retreat to Systematic Theology?

I have mentioned the challenge of seeing theological interpretation as a retreat to the safe confines of systematic theology, which flattens the OT theological testimony or does not sufficiently wrestle with the text's material form. Recent theological interpretations of OT corpora prevent such a caricature. The interpreters selected here offer careful, scholarly, and relevant interpretations that open the OT so that readers can hear God's address. Volumes by Andrew Witt, Csilla Saysell, Andrea Saner, Zoltán S. Schwáb, and Joshua Moon, among others in the Journal for Theological Interpretation Supplement Series, exemplify

36. William P. Brown, "Manifest Diversity: The Presence of God in Genesis," in *Genesis and Christian Theology*, ed. Nathan MacDonald, Mark W. Elliott, and Grant Macaskill (Grand Rapids: Eerdmans, 2012), 3–25.

37. Christopher R. Seitz, *Convergences: Canon and Catholicity* (Waco: Baylor University Press, 2020), 29–82; Seitz, *Elder Testament*; Seitz, *Character of Christian Scripture*. See his foundational essay "The Canonical Approach and Theological Interpretation," in *Canon and Biblical Interpretation*, ed. Craig G. Bartholomew et al., SAHS 7 (Milton Keynes: Paternoster, 2006), 58–110.

38. Seitz, *Convergences*, 11.

sophisticated scholarly appraisals of the OT text, readings at once theologically rich and exegetically sound.[39]

Somewhat different from the supplement volumes of the *Journal for Theological Interpretation*, M. Daniel Carroll R. offers erudite theological reasoning from prophetic texts that destabilizes comfortable social constructs, especially in the Western world. He carefully evaluates three prophetic books (Amos, Isaiah, and Micah) set in dialogue with ethics and situated liberationist readings (and his own social and cultural location as a Guatemalan interpreter). Christian theology, ethics, and the contemporary world are enriched and reenvisioned by Carroll R.'s assessment of these prophetic voices.[40] His is an act of theological imagination: God's address is heard for today regarding current demands of justice, idols in the past and present, and the abiding nature of future hope in the Christian faith.

Briggs employs theological reading and literary studies to inform an exploration of Numbers that opens horizons of Christology (Num. 20), violence (Num. 25), and blessing (Num. 6; 22–24). Briggs takes cues from Hans Frei as well as from ancient and modern readings of the book. He describes his approach as reading "ascriptively," by which he intends a sensitive reading that sees how the narrative re-presents and re-imagines the real world in new ways. Like that of Carroll R., Briggs's is a work of theological imagination. But different from Carroll R., Briggs offers "figural interpretation" of Numbers, in which "key people, places, events, indeed tropes of any kind, as figures of archetypal ways of being, doing, knowing [are] . . . conjoined under the unifying providence of God."[41] He reads the text in and through Jesus Christ, whose identity is present (figurally) in Scripture. The text operates "as witness to the reality of God in Christ, both before and after Christ, that is, in Old and New Testaments, figurally related."[42] Numbers imaginatively presents a world in which the reader journeys with God (e.g., Num. 10–12), and the journey is fresh and unexpected.[43] Reading ascriptively takes seriously the "nature and action of God; indeed it is what allows readers

39. Andrew Carl Witt, *A Voice without End: The Role of David in Psalms 3–14*, JTISup 20 (University Park, PA: Eisenbrauns, 2021); Csilla Saysell, *"According to the Law": Reading Ezra 9–10 as Christian Scripture*, JTISup 4 (University Park, PA: Eisenbrauns, 2012); Andrea D. Saner, *"Too Much to Grasp": Exodus 3:13–15 and the Reality of God*, JTISup 11 (University Park, PA: Eisenbrauns, 2015); Zoltán S. Schwáb, *Toward an Interpretation of the Book of Proverbs: Selfishness and Secularity Reconsidered*, JTISup 7 (University Park, PA: Eisenbrauns, 2012); Joshua N. Moon, *Jeremiah's New Covenant: An Augustinian Reading*, JTISup 3 (University Park, PA: Eisenbrauns, 2011).

40. M. Daniel Carroll R., *The Lord Roars: Recovering the Prophetic Voice for Today* (Grand Rapids: Baker Academic, 2022).

41. Richard S. Briggs, *Theological Hermeneutics and the Book of Numbers as Christian Scripture*, Reading the Scriptures (Notre Dame: University of Notre Dame Press, 2018), 4.

42. Briggs, *Theological Hermeneutics*, 82.

43. Briggs, *Theological Hermeneutics*, 82–83. For his ascriptive reading for Daniel, see Briggs, "A Test Case in Ascriptive Realism: The Quest of the Historical Daniel and Its Complex Relationship to the Practices of Scriptural Interpretation," *JTI* 14, no. 1 (2020): 41–59.

access to ways of talking about the nature and reality of God."[44] Briggs is interested in reading the text for ultimate realities disclosed therein.[45] The benefits of the analysis come in his ability to hold in productive tension the theological claims of the text and the various historical claims made by modern interpreters.

Something similar emerges in Chapman's theological exploration of 1 Samuel.[46] Chapman explores this text so as to hear from God. "In Jewish and Christian tradition, reading the Bible has always involved meditating on its words as if each and every one stood ready to disclose a divine message."[47] But meditation on the text does not lead the interpreter to a predetermined location. Chapman's goal is "not to offer the 'correct' Christian interpretation of an Old Testament book." Indeed, he avers, "I do not think such a thing exists, although I do consider some interpretations better than others." Instead, he hopes "to provide only one way of reading it that honors its historical integrity and literary complexity, while also listening expectantly for how it addresses, confronts, confirms, and deepens a Christian understanding of life before God."[48] While historical questions interweave throughout the commentary, Chapman's theological focus stands central. "At the heart of the Samuel narrative is this question: With the rise of the monarchy, will Israel develop a 'civil religion'?"[49] Questions of personal piety emerge from the reading: the piety of Saul and David, as well as the piety of those who follow God in any age. Moreover, he explores how 1 Samuel depicts Saul and what that depiction might generate for those negotiating life's complexities. Saul's literary presentation offers a pathway to envision life christologically: "In his struggle to die, Saul adumbrates Christ."[50] Chapman goes on to explore how empty ritual emerges as a threat to the life of faith, and finally, how the Davidic legacy can be understood to amplify and/or corrupt Christian faith.[51] Chapman reads Samuel with literary sensitivity that presses toward spiritual concerns beyond historical questions about the monarchy or the events that gave rise to the monarchy. Questions of historicity and the origin of the monarchy in Israel are not unimportant, just not decisive for the interpretation of the book. Rather, 1 Samuel discloses Israel's God, their relationship with this God (especially for Israel's leaders), and the wrestling with the "horizons of tragedy" that mark the human condition before God.[52]

These exemplars of theological interpretation do not read the text to retreat to systematic theology. They attend to the text with historical concern,

44. Briggs, *Theological Hermeneutics*, 5.
45. Briggs, "Test Case," 41–45.
46. Stephen B. Chapman, *1 Samuel as Christian Scripture: A Theological Commentary* (Grand Rapids: Eerdmans, 2016).
47. Chapman, *1 Samuel*, 10.
48. Chapman, *1 Samuel*, 10.
49. Chapman, *1 Samuel*, 16.
50. Chapman, *1 Samuel*, 17.
51. Chapman, *1 Samuel*, 17.
52. Chapman, *1 Samuel*, 217–60.

linguistic precision, care for the Greek and Hebrew text traditions, a deep understanding of the ontology of the OT as God's Word, appropriate engagement with Christian tradition past and present (including historical, moral, and dogmatic theology), and a concern that God's Word might be heard for today's world. Their theological interpretations are rich and varied, engaging a wide array of interests.

Theological Interpretation of the Old Testament and Repristination of Early Christian Interpretation

With the myriad of theological readings of the OT that draw attention to previous modes of interpretation, one might conclude that theological interpretation is a repristination of hermeneutical modes of the past. Daniel Treier speaks of theological interpretation as a "recovery" of Christian reading practices in which the OT is understood with reference to Jesus Christ and the unveiling of the kingdom of God disclosed in the NT. In this way, the OT should not be read apart from the full disclosure of divine action in and through the Messiah, Jesus.[53] "Recovery" also implies reconnection with ancient Christian ways of reading the OT, and several publishing efforts are focused on this "recovery."[54] Here one notes the complexity of theological interpretation over time. It has not always meant the same thing, at least not in practice.[55] This alerts us to the fact that recovery cannot merely be a repristination of previous modes of theological reading.

What holds these diverse practices together is their shared commitment to the ontology of the OT and the needfulness of God's address to be heard in the present. Theological interpretation of the OT, then, remains poly- rather than

53. Daniel J. Treier, *Introducing Theological Interpretation of Scripture: Recovering a Christian Practice* (Grand Rapids: Baker Academic, 2008).

54. E.g., see the following series: Thomas Oden, ed., Ancient Christian Commentary on Scripture (Downers Grove, IL: IVP Academic, 2001–);Thomas Oden, Gerald Bray, and Michael Glerup, eds., Ancient Christian Texts (Downers Grove, IL: IVP Academic, 2009–); Timothy George, ed., Reformation Commentary on Scripture (Downers Grove, IL: IVP Academic, 2011–). Note also the surveys of research in Bartholomew and Thomas, *Minor Prophets*, 7–26; Thomas, *Habakkuk*, 43–58; and monographs such as Hauna T. Ondrey, *The Minor Prophets as Christian Scripture in the Commentaries of Theodore of Mopsuestia and Cyril of Alexandria*, Oxford Early Christian Studies (Oxford: Oxford University Press, 2018); Eugen J. Pentuic, *The Old Testament in Eastern Orthodox Tradition* (Oxford: Oxford University Press, 2014); Mark W. Elliott, *Engaging Leviticus: Reading Leviticus Theologically with Its Past Interpreters* (Eugene, OR: Cascade, 2011); Michael W. Bates, *The Birth of the Trinity: Jesus, God, and Spirit in New Testament and Early Christian Interpretations of the Old Testament* (Oxford: Oxford University Press, 2015); Robert C. Hill, *Reading the Old Testament in Antioch*, The Bible in Ancient Christianity (Atlanta: SBL Press, 2006); Vahan S. Hovhanessian, ed., *The Old Testament as Authoritative Scripture in the Early Churches of the East*, Bible in the Christian Orthodox Tradition 1 (New York: Peter Lang, 2010).

55. Mark W. Elliott, *The Heart of Biblical Theology: Providence Experienced* (London: Routledge, 2016), 3–36.

monochromatic. Hues of allegory, typology, promise-fulfillment, canonical reading, ethical reading, history of reception, and thematic studies of theological themes (and more) color theological interpretation of the OT so that these ancient texts continue to speak.[56]

Are Theological Interpretation and Literary Criticism of the Old Testament the Same?

One can distinguish the *content* of theological interpretation from the tendencies of literary studies, even when both are theologically focused. Tracing biblical ideas or themes in the OT or NT, potentially as a way toward articulating a kind of whole-Bible theology on those respective themes, is commonplace in biblical interpretation. It is possible to assess themes in biblical studies and equate this to theological interpretation. Thematic investigation of covenant, God's kingdom, prophecy, lament, land use, or technology can land in a monograph series designed to elucidate theological themes in the OT.[57] Alternatively, one could address theological topics such as God's body or divine fatherhood/motherhood, divine abode(s), divine emotion(s), divine action, or divine relations to creatures and creation, or any number of other topics, and equally identify these with theological interpretation. The decision to do so is natural; the topics or themes relate to how the OT depicts God.

But God is not, properly speaking, merely a theological theme emerging as a literary concept in the OT.[58] The divine *agent* to whom the text witnesses and from whom the text derives is not a theme, motif, or literary idea. Literary analysis of the OT can and should lead to theological interpretation, but this is not always the case. Literary investigations can serve as on-ramps to the highway of theological interpretation because of the close readings that literary

56. See Geoffrey Boyle, "The Real Presence of Christ in Scripture: A Sacramental Approach to the Old Testament" (PhD diss., St. Michael's College, University of Toronto, 2019), esp. 15–82 and his framing discussion on *Christuszeugnis,* typology, canonical and figural reading, and theological interpretation; cf. Collett, "Reading Forward."

57. See the series New Studies in Biblical Theology (InterVarsity). This series picks up from the older series in the UK, Studies in Biblical Theology (SCM). For theological theme investigations, see the Word Biblical Themes series republished by Zondervan. For monographs dealing with divine realities from a biblical-theological or OT theology framework, see recently Daniel I. Block, *Covenant: The Framework of God's Plan of Redemption* (Grand Rapids: Baker Academic, 2021); Andrew T. Abernethy, *The Book of Isaiah and God's Kingdom: A Thematic-Theological Approach*, NSBT 40 (Downers Grove, IL: IVP Academic, 2016); H. G. L. Peels and S. D. Snyman, eds., *The Lion Has Roared: Theological Themes in the Prophetic Literature of the Old Testament* (Eugene, OR: Pickwick, 2012); Andrew T. Abernethy and Gregory Goswell, *God's Messiah in the Old Testament: Expectations of a Coming King* (Grand Rapids: Baker Academic, 2020); R. W. L. Moberly, *Prophecy and Discernment*, Cambridge Studies in Christian Doctrine 14 (Cambridge: Cambridge University Press, 2006).

58. Thomas, "Old Testament."

study demands.[59] The works of Briggs and Chapman discussed above are recent examples of literary engagements with the OT that are sensitive toward theological understanding.

Conclusion

We have traversed an array of complications to the notion of theological interpretation. Exploration into these complications opens the possibility for more research on theological reading of the OT. We return to the definition with which we began: *Theological interpretation of the OT is, at its most basic calculation, interpretation with a focus on the triune God (theology) and God's address (theological disclosure) for communion with God in all of life.* Without being dogmatically conformist, theological interpretation is properly theological and embraces the ontology of the OT and its theological witness. It offers sustained analysis of the OT text (Hebrew and/or Greek traditions) in its literary, canonical, and cultural contexts. It interprets the OT witness within the full testimony of a two-Testament canon, even while focusing on God's address to be heard for the present. And theological interpretation attends to readings within Christian tradition throughout the past two millennia as they relate to OT texts, precisely because of their embrace of the ontology of the OT and attentiveness to God's address for today. Theological interpretation is a Christian way of reading that is oriented toward that address.

59. David J. H. Beldman, "Literary Approaches and Old Testament Interpretation," in Bartholomew and Beldman, *Hearing the Old Testament*, 67–95.

32

Old Testament Theology

Stephen B. Chapman

The task of OT theology is to say what the Old Testament is about. This task is controversial because scholars disagree over whether (1) the OT is about theology; (2) the OT is about a single theology; (3) the OT is about a theology of its own, apart from the NT and/or Rabbinic Judaism; (4) what the OT is about depends on the scope and order of its books; (5) what the OT is about primarily concerns the history it reflects or the story it tells; and (6) OT theology is more of a descriptive or a normative enterprise. I will take up the first three issues directly and in order, although the discussion will touch on all six. In the process, I will sketch a canonical approach to OT theology that I believe has fruitful potential.

Is There Theology in the Old Testament?

A major fault line in contemporary OT scholarship lies between a history-of-religions approach and a literary approach, between diachronic and synchronic forms of investigation. Most OT scholars wish to combine both impulses in some fashion, yet the impulses continually push against each other. Biblical interpretation traditionally held these two impulses together, but in modernity they pulled apart.[1] Literary scholars of the OT often denounce historical methods as misdirected efforts to replace "the world of the text" with "the world behind the

1. Hans W. Frei, *The Eclipse of Biblical Narrative: A Study in Eighteenth and Nineteenth Century Hermeneutics* (New Haven: Yale University Press, 1974).

text," and those in the history-of-religions camp often make disparaging remarks about "purely synchronic" interpretations and "theologians."

Although some literary scholars might agree with them, resistance to theological interpretation is particularly strong among history-of-religions scholars. I once heard a biblical scholar say, "There is no theology in the Hebrew Bible. Theology is what people did to the Bible later." This kind of sentiment is more often thought than published and more often asserted than argued. It nevertheless represents a strong current in biblical studies, as reflected in the title of a monograph by Konrad Schmid, *Is There Theology in the Hebrew Bible?*[2]

As Schmid rightly notes, answers to this question depend on one's definition of "theology."[3] Schmid adopts a narrow understanding of theology, so he finds less theology in the OT than someone else might. He privileges the philosophical, systematic form of theology known in later Christian tradition and concludes that its absence in the OT entails the absence of theology.[4] Yet it is specious to expect Scholastic-type theology in the OT, and one's definition of theology need not be limited to that type. It certainly does not follow that speaking of theology in the OT is anachronistic. Expand the definition of theology, and much more of it can be identified in the OT.

Schmid actually proceeds to do just that, claiming that while the OT "does not contain theology . . . what it contains is also not simply atheological."[5] But his effort to locate a middle way within this false binary concedes too much to the no-theology view. He describes the OT as "on the way to theology,"[6] only possessing an implicit rather than explicit theology. Schmid also draws a contrast with patently theological statements in the NT such as "God is spirit" (John 4:24), "God is light" (1 John 1:5), and "God is love" (1 John 4:8). He proposes that the NT "developed new ways of speaking and genres that separate it from the [OT] in terms of what later became classified as 'theology.'"[7]

But are such NT statements truly more theological than statements in the OT such as the grace formula of Exod. 34:6–7? "The Lord, the Lord, a God merciful and gracious, slow to anger, and abounding in steadfast love and faithfulness, keeping steadfast love for the thousandth generation, forgiving iniquity and transgression and sin, yet by no means clearing the guilty, but visiting the iniquity of the parents upon the children and the children's children, to the third and the fourth generation" (NRSV). This statement encapsulates the identity of the God of Israel and is just as theological as the NT affirmations cited by

2. Konrad Schmid, *Is There Theology in the Hebrew Bible?*, trans. Peter Altmann, Critical Studies in the Hebrew Bible 4 (Winona Lake, IN: Eisenbrauns, 2015).

3. Schmid, *Is There Theology?*, 3.

4. Schmid, *Is There Theology?*, 48.

5. Schmid, *Is There Theology?*, 48 (emphasis removed).

6. Citing Christoph Levin, "Das Alte Testament auf dem Weg zu seiner Theologie," *ZTK* 105, no. 2 (2008): 125–45.

7. Schmid, *Is There Theology?*, 48.

Schmid. In fact, the grace formula appears at multiple places throughout the OT, giving it the status of a theological touchstone or basic confession within the OT canon.[8] Moreover, the NT testimony includes how God is also the "God of our ancestors" (Acts 22:14), the "God of Israel" (Matt. 15:31), and "Abba, Father" (Rom. 8:15)—that is, the God of the OT.[9]

Or what of a text like "God is a consuming fire" (Deut. 4:24 NIV)? Although metaphorical, it is cited in the NT as a description of God's character (Heb. 12:29). Schmid's distinction with regard to the two Testaments overestimates the philosophical quality of NT belief statements, even as it underestimates the theological nature of OT belief statements.[10] Indeed, if OT theology is framed as the identification and exploration of the OT's belief statements or the OT's presentation of "faith" (as opposed to the "religion of ancient Israel"),[11] then there is theology aplenty.[12]

What Schmid does more successfully in his account of implicit theology in the OT is to emphasize the OT corpus's unique "scribal exegetical character," which features the "reflective interpretation of preexisting religious texts."[13] Here he pinpoints where redaction criticism, inner-biblical exegesis, and OT theology can productively converge. Although he initially dismisses the idea that "the boundaries of the canon" played "a qualitatively decisive role" in this process,[14] his notion of inner-biblical reflection on the nature of earlier traditions seems close to what Brevard Childs meant by "canon consciousness."[15] As the OT corpus grew, the biblical writings themselves gave rise to fresh theological insights and functioned as a guide for the articulation and shaping of those insights.[16] Of course, the historical experiences of the community gave rise to new theological ideas, but those ideas were generated and guided by interaction with preexisting

8. Mark J. Boda, *The Heartbeat of Old Testament Theology: Three Creedal Expressions*, Arcadia Studies in Bible and Theology (Grand Rapids: Baker Academic, 2017), 27–51; Michael P. Knowles, *The Unfolding Mystery of the Divine Name* (Downers Grove, IL: IVP Academic, 2012); Andreas Michel, "Ist mit der 'Gnadenformel' von Ex 34,6 (+7) der Schlüssel zu einer Theologie des Alten Testaments gefunden?," *BN* 118 (2003): 110–23.

9. Brevard S. Childs, *Biblical Theology in Crisis* (Philadelphia: Fortress, 1970), 203.

10. By "belief statements" I have in mind what Gerhard von Rad terms "Israel's own explicit assertions about Jahweh." See von Rad, *Old Testament Theology*, trans. D. M. G. Stalker (New York: Harper & Row, 1962), 1:105.

11. Cf. Werner H. Schmidt, *The Faith of the Old Testament: A History*, trans. John Sturdy (Philadelphia: Westminster, 1983). The latest, eleventh German edition appears as Schmidt, *Alttestamentlicher Glaube* (Göttingen: Vandenhoeck & Ruprecht, 2011).

12. "Faith" is not a native concept in the OT itself, but then neither is "religion." Both are etic (observer) rather than emic (participant) categories.

13. Schmid, *Is There Theology?*, 49.

14. Schmid, *Is There Theology?*, 53.

15. Brevard S. Childs, *Introduction to the Old Testament as Scripture* (Philadelphia: Fortress, 1979), 60.

16. Schmid later discusses canon formation as a "theologizing process." See Schmid, *Is There Theology?*, 99–105.

texts as well. Scripture was a means of revelation already in ancient Israel—not only after the canon was completed but even while being formed.

Konrad Schmid and others are right to say that the OT is not a theological "treatise." But a more expansive view of theology, especially one attentive to the distinctive nature of OT canon formation, will readily discern theological material throughout the OT. Here the summary of Rolf Rendtorff remains apropos: "The Old Testament is a theological book. An account of the 'Theology of the Old Testament' therefore scarcely requires special justification."[17] Schmid quarrels with Rendtorff's second sentence, but he does not finally dispute the first.[18]

Does the Old Testament Have a Single Theology?

A related question is whether the OT has a single theology or theological "center" (German *Mitte*). Here the main challenge confronting any effort "to say what the OT is about" is the diversity of the OT's contents, its smorgasbord of literary genres, historical experiences, and theological viewpoints. Accordingly, the task of OT theology has often been thought to entail the identification of a single theological motif or theme able to ground a framework supple enough to encompass that diversity within some sort of unity. However, efforts to identify a central unifying theme frequently call forth the objection that any attempt to articulate a theological unity will diminish or silence biblical voices perceived to be at a greater distance from the selected center.

As a result, OT theology has moved away from the adoption of a single center to an identification of multiple motifs and themes. Roland Murphy concludes that it is an

> illusion, a chimera, that the Bible has what could be realistically described as a middle, or even a central theme. The basic fact is that neither Testament, nor, consequently, both together, has a distinct middle or center. A Christian might urge Jesus Christ as the center of the New Testament at least. But this literature cannot be reduced to Jesus Christ as "center," without making a mockery of it. One might as well say that God is the center of the Bible . . . but this solves nothing. . . . The Old Testament in particular is far too diversified to be curtailed to an essential center/ theme, no matter how broad (e.g., presence), or how important (e.g., covenant).[19]

Providing indirect support for such a conclusion, Roberto Ouro catalogs almost thirty different proposals for a central organizing theme.[20] The proliferation of

17. Rolf Rendtorff, *The Canonical Hebrew Bible: A Theology of the Old Testament*, trans. David E. Orton, Tools for Biblical Study 7 (Leiden: Deo, 2005), 1.

18. Schmid, *Is There Theology?*, 119.

19. Roland E. Murphy, "Once Again—the 'Center' of the Old Testament," *BTB* 31, no. 3 (2001): 88–89.

20. Roberto Ouro, "The Sanctuary: The Canonical Key of Old Testament Theology," *AUSS* 50, no. 2 (2012): 159–77. He cites a list of fifty proposals in R. M. Davidson, "Back to the

these proposals (and the lack of consensus it represents) indicates a problem with the whole approach.[21]

In response to this methodological dead end, a number of recent theological initiatives have pursued pluralistic approaches to OT theology.[22] Here the problem becomes attempting to identify what if anything holds the various voices of the OT together and if only canonical witnesses should be considered. Gerhard von Rad, author of one of the most important OT theologies in the twentieth century, eventually took the view that an OT theology in the singular ("theology") was impossible. He concludes that "the Old Testament contains not merely one, but quite a number of theologies which are widely divergent both in structure and method of argument."[23] His position has become the default in OT scholarship, so that there are now "theologies" of Genesis, the Priestly source, Second Isaiah, or even individual psalms. John Collins insists, "The God of Job is appreciably different from the God of the Deuteronomist, and either from the God of Daniel."[24] But for all the distinctive features of these traditions, are they really portraying different *Gods*? Of course not. The process of canon formation brought these traditions together. Each one offers a *perspective* on the God of Israel. Still pertinent is the probing review of von Rad's OT theology by Walther Zimmerli, in which he criticizes von Rad's lack of synthetic thinking.[25] The shapers of the canon understood that the God who delivers Israel from Egypt in Exodus is the same God as the Holy One of Israel in Isaiah.[26]

A response to the question of what the OT is about must necessarily observe the profile of the biblical canon, even as that profile changed over time. Moreover, the reflective, inner-biblical expansion of that corpus gave it an internal, tripartite differentiation, so that the OT came to consist of three main subcollections: the Law/Pentateuch, the Prophets, and the Writings. These subcollections are not historical accidents but three communally shaped theological witnesses, discrete yet mutually entangled.

Beginning: Genesis 1–3 and the Theological Center of Scripture," in *Christ, Salvation, and the Eschaton: Essays in Honor of Hans K. LaRondelle*, ed. Daniel Heinz, Jiří Moskala, and Peter M. van Bemmelen (Berrien Springs, MI: Andrews University, 2009), 5–29.

21. Ouro, "Sanctuary," 173. However, Ouro proposes yet another center: sanctuary.

22. Erhard S. Gerstenberger, *Theologies in the Old Testament*, trans. John Bowden (Minneapolis: Fortress, 2002); Georg Fischer, *Theologien des Alten Testaments* (Stuttgart: Katholisches Bibelwerk, 2012).

23. See von Rad, *Old Testament Theology*, 2:414.

24. John J. Collins, *Encounters with Biblical Theology* (Minneapolis: Fortress, 2005), 22.

25. Walther Zimmerli, "Gerhard von Rad, 'Theologie des Alten Testaments,'" *VT* 13, no. 1 (1963): 100–111. Cf. Magne Sæbø, "From 'Unifying Reflections' to the Canon: Aspects of the Traditio-Historical Final Stages in the Development of the Old Testament," in *On the Way to Canon: Creative Tradition History in the Old Testament*, JSOTSup 191 (Sheffield: Sheffield Academic, 1998), 285–307.

26. Gerald Sheppard, "Canonization: Hearing the Voice of the Same God through Historically Dissimilar Traditions," *Int* 36, no. 1 (1982): 21–33 = *ExAud* 1 (1985): 106–14.

From this vantage point, another way of pursuing OT theology is to follow the tripartite lead of the canon. The possibility was recognized by Claus Westermann:

> The structure of the Old Testament in its three parts indicates that the narrative in the Old Testament is determined by the word of God occurring in it and by the response of those for whom God acts and with whom [God] deals. It is therefore the canon of the Old Testament itself which shows us the structure of what happens in the Old Testament in its decisive elements. We have thus found an objective starting point for an Old Testament theology which is independent of any preconceptions about what the most important thing in the Old Testament is and independent of any other prior theological decisions. If one asks what the Old Testament says about God, this threefold structure shows us the way to the answer.[27]

Such a model is certainly not the only approach to OT theology, but by avoiding the hopeless search for a single theological center and the endless rehearsal of sheer theological diversity, a structural-canonical approach holds promise.

Childs sometimes follows this type of approach. In a treatment of "the shape of the obedient life," he moves through sections devoted to the Psalter, wisdom, and the Pentateuch.[28] In a discussion of "life under threat," he organizes his remarks in sections on the Primeval History, the Pentateuch, the Prophets, Daniel and apocalyptic, the Psalms, and wisdom.[29] More significant than the number or order of such canonical groupings is the way of thinking represented by using them to structure theological reflection. Childs identifies these groupings as "canonical guidelines" or "canonical indices." He maintains that "rather than a closed system to be historically described," the shape of the OT canon presents "different dimensions of Israel's faith . . . which lend themselves to a variety of theological construals by modern interpreters."[30] Because the canonical process involved the shaping of not only individual books but "canonical units such as the Torah, Prophets and Writings," and because over time these units influenced each other, the process of canon formation "built in a dimension of flexibility which encourages constantly fresh ways of actualizing the material."[31]

This canonical approach to OT theology resembles a traditional rabbinic mode of working with the Bible. Rabbinic discourse demonstrates a consistent

27. Claus Westermann, *What Does the Old Testament Say about God?*, ed. Friedemann W. Golka (Atlanta: John Knox, 1979), 12.

28. Brevard S. Childs, *Old Testament Theology in a Canonical Context* (Philadelphia: Fortress, 1985), 207–14.

29. Childs, *Old Testament Theology*, 222–32.

30. Childs, *Old Testament Theology*, 207.

31. Childs, *Old Testamant Theology*, 13. Others pursuing OT theology through the shape of the canon include Pablo R. Andiñach, *El Dios que está: Teología del Antiguo Testamento*, EstBíb (Estella, Spain: Verbo Divino, 2014); W. H. Bellinger Jr., *Introducing Old Testament Theology: Creation, Covenant, and Prophecy in the Divine-Human Relationship* (Grand Rapids: Baker Academic, 2022); Stephen G. Dempster, *Dominion and Dynasty: A Biblical Theology of the Hebrew Bible*, NSBT 15 (Downers Grove, IL: InterVarsity, 2003).

appreciation for the HB's threefold form, with rabbis often providing support for a particular judgment from each of the three divisions of the canon rather than only one.[32] As Ben Azzai (2nd cent. CE) describes it, "I thread the words of the Torah onto the Prophets and the words of the Prophets onto the Writings, and the words of the Torah are as joyful as when they were given at Sinai" (Lev. Rabbah 16.4). Such a conception of scriptural interpretation appears to be rooted in liturgical practice, as another early witness details: "The reciter opens with verses from the Torah, and closes with verses from the Torah, and recites from the Prophets and the Writings in between" (t. Rosh Hashanah 2.12[G]).

While not as prominent in the Christian tradition, a sense of the OT's canonical divisions and their usefulness for theological reflection is likewise evident, even in the composition of the NT writings themselves.[33]

The Old Testament on Its Own?

At present, the historical question of whether the OT ever existed on its own cannot be precisely determined. It is unclear that a "closed" OT canon existed at the time of Jesus and the earliest Christians (1st cent. CE). It does appear that an authoritative scriptural corpus was recognized (Josephus, *Ag. Ap.* 1.8),[34] but its boundaries were fuzzy.[35] Late Second Temple Jews and Christians likely read the OT alongside oral (Josephus, *Ant.* 13.297; Matt. 15:1–9; Mark 7:1–13; 1 Cor. 11:2; Gal. 1:14; 2 Thess. 2:15; 3:6) and written traditions (e.g., Sirach, 1 Enoch, Psalms of Solomon) that were eventually left out of the canon (or at least one version of the canon). While the OT was never read separately from the good news of the gospel within the Christian tradition, the writings of the NT also never existed in ignorance of the OT. For the first several generations of the Christian movement, Israel's Bible was the only Scripture that Christians possessed. There is therefore more historical justification for reading the OT apart from the NT than for reading the NT detached from the OT.

Interpreting the OT apart from the NT prevents reading NT realities too quickly into OT texts, and there are two theological reasons why this is appropriate. The first concerns a new sensitivity to the place of Judaism in relation to the OT, particularly after the Holocaust.[36] The second stems from a more com-

32. Stephen B. Chapman, "'A Threefold Cord Is Not Quickly Broken': Interpretation by Canonical Division in Early Judaism and Christianity," in *The Shape of the Writings*, ed. Julius Steinberg and Timothy J. Stone, Siphrut 16 (Winona Lake, IN: Eisenbrauns, 2015), 281–309.

33. Chapman, "Threefold Cord," 298–303.

34. See Stephen G. Dempster, "Old Testament Canons," chap. 11 of the present volume.

35. Stephen B. Chapman, "Second Temple Jewish Hermeneutics: How Canon Is Not an Anachronism," in *Invention, Rewriting, Usurpation: Discursive Fights over Religious Traditions in Antiquity*, ed. Jörg Ulrich, Anders-Christian Jacobsen, and David Brakke, Early Christianity in the Context of Antiquity 11 (Frankfurt: Lang, 2012), 281–96.

36. As Erich Zenger writes, "After Auschwitz the church must read the 'Old Testament' differently." *Das Erste Testament: Die jüdische Bibel und die Christen* (Dusseldorf: Patmos, 1991), 12 (my trans.).

prehensive grasp of biblical hermeneutics within the Christian tradition itself, especially with regard to the relationship between the two Testaments of the Christian Bible.

Rather than insisting, as many Christian theologians and biblical scholars did previously, that early Jewish interpreters misunderstood their own Bible, contemporary scholars conclude instead that Jews and Christians interpreted the OT differently (though also sometimes similarly). "When considered historically, the Bible of Israel is open to two trajectories: the shape of the Mishnah and Talmud on the one side, and the shape of the New Testament on the other. The two-fold outlook means that Israel's Bible 'can be continued and "completed" in different ways. The New Testament represents only one such possibility.'"[37] A valuable "ecumenical" form of OT theology thus consists of articulating the theological base from which both Christianity and Judaism developed their respective traditions of interpretation. A corollary to recognizing the OT's openness to both religious traditions is the realization that the religion of ancient Israel was not identical with either. Judaism and Christianity further extended the religion of Israel and did so with strikingly new accents.[38]

With regard to the OT in Christianity, it is useful once more to look for canonical guidelines. As Adolf von Harnack notes, early Christians could have abandoned the OT altogether, edited it, or added their own commentary directly to it.[39] In the course of its Christian reception, the OT might have received supplements or been rearranged or abridged in some fashion. Yet Israel's

37. Bernd Janowski, "The One God of the Two Testaments: Basic Questions of a Biblical Theology," *ThTo* 57, no. 3 (2000): 306, citing Ulrich Luz, "Ein Traum auf dem Weg zu einer biblischen Theologie: Ein Brief an Peter Stuhlmacher," in *Evangelium–Schriftauslegung–Kirche: Festchrift für Peter Stuhlmacher zum 65. Geburtstag*, ed. Jostein Ådna, Scott J. Hafemann, and Otfried Hofius (Göttingen: Vandenhoeck & Ruprecht, 1997), 283 (Janowski's trans.).

38. A Jewish biblical theology focusing on the HB has recently emerged. Just as in OT theology debates about the relationship between the OT, NT, and later Christian tradition, Jewish scholars disagree about how to interpret the HB in relation to later Jewish writings and rabbinic tradition. See Isaac Kalimi, ed., *Jewish Biblical Theology: Perspectives and Case Studies* (Winona Lake, IN: Eisenbrauns, 2012); Benjamin D. Sommer, "Dialogical Biblical Theology: A Jewish Approach to Reading Scripture Theologically," in *Biblical Theology: Introducing the Conversation*, ed. Leo G. Perdue, Robert Morgan, and Benjamin D. Sommer, The Library of Biblical Theology (Nashville: Abingdon, 2009), 1–53; Marvin A. Sweeney, ed., *Theology of the Hebrew Bible*, vol. 1, *Methodological Studies*, RBS 92 (Atlanta: SBL Press, 2019).

39. Adolf von Harnack, "Appendix II: Forerunners and Rivals of the New Testament," in *The Origin of the New Testament and the Most Important Consequences of the New Creation*, trans. J. R. Wilkinson (London: Williams & Norgate, 1925), 169–83. Such possibilities were real at the time, as indicated by Christian redaction of some "extracanonical" books. See James H. Charlesworth, "Christian and Jewish Self-Definition in Light of the Christian Additions to the Apocryphal Writings," in *Jewish and Christian Self-Definition*, vol. 2, *Aspects of Judaism in the Graeco-Roman Period*, ed. E. P. Sanders (Philadelphia: Fortress, 1981), 27–55.

scripture became the Christian OT without alteration or any official demotion of its scriptural status.[40]

This lack of alteration reflects a stance now expressed in the structure of the Christian Bible as consisting of two Testaments. For Karl Barth, this canonical structure enshrines a biblical hermeneutic in which the OT witnesses to "the time of expectation" and the NT witnesses to "the time of recollection."[41] In between stands Christ. This sense of a "before" and "after" is implicit in the two-Testament canon. A dialectical perspective emerges in which the OT both *is not and is* Christian Scripture.[42] The OT comes from a time prior to the incarnation and does not know of Jesus Christ directly except in prophecies and visions of the future.

However, the OT is perceived to speak providentially and miraculously of the same spiritual realities experienced by Christians.[43] In this sense, the OT is not "pre-Christian." Childs explains:

> The very fact that the Christian canon treasures a portion of the scripture in which the name of Jesus is not mentioned offers an initial warrant for seeking another theological option. The implication of the Old Testament canon, both on a formal and material level, is that the Christian life is still lived between promise and fulfillment, not as a unilinear *heilsgeschichtliche* pattern, but as a description of the essential eschatological dimension of divine redemption. To reflect on God's revelation in the Old Testament is not a pre-Christian stage which has been rendered inoperative by the full revelation in Jesus Christ. Rather, it belongs to the nature of the Christian faith that the perception of God through the witness of the old covenant remains a constitutive stance for Christian theology.[44]

Just like ancient Israel, the Christian church lives between the already and the not yet, a spiritual posture for which the OT gives eloquent, wise, and discerning guidance.[45]

40. Christoph Dohmen and Günter Stemberger, *Hermeneutik der jüdischen Bibel und des Alten Testaments*, 2nd rev. ed., Kohlhammer-Studienbücher Theologie 1.2 (Stuttgart: Kohlhammer, 2019), 11–23.

41. Karl Barth, "The Time of Revelation," in *Church Dogmatics*, vol. I/2, trans. G. W. Bromiley, ed. T. F. Torrance (Edinburgh: T&T Clark, 1956), §14.

42. Cf. the discussion of a "Christian dialectic" involving both Testaments in Henri de Lubac, *Scripture in the Tradition*, trans. Luke O'Neill, Milestones in Catholic Theology (New York: Crossroad, 2000), 173–82.

43. This dimension of traditional Christian understanding opposes the modernist conceit, as critiqued by Kathryn Greene-McCreight ("Introducing Premodern Scriptural Exegesis," *JTI* 4, no. 1 [2010]: 5), that "the OT was 'then' and the NT is 'now.'" Cf. Christopher R. Seitz, *The Character of Christian Scripture: The Significance of a Two-Testament Bible*, STI (Grand Rapids: Baker Academic, 2011).

44. Childs, *Old Testament Theology*, 30.

45. Cf. Don C. Collett, "A Tale of Two Testaments: Childs, Old Testament Torah, and *Heilsgeschichte*," in *The Bible as Christian Scripture: The Work of Brevard S. Childs*, ed. Christopher R. Seitz and Kent Harold Richards, BSNA 25 (Atlanta: Society of Biblical Literature, 2013), 185–219.

The Nature and Task of Old Testament Theology

If OT theology is conceived as the task of describing the religion of ancient Israel, then there is no coherent reason to work with the writings of the OT canon alone or even to privilege written sources over archaeological data. However, if OT theology is framed as the task of exploring the belief statements of the OT corpus, then working within the bounds of the OT canon is inherent to that task, even as it is legitimate to pose the question of how different traditions of the canon's scope (i.e., the number of its books) and order (i.e., its arrangement) might affect such an inquiry. For instance, it seems that the tripartite form of the OT had less influence in Christian tradition than in Jewish tradition, although it clearly had some (Luke 24:44).[46] Christianity received the OT largely in the form of Greek translations (i.e., the Septuagint) in which the deuterocanonical books were included and a tripartite arrangement of the canon was less pronounced.[47] So an OT theology of the Greek OT (or LXX) might be somewhat different from an OT theology of the HB, although much will also be shared in common.

An OT theology focusing on the belief statements of the OT can make use of standard historical methods to identify and explicate those beliefs. Such work has ecumenical potential to involve scholars from different religious traditions in a common descriptive task: Protestants and Catholics, Christians and Jews, even scholars who do not identify as religious. A major challenge, however, is ongoing uncertainty about what is meant by "description," given the postmodern indictment of purportedly neutral description.[48] All description proceeds from prior assumptions and depends on the experience(s) and perspective(s) of the describer.[49] This important insight came into biblical studies from many sources, but above all from feminist biblical criticism.[50]

46. Contra Lee Martin McDonald, "Forming Jewish Scriptures as a Biblical Canon," in *Ancient Jewish and Christian Scriptures: New Developments in Canon Controversy*, ed. John J. Collins, Craig A. Evans, and Lee Martin McDonald (Louisville: Westminster John Knox, 2020), 76–77.

47. Strong contrasts between a threefold Hebrew Bible and a fourfold Greek OT are overstated. Of the three early Christian codices containing the OT, only Vaticanus exhibits something like a fourfold order, with the prophetic books at the end. Alexandrinus and Sinaiticus place the prophetic books in the middle and the poetical books at the end. Worse are contrasts between a threefold Jewish Bible and a fourfold Christian OT. Originally, of course, the Septuagint was a Jewish translation. See Tessa Rajak, *Translation and Survival: The Greek Bible of the Ancient Jewish Diaspora* (Oxford: Oxford University Press, 2009).

48. Sometimes "description" is understood to preclude theological work altogether. E.g., Philip R. Davies, *Whose Bible Is It Anyway?*, 2nd ed. (New York: T&T Clark, 2004).

49. The assumptions of Davies are in this sense no less "confessional."

50. Caroline Vander Stichele and Todd Penner, eds., *Her Master's Tools? Feminist and Postcolonial Engagements of Historical-Critical Discourse*, GPBS 9 (Atlanta: SBL Press, 2005). With regard to OT theology, see Phyllis Bird, "Old Testament Theology and the God of the Fathers: Reflections on Biblical Theology from a North American Feminist Perspective," in *Biblische Theologie: Beiträge des Symposiums "Das Alte Testament und die Kultur der Moderne" anlässlich des 100. Geburtstags Gerhard von Rads (1901–1971) Heidelberg, 18.–21. Oktober*

The fault line between a history-of-religions approach and a synchronic approach is also apparent in the descriptive work of OT theology. In German-language scholarship, OT theology is done mostly in a history-of-religions mode.[51] In English-language scholarship, there is a contrasting effort by some to pursue OT theology in the form of discrete close readings of the received text.[52] A related style of OT theology is essentially synchronic and yet aims at greater comprehensiveness through a persistent attempt to identify encompassing themes, patterns, or principles.[53] Another mainly synchronic form of OT theology explores the biblical traditions as dialogues or conversations.[54] Each group in this methodological divide between the diachronic and the synchronic seeks to acknowledge and incorporate the insights of the other, yet the divide remains.[55]

Ultimately, OT theology must move beyond the "anthropology" of belief statements to genuine theology, for a thoroughly critical OT theology must not only report what ancient Israelites believed but consider whether or not those beliefs are true. This aspect of the task requires normative work, and it naturally takes a more confessional shape. Here as well there are questions and debates. Some scholars insist that an authentically Christian approach to OT theology must proceed exclusively on the basis of normative theological

---

2001, ed. Paul Hanson, Bernd Janowski, and Michael Welker, Altes Testament und Moderne 14 (Münster: LIT, 2005), 69–107. For constructive soundings, see Patricia K. Tull and Jacqueline E. Lapsley, eds., *After Exegesis: Feminist Biblical Theology; Essays in Honor of Carol A. Newsom* (Waco: Baylor University Press, 2015).

51. Michaela Bauks, *Theologie des Alten Testaments: Religionsgeschichtliche und bibelhermeneutische Perspektiven*, Uni-Taschenbücher 4973 (Göttingen: Vandenhoeck & Ruprecht, 2019); Jörg Jeremias, *Theologie des Alten Testaments*, GAT 6 (Göttingen: Vandenhoeck & Ruprecht, 2015); Konrad Schmid, *A Historical Theology of the Hebrew Bible*, trans. Peter Altmann (Grand Rapids: Eerdmans, 2019).

52. Ellen F. Davis, *Opening Israel's Scriptures* (New York: Oxford University Press, 2019); R. W. L. Moberly, *Old Testament Theology: Reading the Hebrew Bible as Christian Scripture* (Grand Rapids: Baker Academic, 2013).

53. Leslie C. Allen, *A Theological Approach to the Old Testament: Major Themes and New Testament Connections* (Eugene, OR: Cascade, 2014); Daniel I. Block, *Covenant: The Framework of God's Grand Plan of Redemption* (Grand Rapids: Baker Academic, 2021); John Goldingay, *Old Testament Theology*, 3 vols. (Downers Grove, IL: IVP Academic, 2003–9); Robin Routledge, *Old Testament Theology: A Thematic Approach* (Downers Grove, IL: IVP Academic, 2008); Bruce K. Waltke with Charles Yu, *An Old Testament Theology: A Canonical and Thematic Approach* (Grand Rapids: Zondervan, 2007). These scholars might dispute the characterization of their work as synchronic, arguing that they instead have a higher appraisal of the historical reliability of the OT's witnesses.

54. Walter Brueggemann, *Theology of the Old Testament: Testimony, Dispute, Advocacy* (Minneapolis: Fortress, 1997); cf. John Kessler, *Old Testament Theology: Divine Call and Human Response* (Waco: Baylor University Press, 2013).

55. Petr Sláma, *New Theologies of the Old Testament and History: The Function of History in Modern Biblical Scholarship*, Beiträge zum Verstehen der Bibel 33 (Zurich: LIT, 2017).

convictions, while others advocate a dialogical approach between Scripture and tradition.[56]

Classically, Christianity read the OT in two directions.[57] This hermeneutical practice is on display in an example like Gregory of Nyssa's *Life of Moses* (4th cent. CE), in which he essentially tells Moses's story twice: "First we shall go through in outline his life as we have learned it from the divine Scriptures. Then we shall seek out the spiritual understanding which corresponds to the history in order to obtain suggestions of virtue."[58] The first retelling is a plain-sense reading in which the biblical story of Moses's life is recounted. The second consists of reexamining the story for ways that it can enrich Christian faith and practice. The first was known in the tradition as *historia* (narrative, story), the second as *theoria* (contemplation, vision).[59]

This bi-directional manner of reading is also implicit in the two-Testament format of the Christian Bible. Plain-sense reading held a primary place in the Christian tradition, moving through the OT corpus literarily and historically from creation to eschaton. The plain sense of the OT is read "forward" toward Christ. This direction of reading can still be understood as broadly historical today, but the modern divide between narrated history and reconstructed history introduced problems for the church that have never been entirely resolved. Moreover, forward reading by itself fails to address the ontological unity to which both Testaments witness (e.g., Isa. 53; John 8:58), especially as that unity has been traditionally understood in Christian theology (above all, in the doctrine of the Trinity).[60]

Therefore, the OT is also read "backward" from the Christ event to the testimony of Israel. This type of retrospective reading perceives figural relationships within the biblical story, which is revealed to be a rhyming history.[61] Such figuralism is sometimes called allegory, sometimes typology, and known

56. Gary A. Anderson, *Christian Doctrine and the Old Testament: Theology in the Service of Biblical Exegesis* (Grand Rapids: Baker Academic, 2017); Robert W. Jenson, *Canon and Creed*, Interpretation (Louisville: Westminster John Knox, 2010); Darren Sarisky, *Reading the Bible Theologically*, Current Issues in Theology (Cambridge: Cambridge University Press, 2019); Kevin J. Vanhoozer, "Toward a Theological Old Testament Theology? A Systematic Theologian's Take on Reading the Old Testament Theologically," in *Interpreting the Old Testament Theologically: Essays in Honor of Willem A. VanGemeren*, ed. Andrew T. Abernethy (Grand Rapids: Zondervan, 2018), 293–317.

57. The terminology of "senses" or "levels" has traditionally been used, but it implies a static "container" theory of hermeneutics. It is therefore preferable to speak of "directions of reading." Cf. Pontifical Biblical Commission, *The Jewish People and Their Sacred Scriptures in the Christian Bible* (Vatican City: Libreria Editrice Vaticana, 2002), II.A.6.

58. Gregory of Nyssa, *The Life of Moses* (New York: HarperOne, 2006), 8.

59. Robert W. Jenson, "Gregory of Nyssa, *The Life of Moses*," *ThTo* 62, no. 4 (2006): 533–37.

60. Don C. Collett, "Reading Forward: The Old Testament and Retrospective Stance," *Pro-Eccl* 24, no. 2 (2015): 178–96.

61. Richard B. Hays, *Reading Backwards: Figural Christology and the Fourfold Gospel Witness* (Waco: Baylor University Press, 2014).

as the "spiritual sense" in contrast to the plain sense. However, the term "spiritual sense" is problematic both because it suggests the application of a second symbolic sense to a first "plain" one and because it implies that the plain sense is not "spiritual."[62]

Reading the OT figurally involves not adding a second sense to the plain sense[63] but rather situating the plain sense of the OT literally and historically within the context of the *entire* Christian Bible. "Far from being in conflict with the literal sense of the biblical stories, figuration or typology was a natural extension of literal interpretation. It was literalism at the level of the whole biblical story and thus of the depiction of the whole of historical reality. Figuration was at once a literary and historical procedure, an interpretation of stories and their meanings by weaving them together into a common narrative referring to a single history and its patterns of meaning."[64] In other words, if Jesus really was the Messiah of Israel, how then must the OT be read?[65]

The Christ event does not change what the OT says, but it does alter an understanding of the substance to which the OT points: "It is not that the coming of Christ gives us extra information on the meaning of OT passages, but that it gives us extra information on the realities that the OT passages refer to."[66] On its own, the OT does not reveal Jesus, but it seems to anticipate him. And in retrospect, the reality of Jesus suffuses the OT, although without leveling and thereby negating the way that God has chosen to advance Israel's story. In Christian understanding, these two directions of reading the OT are distinct but reciprocally implicated, even as they cannot be fused.

OT theology therefore possesses both a descriptive and a normative dimension. Both are necessary; neither should be slighted. Both can be fruitfully pursued as crucial aspects of saying what the OT is about. In this combined task, the main exegetical emphasis should be on attending to the kerygmatic features of the OT or its belief statements. Such belief statements should be construed as broadly as possible so that they include expressions of doubt as well as belief, actions as well as words, poetry as well as prose. The OT canon itself is a kind of belief statement, as are its various books and subcollections. Attending to the structure of the OT canon offers important indices and guidelines for identifying and comparing the variety of belief statements.

62. Jenson, "Gregory," 534, avers, "[Gregory's] distinction between 'story' and 'vision' is *not* a distinction between secular and theological: already in the *historia* God and Moses are both agents" (emphasis original).

63. If this is how "retrospective" reading is understood, then it fails to articulate the ontological unity of both Testaments adequately. So Denis M. Farkasfalvy, "The Pontifical Biblical Commission's Document on Jews and Christians and Their Scriptures: Attempt at an Evaluation," *Communio* 29, no. 4 (2002): 715–37.

64. Frei, *Eclipse of Biblical Narrative*, 2.

65. Luke 24:45; John 5:46.

66. John Goldingay, *Approaches to Old Testament Interpretation*, rev. ed. (Downers Grove, IL: InterVarsity, 1990), 37.

To be sure, the OT does not offer a comprehensive belief "system" that can simply be cataloged and adopted. Instead, it provides a collocation of testimonies from Israel's lived experience before God over many centuries. Yet these testimonies are literarily crafted with a particular audience in mind, so merely paraphrasing the OT's plot will not be enough.[67] There needs to be greater consideration in OT theology of the OT's discourse dimension, the way its contents are formatted, presented, and unfolded for its implied readership.[68] More attention must also be paid to the contemporary situation that OT theology seeks to engage, since "new occasions teach new duties, / time makes ancient good uncouth."[69] Old Testament theology has a pressing obligation to address modern issues more directly rather than sheltering in the comfortable embrace of long ago.[70]

The ongoing task of OT theology can remain vital and beneficial. By its nature, OT theology will always be provisional, tied to its own historical moment, and ultimately elusive. That is no criticism of it, but rather its promise.

67. Stephen B. Chapman, "The How as Well as the What: Canonical Formatting and Theological Interpretation," in *The Identity of Israel's God in Christian Scripture: Essays in Honor of Christopher R. Seitz*, ed. Don Collett, Mark Elliott, and Ephraim Radner, RBS 96 (Atlanta: SBL Press, 2020), 65–80.

68. Richard S. Briggs, *The Virtuous Reader: Old Testament Narrative and Interpretive Virtue*, STI (Grand Rapids: Baker Academic, 2010).

69. From the hymn "Once to Every Man and Nation," by James Russell Lowell. Such engagement will hopefully include more work from the two-thirds world. See, e.g., Kondasingu Jesurathnam, *Old Testament Theology: History, Issues, and Perspectives*, Biblical Hermeneutics Rediscovered 3 (New Delhi: Christian World Imprints, 2016); Bungishabaku Katho, "Faire la Théologie de l'Ancien Testament en Afrique aujourd'hui: Défis et Perspective," *OTE* 23, no. 1 (2010): 82–102.

70. Cf. L. Juliana Claassens and Bruce C. Birch, eds., *Restorative Readings: The Old Testament, Ethics, and Human Dignity* (Eugene, OR: Pickwick, 2015); Terence E. Fretheim, *God and World in the Old Testament: A Relational Theology of Creation* (Nashville: Abingdon, 2005); John W. Rogerson, *A Theology of the Old Testament: Cultural Memory, Communication, and Being Human* (Minneapolis: Fortress, 2010).

Contributors

Samuel L. Boyd
University of Colorado, Boulder

Mark G. Brett
Whitley College, University of Divinity, Melbourne

Aubrey E. Buster
Wheaton College, Illinois

M. Daniel Carroll R. (Rodas)
Wheaton College, Illinois

Stephen B. Chapman
Duke Divinity School

Stephen L. Cook
Virginia Theological Seminary

Matthew J. M. Coomber
St. Ambrose University

Katherine Davis
Sydney Missionary & Bible College, Australian College of Theology

Katharine J. Dell
University of Cambridge

Stephen G. Dempster
Crandall University

Christopher J. Fresch
Bible College of South Australia, Australian College of Theology

Deirdre N. Fulton
Baylor University

Rachelle Gilmour
Trinity College, University of Divinity, Melbourne

Jamie A. Grant
Highland Theological College, University of the Highlands and Islands

H. H. Hardy II
Beeson Divinity School, Samford University

Ralph K. Hawkins
Averett University

Richard S. Hess
Denver Seminary

John W. Hilber
McMaster Divinity College

Brad E. Kelle
Point Loma Nazarene University

Will Kynes
Ajax Health

David T. Lamb
Missio Seminary

Bo H. Lim
Seattle Pacific University

Drew Longacre
Duke University; Scriptura

Tremper Longman III
Westmont College

Sandra L. Richter
Westmont College

Kenneth Ristau
MacEwan University

Jordan J. Ryan
Wheaton College, Illinois

Cynthia Shafer-Elliott
Baylor University

Jason M. Silverman
University of Helsinki

Brent A. Strawn
Duke University

C. A. Strine
University of Sheffield

Heath A. Thomas
Oklahoma Baptist University; Kirby Laing Centre for Public Theology (Cambridge, UK)

Daniel C. Timmer
Puritan Reformed Theological Seminary; Faculté de théologie évangélique (Montreal)

Eric J. Tully
Trinity Evangelical Divinity School

Scripture and Ancient Writings Index

Old Testament

Genesis

Exodus

Leviticus

Numbers

Deuteronomy

Joshua

Judges

1 Samuel

2 Samuel

Medieval Codices and Other Early Texts

Author Index